Learning, Training, and Development in Organizations

Learning, Training, and Development in Organizations

Edited by

Steve W. J. Kozlowski • Eduardo Salas

Routledge
Taylor & Francis Group
New York   London

Routledge
Taylor & Francis Group
270 Madison Avenue
New York, NY 10016

Routledge
Taylor & Francis Group
27 Church Road
Hove, East Sussex BN3 2FA

© 2010 by Taylor and Francis Group, LLC
Routledge is an imprint of Taylor & Francis Group, an Informa business

Printed in the United States of America on acid-free paper
10 9 8 7 6 5 4 3 2

International Standard Book Number: 978-0-8058-5559-3 (Hardback)

For permission to photocopy or use material electronically from this work, please access www. copyright.com (http://www.copyright.com/) or contact the Copyright Clearance Center, Inc. (CCC), 222 Rosewood Drive, Danvers, MA 01923, 978-750-8400. CCC is a not-for-profit organization that provides licenses and registration for a variety of users. For organizations that have been granted a photocopy license by the CCC, a separate system of payment has been arranged.

Trademark Notice: Product or corporate names may be trademarks or registered trademarks, and are used only for identification and explanation without intent to infringe.

Library of Congress Cataloging-in-Publication Data

Kozlowski, Steve W. J.
 Learning, training, and development in organizations / Steve W. J. Kozlowski & Eduardo Salas.
  p. cm.
 ISBN 978-0-8058-5559-3 (hardback)
 1. Organizational learning. 2. Employees--Training of. 3. Active learning. 4. Organizational change. I. Salas, Eduardo. II. Title.

HD58.82.K69 2009
658.3'124--dc22

2008046786

Visit the Taylor & Francis Web site at
http://www.taylorandfrancis.com

and the Psychology Press Web site at
http://www.psypress.com

The Organizational Frontiers Series

The Organizational Frontiers Series is sponsored by the Society for Industrial and Organizational Psychology (SIOP). Launched in 1983 to make scientific contributions to the field, the series has attempted to publish books on cutting-edge theory, research, and theory-driven practice in industrial and organizational psychology and related organizational science disciplines.

Our overall objective is to inform and to stimulate research for SIOP members (students, practitioners, and researchers) and people in related disciplines, including the other subdisciplines of psychology, organizational behavior, human resource management, and labor and industrial relations. The volumes in the Organizational Frontiers Series have the following goals:

Focus on research and theory in organizational science, and the implications for practice.

Inform readers of significant advances in theory and research in psychology and related disciplines that are relevant to our research and practice.

Challenge the research and practice community to develop and adapt new ideas and to conduct research on these developments.

Promote the use of scientific knowledge in the solution of public policy issues and increased organizational effectiveness.

The volumes originated in the hope that they would facilitate continuous learning and a continuing research curiosity about organizational phenomena on the part of both scientists and practitioners.

The Organizational Frontiers Series

SIOP Organizational Frontiers Series

Series Editor

Robert D. Pritchard
University of Central Florida

Kozlowski/Salas: (2009) Learning, Training, and Development in Organizations

Klein/Becker/Meyer: (2008) Commitment in Organizations: Accumulated Wisdom and New Directions

Salas/Goodwin/Burke: (2008) Team Effectiveness in Complex Organizations: Cross-Disciplinary Perspectives and Approaches

Kanfer/Chen/Pritchard: (2008) Work Motivation: Past, Present, and Future

De Dreu/Gelfand: (2008) The Psychology of Conflict and Conflict Management in Organizations

Ostroff/Judge: (2007) Perspectives on Organizational Fit

Baum/Frese/Baron: (2007) The Psychology of Entrepreneurship

Weekley/Ployhart: (2006) Situational Judgment Tests: Theory, Measurement, and Application

Dipboye/Colella: (2005) Discrimination at Work: The Psychological and Organizational Bases

Griffin/O'Leary-Kelly: (2004) The Dark Side of Organizational Behavior

Hofmann/Tetrick: (2003) Health and Safety in Organizations

Jackson/Hitt/DeNisi: (2003) Managing Knowledge for Sustained Competitive Knowledge.

Barrick/Ryan: (2003) Personality and Work

Lord/Klimoski/Kanfer: (2002) Emotions in the Workplace

Drasgow/Schmitt: (2002) Measuring and Analyzing Behavior in Organizations.

Feldman: (2002) Work Careers

Zaccaro/Klimoski: (2001) The Nature of Organizational Leadership

Rynes/Gerhart: (2000) Compensation in Organizations

Klein/Kozlowski: (2000) Multilevel Theory, Research, and Methods in Organizations

Ilgen/Pulakos: (1999) The Changing Nature of Performance

Earley/Erez: (1997) New Perspectives on International I-O Psychology

Murphy: (1996) Individual Differences and Behavior in Organizations

Guzzo/Salas: (1995) Team Effectiveness and Decision Making

Howard: (1995) The Changing Nature of Work

Schmitt/Borman: (1993) Personnel Selection in Organizations

Zedeck: (1991) Work, Families and Organizations

Schneider: (1990) Organizational Culture and Climate

Goldstein: (1989) Training and Development in Organizations

Campbell/Campbell: (1988) Productivity in Organizations

Hall: (1987) Career Development in Organizations

This volume is dedicated to my Mom and Dad, Helena, and Stephen, who taught me the value of learning, to my mentors who taught me how to learn, to my students who taught me how to instill learning in others, to Irv and Paul who pioneered this frontier, and to my wife and son, Georgia and Alex, who help me learn important life lessons every single day!

Steve W. J. Kozlowski

I dedicate this volume to two giants of the training field—Irv Goldstein and Paul Thayer—who have shaped much of what we know and who, in small and big ways, help me learn and think about the science and practice of training.

Eduardo Salas

Contents

Section 1 The Learner, Learning Processes, and Training Outcomes

Section 2 Emerging Issues for Design and Delivery

Series Foreword

This is the 30th book in the Organizational Frontiers Series of books. The overall purpose of the series volumes is to promote the scientific status of the field. Ray Katzell first edited the series. He was followed by Irwin Goldstein, Sheldon Zedeck, and Neal Schmitt. The topics of the volumes and the volume editors are chosen by the editorial board, or individuals propose volumes to the editorial board. The series editor and the editorial board, then, work with the volume editor(s) in planning the volume.

The success of the series is evident in the high number of sales (now over 50,000). Volumes also have received excellent reviews, and individual chapters, as well as volumes, have been cited frequently.

This volume, edited by Steve W. J. Kozlowski and Eduardo Salas, presents current thinking and research on the topic of training, learning, and development in organizations. It is a major synthesis of the new research and thinking and updates us on what is known in this important area. The volume has a number of strengths. Irv Goldstein's classic Organizational Frontiers Series volume on training and development was published in 1989. Since then, as Kozlowski and Salas note in their preface,

> [T]he area has witnessed a shift from research that was predominantly atheoretical to a blossoming of theory that has focused on elaborating the influence of training interventions on *learning processes*, and those theoretical advances have prompted an explosion of theory-driven empirical research.

This volume captures that shift. It gives us a sense of where we have been, what is going on now, and what the future might hold. Another strength is the broad scope of the volume, going beyond just training and learning to include overall development. These topics are approached from a wider variety of different perspectives than usually is found in this topic, and this breadth will increase the impact of the volume. I am especially pleased to have so much space devoted to future research needs. A Frontiers volume should represent the thinking of the best people in the field, and these people should give us the benefit of their ideas on these issues. Such attention to future research can influence the work in this area for years to come.

The editors and chapter authors deserve our gratitude for clearly communicating the nature, application, and implications of the theory and research described in this book. Production of a volume such as this involves the hard work and cooperative effort of many individuals. The editors, the chapter authors, and the editorial board all played important roles in this endeavor. As all royalties from the series volumes are used to help support the Society for Industrial and Organizational Psychology (SIOP), none of the editors or authors received any remuneration. The editors and authors deserve our appreciation for engaging a difficult task for the sole purpose of furthering our understanding of organizational science. We also want to express our gratitude to Anne Duffy, our editor at Psychology Press/Routledge, who has been a great help in the planning and production of the volume.

Robert D. Pritchard
University of Central Florida
Series Editor

Preface

In 1989, Irv Goldstein edited a multiauthored volume entitled *Training and Development in Organizations* for the SIOP Organizational Frontiers Series that helped to stimulate nearly 2 decades of remarkable development for training theory and research. Most notably, the area has witnessed a shift from research that was predominantly atheoretical to a blossoming of theory that has focused on elaborating the influence of training interventions on *learning processes*, and those theoretical advances have prompted an explosion of theory-driven empirical research. This shift in the nature of training and development research is evidenced in commentary appearing in the *Annual Review of Psychology* on training by Salas and Cannon-Bowers, published in 2001, who concluded that there had been a "renaissance" in the field of training over the last decade. The intent for this new volume is to capture this progress and to project forward the continuing and emerging issues that are likely to shape theory and research in this area of endeavor for the next decade and beyond. Moreover, in recognition of the increasing importance of the capacity to acquire knowledge and build human capital to organizational effectiveness, this volume is also designed to broaden and extend the focus beyond training per se to encompass *learning, training,* and *development* in organizations.

Organizing Themes

We see three primary themes that will shape the future of scholarship aimed at enhancing knowledge acquisition and its application in organizations. The first theme centers on the pivotal role that an understanding of the *learner, learning processes,* and *training outcomes* has played in the current "training renaissance." As highlighted previously, we have witnessed a shift in the training paradigm from a simplistic comparison of different techniques to an effort to understand how and why particular techniques are effective. Work in this area has been and will continue to be a key for developing a more sophisticated theoretical foundation to direct research on learning and training that then provides the foundation for training design and delivery.

The second theme concerns new issues for *training design and delivery* given the changing nature of work and organizations. Many traditional training approaches assume routine tasks, predictable work settings, and significant instructor–trainee face-to-face interaction in the classroom. Yet, work is increasingly complex, entailing greater emphasis on expertise and cognitive skills. It is increasingly dynamic, placing a premium on the adaptation of knowledge and skills to novel situations and problems. Furthermore, advances in technology and connectivity (e.g., computer simulation and Web-based training) are pushing more and more training out of the classroom and into the workplace, distributing it in time and space, and necessitating a more active role for the learner in the training process. These trends are changing the way we think about the nature of training and where and how it is delivered, and they create a need for new approaches for instructional design and delivery.

The third theme focuses on *learning and development in the organizational context, across levels, and over time.* Organizations are beginning to realize that knowledge and learning are major, if not the only, sources of true competitive advantage in a rapidly changing, unpredictable global economy. Thus, in the broader context of the organization system and the life course of a career, there is a need to understand how learning can be fostered as an informal, not merely formal, process; how learning and development can be promoted as continuous lifelong endeavors; and how learning and knowledge can be leveraged and captured via systems that cut across multiple levels of the organization to unite the micro, meso, and macro antecedents, processes, and consequences of learning, training, and development. Finally, we close the book with a consideration of how training and development research has progressed, where it needs to go, and what specific areas and issues are primary targets for research attention, and a peek "over the horizon" for some possible future developments.

These themes provide the structure for organizing the volume. We hope you find them to be thought provoking and stimulating:

The learner, learning processes, and training outcomes

Emerging issues in training design and delivery

The organizational context, levels, and time

Reflection and future directions

Steve W. J. Kozlowski
Michigan State University

Eduardo Salas
University of Central Florida

About the Contributors

Rebecca Beard has 20+ years experience consulting with many organizations, including numerous Fortune 500 companies, not-for-profits, and the military, helping them identify learning needs and clarify the learning offer required to meet those needs. She has conducted and managed individual and team development efforts from early diagnosis and needs analysis through design, delivery, and evaluation. Beard is the executive vice president and cofounder of The Group for Organizational Effectiveness, Inc., an Albany, New York–based consulting and research firm. She received her M.S. in psychology from Old Dominion University in Norfolk, Virginia, in 1982 and was part of the team that won SIOP's 2007 M. Scott Meyers Award for applied research.

Margaret E. Beier is assistant professor at Rice University, Houston, Texas. She received her Ph.D. in industrial and organizational psychology from the Georgia Institute of Technology in 2003. Beard's research is broadly focused on intellectual development through the life span. Specific topics include investigation of cognitive ability, age, gender, and personality and motivational traits as related to job and training performance in both organizations and educational settings. Her research combines elements of cognitive psychology, industrial-organizational psychology, and human factors. A main focus of her current research involves investigating how to best design training for older learners. She is on the editorial board of *Journal of Experimental Psychology: Applied*, and she has authored numerous book chapters and journal articles. Her work has appeared in *Intelligence, Psychological Bulletin, Journal of Educational Psychology, Journal of Experimental Psychology: Applied, Journal of Experimental Psychology: General, Journal of Personality and Social Psychology*, and *Psychology and Aging*.

Bradford S. Bell is an associate professor of human resource studies in the School of Industrial and Labor Relations at Cornell University. He received his B.A. in psychology from the University of Maryland at College Park and his M.A. and Ph.D. in industrial and organizational psychology from Michigan State University. Dr. Bell's research interests include training and development, team development and effectiveness, and organizational justice. His research has appeared in the *Journal of Applied Psychology, Personnel Psychology, Human Resource Management, Human Resource Development Quarterly, International Journal of Human Resource Management, Group and Organization Management*, and the *International*

Journal of Selection and Assessment. In addition, Dr. Bell has published numerous chapters that have appeared in edited research volumes.

Clint Bowers holds M.A. and Ph.D. degrees in psychology from the University of South Florida, Tampa. He is currently a professor of psychology at the University of Central Florida. He is also chief scientist of the Applied Cognition and Training in Virtual Environments laboratory at the university's Institute for Simulation and Training. Dr. Bowers' research career has focused on optimizing technology-enabled learning in high-performance environments. He has received more than $8 million of external funding from agencies such as the Federal Aviation Administration, the Office of Naval Research, the Robert Wood Johnson Foundation, and the National Science Foundation. Dr. Bowers has been an active researcher, with over 100 publications in scholarly journals, books and technical reports, and numerous professional presentations. He is a fellow of the American Psychological Association and has served on a number of editorial boards and review panels.

Jan Cannon-Bowers holds M.A. and Ph.D. degrees in industrial-organizational psychology from the University of South Florida, Tampa. She recently left her position as the U.S. Navy's senior scientist for training systems to join the Institute for Simulation and Training at the University of Central Florida (UCF), Orlando, as an associate professor and senior research associate. As the team leader for advanced training research for the Navy, she was involved in a number of research projects directed toward improving performance in complex environments. She was also instrumental in the formation of the Navy's new Human Performance Center as part of her work for the chief of naval operations in his Revolution in Navy Training. At UCF, Dr. Cannon-Bowers is continuing her work in technology-enabled learning and synthetic learning environments. Her goal is to leverage and transition the U.S. Department of Defense's sizable investment in modeling, simulation, and training to other areas such as medicine, entertainment, workforce development, and education. To date, she has been awarded several grants to support this work, including awards by the National Science Foundation and Office of Naval Research related to game-based training. Dr. Cannon-Bowers has been an active researcher, with over 100 publications in scholarly journals, books and technical reports, and numerous professional presentations. She is also on the editorial boards of several scholarly journals. She has received numerous awards for her work, and is on the Board of Directors of the Society for Medical Simulation and advisor to the national Serious Games Initiative. Currently, Dr. Cannon-Bowers is working with UCF's newly formed College of Medicine to help integrate simulation into the curriculum.

Georgia T. Chao, Ph.D., is an associate professor of management at Michigan State University. She has a B.S. in psychology from the University of Maryland and M.S. and Ph.D. in industrial-organizational psychology from the Pennsylvania State University. Her primary research interests lie in the areas of organizational socialization and work adjustment, cultural influences on organizational behavior, mentoring, and career development. In 1995, Dr. Chao received the Outstanding Publication Award in Organizational Behavior from the Academy of Management. In that publication, she was the lead author and principal investigator of a 5-year study on the content and consequences of organizational socialization. Dr. Chao's international activities include visiting professorships in Bond University, Australia; Zhejiang University, China; and Tamkang University, Taiwan. She served as chair to the American Psychological Association's Committee on International Relations in Psychology and directed a mentoring program for APA's early career psychologists. In addition, she served on the Executive Committees of three divisions in the Academy of Management, the Executive Committee of the Society for Industrial and Organizational Psychology, and the Council for APA. She serves on four editorial boards and is a fellow of the American Psychological Association and the Society for Industrial and Organizational Psychology.

Gilad Chen is an associate professor of management and organization in the Robert H. Smith School of Business at the University of Maryland. He received his doctoral degree in industrial-organizational psychology from George Mason University in 2001. His research on work motivation, learning and adaptation, teams, and leadership has appeared in such journals as *Academy of Management Journal, Journal of Applied Psychology, Organizational Behavior and Human Decision Processes, Personnel Psychology,* and *Research in Organizational Behavior,* and has been funded by the U.S. Army Research Institute. He is a recipient of several research awards, including the 2008 Cummings Scholar Award for early- to mid-career scholarly achievement (from the Organizational Behavior Division of the Academy of Management), and the 2007 Society for Industrial and Organizational Psychology's Distinguished Early Career Contributions Award. He is currently serving as associate editor for the *Journal of Applied Psychology.*

Nancy J. Cooke is a professor of applied psychology at Arizona State University at the Polytechnic Campus and is science director of the Cognitive Engineering Research Institute in Mesa, Arizona. She is also editor-in-chief of *Human Factors.* Dr. Cooke received a B.A. in psychology from George Mason University in 1981 and received her M.A. and Ph.D. in cognitive psychology from New Mexico State University in 1983 and 1987, respectively. Her research interests include the study of individual and team cognition and its application to the development of cognitive- and knowledge-engineering methodologies, homeland security systems, remotely operated vehicles, and emergency response systems. In particular, Dr. Cooke specializes in the development, application, and evaluation of methodologies to elicit and assess individual and team cognition. Her most recent work includes empirical and modeling efforts to understand the acquisition and retention of team skill and the measurement of team coordination and team situation awareness, especially through the analysis of communication. This work is funded primarily by the Air Force Research Laboratory and the Office of Naval Research. Dr. Cooke has organized annual workshops on the human factors of unmanned aerial vehicles since 2004; has coedited *Human Factors of Remotely Operated Vehicles* (published by Elsevier) and *The Best of Human Factors* (with Eduardo Salas and published by HFES); and has coauthored (with Frank Durso) *Stories of Modern Technology Failures and Cognitive Engineering Successes* (published by Taylor & Francis).

Stephen M. Fiore, Ph.D., is faculty with the University of Central Florida's Cognitive Sciences Program in the Department of Philosophy and director of the Cognitive Sciences Laboratory at UCF's Institute for Simulation and Training. He earned his Ph.D. degree (2000) in cognitive psychology from the University of Pittsburgh, Learning Research and Development Center. He maintains a multidisciplinary research interest that incorporates aspects of cognitive, social, and organizational sciences in the investigation of learning and performance in individuals and teams. He is coeditor of recent volumes on *Team Cognition* (2004) and on *Distributed Learning* (2007) as well as recent journal special issues on human learning and performance. Dr. Fiore has published in the areas of learning, memory, and problem solving at the individual and group levels. As principal investigator, coprincipal investigator, or senior personnel; he has helped to secure and manage research funding from organizations such as the National Science Foundation, the Transportation Security Administration, the Office of Naval Research, and the Air Force Office of Scientific Research.

J. Kevin Ford is a professor of psychology at Michigan State University. His major research interests involve improving training effectiveness through efforts to advance our understanding of training needs assessment, design, evaluation, and transfer. Dr. Ford also concentrates on building continuous learning and improvement orientations within organizations. He is an active consultant with private industry and the public sector on training, leadership, and organizational change issues. He is a fellow of the American Psychological Association and the Society for Industrial and Organizational Psychology. He received his B.S. in psychology from the University of Maryland and his M.A. and Ph.D. in psychology from the Ohio State University. Further information about Kevin and his research and consulting activities can be found at http://www.io.psy.msu. edu/jkf.

Irwin Goldstein came to the University of Maryland at College Park in 1966 and served as professor and chair from 1981 to 1991. In 1991, he was selected to be dean of the College of Behavioral and Social Sciences. In 2001, he was awarded the University of Maryland President's Medal for "extraordinary contributions to the intellectual, cultural and social life of the University." In 2003, he was selected to serve as vice chancellor for academic affairs for the 13 campuses of the University System of Maryland. Dr. Goldstein's research career as an industrial-organizational psychologist has focused on issues facing individuals, such as how they are selected and promoted, how they are trained by organizations, and how the climate of the organizations affects human resources practices. He also has a strong interest in understanding and resolving the constraints that affect people who live in organizations, such as the problems of race and gender discrimination. In these roles, he has served as a consultant to both public and private sector organizations. He has served as an associate editor of the *Journal of Applied Psychology* and the *Human Factors Journal* and as editor of the Frontiers Book Series for the Society for Industrial and Organizational Psychology. In 1992, he received the Distinguished Service Award from the Society for Industrial and Organizational Psychology. In 1995, he received the Swanson Award for Research Excellence from the American Society for Training and Development. Dr. Goldstein has also been honored by being elected to serve as president of the Society for Industrial and Organizational Psychology.

Stanley M. Gully is a member of the faculty in the Department of Human Resource Management in the School of Management and Labor Relations at Rutgers University. He has authored or presented numerous papers, research articles, and book chapters on a variety of topics. His work has appeared in *Research in Personnel and Human Resources Management, Journal of Applied Psychology, Organizational Behavior and Human Decision Processes, Journal of Organizational Behavior,* and *Organizational Research Methods,* among other outlets. Stan earned his master's and Ph.D. degrees in industrial-organizational psychology from Michigan State University. He has taught courses at the undergraduate, master's, Ph.D., and executive master's level, covering content such as organizational learning and innovation, recruiting and staffing, strategic human resource management, training and development, and leadership. He has taught using traditional and hybrid technologies in the United States, Singapore, and Indonesia. Stan has won awards for the quality of his research, teaching, and service, and he has served on the editorial boards of *Journal of*

Applied Psychology, Academy of Management Journal, Journal of Management, and *Journal of Organizational Behavior.* His applied work includes, but is not limited to, management at a major parcel delivery firm, assessment of the effectiveness of an employer branding initiative, design of various training programs, and evaluation of recruiting source effectiveness. His research interests include strategic recruiting, leadership and team effectiveness, training, and organizational learning.

Jaclyn M. Jensen is an assistant professor of management at the George Washington University School of Business. She currently teaches introductory human resource management for undergraduates and managing human capital for MBA students. Dr. Jensen's research focuses on counterproductive work behavior, organizational justice, and organizational learning. Her research has been published in *Organizational Behavior and Human Decision Processes* and the *International Journal of Conflict Management,* as well as in several book chapters. She received her Ph.D. and M.A. in industrial-organizational psychology from Michigan State University and holds a B.S. in psychology from the Ohio State University.

Ruth Kanfer received her Ph.D. in 1981 from Arizona State University. She completed a postdoctoral fellowship in quantitative psychology at the University of Illinois (1981–1983), and served on the faculty at the University of Minnesota from 1984 to 1997. She has been at the Georgia Institute of Technology since 1997, where she is currently on the faculty of the School of Psychology. Her research interests are in motivation and self-regulation in the context of complex skill training, job performance, team performance, employee development, and job search and reemployment. She is author of over 60 articles and chapters on these topics, and she is coeditor of *Learning, Motivation, and Methodology* (1989) and two SIOP Frontier Series books, *Emotions in the Workplace* (2002) and *Work Motivation* (2008). She received the 2007 Distinguished Scientific Contribution Award and the 2006 William R. Owens Scholarly Achievement Award from the Society for Industrial and Organizational Psychology, the 1989 Organizational Psychology Division Outstanding Publication of the Year from the Academy of Management, and the 1989 Distinguished Scientific Award for an Early Career Contribution in Applied Research from the American Psychological Association. She has served on the Academy of Management Board of Governors and has served on nine journal editorial boards, including those of the *Journal of Applied Psychology, Organizational Behavior and Human Decision Processes, Applied Psychology: An International Review,* and the *Journal of Management.* Her research has been funded by the National Science Foundation, the U.S. Office of Naval Research, the U.S. Air Force Office of Scientific Research, the National Institutes of Health, the Spencer Foundation, the American Council of Learned Societies, the

Georgia Department of Labor, and private organizations. She is a fellow in the Society for Industrial and Organizational Psychology, the American Psychological Association, and the American Psychological Society.

Steve W. J. Kozlowski, Ph.D., is a professor of organizational psychology at Michigan State University. His research program is focused on active learning, self-regulation, and adaptive performance; simulation-based training; enhancing team learning and effectiveness; and the critical role of team leaders in the development of adaptive teams. The goal of this programmatic work is to generate actionable theory, research-based principles, and deployable tools to facilitate the development of adaptive individuals, teams, and organizations. His research has been supported by the Air Force Office of Scientific Research, the Army Research Institute for the Behavioral and Social Sciences, and the Naval Air Warfare Center Training Systems Division, among others. Dr. Kozlowski is editor (and former associate editor) for the *Journal of Applied Psychology*. He has served on the editorial boards of the *Academy of Management Journal, Human Factors*, the *Journal of Applied Psychology,* and *Organizational Behavior and Human Decision Processes*. He is a fellow of the American Psychological Association, the Association for Psychological Science, the International Association for Applied Psychology, and the Society for Industrial and Organizational Psychology. Dr. Kozlowski received his B.A. in psychology from the University of Rhode Island, and his M.S. and Ph.D. degrees in organizational psychology from the Pennsylvania State University.

Kurt Kraiger is a professor of psychology at Colorado State University. He is also the director of the university's Center for Organizational Excellence, through which he works to forge strategic partnerships between university faculty and graduate students with businesses and agencies in Colorado and the Rocky Mountain region. Dr. Kraiger is a fellow of the Society for Industrial and Organizational Psychology. He is a noted expert on training and training evaluation, having edited two books and published or presented over 130 papers on training and related topics. He is also actively engaged in research on learning in ill-structured environments (e.g., computer-based training and through mentoring programs). Dr. Kraiger also has a long history of consulting with organizations in problem areas related to training, selection, competency modeling, and organizational attitudes.

John Mathieu is a professor and the department head of management at the University of Connecticut (UConn). He also holds the Cizik Chair in Management at UConn. His primary areas of interest include models of training effectiveness, team and multiteam processes, and cross-level models of organizational behavior. He has conducted work with several

Fortune 500 companies, the armed services (i.e., the U.S. Army, Navy, and Air Force), federal and state agencies (e.g., the National Research Council [NRC], National Aeronautics and Space Administration [NASA], Federal Aviation Administration [FAA], U.S. Department of Transportation [DOT]), and numerous public and private organizations). Dr. Mathieu has over 80 publications and 175 presentations at national and international conferences, and has been a principal investigator or coprincipal investigator on over $5 million in grants and contracts. He is a fellow of the American Psychological Association as well as the Society for Industrial and Organizational Psychology, and a member of the Academy of Management. He serves on numerous editorial boards and has guest edited special volumes of top-level journals. He holds a Ph.D. in industrial-organizational psychology from Old Dominion University.

Richard E. Mayer is professor of psychology at the University of California, Santa Barbara (UCSB), where he has served since 1975. He received a Ph.D. in psychology from the University of Michigan in 1973, and served as a visiting assistant professor of psychology at Indiana University from 1973 to 1975. His research interests are in educational and cognitive psychology. His current research involves the intersection of cognition, instruction, and technology with a special focus on multimedia learning and computer-supported learning. He is past president of the Division of Educational Psychology of the American Psychological Association, former editor of *Educational Psychologist* and former coeditor of *Instructional Science*, former chair of the UCSB Department of Psychology, and the year 2000 recipient of the E. L. Thorndike Award for career achievement in educational psychology. He is the winner of the 2008 Distinguished Contribution of Applications of Psychology to Education and Training Award from the American Psychological Association. He was ranked number 1 as the most productive educational psychologist for 1991–2001 (*Contemporary Educational Psychology*, vol. 28, pp. 422–430). Currently, he is vice president for Division C (Learning and Instruction) of the American Educational Research Association. He is on the editorial boards of 14 journals, mainly in educational psychology. He has served on a local school board in Goleta, California, since 1981. He is the author of more than 390 publications, including 23 books, such as *Multimedia Learning* (2009), *Learning and Instruction* (2008), *E-Learning and the Science of Instruction* (with R. Clark, 2008), and the *Cambridge Handbook of Multimedia Learning* (editor, 2005).

Laurel McNall is an assistant professor of psychology at the College at Brockport, State University of New York. While working as a consultant for the Group for Organizational Effectiveness in Albany, New York, she earned her Ph.D. in industrial-organizational psychology from the University at Albany, State University of New York, in 2005. Her current research interests include electronic performance monitoring, job attitudes, and the work–family interface.

Stephanie M. Merritt is assistant professor of industrial-organizational psychology at the University of Missouri–St. Louis. She received her Ph.D. from Michigan State University in 2007. Her research interests include organizational attitudes and attitude–behavior links as well as human–computer interaction.

Janice C. Molloy is an assistant professor of human resource management at Michigan State University's School of Labor and Industrial Relations. Her doctorate is from the Ohio State University's Fisher College of Business and focused on business strategy and psychometrics. Janice applies these specialties to integrate economic and psychological views of human capital in her strategic human resource management research.

Raymond A. Noe is the Robert and Anne Hoyt Designated Professor of Management in the Department of Management and Human Resources at the Ohio State University. He received his B.S. in psychology from the Ohio State University and his M.A. and Ph.D. in psychology from Michigan State University. Professor Noe's teaching and research interests are in human resource management, organizational behavior, and training and development. He has published articles on training motivation, employee development, work and nonwork issues, mentoring, Web-based recruiting, and team processes.

Michael A. Rosen is a doctoral candidate in the Applied Experimental and Human Factors Psychology Program at the University of Central Florida and a graduate researcher at the Institute for Simulation and Training. He has coauthored over 60 journal articles, book chapters, and conference papers related to teams, decision making and problem solving, performance measurement, and simulation-based training.

Eduardo Salas is University Trustee Chair and Pegasus Professor of Psychology at the University of Central Florida (UCF) and program director for the Human Systems Integration Research Department at UCF's Institute for Simulation and Training. Salas is a fellow of the American Psychological Association (SIOP and Divisions 19, 21, and 49), the Human Factors and Ergonomics Society, and the Association for Psychological Science. He was editor of *Human Factors* in 2000–2004. For 15 years, he was a senior research psychologist and head of the Training Technology Development Branch of Naval Air Systems Command (NAVAIR) Orlando. Salas served as a principal investigator for numerous R&D programs focusing on teamwork, team training, simulation-based training, decision making under stress, learning methodologies, and performance assessment. He helps organizations foster teamwork, design and implement team training strategies, facilitate training effectiveness, manage decision making under stress, develop performance measurement tools, and design learning and simulation-based environments. Salas has coauthored more than 330 journal articles and book chapters and has coedited 20 books. He has served as an editorial board member for numerous journals and is an associate editor of the *Journal of Applied Psychology*. He received a Ph.D. in industrial and organizational psychology from Old Dominion University in 1984.

Scott I. Tannenbaum is president of the Group for Organizational Effectiveness (GOE), an Albany, New York-based boutique consulting and research firm he founded in 1987 that has provided consulting and research support to over 250 organizations, including 75+ Fortune and Global 1000 companies. Formerly a tenured business school professor, Scott is a fellow of SIOP. His scientific-academic accomplishments include 50+ publications, 100+ presentations, and 5+ research or teaching awards. He has reviewed for 20 professional journals, and has served as a principal investigator or scientist on a wide range of funded research efforts. He holds a Ph.D. in industrial-organizational psychology from Old Dominion University.

Paul Tesluk (Ph.D. and M.S. industrial-organizational psychology, Penn State University; B.S., Cornell University) is Tyser Professor of Organizational Behavior and Human Resource Management at the Robert H. Smith School of Business at the University of Maryland, College Park, and codirector of the Center for Human Capital, Innovation and Technology (HCIT), also at the Robert H. Smith School of Business. His research focuses on strategies to enhance team effectiveness and innovation, the development of management and leadership talent, and organizational culture and climate in organizations transitioning to high-involvement workplace systems. He has published more than 30 articles and book chapters on these topics and has received awards from the Society for Industrial and Organizational Psychology for his research on work team effectiveness and work experience and leadership development. He is currently on the editorial boards of several of the field's leading journals.

Paul W. Thayer is an industrial-organizational psychologist and independent consultant. He is a professor emeritus of psychology at North Carolina State University, where he was head of the department from 1977 to 1992. Before that, he worked at the Life Insurance Marketing and Research Association for 21 years, rising from training researcher through research vice president to senior vice president. He has been a consultant for many arms of federal and state governments, many firms, and hundreds of insurance companies. He received his Ph.D. in psychology from Ohio State University. He has been author or coauthor of dozens of articles on selection, training, job design, and related areas, and (with McGehee) the classic text *Training in Business and Industry*. He is a fellow of the American Association for the Advancement of Science, the Association for Psychological Science, the American Psychological Association, and the Society for Industrial and Organizational Psychology (SIOP). He has held all elective offices of SIOP, including president, and is recipient of its Distinguished Professional Practice Award and Distinguished Service Award. He served on the editorial board of *Personnel Psychology* from 1967 to 1996, and is currently on the Book Review Board. He is president of the SIOP Foundation, and serves on the Technical Advisory Board of Previsor, a consulting firm providing selection services on the Internet. He was an associate editor of *Historical Perspectives in Industrial and Organizational Psychology*, edited by Laura Koppes. He claims to be retired.

Section 1

The Learner, Learning Processes, and Training Outcomes

One of the key hallmarks of training and development research in the 1990s has been the shift from simplistic atheoretical research (e.g., "Is A training better than B training?") to theoretically driven research that endeavors to elucidate learning processes and to understand the effects of interventions, individual differences, and their interaction—via learning processes—on a range of multidimensional training outcomes. Thus, the focus of this section encompasses individual differences and aptitude–treatment interactions, motivation and self-regulated learning, and advances in the ways that researchers can track the effects of training and individual differences on a broad array of learning outcomes.

Chapter 1 by Gully and Chen, "Individual Differences, Attribute–Treatment Interactions, and Training Outcomes," addresses the growing literature identifying important individual difference characteristics that influence learning processes (e.g., cognitive ability, metacognitive ability, goal orientation, and personality), the ways in which these individual differences can interact with training interventions to yield differential effects on training outcomes, and the theoretical and research advances that will be needed to make progress in this emerging area of work.

Chapter 2 by Beier and Kanfer is entitled "Motivation in Training and Development: A Phase Perspective." From a theoretical perspective, one of the major advances of the past decade had been our improved understanding of skill acquisition and learning processes through the self-regulation of intention, action, and emotion. This chapter considers theory and research advances, and new directions for work, in the broad area of learning as a motivated process, with the regulation of attention, effort, and emotion as important determinants of learning.

In Chapter 3, "Experts at Work: Principles for Developing Expertise in Organizations," Salas and Rosen unpack the implications of the nature of expertise for training and development. There has been a tremendous amount of research on the nature of expertise and how it is that experts

1

do what they do. Much of that knowledge has not been used by organizational psychologists in the design or delivery of training systems. This chapter discusses how research findings from the study of expert performance can help in the design, delivery, and implementation of training and learning systems.

Chapter 4 is by Ford, Kraiger, and Merritt, who provide "An Updated Review of the Multidimensionality of Training Outcomes: New Directions for Training Evaluation Research." No consideration of the advances in training research over the last decade would be complete without acknowledging the contribution made by the expanded conceptualization of training outcomes. This chapter considers advances in the treatment of training outcomes (e.g., interrelationships, validity, and evaluation issues) in light of research findings over the last decade. The goal is to update, integrate, refine, and expand further the conceptualization of training outcomes, with an eye toward simulating new research.

1

Individual Differences, Attribute–Treatment Interactions, and Training Outcomes

Stan Gully
Rutgers University

Gilad Chen
University of Maryland

Researchers and practitioners have long been aware of the important role that individual differences play in determining learning and training outcomes (for a review, see Ackerman & Heggestad, 1997). In 1984, Hunter and Hunter conducted a meta-analysis that included predictors of training performance. Their results showed that training success was predicted by peer ratings (r = .35), biodata (r = .30), college GPA (r = .30), and the Strong Interest Inventory (r = .18) (Hunter & Hunter, 1984). These findings indicated that individual characteristics played a key role in determining training success. However, their work focused on predictors of job success instead of individual characteristics related to training success. Thus, it had limited application to the development of new theories about individual differences and training outcomes.

Several theoretical frameworks and empirical investigations of training success later focused more explicitly on individual differences. For example, Noe (1986) included locus of control, career and job attitudes, and trainee motivation as key determinants of training effectiveness. Baldwin and Ford (1988) included trainee characteristics such as ability, personality, and motivation in their model of determinants of training transfer. As Baldwin and Ford noted, a variety of trainee characteristics thought to affect transfer had been suggested, but "empirical investigations of ability, personality, and motivational effects on training and transfer outcomes are quite limited" (p. 68). Awareness of the important role of individual differences is supported further by their inclusion in (person) needs analysis (Goldstein & Ford, 2002).

Despite previous work, gaps in our understanding exist and opportunities for research abound. In 1992, Tannenbaum and Yukl noted that research on trainee characteristics had focused more attention on selecting trainees who would pass training rather than designing programs to match trainee attributes or understanding how trainee characteristics improved training effectiveness. Colquitt, LePine, and Noe (2000) and Salas and Cannon-Bowers (2001) noted that research on trainee characteristics had proliferated in the preceding decade, but the assessment of trainees' personality characteristics during needs analysis was still a neglected or ignored issue. They also called for the expansion of personality variables in training research to include emotions, adaptability, trait goal orientation, and other Big Five variables.

There are a number of reasons that much work on the topic remains needed. First, the role of individual differences is often given secondary attention. For example, training texts devote entire chapters to needs analysis, design, implementation, and evaluation, yet most include individual differences as ancillary material. Rarely is it treated as a topic in its own right. Second, much work has taken a piecemeal approach, incorporating one or relatively few individual differences into theoretical frameworks and empirical studies. There are few or no comprehensive frameworks that help us understand how, why, and when particular individual differences are likely to promote learning. Third, much empirical work has focused on relational or predictive relationships rather than a theoretical understanding of why observed relationships exist. Fourth, ability has received the most attention in training studies. Less work has focused on other, noncognitive trainee attributes and attitudes (Noe, 1986; Salas & Cannon-Bowers, 2001). Fifth, researchers generally have not focused on explanatory mechanisms that mediate the effects of individual differences on training outcomes. When such mechanisms have been invoked, they often focus on training motivation, expectancy, and self-efficacy. Although clearly relevant, other intervening mechanisms are likely to exist. Finally, most work has not considered how individual differences interact with training design and contextual factors to influence training outcomes. Both Campbell and Kuncel (2002) and Tannenbaum and Yukl (1992) noted that although they may be important, the potential of such interactions to be useful in organizational training applications remains unfulfilled.

Accordingly, the time is ripe for a framework devoted to understanding how individual differences influence training outcomes. Theory (e.g., Mathieu & Martineau, 1997; Smith, Ford, & Kozlowski, 1997) and research (e.g., Ford, Smith, Weissbein, Gully, & Salas, 1998; Kozlowski & Bell, 2006) indicate that trainees are active participants in the training process (see also Bell & Kozlowski, this volume). Trainees actively regulate their motivation, emotion, and learning processes. They decide what to attend to, determine how much effort they will devote, and actively engage themselves in, or disengage themselves from, training (see Beier & Kanfer, this volume). Trainees are ultimately responsible for applying and transferring trained skills to the work environment. It seems self-evident that individual differences will influence regulatory and motivational processes that determine whether trained content is learned, retained, applied, and transferred to the work context. Unfortunately, most previous work on individual differences has not focused on understanding the mechanisms that connect them to training outcomes. This is problematic because without a better understanding of the intervening mechanisms, it is difficult to know which individual differences matter and when they are likely to have influence. We suggest that in addition to the main effects on training outcomes observed in previous work, the effects of individual differences are dependent on training design features and contextual influences.

Theoretical Framework

The purpose of this chapter is to address these gaps by introducing a framework that includes a broad variety of individual differences and explanatory mechanisms (see Figure 1.1). This framework is used to introduce and discuss both main effects and aptitude– or attribute–treatment interactions (ATIs). Finally, we explore implications of the framework for theory, future research, and applied practice.

Training outcomes of interest are drawn from the work of Kraiger, Ford, and Salas (1993) and Ford and Kraiger (this volume). These include cognitive, behavioral, and affective and motivational outcomes. Cognitive

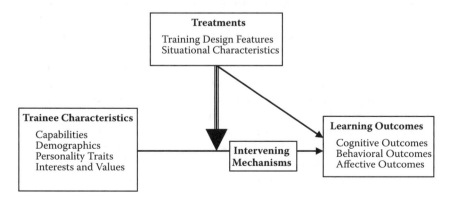

FIGURE 1.1
Guiding framework.

outcomes include declarative, procedural, and strategic knowledge as well as the structure and organization of such knowledge. It also includes cognitive transfer, which is the ability to apply previously learned knowledge to new situations or contexts. Affective and motivational outcomes include satisfaction, self-efficacy, and expectancy, as well as perceived utility of training. Attitudinal outcomes include changes in attitudes toward tasks, jobs, or others. Behavioral outcomes include skill development, automaticity, and maintenance. Behavioral outcomes also include skill generalization and adaptability, which encompasses transfer of training (Baldwin & Ford, 1988).

Treatments are broadly defined to include training design features and contextual or situational characteristics of the training system. Training design features include sequencing, complexity, delivery mode, and goals of the training content. Situational characteristics include work environment features such as the reward system, climate to support training transfer, and climate of support for skills updating. Research evidence supports the notion that both individual and situation factors influence training outcomes (e.g., Tesluk, Farr, Mathieu, & Vance, 1995). For additional discussions pertaining to training methods and contextual influences on learning processes, see the chapters by Cannon-Bowers and Bowers, Mathieu and Tesluk, Cooke and Fiore, and Mayer in this volume.

Individual differences include demographics and relatively enduring trainee characteristics that influence cognition, motivation, and behavior such as personality, interests, and cognitive capabilities. Although individual differences may evolve or be somewhat malleable over longer periods of time, the characteristics of interest are somewhat stable, exerting influence during and throughout the entire training process, including transfer. Thus, statelike, transient, and more malleable individual differences such as mood, task-specific self-efficacy, and motivation to learn are not reviewed in the framework except where relevant as part of the intervening mechanisms that connect the more distal individual difference variables to the outcomes of interest (e.g., Chen, Gully, Whiteman, & Kilcullen, 2000).

Individual differences are grouped into four general categories: (a) capabilities, (b) demographics, (c) personality traits, and (d) values and interests. Capabilities include general mental ability and specific talents, capabilities, or skills. Demographics refer to physical and observable characteristics of the individual such as sex, ethnicity, and age. Personality traits include umbrella traits such as the Big Five, as well as self-concept traits such as goal orientation, general self-efficacy, self-esteem, and locus of control. Values and interests include career orientation, vocational interests, and education.

We suggest that the impact of individual differences on training outcomes is transmitted through intervening process mechanisms. Snow

(1998) argued that process explanations of aptitude theory were perhaps the most important issue underlying theory-oriented aptitude research. Similarly, despite some progress, several authors have noted recently that more work is needed to identify the connections between training design, trainee characteristics, and learning processes and outcomes (e.g., Bell & Kozlowski, 2008; Debowski, Wood, & Bandura, 2001; Gully, Payne, Koles, & Whiteman, 2002; Heimbeck, Frese, Sonnentag, & Keith, 2003; Keith & Frese, 2005; Kozlowski & Bell, 2006).

We propose that intervening mechanisms include (a) information-processing capacity, (b) attentional focus and metacognitive processing, (c) motivation and effort allocation, and (d) emotional regulation and control. Thus, training outcomes are determined by a combination of mechanisms that influence how people process information, focus their attention, direct their effort, and manage their affect during learning (Ackerman & Kanfer, 2004; Ackerman, Kanfer, & Goff, 1995; Kanfer, Ackerman, & Heggestad, 1996; Kozlowski, Toney, et al., 2001). These are consistent with other models of self-regulation that emphasize the roles of self-monitoring, self-evaluation, and self-reaction in the reallocation of attention and effort to move closer toward goal accomplishment (Ackerman & Kanfer; Bandura, 1997; Kanfer & Ackerman, 1989). Chapters by Beier and Kanfer and by Bell and Kozlowski (this volume) consider the roles of self-regulatory mechanisms in learning more fully. We will briefly review them here, but our main focus is on reviewing the influences of various individual differences on learning outcomes and mechanisms.

First, *information-processing capacity* involves the manner in which individuals process and organize information during learning. It is often argued that general intelligence, or *g*, influences information-processing capacity and, as a result, is a key determinant of training outcomes (Ree, Carretta, & Teachout, 1995). Information-processing capacity also helps explain differences between experts and novices on task learning and performance, as experts process and organize information more efficiently and accurately than novices (Chase & Simon, 1973; Chi, Glaser, & Rees, 1982). Age also explains differences in information-processing capacity. As noted by Kanfer and Ackerman (2004), relative to younger adults, older adults tend to have access to a wider amount and variety of information (i.e., greater crystallized intelligence, or *gc*), but are also less able to process novel information quickly (i.e., lower fluid intelligence, or *gf*). Clearly, individuals vary in the manner in which they process information, and the effects of individual differences such as ability, task experience, and age are likely to occur in part through differences in information-processing capabilities.

A second intervening mechanism includes *attentional focus and metacognitive processing*. Attentional focus refers to the cognitive resources engaged and applied to particular aspects of the task or task environment.

For example, trainees can focus on learning declarative knowledge or procedural knowledge, or they can engage in off-task ruminations about their abilities (or lack thereof). These different types of attentional focus redirect cognitive capabilities, which can impede or enhance the acquisition of task-related knowledge or skills (Kanfer & Ackerman, 1989). A related concept is *metacognition*, which refers to planning, monitoring, and revising goal-appropriate behaviors and self-monitoring of one's cognitive functions (Brown, Bransford, Ferrara, & Campione, 1983; Cannon-Bowers, Rhodenizer, Salas, & Bowers, 1998). Attentional focus and metacognitive processing are distinguished from information processing because they highlight what trainees attend to rather than how they process information. Trainees are not passive recipients of training interventions. Instead, trainees actively engage in or disengage from the training environment and alter what they attend to and what they plan to do before, during, and after the training experience (e.g., Kozlowski & Bell, 2006). This enables learners to become active in their learning rather than merely being passive recipients of instruction. Individuals with greater metacognitive skills learn more effectively because they are better able to monitor their progress, identify problems, and adjust their learning approach dynamically (Ford et al., 1998).

A third intervening mechanism is *motivation and effort allocation*. Training motivation can be conceptualized as the direction, effort, intensity, and persistence that trainees apply to learning-oriented activities before, during, and after training (Kanfer, 1990; Tannenbaum & Yukl, 1992). Research has repeatedly demonstrated the potent effects of motivation and effort allocation on learning, retention, and application of knowledge and skills (Baldwin & Ford, 1988; Colquitt et al., 2000; Kanfer & Ackerman, 1989; Martocchio & Webster, 1992; Mathieu, Tannenbaum, & Salas, 1992; Noe, 1986; Phillips & Gully, 1997; Quiñones, 1995; Tannenbaum & Yukl). Self-efficacy is a key factor influencing motivation. Salas and Cannon-Bowers (2001) noted that self-efficacy consistently leads to more positive training outcomes (Mathieu, Martineau, & Tannenbaum, 1993; Martocchio, 1994; Martocchio & Webster, 1992; Quiñones; Stevens & Gist, 1997).

A fourth intervening mechanism is *emotional regulation and control*. This refers to the use of emotional regulatory processes to control anxiety and other negative emotional reactions during task engagement and learning and to the generation of positive emotional reactions during and after training (Kanfer et al., 1996; Kanfer & Heggestad, 1997). Research supports the notion that emotional control is an important intervening mechanism. Negative emotions, such as anxiety and frustration, are distracting, diverting attentional resources from on-task activities and making learning difficult, especially in the early stages of training when cognitive demands are high (Kanfer et al., 1996). Anxiety results in diminished learning, training performance, and other training outcomes (e.g., Chen et al., 2000;

Colquitt et al., 2000; Martocchio, 1994; Webster & Martocchio, 1993). Keith and Frese (2005) found that emotion control, along with metacognition, mediated the effects of different types of error management training on performance outcomes. Although relatively unstudied, it is also possible that emotional regulation and control are necessary to manage distracting positive emotions.

In sum, we suggest that the entire set of intervening mechanisms captures most of the ways through which individual differences and treatments are likely to influence training outcomes (Ackerman & Kanfer, 2004; Bell & Kozlowski, 2008; Kozlowski & Bell, 2006). It also appears that some or all of these mechanisms may be equally relevant in team-training contexts (Chen, Thomas, & Wallace, 2005). Although not comprehensive, this serves as a useful starting framework for understanding when, how, and why various individual differences are likely to influence training outcomes. The next section will begin by reviewing the main effects of individual differences on training outcomes. When relevant, intervening mechanisms will be described or included.

Main Effects of Individual Differences

General Cognitive Ability

General cognitive ability, or g, is the capacity to rapidly and fluidly acquire, process, and apply information. It involves the performance of higher mental processes including reasoning, remembering, understanding, and problem solving. It has also been defined simply as the ability to learn (Hunter, 1986). It is associated with the increased ability to acquire, process, and synthesize information, allowing for more rapid acquisition, application, and generalization of knowledge to new domains. The strong association between measures of g and performance in a wide variety of task domains is one of the most consistent findings in our field (Hunter & Hunter, 1984; Ree et al., 1995). Cognitive ability is one of the most frequently examined individual difference variables in training studies.

Cognitive ability is a consistently strong predictor of learning and performance, especially on complex or challenging tasks (Hunter, 1986; Hunter & Hunter, 1984; Ree & Earles, 1991; Thomas & Mathieu, 1994). The general conclusion of both qualitative (Salas & Cannon-Bowers, 2001) and quantitative reviews (Colquitt et al., 2000) is that g matters to training success. Ackerman et al. (1995) determined that cognitive ability accounted for nearly 50% of the variance in task performance on a complex radar control simulation. Ree et al. (1995) found that ability directly influenced the development of job knowledge and influenced performance on work samples through job knowledge. Similarly, Lievens, Harris, Van Keer, and Bisqueret (2003) found cognitive ability was significantly associated with language acquisition in a cross-cultural training program in Japan. Colquitt et al. (2000) found cognitive ability was correlated with declarative knowledge ($r = .69$), skill acquisition ($r = .38$), transfer ($r = .43$), and posttraining self-efficacy ($r = .22$). Phillips and Gully (1997) and Chen et al. (2000) demonstrated that cognitive ability has influences on learning performance both directly and indirectly through motivationally related variables such as self-efficacy and goals. Clearly, cognitive ability matters in training contexts. Trainees who have high cognitive ability tend to learn more, acquire more skills, and transfer training. They also tend to be more efficacious regarding the ability to perform, and therefore have greater motivation.

Kanfer and Ackerman (1989) argued that g provides a pool of resources that can be allocated to on- and off-task cognitions, and suggested that trainees with more g can handle more off-task cognitions and demands because they have a greater pool from which to draw. An alternative school of thought proposes that people can have multiple "pools" of resources that influence their ability to perform multiple tasks simultaneously. DeShon, Brown, and Greenis (1996) found that performance on one task does not necessarily interfere with performance on a second task, supporting the idea that people don't have a single pool of resources. Although theorizing and research in this area are just beginning, most researchers agree that cognitive ability provides the basis for execution of a set of goals or strategies. As a result, cognitive ability may interact with other variables such as motivation and personality. Indeed, Yeo and Neal (2004) found that trainees' cognitive ability interacted with effort and practice to influence learning performance, such that the within-person positive relationship between effort and performance increased with practice more quickly for high-ability trainees as opposed to low-ability ones.

A limited amount of research has examined whether cognitive ability interacts with goal orientation to predict learning outcomes. Bell and Kozlowski (2002b) found that learning goal orientation (LGO) was positively related to self-efficacy and performance for high-ability individuals but unrelated or modestly negatively related to self-efficacy and performance for low-ability individuals. In contrast, performance goal orientation (PGO) was positively related to self-efficacy for high-ability individuals but negatively related for low-ability individuals, and negatively related to performance for high-ability individuals but generally unrelated for low-ability individuals.

Several conclusions can be drawn from previous findings. First, cognitive ability matters for training effectiveness. Second, cognitive ability appears to influence training outcomes through both information-processing and motivational pathways. Additionally, g may influence training outcomes by enhancing metacognition, attentional focus, and emotional regulation through the availability of resources that can be allocated to these various activities. Third, cognitive ability may interact with other individual differences to influence training outcomes. More research is needed to better establish why and when *g* promotes learning.

Cognitive ability tells only part of the story. Ackerman (1986) proposed that the effects of *g* on task performance would vary and diminish over time and that other, more specific, capabilities would become increasingly important. His research supported these hypotheses. Perceptual speed is an increasingly potent predictor of task performance as tasks became increasingly automatized, even on complex tasks. Different types of information processing occur at various stages of skill acquisition (Ackerman, 1992).

Specific Abilities, Talents, and Skills

Metacognitive and Self-Regulatory Ability

Metacognition is one's awareness of and control over cognitions (Cannon-Bowers et al., 1998; Flavell, 1979). It includes the ability to develop a plan for achieving a goal and evaluating one's effectiveness of reaching that goal. Metacognition involves planning, monitoring, and revising goal-appropriate behavior (Brown et al., 1983; Ford et al., 1998). Trainees with greater metacognitive skills should learn more effectively because they are better able to monitor their progress, identify areas requiring improvement, and adjust their learning accordingly.

Research has established that metacognition, and related processes such as self-regulation, are important determinants of learning and performance (Bell & Kozlowski, 2008; Ford et al., 1998; Kozlowski & Bell, 2006). It also appears that metacognition may be trainable and amenable to training design factors (Bell & Kozlowski, 2002a, 2002b, 2008; Dunlosky, Kubat-Silman, & Hertzog, 2003; Keith & Frese, 2005; Kozlowski & Bell; Schmidt & Ford, 2003). Radosevich, Vaidyanathan, Yeo, and Radosevich (2004) found that as LGO increased, cognitive resource allocation and cognitive self-regulation also increased. Also, goals were revised downward in response to negative performance feedback. These, and similar findings, suggest that metacognition is a flexible and malleable skill. It is also possible, however, that individuals have relatively stable differences in metacognitive ability (MCA). Metacognition is an umbrella term that subsumes awareness of self-knowledge, self-monitoring, and self-directed learning. Research in other personality and ability domains suggests that some individuals are more open to self-reflection (e.g., self-monitoring; Snyder, 1974) and have greater capacity to engage attentional resources to such activities (Kanfer & Ackerman, 1989).

Some evidence suggests that MCA contributes to learning. Veenman and Spaans (2005), using secondary school students, found that metacognitive skill outweighed intelligence as a predictor of learning. They also found that it develops alongside intellectual ability but is not fully dependent on it. Schraw and Dennison (1994) found further that MCA related to reading comprehension and test performance. Using the Motivational Strategies for Learning Questionnaire (MSLQ), Pintrich and DeGroot (1990) have found similar results, although their measure does not explicitly focus on malleable versus stable elements of MCA.

Although promising, much work remains to be done to establish whether metacognitive ability is a stable individual difference variable and, if so, whether it is distinguishable from other individual differences such as cognitive ability, openness, self-concept traits, and self-monitoring. However, initial evidence suggests that MCA is worthy of additional investigation.

Tacit Intelligence

Sternberg (1996) noted that people who do well on tests sometimes do not do as well in real-world situations, and vice versa. In response, Sternberg (1996) has proposed a "triarchy" of abilities including analytical, creative, and practical capabilities. Analytical abilities most closely resemble general cognitive ability. They are abilities that enable reasoning, processing information, and solving problems. They include abilities that are used to analyze, evaluate, judge, compare, and contrast. Creative abilities are those used to create, discover, invent, and imagine. High-creative-ability individuals can use past experiences to achieve insight and deal with new situations. They are also good at combining seemingly unrelated facts to form new ideas. Practical abilities relate to individuals' ability to select, adapt in relation to, and shape their real-world environment. It includes tacit knowledge as well as skills that are used to utilize, activate, apply, and implement. Sternberg (1996) argued that successful people are not necessarily high in all three of these abilities but can find a way to best utilize whatever pattern of abilities they may have. He also argued (Sternberg, 1996) that all of these abilities can be further developed.

There is much controversy surrounding Sternberg's ideas (e.g., Gottfredson, 2001, 2003; Sternberg, 2003), but Sternberg (2003) has conducted a number studies to attempt to further validate and support his ideas. Cianciolo et al. (2006) conducted three studies involving tacit-knowledge inventories using diverse samples. Results supported the conclusion that the new tacit-knowledge inventories were reliable and valid assessments of practical intelligence. Cianciolo et al. (2006) also argued that practical intelligence and general intelligence are not the same construct, although some overlap was found. Hedlund, Wilt, Nebel, Ashford, and Sternberg (2005) found that measures of practical intelligence, including skill-based and knowledge-based dimensions, predicted master of business administration (MBA) success inside and outside the classroom beyond the Graduate Management Admission Test (GMAT) and undergraduate grade point average (GPA). It is possible that creative, practical, and analytical intelligence provides access to different types of knowledge and engages different pathways through which learning and performance occur. Future research is necessary to further evaluate and disentangle these relationships.

Job-Specific Aptitudes

Jobs and tasks require distinct and specific sets of knowledge, skills, and abilities. There is evidence that job knowledge, job experience, and job-specific aptitudes may determine training success beyond other individual difference factors. Ackerman and Heggestad (1997) found evidence of communalities across intelligence, personality, and interests. They identified four trait–ability complexes, including social, clerical and conventional, science and math, and intellectual and cultural dimensions, that are associated with learning and career development (Ackerman, 2003; Ackerman & Beier, 2003). Hattrup and Schmitt (1990) found that job-specific aptitudes and skills such as table reading, technical reading, industrial math, and following directions were highly correlated with task performance measures for apprentices performing manufacturing tasks. Driskell, Hogan, Salas, and Hoskin (1994) found that the Armed Services Vocational Aptitude Battery (ASVAB) predicted success in naval basic electricity and electronic training. Similarly, using a sample of 891 automotive and 522 helicopter mechanics, Mayberry and Carey (1997) found that a mechanical maintenance composite of the ASVAB predicted hands-on performance, job knowledge, and training grades quite well. Additionally, job experience was important for predicting job performance. Earles and Ree (1992) examined the validity of the ASVAB for predicting grades of 88,724 U.S. Air Force recruits in 150 military technical schools. The Arithmetic Reasoning section of the ASVAB was found to be the most valid subtest. Across all jobs and within the job categories, the Electronics composite or the General composite was the most valid composite.

It seems logical that job-specific aptitudes should be strongly related to training outcomes, yet this issue is still being debated. For example, Hunter (1986) and Ree and Earles (1991) found that specific abilities provided little incremental prediction of performance or training success beyond a general ability composite. However, research and theoretical reviews suggest that specific interest and aptitude composites may be useful for understanding training and performance outcomes (Ackerman & Heggestad, 1997; Hartigan & Wigdor, 1989). It seems that in certain training contexts, job-specific abilities may contribute to the prediction of training success beyond g, but the mechanisms through which and the conditions under which it occurs have been relatively unexplored.

Job Knowledge and Work Experience

Job-specific knowledge, expertise, and work experience are not identical, but they are strongly related. As individuals acquire more work experience, they also develop more expertise and job knowledge (Schmidt, Hunter, & Outerbridge, 1986). Job knowledge is a potent predictor of training success and performance (Hunter, 1986; Ree et al., 1995; Schmidt et al., 1986). Schmidt et al. created and tested a model for predicting job performance that included cognitive ability, job knowledge, and work sample performance. They found that the effect of cognitive ability on job performance was almost completely mediated by job knowledge. Similarly, Schmidt and Hunter (1998) found that measures of job knowledge significantly increased the prediction of performance beyond measures of cognitive ability. Schmidt and Hunter also noted that too few studies investigating the relationship between job knowledge and training performance were available to include in their meta-analysis.

Ree et al. (1995) tested a causal model of the relationship between general cognitive ability and prior job knowledge on subsequent job knowledge acquisition and work sample performance during training. Participants included 3,428 U.S. Air Force officers in pilot training. Results showed that ability directly influenced the acquisition of job knowledge and indirectly influenced work sample performance through job knowledge. Prior job knowledge had little influence on subsequent job knowledge, but it directly influenced early work sample performance. Early training job knowledge influenced subsequent knowledge and work sample performance. Finally, early work sample performance strongly influenced subsequent work sample performance.

Wolf, London, Casey, and Pufahl (1995) examined the behavior and outcomes of 72 displaced engineers in a semester-long previous retraining program in technology management. They found experience interacted with career motivation to influence training outcomes. Specifically, experience was positively related to previous training behaviors for highly motivated individuals. However, low career motivation had a particularly negative effect on training behaviors for the most experienced individuals.

Expertise is likely to influence training success. Chase and Simon (1973) exposed expert and novice chess players to 25 chess pieces for 5 to 10 seconds. They then asked participants to try to recreate the placement of the pieces. When pieces were placed in meaningful patterns, experts correctly placed 90% of the pieces, whereas novices could only place 20%. However, when pieces were distributed randomly over the board, expert performance dropped to the same level as that of novices. Similar research has replicated the finding in a number of other domains (e.g., Chi et al., 1982). Experts show superior performance within their domain of expertise, but not for other areas of performance. This suggests that experts do not process and store information in the same way as do novices and that knowledge and expertise are domain specific to some degree.

These findings indicate that job knowledge, expertise, and job experience are strong determinants of performance and training success in a variety of environments. It also appears that experience may interact with other individual differences to influence training outcomes. It is therefore surprising that more research has not incorporated these variables. More research is needed to further elucidate how experience, expertise, and knowledge influence training motivation and outcomes. For example, experience and job knowledge may be negatively related to training motivation when trainees are presented with a basic training program.

Emotional Intelligence

Research on emotional intelligence (EI) has exploded, gaining such momentum that there have been concerns about faddism (Murphy & Sideman, 2006). EI is a multidimensional form of interpersonal capability that includes the ability to perceive and express emotions, to understand and use them, and to manage emotions in oneself and other people (Mayer & Salovey, 1993, 1997). Goleman (1998) defined EI as "the capacity for recognizing our own feelings and those of others, for motivating ourselves, and for managing emotions well in ourselves and in our relationships" (p. 317). He described five dimensions of EI: three personal competencies (self-awareness, self-regulation, and motivation) and two social competencies (empathy and social skills). Huy (1999) and Jordan, Ashkanasy, and Hartel (2002) made EI a central component of their theoretical frameworks. Huy suggested that emotional capabilities operate at multiple levels to influence change in organizations. Jordan and colleagues (2002) proposed that EI moderates employee emotional reactions to job insecurity and their coping with associated stresses. There is some evidence that components of EI are malleable skills that can be developed (e.g., Dulewicz & Higgs, 2004). Boyatzis, Stubbs, and Taylor (2002) suggested that EI competencies can be developed in MBA students, but not with a typical MBA curriculum.

Much controversy surrounds the notion of EI (Locke, 2005). Several have argued that its theoretical conceptualization is unclear because it is overly broad and inclusive and lacks specificity in content. It encompasses both static trait components and malleable state components. It is not clear if it is simply a learned skill or an innate capability. Also, several researchers have argued that EI is simply a surrogate for general cognitive ability and other well-established personality traits. For example, Schulte, Ree, and Carretta (2004) found a large multiple correlation between EI and gender, agreeableness, and *g*. The authors concluded that the uniqueness of EI as a construct is questionable and its potential for advancing our understanding of human performance may be limited. On the other hand, a number of studies have provided evidence for the construct validity of EI (Cote & Miners, 2006; Fox & Spector, 2000; Law, Wong, & Song, 2004; Tett & Fox, 2006; Van Rooy & Viswesvaran, 2004; Van Rooy, Viswesvaran, & Pluta, 2005). For instance, Law et al. (2004) demonstrated that EI was related to yet distinct from personality dimensions. Also, they demonstrated that various measures of EI provided incremental predictive power to the prediction of life satisfaction and job performance, even after controlling for Big Five personality dimensions.

There is also initial evidence that EI plays a role in predicting learning performance. Using a sample of secondary school students, Petrides, Frederickson, and Furnham (2004) found trait EI moderated the relationship between cognitive ability and academic performance. Additionally, those with high trait EI scores were less likely to be absent or excluded from school. Most of these trait EI effects remained after controlling for personality. Austin and colleagues (Austin, Evans, Goldwater, & Potter, 2005) examined the predictive usefulness of EI for exam performance of first-year medical students. They found EI was positively related to exam performance early in the year, but there was no association between EI and exam performance later in the year. Also, high-EI students reported more positive feelings about a communication skills exercise in the study.

It appears that, although controversies abound, EI is distinct from other ability and personality trait measures. There is some ambiguity about the degree to which EI is considered a malleable and trainable set of skills or competencies versus a stable set of personality traits or emotional abilities. EI relates to job performance, adjustments to stressful situations, and prosocial behaviors. It may interact with cognitive ability to influence learning and adjustment. There is very limited work done on the role of EI as a predictor of training outcomes. The degree to which it will demonstrate unique variance beyond other individual difference measures such as trait metacognitive ability, self-monitoring, or self-concept traits remains unknown. Previous findings suggest that EI is worthy of additional investigation as a determinant of training success.

Demographics

Demographics refer to physical and observable characteristics of trainees, including gender, ethnicity, and age. In many cases, demographics are alternative indicators of other underlying variables. For example, ethnicity and race may serve as indirect indicators of exposure to prejudice, previous job opportunities, and cultural values. Similarly, gender may serve as a proxy for interests, self-beliefs when performing traditional gender role jobs (e.g., nursing and plumbing), or differences in leadership style. Age can be an indicator of generational differences as well as differences in knowledge, work experience, and fluid or crystallized intelligence. For every demographic variable, there are a multitude of underlying explanatory variables. It is always preferable to assess the underlying causal variables, but this is not always possible. Thus, gender, ethnicity, age, and other demographic variables are worthy of study in their own right.

Gender

Gender can have a variety of effects in training and learning environments, in part by influencing motivational processes and emotional regulation. Research has shown that girls and women tend to get higher grades in high school and college (Dwyer & Johnson, 1997), yet they tend to score lower than boys and men on high-stakes tests like AP exams (Ackerman, Bowen, Beier, & Kanfer, 2001). It is difficult to reconcile these patterns unless one considers the issue of emotional regulation. Kanfer and Heggestad (1997) suggested that gender might be related to motivational traits and skills that explain observed gender-related differences. It is possible that the different patterns of performance across gender on grades and tests could be due to differences in emotional control skills. In a study of the impact of training on salary negotiation skills, Stevens, Bavetta, and Gist (1993) found that women tended to negotiate lower salaries than men following initial training, but controlling for goals eliminated this difference. After supplemental training, gender differences were reduced for self-management trainees only, and this effect appeared to occur through changes in perceived control over the negotiation. These results point to the important role of emotional control and regulation.

Similarly, gender can influence motivation through cognitive investments in learning. In a study investigating determinants of knowledge across physical sciences–technology, biology–psychology, humanities, and civics domains, Ackerman and colleagues (2001) found gender differences favoring males in test scores for most knowledge domains. Accounting for fluid intelligence (*Gf*) *and* crystallized intelligence (*Gc*) and nonability factors reduced gender differences (Ackerman et al., 2001). They argued that the results are consistent with the view that knowledge development is a result of investments in cognitive resources, and these investments seem to be at least partially influenced by gender. Ong and Lai (2006) investigated gender differences in e-learning acceptance using employees from an industrial park in Taiwan. They found that computer self-efficacy, perceived usefulness, perceived ease of use, and behavioral intentions to use e-learning were all higher for males than females. Additionally, females were more strongly influenced by perceptions of computer self-efficacy and ease of use. In a related study, Venkatesh, Morris, and Ackerman (2000) examined gender differences in the individual adoption and sustained usage of technology in the workplace. They found that men were more influenced by their attitude toward using the new technology than women, whereas women were more strongly influenced by subjective norms and perceived behavioral control. Loss of control can be interpreted as threatening and anxiety producing. Using employees of a U.S. telecom company, Zhang (2005) found women felt more anxiety about using the Internet and perceived the Internet as being less useful than did men.

These studies indicate that gender may influence training outcomes through all four intervening mechanisms. Information processing may be influenced by background knowledge and crystallized intelligence, attentional focus may be influenced by perceived control, motivation through background interests, and emotional regulation through anxiety and related trait differences. Together, these factors may be instrumental in determining training outcomes for males and females. Additionally, these effects may be pronounced in particular training contexts that highlight gender or gender-related differences such as leadership, diversity, sexual harassment, and technology. Depending on the training content and context, either males or females may exhibit superior training performance as a result of the four intervening variables.

Race, Nationality, and Ethnicity

Other than diversity training, research on the effects of race, nationality, and ethnicity on training outcomes appears relatively scarce. This is surprising given the large body of research that has established differences in cultural values (Gelfand, Erez, & Zeynep, 2007), learning-related motivations (Eaton & Dembo, 1997), test-taking performance (Chan, Schmitt, DeShon, Clause, & Delbridge, 1997; Steele, 1997), pay differences in organizations (Joshi, Liao, & Jackson, 2006), and well-being (Contrada et al., 2001). Despite the dearth of research, we may be able to extrapolate expected main effects from findings in the areas of diversity training and applicant reactions to test taking.

Kossek and Zonia (1993) and Mor Barak, Cherin, and Berkman (1998) found that White women and racial minorities reacted more favorably to the implementation of diversity training than did White men. Similarly, Chung and Gully (2004) found that previous exposure to discriminatory experiences was positively correlated with receptiveness to diversity training initiatives. These findings suggest that demographic backgrounds and multicultural experiences may influence reactions to and attitudes toward training (Kossek & Zonia; Mor Barak et al., 1998; Sanchez & Medkik, 2004). The processes through which these demographic characteristics may influence training outcomes remain relatively unexplored, but Chung and Gully (2004) provided evidence that it may occur at least in part through motivational processes related to self-efficacy, perceived utility of training, and intentions to use training content. This is consistent with the work from Eaton and Dembo (1997), which showed that the effects of ethnicity on academic performance occurred in part due to fear of failure and self-efficacy.

People from minority backgrounds are more likely to feel stress, perceive discrimination (Contrada et al., 2001), and feel threatened by stereotypes (Steele & Aronson, 1995). In the realm of test taking, they are less likely to feel tests are relevant, less likely to feel the situation is fair, and more likely to be concerned about performance. Steele (1997) argued that, due to awareness of subgroup differences on standardized tests, the administration of such tests produces a stereotype threat that creates frustration among minority test takers and correspondingly lower test scores. Additionally, this threat lowers expectations and effort, thus producing lower scores among individuals affected by the stereotype threat. Together, these factors can lead to differences in test-taking performance (Arvey, Strickland, Drauden, & Martin, 1990; Chan et al., 1997; Ployhart, Ziegert, & McFarland, 2003). Supporting these ideas, Ployhart et al. (2003) found that individual differences in perceptions of stereotype threat were related to lower perceived face validity, lower test-taking motivation, and higher anxiety. Schmit and Ryan (1997) found that African Americans were more likely to withdraw from a selection process and that comparative anxiety, motivation, and literacy scales predicted withdrawal.

It seems possible, even likely, that such effects may exist in difficult, challenging, or high-stakes training environments. A central concern in test-taking performance is the role of perceived fairness and test relevance (Schmitt & Chan, 1999). Similarly, motivation and performance may flag if training is perceived as unfair (Quiñones, 1995) or irrelevant (Alliger, Tannenbaum, Bennett, Traver, & Shotland, 1997). In situations in which the training may highlight racial differences (e.g., diversity training) or evoke stereotype threat (e.g., expert skills training with high-stakes evaluation), ethnic, racial, or national demographics are likely to influence training outcomes. This may occur not only through influences on motivational processes but also through impacts on attentional focus and emotional regulation.

Age

Using meta-analytic techniques, Waldman and Avolio (1986) found an overall positive relationship between age and job performance, whereas McEvoy and Cascio (1989) found no overall significant relationship between age and job performance. Although focused on performance, these findings have implications for the expected effects of age in training contexts. The influence of age in training environments has been studied more than most other demographic variables. Warr and Bunce (1995) found that age was negatively associated with learning scores in an open learning program for managerial skills. In a comprehensive integrative meta-analysis of training outcomes, Colquitt et al. (2000) found older trainees demonstrated lower motivation, reduced learning, and less posttraining self-efficacy in comparison to younger trainees. This evidence suggests that age has a negative relationship with learning, and part of its influence may be transmitted through motivational variables and processes.

Fluid and crystallized intelligence provide a partial resolution to these conflicting findings because they show different patterns of development as age increases (Kanfer & Ackerman, 2004). Speed of processing slows as age increases (Hertzog, 1989), so Gf is expected to go down, whereas Gc is expected to stay level or even increase (Cattell, 1987). Gc is correlated with knowledge, which is a key to effective job performance. Gf is likely to be most important on jobs requiring high levels of intense, rapid processing of information (e.g., air traffic controller), whereas Gc is likely to be relevant for jobs in a wide variety of domains (e.g., managerial positions).

Beier and Ackerman (2005) investigated learning about two topics: cardiovascular disease and xerography. They found prior knowledge to be an important determinant of learning. They also found age to be positively related to prior knowledge as a direct effect and as an indirect effect through experience and Gc. They previously found similar effects for current-events knowledge (Beier & Ackerman, 2001). Age was positively related to current-events knowledge. Moreover, Gf was a less effective predictor of knowledge levels than was Gc. Prior knowledge and Gc are important for new knowledge acquisition, and age is positively related to both. Ackerman and Beier (2006) found, in a study involving learning about financial issues, that Gc was a stronger predictor than Gf of domain knowledge prior to learning, and nonability traits added incremental predictive validity. After learning, Gf showed an increase in the prediction of domain knowledge, but the final correlation did not exceed Gc.

Theories of personality generally assume stability in traits such as conscientiousness, but emerging evidence suggests that age is related to changes in personality. In particular, agreeableness and conscientiousness seem to show increases with age, whereas extroversion, neuroticism, and openness show declines (Jones & Meredith, 1996; Warr, Miles, & Platts,

2001). As will be discussed later, conscientiousness is positively associated with a variety of work outcomes, including training performance.

Together, these findings suggest that age is positively related to important variables, including conscientiousness and *Gc*, which are strong predictors of learning. These relationships ameliorate some of the negative effects of aging that result from reductions in *Gf*. Findings are consistent with a cognitive investment theory of adult intellect, which views intellectual development as an evolving outcome of intelligence-as-process, personality, and interests, leading to *Gc* and domain-specific knowledge (Kanfer & Ackerman, 2004).

Age is clearly related to learning and training outcomes in a variety of ways, and some of its effect is transmitted through differences in information processing. However, age also appears to be negatively related to motivational variables and processes that positively relate to learning and skill development. Reed, Doty, and May (2005) found negative relationships between age and computer self-efficacy, and Zhang (2005) found age to be positively related to anxiety about using the Internet and negatively related to perceived usefulness of the Internet. Gist, Rosen, and Schwoerer (1988) examined the influence of training design and age on training outcomes for computer software skills. Although training design had separate influences, older trainees exhibited significantly lower performance than did young trainees in both modeling and tutorial training conditions.

These findings are consistent with the Colquitt et al. (2000) results indicating that age has a negative impact on important motivational processes and variables. It is likely that age is related to anxiety and other emotional regulatory variables, particularly in a complex or technologically oriented setting. Both *Gf* and *Gc* are positively related to learning and performance in training environments, but age is negatively related to *Gf*. It is possible that older trainees have concerns about their ability to rapidly process new complex information and, as a result, suffer from a variation of the stereotype threat that ethnic minorities may experience. Consistent with this view, Maurer and colleagues (Maurer, 2001; Maurer, Weiss, & Barbeite, 2003) argued that older workers may not participate in learning and development activities as much as younger workers, in part due to a decline in self-efficacy. When faced with challenging tasks, perhaps older trainees are more likely to become disengaged and have to allocate resources to managing emotions and off-task cognitions. Beliefs in one's skill adequacy influence decisions to exert and maintain effort, particularly in the face of challenges. It is possible that *Gf* and *Gc* have both direct and indirect effects on learning and performance, and part of their influence may be exerted through attentional focus, metacognition, and emotional regulation.

Hertzog (2002) argued that older adults might benefit from metacognitive training which would enhance learning strategies and knowledge acquisition. Metacognitive training could also help to reduce disruptive off-task cognitions and enhance emotional regulation. Dunlosky et al. (2003) found that training older adults to use metacognitive skills and self-regulatory strategies resulted in superior training gains.

Taken as a whole, these results suggest that although age is generally negatively related to learning and skill acquisition in a training environment, particularly for complex or technologically oriented content, age can also have positive effects on key determinants of training success. Specifically, *Gc* tends to stay flat or increase with age, and domain-specific knowledge tends to be greater. However, these positive effects tend to be offset by reduced motivation, increased off-task cognitions, and increased need for emotional regulation as older trainees deal with reduced efficacy, increased anxiety, and diminished attentional focus. Older adults may benefit from self-paced learning environments, which may allow additional time and remediation for declines in *Gf* abilities in knowledge acquisition. Additionally, trainers must consider the use of self-regulatory and metacognitive interventions to address the persistent negative effects of heightened anxiety and reduced confidence.

Personality Traits

Big Five

The Big Five is one of the more established personality frameworks, containing the dimensions of extroversion, emotional stability, agreeableness, conscientiousness, and openness to experience (Barrick & Mount, 1991). Extroversion is associated with being sociable, assertive, talkative, and energetic. Emotional stability is associated with not being anxious, depressed, angry, embarrassed, or insecure; its inverse is neuroticism. Agreeableness is associated with being polite, flexible, trusting, cooperative, forgiving, and tolerant. Conscientiousness is associated with being careful, thorough, responsible, organized, and planful. It also includes being hardworking, achievement oriented, and persistent. The final dimension, intellectence (or openness to experience), is associated with being imaginative, cultured, curious, broad-minded, and artistically sensitive.

Barrick and Mount (1991) conducted a comprehensive meta-analysis evaluating the relationship between the Big Five dimensions and job performance, including training proficiency. Extroversion ($\rho = .26$), conscientiousness ($\rho = .23$), and openness ($\rho = .25$) were relatively strongly related to training proficiency, whereas emotional stability ($\rho = .07$) and agreeableness were less strongly related ($\rho = .10$). These findings demonstrate the importance of extroversion, conscientiousness, and openness for trainee outcomes. Recent research suggests that more complicated relationships might exist. Using a flight simulator training program, Herold,

Davis, Fedor, and Parsons (2002) found a positive main effect for openness but no main effect for conscientiousness. In their meta-analysis, Colquitt et al. (2000) found conscientiousness was positively related to motivation to learn but was negatively related to skill acquisition.

Examining the intervening mechanisms helps to clarify why varying results have been observed. Dispositions influence training outcomes through attentional focus, motivation, and emotional regulation. Judge and Ilies (2002) found that emotional stability and conscientiousness were the strongest and most consistent correlates of performance motivation in their meta-analysis. Dispositions are associated with differences in proximal motivational states, self-set goals, assessments of situations, interpretations of situations, and reactions to these interpretations, including anxiety (Chen et al., 2000; Herold et al., 2002; Kanfer & Heggestad, 1997). Conscientiousness subsumes need for achievement, and conscientious individuals should set more challenging goals and be more committed to them (Barrick, Mount, & Strauss, 1993; Hollenbeck & Klein, 1987). Martocchio and Judge (1997) and Colquitt and Simmering (1998) found highly conscientious individuals were more efficacious. Martocchio and Judge suggested that previous counterintuitive results involving conscientiousness might be due to the tendency of highly conscientious individuals to be self-deceptive regarding their actual learning progress. Highly conscientious individuals might also engage in more internal self-regulatory activity (e.g., self-monitoring and self-evaluation), which detracts from their on-task attention (e.g., Kanfer & Ackerman, 1989). Supporting both points, LePine, Colquitt, and Erez (2000), using an experimental learning task, found that some aspects of conscientiousness, including dependability, order, and dutifulness, can reduce performance when adaptability to changing task conditions is important. It is possible that the subdimensions of conscientiousness, such as achievement striving and perseverance, need to be examined separately to better understand why and when conscientiousness influences training outcomes (Herold et al.).

Emotional stability can be linked to training outcomes through its potential impact on anxiety. Less stable (and more neurotic) individuals are more likely to have negative emotional reactions in training contexts, including increased anxiety. Chen et al. (2000) and Martocchio (1994) observed negative relationships between anxiety and learning outcomes. Colquitt et al.'s (2000) meta-analysis indicated that anxiety was negatively related to all training outcomes. The anxiety associated with low emotional stability may affect performance by diverting attentional focus, thus reducing the resources available for "on-task" learning (Kanfer & Ackerman, 1989; Kanfer & Heggestad, 1997). Overall, lower emotional stability may result in reductions in attention focus, less ability to engage in metacognition, and reduced motivation overall, in part through reductions in self-efficacy. Consistent with Barrick and Mount's (1991) findings, one would expect high emotional stability to be positively related to training outcomes through reductions in anxiety, enhanced attentional focus, and higher levels of motivation.

Openness to new experiences, or intellectence, is likely to be positively related to training outcomes because more open individuals are, by definition, more receptive to experiencing and learning new things. As a result, they are more likely to maintain attentional focus on learning and sustaining motivation when learning becomes challenging. Beier and Ackerman (2001) found openness to experience and self-concept were positively related to current-events knowledge. Lievens et al. (2003) found openness of European managers to be related to cross-cultural training performance in Japan. Major, Turner, and Fletcher (2006) found openness to be related to motivation to learn, which in turn was related to development activities.

Extroversion appears to be unrelated to ability (Wolf & Ackerman, 2005) and positively related to development and training outcomes (Barrick & Mount, 1991; Major et al., 2006). Extroversion may be related to training outcomes because extroverted individuals are more energetic, talkative, assertive, and sociable. Extroverted individuals may be better able to maintain an outward focus, enabling learning. Other than Web-based or computer programs, many training programs include some component of interpersonal interaction. To the degree that training and learning require social interaction, extroversion is likely to facilitate and enhance such interactions, reducing anxiety and increasing motivation to learn.

Overall, three of the Big Five personality traits appear to be reliably related to training outcomes. Evidence suggests extroversion and openness are good predictors of training success, whereas the evidence for conscientiousness appears to be mixed (e.g., Colquitt et al., 2000). It is possible that conscientiousness affects the intervening variables in countervailing ways such that it enhances motivation and persistence, but it reduces attentional focus and metacognition. Future research should clarify the effects of the Big Five and their underlying dimensions on information processing, metacognition, motivation, and emotional regulation.

Self-Concept Traits

Self-concept refers to a person's perceptions of him or herself (Ackerman, 1997; Shavelson, Hubner, & Stanton, 1976). It is formed through experience and interactions with others and through interpretations of one's environment. It is especially influenced by evaluations by significant others, reinforcements, and attributions for one's own behavior. Self-concept is "organized, multifaceted, hierarchical, stable, developmental, evaluative, and differentiable" (Shavelson et al., 1976, p. 411). Self-concept traits are related to other personality measures but contain distinct components including self-evaluation, self-worth, and self-determination that only partially overlap with other frameworks such as the Big Five. They include goal orientation, general self-efficacy, self-esteem, and locus of control.

It should be noted that recent work by Judge and colleagues (e.g., Judge & Bono, 2001) argued that general self-efficacy, self-esteem, and locus of control, together with emotional stability, capture a higher order construct, which they termed *core self-evaluations*. However, to date the majority of training-related research on self-evaluations treated these constructs separately, and, as we indicate below, there is also evidence that some core self-evaluation traits relate to learning through somewhat distinct mechanisms.

Goal Orientation

Learning goal orientation (LGO) involves a desire to increase task mastery or competence, whereas a performance goal orientation (PGO) reflects a desire to demonstrate high ability and to be positively evaluated by others (Dweck, 1986; Farr, Hofmann, & Ringenbach, 1993; Gully & Phillips, 2005; VandeWalle, 1997). Individuals high in PGO believe ability is demonstrated by outperforming others, exceeding normative standards, and achieving success with limited effort. They may also have an increased fear of failure and negative evaluations by others (VandeWalle, 1997). In contrast, learning goal–oriented individuals are interested in developing new skills, understanding and improving their work, improving their competence, and achieving task mastery based on self-referenced standards (Button, Mathieu, & Zajac, 1996; Farr et al., 1993; VandeWalle, 1997). The focus of LGO is on task mastery, including learning through experimentation and failure (Dweck, 1986). The notions of LGO and PGO originated in research on childhood learning, but the effects of LGO and PGO have been established with adults in work settings (Gully & Phillips, 2005; Martocchio, 1994; Potosky & Ramakrishna, 2002). In a recent meta-analysis, Payne, Youngcourt, and Beaubien (2007) determined LGO and PGO were relatively uncorrelated with each other and uncorrelated with ability. LGO was moderately correlated with conscientiousness, openness, and self-esteem, whereas PGO was not.

LGO and PGO have been found to be related to a number of processes and outcomes relevant to training contexts. Goal orientations influence perceptions of task complexity (Mangos & Steele-Johnson, 2001). High LGO has been positively related to feedback seeking (Payne et al., 2007; VandeWalle & Cummings, 1997; VandeWalle, Ganesan, Challagalla, & Brown, 2000), complex learning strategies (Fisher & Ford, 1998; Payne et al., 2007), and adaptive performance (Kozlowski, Gully, et al., 2001). Higher LGO individuals make greater use of metacognitive strategies

(Ford et al., 1998), have greater motivation to learn (Colquitt & Simmering, 1998), and set higher goals, including those for development (Brett & VandeWalle, 1999; Phillips & Gully, 1997). The increased motivation of high-LGO individuals may be due in part to greater self-efficacy (Bell & Kozlowski, 2002b; Kozlowski, Gully, et al., 2001; Phillips & Gully, 1997; Potosky & Ramakrishna, 2002). Self-efficacy, in turn, positively influences goals and performance even after controlling for ability (Chen et al., 2000; Kozlowski, Gully, et al., 2001; Phillips & Gully, 1997; Potosky & Ramakrishna, 2002). These relationships generally result in greater levels of learning, knowledge development, skill acquisition, and performance (e.g., Bell & Kozlowski, 2002b). However, negative effects of LGO on learning have also been found (Brown, 2001).

In general, LGO is associated with positive learning and training outcomes. Higher LGO individuals maintain attentional focus, engage in more metacognition, sustain motivation, have higher self-efficacy, and have less anxiety than those lower in LGO. Learning-oriented individuals like high-effort experiences, which characterize most novel situations. Learning-oriented individuals welcome opportunities to develop new skills, understand and improve their work, and improve their level of competence (Farr et al., 1993).

People high in PGO have been found to choose less subjectively difficult and challenging tasks and to not choose those that might threaten their perceived level of normative competence, whereas people high in LGO are more likely to choose subjectively difficult tasks and to persist in the tasks they choose (Farr et al., 1993; Gully & Phillips, 2005). High-PGO individuals, particularly those with a fear of failure, are less likely to seek feedback (Payne et al., 2007; VandeWalle & Cummings, 1997) and have lower motivation to learn (Colquitt & Simmering, 1998). PGO may reduce motivation because it can be negatively related to self-efficacy, especially when fear of failure is high (Payne et al., 2007; Phillips & Gully, 1997). It increases anxiety, which also reduces self-efficacy (Chen et al., 2000). However, Hofmann (1993) found that having high PGO was not necessarily dysfunctional. PGO was positively related to performance, but it was also positively related to task-related cognitive interference, which was negatively related to performance. Thus, PGO had countervailing effects on performance.

It appears that LGO and PGO have important effects on outcomes relevant to training contexts. LGO generally results in more positive training outcomes, whereas PGO is either unrelated or negatively related to training outcomes. In particular, PGO, with a focus on avoidance of failure, appears to result in greater anxiety, lower efficacy, and less feedback seeking. These results indicate that understanding the intervening mechanisms will allow better prediction of how LGO and PGO influence training. It should also be noted that patterns found in U.S. and Western samples may not immediately generalize to other cultures. Lee, Tinsley, and Bobko (2003) found that although U.S. college students consider LGO and PGO as distinguishable concepts, students in Hong Kong do not distinguish them as much (r = .71).

General Self-Efficacy and Self-Esteem

General self-efficacy (GSE) is considered a stable trait-like construct that captures the generality dimension of self-efficacy (Chen, Gully, & Eden, 2001). GSE is defined as "one's belief in one's overall competence to effect requisite performances across a wide variety of achievement situations" (Eden, 2001, p. 75). It is a self-evaluation of one's fundamental ability to cope, perform, and be successful (Judge & Bono, 2001). GSE is more stable and resistant to the influences of such factors as past performance and vicarious experience than self-efficacy (Chen et al., 2001), and is somewhat distinct from global self-esteem (Chen, Gully, & Eden, 2004). *Global self-esteem* refers to one's feelings of self-worth and an individual's liking or disliking of him or herself (Brockner, 1988; Chen et al., 2004). Self-esteem is a general construct that captures affective components of self-evaluation (Betz & Klein, 1996; Brown, 1998; Gardner & Pierce, 1998). Research by Chen et al. (2004) suggested that GSE is relatively more strongly related to motivational mechanisms such as specific self-efficacy, self-set goals, and effort allocation, whereas self-esteem is relatively more strongly related to emotional mechanisms, such as state anxiety and emotion regulation.

Chen et al. (2000) conducted two field studies in an academic setting to test a model incorporating stable individual differences such as cognitive ability, GSE, and goal orientation. They found that, after controlling for ability and goal orientation, GSE related to learning performance primarily through task-specific self-efficacy and self-set goals. These relationships suggest that GSE is a useful self-evaluation construct for understanding learning and training effectiveness. It also appears that GSE may influence training outcomes by affecting motivational regulation, such as effort allocation, metacognitive processes, self-efficacy, and self-set goals (Chen et al., 2004). Although there is ample opportunity to further illuminate how GSE operates in training contexts, there is sufficient research to suggest that it is an important variable for understanding training outcomes. Finally, there is more limited research on self-esteem in training environments. However, research shows that self-esteem is related to job performance (Judge & Bono, 2001) and can operate to influence learning through emotion regulation and state anxiety (Chen et al., 2004). This work suggests that emotional regulation is a key pathway through which self-esteem may influence learning.

Locus of Control

Locus is another traitlike self-evaluation characteristic, which reflects the degree to which one generally perceives events to be under his or her control (internal locus) or under the control of others (external locus; Rotter, 1990). An external locus of control is related to passivity and learned helplessness (Rotter, 1992), and an internal locus has been positively related to self-efficacy (Phillips & Gully, 1997). Research supports the notion that locus is an important determinant of training outcomes. Noe (1986) argued that trainees with a greater internal locus of control would have more positive attitudes toward training because they believe training is more likely to be useful and beneficial. Noe and Schmitt (1986) tested and supported this hypothesis. Phillips and Gully found internal locus to be positively related to self-efficacy, whereas Silver, Mitchell, and Gist (1995) found internal locus was more strongly related to skill acquisition than to pretraining self-efficacy. Colquitt et al. (2000) found internal locus was strongly related to motivation to learn, whereas external locus was moderately related to declarative knowledge and transfer.

These findings suggest that locus is an important determinant of training outcomes, but the effects of locus may be mixed (Colquitt et al., 2000). It is possible that inconsistencies in observed patterns are due to countervailing effects of the intervening mechanisms. Specifically, although internal-locus trainees have higher motivation, it is also possible that they are more internally focused, reducing the usefulness of a given training program.

Interests, Values, and Styles

Interests, values, and styles include a wide variety of general individual difference variables that capture involvement, valuation, and a generalized approach toward careers, jobs, learning preferences, and vocational interests. They include career orientation, vocational interests, and cognitive style. Surprisingly, we did not find much research on training outcomes in these areas. Even in the broad and inclusive area of vocational interests, over 50 years of published studies suggest that theory-based hypothesis testing may be relatively rare (Hogan & Blake, 1999).

Vocational and Career Interests

Colquitt et al. (2000) found career-related variables such as job involvement, organizational commitment, career planning, and career exploration were related to a variety of training outcomes. Holland (1997) proposed a six-dimensional vocational model with six dimensions that represent characteristics of the work environment, personality traits, and interests of working people. These dimensions are realistic (building, practical, hands-on, tool oriented, and physical), investigative (analyzing, intellectual, and scientific), artistic (creating, original, independent, and chaotic), social (supporting, helping, cooperative, and healing), enterprising (persuading, leadership, and competitive), and conventional (detail oriented, organizing, and clerical). Gottfredson (1980) found support for the validity of Holland's occupational typology for describing work activities, general training requirements, and rewards.

Holland (1997) viewed vocational interests as an expression of personality. It appears that there is some overlap between the six dimensions and other personality frameworks such as the Big Five (Hogan & Blake, 1999). Given the pervasive effects of personality on learning, motivation, and performance, it seems reasonable to expect that vocational interests may have similar effects. In particular, Hogan and Hogan (1991) reviewed the literature on personality, vocational interests, and occupational performance. They found that the pattern of personality variables associated with occupational success depends on the occupation as organized by Holland's framework. Success in artistic occupations depends on high scores for openness along with low scores for conscientiousness. Success in conventional occupations depends on low scores for openness and high scores for conscientiousness. Blake and Sackett (1999) found distinctive patterns associating the Big Five and Holland's typology.

It seems logical that interests in a particular area would lead to more positive training outcomes by enhancing attentional focus and increasing motivation. This is some evidence to support the notion that interests, values, and styles may matter to training outcomes. Gellatly, Paunonen, Meyer, Jackson, and Goffin (1991) found that measures of vocational interest predicted several performance criteria, including effectiveness in training. Ralston, Borgen, Rottinghaus, and Donnay (2004) found that basic interest scales of the Strong Interest Inventory (a vocational interest scale) predicted choice of major field of education or training beyond measures of the six Holland themes.

Ackerman and colleagues (Ackerman & Beier, 2003; Ackerman & Heggestad, 1997) found a small set of trait complexes to be differentially related to career choices and adult intellectual development. Distinguishing between intelligence as maximal performance and intelligence as typical performance, Ackerman and Heggestad (1967) reviewed theories of personality, intelligence, and interest. They identified relationships across personality constructs, vocational interests, and intellectual interests that provided a basis for conducting a meta-analysis. Findings indicate that personality, intelligence, and interests focus on four key trait complexes: social, clerical and conventional, science and math, and intellectual and cultural. These four complexes result from the development of abilities through the investment of cognitive effort as a result of personality. As abilities are developed, interests evolve.

The implications of these results for training outcomes seem clear. Individuals who are interested in, and have vocational aptitude for, a particular career are more likely to maintain motivation and attentional focus in training relevant to their career. Research on personality suggests that it operates to influence more proximal processes and states to influence learning and training outcomes. Given the observed overlap between personality, ability, and interests, it seems reasonable to expect that vocational interests will have similar effects, although they may be more pronounced. Interests are associated with abilities in a given area, so they may also influence information processing in training environments. More interested individuals should process content more effectively.

Learning or Cognitive Style

Learning styles or *cognitive styles* refer to individuals' differences and preferences in how they process information when problem solving, learning, or engaging in other similar activities (Liu & Ginther, 1999; Robertson, 1985; Sadler-Smith, 1997; Sternberg & Zhang, 2001; Zhang & Sternberg, 2006). There are numerous typologies, measures, and models that capture these differences and preferences (Sternberg & Zhang, 2001). Most of these approaches have focused on child learning, but there is evidence that these differences are important for adults as well (Sternberg & Zhang, 2001). First, field independence or dependence (FID; Witkin, 1979) involves the ability to distinguish key elements from confusing or distracting backgrounds, particularly visual ones. High-field-independent people see objects as distinctly separate from their environment and are better able to develop and manage cognitive restructuring skills. However, they seem less able to develop and manage interpersonal skills. In contrast, high-field-dependent individuals see their surroundings in a global context and are often incapable of disconnecting specific objects from their environment. They are better able to develop and manage interpersonal skills but less able to develop and manage cognitive restructuring skills. Witkin, Moore, Goodenough, and Cox (1977) found high-field-independent people were more intrinsically motivated and preferred individualized learning. Field-dependent people were more extrinsically motivated and preferred cooperative learning.

In a second approach, Riding and Cheema (1991) suggested that most of the previous work on learning styles has focused on two important dimensions: (a) holist versus analyst, and (b) verbalizer versus imager. Holists look at a situation in its entirety, whereas analysts will focus on one or two aspects at a time and see a situation as a collection of separate elements (Liu & Ginther, 1999). Intermediates blend both. *Verbalizer* and *imager* refer to the modality in which information is presented. They are also associated with attentional focus. Imagers tend to be internal and passive, whereas verbalizers tend to be external and stimulated (Liu & Ginther, 1999; Riding & Cheema; Sadler-Smith, 1997).

A third approach has been to focus on preference for sensory modality. According to Bissell, White, and Zivin (1971), a sensory modality is a system that interacts with the environment through one of the basic senses. The most important sensory modalities are visual (learning by seeing), auditory (learning by hearing), and kinesthetic (learning by doing). According to Dunn and Dunn (1979), about 20–30% of American students are auditory; about 40% are visual; and the remaining 30–40% are either tactual-kinesthetic, visual-tactual, or some combinations of the above major senses. There is also the reading and writing modality (learning by processing text) that is sometimes included in sensory modality.

The fourth approach, the Kolb Learning Style Inventory, is one of the more dominant approaches to categorizing cognitive styles (Tennant, 1988). Kolb's model has been found to be effective in some language-teaching activities (Kolb, 1984). According to Kolb, the four basic learning modes are defined as active experimentation (AE), reflective observation (RO), concrete experience (CE), and abstract conceptualization (AC). In addition, the learning process is considered from two dimensions: active-passive and concrete-abstract.

Kolb (1984) argued that there are four basic learning styles: converger, diverger, assimilator, and accommodator. Convergers depend primarily on active experimentation and abstract conceptualization to learn. People with this style are superior in technical tasks and problems and inferior in social and interpersonal matters. Divergers depend primarily on concrete experience and reflective observation. People with this style tend to organize concrete situations from different perspectives and to structure their relationships into a meaningful whole. They are superior in generating alternative hypotheses and ideas, and tend to be imaginative, and people or feeling oriented. Assimilators depend on abstract conceptualization and reflective observation. These individuals tend to be more concerned about abstract concepts and ideas, and less concerned about people. However, they also tend to focus on the logical soundness and preciseness of the ideas, rather than their practical values; they tend to choose to work in research and planning units. Finally, accommodators rely mainly on active experimentation and concrete experience, and focus on risk taking, opportunity seeking, and action. People with an accommodator style tend to deal with people easily; they tend to specialize in action-oriented jobs, such as marketing and sales. According to Kolb, the above patterns connected with these four basic learning styles are exhibited consistently at various levels of behavior, from personality type to some specific task-oriented skills and performance, such as professional career and current job role.

Although much has been written about cognitive styles, there are many gaps in our current understanding. First, there are many differences in how styles are conceptualized (Cassidy, 2004; Dunn, DeBello, Brennan, Krimsky, & Murrain, 1981). Second, there have been numerous criticisms of the measures and the underlying theory (Towler & Dipboye, 2003). Many of the measures are ipsative in nature, causing a variety of statistical and inferential problems, and many show low reliability (e.g., Duff & Duffy, 2002; Newstead, 1992; Wilson, 1986). Third, most research has focused on children. Less work has focused on how cognitive styles influence adult learning. Fourth, it remains unclear how and when cognitive styles will predict training outcomes beyond personality, self-concept traits, and ability. Fifth, very little research on cognitive styles has been applied to training settings. This may be due in part to the limited availability of high-quality measures.

Despite these concerns and limitations, evidence suggests that cognitive and learning styles may be important for understanding human behavior and performance in a variety of contexts, including adult learning contexts (Anis, Armstrong, & Zhul, 2004; Sternberg & Zhang, 2001; Zhang & Sternberg, 2006). Jamieson (1992) found, using a sample of 46 adult international students of an English as a Second Language program, that field independence was related to a high score on all language measures. Using a sample of adult undergraduates enrolled in a management course, Liegle and Janicki (2006) found that learning style predicted behaviors in a Web-based learning system. Learners classified as *Explorers* tended to "jump" more and created their own path of learning (learner control), whereas subjects classified as *Observers* tended to follow the suggested path by clicking on the Next button (system control). In addition, test scores for explorers who did jump around were higher than for explorers who did not jump, whereas, conversely, observers who did not jump scored higher than observers who did jump. Using 165 employees from a large U.S. financial institution, Buch and Bartley (2002) found learning style, as measured by the Kolb learning style instrument, predicted preference for training delivery mode. Convergers showed a stronger preference for computer-based delivery, and assimilators showed a stronger preference for print-based delivery. Results also revealed an overall preference for classroom-based delivery regardless of learning style.

Towler and Dipboye (2003) developed the learning style orientation measure to address some of the concerns noted earlier. Specifically, they began with a critical incidents methodology to identify key styles and preferences for learning. They then validated their measure using two samples and demonstrated that learning style orientations (LSOs) predicted preferences for instructional methods beyond the Big Five. They identified five key factors: discovery learning, which is an inclination for exploration during learning; experiential learning, which is a desire for hands-on approaches to instruction; observational learning, which indicates preference for external stimuli such as demonstrations and diagrams to help facilitate learning; structured learning, which is a preference for processing strategies such as taking notes, writing down task steps, and so forth; and group learning, which involves a preference to work with others while learning. Future research should further explore the relationship of LSOs to training outcomes in employee contexts.

Despite the tremendous amount of work in the area, research in the area of individual differences in cognitive and learning style preferences seems ripe for new ideas, theoretical frameworks, and measures. Currently, there is incredible breadth in the approaches used to capture cognitive style, but very little work has applied it to better understanding training effectiveness in adult contexts. Additionally, the work is fragmented, and problems with measurement abound. It seems likely that cognitive styles will influence all of the proposed intervening mechanisms, including information processing, metacognition, motivation, and emotional regulation. It is particularly important to consider these issues as training systems become more Web-based, and potentially more reliant on metacognitive and motivational processes of the trainee.

Attribute–Treatment Interactions (ATIs)

The preceding section examined the main and interacting effects of individual differences on training outcomes and related intervening mechanisms. A more limited amount of research has examined how individual differences interact with treatments to influence training effectiveness. We first provide a historical perspective on the issue of attribute– or aptitude–treatment interactions (ATIs). We also broaden the notion of ATIs to include general attributes of trainees. Next, we define *treatment* to include training design factors as well as contextual characteristics of the training environment. Finally, we review empirical evidence on ATIs, with a particular focus on intervening mechanisms and training outcomes.

History of ATIs

Lee Cronbach's famous 1957 American Psychological Association presidential address was one of the first clear calls for investigations of how individual differences might interact with treatments to influence learning outcomes. He argued that researchers were segmented into two distinct groups, experimenters and correlators (Cronbach, 1957). Experimenters were interested in the variation they themselves created, whereas correlators were interested in the already existing variation between individuals and groups. Cronbach called for the integration of correlational and experimental disciplines using the concept of ATIs. He saw a future in which we would ultimately design treatments to fit groups of individuals with particular aptitude patterns rather than focus on fitting the average individual. Cronbach also suggested we should seek out the aptitudes that differentially responded to (or interacted with) modifiable aspects of a given treatment. He felt that unless one treatment was clearly best for everyone, treatments should be differentiated in such a way as to maximize their interaction with aptitudes (Cronbach).

Cronbach and his colleague, Snow, used a broad definition of *aptitudes* to include cognitive, affective, and conative characteristics. Snow (1991) stated that aptitudes "should refer to any measurable person characteristic hypothesized to be propaedeutic to successful goal achievement in the treatment(s) studied; propaedeutic means needed as preparation for response to treatment" (p. 205). According to this view, an aptitude is a complex set of personal characteristics identified before and during treatment that accounts for a person's outcomes from a particular treatment. This usage of the term is not limited to intelligence or some fixed list of differential abilities (Kyllonen & Lajoie, 2003). It includes personality and motivational differences along with styles, attitudes, and beliefs.

During the 1960s and 1970s, Cronbach and colleagues (Cronbach & Snow, 1977) searched intensely for ATIs using a variety of aptitudes and instructional treatments. They were looking for evidence that showed regression slopes predicting outcomes using aptitudes varied from one treatment to another. For example, they searched for ATIs by assigning people who had low spatial ability and high verbal ability to one treatment and people with the opposite set of aptitudes to another treatment. The treatments were designed to optimize learning for a particular set of aptitudes. They found limited evidence for ATI effects across multiple studies. A spatial pretest, for example, inconsistently predicted outcomes from instruction filled with diagrams (Cronbach, 1989; Shavelson, 2003). Successive studies employing the same treatment variable found different relationships between aptitude and outcomes. Cronbach surmised that the inconsistency came from unidentified interactions. Cronbach (1975) eventually revisited his presidential address and stated that ATIs were far more complex, rapidly changing, and context bound than he had imagined. He was less sure that general principles or guidelines about instructional design could be identified. He concluded that "troubles do not arise because human events are in principle unlawful … the trouble, as I see it, is that we cannot store up generalizations and constructs for ultimate assembly into a network" (Cronbach, 1975, p. 123).

Despite these challenges, some consistent patterns were found. The strongest ATIs involved general ability (Cronbach & Snow, 1977). Students with above average ability benefited more from instruction that provided them with opportunities to have responsibility and control over their learning experience than those with below average ability, whereas lower ability students seemed to profit more from highly structured learning environments. Also, some evidence showed that learning outcomes were better when the instructor's presentation was adapted to student aptitude and personality (Cronbach & Snow, 1977). According to Snow (1989, 1991), the best instruction involves treatments that differ in structure and completeness in conjunction with an appreciation of the high or low ability of students. Highly structured treatments (e.g., high external control, and/or explicit sequences and components) seem to help students with low ability but hinder those with high abilities (relative to low-structure treatments). Similar effects were found when the effects of high and low structure in instructional treatments were contrasted using test anxiety as aptitude. Highly anxious students demonstrate better performance with externally imposed structure but perform less effectively with low structure.

Our review that follows builds on the theoretical framework formulated by Cronbach and Snow (1977), but it has several distinguishing characteristics. First, we specifically focus on training and learning outcomes of adult learners. Second, we are particularly interested in processes and outcomes relevant to work environments so our conceptualization of treatments explicitly includes organizational contextual effects such as transfer climate and supervisory attitudes. Third, we are focused on stable individual differences, not malleable ones. This is distinct from how Cronbach and Snow defined aptitudes. Fourth, despite Cronbach and Snow's broad definition of the term, *aptitude* is often construed as being synonymous with ability. We include ability, but we also focus on other characteristics such as personality, gender, and other demographics. To highlight these differences, we prefer to use the term *attribute* rather than *aptitude* to indicate that we are focused on broad and stable features of trainees.

The concept of attribute–treatment interaction is based on the notion that some instructional strategies, training designs, delivery systems, and contexts (treatments) are more or less effective for particular individuals depending upon their specific characteristics. As a theoretical framework, ATI proposes that optimal training outcomes result when trainees exhibit maximal fit with the training environment (which includes content, delivery, and context). This is much like the person–environment fit research that suggests optimal individual and organizational outcomes occur when employees fit the job, unit, and organization in supplementary and complementary ways (Cable & Edwards, 2004; Edwards, Cable, Williamson, Lambert, & Shipp, 2006).

Treatments

There are numerous kinds of treatments that exist in a training system. Treatments include aspects of content, training design, goals, feedback, delivery systems, leadership support, rewards, and climate of the transfer environment. Also, the social structure of the training system is of interest as well. Delivering training to groups involves different processes and systems from delivering to individuals. These issues are covered in more detail in the chapters by Cannon-Bowers and Bowers, Mathieu and Tesluk, Cooke and Fiore, and Mayer in this volume. Here, we highlight several key findings that set the stage for discussing ATIs in the next section.

Training Content, Goals, and Feedback

The content, goals, and feedback of training will affect the information processing, attentional focus, metacognition, motivation, and emotional responses of trainees (e.g., Mathieu et al., 1992). Content alone, like diversity training, can engage these processes (Chung & Gully, 2004). Additionally, the nature of the goals and feedback provided will influence self-regulation. Kozlowski and Bell (2006), for instance, used a complex computer-based simulation to examine the effects of goal frame, goal content, and goal proximity on self-regulatory activities of 524 trainees. Results indicated that all three had a significant effect on self-regulation, with goal content exhibiting the greatest influence. Similarly, research by Frese et al. (1991) and Keith and Frese (2005) demonstrated that the framing of errors influences regulation. When errors are framed as a natural, instructive part of the learning process and performance evaluation is deemphasized, individuals are more likely to adopt a mastery orientation (Ivancic & Hesketh, 1995–1996). In contrast, telling trainees to avoid errors and framing them negatively create regulatory processes that detract from learning (Frese et al., 1991; Keith & Frese, 2005). As described in Bell and Kozlowski (2008), Kanfer and Ackerman (1990) showed that trainees given emotion control instructions reported less negative affect and higher levels of performance. These effects were most apparent early, when attentional demands were greatest and trainees most likely to fail. Kozlowski, Gully et al. (2001) demonstrated that mastery and performance goals engaged different regulatory processes and learning outcomes. These, and related findings, demonstrate that training content, goals, instructions, and feedback affect the intervening mechanisms.

Design Approaches

There are numerous approaches that can be considered during the design of training. For example, repetitive exposure to content can yield overlearning and skill automaticity (Arthur et al., 1998). Also, training can be sequenced from simple to more complex components. The usefulness of both approaches may depend on the expertise and experience of the trainees. Some training approaches provide learners with a great deal of control or allow trainees to engage in discovery learning. Training design features have been shown to be related to training effectiveness criteria (Arthur, Bennett, Edens, & Bell, 2003). The effectiveness of these approaches will be contingent on the ability of trainees to effectively manage self-regulation, process information in an unstructured setting, and remain open to new ideas or approaches to learning (see Arthur et al., 2003, for a meta-analytic review of training design features).

Training Context

The training context includes a broad set of factors including reward and feedback systems, climate in the work unit and organization, leadership support, and general social environment. In one of the earliest studies that examined climate and skill development, Kozlowski and Hults (1987) assessed the effect of an organizational climate that supported technical updating using 447 engineers and 218 supervisors. They found a climate that supported skills updating was related to supervisory ratings of technical performance, updating orientation, and skills. Leadership support, organizational support, feedback, rewards, and resources were important variables that contributed to a climate of support for skills updating. Additionally, Kozlowski and Doherty (1989) found that leaders play a critical role in the development of perceptions of unit and organizational climate.

Baldwin and Ford (1988) argued that characteristics of the work environment such as leader and peer support, situational constraints, and opportunities to use knowledge and skills would influence transfer. Research has supported some of these connections. Mathieu and colleagues (1992, 1993) found that situational constraints can reduce training outcomes or impede transfer. Rouiller and Goldstein (1993) investigated the effect of climate on training transfer in a chain of fast-food restaurants. The transfer climate included situational cues that reminded trainees of their training or provided them with opportunities to use their training and consequences that supported or rewarded transfer. They demonstrated that organizational climate significantly predicted whether trainees transferred learned skills. Tracey, Tannenbaum, and Kavanagh (1995) replicated and extended Rouiller and Goldstein's work. They showed that organizational climate and culture were directly related to posttraining behaviors. Using data collected in supermarkets, Tracey et al. (1995) found continuous-learning culture and transfer climate were related to posttraining behaviors, even after controlling for pretraining performance and knowledge. More recently, Tracey and Tews (2005) provided evidence that a measure of general training climate is related to important training outcomes. Colquitt et al. (2000) found evidence for both direct and indirect effects of transfer climate on transfer.

Contextual effects are not limited to posttraining environments. Pretraining factors can affect training outcomes (Mathieu & Martineau, 1997; Webster & Martocchio, 1995). For example, Tracey, Hinkin, Tannenbaum, and Mathieu (2001) found work environment characteristics related positively to both pretraining efficacy and motivation, as well as other outcomes. Similarly, Quiñones (1995) showed that framing training as advanced or remedial affected motivation and learning, and Martocchio (1992) showed that labeling the training assignment as an "opportunity" had similar effects. Previous experiences with training (e.g., prior negative events) also affect learning and retention (see Salas & Cannon-Bowers, 2001). Chung and Gully (2004) demonstrated that pretraining backgrounds and demographics can affect pretraining efficacy, motivations, and intentions to transfer. These findings, and others, are supportive of the important role that the pretraining context plays, but Salas and Cannon-Bowers (2001) pointed out that much more work is needed in this area.

Several points can be gleaned from this discussion. First, organizational factors clearly influence learning processes and training outcomes, including transfer. Second, leadership and peer support are crucial for enhancing transfer. Third, aspects of the human resource management system, such as feedback and rewards, are likely to influence the development of a training or transfer climate. Prior work on training design features and situational characteristics sets the foundation for understanding how and what treatments may interact with individual differences to affect training outcomes.

ATI Findings

The most surprising thing about previous research on ATIs is how little work has been done (Campbell & Kuncel, 2002). Theory and research support the idea that individual characteristics are likely to interact with various aspects of the training system. Anyone who has ever taught a class has experienced the effect of ATIs. It is common to see completely different reactions and learning by some subset of students even given the exact same stimuli (instructor, materials, and delivery). This section will briefly review the empirical findings related to ATIs.

Demographics

Environments in which trainees have control may exhibit differential effects for males and females, depending on training content. Gray (1987) found no performance differences for gender in learning control environments, but some researchers have found gender differences in preferences for learner control (DeRouin, Fritzsche, & Salas 2005a; Hintze, Mohr, & Wenzel, 1988; Ross, Morrison, & O'Dell, 1989). Using a sample of dental students, Hintze et al. (1988) found males preferred learner-controlled structures more than females. Similarly, Ross et al. (1989) used undergraduates to study the uses and effects of learner control during statistics lessons. They found males chose sports examples more often than did females, and females chose education examples more than males. In addition, females were significantly more likely to change their context selections across lessons. Cross (2001) found that men and women graduate students were similar in Graduate Record Examination (GRE) scores and grades, but women evaluated their abilities related to intelligence lower than did men. Female graduate students whose self-evaluation of abilities is low are most vulnerable to nonsupportive learning environments. Female engineering students who were more focused on social interdependence were more influenced by social support in the academic environment than those with social independence (Cross & Vick, 2001). Female college students, even those who select math-intensive majors, have difficulty associating math with their self-identity if they implicitly stereotype mathematics as masculine (Lips, 2004; Nosek, Banaji, & Greenwald, 2002). The interaction of gender with masculine and feminine stereotypes in training environments is consistent with Heilman's (1983) lack of fit model. When self-perceptions or perceptions of others are inconsistent with the perceived masculine and feminine stereotypes associated with a given context, negative attributions and outcomes are likely to result. Limited work has explored these and related issues, but there is a strong likelihood that gender will interact with contextual features of training that elicit or inhibit sex-based stereotypes.

Relatively little work has explored the effects of race on training outcomes. The work that has been done has typically focused on diversity training. Sanchez and Medkik (2004) found that ethnicity interacted with diversity training to influence differing perceptions and reactions to the trained content. According to the authors, non-White coworkers may have higher levels of resentful demoralization, leading to potentially negative outcomes. Similarly, Linnehan, Chrobot-Mason, and Konrad (2006) found supervisor race and trainee race interacted with other variables to influence outcomes of diversity initiatives. People of color with a high ethnic identity achievement with a supervisor of color were more likely to have positive views of subjective norms toward inclusive behavior, understanding others, and treating others with respect than people of color with low ethnic identity achievement. Roberson, Kulik, and Pepper (2001) found racial composition of training groups influenced responses to training when trainees had prior experience with training. However, composition did not matter to trainees without prior experience.

Clearly, race of trainees matters in *diversity* training environments. However, much less is known about how race may interact with treatments to affect outcomes in other training contexts. We know, however, that race can influence motivation, perceptions, and affect in high-stakes testing environments. It seems likely that it can have similar effects in high-stakes training environments, particularly in situations that evoke stereotypes or stereotype threat. Much more research is needed to evaluate these and other possibilities.

Trainee age has the potential to interact with various training system characteristics to affect outcomes through multiple intervening variables. Relatively few studies have examined the influence of age as an interacting variable. Webster and Martocchio (1993) found that labeling training as play resulted in higher motivation to learn and more knowledge for younger employees than older employees. In contrast, no differences were found due to age when training was labeled as work. This could be due to the fit between the framing of the training and the motivational tendencies of younger employees.

Training contexts that require differing levels and types of information processing will likely interact with age to influence outcomes because of differences in *Gf* and *Gc*. Additionally, training that elicits age-based stereotype threat (e.g., intense use of technology) may also stimulate differential outcomes based on age. However, relatively little research has explored these possibilities.

Big Five Personality Traits

Much work has been done on the main effects of personality on training outcomes, but relatively little has explored interactive effects of frameworks such as the Big Five. Using a sample of 91 pilot trainees, Herold et al. (2002) investigated the interactive effects between early training performance and conscientiousness, emotional stability, and openness on later training outcomes. They found openness had a main effect on later training performance, but conscientiousness and emotional stability interacted with early training performance. Specifically, when early performance was strong, conscientiousness had little impact, but when early performance was problematic, only highly conscientious trainees performed better later. Additionally, when early performance was weak, emotional stability had little influence on later performance, but when early performance was strong, only emotionally stable trainees performed well later. Stewart, Carson, and Cardy (1996) examined the interactive effects of conscientiousness and self-leadership training on employee behavior using 130 hotel and resort employees. They found that less conscientious employees who received self-leadership training increased their self-directed behavior more than highly conscientious employees.

Finally, Gully et al. (2002) found that the traits of conscientiousness and openness interacted with training interventions that encouraged errors. Specifically, for trainees who were high, as opposed to low, on openness to experience, error encouragement training instructions more positively related to knowledge and skill acquisition and self-efficacy relative to error avoidance training instructions. Also, for trainees with high, as opposed to low, levels of conscientiousness, error encouragement training instructions more negatively affected self-efficacy relative to error avoidance training instructions. These studies suggest that Big Five personality traits interact with various training features to influence various mechanisms that promote learning as well as learning outcomes.

Self-Concept Traits

Self-concept traits such as goal orientation, GSE, self-esteem, and locus of control may also interact with aspects of the learning and training environment to affect training outcomes. Chen et al. (2001) found previous exam performance was more strongly related to subsequent self-efficacy for low-GSE individuals than high-GSE individuals. Likewise, research by Eden and colleagues (Eden & Aviram, 1993; Eden & Zuk, 1995) suggests that training interventions directed at boosting trainees' task-specific self-efficacy were more effective among trainees with low, rather than high, GSE.

Bell and Kozlowski (2008) found dispositional goal orientation and ability moderated the relationship between training mastery inductions, instructions to explore, and outcomes of active-learning training. Brown (2001) found performance goal orientation interacted with self-efficacy to affect the amount of practice learners chose to complete. Trainees with a high performance goal orientation and high self-efficacy engaged in more practice than trainees with a high performance orientation and low self-efficacy (Brown, 2001; DeRouin, Fritzsche, & Salas, 2005b). Schmidt and Ford (2003) demonstrated that metacognitive interventions enhanced metacognitive activity for trainees with low performance avoidance orientations, but resulted in lower metacognitive activity among highly avoidant learners.

Given that training design and content can affect difficulty, consistency, and complexity, it is likely that goal orientation will interact with such training design and content elements. Indeed, Steele-Johnson, Beauregard, Hoover, and Schmidt (2000) found goal orientation interacted with task characteristics, such as difficulty and consistency, to influence satisfaction, self-efficacy, and intrinsic motivation. Similarly, Martocchio and Hertenstein (2003) found learning orientation and training goal orientation contexts interacted to affect posttraining self-efficacy. Specifically, they observed significantly higher self-efficacy ratings when learning orientation and goal orientation contexts were most similar than in situations where learning orientation and goal orientation contexts were most dissimilar.

Heimbeck et al. (2003) found that prove and avoid goal orientations interacted with different instructions for handling errors to influence training outcomes. When trainees were told to avoid errors, they found that trainees with high prove (and avoidance) goal orientations showed higher performance than those with low prove (and avoidance) goal orientations. Davis, Carson, Ammeter, and Treadway (2005) found that learning and performance orientations interacted with feedback specificity to predict initial and subsequent performance. The effect of feedback specificity on initial performance was greatest for individuals low in learning orientation, and the effect of feedback specificity on subsequent performance was greatest for individuals high in performance orientation. These studies support the idea that trainees perform better when the training conditions provide better fit to trainee personalities and orientations.

In the only study to investigate interactions between goal orientations and updating climate perceptions, Potosky and Ramakrishna (2002) found individual learning orientation interacted with perceptions of a supportive organizational climate for updating to affect learning self-efficacy and job performance. Higher levels of self-efficacy and performance were observed when individuals had a high learning orientation and perceived a supportive climate for updating skills. The obvious conclusion of this set of studies is that the appropriate training content, design, delivery, and context are likely to depend on the goal orientations of trainees.

Interests, Values, and Styles

Shute and Towle (2003) investigated how individual preferences for initial exploration interacted with two different learner control environments using a sample of 300 high school graduates. One instructional system provided information about rules and concepts to the learner, and the other required the learner to derive concepts and rules on his or her own. During early exposure to the learning environment, they found some learners spent a lot of time exploring the computer environment, whereas others tended to go right to the problems, with minimal amounts of time spent exploring. Results showed that exploratory learners learned more if they were assigned to the discovery environment and less exploratory learners learned more in the structured environment. Similarly, Burwell (1991) found field-independent learners performed better in program-controlled settings and field-dependent learners per-formed better in learner-controlled environments. These results indicate that providing learner control that fits individual learning styles can lead to better learning outcomes (DeRouin, Fritzsche, & Salas, 2005b).

Martocchio and Webster (1992) demonstrated that cognitive playful-ness (CP) interacted with training design to influence training outcomes. *Cognitive playfulness* refers to the capacity to be guided by internal moti-vation, to be oriented toward intellectual exploration of process, to be able to self-impose goals, to be free from externally imposed rules, and to be actively involved without regard to ulterior motives. They used a sample of 68 administrative employees to demonstrate that CP inter-acted with positive and negative feedback to influence training outcomes. There was a main effect of CP such that employees lower in CP showed lower test performance than those higher in CP. An interaction was also observed. When feedback was negative, employees low in CP did substan-tially worse than employees in any other condition. When feedback was positive, employees high in CP did better than employees in any other condition, but employees low in CP performed substantially better in the positive feedback condition than in the negative feedback condition.

This is some evidence that interests, values, and learning styles will interact with training design and context factors, but the research to date is limited. Visually oriented learners appear to benefit more from visual content than verbally oriented learners. Similarly, verbal learners seem to benefit more from textual and oral content than visual learners. Research using children and adolescent learners on these topics has been mixed but generally supportive. It is clear from the preceding findings that some trainees are likely to prefer structured environments, whereas others will prefer exploratory environments. These preferences appear to interact with discovery versus structured training design. The implications of these findings are important for Internet-based training environments.

Capabilities

As early as 1975, it was recognized that although general ability had a strong positive relationship with learning and training outcomes, the steepness of the slope depended on the learning system used. Cronbach (1975) stated that "the regression of outcome onto general ability tends to be relatively steep when the instruction requires the learner to actively transform information, and it tends to be shallow when the demands are less" (p. 119). He also noted that although this was the general pattern, a number of studies provided conflicting findings. Snow (1986) suggested that students with lower levels of ability typically benefit from tightly structured lessons, whereas students with higher levels of ability tend to perform better in less structured environments.

Research has supported Cronbach's (1975) and Snow's (1986, 1991, 1998) arguments. Using meta-analytic techniques on studies involving children and college students, Whitener (1989) obtained support for the idea that ability interacted with instructional systems to influence learning outcomes. Goska and Ackerman (1996) found that training similarity to transfer tasks and training duration yielded differences in transfer outcomes. They also found that ability moderated relationships such that learners of higher ability were better able to apply what was learned in the more distant-transfer training situation than were those of lower ability.

Gully et al. (2002) found ability interacted with error training instructions to influence performance and self-efficacy. Specifically, high-ability learners had better performance and higher self-efficacy when given no specific instructions on how to handle errors or when told to use errors as an opportunity to learn. In contrast, low-ability learners had lower performance and lower self-efficacy when told to use errors as an opportunity to learn. Bell and Kozlowski (2008) obtained related findings. They conducted a comprehensive study of the cognitive, motivational, and emotion processes involved in active learning and evaluated how training design elements and individual differences influenced these processes. They found that cognitive ability interacted with proceduralized versus exploratory training instruction to influence metacognitive activity. Low-ability learners displayed similar levels of metacognitive activity under both instructional conditions, but high-ability learners displayed significantly higher levels of metacognitive activity when given exploratory instruction than when given proceduralized instruction. DeRouin, Fritzsche, & Salas (2005b) argued that higher ability learners and learners who are more familiar with computers may enjoy more sequence control in computer-based instruction than others (Gray, 1989; Hintze et al., 1988, cited in DeRouin, Fritzsche, & Salas, 2005b). Also, greater performance differences have been found between higher and lower ability learners in learner control conditions. Thus, it appears that the interaction between cognitive ability and structure of training design is one of the more robust findings in the ATI literature. Low-ability learners seem to benefit from more structure and less discovery-based exploration, whereas high-ability learners seem to profit from less structure and more self-guided exploration.

Because experience will generate different levels of familiarity, knowledge, and expertise, one can surmise that it will likely interact with training design and context elements. DeRouin, Fritzsche, & Salas (2005b) concluded that experience is a moderator of the relationship between learner control design factors and learning outcomes. Studies measuring experience as prior achievement, knowledge, computer familiarity, GPA, and education level have found that in general, learners with greater experience outperform learners with less experience.

They have also noted ATIs such that less experienced learners perform less well under learner control conditions than under more structured conditions. However, Brown (2001) found that education level and computer experience did not predict the selection of learner control options. In contrast, Gay (1986) found high experience was associated with less time spent on instruction, especially under learner control conditions (DeRouin, Fritzsche, & Salas, 2005b).

Using a sample of 32 private pilots, Smith-Jentsch, Jentsch, Payne, and Salas (1996) found previous negative flight experiences were associated with increased pilot assertiveness ratings for pilots who received assertiveness training, but negative experiences were unassociated with assertiveness ratings for untrained pilots. The findings may indicate that previous experiences create a motivational readiness to learn for certain types of training programs.

It is clear that capability, broadly construed to include general and specific abilities and experiences, interacts with training design elements and context to affect training outcomes. General ability appears to enhance the capacity to process complex information and infer underlying principles and ideas through exploration and under conditions of limited structure. Experience appears to have mixed effects, depending on the content and design of the training. It is easy to envision how trainees with high levels of experience might be demotivated when exposed to basic training, but the same trainees may be engaged by advanced, complex, or challenging training. Relatively little research has explored these important ATIs, but the initial evidence is compelling.

Discussion and Conclusions

As our review suggests, research on the roles of individual differences in training effectiveness has been vast. Within each individual difference cluster we reviewed, there are numerous studies considering the impact of specific individual differences and both mediating mechanisms and training outcomes. There has also been an increasing amount of training-related research on ATIs, although much work remains in this area. However, as we highlighted throughout our review, numerous areas remain where additional theory development and empirical research are needed. Thus, we close our chapter with a few observations regarding what we view as the most important areas where additional work on the roles of individual differences and ATIs in training effectiveness is needed (we also summarize these areas in Table 1.1).

TABLE 1.1

Summary of Directions for Future Research

Research Domain	Research Needs and Directions
Individual differences' effects on learning	1. Explore the unique and combined influences of diverse individual differences across cognitive and noncognitive domains on learning outcomes.
	2. Examine the unique mechanisms linking different individual differences to learning outcomes.
	3. Consider the potential for countervailing mechanisms linking individual differences to learning outcomes.
ATI effects on learning	1. Explore a greater number of possible ATI effects across combinations of individual differences and treatments or situations.
	2. Build on P–E fit theories to develop stronger theories of ATIs, which consider how treatments and situations either accentuate or attenuate certain individual difference effects.
	3. Consider more distal criteria, such as transfer of training, in ATI research.
	4. Examine ATIs consisting of situational characteristics not explicitly tied to training (e.g., organizational or group climate) when studying proximal training criteria (e.g., skill or knowledge acquisition).
	5. Study ATIs consisting of training design features when studying more distal training criteria (e.g., transfer performance).
	6. Use high-quality measures and sufficient sample size to have the power to detect ATIs when studying them.

To begin with, our review indicates relatively few attempts to integrate among different and related individual differences. Individual differences within and across domains are often related to each other. Indeed, a recent large-scale meta-analytic review of individual differences in personality traits, abilities, and interests by Ackerman and Heggestad (1997) found substantial overlap across the three individual difference domains, which formed four distinct trait complexes, or clusters of individual difference traits. For instance, individual differences in crystallized intelligence (*Gc*), openness to experience, and investigative and artistic interests formed a single intellectual-cultural trait complex. Ackerman and Heggestad's research suggests that prior findings pertaining to specific individual differences' effects may have masked the impact of more complex individual difference clusters or complexes.

Thus, more research is needed to learn about the unique and overlapping influences of individual differences on learning processes and training outcomes. Such research will clearly have to balance potential trade-offs between bandwidth and fidelity of individual difference predictors (cf. Cronbach, 1956). On the one hand, broader individual differences complexes can predict training outcomes to a greater extent and help integrate among seemingly disparate theories of individual differences. On the other hand, reliance on trait complexes with greater "bandwidth" can sometimes mask important differences in the theoretical mechanisms linking individual differences to training outcomes. For example, although GSE and self-esteem relate to a core self-evaluation cluster, findings by Chen et al. (2004) indicate that these highly related individual differences relate to performance through somewhat different mechanisms. Nonetheless, clearly more research is needed on both the classification of individual difference clusters and the distinct and similar mechanisms through which individual differences influence training-related phenomena.

With respect to mediating mechanisms, it is important to consider the various pathways through which individual differences differentially affect learning outcomes. Considering mediating mechanisms can also shed more light on variation in observed findings to date, as certain individual difference constructs may affect learning outcomes by triggering intervening mechanisms with countervailing effects on learning outcomes. For example, performance goal orientation may have positive effects on outcomes by enhancing attentional focus and motivation, but it may also result in distracting off-task ruminations about the likelihood of failure, resulting in greater need for emotional control and anxiety reduction. These effects can be enhanced or diminished in part through the treatments that are part of the training context. It is important to identify the most likely intervening variables for a given situation and include them as part of the training design, delivery, and evaluation process.

Regarding ATI effects, our review highlights several conclusions. First, relative to research on main effects of individual differences, far less research has been examined on possible ATIs. In part, this can perhaps be attributable to the large number of possible ATI combinations of individual differences and situations. Paucity in published ATI research can also be due to the difficulty inherent in detecting interaction effects, which are notoriously low in statistical power. High-quality measures and large sample sizes will be necessary to detect the ATIs that exist. What is perhaps most needed at this point is strong theoretical guidance regarding which individual differences should be combined with which situational factors to produce particular learning mechanisms and training outcomes.

Second, it is perhaps surprising that few attempts have been made to integrate ATI research with other postulations of person–situation interactions. It seems that a more explicit integration between ATI research and person–environment (P–E) fit theory is particularly warranted, as both areas of research seek to delineate situational boundaries for person-level relationships. Building on principles of complementary and supplementary fit (Cable & Edwards, 2004), researchers can identify particular situational characteristics that either attenuate or accentuate proposed individual differences effects. Complementary fit occurs when the environment compensates for an individual's weakness or shortcoming, or when an individual provides an asset the environment would not otherwise possess. For instance, training programs that provide more opportunities for "small wins" (incremental skill development) and plenty of positive encouragement may fit older trainees better than younger trainees, given that older trainees tend to have lower learning self-efficacy (cf. Maurer, 2001; Maurer et al., 2003). In contrast, supplementary fit exists when the environment adds to the individuals something the individuals already possess, or vice versa. For instance, training programs that encourage trainees to explore, or even make errors, during training work particularly well for individuals high on openness to experience (e.g., Gully et al., 2002).

Finally, it is interesting to note that the majority of ATI research has focused on either mediating learning processes (e.g., information processing, and self-regulation) or proximal learning outcomes (e.g., knowledge acquisition) as the dependent variables, and that the majority of this research has focused on training design features (e.g., training goal frame or instructions) as the situational moderators, as opposed to situational factors not specifically tied to training (e.g., leader support, and group climate). In contrast, several non-ATI studies have also shown that posttraining group and leadership climate and opportunity to perform account for more distal transfer of training effectiveness (e.g., Ford et al., 1992; Rouiller & Goldstein, 1993; Smith-Jentsch et al., 2001; Tesluk et al., 1995; Tracey et al., 1995). As such, it is important to extend ATI research to include more distal outcomes and a greater variety of training-specific and more general situational moderators. Such research will clearly enhance our understanding of whether and how individual differences operate differently to influence training-related outcomes in response to different training design features as well as the broader sociotechnical context in which they work.

The practical implications are many. Here are three. First, we must recognize that one size does not fit all. Certain types of training work better for some people than others. For example, e-learning, an instructional strategy for imparting needed knowledge, skills, and attitudes in organizations through technological means, is here to stay (DeRouin, Fritzsche, & Salas, 2005b). As society increasingly turns to technology to deliver training, trainees have acquired more control over when, why, what, and how they learn. As noted earlier, many trainee characteristics can enhance or impede learning and transfer in such learner control situations. Shute and

Towle (2003) argued that technology has now reached the point where we can capitalize on ATI effects to better design training to fit trainees' needs. However, this requires a thoughtful analysis of the types of technological interventions that would be required to best suit some set of individual characteristics. Second, we have to think more carefully about supplementary and complementary fit of trainees with training design features and with their broader work environment. At least some of the individual differences we have discussed are likely to interact with the training climate and culture, peer and leader support of training, reward systems, and so forth. This suggests we have to be more cognizant of the types of people we put through training, the design features we incorporate, and the support mechanisms in place in the broader context. Third, if individual differences matter, then it is critical to assess trainee background, ability, and personality during training needs analysis. Colquitt et al. (2000) suggested that these types of assessments are frequently neglected or ignored during person analysis.

In conclusion, it is apparent that it is critical to consider individual differences when developing, designing, implementing, and evaluating any training or instructional system. Trainees are active participants in learning and transfer, and the unique characteristics of each trainee will influence what happens during the training process. Individual differences matter, and they interact with training features and the broader environment to affect outcomes. Given the amount of money invested in training by organizations, it seems appropriate to give individual differences their due attention. People are complex, and training is made more complex by virtue of their involvement. Our theories and practices should reflect this reality.

References

Ackerman, P. L. (1986). Individual differences in information processing: An investigation of intellectual abilities and task performance during practice. *Intelligence, 10*(2), 101–139.

Ackerman, P. L. (1992). Predicting individual differences in complex skill acquisition: Dynamics of ability determinants. *Journal of Applied Psychology, 77*(5), 598–614.

Ackerman, P. L. (1997). Personality, self-concept, interests, and intelligence: Which construct doesn't fit? *Journal of Personality, 65*(2), 171–204.

Ackerman, P. L. (2003). Aptitude complexes and trait complexes. *Educational Psychologist, 38*, 85–93.

Ackerman, P. L., & Beier, M. E. (2003). Intelligence, personality, and interests in the career choice process. *Journal of Career Assessment, 11*(2), 205–218.

Ackerman, P. L., & Beier, M. E. (2006). Determinants of domain knowledge and independent study learning in an adult sample. *Journal of Educational Psychology, 98*(2), 366–381.

Ackerman, P. L., Bowen, K. R., Beier, M., & Kanfer, R. (2001). Determinants of individual differences and gender differences in knowledge. *Journal of Educational Psychology, 93*(4), 797–825.

Ackerman, P. L. & Heggestad, E. D. (1997). Intelligence, personality, and interests: Evidence for overlapping traits. *Psychological Bulletin, 121*(2), 219–245.

Ackerman, P. L., & Kanfer, R. (2004). Cognitive, affective, and conative aspects of adult intellect within a typical and maximal performance framework. In D. Y. Dai & R. J. Sternberg (Eds.), *Motivation, emotion, and cognition: Integrated perspectives on intellectual functioning* (pp. 119–141). Mahwah, NJ: Lawrence Erlbaum Associates.

Ackerman, P. L., Kanfer, R., & Goff, M. (1995). Cognitive and noncognitive determinants and consequences of complex skill acquisition. *Journal of Experimental Psychology: Applied, 1*, 270–304.

Alliger, G. M., Tannenbaum, S. I., Bennett, W., Jr., Traver, H., & Shotland, A. (1997). A meta-analysis of the relations among training criteria. *Personnel Psychology, 50*(2), 341–358.

Anis, M., Armstrong, S. J., & Zhul, Z. (2004). The influence of learning styles on knowledge acquisition in public sector management. *Educational Psychology, 24*(4), 549–571.

Arthur, W., Jr., Bennett, W., Jr., Edens, P. S., & Bell, S. T. (2003). Effectiveness of training in organizations: A meta-analysis of design and evaluation features. *Journal of Applied Psychology, 88*, 234–245.

Arthur, W., Jr., Bennett, W., Jr., Stanush, P. L., & McNelly, T. L. (1998). Factors that influence skill decay and retention: A quantitative review and analysis. *Human Performance, 11*, 57–101.

Arvey, R. D., Strickland, W., Drauden, G., & Martin, C. (1990). Motivational components of test taking. *Personnel Psychology, 43*, 695–716.

Austin, E. J., Evans, P., Goldwater, R., & Potter, V. (2005). A preliminary study of emotional intelligence, empathy and exam performance in first year medical students. *Personality and Individual Differences, 39*(8), 1395–1405.

Baldwin, T. T., & Ford, J. K. (1988). Transfer of training: A review and directions for future research. *Personnel Psychology, 41*, 63–103.

Bandura, A. (1997). *Self-efficacy: The exercise of control.* New York: Freeman.

Barrick, M. R., & Mount, M. K. (1991). The Big Five personality dimensions and job performance: A meta-analysis. *Personnel Psychology, 44*, 1–26.

Barrick, M. R., Mount, M. K., & Strauss, J. P. (1993). Conscientiousness and performance of sales representatives: Test of the mediating effects of goal setting. *Journal of Applied Psychology, 78*, 715–722.

Beier, M. E., & Ackerman, P. L. (2001). Current-events knowledge in adults: An investigation of age, intelligence, and nonability determinants. *Psychology and Aging, 16*(4), 615–628.

Beier, M. E., & Ackerman, P. L. (2005). Age, ability, and the role of prior knowledge on the acquisition of new domain knowledge: Promising results in a real-world learning environment. *Psychology and Aging, 20*(2), 341–355.

Bell, B. S., & Kozlowski, S. W. J. (2002a). Adaptive guidance: Enhancing self regulation, knowledge, and performance in technology-based training. *Personnel Psychology, 55,* 267–306.

Bell, B. S., & Kozlowski, S. W. J. (2002b). Goal orientation and ability: Interactive effects on self-efficacy, performance, and knowledge. *Journal of Applied Psychology, 87,* 497–505.

Bell, B. S., & Kozlowski, S. W. J. (2008). Active learning: Effects of core training design elements on self-regulatory processes, learning, and adaptability. *Journal of Applied Psychology, 93,* 296–316.

Betz, N. E., & Klein, K. L. (1996). Relationships among measures of career self-efficacy, generalized self-efficacy, and global self-esteem. *Journal of Career Assessment, 4,* 285–298.

Bissell, J., White, S., & Zivin, G. (1971). Sensory modalities in children's learning. In G. S. Lesser (Ed.), *Psychology and educational practice* (pp. 130–155). Glenview, IL: Scott, Foresman.

Blake, R. J., & Sackett, S. A. (1999). Holland's typology and the Five-Factor model: A rational-empirical analysis. *Journal of Career Development, 7,* 251–288.

Boyatzis, R. E., Stubbs, E. C., & Taylor, S. N. (2002). Learning cognitive and emotional intelligence competencies through graduate management education. *Academy of Management Learning and Education, 1*(2), 150–162.

Brett, J. F., & VandeWalle, D. (1999). Goal orientation and goal content as predictors of performance in a training program. *Journal of Applied Psychology, 84*(6), 863–873.

Brockner, J. (1988). *Self-esteem at work: Research, theory, and practice.* Lexington, MA: Lexington.

Brown, A. L., Bransford, J. D., Ferrara, R. A., & Campione, J. C. (1983). Learning, remembering, and understanding. In J. H. Flavell & E. M. Markman (Eds.), *Handbook of child psychology* (4th ed., Vol. 3, pp. 77–166). New York: Wiley.

Brown, J. D. (1998). *The self.* New York: McGraw-Hill.

Brown, K. G. (2001). Using computers to deliver training: Which employees learn and why? *Personnel Psychology, 54*(2), 271–296.

Buch, K., & Bartley, S. (2002). Learning style and training delivery mode preference. *Journal of Workplace Learning, 14*(1), 5–10.

Burwell, L. B. (1991). The interaction of learning styles with learner control treatments in an interactive videodisc lesson. *Educational Technology, 31,* 37–43.

Button, S. B., Mathieu, J. E., & Zajac, D. M. (1996). Goal orientation in organizational research: A conceptual and empirical foundation. *Organizational Behavior & Human Decision Processes, 67*(1), 26–48.

Cable, D. M., & Edwards, J. R. (2004). Complementary and supplementary fit: A theoretical and empirical integration. *Journal of Applied Psychology, 89*(5), 822–834.

Campbell, J. P., Kuncel, N. R., Sinangil, H. K., & Viswesvaran, C. (2002). Individual and team training. In N. Anderson, D. S. Ones, et al. (Eds.), *Handbook of industrial, work and organizational psychology* (Vol. 1, pp. 278–312). London: Sage.

Cannon-Bowers, J. A., Rhodenizer, L., Salas, E., & Bowers, C. A. (1998). A framework for understanding pre-practice conditions and their impact on learning. *Personnel Psychology, 51,* 291–320.

Cassidy, S. (2004). Learning styles: An overview of theories, models, and measures. *Educational Psychology, 24*(4), 419–444.

Cattell, R. B. (1987). *Intelligence: Its structure, growth, and action.* New York: Elsevier.

Chan, D., Schmitt, N., DeShon, R. P., Clause, C. S., & Delbridge, K. (1997). Reactions to cognitive ability tests: The relationships between race, test performance, face validity perceptions, and test-taking motivation. *Journal of Applied Psychology, 82,* 300–310.

Chase, W. G., & Simon, H. A. (1973). The mind's eye in chess. In W. G. Chase (Ed.), *Visual information processing* (pp. 215–281). New York: Academic Press.

Chen, G., Gully, S. M., & Eden, D. (2001). Validation of a new general self-efficacy scale. *Organizational Research Methods, 4,* 62–83.

Chen, G., Gully, S. M., & Eden, D. (2004). General self-efficacy and self-esteem: Toward theoretical and empirical distinction between correlated self-evaluations. *Journal of Organizational Behavior, 25,* 375–395.

Chen, G., Gully, S. M., Whiteman, J. A., & Kilcullen, B. N. (2000). Examination of relationships among trait-like individual differences, state-like individual differences, and learning performance. *Journal of Applied Psychology, 85,* 835–847.

Chen, G., Thomas, B., & Wallace, J. C. (2005). A multilevel examination of the relationships among training outcomes, mediating regulatory processes, and adaptive performance. *Journal of Applied Psychology, 90*(5), 827–841.

Chi, M. T. H., Glaser, R., & Rees, E. (1982). Expertise in problem solving. In R. J. Sternberg (Ed.), *Advances of the psychology of human intelligence* (Vol. 1, pp. 7–75). Hillsdale, NJ: Lawrence Earlbaum Associates.

Chung, Y., & Gully, S. M. (2004, April). The influence of previous discrimination experiences and dyadic dissimilarity on trainees' pre-training expectations and diversity attitudes. In C. T. Kulik (Chair) & B. M. Ferdman (Discussant), *Individual differences in diversity initiatives.* Symposium conducted at the 19th Annual Conference of the Society for Industrial and Organizational Psychology, Chicago.

Cianciolo, A. T., Grigorenko, E. L., Jarvin, L., Gil, G., Drebot, M. E., & Sternberg, R. J. (2006). Practical intelligence and tacit knowledge: Advancements in the measurement of developing expertise. *Learning and Individual Differences, 16*(3), 235–253.

Colquitt, J. A., LePine, J. A., & Noe, R. A. (2000). Toward an integrative theory of training motivation: A meta-analytic path analysis of 20 years of research. *Journal of Applied Psychology, 85*(5), 678–707.

Colquitt, J. A., & Simmering, M. J. (1998). Conscientiousness, goal orientation, and motivation to learn during the learning process: A longitudinal study. *Journal of Applied Psychology, 83,* 654–665.

Contrada, R. J., Ashmore, R. D., Gary, M. L., Coups, E., Egeth, J. D., Sewell, A., et al. (2001). Measures of ethnicity-related stress: Psychometric properties, ethnic group differences, and associations with well-being. *Journal of Applied Social Psychology, 31*(9), 1775–1820.

Cote, S., & Miners, C. T. H. (2006). Emotional intelligence, cognitive intelligence, and job performance. *Administrative Science Quarterly, 51*(1), 1–28.

Cronbach, L. J. (1956). Assessment of individual differences. *Annual Review of Psychology, 7,* 173–196.

Cronbach, L. J. (1957). The two disciplines of scientific psychology. *American Psychologist, 12,* 671–684.

Cronbach, L. J. (1975). Beyond the two disciplines of scientific psychology. *American Psychologist, 30*(2), 116–127.

Cronbach, L. J. (1989). Lee J. Cronbach. In G. Lindzey (Ed.), *A history of psychology in autobiography* (Vol. 8, pp. 64–93). Stanford, CA: Stanford University Press.

Cronbach, L. J., & Snow, R. E. (1977). *Aptitudes and instructional methods: A handbook for research on interactions.* New York: Irvington.

Cross, S. E. (2001). Training the scientists and engineers of tomorrow: A person-situation approach. *Journal of Applied Social Psychology, 31*(2), 296–323.

Cross, S. E., & Vick, N. V. (2001). The interdependent self-construal and social support: The case of persistence in engineering. *Personality and Social Psychology Bulletin, 27,* 820–832.

Davis, W. D., Carson, C. M., Ammeter, A. P., & Treadway, D. C. (2005). The interactive effects of goal orientation and feedback specificity on task performance. *Human Performance, 18*(4), 409–426.

Debowski, S., Wood, R. E., & Bandura, A. (2001). Impact of guided exploration and enactive exploration on self-regulatory mechanisms and information acquisition through electronic search. *Journal of Applied Psychology, 86,* 1129–1141.

DeRouin, R. E., Fritzsche, B. A., & Salas, E. (2005a). E-learning in organizations. *Journal of Management, 31*(6), 920–940.

DeRouin, R. E., Fritzsche, B. A., & Salas, E. (2005b). Learner control and workplace e-learning: Design, person, and organizational issues. In J. Martocchio (Ed.), *Research in personnel and human resources management* (Vol. 24, pp. 181–214). Greenwich, CT: JAI/Elsevier Science.

DeShon, R. P., Brown, K. G., & Greenis, J. L. (1996). Does self-regulation require cognitive resources? Evaluation of resource allocation models of goal setting. *Journal of Applied Psychology, 81,* 595–608.

Driskell, J. E., Hogan, J., Salas, E., & Hoskin, B. (1994). Cognitive and personality predictors of training performance. *Military Psychology, 6*(1), 31–46.

Duff, A., & Duffy, T. (2002). Psychometric properties of Honey and Mumford's Learning Styles Questionnaire. *Personality and Individual Differences, 33,* 147–163.

Dulewicz, V., & Higgs, M. (2004). Can emotional intelligence be developed? *International Journal of Human Resource Management, 15*(1), 95–111.

Dunlosky, J., Kubat-Silman, A., & Hertzog, C. (2003). Training metacognitive skills improves older adults' associative learning. *Psychology and Aging, 18,* 340–345.

Dunn, R., DeBello, T., Brennan, P., Krimsky, J., & Murrain, P. (1981). Learning style researchers define differences differently. *Educational Leadership, 38,* 327–374.

Dunn, R. S., & Dunn, K. J. (1979). Learning styles/teaching styles: Should they … can they … be matched? *Educational Leadership, 36,* 238–244.

Dweck, C. S. (1986). Motivational processes affecting learning. *American Psychologist, 41,* 1040–1048.

Dwyer, C. A., & Johnson, L. M. (1997). Grades, accomplishments, and correlates. In W. W. Willingham & N. S. Cole (Eds.), *Gender and fair assessment* (pp. 127–156). Mahwah, NJ: Lawrence Erlbaum Associates.

Earles, J. A., & Ree, M. J. (1992). The predictive validity of the ASVAB for training grades. *Educational and Psychological Measurement, 52*(3), 721–725.

Eaton, M. J., & Dembo, M. H. (1997). Differences in the motivational beliefs of Asian American and non-Asian students. *Journal of Educational Psychology, 89*(3), 433–440.

Eden, D. (2001). Means efficacy: External sources of general and specific subjective efficacy. In M. Erez, U. Kleinbeck, & H. Thierry (Eds.), *Work motivation in the context of a globalizing economy* (pp. 73–86). Hillsdale, NJ: Lawrence Erlbaum Associates.

Eden, D., & Aviram, A. (1993). Self-efficacy training and speed of reemployment: Helping people help themselves. *Journal of Applied Psychology, 78*, 352–360.

Eden, D., & Zuk, Y. (1995). Seasickness as a self-fulfilling prophecy: Raising self-efficacy to boost performance at sea. *Journal of Applied Psychology, 80*, 628–635.

Edwards, J. R., Cable, D. M., Williamson, I. O., Lambert, L. S., & Shipp, A. J. (2006). The phenomenology of fit: Linking the person and environment to the subjective experience of person-environment fit. *Journal of Applied Psychology, 91*(4), 802–827.

Farr, J. L., Hofmann, D. A., & Ringenbach, K. L. (1993). Goal orientation and action control theory: Implications for industrial and organizational psychology. In C. L. Cooper & I. T. Robertson (Eds.), *International review of industrial and organizational psychology* (pp. 193–232). New York: Wiley.

Fisher, S. L., & Ford, J. K. (1998). Differential effects of learner effort and goal orientation on two learning outcomes. *Personnel Psychology, 51*, 397–420.

Flavell, J. H. (1979). Metacognition and cognitive monitoring: A new area of cognitive-developmental inquiry. *American Psychologist, 34*, 906–911.

Ford, J. K., Smith, E. M., Weissbein, D. A., Gully, S. M., & Salas, E. (1998). Relationships of goal orientation, metacognitive activity, and practice strategies with learning outcomes and transfer. *Journal of Applied Psychology, 83*(2), 218–233.

Fox, S., & Spector, P. E. (2000). Relations of emotional intelligence, practical intelligence, general intelligence, and trait affectivity with interview outcomes: It's not all just 'G'. *Journal of Organizational Behavior, 21*, 203–220.

Frese, M., Brodbeck, F. C., Heinbokel, T., Mooser, C., Schleiffenbaum, E., & Thiemann, P. (1991). Errors in training computer skills: On the positive function of errors. *Human–Computer Interaction, 6*, 77–93.

Gardner, D. G., & Pierce, J. L. (1998). Self-esteem and self-efficacy within the organizational context. *Group and Organization Management, 23*, 48–70.

Gay, G. (1986). Interaction of learner control and prior understanding in computer-assisted video instruction. *Journal of Educational Psychology, 78*, 225–227.

Gelfand, M. J., Erez, M., & Zeynep, A. (2007). Cross-cultural organizational behavior. *Annual Review of Psychology, 58*, 479–514.

Gellatly, I. R., Paunonen, S. V., Meyer, J. P., Jackson, D. N., & Goffin, R. D. (1991). Personality, vocational interest, and cognitive predictors of managerial job performance and satisfaction. *Personality and Individual Differences, 12*(3), 221–231.

Gist, M., Rosen, B., & Schwoerer, C. (1988). The influence of training method and trainee age on the acquisition of computer skills. *Personnel Psychology, 41*(2), 255–265.

Goldstein, I. L., & Ford, J. K. (2002). *Training in organizations: Needs assessment, development, and evaluation* (4th ed.). Pacific Grove, CA: Wadsworth/Thompson.

Goleman, D. (1998). *Working with emotional intelligence.* New York: Bantam.

Goska, R. E., & Ackerman, P. L. (1996). An aptitude-treatment interaction approach to transfer within training. *Journal of Educational Psychology, 88*(2), 249–259.

Gottfredson, L. S. (1980). Construct validity of Holland's occupational typology in terms of prestige, census, Department of Labor, and other classification systems. *Journal of Applied Psychology, 65*(6), 697–714.

Gottfredson, L. S. (2001). Review of *Practical Intelligence in Everyday Life* by R. J. Sternberg et al. *Intelligence, 29*, 363–365.

Gottfredson, L. S. (2003). On Sternberg's "Reply to Gottfredson." *Intelligence, 31*(4), 415–424.

Gray, S. H. (1987). The effect of sequence control on computer assisted learning. *Journal of Computer-Based Instruction, 14*, 54–56.

Gray, S. H. (1989). The effect of locus of control and sequence control on computerized information retrieval and retention. *Journal of Educational Computing Research, 5*, 459–471.

Gully, S. M., Payne, S. C., Koles, K. L. K., & Whiteman, J. K. (2002). The impact of error training and individual differences on training outcomes: An attribute-treatment interaction perspective. *Journal of Applied Psychology, 87*(1), 143–155.

Gully, S. M., & Phillips, J. M. (2005). A multilevel application of learning and performance orientations to individual, group, and organizational outcomes. In J. Martocchio (Ed.), *Research in personnel and human resources management* (Vol. 24, pp. 1–51). Greenwich, CT: JAI/Elsevier Science.

Hartigan, J. A., & Wigdor, A. K. (1989). (Eds.), *Fairness in employment testing.* Washington, DC: National Academy Press.

Hattrup, K., & Schmitt, N. (1990). Prediction of trades apprentices' performance on job sample criteria. *Personnel Psychology, 43*, 453–466.

Hedlund, J., Wilt, J. M., Nebel, K. L., Ashford, S. J., & Sternberg, R. J. (2005). Assessing practical intelligence in business school admissions: A supplement to the graduate management admissions test. *Learning and Individual Differences, 16*(2), 101–127.

Heilman, M. E. (1983). Sex bias in work settings: The lack of fit model. *Research in Organizational Behavior, 5*, 269–298.

Heimbeck, D., Frese, M., Sonnentag, S., & Keith, N. (2003). Integrating errors into the training process: The function of error management instructions and the role of goal orientation. *Personnel Psychology, 56*(2), 333–361.

Herold, D. M., Davis, W., Fedor, D. B., & Parsons, C. K. (2002). Dispositional influences on transfer of learning in multistage training programs. *Personnel Psychology, 55*(4), 851–869.

Hertzog, C. (1989). Influences of cognitive slowing on age differences in intelligence. *Developmental Psychology, 25*, 636–651.

Hertzog, C. (2002). Metacognition in older adults: Implications for application. In T. J. Perfect & B. L. Schwartz (Eds.), *Applied Metacognition* (pp. 169–196). Cambridge, UK: Cambridge University Press.

Hintze, H., Mohr, H., & Wenzel, A. (1988). Students' attitudes towards control methods in computer-assisted instruction. _Journal of Computer Assisted Learning_, 4(1), 3–10.

Hofmann, D. A. (1993). The influence of goal orientation on task performance: A substantively meaningful suppressor variable. _Journal of Applied Social Psychology_, 23, 1827–1846.

Hogan, R., & Blake, R. (1999). John Holland's vocational typology and personality theory. _Journal of Vocational Behavior_, 55, 41–56.

Hogan, R., & Hogan, J. (1991). Personality and status. In D. G. Gilbert & J. J. Conley (Eds.), _Personality, social skills, and psychopathology_ (pp. 137–154). New York: Plenum.

Holland, J. L. (1997). _Making vocational choices._ Odessa, FL: Psychological Assessment Resources.

Hollenbeck, J. R., & Klein, H. J. (1987). Goal commitment and the goal setting process: Problems, prospects and proposals for future research. _Journal of Applied Psychology_, 74, 18–23.

Hunter, J. E. (1986). Cognitive ability, cognitive aptitudes, job knowledge, and job performance. _Journal of Vocational Behavior_, 29, 340–362.

Hunter, J. E., & Hunter, R. F. (1984). Validity and utility of alternative predictors of job performance. _Psychological Bulletin_, 96, 72–98.

Huy, Q. N. (1999). Emotional capability, emotional intelligence, and radical change. _Academy of Management Review_, 24(2), 325–345.

Ivancic, K., & Hesketh, B. (1995–1996). Making the best of errors during training. _Training Research Journal_, 1, 103–125.

Jamieson, J. (1992). The cognitive styles of reflection/impulsivity and field independence/dependence and ESL success. _Modern Language Journal_, 76(4), 491–501.

Jones, C. J., & Meredith, W. (1996). Patterns of personality change across the life span. _Psychology and Aging_, 11, 57–65.

Jordan, P. J., Ashkanasy, N. M., & Hartel, C. E. J. (2002). Emotional intelligence as a moderator of emotional and behavioral reactions to job insecurity. _Academy of Management Review_, 27(3), 361–372.

Joshi, A., Liao, H., & Jackson, S. E. (2006). Cross-level effects of workplace diversity on sales performance and pay. _Academy of Management Journal_, 49(3), 459–481.

Judge, T. A., & Bono, J. E. (2001). Relationship of core self-evaluations traits—self-esteem, generalized self-efficacy, locus of control, and emotional stability—with job satisfaction and job performance: A meta-analysis. _Journal of Applied Psychology_, 86(1), 80–92.

Judge, T. A., & Ilies, R. (2002). Relationship of personality to performance motivation: A meta-analytic review. _Journal of Applied Psychology_, 87(4), 797–807.

Kanfer, R. (1990). Motivation and individual differences in learning: An integration of developmental, differential and cognitive perspectives. _Learning and Individual Differences_, 2, 221–239.

Kanfer, R., & Ackerman, P. L. (1989). Motivation and cognitive abilities: An integrative/aptitude-treatment interaction approach to skill acquisition. _Journal of Applied Psychology_, 74(4), 657–690.

Kanfer, R., & Ackerman, P. L. (1990). *Ability and metacognitive determinants of skill acquisition and transfer* (Air Force Office of Scientific Research Final Report). Minneapolis, MN: Air Force Office of Scientific Research.

Kanfer, R., & Ackerman, P. L. (2004). Aging, adult development and work motivation. *Academy of Management Review, 29,* 1–19.

Kanfer, R., Ackerman, P. L., & Heggestad, E. D. (1996). Motivational skills and self-regulation for learning: A trait perspective. *Learning and Individual Differences, 8,* 185–209.

Kanfer, R., & Heggestad, E. D. (1997). Motivational traits and skills: A person-centered approach to work motivation. In L. L. Cummings & B. M. Staw (Eds.), *Research in organizational behavior* (Vol. 19, pp. 1–56). Greenwich, CT: JAI.

Keith, N., & Frese, M. (2005). Self-regulation in error management training: Emotion control and metacognition as mediators of performance effects. *Journal of Applied Psychology, 90*(4), 677–691.

Kolb, D. A. (1984). *Experiential learning: Experience as the source of learning and development.* Englewood Cliffs, NJ: Prentice Hall.

Kossek, E. E., & Zonia, S. (1993). Assessing diversity climate: A field study of reactions to employer efforts to promote diversity. *Journal of Organizational Behavior, 14,* 61–81.

Kozlowski, S. W. J., & Bell, B. S. (2006). Disentangling achievement orientation and goal setting: Effects on self-regulatory processes. *Journal of Applied Psychology, 91*(4), 900–916.

Kozlowski, S. W., & Doherty, M. L. (1989). Integration of climate and leadership: Examination of a neglected issue. *Journal of Applied Psychology, 74*(4), 546–553.

Kozlowski, S. W. J., Gully, S. M., Brown, K. G., Salas, E., Smith, E. M., & Nason, E. R. (2001). Effects of training goals and goal orientation traits on multidimensional training outcomes and performance adaptability. *Organizational Behavior and Human Decision Processes, 85,* 1–31.

Kozlowski, S. W. J., & Hults, B. M. (1987). An exploration of climates for technical updating and performance. *Personnel Psychology, 40*(3), 539–563.

Kozlowski, S. W. J., Toney, R. J., Mullins, M. E., Weissbein, D. A., Brown, K. G., & Bell, B. S. (2001). Developing adaptability: A theory for the design of integrated-embedded training systems. In E. Salas (Ed.), *Advances in human performance and cognitive engineering research* (Vol. 1, pp. 59–123). Amsterdam: JAI/Elsevier Science.

Kraiger, K., Ford, J. K., & Salas, E. (1993). Application of cognitive, skill-based, and affective theories of learning outcomes to new methods of training evaluation. *Journal of Applied Psychology, 78,* 311–328.

Kyllonen, P. C., & Lajoie, S. P. (2003). Reassessing aptitude: Introduction to a special issue in honor of Richard E. Snow. *Educational Psychologist, 38,* 79–83.

Law, K. S., Wong, C. S., & Song, L. J. (2004). The construct and criterion validity of emotional intelligence and its potential utility for management studies. *Journal of Applied Psychology, 89*(3), 483–496.

Lee, C., Tinsley, C., & Bobko, P. (2003). Cross-cultural variance in goal orientations and their effects. *Applied Psychology, 52*(2), 272–297.

Liegle, J. O., & Janicki, T. N. (2006). The effect of learning styles on the navigation needs of Web-based learners. *Computers in Human Behavior, 22*(5), 885–898.

LePine, J. A., Colquitt, J. A., & Erez, M. (2000). Adaptability to changing task contexts: Effects of general cognitive ability, conscientiousness, and openness to experience. *Personnel Psychology, 53*, 563–593.

Lievens, F., Harris, M. M., Van Keer, E., & Bisqueret, C. (2003). Predicting cross-cultural training performance: The validity of personality, cognitive ability, and dimensions measured by an assessment center and a behavior description interview. *Journal of Applied Psychology, 88*(3), 476–489.

Linnehan, F., Chrobot-Mason, D., & Konrad, A. M. (2006). Diversity attitudes and norms: The role of ethnic identity and relational demography. *Journal of Organizational Behavior, 27*(4), 419–442.

Lips, H. M. (2004). The gender gap in possible selves: Divergence of academic self-views among high school and university students. *Sex Roles, 50*, 357–371.

Liu, Y., & Ginther, D. (1999). Cognitive styles and distance education. *Online Journal of Distance Learning Administration, 2*(3). State University of West Georgia, Distance Education. Retrieved January 24, 2009, from http://www.westga.edu/~distance/ojdla/

Locke, E. A. (2005). Why emotional intelligence is an invalid concept. *Journal of Organizational Behavior, 26*(4), 425–431.

Major, D. A., Turner, J. E., & Fletcher, T. D. (2006). Linking proactive personality and the Big Five to motivation to learn and development activity. *Journal of Applied Psychology, 91*(4), 927–935.

Mangos, P. M., & Steele-Johnson, D. (2001). The role of subjective task complexity in goal orientation, self-efficacy, and performance relations. *Human Performance, 14*(2), 169–186.

Martocchio, J. (1992). Microcomputer usage as an opportunity: The influence of context in employee training. *Personnel Psychology, 45*, 529–552.

Martocchio, J. (1994). Effects of conceptions of ability on anxiety, self-efficacy, and learning in training. *Journal of Applied Psychology, 79*, 819–825.

Martocchio, J. J., & Hertenstein, E. J. (2003). Learning orientation and goal orientation context: Relationships with cognitive and affective learning outcomes. *Human Resource Development Quarterly, 14*(4), 413–434.

Martocchio, J. J., & Judge, T. A. (1997). Relationship between conscientiousness and learning in employee training: Mediating influences of self-deception and self-efficacy. *Journal of Applied Psychology, 82*, 764–773.

Martocchio, J. J., & Webster, J. (1992). Effects of feedback and cognitive playfulness on performance in microcomputer software training. *Personnel Psychology, 45*(3), 553–578.

Mathieu, J. E., & Martineau, J. W. (1997). Individual and situational influences on training motivation. In J. K. Ford (Ed.), *Improving training effectiveness in work organizations* (pp. 193–221). Mahwah, NJ: Lawrence Earlbaum Associates.

Mathieu, J. E., Martineau, J. W., & Tannenbaum, S. I. (1993). Individual and situational influences on the development of self-efficacy: Implications for training effectiveness. *Personnel Psychology, 46*, 125–147.

Mathieu, J. E., Tannenbaum, S. I., & Salas, E. (1992). Influences of individual and situational characteristics on measures of training effectiveness. *Academy of Management Journal, 35*, 828–847.

Maurer, T. J. (2001). Career-relevant learning and development, worker age, and beliefs about self-efficacy for development. *Journal of Management, 27*(2), 123–140.

Maurer, T. J., Weiss, E. M., & Barbeite, F. G. (2003). A model of involvement in work-related learning and development activity: The effects of individual, situational, motivational, and age variables. *Journal of Applied Psychology, 88*(4), 707–724.

Mayberry, P. W., & Carey, N. B. (1997). The effect of aptitude and experience on mechanical job performance. *Educational and Psychological Measurement, 57*(1), 131–149.

Mayer, J. D., & Salovey, P. (1993). The intelligence of emotional intelligence. *Intelligence, 17*, 433–442.

Mayer, J. D., & Salovey, P. (1997). What is emotional intelligence? In P. Salovey & D. J. Sluyter (Eds.), *Emotional development and emotional intelligence.* New York: Basic Books.

McEvoy, G. M., & Cascio, W. F. (1989). Cumulative evidence of the relationship between employee age and job performance. *Journal of Applied Psychology, 74*, 11–17.

Mor Barak, M. E., Cherin, D. A., & Berkman, S. (1998). Organizational and personal dimensions in diversity climate: Ethnic and gender differences in employee perceptions. *Journal of Applied Behavioral Science, 34*(1), 82–104.

Murphy, K. R., & Sideman, L. (2006). The fadification of emotional intelligence. In K. R. Murphy (Ed.), *A critique of emotional intelligence: What are the problems and how can they be fixed?* (pp. 283–299). Mahwah, NJ: Lawrence Earlbaum Associates.

Newstead, S. E. (1992). A study of two "quick-and-easy" methods of assessing individual differences in student learning. *British Journal of Educational Psychology, 62*(3), 299–312.

Noe, R. A. (1986). Trainees' attributes and attitudes: Neglected influences on training effectiveness. *Academy of Management Review, 11*, 736–749.

Noe, R. A., & Schmitt, N. (1986). The influence of trainee attitudes on training effectiveness: Test of a model. *Personnel Psychology, 39*, 497–523.

Nosek, B. A., Banaji, M. R., & Greenwald, A. G. (2002). Math = male, me = female, therefore math [not equal to] me. *Journal of Personality and Social Psychology, 83*, 44–59.

Ong, C., & Lai, J. (2006). Gender differences in perceptions and relationships among dominants of e-learning acceptance. *Computers in Human Behavior, 22*(5), 816–829.

Payne, S. C., Youngcourt, S. S., & Beaubien, J. M. (2007). Meta-analytic examination of the goal orientation nomological net. *Journal of Applied Psychology, 92*, 128–150.

Petrides, K. V., Frederickson, N., & Furnham, A. (2004). The role of trait emotional intelligence in academic performance and deviant behavior at school. *Personality and Individual Differences, 36*(2), 277–293.

Phillips, J. M., & Gully, S. M. (1997). The role of goal orientation, ability, need for achievement, and locus of control in the self-efficacy and goal setting process. *Journal of Applied Psychology, 82*, 792–802.

Pintrich, P. R., & DeGroot, E. V. (1990). Motivational and self-regulated learning components of classroom academic performance. *Journal of Educational Psychology, 82*, 33–40.

Ployhart, R. E., Ziegert, J. C., & McFarland, L. A. (2003). Understanding racial differences on cognitive ability tests in selection contexts: An integration of stereotype threat and applicant reactions research. *Human Performance, 16*(3), 231–259.

Potosky, D., & Ramakrishna, H. V. (2002). The moderating role of updating climate perceptions in the relationship between goal orientation, self-efficacy, and job performance. *Human Performance, 15*(3), 275–297.

Quiñones, M. A. (1995). Pretraining context effects: Training assignment as feedback. *Journal of Applied Psychology, 80*, 226–238.

Radosevich, D. J., Vaidyanathan, V. T., Yeo, S., & Radosevich, D. M. (2004). Relating goal orientation to self-regulating processes: A longitudinal field test. *Contemporary Educational Psychology, 29*, 207–229.

Ralston, C. A., Borgen, F. H., Rottinghaus, P. J., & Donnay, D. A. C. (2004). Specificity in interest measurement: Basic Interest Scales and major field of study. *Journal of Vocational Behavior, 65*(2), 203–216.

Ree, M. J., Carretta, T. R., & Teachout, M. S. (1995). Role of ability and prior knowledge in complex training performance. *Journal of Applied Psychology, 80*(6), 721–730.

Ree, M. J., & Earles, J. A. (1991). Predicting training success: Not much more than *g*. *Personnel Psychology, 44*, 321–332.

Reed, K., Doty, D. H., & May, D. R. (2005). The impact of aging on self-efficacy and computer skill acquisition. *Journal of Managerial Issues, 17*(2), 212–228.

Riding, R., & Cheema, I. (1991). Cognitive styles: An overview and integration. *Educational Psychology, 11*(3–4), 193–215.

Roberson, L., Kulik, C. T., & Pepper, M. B. (2001). Designing effective diversity training: Influence of group composition and trainee experience. *Journal of Organizational Behavior, 22*(8), 871–885.

Robertson, I. T. (1985). Human information-processing strategies and style. *Behavior and Information Technology, 4*(1), 19–29.

Ross, S. M., Morrison, G. R., & O'Dell, J. K. (1989). Uses and effects of learner control of context and instructional support in computer-based instruction. *Educational Technology Research and Development, 37*(4), 29–39.

Rotter, J. B. (1990). Internal versus external control of reinforcement: A case history of a variable. *American Psychologist, 45*, 489–493.

Rotter, J. B. (1992). "Cognates of personal control: Locus of control, self-efficacy, and explanatory style": Comment. *Applied and Preventive Psychology, 1*, 127–129.

Rouiller, J. Z., & Goldstein, I. L. (1993). The relationship between organizational transfer climate and positive transfer of training. *Human Resource Development Quarterly, 4*(4), 377– 390.

Sadler-Smith, E. (1997). "Learning style": Frameworks and instruments. *Educational Psychology, 17*(1–2), 51–63.

Salas, E., & Cannon-Bowers, J. A. (2001). The science of training: A decade of progress. *Annual Review of Psychology, 52*, 471–499.

Sanchez, J. I., & Medkik, N. (2004). The effects of diversity awareness training on differential treatment. *Group & Organization Management, 29*, 517–536.

Schmidt, A. M., & Ford, J. K. (2003). Learning within a learner control training environment: The interactive effects of goal orientation and metacognitive instruction on learning outcomes. *Personnel Psychology, 56*(2), 405–429.

Schmidt, F. L., & Hunter, J. E. (1998). The validity and utility of selection methods in personnel psychology: Practical and theoretical implications of 85 years of research findings. *Psychological Bulletin, 124*(2), 262–274.

Schmidt, F. L., Hunter, J. E., & Outerbridge, A. N. (1986). Impact of job experience and ability on job knowledge, work sample performance, and supervisory ratings of job performance. *Journal of Applied Psychology, 71*(3), 432–439.

Schmit, M. J., & Ryan, A. M. (1997). Applicant withdrawal: The role of test-taking attitudes and racial differences. *Personnel Psychology, 50*(4), 855–876.

Schmitt, N., & Chan, D. (1999). The status of research on applicant reactions to selection tests and its implications for managers. *International Journal of Management Reviews, 1*, 45–62.

Schraw, G., & Dennison, R. S. (1994). Assessing metacognitive awareness. *Contemporary Educational Psychology, 19*, 460–475.

Schulte, M. J., Ree, M. J., & Carretta, T. R. (2004). Emotional intelligence: Not much more than g and personality. *Personality and Individual Differences, 37*(5), 1059–1068.

Shavelson, R. J. (2003). Lee J. Cronbach. *Proceedings of the American Philosophical Society, 147*(4), 379–385.

Shavelson, R. J., Hubner, J. J., & Stanton, G. C. (1976). Self-concept: Validation of construct interpretations. *Review of Educational Research, 46*, 407–441.

Shute, V., & Towle, B. (2003). Adaptive e-learning. *Educational Psychologist, 38*, 105–114.

Silver, W. S., Mitchell, T. R., & Gist, M. E. (1995). Responses to successful and unsuccessful performance: The moderating effect of self-efficacy on the relationship between performance and attributions. *Organizational Behavior and Human Decision Processes, 62*, 286–299.

Smith, E. M., Ford, J. K., & Kozlowski, S. W. J. (1997). Building adaptive expertise: Implications for training design strategies. In M. A. Quiñones & A. Ehrenstein (Eds.), *Training for a rapidly changing workplace* (pp. 89–118). Washington, DC: American Psychological Association.

Smith-Jentsch, K. A., Jentsch, F. G., Payne, S. C., & Salas, E. (1996). Can pretraining experiences explain individual differences in learning? *Journal of Applied Psychology, 81*(1), 110–116.

Smith-Jentsch, K. A., Salas, E., Brannick, M. T. (2001). To transfer or not to transfer? Investigating the combined effects of trainee characteristics, team leader support, and team climate. *Journal of Applied Psychology, 86*, 279–292.

Snow, R. E. (1986). Individual differences and the design of educational programs. *American Psychologist, 41*, 1029–1039.

Snow, R. E. (1989). Aptitude-treatment interaction as a framework for research on individual differences. In P. Ackerman, R. J. Sterberg, & R. Glaser (Eds.), *Learning and individual differences.* New York: Freeman.

Snow, R. E. (1991). Aptitude-treatment interaction as a framework for research on individual differences in psychotherapy. *Journal of Consulting and Clinical Psychology, 59*(2), 205–216.

Snow, R. E. (1998). Abilities as aptitudes and achievements in learning situations, In J. J. McArdle & R. W. Woodcock (Eds.), *Human cognitive abilities in theory and practice* (pp. 93–112). Mahwah, NJ: Lawrence Earlbaum Associates.

Snyder, M. (1974). Self-monitoring of expressive behavior. *Journal of Personality and Social Psychology, 30,* 526–537.

Steele, C. M. (1997). A threat in the air: How stereotypes shape intellectual identity and performance. *American Psychologist, 52,* 613–629.

Steele, C. M., & Aronson, J. (1995). Stereotype threat and the intellectual test performance of African Americans. *Journal of Personality and Social Psychology, 69,* 797–811.

Steele-Johnson, D., Beauregard, R. S., Hoover, P. B., & Schmidt, A. M. (2000). Goal orientation and task demand effects on motivation, affect, and performance. *Journal of Applied Psychology, 85*(5), 724–738.

Sternberg, R. J. (1996). *Successful intelligence.* New York: Simon & Schuster.

Sternberg, R. J. (2003). Our research program validating the triarchic theory of successful intelligence: Reply to Gottfredson. *Intelligence, 31*(4), 399–413.

Sternberg, R. J., & Zhang, L. (Eds.). (2001). *Perspectives on thinking, learning, and cognitive styles.* Mahwah, NJ: Lawrence Earlbaum Associates.

Stevens, C. K., Bavetta, A. G., & Gist, M. E. (1993). Gender differences in the acquisition of salary negotiation skills: The role of goals, self-efficacy, and perceived control. *Journal of Applied Psychology, 78,* 723–735.

Stevens, C. K., & Gist, M. E. (1997). Effects of self-efficacy and goal orientation on negotiation skill maintenance: What are the mechanisms? *Personnel Psychology, 50,* 995–1015.

Stewart, G. L., Carson, K. P., & Cardy, R. L. (1996). The joint effects of conscientiousness and self-leadership training on employee self-directed behavior in a service setting. *Personnel Psychology, 49*(1), 143–164.

Tannenbaum, S., & Yukl, G. (1992). Training and development in work organizations. In M. R. Rosenzweig & L. W. Porter (Eds.), *Annual review of psychology* (Vol. 43, pp. 399–441). Palo Alto, CA: Annual Reviews.

Tennant, M. (1988). *Psychology and adult learning.* London: Routledge.

Tesluk, P. E., Farr, J. L., Mathieu, J. E., & Vance, R. J. (1995). Generalization of employee involvement training to the job setting: Individual and situational effects. *Personnel Psychology, 48,* 607–632.

Tett, R. P., & Fox, K. E. (2006). Confirmatory factor structure of trait emotional intelligence in student and worker samples. *Personality and Individual Differences, 41*(6), 1155–1168.

Thomas, K. M., & Mathieu, J. E. (1994). Role of causal attributions in dynamic self-regulation and goal processes. *Journal of Applied Psychology, 79,* 812–818.

Towler, A., & Dipboye, R. L. (2003). Development of a learning style orientation measure. *Organizational Research Methods, 6,* 216–235.

Tracey, J. B., Hinkin, T. R., Tannenbaum, S. I., & Mathieu, J. E. (2001). The influence of individual characteristics and the work environment on varying levels of training outcomes. *Human Resource Development Quarterly, 12,* 5–24.

Tracey, J. B., Tannenbaum, S. I., & Kavanagh, M. J. (1995). Applying trained skills on the job: The importance of the work environment. *Journal of Applied Psychology, 80,* 239–252.

Tracey, J. B., & Tews, M. J. (2005). Construct validity of a general training climate scale. *Organizational Research Methods, 8*(4), 353–374.

VandeWalle, D. (1997). Development and validation of a work domain goal orientation instrument. *Educational and Psychological Measurement, 57*, 995–1015.

VandeWalle, D., & Cummings, L. L. (1997). A test of the influence of goal orientation on the feedback-seeking process. *Journal of Applied Psychology, 82*, 390–400.

VandeWalle, D., Ganesan, S., Challagalla, G. N., & Brown, S. P. (2000). An integrated model of feedback-seeking behavior: Disposition, context, and cognition. *Journal of Applied Psychology, 85*, 996–1003.

Van Rooy, D. L., & Viswesvaran, C. (2004). Emotional intelligence: A meta-analytic investigation of predictive validity and nomological net. *Journal of Vocational Behavior, 65*(1), 71–95.

Van Rooy, D. L., Viswesvaran, C., & Pluta, P. (2005). An evaluation of construct validity: What is this thing called emotional intelligence? *Human Performance, 18*(4), 445–462.

Veenman, M. V. J., & Spaans, M. A. (2005). Relation between intellectual and metacognitive skills: Age and task differences. *Learning and Individual Differences, 15*(2), 159–176.

Venkatesh, V., Morris, M. G., & Ackerman, P. L. (2000). A longitudinal field investigation of gender differences in individual technology adoption decision-making processes. *Organizational Behavior and Human Decision Processes, 83*(1), 33–60.

Waldman, D. A., & Avolio, B. J. (1986). A meta-analysis of age differences in job performance. *Journal of Applied Psychology, 71*, 33–38.

Warr, P., & Bunce, D. (1995). Trainee characteristics and the outcomes of open learning. *Personnel Psychology, 48*(2), 347–375.

Warr, P., Miles, A., & Platts, C. (2001). Age and personality in the British population between 16 and 64 years. *Journal of Occupational and Organizational Psychology, 74*, 165–199.

Webster, J., & Martocchio, J. J. (1993). Turning work into play: Implications for microcomputer software training. *Journal of Management, 19*(1), 127–146.

Webster, J., & Martocchio, J. J. (1995). The differential effects of software training previews on training outcomes. *Journal of Management, 21*(4), 757–787.

Whitener, E. M. (1989). A meta-analytic review of the effect of learning on the interaction between prior achievement and instructional support. *Review of Educational Research, 59*, 65–86.

Wilson, D. K. (1986). An investigation of the properties of Kolb's Learning Style Inventory. *Leadership & Organization Development Journal, 7*(3), 3–15.

Witkin, H. A. (1979). Socialization, culture and ecology in the development of group and sex differences in cognitive style. *Human Development, 22*(5), 358–372.

Witkin, H. A., Moore, C. A., Goodenough, D. R., & Cox, P. W. (1977). Field dependent and field independent cognitive styles and their educational implications. *Review of Educational Research, 47*, 1–64.

Wolf, M. B., & Ackerman, P. L. (2005). Extraversion and intelligence: A meta-analytic investigation. *Personality and Individual Differences, 39*(3), 531–542.

Wolf, G., London, M., Casey, J., & Pufahl, J. (1995). Career experience and motivation as predictors of training behaviors and outcomes for displaced engineers. *Journal of Vocational Behavior, 47*(3), 316–331.

Yeo, G. B., & Neal, A. (2004). A multilevel analysis of effort, practice, and performance: Effects of ability, conscientiousness, and goal orientation. *Journal of Applied Psychology, 89,* 231–247.

Zhang, L., & Sternberg, R. J. (2006). *The nature of intellectual styles.* Mahwah, NJ: Lawrence Earlbaum Associates.

Zhang, Y. (2005). Age, gender, and Internet attitudes among employees in the business world. *Computers in Human Behavior, 21*(1), 1–10.

2

Motivation in Training and Development: A Phase Perspective

Margaret E. Beier
Rice University

Ruth Kanfer
Georgia Institute of Technology

Introduction

For decades, interest in training motivation focused primarily on the determinants and consequences of motivational processes in the context of formal training environments. Building on a continuing stream of theory and research on learning motivation in educational psychology (e.g., Pintrich, 2003), industrial-organizational (IO) scientists focused on the identification of personal (e.g., need for achievement, and cognitive abilities) and situational (e.g., goal type, and provision of feedback) factors that influence goal choice, attentional effort, task interest, persistence during learning, and their effects on learning outcomes (e.g., knowledge and performance; e.g., see Goldstein, 1991; Noe, 1986; Tannenbaum & Yukl, 1992).

Recently, however, new trends in the changing nature of work and workforce composition have substantially broadened the field. Demographic developments such as increased workforce diversity, and changes in the way people approach work such as career sequencing (i.e., reentering the workforce after a leave), have led to the proliferation of a variety of continuous learning opportunities and a widespread acceptance of the notion of lifelong learning to prevent skill obsolescence and promote career progress. Adult learning opportunities—delivered via the Internet, at satellite locations, or at organizationally developed "universities"—abound. The growth of diverse methods for developing adult knowledge and skills has brought about a corresponding new interest in how motivation operates, in concert with other personal and situational factors, to affect who participates in training and how motivation and learning in training affect work behaviors, job performance, work attitudes, and career success.

Changes in technology and connectivity have impacted both what is trained and the way that training is delivered. A central concern, for example, is the proliferation of e-learning (Galagan, 2000), defined as the use of computers and networking to deliver training (DeRouin, Fritzsche, & Salas, 2004; Welsh, Wanberg, Brown, & Simmering, 2003). Many organizations are adopting e-learning strategies for their training and development programs because of the apparent benefits to this approach, which include allowing for synchronous or asynchronous training, easy off-site training, and increased learner control—control over the training residing with the learner as opposed to a trainer. For example, e-learning environments with high learner control would give learners control over the content they examine, the pace of the training, and even the sequencing of the information presented. However, these features may also potentially affect motivational processes involved in selecting training goals, striving toward learning in the training environment, and transfer. E-learning is but one example of the changes in the landscape of the workplace that will influence the direction of future research on training and motivation.

The purpose of this chapter is to provide a selective review of recent advances in motivation theory and research in the context of training and development. Although there are many theories of motivation, there is no single theory applicable to all situations (Mitchell & Daniels, 2003), and this diversity of theoretical approaches in the area of motivation for learning is readily apparent in both educational psychology and IO. Our goal here is not to provide a unified, comprehensive theory of motivation as it relates to learning in training and development activities. Other researchers have provided comprehensive and empirically based models of this process elsewhere (Colquitt, LePine, & Noe, 2000; also see Kanfer, 1990; Mitchell & Daniels [2003] for comprehensive reviews of motivational theory in I/O psychology). Rather, our intention is to review current theoretical approaches and research and to provide a framework that will be useful for practitioners and researchers alike for understanding the motivational issues relevant to training and development activities.

This chapter is organized in three major sections. We begin by providing a heuristic framework for understanding relevant motivational processes in the context of work training and development. We then discuss current theory and research within this framework. Next, we discuss special considerations for motivation in training for special populations such as older workers and teams and propose an agenda for future research.

A Stage Model of the Training Process

The first question to be addressed in the application of motivation theories to applied contexts is "Motivation for what?" In this chapter, we are broadly concerned with an individual's motivation for work-related skill training and development. Included in this domain is an array of criteria, ranging from the choice to participate in training, learning outcomes in formal training and informal development opportunities, and subsequent changes in work attitudes and job performance. Motivation in training may be broadly organized in terms of a heuristic stage model that approximates the individual's experience. Specifically, we posit a dynamic, three-stage model that begins with motivation for training and continues through motivation during the learning process and, finally, to motivation for transfer. The use of a recursive, interrelated phase model has two potential advantages. First, the model allows for an examination of the qualitatively different motivational processes relevant at each stage. Second, by representing motivation as a temporal, cumulative set of processes, we may more clearly explicate how and when prior events might influence downstream training outcomes and how downstream outcomes may alter the individual's propensity for further training.

Our proposed metamodel for motivation in work training and development is graphically depicted in Figure 2.1. As shown, motivational

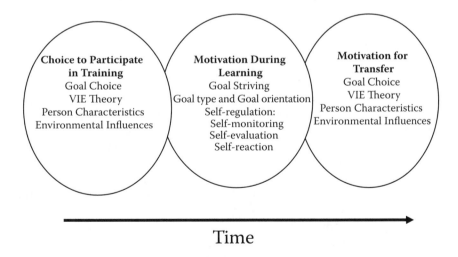

FIGURE 2.1
Stage model of motivation in training and learning activities.

processes relevant to learning and training are distinguished in terms of three successive stages: (a) motivation to participate in training, (b) motivation during learning and training, and (c) motivation for transfer of knowledge and skills to the work environment. Although the model depicts a temporal ordering of the three stages, the stages are not discrete—that is, outcomes at each stage are posited to influence the other stages of the process.

In each phase, motivation is conceptualized as a resource allocation process that influences the direction, intensity, and persistence of behavior (Campbell & Pritchard, 1976; Kanfer & Ackerman, 1989). In the first stage, motivation is posited to play a critical role in the choice to pursue, initiate, and respond to training and developmental opportunities. During training, self-regulatory processes and the environment importantly affect the intensity and persistence of attentional effort directed toward learning and performance. In the third stage, motivation for transfer is posited to affect the initiation and deployment of knowledge and skills in the work context (Kanfer, 1990). Although other stage models (Cole, Harris, & Feild, 2004) and models of the predictors and determinants of learning relevant to motivation (Colquitt et al., 2000) are more elaborate, the proposed model provides a complementary, macro level of analysis that may be integrated with extant models focused on microanalytic processes operative at different phases. Dominant theoretical perspectives and critical empirical research within each stage in the framework are discussed below.

Stage 1: Training Participation

Our model recognizes that adult motivation for training and development typically begins before the first training session takes place. We expect that motivational forces operative in the choice to participate in training have important consequences for training. Employees who take the initiative to seek training opportunities, for example, may approach learning differently than employees who respond to unsolicited or compulsory invitations to participate in training. Invitations to participate in training may range from general notices to specific requests made by supervisors or other organizational personnel. In these contexts, as we discuss next, the type and specificity of information provided about the content and format of training can importantly influence intentions to attend training.

The primary focus in the pretraining stage is on the decision to participate. Expectancy value theories, with their emphasis on choice, are thus likely to be most useful for predicting the decision to participate in training. These theories generally include at least three determinants of goal choice and action: (a) the value the person places on the outcomes associated with training, (b) the instrumentality of training performance to desired outcomes (e.g., certification), and (c) the expectation that effort will lead to successful performance (Kanfer, 1990; Vroom, 1964). Although there are many variations of expectancy theorizing in the work motivation literature (e.g., theory of reasoned action [Fishbein & Ajzen, 1975], and valence, instrumentality, expectancy [VIE] theory [Vroom]), all formulations share the notion that the participation or choice decision involves cognitive processes and rational decision making. In IO psychology, the popularity of VIE theories has waned over the years, most likely because of untenable assumptions about rationality of decision-making processes and the mental calculations that precede goal choice. Nevertheless, expectancy conceptualizations of motivated action continue to provide a useful rubric for understanding goal choice in training and development (Mathieu & Martineau, 1997; Noe, 1986). In particular, empirical research using expectancy formulations has generally shown the value of this approach—motivational force is higher when trainees value the outcomes associated with success in the training program, believe that performance in training will lead to the desired outcome, and believe effort will lead to performance in training (see Mathieu, Tannenbaum, & Salas, 1992). Application of this conceptualization to the training context indicates two broad categories of variables that influence judgments of valence, instrumentality, expectancy, and, in turn, the choice to attend training, namely, trainee characteristics and the organizational context.

Trainee Characteristics

An individual's general level of motivation for learning is perhaps the most straightforward predictor of the likelihood that a person will participate in training and development activities. Motivation to learn can be broadly conceived of as the value that an individual places on learning and development activity, and has indeed been found to be positively related to participation (e.g., Birdi, Allan, & Warr, 1997; Noe & Schmitt, 1986; Noe & Wilk, 1993). In addition to measuring motivation to learn directly, personality traits such as typical intellectual engagement (TIE, a measure of intellectual engagement in typical performance situations; Goff & Ackerman, 1992) and openness to experience (a personality trait associated with intellect and culture; Goldberg, 1993) represent relatively stable individual differences in a person's general tendency to engage in intellectually enriching activities. Empirical studies of the relations between these traits and existing knowledge in adults demonstrate that there is indeed a significant positive relation, suggesting that these broad trait characteristics represent motivation for intellectually enriching activities that result in learning over the life span (Ackerman, 2000; Beier & Ackerman, 2001, 2003).

Empirical research on additional person-related antecedents of motivation for work-related learning, such as job involvement (the importance of the job to the individual), organizational and job commitment, and individual differences in personality traits such as conscientiousness (a personality trait related to dependability and need for achievement; Goldberg, 1993), shows that these factors are generally positively related to motivation for learning and the choice to engage in training activities (Colquitt & Simmering, 1998; Mathieu et al., 1992; Noe, 1986; Noe & Schmitt, 1986; Noe & Wilk, 1993; Tracey, Hinkin, Tannenbaum, & Mathieu, 2001). However, the effects of these antecedents on the choice to attend training are neither very strong nor consistent (e.g., Mathieu et al., 1992), perhaps because these variables do not directly consider the content or purpose of the training or the organizational environment. For example, individuals may maintain strong general interest in learning but show little interest in participating in work safety training if they perceive the training to be redundant and/or of little personal relevance. Perceptions of the current work and organizational environment may also influence the valence that an individual places on training or developmental opportunities. Factors such as perceived need for training and perceived training utility have been examined to link the person and characteristics more closely to the training experience and organizational context. Perhaps not surprisingly, because they are directly related to perceptions of the instrumentality of the training program, perceived utility and perceived need for training have been shown to be important mediators of the relation between person characteristics and training opportunities that affect the choice to attend training (Ford & Noe, 1987; Guthrie & Schwoerer, 1994).

Research also shows that the choice to attend training is influenced by an individual's perception of how effective he or she will be at learning during training (Colquitt et al., 2000; Noe & Wilk, 1993; Tracey et al., 2001). Task-specific self-efficacy is a prospective judgment about one's capabilities for successful performance in a specific situation (Bandura, 1977; Gist & Mitchell, 1992). Research on self-efficacy and training participation indicates that this variable has an effect through perceived utility of training (Guthrie & Schwoerer, 1994) and through motivation for training (Colquitt et al., 2000; Noe & Wilk, 1993; Tracey et al., 2001). Unlike other person-related variables discussed above (e.g., job involvement and job commitment), where the results are somewhat equivocal (Mathieu et al., 1992), research has consistently shown that self-efficacy is an important determinant of training motivation.

Current trends in the delivery of training (e-learning) may also affect self-efficacy for learning. For example, Welsh et al. (2003) pointed out that learners with low self-efficacy for technology use may be unwilling to participate in training when they believe that the training delivery method will present a difficult barrier to successful learning outcomes. This suggests that organizations can potentially increase learner self-efficacy and affect the choice to attend training by making e-learning experiences easy to navigate, providing help when needed, and making trainees aware of support resources available for successful completion of the training program. In other words, organizations may influence self-efficacy for training by modifying elements in the training context. Contextual influences on motivation to participate in training will be discussed next.

Contextual Influences

The organizational climate provides information to employees about the instrumentality of training and development activities for obtaining desired outcomes and is an important determinant of motivation to attend training (Noe, 1986; Quiñones, 1995, 1997). Quiñones (1997) identified three general categories of the training context that are important for training outcomes as follows: (a) the trainee's involvement in the decision to participate in training, (b) the organizational climate, and (c) the framing of training. We will not restate Quiñones' comprehensive summary of these contextual influences of motivation here. Rather, we will focus on updating his framework with current research findings and practical considerations.

Voluntary Versus Mandated Training

It is widely assumed that volunteering for training is a behavioral manifestation of training motivation, and research has generally supported this idea. The results of several studies show that employees are more motivated to attend training when they make the choice to attend training (Baldwin, Magjuka, & Loher, 1991; Guerrero & Sire, 2001; Hicks & Klimoski, 1987; Mathieu et al., 1992). Findings by Baldwin et al. (1991) also illustrate one important caveat to this finding—organizations that provide employees the choice to attend specific training programs must be prepared to honor the employee's choice, or risk decreasing motivation for training and negatively affecting learning during training.

Although voluntary choice to participate in training has been long regarded as having a beneficial influence on motivation during training, recent research suggests that compulsory attendance may also exert a *positive* influence on training motivation. Tsai and Tai (2003) found that training motivation among bank employees in Taiwan was positively related to the assignment of mandatory training. This relationship was mediated by the perceived importance of the training. While these findings appear inconsistent with previous results, they underscore two potentially important considerations in evaluating the impact of compulsory training on motivation for training. First, cultural influences may interact with the compulsory nature of training. For example, power distance is a cultural dimension that describes the extent to which a less powerful member of an organization is socialized toward obedience and accepts the unequal distribution of power (Hofstede & McCrae, 2004). Because the Tsai and Tai study was conducted in Taiwan, a country that would rank high on the power distance scale relative to the United States, employees might have been more motivated to attend mandated training than they might be in the United States. Second, it could be that the compulsory nature of the training essentially framed the training experience by communicating the importance of the experience, which helped employees set expectations (Tannenbaum, Mathieu, Salas, & Cannon-Bowers, 1991). We will discuss the importance of framing next.

Framing of Training

Training opportunities for job incumbents do not occur in a vacuum. Organizational personnel (e.g., coworkers and supervisors) and organizational events (e.g., performance appraisals, personnel changes, and restructuring) provide cues from which trainees construct schemas about the content, target, and potential value of training experiences—cues that in turn *frame* the training situation (Quiñones, 1997). The motivational impact of framing is assumed to occur through the provision of information that helps trainees develop expectations about the training experience. Realistic expectations are important—research shows that when expectations are fulfilled, motivation for subsequent training is increased, as are organizational commitment and self-efficacy for learning (Tannenbaum et al., 1991). Elements as simple as the label or title assigned to the training, and the description of the training (e.g., positioning training as an opportunity, remedial, or advanced; Martocchio, 1992; Quiñones, 1995), provide the frame for the training experience.

Framing may be particularly important in motivation for training directed toward the development of behaviors that reflect organizational values, such as tolerance for diversity and sexual harassment training. Such training is often compulsory for job incumbents and may involve discussion of attitudes toward sensitive topics. If trainees feel threatened by the training content, they may reject opportunities to learn and/or may retaliate (e.g., by creating backlash—an unpleasant environment for diverse groups; Holladay, Knight, Paige, & Quiñones, 2003) undermining the very purpose of the training. Research in this area suggests that straightforward training titles (e.g., diversity training versus building human relations) enable trainees to more easily set appropriate expectations about the content of the training (Holladay et al., 2003).

Setting learner expectations about the content and process of training is also potentially important in e-learning environments (DeRouin et al., 2004). Because learners may be new to the e-learning environment, the organization can help set learner expectations about the e-learning experience by explaining how e-learning differs from traditional training experiences and, perhaps most importantly, how e-learning may seem more difficult than traditional learning experiences because of increased learner control. For example, in a study of Web-based versus classroom-based learning, Maki and Maki (2002) found that students enrolled in a Web-based course rated the workload associated with the course significantly higher than students taking the same course in lecture format. Even though the students in the Web-based course learned more over the course of the semester than those in the lecture format, students in the lecture format were more satisfied with the course at the end of the semester. Although not examined directly in this study, it may not be the extra effort per se, but rather that individuals in the Web-based course did not expect the extra effort. Indeed, research shows that setting trainee expectations with a realistic preview of the training experience can significantly increase motivation for training and other positive training outcomes, even when the preview describes the training as involving more work relative to another description (Hicks & Klimoski, 1987). These findings highlight the importance of communicating or framing the training experience such that potential trainees set appropriate and realistic expectations. For example, if learners do not anticipate the effects of increased learner control in the e-learning environment, inaccurate perceptions could influence trainee expectations and have a negative effect on motivation for learning during training, self-efficacy, and motivation to participation in e-learning in the future.

Organizational Climate

Several studies show that the organizational climate can potentially affect motivation for training and development activities as well as learning outcomes (Kozlowski & Farr, 1988; Kozlowski & Hults, 1987; Mathieu & Martineau, 1997; Maurer & Tarulli, 1994; Noe & Wilk, 1993; Tannenbaum & Yukl, 1992). Positive organizational climates for learning generally enhance self-confidence for learning, and enhance beliefs that favorable outcomes will result from participating in training or development activities (Mathieu & Martineau, 1997). Organizational climate as it relates to training includes factors such as trainee perceptions regarding company rules and policies about training and development activity; perceptions of the organization's general orientation toward learning and development, which also include perceptions of the resources available for training and development (e.g., is the organization a "learning organization"; Yang, Watkins, & Marsick, 2004); and perceptions of supervisor and coworker support for learning (Kozlowski & Farr, 1988; Kozlowski & Hults, 1987).

Organizational climate, especially as it relates to the training environment, potentially influences motivation for e-learning as well as learning outcomes in e-learning environments in important ways. For example, both traditional and e-learning training environments generally involve training at the workplace and require that trainees invest time and attention to the training tasks. In the e-learning format, however, the trainee selects when training takes place and must manage work and learning demands. Brown (2005) examined the impact of situational factors, such as supervisor and coworker support and job characteristics (e.g., autonomy and workload), on amount of time spent on an e-learning activity (intranet-based software training). Results obtained showed that time spent on training was related to performance gains. In addition, however, the trainee's workload exerted a significant detrimental influence on time spent on training. These findings highlight the importance of fostering an organizational climate that provides support for e-learning activities (e.g., reduction in workload to ensure ample time to participate in the training without interruption).

Summary

Motivational processes prior to the onset of training set the stage for motivational processes that occur during and after the training period. Consistent with expectancy-based formulations of motivation, research to date has shown that the decision to participate in training is importantly influenced by perceived self-efficacy for learning (expectancies), the perceived costs and benefits of training for work outcomes (instrumentalities), and the perceived attractiveness of these outcomes for job and career success (valence). Personal, contextual, and organizational factors influence the decision process. Personal attributes, most notably the individual's self-efficacy or confidence for learning, represent potentially important determinants of willingness to train using new training technologies, such as e-learning. Contextual factors, such as framing and the training description, also appear to represent potent influences on the decision to train through their influence on training expectations regarding effort and instrumentality and on self-efficacy. Organizational factors, such as climate and social support, influence motivation to participate in training through their effects on percepts of efficacy and the utility of training outcomes for on-the-job and career performance.

Stage 2: Motivation During Learning

Over the past two decades, scientists have been studying the specific motivational processes involved in skill acquisition and learning in organizational and educational contexts (e.g., see Kanfer & Ackerman, 1989; Pintrich, 2003). This research has informed the science of training in IO psychology and has led to an explosion of theories, topics, and empirical studies over the last decade. The second stage of our model focuses on the motivational processes that influence training outcomes, including knowledge and skill acquisition, attitude change, and behavior change.

The decision to engage in training provides a broad purpose or objective for action and sets the stage for motivational processes during training. In training, individuals engage in specific goal-directed activities, set proximal learning goals, monitor interim learning outcomes, evaluate goal progress, adjust allocation of personal resources, and update self-percepts of competencies. In accord with the work motivation literature, theory and research directed toward understanding and remediating motivation in this phase of training are generally subsumed under the broad class of processes involved in goal striving. Relevant topics include goal type and an individual's goal orientation and self-regulatory processes such as self-monitoring, self-evaluation, and self-reaction (Kanfer & Ackerman, 1989). In this section, we review recent trends in theory and research investigating the impact of self-efficacy and goal characteristics on learning and performance during training.

Metacognition

As Flavell (1979) noted, self-regulation involves metacognition (e.g., thinking about your thinking), and so represents a critical concept for learning. There are two components to metacognitive activity: monitoring and control. *Metacognitive monitoring* refers to the subjective assessment of one's own cognitive processes and knowledge. *Metacognitive control* refers to the processes that regulate cognitive processes in behavior (Koriat, Ma'ayan, & Nussinson, 2006). In the context of learning and training, metacognitive monitoring includes evaluating one's learning and task, and predicting outcomes; metacognitive control includes decisions about where to allocate resources and intensity and speed of work (Schmidt & Ford, 2003).

Much research on the importance of metacognition in learning has been conducted in e-learning environments, mainly because the absence of a trainer in these environments makes metacognitive activity (i.e., monitoring and control) crucial for success. Research has shown that metacognitive skill can be effectively trained through embedding metacognitive instruction into computer-based training (Aleven & Koedinger, 2002) or through explicit instruction on effective metacognitive strategies provided before the e-learning activity (Schmidt & Ford, 2003). The implication of these findings is that training on self-regulatory skills that encompass metacognition (either incorporated directly into the training module or conducted outside of the module) can go a long way to improving learning in training, especially when the training environment is one that includes increased learner control.

Goal Orientation

Goal orientation refers to the purpose or underlying focus an individual adopts when pursuing goals in an achievement context. Specifically, it addresses whether an individual is likely to focus on the process of learning (i.e., mastery orientation) or whether he or she is likely to focus on outcomes (i.e., performance orientation; Dweck, 1986). Because goal orientation directs self-regulatory processes during goal striving, it can be considered an antecedent of metacognitive activity (Schmidt & Ford, 2003). Persons high in mastery orientation, for example, are more likely to adopt learning goals that emphasize task competence and mastery. In contrast, persons high in performance goal orientation are posited to adopt performance goals that focus on demonstrating competence or avoiding a show of incompetence (Dweck, 1986).

Theory and research on the impact of goal orientation have conceptualized orientation as both a motivational trait and a motivational state induced in the training context. For example, in a study by Kozlowski and Bell (2006), goal orientation was induced through goal content (i.e., mastery goals focused on learning how to execute a task, and performance goals focused on achieving a certain score on the task) and goal frame (i.e., mastery frames encouraged participants to use practice as an opportunity to develop skills as opposed to performance frames that encouraged demonstrations of competence). This research showed that goal content accounted for more variance in trainee self-regulatory activity than goal frame and that self-regulatory processes were most improved when the goal frame and content were congruent and focused on mastery. Although individual differences in trait goal orientation were also measured in this study, Kozlowski and Bell (2006) found that the goal manipulations had an effect on self-regulatory activities during training over and above individual differences in goal orientation.

Recently, DeShon and Gillespie (2005) reviewed the goal orientation literature and examined the question of whether goal orientation is best conceptualized as a state or a trait. They proposed an action theory of goal orientation that conceptualizes this construct as a tendency toward a certain orientation in the context of the action required by a particular situation. For example, in the context of training and development activity (i.e., a situation where the appropriate action would be to explore problems, get feedback, and allocate resources toward learning), a mastery orientation would be most appropriate. Researchers working in this area have recently begun to study task and personal characteristics that may interact with goal orientation to influence learning outcomes in training. Specifically, task characteristics such as perceived complexity and stage in the skill acquisition process are potentially important considerations for understanding the relation between goal orientation and learning in training. Personal characteristics such as cognitive ability and self-efficacy are also potentially important moderators of the goal orientation–learning relation.

The basis for much of the research on the importance of task complexity and novelty on the goal orientation–performance relation came from the skill acquisition literature. In a classic study of skill acquisition on an air traffic control task, Kanfer and Ackerman (1989) found that focusing on an outcome-oriented goal was detrimental to learning a new skill because it required cognitive resources that were thus diverted from learning. Similarly, researchers working in the area of skill acquisition have begun to understand how different types of goals and goal orientations interact with task complexity and task novelty to influence learning in training. Latham and colleagues (Seijts & Latham, 2001; Seijts, Latham, Tasa, & Latham, 2004; Winters & Latham, 1996) conducted a series of studies that examined mastery and performance goals and learning on a complex business simulator. They found that the induction of performance goals (i.e., goals focused on obtaining a certain score on the simulator) was detrimental to initial stages of learning relative to a mastery goal induction (i.e., goals focused on learning the process). In these studies, when the task was relatively simple, performance goals were productive—suggesting that focusing on performance, when the task is easily learned, can be beneficial to performance.

Steele-Johnson, Beauregard, Hoover, and Schmidt (2000) also found that participants scoring high on performance orientation outperformed those scoring high on mastery orientation when the task to be learned was simple, but they did not find a benefit of mastery orientation for learning when the task was complex. Yeo and Neal (2004) found that participants with high mastery orientation demonstrated greater skill at the end of practice when they also had low performance orientation. When participants were high in both mastery and performance orientations, performance at the end of practice suffered. Yeo and Neal's findings suggest that focusing on both learning the skills (i.e., mastery orientation) and demonstrating competence (i.e., performance orientation) will interfere with skill acquisition perhaps because of the cognitive resources required to self-regulate learning and performance simultaneously (e.g., Kanfer & Ackerman, 1989).

Individual differences in goal orientation also appear to interact with cognitive ability to influence learning outcomes. In a study of learning a computerized navy radar simulation, mastery orientation was positively related to performance in training for those high in cognitive ability, but slightly negatively related to performance for those lower in ability (Bell & Kozlowski, 2002). Bell and Kozlowski also found that those high in ability learned less when they were also high in performance orientation. It may be that trainees high in performance orientation were unwilling to select challenging learning tasks in training because they wanted to demonstrate competence. This finding suggests that perceptions of how effective one will be at the task (i.e., task-specific self-efficacy) may mediate the relation between goal orientation and performance.

Indeed, there is evidence that self-efficacy does mediate the relation between goal orientation and performance in learning environments through self-set goals (Chen, Gully, Whiteman, & Kilcullen, 2000). The effect of goal orientation and self-efficacy on performance also seems to depend on task complexity. Mangos and Steele-Johnson (2001) examined learning and performance on a complex scheduling task. Similar to Bell and Kozlowski (2002), when the task was perceived to be easy, performance orientation and self-efficacy were positively related to performance at the end of training. Although Mangos and Steele-Johnson did not find effects for mastery orientation, their results emphasize the role that perceptions of complexity and self-efficacy play in the relation between performance orientation and learning in training.

Similar results have also been found in the area of e-learning. Brown (2001) examined goal orientation and self-efficacy as predictors of time on task, practice level, and knowledge gained for a learner-controlled intranet environment in an organization. He found that those who practiced the least were learners high in performance orientation and low in self-efficacy for learning. Those who practiced the most were those high in self-efficacy and also high in performance orientation. Brown's findings are consistent with the position that those who are high in performance orientation will engage in tasks when they feel competent at the task, but will avoid tasks they perceive will demonstrate their incompetence. In total, these findings suggest that the relation between goal orientation and learning in training is not straightforward—it is likely to depend on situational factors such as task complexity, the stage of the skill acquisition, and the type of goals the individual is pursuing. It will also depend on personal characteristics like cognitive ability and an individual's self-efficacy for achieving the task.

Summary

Motivation during training is best conceptualized as including goal-striving processes such as self-monitoring, self-evaluation, and self-reaction. Consistent with this perspective, in the learning and training domain, metacognition, goal orientation, and self-efficacy represent important theoretical approaches that provide meaningful predictions for learning outcomes during this stage of training. Specifically, research to date has shown that performance in training is influenced by the type of goals adopted by the learner (e.g., mastery or performance), individual differences in goal orientation, and self-regulatory mechanisms such as self-efficacy and metacognition. Recent research has also examined how the design of the training interventions can influence trainee use of self-regulatory skills and influence learning outcomes. Specifically, researchers have shown that incorporating instructional sets to encourage metacognitive activity can significantly and positively affect training outcomes. Self-regulatory processes are likely to be especially important in situations where trainees experience high learner control. Thus, we expect theory and research in this area to continue to grow along with the proliferation of e-learning over the coming decade.

Stage 3: Motivation for Transfer

From an organizational perspective, the transfer and utilization of skills and knowledge acquired during training back to the job represent crucial aspects of training effectiveness. Traditionally, the focus of empirical research on transfer has examined the conditions of practice and training design that are most likely to lead to transfer of skills (e.g., Baldwin & Ford, 1988; Schmidt & Bjork, 1992). Although there is no question that these factors do affect transfer, there are also important motivational processes at play during this posttraining phase—the third stage in our model. According to Baldwin and Ford (1988), there are two conditions for transfer, "(1) generalization of material learned in training to the job context, and (2) maintenance of the learned material over a period of time on the job" (p. 64).

Because transfer of training potentially affects organizational effectiveness and individual job performance, different levels of analysis are appropriate to consider when conducting research on transfer. However, different levels of analysis have been rarely considered in training research until recently (Kozlowski, Brown, Weissbein, Cannon-Bowers, & Salas, 2000). Rather, most research to date has focused on what Kozlowski et al. (2000) called *horizontal transfer*—transfer across different settings or contexts at the same level (e.g., the relation between an individual's performance in training and his or her performance back on the job). Vertical transfer is concerned with linking individual training outcomes to higher levels of the organizational (i.e., team or organizational effectiveness; Kozlowski et al., 2000). Most of our discussion will be focused on motivational components of horizontal transfer, as that is the topic of much research. Motivational processes relevant for vertical transfer will be further discussed below (in our discussion of teams). Although transfer is temporally distant from the choice to attend training, many of the motivational processes relevant in Stage 1 of our model are also important in Stage 3. VIE models frame the choice to attend training in Stage 1; in Stage 3, similar concerns about valence, instrumentality, and expectancy will also influence the choice to transfer skills learned in training back on the job. The organizational climate, characteristics of the job, the support of the manager, and person-related variables such as self-efficacy are all potential influences on transfer. For example, the probability of transfer is higher for workers who perceive that a desired outcome is related to the use of trained skills on the job. At the same time, skills learned in training are less likely to be used at work if the job is not designed to accommodate new skills or if a supervisor does not support their use. Similarly, a trainee who does not believe that he or she can effectively perform the trained tasks at the end of training will probably show a low level of motivation for performing the trained task on the job. Two motivational factors relevant to transfer that have received substantial research attention are discussed below: posttraining self-efficacy, and the organizational climate.

Self-Efficacy

An important motivational component related to the transfer of trained skills is how effectively a trainee feels he or she can perform the trained tasks at the end of training. Posttraining self-efficacy was identified by Kraiger, Ford, and Salas (1993) as a potentially important affective outcome of the training experience related to transfer—an idea that has been supported by empirical research. For example, research has demonstrated that posttraining self-efficacy is related to transfer in situations requiring near transfer (i.e., transfer to a task identical to the trained task; Barnett & Ceci, 2002; Martocchio, 1992; Mathieu et al., 1992). Recently, researchers have also examined the determinants of adaptive or far transfer. Adaptive transfer is transfer to a task that is not identical to the trained task, but instead is a generalization or adaptation of the task. It involves using information learned in training to generate new approaches to solving problems that might include, for example, application of knowledge learned in computer software training to solve a difficult problem with the software that was not trained (e.g., Barnett & Ceci; Smith, Ford, & Kozlowski, 1997). Findings suggest that posttraining self-efficacy is also important in situations of far or adaptive transfer (i.e., Ford, Smith, Weissbein, Gully, & Salas, 1998; Holladay & Quiñones, 2003; Kozlowski et al., 2001). The implications of these findings are that, in addition to ensuring that trainees have the intended skills when exiting a training program, organizations should also be concerned that trainees perceive that they have the skills and can effectively use the skills on the job.

E-learning may also potentially affect the development of posttraining self-efficacy. Self-efficacy is posited to develop through perceptions of mastery experiences with a task, vicarious experiences (modeling), verbal persuasion, and psychological arousal (e.g., anxiety; Bandura, 1977; Gist & Mitchell, 1992). During training, self-efficacy is influenced by these factors. For example, increased self-efficacy would be expected when an individual masters a task in training, observes others who are successful during training, receives positive encouragement to persist during training, and perceives little anxiety associated with task performance during training.

While e-learning may provide opportunities to develop mastery with the task during the training experience, and to perceive physiological responses to task performance, research studies suggest that learners perceive e-learning experiences to be more difficult and less satisfying than traditional learning experiences (Maki & Maki, 2002). This perception of difficulty may affect the development of posttraining self-efficacy by negatively influencing perceptions of task mastery beyond the training context. Also, asynchronous e-learning activities may not provide the vicarious learning or positive encouragement and persuasion experiences (prevalent in traditional training environments) that would support enduring percepts of self-efficacy. Whether or not these more interpersonal determinants of self-efficacy are truly different in an e-learning experience versus a traditional training experience represents an important question for future empirical research. With the proliferation of e-learning in organizations, the next 10 years will certainly bring additional research on how motivational processes affect transfer differently when training is delivered electronically versus traditionally.

Organizational Climate

Many of the same factors related to organizational context that affect the choice to attend training have also been found to influence likelihood of transfer (Quiñones, 1997). For example, characteristics of the job itself are important for transfer. Jobs that are flexible enough to accommodate the application of new skills learned in training will facilitate transfer (Ford, Quiñones, Sego, & Sorra, 1992). Research also shows that the organizational climate—which would include support for the transfer of specific skills learned on the job as well as a more general culture that supports continuous learning—can increase the probability that skills and knowledge acquired in training will be transferred back to the job and will influence job performance post training (Kozlowski & Farr, 1988; Kozlowski & Hults, 1987; Rouiller & Goldstein, 1993; Tracey, Tannenbaum, & Kavanagh, 1995). A transfer of training climate, as outlined by Rouiller and Goldstein (1993), includes factors such as encouragement from supervisors and coworkers, characteristics of the job that allow for using skills learned in training, and the feedback received from the environment. A continuous learning culture as defined by Tracey et al. (1995) includes a more general assessment of the support provided by the organizational culture for the acquisition of knowledge and skills through many means (not only through training). Tracey et al. (1995) have found that these two facets of the organizational climate (i.e., transfer of training climate and continuous learning culture) are separable. Many researchers have posited that the organizational climate moderates the relation between training outcomes and transfer back to the job, a position that has received mixed support from the empirical literature (Kozlowski et al., 2000). Rather, most research has found a direct effect of training outcomes to transfer (Tracey et al., 1995), although see Ford et al. (1992) for evidence of a moderating influence of organizational context.

New developments in the delivery of training will also potentially affect the likelihood of transfer. Although organizations that use e-learning extensively may be communicating to their employees that they support skill updating, asynchronous e-learning, where trainees can participate in training at their convenience, may make it more difficult for managers to keep abreast of employee training progress and program completion. In these cases, managerial support of the transfer of skills may be lacking simply because the manager is not aware that the employee has been trained (Welsh et al., 2003). Effective transfer of training in e-learning contexts may thus require increased communication relative to training in traditional contexts.

Summary

Many of the same motivational processes relevant at Stage 1 (choice to attend training) are also relevant at Stage 3 (transfer). Theoretical models such as VIE theory can explain why some individuals make a choice to transfer skills learned on the job and others do not. Research on motivational issues in transfer of training also highlights the importance of posttraining self-efficacy for transfer as well as organizational and job-related factors such as transfer of training climate, continuous learning culture, and job characteristics. Changes in the way that training is delivered will necessitate an understanding of how a shift toward a learner-controlled environment will influence the motivational processes important in transfer such as posttraining self-efficacy and organizational support. It is perhaps also important to note that Stage 1 and Stage 3 of our model are linked in that reactions to training that affect transfer at Stage 3 (i.e., how effective, relevant, and valuable a trainee perceives that training was) will also influence the choice to participate in subsequent training opportunities.

Special Populations and an Agenda for Future Research

Current changes in the demographic makeup of the workforce and the movement toward team-based work will potentially have significant impacts on the motivational processes involved in training. As of this writing, there are two major shifts in the workforce that are of great concern and interest to IO psychology in general and, more to the point, to scientists working in the areas of training and motivation. The first topic is related to the graying of the American workforce. A small but growing literature suggests important age-related differences in motivation to participate in training, conditions that maximize learning, and motivation to utilize newly learned information and skills on the job. The second topic pertains to the shift in the way work is accomplished in organizations— the move from individual jobs to team-based work. In this section, we will discuss these changes in the American workforce and how they will influence the agenda for future research in training motivation. We will also discuss other topics that we believe will be paramount in the research agenda on training motivation and age. These are e-learning and emotion in training motivation. Our research agenda is summarized in Table 2.1.

Age

According to the U.S. Bureau of Labor Statistics (2006), by the year 2010, nearly half of the U.S. workforce will be 45 years or older. By 2012 the largest group of workers in the United States will be 45–54 years old, the percentage of workers between the ages of 35 and 44 will shrink, and the group of workers younger than 35 will grow at a rate slower than the overall growth of the labor force (reflecting the birth dearth following the baby boom). Although research on the impact of these demographic trends on training motivation is still sparse, a growing number of studies suggest that age-related differences in cognitive and noncognitive traits importantly affect motivation for, during, and following training experiences.

To date, the bulk of theory and research on age-related differences in training has focused on the implications of well-documented changes in cognitive abilities across the life span as they affect learning outcomes (Ackerman, 1996; Cattell, 1987). Evidence from the cognitive aging literature indicates that fluid abilities (commonly denoted as Gf); Ackerman, 1996; Horn & Cattell, 1966) such as working memory, abstract reasoning, and novel problem solving decline with advancing age (Ackerman, 2000; Schaie, 1996). Practically, this decline in Gf has often been associated with greater difficulty in novel, complex learning tasks and longer time to training proficiency (Ackerman & Kyllonen, 1991). In contrast, crystallized abilities (commonly denoted as Gc; see Ackerman, 1996; Horn &

TABLE 2.1

Summary of Proposed Agenda for Future Research in Motivation and Training

Topic	Initiative

Age	• Examination of differences in motivational processes in training for older and younger learners
	    • Perception of effort involved in learning new skills
	    • Influence of time orientation on motivation for learning job-related skills
	    • Reactions to environments that include learner control

E-learning	• Influence of perceptions of difficulty associated with learner control on motivation for learning. • Does increased learner control interact with ability to affect motivation during training, self-efficacy, and willingness to participate in e-learning in the future? • Exploration of potential differences between e-learning and traditional training in terms of the influence of the organizational climate and support for training. • Further investigation of the importance of self-regulation and metacognition in e-learning environments. • Investigation into the development of self-efficacy in e-learning environments versus traditional learning environments.
Emotion	• The role of emotion in motivation for training, learning during training (e.g., emotion control skills), and transfer.
Teams	• Investigation of the motivational processes that might influence vertical transfer relative to horizontal transfer. • Investigation of the influence of group processes of existing teams on training motivation.

Cattell, 1966) represent the knowledge acquired through education and experience. Cross-sectional and longitudinal studies indicate that, in contrast to Gf, Gc tends to be relatively stable or even increase over the adult life span at least through the working years—until about age 70 (Ackerman, 2000; Schaie, 1996). Although Gf abilities are generally considered the primary mechanism through which new knowledge is acquired, recent studies of adult learning suggest that Gc abilities are also important in knowledge acquisition (Beier & Ackerman, 2005). This finding is in line with recommendations for designing training interventions for older learners (Sterns & Doverspike, 1989) and suggests that age-related differences in training outcomes may be attenuated by training that builds upon the older learner's extensive knowledge.

Empirical research in IO psychology on the age–training relation has generally taken a descriptive approach (Birdi et al., 1997; Kubeck, Delp, Haslett, & McDaniel, 1996). Findings indicate a negative relation between age and learning outcomes in training (Kubeck et al., 1996), that older workers are less likely to participate in training opportunities than are younger workers (Birdi et al., 1997), and that older workers may be more likely to experience anxiety when faced with training that employs new delivery technologies than younger workers (Kelley & Charness, 1995). Although most of these studies suggest a fairly bleak picture of aging and training motivation, some researchers have found that motivation for training and development does not always decline with advancing age. For example, Simpson, Greller, and Stroh (2002) found that although older workers were less likely to participate in organizationally sponsored training activities, they were more likely to participate in nonwork development activities than younger workers. The Simpson et al. (2002) findings suggest that age-related differences in goals, motives, and motivation processes may also account for age-related differences in training outcomes.

Recently, Kanfer and Ackerman (2004) proposed a model that attempts to understand age-related changes in the context of four patterns of age-related changes in cognitive and noncognitive traits, namely, (a) decline in Gf, (b) growth of Gc, (c) motive discontinuity, and (d) motive and interest reorganization. Consistent with cognitive theories of aging, Kanfer and Ackerman suggested that the gradual decline in Gf associated with aging may affect motivation through its influence on the perceived effort–performance relation and self-efficacy for learning. For example, it is likely that older workers will estimate that a significant amount of effort is necessary to obtain desired outcomes through training and development activity. That is, older adults are likely to perceive declines in their own working memory ability and processing speed that, coupled with personal exemplars of difficult learning experiences (e.g., problems experienced when learning a new computer program), may have a negative influence on motivation. On the other hand, training content that builds on previously acquired knowledge and training formats that promote a strong sense of self-efficacy may promote effective learning among older workers.

Kanfer and Ackerman (2004) summarized a growing body of evidence to suggest that motives for action also shift across the life span. Carstensen (1998), for example, suggested that individuals shift their orientation around midlife from more instrumental goals to satisfaction of affective goals. McAdams and de St. Aubin (1998) further suggested that generativity motives tend to first emerge and take an increasingly important priority around midlife. Kanfer and Ackerman (2004) suggested that the shift in motives across the life span affects the perceived utility of performance, such that training outcomes that provide intrinsic and affiliative outcomes have higher valence. From a practical perspective, motive discontinuities and reorganization across the life span suggest several implications for motivation related to training. For example, older individuals are less likely to participate in training that involves new skills that cannot be conceptualized as immediately relevant to the current work role or training that does not afford opportunities for achievement of intrinsic, affiliative, or security-related goals. This may explain why older adults have been found to be less likely to participate in work-related development activities (Birdi et al., 1997), but still participate in non-work-related development (Simpson et al., 2002). Specifically, the decreased motivation for job-related training is potentially a reflection of the assessment of diminished payoff associated with developing work-related skills. However, non-job-related development may still be interesting to this group of workers because retirement may represent a relatively long period of time during which they can continue to develop intellectually.

In summary, training among midlife and older workers is becoming a reality that organizations will have to face in the relative short term. The shrinkage of younger workers in the labor pool will necessitate the training and retraining of older workers for new jobs or for new opportunities within the same job. Because of the well-researched and well-documented changes in the trajectories of cognitive abilities over the life span, we know that training interventions may have to be designed differently to accommodate differences in working memory ability, speed of processing, and knowledge acquired through education and experience between younger and older learners. However, very little is known about the motivational processes associated with training for older workers. Kanfer and Ackerman (2004) provided a number of propositions related to age and motivation that are directly relevant to the study of motivational processes related to training. Their analysis suggests that organizations may need to provide stronger performance incentives to spur midlife workers to develop new skills compared to younger workers due to perceptions of the effort involved in learning a new skill and perceptions of the diminished return on investment in training. Surprisingly, the research agenda on the topic of age and motivation in IO psychology is relatively undeveloped—with no empirical studies to date that address the propositions laid out by Kanfer and Ackerman.

The demographic changes discussed above put age in the forefront of our research agenda for motivation in training. As part of this agenda, there are a number of questions about the age and motivation for training relation that appear ripe for research. First, we know very little about how the perceptions of the effort required to learn new skills are different for older versus younger learners. Perhaps more importantly, we know little about how these perceptions influence the motivation to participate in training and influence self-regulatory processes during learning. Because the aging of the workforce coincides with the proliferation of e-learning, this area of research would seem especially important. As previously discussed, e-learning experiences can seem more effortful than more passive learning experiences because of increased learner control. Add to this the aging learner's estimation of how effortful learning will be in this context, and motivation for training may be significantly reduced. Research conducted in this area would have implications related to designing e-learning activities for ease of use and designing training to meet the unique cognitive qualities of older learners (i.e., self-paced, related to existing knowledge, and fewer demands on working memory; Beier & Ackerman, 2005).

Teams

Over the past decade, the workplace has experienced a shift from individual jobs to team-based work (Cohen & Bailey, 1997), and scientists in IO psychology are working to understand how theories and research applied at an individual level of analysis fit into a team-based structure (Kozlowski & Bell, 2003). The topic of training is no exception. Researchers in this area have identified the optimal team composition in terms of traits for increased team learning in training (i.e., high team cognitive ability is positively related to team training performance, and high team agreeableness is negatively related; Ellis, Hollenbeck, Ilgen, Porter, & West, 2003) and best practices associated with team training (e.g., Salas, Burke, & Cannon-Bowers, 2002). Recently, researchers have also begun investigating team-level motivational processes (see Chen & Kanfer, 2006, for a discussion of team motivation) and, more specifically, the motivational processes involved in team training environments (Bunderson & Sutcliffe, 2003; Chen, Thomas, & Wallace, 2005; DeShon, Kozlowski, Schmidt, Milner, & Wiechmann, 2004). Preliminary theory and research in this area have been concerned with the similarity between team- and individual-level motivational processes involved in goal choice and goal striving. Marks, Mathieu, and Zaccaro (2001) developed a taxonomy of team processes that somewhat mirrors the motivational processes of goal choice and goal striving at individual levels of analysis. Transition processes as defined by Marks et al. (2001) are most similar to goal choice in that they include mission analysis formulation and planning, and goal specification. Action processes are the team-level processes that most resemble motivational processes involved in goal striving such as monitoring the team's progress toward the goal, monitoring systems, backup behavior, and coordination.

The similarity between group- and team-level motivational processes in team training environments has been confirmed through a handful of empirical studies. DeShon et al. (2004) examined the effects of both individual- and team-level motivational processes on individual- and team-level outcomes of performance at the end of training. They found that most of the team-level variables (e.g., team goal orientation and team self-efficacy) showed the same pattern of relationships with outcomes as the individual-level variables. Chen et al. (2005) also examined individual- and team-level outcomes for performance on an adaptive task (i.e., they examined the generalizability of the skills learned in training) and found, as did DeShon et al., that the individual- and team-level motivational processes were similar.

Recently researchers have begun to investigate how transfer of training is best conceptualized and examined in team environments (Kozlowski et al., 2000). Horizontal transfer is transfer on one level of analysis and represents the type of transfer that we have previously discussed. An examination of vertical transfer, on the other hand, recognizes that individual levels of performance at the end of a training program influence higher levels of performance—performance relevant to team and organizational success. Kozlowski et al. (2000) discussed the importance of understanding vertical transfer, especially when performance of the team relies on the integration of a diverse set of tasks performed by each team member (e.g., an airline crew or a surgical team). In these cases, training will not only involve teaching each individual a specific skill but also entail the coordination and integration of diverse skills that will lead to team performance. Failure of one individual to meet the needs of the team can, in these cases, result in failure of the entire team (an example given by Kozlowski et al., 2000, is of a surgical team—if the anesthesiologist fails in his or her task, the entire team fails, regardless of how well other team members perform). Influence on motivation for training and vertical transfer may thus be different for these types of teams than it is for individuals. Specifically, because use of a new skill would directly impact success of the team, it may be that teammate support is a more potent predictor of transfer that would be coworker or manager support for use of a trained skill when the question pertains to horizontal transfer. Team members, for example, may be less supportive of the use of a new skill learned in training if use of that new skill threatens the success of the team, but may be quite supportive when use of the trained skill is likely to lead to team success. Motivational processes relevant to training and transfer within teams are still a relatively untapped area of research, but questions like these will undoubtedly be posed and answered within the next few years.

In summary, early work in this area suggests that individual-level findings regarding motivational processes involved in individual-level training are generalizable to teams. Like the topic of aging, teams are an important entry on the research agenda of motivational processes in training. It would be interesting if this research examined motivational processes associated with preexisting teams. Research done to date has been conducted in laboratories with teams assembled for experimental purposes, teams that lack the interpersonal interaction and history that may affect motivation in preexisting teams. Existing relationships within the team, collaborative styles, cohesion, and collective confidence (Marks et al., 2001) might potentially influence team training motivation when the choice is made to attend training, during learning, and during the decision to transfer skills learned in training back on the job. To date, we know very little about how the interpersonal interactions inherent in teams influence motivational processes related to training and learning.

Additional Areas for Future Research

Here, we cover additional topics that we expect will be on the agenda for training motivation research in the coming decade.

E-Learning

Throughout the chapter, we have discussed important research findings regarding e-learning and motivational processes in training, which are summarized on Table 2.1. Important areas for future research in this domain will include understanding the effects of increased learner control on perceptions of effort and self-efficacy and how these factors influence motivation for training and learning outcomes. Contextual factors such as organizational support for e-learning and framing e-learning experiences are also potentially important influences on the decision to attend training and the decision to transfer skills learned in training back on the job.

Emotion and Training Motivation

In our review of the literature, we found few studies that explicitly addressed the role of emotion in training motivation. Emotion will potentially influence all three stages of our model. Emotional responses or affective traits could influence valence, instrumentality, and expectancy ratings relevant to the choice to attend training and the choice to transfer skills learned in training back on the job. Self-regulatory processes associated with goal striving are also potentially importantly influenced by emotion and emotion control skills (e.g., Kanfer & Ackerman, 1996; Keith & Frese, 2005). Building upon Kuhl's (1985) distinction between emotion and motivation control strategies for self-regulation, Kanfer and Ackerman (1996) conducted two studies investigating the influence of emotion control strategy training on skill acquisition of an air traffic controller simulation task. Across both studies, emotion control training exerted a significant beneficial effect on error frequency, particularly for lower ability trainees. In the first study, where supplementary emotion control instructions were provided, lower ability trainees committed fewer errors throughout training. In the second study, investigating the transfer effects of emotion control instructions during pretraining, earlier emotion control training had a beneficial effect on error reduction during the initial phase of the transfer task. The pattern of results provides support for the notion that negative emotional processing debilitates performance though its effects on both speed (keystrokes) and accuracy (errors) of performance. Instructional methods that reduce negative emotional processing, such as emotion control training, were shown to be particularly useful in contexts where the attentional demands of the task were greatest and errors most likely (e.g., among lower ability trainees, or during the early phase of complex skill training).

Research on error training also highlights the potential importance of emotions on motivation and learning in training. Specifically, Heimbeck, Frese, Sonnentag, and Keith (2003) used error encouragement training instructions with the goal of decreasing the negative affect associated with making errors in training. A follow-up study by Keith and Frese (2005) indicated that emotion control and metacognitive skills were the mechanisms through which error management instructions influence training outcomes. Consistent with findings by Kanfer and Ackerman (1996), Heimbeck et al. (2003) found that error encouragement instructions, when paired with a less structured task (i.e., a task that allowed for some level of exploration so the learner could make errors), positively influenced performance in training. Lest one think it was the loosening of the didactic nature of the training that caused the increase in learning for the error encouragement trainees, Heimbeck et al. found that trainees who received error management training without the error encouragement instructions were likely to do about the same in training as trainees who received the error avoidance instructions. These findings suggest that positive and negative affect are important influences of learning during training and that elements of the training experience can influence affect during learning. Additional research is warranted to further understand affective influences on the choice to attend training, to transfer skills learned in training back on the job, and to further explore the relations among emotions and self-regulatory processes during the training experience.

Summary

A perusal of the scientific literature on the topic of motivation in the context of organizationally sponsored training suggests that there has been substantial progress over the past few decades. Research in more established areas, such as motivation during training, has advanced beyond the influence of different methods to a more comprehensive understanding of how individual characteristics, including training goals, abilities, and self-regulatory skills, may influence and interact with training methods. Continuing research on the transfer of training gains to the work environment has broadened to consider the contextual characteristics, such as work unit climate and managerial support, as they affect transfer of training.

Most notably, however, is the emergence of new programs of research in previously neglected or unidentified areas, including motivation for training, motivation in the context of team training, motivation in e-learning, and training motivation in special populations. Findings to date in these areas provide a more complete picture of the general and specific factors that may affect motivation in the context of adult learning in the workplace. From a theoretic perspective, these new areas offer unique opportunities for theory testing and development. From a practical perspective, the new growth in the field enables the development of scientifically driven methods and procedures for meeting new challenges brought about by the dynamics of the global environment. As such, the prospects for learning more about and enhancing training motivation appear more promising than ever.

References

Ackerman, P. L. (1996). A theory of adult intellectual development: Process, personality, interests, and knowledge. *Intelligence, 22,* 227–257.

Ackerman, P. L. (2000). Domain-specific knowledge as the "dark matter" of adult intelligence: Gf/Gc, personality and interest correlates. *Journal of Gerontology: Psychological Sciences, 55B,* P69–P84.

Ackerman, P. L., & Kyllonen, P. C. (1991). Trainee characteristics. In J. E. Morrison (Ed.), *Training for performance: Principles of applied human learning* (pp. 193–229). Hoboken, NJ: Wiley & Sons.

Aleven, V. A. W. M. M., & Koedinger, K. R. (2002). An effective metacognitive strategy: Learning by doing and explaining with a computer based tutor. *Cognitive Science, 26,* 147–179.

Baldwin, T. T., & Ford, J. K. (1988). Transfer of training: A review and directions for future research. *Personnel Psychology, 41,* 63–105.

Baldwin, T. T., Magjuka, R. J., & Loher, B. T. (1991). The perils of participation: Effects of choice of training on trainee motivation and learning. *Personnel Psychology, 44,* 51–65.

Bandura, A. (1977). Self-efficacy: Toward a unifying theory of behavioral change. *Psychological Review, 84,* 191–215.

Barnett, S. M., & Ceci, S. J. (2002). When and where to we apply what we learn? A taxonomy for far transfer. *Psychological Bulletin, 128,* 612–637.

Beier, M. E., & Ackerman, P. L. (2001). Current-events knowledge in adults: An investigation of age, intelligence, and nonability determinants. *Psychology and Aging, 16,* 615–628.

Beier, M. E., & Ackerman, P. L. (2003). Determinants of health knowledge: An investigation of age, gender, abilities, and interests. *Journal of Personality and Social Psychology, 84*, 439–448.

Beier, M. E., & Ackerman, P. L. (2005). Age, ability, and the role of prior knowledge on the acquisition of new domain knowledge: Promising results in a real-world learning environment. *Psychology and Aging, 20*, 341–355.

Bell, B. S., & Kozlowski, S. W. J. (2002). Goal orientation and ability: interactive effects on self-efficacy, performance, and knowledge. *Journal of Applied Psychology, 87*, 497–505.

Birdi, K., Allan, C., & Warr, P. (1997). Correlates and perceived outcomes of four types of employee development activity. *Journal of Applied Psychology, 82*, 845–857.

Brown, K. G. (2001). Using computers to deliver training: Which employees learn and why? *Personnel Psychology, 54*, 271–296.

Brown, K. G. (2005). A field study of employee e-learning activity and outcomes. *Human Resources Development Quarterly, 16*, 465–480.

Bunderson, J., & Sutcliffe, K. (2003). Management team learning orientation and business unit performance. *Journal of Applied Psychology, 88*, 552–560.

Campbell, J. P., & Pritchard, R. D. (1976). Motivation theory in industrial and organizational psychology. In M. D. Dunnette (Ed.), *Handbook of industrial and organizational psychology* (pp. 63–130). Chicago: Rand McNally.

Carstensen, L. L. (1998). A life-span approach to social motivation. In J. Heckhausen & C. S. Dweck (Eds.), *Motivation and self-regulation across the lifespan* (pp. 341–364). New York: Cambridge University Press.

Cattell, R. B. (1987). *Intelligence: Its structure, growth, and action.* New York: Elsevier.

Chen, G., Gully, S. M., Whiteman, J. A., & Kilcullen, R. N. (2000). Examination of relationships among trait-like individual differences, state-like individual differences, and learning performance. *Journal of Applied Psychology, 85*, 835–847.

Chen, G., & Kanfer, R. (2006). Toward a systems theory of motivated behavior in work teams. *Research in Organizational Behavior, 27*, 223–267.

Chen, G., Thomas, B., & Wallace, J. C. (2005). A multilevel examination of the relationships among training outcomes mediating regulatory processes, and adaptive performance. *Journal of Applied Psychology, 90*, 827–841.

Cohen, S. G., & Bailey, D. E. (1997). What makes teams work: Group effectiveness research from the shop floor to the executive suite. *Journal of Management, 23*, 239–290.

Cole, M. S., Harris, S. G., & Feild, H. S. (2004). Stages of learning motivation: Development and validation of a measure. *Journal of Applied Social Psychology, 34*, 1421–1456.

Colquitt, J. A., LePine, J. A., & Noe, R. A. (2000). Toward an integrative theory of training motivation: A meta-analytic path analysis of 20 years of research. *Journal of Applied Psychology, 85*, 678–707.

Colquitt, J. A., & Simmering, M. J. (1998). Conscientiousness, goal orientation, and motivation to learn during the learning process: A longitudinal study. *Journal of Applied Psychology, 83*, 656–665.

DeRouin, R. E., Fritzsche, B. A., & Salas, E. (2004). Optimizing e-learning: Research-based guidelines for learner-controlled training. *Human Resources Management, 43*, 147–162.

DeShon, R. P., & Gillespie, J. Z. (2005). A motivated action theory account of goal orientation. *Journal of Applied Psychology, 90,* 1096–1127.

DeShon, R. P., Kozlowski, S. W. J., Schmidt, A. M., Milner, K. R., & Wiechmann, D. (2004). A multiple-goal, multilevel model of feedback effects on the regulation of individual and team performance. *Journal of Applied Psychology, 89,* 1035–1056.

Dweck, C. S. (1986). Motivational processes affecting learning. *American Psychologist, 41,* 1040–1048.

Ellis, A. P. J., Hollenbeck, J. R., Ilgen, D. R., Porter, C. O. L. H., & West, B. J. (2003). Team learning: Collectively connecting the dots. *Journal of Applied Psychology, 88,* 821–835.

Fishbein, M., & Ajzen, I. (1975). *Belief, attitude, intention, and behavior: An introduction to theory and research.* Reading, MA: Addison-Wesley.

Flavell, J. H. (1979). Metacognition and cognitive monitoring: A new area of cognitive-developmental inquiry. *American Psychologist, 34,* 906–911.

Ford, J. K., & Noe, R. A. (1987). Self-assessed training needs: The effects of attitudes toward training, managerial level, and function. *Personnel Psychology, 40,* 39–53.

Ford, J. K., Quiñones, M. A., Sego, D. J., & Sorra, J. S. (1992). Factors affecting the opportunity to perform trained tasks on the job. *Personnel Psychology, 45,* 511–527.

Ford, J. K., Smith, E. M., Weissbein, D. A., Gully, S. M., & Salas, E. (1998). Relationship of goal orientation, metacognitive activity, and practice strategies with learning outcomes and transfer. *Journal of Applied Psychology, 83,* 218–233.

Galagan, P. A. (2000, December). The e-learning revolution. *Training and Development, 54,* 24–30.

Gist, M. E., & Mitchell, T. R. (1992). Self-efficacy: A theoretical analysis of its determinants and malleability. *Academy of Management Review, 17,* 183–211.

Goff, M., & Ackerman, P. L. (1992). Personality-intelligence relations: Assessment of typical intellectual engagement. *Journal of Educational Psychology, 84,* 537–552.

Goldberg, L. R. (1993). The structure of phenotypic personality traits. *American Psychologist, 48,* 26–34.

Goldstein, I. L. (1991). Training in work organizations. In M. D. Dunnette & L. M. Hough (Eds.), *Handbook of industrial and organizational psychology* (Vol. 2, 2nd ed., pp. 507–620). Palo Alto, CA: Consulting Psychologists Press.

Guerrero, S., & Sire, B. (2001). Motivation to train from the workers' perspective: Example of French companies. *International Journal of Human Resource Management, 12,* 988–1004.

Gutherie, J. P., & Schwoerer, C. E. (1994). Individual and contextual influences on self-assessed training needs. *Journal of Organizational Behavior, 15,* 405–422.

Heimbeck, D., Frese, M., Sonnentag, S., & Keith, N. (2003). Integrating errors into the training process: The function of error management instructions and the role of goal orientation. *Personnel Psychology, 56,* 333–361.

Hicks, W. D., & Klimoski, R. J. (1987). Entry into training programs and its effects on training outcomes: A field experiment. *Academy of Management Journal, 30,* 542–552.

Hofstede, G., & McCrae, R. R., (2004). Personality and culture revisited: Linking traits and dimensions of culture. *Cross-Cultural Research, 38,* 52–88.

Holladay, C. L., Knight, J. L., Paige, D. L., & Quiñones, M. A. (2003). The influence of framing on attitudes toward diversity training. *Human Resources Development Quarterly, 14,* 245–263.

Holladay, C. L., & Quiñones, M. A. (2003). Practice variability and transfer of training: The role of self-efficacy generality. *Journal of Applied Psychology, 88,* 1094–1103.

Horn, J. L., & Cattell, R. B. (1966). Refinement and test of the theory of fluid and crystallized general intelligence. *Journal of Educational Psychology, 57,* 253–270.

Kanfer, R. (1990). Motivation theory in industrial and organizational psychology. In M. Dunnette & L. M. Hough (Eds.), *Handbook of industrial and organizational psychology* (Vol. 1, 2nd ed., pp. 75–150). Palo Alto, CA: Consulting Psychologists Press.

Kanfer, R., & Ackerman, P. L. (1989). Motivation and cognitive abilities: An integrative/aptitude-treatment interaction approach to skill acquisition. *Journal of Applied Psychology, 74,* 657–690.

Kanfer, R., & Ackerman, P. L. (1996). A self-regulatory skills perspective to reducing cognitive interference. In I. G. Sarason, G. R. Pierce, & B. R. Sarason (Eds.), *Cognitive interference: Theories, methods, and findings* (pp. 153–171). Mahwah, NJ: Erlbaum.

Kanfer, R., & Ackerman, P. L. (2004). Aging, adult development, and work motivation. *Academy of Management Review, 29,* 440–458.

Keith, N., & Frese, M. (2005). Self-regulation in error management training: Emotion control and metacognition as mediators of performance effects. *Journal of Applied Psychology, 90,* 677–691.

Kelley, C. L., & Charness, N. (1995). Issues in training older adults to use computers. *Behaviour & Information Technology, 14,* 107–120.

Koriat, A., Ma'ayan, H., & Nussinson, R. (2006). The intricate relationship between monitoring and control in metacognition: Lessons for the cause-and-effect relation between subjective experience and behavior. *Journal of Experimental Psychology: General, 135,* 36–69.

Kozlowski, S. W. J., & Bell, B. S. (2003). Work groups and teams in organizations. In W. C. Borman, D. R. Ilgen, & R. J. Klimoski (Eds.), *Handbook of psychology: Volume 12. Industrial and organizational psychology* (pp. 225–254). Hoboken, NJ: Wiley.

Kozlowski, S. W. J., & Bell, B. S. (2006). Disentangling achievement orientation and goal setting: Effects on self-regulatory processes. *Journal of Applied Psychology, 91,* 900–916.

Kozlowski, S. W. J., Brown, K. G., Weissbein, D. A., Cannon-Bowers, J. A., & Salas, E. (2000). A multilevel approach to training effectiveness: Enhancing horizontal and vertical transfer. In K. J. Klein & S. W. J. Kozlowski (Eds.), *Multilevel theory, research, and methods in organizations* (pp. 157–210). Mahwah, NJ: Erlbaum.

Kozlowski, S. W. J., & Farr, J. L. (1988). An integrative model of updating and performance. *Human Performance, 1,* 5–29.

Kozlowski, S. W. J., Gully, S. M., Brown, K. G., Salas, E., Smith, E. M., & Nason, E. R. (2001). Effects of training goals and goal orientation traits on multidimensional training outcomes and performance adaptability. *Organizational Behavior and Human Decision Processes, 85*, 1–31.

Kozlowski, S. W. J., & Hults, B. M. (1987). An exploration of climates for technical updating and performance. *Personnel Psychology, 40*, 539–563.

Kraiger, K., Ford, J. K., & Salas, E. (1993). Application of cognitive, skill-based, and affective theories of learning outcomes to new methods of training evaluation. *Journal of Applied Psychology Monograph, 78*, 311–328.

Kubeck, J. E., Delp, N. D., Haslett, T. K., & McDaniel, M. A. (1996). Does job-related training performance decline with age? *Psychology and Aging, 11*, 92–107.

Kuhl, J., & Beckmann, J. (Eds.) (1985). *Action control, from cognition to behavior: From cognition to behavior*. New York: Springer-Verlag.

Maki, W. S., & Maki, R. H. (2002). Multimedia comprehension skill predicts differential outcomes of Web-based and lecture courses. *Journal of Experimental Psychology: Applied, 8*, 85–98.

Mangos, P. M., & Steele-Johnson, D. (2001). The role of subjective task complexity in goal orientation, self-efficacy and performance relations. *Human Performance, 14*, 169–186.

Marks, M. A., Mathieu, J. E., & Zaccaro, S. J. (2001). A temporally based framework and taxonomy of team processes. *Academy of Management Review, 26*, 356–376.

Martocchio, J. J. (1992). Microcomputer usage as an opportunity: The influence of context in employee training. *Personnel Psychology, 45*, 529–552.

Mathieu, J. E., & Martineau, J. W. (1997). Individual and situational influences on training motivation. In J. K. Ford & Associates (Eds.), *Improving training effectiveness in work organizations*. Mahwah, NJ: Erlbaum.

Mathieu, J. E., Tannenbaum, S. I., & Salas, E. (1992). Influences of individual and situational characteristics on measures of training effectiveness. *Academy of Management Journal, 35*, 828–847.

Maurer, T. J., & Tarulli, B. A. (1994). Investigation of perceived environment, perceived outcome, and person variables in relationship to voluntary development activities by employees. *Journal of Applied Psychology, 79*, 3–14.

McAdams, D. P., & de St. Aubin, E. (Eds.) (1998). *Generativity and adult development*. Washington, DC: American Psychological Association.

Mitchell, T. R., & Daniels, D. (2003). Motivation. In W. C. Borman, D. R. Ilgen, & R. J. Klimoski (Eds.), *Handbook of psychology: Volume 12. Industrial and organizational psychology* (pp. 225–254). Hoboken, NJ: Wiley.

Noe, R. A. (1986). Trainees' attributes and attitudes: Neglected influences on training effectiveness. *Academy of Management Review, 11*, 736–749.

Noe, R. A., & Schmitt, N. (1986). The influence of trainee attitudes on training effectiveness: Test of a model. *Personnel Psychology, 39*, 497–523.

Noe, R. A., & Wilk, S. L. (1993). Investigation of the factors that influence employees' participation in development activities. *Journal of Applied Psychology, 78*, 291–302.

Pintrich, P. R. (2003). A motivational science perspective on the role of student motivation in learning and teaching contexts. *Journal of Educational Psychology, 95*, 667–686.

Quiñones, M. A. (1995). Pretraining context effects: Training assignment as feedback. *Journal of Applied Psychology, 80*, 226–238.

Quiñones, M. A. (1997). Contextual influences on training effectiveness. In M. A. Quiñones & A. Ehrenstein (Eds.), *Training for a rapidly changing workplace: Applications of psychological research* (pp. 177–199). Washington, DC: American Psychological Association.

Rouiller, J. Z., & Goldstein, I. L. (1993). The relationship between organizational transfer climate and positive transfer of training. *Human Resource Development Quarterly, 4*, 377–390.

Salas, E., Burke, C. S., & Cannon-Bowers, J. A. (2002). What we know about designing and delivering team training: Tips and guidelines. In K. Kraiger (Ed.), *Creating, implementing, and managing effective training and development: State-of-the-art lessons for practice* (pp. 234–259). San Francisco: Jossey-Bass.

Schaie, K. W. (1996). *Intellectual development in adulthood: The Seattle longitudinal study*. New York: Cambridge University Press.

Schmidt, A. M., & Ford, J. K. (2003). Learning within a learner control training environment: The interactive effects of goal orientation and meta-cognitive instruction on learning outcomes. *Personnel Psychology, 56*, 405–429.

Schmidt, R. A., & Bjork, R. A. (1992). New conceptualizations of practice: Common principles in three paradigms suggest new concepts for training. *Psychological Science, 3*, 207–217.

Seijts, G. H., & Latham, G. P. (2001). The effect of distal learning, outcome, and proximal goals on a moderately complex task. *Journal of Organizational Behavior, 22*, 291–302.

Seijts, G. H., Latham, G. P., Tasa, K., & Latham, B. W. (2004). Goal setting and goal orientation: An integration of two different yet related literatures. *Academy of Management Journal, 47*, 227–239.

Simpson, P. A., Greller, M. M., & Stroh, L. K. (2002). Variations in human capital investment activity by age. *Journal of Vocational Behavior, 61*, 109–138.

Smith, E. M., Ford, J. K., & Kozlowski, S. W. J. (1997). Building adaptive expertise: Implications for training design strategies. In M. A. Quiñones & A. Ehrenstein (Eds.), *Training for a rapidly changing workplace: Applications of psychological research* (pp. 89–118). Washington, DC: American Psychological Association.

Steele-Johnson, Beauregard, R. S., Hoover, P. B., & Schmidt, A. M. (2000). Goal orientation and task demand effects on motivation, affect, and performance. *Journal of Applied Psychology, 85*, 724–738.

Sterns, H. L., & Doverspike, D. (1989). Aging and the training and learning process. In I. L. Goldstein & Associates (Eds.), *Training and development in organizations* (pp. 299–332). San Francisco: Jossey-Bass.

Tannenbaum, S. I., Mathieu, J. E., Salas, E., & Cannon-Bowers, J. A. (1991). Meeting trainees' expectations: The influence of training fulfillment on the development of commitment, self-efficacy, and motivation. *Journal of Applied Psychology, 76*, 759–769.

Tannenbaum, S. I., & Yukl, G. (1992). Training and development in work organizations. *Annual Review of Psychology, 43*, 399–441.

Tracey, J. B., Hinkin, T. R., Tannenbaum, S., & Mathieu, J. E. (2001). The influence of individual characteristics and the work environment on varying levels of training outcomes. *Human Resources Development Quarterly, 12*, 5–23.

Tracey, J. B., Tannenbaum, S. I., & Kavanagh, M. J. (1995). Applying trained skills on the job: The importance of the work environment. *Journal of Applied Psychology, 80*, 239–252.

Tsai, W. C., & Tai, W. T. (2003). Perceived importance as a mediator of the relationship between training assignment and training motivation. *Personnel Review, 32*, 151–163.

U.S. Bureau of Labor Statistics (2006, February). *Occupational outlook handbook, 2006–07 Edition*. Bulletin No. 2600. Washington, DC: U.S. Department of Labor.

Welsh, E. T., Wanberg, C. R., Brown, K. G., & Simmering, M. J. (2003). E-learning: Emerging uses, empirical results and future directions. *International Journal of Training and Development, 7*, 245–258.

Winters, D., & Latham, G. P. (1996). The effects of learning versus performance goals on a simple versus a complex task. *Group and Organizational Management, 21*, 236–250.

Vroom, V. (1964). *Work and motivation*. Chichester, UK: Wiley.

Yang, B., Watkins, K. E., & Marsick, V. J. (2004). The construct of the learning organization: Dimensions, measurement, and validation. *Human Resources Development Quarterly, 15*, 31–55.

Yeo, G. B., & Neal, A. (2004). A multilevel analysis of effort, practice, and performance: Effects of ability, conscientiousness, and goal orientation. *Journal of Applied Psychology, 89*, 231–247.

3

Experts at Work: Principles for Developing Expertise in Organizations

Eduardo Salas
University of Central Florida

Michael A. Rosen
University of Central Florida

Introduction

A recent report by the National Academies' Committee on Science, Engineering, and Public Policy (COSEPUP; 2006) documented a stark state of affairs for U.S.-based companies. In short, there are many challenges facing the competitiveness of the United States and its world leadership position in the realm of science and technology stemming from a national inadequacy in the development of prospective employees. The COSEPUP report concluded that there is an erosion of expertise in mathematics, science, and engineering that threatens the long-term position of the United States in the world economy. This erosion of knowledge and skills is caused by losses of expertise through the retirement of experienced employees as well as insufficient development of replacements for the wealth of expertise exiting the workforce. This trend has immediate, not distant, consequences. Bill Gates openly commented on the lack of available applicants with adequate training to fill positions in the United States: "The jobs are there, and they are good-paying jobs, but we don't have the same pipeline" (Gates, cited in Vise, 2005, p. E05). The COSEPUP report recommended changes in federal government policies to correct this trend of declining expertise on a national level.

Similarly, we argue that organizations too must attend to the internal development and maintenance of expertise within their ranks to remain competitive. This issue of a waning supply of expertise is not limited to technology-based industries. The recent American Society for

Training and Development (ASTD) *Annual Review of Trends in Workplace Learning and Performance* (2006) reported a 10-year trend of increased investment in employee development and training. This can be seen as one indicator of a heightened need to develop and maintain the expertise within the ranks of modern organizations. Expertise is a form of human capital that requires investment in resources to develop and that pays dividends in productivity (Mieg, 2006). Consequently, within an organization, the focus on developing expertise should not be limited to science and technology, but should include expertise of all varieties important to organizational performance. Organizations must concern themselves not only with the emerging sources of technical expertise abroad but also with their domestic competition's ability to generate and exploit the expertise of its employees. To that end, a better understanding of expertise is in order, a need this chapter is intended to address.

Expertise is the product of high levels of motivation, effective learning, development, training, and experience and is characterized by performance levels at the uppermost ranges within a domain. Experts and the processes by which they develop have received much attention from contemporary researchers. The recent publication of the first handbook of expertise (Ericsson, Charness, Feltovich, & Hoffman, 2006) is a significant marker in the development of the field of expertise research. This signifies that a "critical mass"—a body of knowledge—of theoretical frameworks and models, empirical findings, and methods specialized to the study of expertise and expert performance has been realized (Ericsson, 2006).

In light of the above, the overall purpose of this chapter is to provide an entry point for industrial-organizational psychologists working to develop the knowledge and skills of personnel within organizations to this relatively untapped wealth of knowledge—the expertise literature. Therefore, this chapter sets out to meet three goals. First, we will review the current scientific understanding of expertise, including definitions and descriptions of what expertise is as well as how it is developed. Second, we develop a set of principles for the development of expertise in organizations based upon the theoretical and empirical expertise literature. Third, we conclude this chapter with a discussion of future directions for the study and development of expertise in organizations.

The Nature and Acquisition of Expertise

Researchers and the general public have long been fascinated with experts. Eminent scientists, musicians, artists, and athletes are captivating figures, often inspiring historiographic research into the details of their lives and their journeys toward eminence. However, the scientific investigation of the psychological and physiological processes involved in the production of superior performance is relatively new. A significant challenge to developing a science of expertise is the variety of types of expertise across different domains (Ericsson & Smith, 1991). This section is devoted to exploring factors that, in varying degrees, contribute to expertise and superior performance across domain boundaries as well as global factors that contribute to the development of expertise. Before we turn to the properties, characteristics, and development of expertise, it is necessary to provide some general definitions to frame the discussion.

What Is Expertise?

The *American Heritage Dictionary* (2000) defined expertise as "skill or knowledge in a particular area." This deceptively simple conceptualization of expertise has been interpreted through various lenses. The modern theoretical understanding of expertise has passed through a series of stages (Holyoak, 1991) beginning with the idea that expertise is the application of general reasoning strategies (Newell & Simon, 1972). Expertise was viewed as a function of skill with using a relatively small number of heuristic searches (e.g., means–ends analysis, and hill climbing; Hayes, 1989) in a problem space. This approach was quickly found to be limited in that empirical findings suggested that domain knowledge played a major role in expert performance (Chase & Simon, 1973; de Groot, 1946/1978). This gave rise to the knowledge-based view of expertise; experts use domain-specific knowledge, inference patterns, and skilled memory, whereas novice performance is characterized by non-domain-dependent heuristics. Within this very general approach, explanations of the nature of expertise have been couched in terms of factors such as the amount and organization of knowledge (Chase & Simon, 1973; Chi, Glaser, & Rees, 1982; Larkin, McDermott, Simon, & Simon, 1980), specialized analytical reasoning strategies, skills, and heuristics (Anzai, 1991; Charness, 1989; Dorner & Scholkopf, 1991; Schunn & Anderson, 1999; Schunn, McGregor, & Saner, 2005), individual differences in intelligence and creativity (Simonton, 1996, 2003), acquired memory skills (Chase & Ericsson, 1982; Ericsson & Kintsch, 1995), physiological adaptation (Ericsson & Lehman, 1996), and practice, automaticity, and skilled performance (Anderson, 1982). This breadth of dimensions used to articulate the nature of expertise has come to be viewed as a "prototype" of expertise, with each of the separate aspects manifested to varying degrees in different domains (Hoffman, Feltovich, & Ford, 1997; Holyoak, 1991; Sternberg, 1997) as task requirements in these varied domains dictate the mechanisms needed for expert performance. In this way, expertise is psychological and physiological adaptation to task constraints (Ericsson & Lehman, 1996). People who have attained expert levels of performance for a domain of tasks have developed specialized mechanisms (e.g., memory skill, reasoning strategies, and metacognition skills) fitted to that task that allow for superior performance. Therefore, expertise is a difference in the type of performance processes used and not just elevated levels of performance outcomes achieved via optimal execution of the same performance processes used by novices. We will discuss the characteristics of expertise in more detail in later sections.

Adaptive and Routine Expertise

An important distinction can be drawn between routine and adaptive expertise (Hatano & Inagaki, 1986). Specifically, routine expertise can be thought of as the skill acquisition component of expertise in that routine experts are capable of superior and reproducible performance in terms of speed, accuracy, and automaticity on familiar tasks but generally lack the ability to transfer their skills to new tasks or problems (Hatano & Inagaki, 1986). Expertise of this variety comes at a cost (Sternberg, 1996). Specifically, high levels of adaptation to a particular set of task constraints can induce rigidity of performance (Sternberg & Frensch, 1991); that is, if the task constraints change, the expert may no longer be able to produce superior levels of performance. This result is characteristic of routine expertise. Conversely, adaptive expertise involves the ability to invent new procedures and adjust to variations in the task. What separates adaptive from routine experts is a conceptual understanding of the domain (Barnett & Koslowski, 2002; Hatano & Inagaki, 1986), and, consequently, the development of routine versus adaptive expertise is characterized as the difference between the accretion of skill and learning with understanding. A deep understanding of the concepts involved in task performance allows adaptive experts to exhibit expert performance in domains with inherent variation in task constraints (Feltovich, Spiro, & Coulson, 1997).

Developing Expertise

Another approach to the issue of defining expertise is to look at the process of becoming an expert. Although there are multiple views on this issue, Dreyfus and Dreyfus (1986) provided a five-stage model of skill acquisition and the development of expertise that is most applicable to the types of ill-defined tasks and problems that comprise work in modern knowledge-driven organizations. The first stage of the model, the novice, consists of performance characterized by manipulation of context-free information by context-free rules. That is, the novice applies precise and explicitly stated rules to clearly and objectively defined elements of the situation. Attending to a limited and clearly defined set of features in the environment and using a universally applied set of rules allow the novice to perform without an overall or coherent understanding of the entire task and context. The learner advances to the second stage, advanced beginner, through extensive experience with different real-world situations. The advanced beginner performs reasonably well and does so by applying more complex rules as well as by beginning to use situational features of the environment in task performance. In contrast to context-free features, situational features are difficult to objectively and explicitly articulate by the learner or the trainer or mentor. As more experience is accumulated and more situational features are recognized, the learner progresses into the competent stage of expertise. This is typified by someone who is able to manage the complexity of numerous situational features in terms of goals and plans. That is, the importance of some features will change depending on the presence or absence of others; the competent performer decides how to extract meaning from the context in relation to relevant goals and plans. These goals and plans must be consciously adopted by the competent performer, a process that usually requires large amounts of effort and deliberation. The fourth stage of expertise, the proficient performer, is characterized by a shift in situation perception. The proficient performer sees situations as complete wholes and uses these patterns without decomposing them into their constituent features (i.e., holistic similarity recognition; Dreyfus & Dreyfus, 1986, p. 28). In this way, the proficient performer rapidly understands and organizes the task in a specific situation; however, he or she must still analytically reason about what to do. In the fifth stage, the expert performer rapidly and effortlessly assesses the situation and decides what to do. Dreyfus and Dreyfus summarized an expert's performance under normal conditions enabled by large amounts of experience: "Experts don't solve problems and don't make decisions; they do what normally works" (pp. 30–31).

In general, shifts from one stage to the next in the Dreyfus model depend on changes in one of two nonorthogonal dimensions. First, moving from novice to expert means changing from relying on abstract and explicit rules to guiding performance by drawing on past experience. Second, the development of expertise entails a change in the perception and understanding of a situation from a fragmented perception where discrete and equivalent "bits" of the environment are evaluated to a more holistic perception of the environment. Dreyfus and Dreyfus' five-stage model has received empirical support within complex and ill-defined work domains such as nursing (see Benner, 1982, 1984).

Who Is an Expert?

The accurate identification of experts is crucial to the development of the science of expertise and learning, and to the development and optimal use of expertise within organizations. It is simple to assume that an expert is someone who exhibits the characteristics of expertise, including reliably superior performance; however, the process of identifying experts in many workplace settings is often more complicated than this for two main reasons. First, it is difficult to determine reliable and consistent expert performance in domains characterized by ill-defined problems and tasks with unstable dynamic structures, such as those found in many modern organizational settings. This difficulty is rooted in a lack of readily available "gold standards" of performance by which to make evaluations. Second, non-performance-based significations of expertise (e.g., social attributions, seniority, and certifications) are prevalent yet do *not* reliably predict expert performance (Camerer & Johnson, 1991). Two examples of approaches to evaluating expertise along these dimensions for ill-defined tasks are discussed below.

The Cochran–Weiss–Shanteau (CWS) Index of expertise is a ratio of two necessary but insufficient characteristics of expertise that provides an empirical and relative measure of expertise in domains where gold standards are unavailable (Weiss & Shanteau, 2003). Specifically, the CWS Index of expertise is based on the idea that experts must (a) be able to discriminate between stimuli within their domain of expertise (Hammond, 1996), and (b) exhibit high levels of internal consistency of discrimination judgments over time (Einhorn, 1974). Through a process of eliciting discrimination judgments on a set of stimuli from a specific domain, scores for discrimination ability and consistency can be calculated. The ratio of discrimination over inconsistency (the CWS Index) can then be used to evaluate expertise; larger ratios indicate higher levels of expertise (i.e., more accurate and consistent discrimination judgments of stimuli). The CWS Index has been shown to be a useful evaluation of expertise in making judgments in such domains as medical diagnosis, personnel selection, auditing, dynamic decision-making tasks, and livestock judging (Shanteau, Friel, Thomas, & Raacke, 2005; Shanteau, Weiss, Thomas, & Pounds, 2003; Weiss & Shanteau, 2003).

More in line with definitions of expertise based on social selection (Agnew, Ford, & Hayes, 1997; Mieg, 2001), Stein (1997) proposed that expertise can be conceived of as a product of social context as well as individual skills and, consequently, that elements of expertise can be measured within an organizational context via multidimensional scaling techniques or network analysis. These methods provide insight into social attributions of expertise within an organization—knowledge about the perception of "who knows what" (Stein, 1992). Although there is a substantial amount of research indicating that non-performance-based evaluations of expertise are often erroneous (Camerer & Johnson, 1991), the social attribution of expertise is an important topic in its own right. For example, a group's performance and decision-making effectiveness are closely tied to its ability to recognize the actual performance-based expertise levels of its members and weight task inputs accordingly (Bonner, 2004; Faraj & Sproull, 2000; Hollenbeck et al., 1995), regardless of the degree of role specialization (Hollenbeck, Colquitt, Ilgen, LePine, & Hedlund, 1998). This ability becomes increasingly important as the task grows in complexity (Libby, Trotman, & Zimmer, 1987). Essentially, greater consistency between subjective evaluations of expertise and actual levels of expert performance yield better group performance outcomes.

In sum, expertise comprises an individual's ability to perform repeatedly and reliably at high levels on a specific set of tasks within the boundaries of a domain. A wide variety of mechanisms have been identified as mediating the processes of expert performance. The types of mechanisms acquired in the development of expertise depend on task constraints, and, therefore, expertise is best viewed as cognitive, behavioral, and attitudinal adaptations to the demands of the performance domain. Although expertise can only truly be defined in terms of performance, social attributions of expertise (e.g., perceptions of expertise, certifications, and status) within an organization can have significant ramifications on the performance of groups and teams. Proceeding from this general discussion of the nature of expertise, we now advance a descriptive and organizational framework of an array of mechanisms that have been found to mediate expert performance across domains.

A Framework of Expertise

Based on the investigations of experts in numerous domains, a number of general characteristics of expertise can be synthesized (see Bedard & Chi, 1992; Chi, 2006; Feltovich, Prietula, & Ericsson, 2006; Glaser, 1987; Glaser & Chi, 1988; Hoffman et al., 1997). These characteristics are presented as a framework of expertise in Figure 3.1 and described below. This framework is best understood from the "prototype of expertise" approach described earlier, where each factor in the framework enables expert performance to varying degrees depending on task constraints. Additionally, many of these factors are highly interrelated (e.g., knowledge organization facilitates pattern recognition). We present this framework in two subsections: first the elements of the prototype of expertise, and subsequently the development and maintenance of expertise. Thus, this framework illustrates the main mechanisms by which experts produce reliably superior performance as well as the means by which experts develop these performance mechanisms.

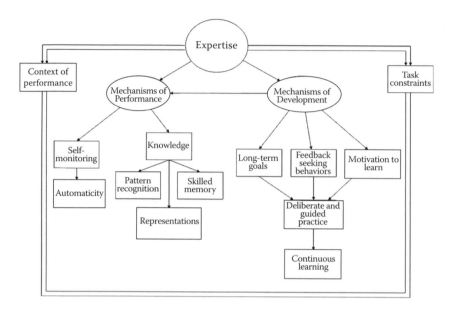

FIGURE 3.1
A framework of the components of expertise and its development.

What Are the Characteristics of Expertise?

Context and Task Constraints: Experts Are Masters of Their Domain

The first aspect of our framework is context and task constraints. Expertise is highly specific to the domain of expertise (Vicente & Wang, 1998; Voss & Post, 1988). Because expertise is extreme adaptation to task constraints (Ericsson & Lehman, 1996), it is inherently fragile (Huguenard, Prietula, & Lerch, 1990). Expertise in one domain does not generalize to another, even when tasks share many similarities (Eisenstadt & Kareev, 1979), and expertise can break down when the task constraints change. This is true of tasks involving cognitive or psychomotor skills. In addition to being limited to a specific domain, expert performance is often dependent upon contextual cues within that domain (Chi, 2006). For example, experts use aspects of contextual information to help them make decisions. These aspects of context are not necessarily causally related to the phenomenon, but nonetheless, through experience experts are able to develop sensitivity to patterns of cues that correlate with the problem at hand. This gives experts an advantage when the performance episode occurs in a familiar context (Hobus, Schmidt, Boshuizen, & Patel, 1987). For these reasons, it has been argued that "when studying expertise, the minimum unit of analysis is the 'expert in context'" (Hoffman et al., 1997, p. 553). This means that expert performance is inextricably linked not only to the task constraints but to the context of performance as well. Thus, our framework depicts context and task constraints as encompassing the mechanisms contributing to expertise and expert performance at large.

Knowledge: Experts Know More!

Of course, the domain limitations of expertise are not surprising given the importance of domain-related knowledge (Chase & Simon, 1973; de Groot, 1946/1978). Simply put, experts know more about their domain than non-experts. Although this may appear to be a definitional truism, this point is nuanced and multifaceted. To explicate this relationship, it is useful to discuss human long-term memory in terms of a semantic network. From this perspective, concepts are taken to be nodes connected by links or relations between concepts, and cognitive processing (such as memory retrieval) operates by traversing these links (Baddeley, 1997; Quillian, 1969). The knowledge advantage of experts can subsequently be conceptualized as a larger semantic network (for a particular domain). Experts have more concepts (nodes); however, experts do not differ from novices solely in terms of knowledge quantity. There are striking differences in terms of the organization of knowledge between experts and novices. Specifically, the expert's knowledge is organized around deeper conceptual relationships with more robust connections between units of knowledge (Bordage & Zacks, 1984). For example, Chi, Feltovich, and Glaser (1981) showed that when classifying physics problems, novices tended to categorize problems based on superficial aspects (e.g., the objects involved in the problem), whereas experts classified problems based on principles and methods used to solve the problem (e.g., applicable laws of physics). In addition to a more conceptual organization of knowledge, experts maintain a greater amount of "cross-referencing" of their knowledge, whereas novices have fewer and weaker links between aspects of their knowledge. In a medical reasoning task, Feltovich, Johnson, Moller, and Swanson (1984) found that experts' knowledge of diseases had a rich network of connections linking diseases by shared symptoms, whereas novices' knowledge was fixed by the most salient features of each individual disease in isolation from others. Therefore, the expert's domain-related knowledge base is more complex than the novice's due to a greater size (or amount) of knowledge, a deeper conceptual quality of knowledge, and a greater density of interrelations between concepts (Chi & Ohlsson, 2005). This more complex and robust knowledge base increases the ability of the expert to learn more task-related knowledge; that is, the more a person knows about a domain of expertise, the easier it becomes to learn even more about that domain (Hambrick, 2003).

Pattern Recognition: Experts See the World in Patterns

Expertise involves the perception of larger and more meaningful patterns in the environment (Egan & Schwartz, 1979; Engle & Bukstel, 1978;

Hogarth, 2001). The more robust base of knowledge held by the expert affords efficient performance through pattern recognition. This advantage is limited to the domain of expertise because it does not involve an underlying superiority of perceptual abilities in general, but is an artifact of superior organization of domain knowledge and the development of memory skills specialized to the task constraints of the domain (Ericsson & Kintsch, 1995). For example, Lesgold and colleagues (1988) found that expert radiologists are able to detect patterns and nuances in cue configurations in X-ray films that novice radiologists could not.

This conceptualization of expert performance produced through increased pattern recognition ability and an extensive knowledge base was a central component of the first general theory of expertise, proposed by Simon and Chase (1973). This theory, commonly referred to as *chunking theory*, was firmly rooted in the highly influential work of de Groot (1946/1978) on world-class chess players. His research revealed that expert chess players did not differ from more novice players in terms of basic memory capacity or speed of thought. Instead, greater chess skill in the expert was realized through prior experience with and knowledge of chess. This finding fit well with assumptions of the burgeoning human information processing (HIP) theory (Newell & Simon, 1972), specifically, that normal adults do not vary significantly in working memory capacity, attentional resources, and other cognitive capacities. Synthesizing the work of de Groot and others with HIP theory, Simon and Chase (1973) proposed that expertise is the product of prolonged experience with a domain that allows an individual to acquire a large collection of increasingly complex patterns (of chess pieces) or "chunks" (Miller, 1956). Once these chunks have been acquired, they are used to retrieve associated actions (chess moves) when they are perceived again, thus eliminating the need for an extensive search of memory or analytical reasoning about what move should be made. This ability to store complex patterns allows for the rapid perception and response selections that are characteristic of expert performance and is viewed in chunking theory as the primary mechanism of expert performance; the role of thinking ahead is minimized (Gobet & Simon, 1996).

The importance of the pattern recognition mechanism of expertise has been reinforced by investigations of real-world decision making where characteristics of the environment make the application of formal decision analyses unrealistic or even impossible (Klein, Orasanu, & Calderwood, 1993). These investigations, collectively carried out under the title *naturalistic decision making* (Zsambok & Klein, 1997), examine decision makers in domains such as medicine, the military, and firefighting, where high levels of time pressure, uncertain dynamic environments, ill-structured problems, shifting goals, and high-stakes outcomes define the operational context

(Orasanu & Connolly, 1993). In these conditions, expert decision makers do not evaluate multiple decision options. Instead, they engage in recognition primed decision making (RPD; Klein, 1993). RPD is characterized by the retrieval of action options, goals, and expectations for a decision based on the expert's dynamic experience of a situation. That is, expert decision makers use environmental cues associated with a prototype or analogue of their present situation to retrieve a single decision alternative that has worked in previous similar situations (Klein, 1993, 1998). Expert decision makers are able to employ mental simulation of the retrieved decision alternative in order to diagnose the retrieved solution's fit with the current situation and modify it if need be (Hutton & Klein, 1999).

Representations: Experts Understand the Task Domain at a Deeper Level

Related to but distinct from experts' increased pattern recognition ability and more abstractly and functionally organized knowledge base is experts' ability to create better representations of situations and problems. Experts create representations of available information in the environment that are deeper than those of novices, who tend to build superficial representations of problems (Glaser & Chi, 1988). Essentially, the expert representation is more functional and abstract than that of the novice (Feltovich et al., 2006). Representations with these characteristics afford several advantages, including aiding the recall of relevant information, facilitating the integration of environmental cues, guiding the process of determining what information is important to the problem at hand, aiding analogical reasoning, and supporting the evaluation of possible problem solutions (Zeitz, 1997). The more ill defined a problem is, the greater the difference between expert and novice problem representations becomes (Bedard & Chi, 1992). This is evidenced by the empirical findings that experts spend more time creating problem (or situation) representations than novices (Chi et al., 1981; Van Gog, Paas, & Van Merrienboer, 2005). For example, Randel and colleagues (1996) found that expert electronic warfare technicians in the U.S. Navy spend more time analyzing the situation in a naturalistic decision-making task than novices. The novice technicians spent considerably more time evaluating possible courses of action. For the expert, building a model or representation of the problem is central to task performance. Once the situation is represented, the expert can use his or her highly develop pattern recognition skills afforded by the robust knowledge base to retrieve and adapt courses of action to the present context. Better representations of the situation will lead to more effective pattern recognition and mental simulation outcomes (i.e., the process of retrieving information appropriate to the present situation will be facilitated; the evaluation of the retrieved information's fit with the current situation will be improved).

Memory Skill: Experts Manage Incoming Information—They Encode Better,
Retrieve Better, and Make Associations

The complexity of many domains can exceed the basic limitations on human information processing such that representing all of the essential information of a situation necessary for pattern recognition may outstrip an individual's working memory capacity. However, as noted, experts develop adaptations that allow them to overcome this limitation. The finding that scores on tests of short-term memory (STM) could be greatly improved with practice (Chase & Ericsson, 1981, 1982; Ericsson, 1985) led to the theory of skilled memory (Chase & Ericsson, 1981, 1982; Ericsson & Staszewski, 1989) and ultimately to the theory of long-term working memory (LTWM; Ericsson & Delaney, 1998, 1999; Ericsson & Kintsch, 1995). LTWM theory asserts that experts develop skills for rapid storage and retrieval of information into long-term memory (LTM) that effectively increase the capacity of working memory without changing the tempo-rary storage capacity of STM. Essentially, "cognitive processes are viewed as a sequence of stable states representing end products of processing" (Ericsson & Kintsch, 1995, p. 211), and, by means of acquired memory skills, these end products can be stored in LTM and kept directly, reliably, and efficiently accessible through retrieval cues held in short-term work-ing memory (STWM). This is consistent with findings showing that for novices, working memory (WM) capacity is more predictive than LTWM skill of levels of performance on complex cognitive tasks, whereas the converse is true of experts (Sohn & Doane, 2003, 2004). This means that before individuals develop LTWM skills for a particular task, their perfor-mance is bound by limitations of transient storage in STM, a capacity that does not increase with practice (Oberauer, 2006).

The type of memory skill developed (e.g., encoding strategies, retrieval structures, and associations with prior knowledge) is determined by the demands placed on WM by the specific task (Ericsson & Kintsch, 1995). This explains the domain specificity of expert memory performance. Just as individuals must learn the basic procedures for successfully complet-ing a task, they must also develop strategies for encoding and retrieving information from LTM. Developing effective memory skills requires an understanding of the task constraints as the individual must be able to anticipate the retrieval demands involved in task performance (Ericsson & Kintsch, 1995). Tasks vary greatly in terms of memory demands. Mental calculation does not require that intermediate calculations be stored for long durations, and therefore cue-based retrievals that focus on the most recent information will be optimal. Conversely, tasks that demand large amounts of information remain durably stored and readily accessible for times exceeding the limitations of STWM (e.g., expert memory of waiters for menu orders, and text comprehension; Ericsson & Kintsch, 1995) and will require more elaborative encoding.

Automaticity: Experts Have Adaptive Automation

Experts achieve automaticity in the basic skills of their domain (Gentner, 1988; Lesgold et al., 1988). They automate many aspects of their performance processes that, for novices, require conscious and effortful control (Sternberg, 1997). *Automaticity* is a broad term used to describe changes in attentional requirements, conscious and unconscious control, and the speed and accuracy of task performance that sometimes accompanies extensive learning (Moors & De Houwer, 2006). In general, automated cognitive processes are faster, less effortful, more autonomous, and less available to conscious control than nonautomated processes (Logan, 1988). Additionally, automated processes are more rigid or stereotypic. Automaticity develops for tasks in consistent environments, where cue configurations appear in a predictable way so that responses can be reliably mapped to stimuli across performance episodes (Logan, 1988). With large amounts of practice designed to increase performance, the speed and smoothness of cognitive operations increase, and the amount of cognitive resources required to carry out the processes decreases. In relation to enabling higher order cognitive processes, automaticity is a means to overcome the physiological limitations of human information processing (Salthouse, 1991). As the basic elements of a task become automated, the expert yields a greater balance of cognitive resources that can be allocated to higher level processes such as self-monitoring and more complex aspects of task performance. For example, expert typists are able to recite nursery rhymes while typing (Shaffer, 1975), and reading comprehension is dependent on the low-level processes of encoding and decoding letters and words (Wagner & Stanovich, 1996). In this way, complex skill acquisition can be thought of as incremental building of automaticity in low-level task processes (Salthouse, 1986).

Metacognition and Self-Regulation: Experts Monitor Their Processes

Although experts develop automaticity in the basic task components of their domain, they do not lose the ability to monitor their performance processes. In fact, self-monitoring and metacognitive skills are essential components of expertise (Feltovich et al., 2006; Glaser & Chi, 1988; Sternberg, 1998). Metacognitive abilities are enhanced by the expert's increased level of automaticity in low-level task components as more cognitive resources are available for self-regulation (Glaser, 1987). Metacognition is the knowledge about one's own knowledge, cognitive processes, and performance (Flavell, 1979). It is essential to expert performance as well as to the development of expertise. First, the expert's ability to maintain awareness of his or her knowledge and task performance processes while engaged in the task allows the expert to evaluate his or her understanding of the situation; determine when the available information is inconsistent, unreliable, or incomplete; and decide when to continue analyzing a situation and retrieving additional information (Cohen, Freeman, & Thompson, 1998; Cohen, Freeman, & Wolf, 1996). Second, from a developmental perspective, metacognition during task performance is necessary for improving performance processes. The developing expert must be aware of his or her performance processes in order to make adjustments and improvements. Experts are better at detecting their errors, why the error has occurred, and when they need to evaluate their problem solutions (Glaser & Chi, 1988), factors that improve both the development of expertise and task performance. Additionally, the use of self-evaluation and self-monitoring has been shown to reduce the effects of acute stress on task performance (Baumann, Sniezek, & Buerkle, 2001), a means by which experts maintain high levels of performance when faced with high-stress conditions.

There are three general elements of self-regulation, specifically, the self-regulation of the environment surrounding task performance, of one's internal cognitive and affective states and processes, and of the behavioral processes of task performance (Bandura, 1986). All three of these have been identified as crucial aspects of expertise in three phases of a self-regulatory cycle: forethought, performance control, and self-reflection (Zimmerman, 2006; Zimmerman & Campillo, 2003). During the forethought, or preperformance planning, phase, experts engage in goal setting. The expert's goal setting involves a combination of both process and outcome goals, whereas novices tend to focus more strictly on setting outcome goals. The expert effectively selects strategies, or means to reach the set goals. During task performance, experts engage in monitoring, evaluation, and attentive guidance of their own performance (Zimmerman, 2006). Experts use such methods as self-instruction, the use of imagery, the application of task strategies, effective time management, seeking help and feedback from others, and structuring their environment to facilitate learning and performance. Most essentially, the experts are able to more effectively observe and record their own performance processes (Kitsantas & Zimmerman, 2002). This record of performance feeds into self-evaluation during the self-reflective phase. Here, experts evaluate their performance in relation to set criteria. The selection of appropriate criteria is essential to evaluating performance in a way that further develops expertise. If a performance criterion is set too high, motivation can be diminished; and, conversely, if the criteria are not challenging, performance gains are not likely (Locke & Latham, 2002).

How Is Expertise Developed and Maintained?

Like most developmental phenomenon, the acquisition of expertise can be viewed as a differentially weighted interaction between inherent capabilities (nature) and training and experience (nurture) (Ericsson & Lehmann, 1996), and, in fact, a good deal of recent expertise research has focused on ascertaining the relative weights of this interaction. That is, to what degree is expert performance a function of appropriate forms of practice rather than innate talent (Shiffrin, 1996)? Although both perspectives have their advocates, the experience-based view perspective has received the most empirical support. The simplest version of this view holds that expertise is a function of years of experience in the domain of expertise. However, the empirical link between experience in a field and levels of performance is weak at best (Bedard, 1991; Bonner & Pennington, 1991; Ericsson & Lehman, 1996; Quiñones, Ford, & Teachout, 1995), suggesting that experience in general is not enough to increase performance to expert levels. This section provides a description of the characteristics of practice and experience and of the learner (feedback-seeking behavior, long-term goals, and motivation) that contribute to the development of expertise.

Deliberate and Guided Practice: Experts Engage in Deliberate and Guided Practice

In domains with long-established traditions of skill development and instruction (e.g., sports and the performing arts in particular), training programs are developed by experienced coaches and teachers. These instructors individualize practice opportunities for a particular student's place in the continuum of development from novice to expert (Ericsson & Charness, 1994). These training programs utilize repetition to fine-tune specific aspects of performance. Activities that most effectively increase performance levels are collectively known as *deliberate practice*—a "highly structured activity, the explicit goal of which is to improve performance" (Ericsson, Krampe, & Tesch-Romer, 1993, p. 368). There are four conditions that must be met for an activity to be classified as deliberate practice and result in optimal performance improvement (Ericsson et al., 1993): (a) Learners must engage in repetitive performance of the same task or similar tasks with minor variations, (b) learners should receive immediate feedback that can be used to modify performance, (c) the task should build on the learners' preexisting knowledge so that it can be understood in a brief period of time, and (d) the learner should be motivated to exert the required effort to improve performance.

Although the theory of deliberate practice most readily explains expert performance in domains where individuals train extensively· for a specific performance (e.g., sports or music), it has relevance for modern organizations as well. Sonnentag and Kleine (2000) argued that deliberate practice activities in a work context may look substantially different from those witnessed in such disciplines as sports and the arts. Specifically, they stated that

> deliberate practice may not comprise extensive rehearsal of difficult tasks and sub tasks or the refinement of isolated processes, but a wide range of activities such as extensive preparation of task accomplishment, gathering information from domain experts, or seeking feedback. (Sonnentag & Kleine, 2000, p. 89)

They differentiated between two types of task-supporting behavior. Behavior engaged in to increase immediate task performance is supportive, but it is not deliberate practice because its purpose is not to develop performance abilities in a global or long-term sense. Behaviors engaged in on a regular basis during task performance that serve the additional purpose of improving competence over the long run can rightly be considered as deliberate practice activities.

Continuous Learning: Experts Take the Long View of Development

As detailed above, the path to excellence requires large amounts of effort and copious amounts of experience that have been specifically designed to afford the optimal conditions for increasing performance. The development and subsequent maintenance of expertise require such intensive effort over such a prolonged period of time that they are best viewed as lifelong challenges. Although expertise can be viewed as the product of successful training and experience, it is never a final product. As surely as effort was involved in developing the abilities of expert performance, effort is involved in the maintenance of expert performance. Krampe and Ericsson (1996) found that aging experts are able to maintain high levels of performance in domain-specific tasks despite suffering the normal age-related decline in general processing speed. These aging experts were able to do so by maintaining deliberate practice activities. Therefore, continued engagement in deliberate practice is necessary to maintain high levels of performance (see Krampe & Charness, 2006).

Motivation: Experts Want to Learn—All the Time

Motivation is perhaps the most important component of expertise presented in this framework. Sternberg (1998) placed motivation at the center of his model of developing expertise. In this model, various types of extrinsic and intrinsic motivation (e.g., achievement and self-efficacy motivation) are viewed as indispensable to the development of expertise as these are the forces that drive individuals to learn and develop their abilities. In reports of her investigations of children with precocious abilities in the visual arts, Winner (1996) described what she called the "rage to master," an intense drive to master a specific domain of performance. Glaser (1987) spoke of the development of expertise in terms of a shift in the agency of learning. That is, as performance improves, there is a change in the driving force behind learning activities. As development proceeds, a learner progresses through three general phases. The first stage is characterized by external support, wherein parents, teachers, coaches, and the like provide scaffolding and help to organize the environment so that it is optimal for learning. The second stage is a transition period, where external support begins to wane. External scaffolding is replaced with apprenticeship-style learning and guided practice that foster self-monitoring and regulation. This feeds into the final stage of development—self-regulated learning. Here, learners take control of the learning environment, build and engage in challenging practice opportunities, and receive feedback on and diagnose their own performance. External support is limited and characterized by asking for advice from mentors, coaches, competitors, and the like. From this high-level view of the course of developing expertise, it is apparent that a strong motivation to learn is key to developing and engaging in learning activities without external support, supervision, or acute pressure to do so. It is the driving force that sustains practice activities and ensures that the learner continues to improve after formally structured training ends and external supports are removed.

Four types of motivation have been identified as being especially important to the development of expertise (Zimmerman, 2006). First, self-efficacy beliefs (i.e., a person's belief in his or her ability to perform effectively) are important in that higher self-efficacy leads to a learner setting higher goals and being more committed to reaching those goals (Cleary & Zimmerman, 2001; Locke & Latham, 2002; Zimmerman, Bandura, & Martinez-Pons, 1992). Second, learners' goal orientations have a large impact on their development. For instance, focusing on outcome or performance goals can have a deleterious effect on development when the acquisition of skill is the primary objective. In this situation, setting a challenging learning goal will draw attention away from the end result and place it on the exploration and development of effective performance strategies (Seijts & Latham, 2005). Learning goals are associated with higher levels of cognitive engagement (Graham & Golen, 1991). Third, experts tend to value the ultimate outcomes of the development process; they are motivated by an attraction to positive outcomes and not an attempt to avoid negative outcomes (Pintrich, 2000). Fourth, experts tend to value the task in and of itself (Karniol & Ross, 1977), and they tend to continue performing the task and striving for improvement even in the absence of immediate rewards (Kitsantas & Zimmerman, 2002).

Long-Term Goals: Experts Have Long-Term Goals

The 10-year rule (i.e., the recurring trend that expert performance in classically studied domains requires approximately 10 years of sustained training) in the development of expertise highlights the importance of having long-term goals when pursuing expert levels of performance. Developing experts cannot focus solely on immediate performance improvements or on reaching some static level of performance. Specifically, experts must value the process of becoming an expert—the process of continuous learning and adaptation to changing task constraints. There has been increasing support for the notion of maintaining learning goals in comparison to outcome or performance goals when engaged in activities focused on developing knowledge and skills (Seijts & Latham, 2005). A learning goal focuses the learner's attention on discovering new performance processes or modifying existing performance processes instead of focusing on outcomes. This builds the type of understanding that is characteristic of adaptive expertise (i.e., the ability to alter or invent new procedures) as well as avoids the potential damage to motivation and self-efficacy caused by a unitary focus on near-term performance outcomes. Therefore, experts take the long view of the learning process; they maintain long-term learning goals.

Feedback Seeking: Experts Seek Diagnostic Feedback

Developing experts must receive feedback in order to make the adjustments to their performance processes that enable higher levels of performance to be reached. Feedback is instrumental to the learning process in general and to deliberate practice in particular. Sonnentag (2000) found that expert performers actively sought more feedback from colleagues in comparison to moderate performers in technical jobs (e.g., software design and engineering). Developing experts must proactively seek input from individuals with higher levels of expertise. Self-motivated feedback-seeking behavior on the part of the learner is critical to the development of expertise. In addition to seeking feedback on their own performance, experts use narratives to learn from the mistakes and successes of others. Although the use of narrative by experts is a relatively new research topic, it promises to inform our understanding of how experts make sense of and learn from experiences in complex organizational environments (Fiore, McDaniel, Rosen, & Salas, 2007; Snowden, 1999).

In sum, this framework presents an overview of the mechanisms that mediate expert performance and the process of developing expertise in various domains. The specific attributes of expertise in any one particular domain are the product of a long development process through which learners adapt their performance processes to task domains through frequent and consistent deliberate practice activities. The following section provides a set of principles for developing expertise in organizations. These principles are offered as a preliminary guide to the process of applying the expertise literature to the tasks faced by industrial and organizational psychologists.

Principles for Developing Expertise at Work

For researchers and practitioners in the field of training, a main goal is to improve the methods by which we are able to produce skilled workers. The ideal end product is more people performing at higher levels. In the preceding sections, we presented a general framework of the mechanisms of expert performance and development. In this section, we offer a set of preliminary principles for leveraging the expertise literature into guidance for organizations attempting to develop experts. These principles are organized around the five elements of the "mechanisms of development" in our framework presented earlier.

Deliberate and Guided Practice

What types of training programs are required to develop experts within organizations? What are the central characteristics of such programs? The expertise literature is clear; expertise is a lifelong challenge requiring learners to commit to frequent and consistent practice of skills. Much of the learning that will be done in such a pursuit naturally occurs outside of formalized training programs. Self-guided (or self-monitored; Glaser, 1996) learning drives much of the progress toward expertise, especially in later phases of development. In organizational contexts, these activities may be less distinguishable from work performance than in classically studied domains of expertise (e.g., chess or sports). Deliberate practice is separate from work performance; however, the experience of work practice can be maximized by applying aspects of the features that make deliberate practice so effective. An essential feature of deliberate practice is feedback, and more specifically, feedback that is diagnostic of performance processes. Diagnostic feedback allows learners to determine the causes of both effective and ineffective performance. This information drives the learner's adjustment of performance processes necessary for producing higher levels of performance outcomes. An example of this is the retrospective review of patient data by physicians. These medical doctors attempt to replay their diagnostic reasoning to detect shortcomings in their processes and knowledge base. This activity drives the development of skill. Therefore, the first principle advanced seeks to leverage work experiences into learning experiences:

Principle 1: Enable learning and development through diagnostic feedback of work performance.

"The principal challenge for attaining expert performance is that further improvements require continuously increased challenges that raise the performance beyond its current level" (Ericsson, 2003b, p. 116). In an organizational context, this means that personnel must be able to engage in activities beyond their current levels of competence. Avoidance of adverse outcomes for the organization (e.g., increased likelihood of errors, or decrease in safety) caused by such activity in the course of job performance limits the ability of learners to engage in task performance outside of their skill level. Various strategies can be used to address this obstacle (e.g., providing simulations of various fidelities), but developing experts need to engage in tasks that are just outside of their current skill level without fear of causing harm to individuals or incurring negative effects for the organization. This means that learners will need skill-building activities to engage in that are outside of their work performance. Therefore, the following two principles are advanced.

Principle 2: Provide safe environments to make mistakes.

Principle 3: Provide opportunities for practice inside and outside of work performance.

There is no doubt that a large portion of the developing expert's knowledge and skill acquisition occurs informally in the organization (e.g., on-the-job training, coaches, and mentors; Chao, 1997); however, the value of formalized learning can be maximized with the use of training tools. For example, Cornford and Athanasou (1995) attributed the relatively small number of occupational experts in the workforce to a reliance on "experience" and a lack of emphasis on training programs that push skill levels to the highest levels. To maximize the return on investment of training programs designed to build expertise, prepractice tools should be provided to learners (Cannon-Bowers, Rhodenizer, Salas, & Bowers, 1998). There are a variety of tools available (e.g., advanced organizers, attentional advice, goal orientation, and pretraining briefs), and each of these operates via different mechanisms to assist the learner in maximizing the training opportunity and integrating the newly trained skills and knowledge with preexisting knowledge and skills.

Principle 4: Provide prepractice tools for learning activities.

Principle 5: Draw explicit connections between new and previously held knowledge and skills.

When developing experts are engaged in learning activities outside of their present skill levels, the use of guided errors can help to develop awareness of performance processes and expedite learning. With this approach, learners are guided into and out of faulty performance processes. This process is associated with higher levels of performance (accuracy and efficiency) as well as higher self-efficacy (Lorenzet, Salas, & Tannenbaum, 2005). An additional approach is to provide learning activities with a range of variations in the task. These variations will lead to more adaptive expertise, the ability to transfer to a wider variety of situations (Holladay & Quiñones, 2003).

Principle 6: Use guided errors to accelerate learning and conceptual understanding.

Principle 7: Provide variability in learning activities.

What are the issues involved in measuring and diagnosing expert performance in organizations? As discussed earlier, the accurate identification of expertise is important within an organization. The accurate identification of expertise improves group and team outcomes. Additionally, the identification of experts is essential to the success of coaching or mentoring programs. General findings within the expertise literature (Camerer & Johnson, 1991) resonate with industrial and organizational psychology literature (Quiñones et al., 1995) in that years of experience or certifications and other social attributions are poor predictors of performance levels. Therefore, when evaluating expertise within an organization for any reason, consistently and reliably superior performance on objective, representative tasks of a domain is the gold standard by which expertise should be evaluated.

Principle 8: Objective performance is the "brass ring" for evaluating expertise.

Continuous Learning

Given the domain specificity of expertise and the ever increasing rate of change in the skills necessary for varieties of performance within organizations, learners need guidance in selecting the skills and knowledge domains they should be developing over time. In the spirit of the great one, Wayne Gretzky, learners should be skating to where the puck will be, not to where it is. Information about the direction of the planned or likely future course of the organization can be used by learners to direct their self-guided learning. By delineating what is or likely will be of value, the chances of an individual developing rigid and obsolete expertise is decreased. Therefore, the following proposition is advanced:

> Principle 9: Provide information on likely future directions for the organization and skill sets and knowledge bases of value to the organization.

Optimal learning environments and deliberate practice activities have very specific characteristics. By providing personnel with an overarching framework of how to develop their own expertise, organizations can support the development of self-monitored learning on the part of developing experts. The training and support needs of an individual will change throughout the course of development, and the organization should be responsive to this. Beginners need scaffolding and more formalized structuring of the learning environment. Intermediate learners need help in developing the self-monitoring skills necessary to continue with higher levels of skill and knowledge development. Advanced learners need access to mentors, coaches, and competitors for feedback, advice, help, and guidance with practice activities. This leads to the following propositions:

> Principle 10: Support changing learning needs throughout the course of development.
>
> Principle 10a: Provide "phase-appropriate" scaffolding for beginning learners.
>
> Principle 10b: Provide training on independent learning and self-monitoring for intermediate learners.
>
> Principle 10c: Provide access to guidance from mentors for advanced learners.

Motivation to Learn and Long-Term Goals

How can organizational interventions affect the motivation to become an expert? The literature is clear on the role of motivation in developing expertise—the appropriate amount and focus of motivation are critical to learning efforts extended over long durations of time. There are several implications from the expertise literature on what organizations can do to foster the motivation of their employees and direct it toward learning objectives. In terms of reward systems, organizations can focus on performance improvements instead of reinforcing performance levels. Rewarding a particular level of performance will work to develop an asymptote at that level of performance. If the major reward is given for improvement of performance levels, that will create motivation for continuous development. Additionally, organizations can invest in the development of the self-efficacy of their employees. Focusing developing experts' attitudes toward learning and their development of self-efficacy is an important step in a long-term development process. Learners with high self-efficacy are more likely to engage and sustain in prolonged endeavors of learning. This can be approached in several ways, including framing learning and training experiences so that they are perceived as promoting excellence versus remediating poor performance (Quiñones, 1995). Additionally, learning goals should be reinforced by the organizational policy and culture. Learning goals are positively associated with higher levels of motivation to learn, whereas outcome goals have an inverse relationship with motivation to learn (Colquitt & Simmering, 1998). Additionally, learners should have choices in the course of their development. This increases the satisfaction and motivation of employees in their own development (Deci & Ryan, 1985; London & Smither, 1999; Pritchard, 1995). This type of "empowering" work environment will encourage employees to take learning into their own hands, an increasingly important factor as learners reach higher levels of development. With these points considered, the following principles can be advanced:

Principle 11: Reward performance improvements instead of performance levels.

Principle 12: Frame learning experiences to improve self-efficacy.

Principle 13: Reinforce learning goals.

Principle 14: Create "empowering" work environments.

Feedback Seeking

How can feedback be generated that assists people to continue their development? As previously discussed, feedback must be diagnostic. That is, it must include information about performance processes as well as outcomes. In relation to outcomes, individuals must have a way of gauging organizational expectations and performance criteria. This must be provided on a level of granularity that enables the learner to evaluate his or her own performance.

Principle 15: Provide organizational goals and performance criteria at a level that enables feedback.

Principle 16: Encourage feedback-seeking behaviors.

Principle 17: Provide feedback that affords the diagnosis—the determination of causes—of performance.

Research Needs: The Road Ahead

It is an exciting time for the field of expertise studies, and it is the intent of this chapter to bring some of that excitement (and knowledge base) to the organizational context. Through the discussion of definitions, framework, and principles presented in this chapter, two points become salient. First, there is a large and ever increasing amount of theoretical and empirical work on the nature of expertise and its development, emphasizing that expertise is acquired and not a product of innate talent. Second, although some implications of this work are clear for organizational contexts, there is much to be done in "mining" the expertise literature for guiding organizational practices related to training and development. We have outlined much of the existing literature on this topic, but the picture is far from complete. Much of the systematic and scientific expertise literature involves domains and tasks that are tightly constrained (i.e., they involve a stable task structure with clear boundaries to the domain). This is frequently not the case in organizations. The expertise literature has been applied in complex real-world environments resulting in promising successes (e.g., Salas & Klein, 2001). However, an overarching research need is a better understanding of what findings from the expertise literature developed around tightly constrained tasks generalize to organizational contexts. Within this broad research need, we next provide a set of four general questions and associated specific issues that need to be addressed more fully than is presently possible with available research. These questions and issues are summarized in Table 3.1.

First, how do you structure experience at work to develop expertise? How can you leverage daily opportunities for practice and learning into continuous development and pursuit of the lifelong challenge of expertise? Given the importance of informal learning and the necessity of large amounts of daily practice activities to attain expert levels of performance, this is an especially critical research issue. Workers in modern organizations do not have the resources in time or practice activities to cleanly separate learning from performance, as is the case in more traditional domains of expertise. Therefore, understanding how performance on the job can be

TABLE 3.1

Summary of Research Agenda

Research Question	Research Needs
1. How do you structure experience at work to develop expertise?	• An understanding of how daily work activities can be maximized as learning opportunities • Methods for maximizing the effectiveness of coaching and mentoring • Guidance in balancing informal and formal learning to maximize expertise development • Articulating the types and degrees of training variability that contribute to the development of expertise
2. What are the individual characteristics that lead to expertise?	• Methods for capturing and developing the "rage to master" (i.e., the high levels of motivation needed for sustained development) • A better understanding of effective feedback-seeking behavior and how to develop it
3. What metrics need to be developed in order to diagnose expert performance?	• Methods for identifying experts for coaching and mentoring and matching these experts with developing experts • Methods for generating diagnostic feedback from work activities • Methods for understanding change in performance over time when the demands of the task change over time
4. What organizational variables facilitate or hinder the development of expertise?	• An understanding of how to set and articulate organizational goals in a way that affords diagnostic feedback • Methods for forecasting knowledge and skill sets that will be useful to the organization in the future • The development of reward systems that balance immediate performance and long-term development

maximized as a learning opportunity is essential. For example, how can formal and informal learning be leveraged and balanced to achieve maximum learning and development? Coaching and mentoring are critical to the development of more advanced learners, but a better understanding is needed of how to match developing experts with more proficient performers. This is related to measurement issues in that coaches and mentors should be selected based on performance levels; however, there are likely interpersonal factors that will influence the effectiveness of the relationship. Of course, formal training has a role in the development of expertise. A critical need here is a better understanding of what types and degrees of variability in learning activities are appropriate for a given domain.

Second, what are the individual characteristics that lead to expertise? It has been strongly argued that expertise is a function of time spent in purposeful skill acquisition activities and not of talent. However, we know that motivation to learn is essential for persevering in these activities over years of development. Therefore, an important research question is, how do we capture the "rage to master"? Because the development of expertise involves maintaining the direction of high levels of energy toward long-term goals over many years, it is unclear to what degree external factors are influential in maintaining these levels of motivation. In fact, experts tend to persist with practice activities in the absence of external reward. So, can the rage to master be developed effectively, and if so, how? If not, how can individuals be selected who are capable of maintaining motivation directed at long-term learning goals? Similarly, we know that feedback-seeking behavior is a critical component of building expertise, but we do not have a detailed understanding of what drives this process, of why some people actively seek feedback about their performance and others do not. A more nuanced understanding of what types of feedback-seeking behaviors are most effective and how to develop these within personnel is called for as well.

Third, what metrics do we need to develop in order to diagnose expert performance? The measurement and identification of expert performance are essential for providing the feedback necessary for guided practice. In traditional expertise domains (e.g., chess or sports), this task is relatively simple when compared to the ill-defined tasks in organizations. Given that performance measurement and the associated criterion problems are long-standing issues, what are the best ways to generate diagnostic feedback in organizational contexts? If diagnostic feedback can be tied to the measurement of daily work activities, this would help to maximize learning from task performance, a critical need given the limitations on time that can be devoted to pure practice activities. To complicate matters, tracking the development of expertise over years requires assessing growth and change over time, which will frequently have to be considered in the context of changing task constraints (i.e., assessing change in performance in a job whose performance demands change).

Fourth, what organizational variables facilitate or hinder the development of expertise? What are the characteristics of an organization that afford the development of expertise within its staff? As discussed in the introduction of this chapter, organizations are spending more on employee development, but formal training and development programs are only one facet of creating experts. Therefore, understanding how an organization can configure itself to build expertise is a topic of great importance. Because of the importance of high levels of motivation sustained over long periods of time to the development of expertise, organizational reward systems play a critical role. There is a need here for a better understanding of how to balance reinforcement of immediate performance (which is the near-term necessity) and long-term learning goals (which are necessary to build and maintain expertise and future levels of performance). Frequently, these goals may be at odds with one another. So, how can organizations effectively manage these competing goals? Related to this is the ability of the organization to set goals that are macro enough to guide the organization and yet of a fine enough granularity that they afford feedback on individual performance. Because the organization must adapt to a changing economy, the expertise of its personnel must adapt as well. How can organizations provide meaningful guidance to its employees on what knowledge and skill sets they should be developing to prepare for future organizational needs?

The overarching theories of expertise and its acquisition are likely applicable in many organizations; however, the task constraints within an organization will dictate the specifics of the development process. It is likely that the organizational sciences will need to build from and adapt to the extant theories of expertise in order to synthesize more guidance for developing interventions, programs, and mechanisms for developing, maintaining, and retaining the expertise of its personnel.

Concluding Remarks

We live in a flat world now, a world where those who learn the fastest and those who know more win. And so expertise, its nature, and its development are crucial to organizations. Organizations that develop experts, those that motivate the acquisition of expert performance, those that provide opportunities for learning and development, those that create mechanisms and initiatives to develop expertise, and those that value human capital at its best will thrive. We hope that this chapter motivates organizations to reach out to the expertise literature. We hope this will motivate scholars to cultivate robust research agendas and to generate evidence-based principles on how to develop, promote, motivate, and refine expertise in organizations.

Acknowledgments

We would like to thank Steve Kozlowski for his comments on an earlier version of this chapter. The views herein are those of the authors and do not necessarily reflect those of the organizations with which they are affiliated or their sponsoring agencies. Writing this chapter was partially supported by Grant No. SBE0350345 from the National Science Foundation awarded to Eduardo Salas and Stephen M. Fiore; by Grant No. SES0527675 from the National Science Foundation awarded to Glenn Harrison, Stephen M. Fiore, Charlie Hughes, and Eduardo Salas; and by the Office of Naval Research Collaboration and Knowledge Interoperability (CKI) Program and ONR MURI Grant No. N000140610446.

References

Agnew, N. M., Ford, K. M., & Hayes, P. J. (1997). Expertise in context: Personally constructed, socially selected and reality relevant? In P. J. Feltovich, K. M. Ford, & R. R. Hoffman (Eds.), *Expertise in context* (pp. 219–244). Menlo Park, CA: AAAI Press/MIT Press.

Anderson, J. R. (1982). Acquisition of cognitive skill. *Psychological Review, 89*(4), 369–406.

Anzai, Y. (1991). Learning and use of representations for physics expertise. In K. A. Ericsson and J. Smith (Eds.), *Toward a general theory of expertise: Prospects and limits* (pp. 64–92). Cambridge: Cambridge University Press.

Baddeley, A. (1997). *Human memory: Theory and practice.* New York: Psychology Press.

Bandura, A. (1986). *Social foundations of thought and action: A social cognitive theory.* Englewood Cliffs, NJ: Prentice Hall.

Barnett, S. M., & Koslowski, B. (2002). Adaptive expertise: Effects of type of experience and the level of theoretical understanding it generates. *Thinking and Reasoning, 8*(4), 237–267.

Baumann, M. R., Sniezek, J. A., & Buerkle, C. A. (2001). Self-evaluation, stress, and performance: A model of decision making under acute stress. In E. Salas & G. Klein (Eds.), *Linking expertise and naturalistic decision making* (pp. 139–158). Mahwah, NJ: Lawrence Erlbaum Associates.

Bedard, J. (1991). Expertise and its relation to audit decision quality. *Contemporary Accounting Research, 8*, 198–222.

Bedard, J., & Chi, M. T. H. (1992). Expertise. *Current Directions in Psychological Science, 1*(4), 135–139.

Benner, P. (1982). From novice to expert. *American Journal of Nursing, 82*(3), 402–407

Benner, P. (1984). *From novice to expert: Excellence and power in clinical nursing practice.* Reading, MA: Addison Wesley.

Bonner, B. L. (2004). Expertise in group problem solving: Recognition, social combination, and performance. *Group Dynamics: Theory, Research, and Practice, 8*(4), 277–290.

Bonner, S. E., & Pennington, N. (1991). Cognitive processes and knowledge as determinants of auditor expertise. *Journal of Accounting Literature, 10*, 1–50.

Bordage, G., & Zacks, R. (1984). The structure of medical knowledge in the memories of medical students and general practitioners: Categories and prototypes. *Medical Education, 18*, 406–416.

Camerer, C. F., & Johnson, E. J. (1991). The process-performance paradox in expert judgement: How can experts know so much and predict so badly? In K. A. Ericsson & J. Smith (Eds.), *Toward a general theory of expertise: Prospects and limits* (pp. 195–217). Cambridge: Cambridge University Press.

Cannon-Bowers, J., Rhodenizer, L., Salas, E., & Bowers, C. A. (1998). A framework for understanding pre-practice conditions and their impact on learning. *Personnel Psychology, 51*(2), 291–320.

Chao, G. T. (1997). Unstructured training and development: The role of organizational socialization. In J. K. Ford (Ed.), *Improving training effectiveness in work organizations*. Mahwah, NJ: Lawrence Erlbaum Associates.

Charness, N. (1989). Expertise in chess and bridge. In D. Klahr & K. Kotovsky (Eds.), *Complex information processing: The impact of Herbert A. Simon* (pp. 183–208). Hillsdale, NJ: Lawrence Erlbaum Associates.

Chase, W. G., & Ericsson, K. A. (1981). Skilled memory. In J. R. Anderson (Ed.), *Cognitive skills and their acquisition* (pp. 141–189). Hillsdale, NJ: Lawrence Erlbaum Associates.

Chase, W. G., & Ericsson, K. A. (1982). Skill and working memory. In G. H. Bower (Ed.), *The psychology of learning and motivation* (Vol. 16, pp. 1–58). Hillsdale, NJ: Lawrence Erlbaum Associates.

Chase, W. G., & Simon, H. A. (1973). Perception in chess. *Cognitive Psychology, 4*, 55–81.

Chi, M. T. H. (2006). Two approaches to the study of experts' characteristics. In K. A. Ericsson, N. Charness, R. Hoffman, & P. J. Feltovich (Eds.), *The Cambridge handbook of expertise and expert performance* (pp. 21–30). New York: Cambridge University Press.

Chi, M., Feltovich, P., & Glaser, R. (1981). Categorization and representation of physics problems by experts and novices. *Cognitive Science, 5*, 121–152.

Chi, M., Glaser, R., & Rees, E. (1982). Expertise in problem solving. In R. J. Sternberg (Ed.), *Advances in the psychology of human intelligence* (Vol. 1, pp. 7–75). Hillsdale, NJ: Lawrence Erlbaum Associates.

Chi, M. T. H., & Ohlsson, S. (2005). Complex declarative learning. In K. J. Holyoak & R. G. Morrison (Eds.), *The Cambridge handbook of thinking and reasoning* (pp. 371–399). New York: Cambridge University Press.

Cleary, T. J., & Zimmerman, B. J. (2001). Self-regulation differences during athletic practice by experts, non-experts, and novices. *Journal of Applied Sport Psychology, 13*, 61–82.

Cohen, M. S., Freeman, J. T., & Thompson, B. (1998). Critical thinking skills in tactical decision making: A model and a training strategy. In J. Cannon-Bowers & E. Salas (Eds.), *Making decisions under stress: Implications for individual and team training* (pp. 155–189). Washington, DC: APA Press.

Cohen, M. S., Freeman, J. T., & Wolf, S. (1996). Meta-recognition in time stressed decision making: Recognizing, critiquing and correcting. *Human Factors, 38*, 206–219.

Colquitt, J. A., & Simmering, M. J. (1998). Conscientiousness, goal orientation, and motivation to learn during the learning process: A longitudinal study. *Journal of Applied Psychology, 83*(4), 654–665.

Committee on Science, Engineering, and Public Policy (COSEPUP). (2006). *Rising above the gathering storm: Energizing and employing America for a brighter economic future*. Washington, DC: National Academy of Sciences.

Cornford, I., & Athanasou, J. (1995). Developing expertise through training. *Industrial and Commercial Training, 27*(2), 10–18.

Deci, E. L., & Ryan, R. M. (1985). *Intrinsic motivation and self-determination in human behavior*. New York: Springer.

de Groot, A. (1978). *Thought and choice in chess* (2nd ed.). The Hague, The Netherlands: Mouton de Gruyter. (Originally published in 1946)

Dorner, D., & Scholkopf, J. (1991). Controlling complex systems; or, expertise as "grandmother's know-how." In K. A. Ericsson & J. Smith (Eds.), *Toward a general theory of expertise: Prospects and limits* (pp. 218–239). Cambridge: Cambridge University Press.

Dreyfus, H. L., & Dreyfus, S. E. (1986). *Mind over machine: The power of human intuition and expertise in the era of the computer*. New York: Free Press.

Egan, D. E., & Schwartz, B. J. (1979). Chunking in recall of symbolic drawings. *Memory and Cognition, 7*, 149–158.

Einhorn, H. J. (1974). Expert judgement: Some necessary conditions and an example. *Journal of Applied Psychology, 59*, 562–571.

Eisenstadt, M., & Kareev, Y. (1979). Aspects of human problem solving: The use of internal representations. In D. A. Norman & D. E. Rumelhart (Eds.), *Exploration in cognition*. San Francisco: Freeman.

Engle, R. W., & Bukstel, L. (1978). Memory processes among bridge players of differing expertise. *American Journal of Psychology, 91*, 673–689.

Ericsson, K. A. (1985). Memory skill. *Canadian Journal of Psychology, 39*, 188–231.

Ericsson, K. A. (1988). Analysis of memory performance in terms of memory skill. In R. J. Sternberg (Ed.), *Advances in the psychology of human intelligence* (Vol. 5, pp. 137–179). Hillsdale, NJ: Lawrence Erlbaum Associates.

Ericsson, K. A. (2003b). The search for general abilities and basic capacities: Theoretical implications from the modifiability and complexity of mechanisms mediating expert performance. In R. J. Sternberg & E. L. Grigorenko (Eds.), *The psychology of abilities, competencies, and expertise* (pp. 93–125). New York: Cambridge University Press.

Ericsson, K. A. (2006). An introduction to Cambridge handbook of expertise and expert performance: Its development, organization, and content. In K. A. Ericsson, N. Charness, P. J. Feltovich, & R. R. Hoffman (Eds.), *The Cambridge handbook of expertise and expert performance* (pp. 3–19). New York: Cambridge University Press.

Ericsson, K. A., & Charness, N. (1994). Expert performance: Its structure and acquisition. *American psychologist, 49*(8), 725–747.

Ericsson, K. A., Charness, N., Feltovich, P. J., & Hoffman, R. R. (Eds.). (2006). *The Cambridge handbook of expertise and expert performance*. New York: Cambridge University Press.

Ericsson, K. A., & Delaney, P. F. (1998). Working memory and expert performance. *Working Memory and Thinking*, 93–114.

Ericsson, K. A., & Delaney, P. F. (1999). Long-term working memory as an alternative to capacity models of working memory in everyday skilled performance. In A. Miyake and P. Shah (Eds.). *Models of working memory: Mechanisms of active maintenance and executive control* (pp. 252–297), Cambridge, UK: Cambridge University Press.

Ericsson, K. A., & Kintsch, W. (1995). Long-term working memory. *Psychological Review, 102*(2), 211–245.

Ericsson, K. A., Krampe, R. T., & Tesch-Romer, C. (1993). The role of deliberate practice in the acquisition of expert performance. *Psychological Review, 100*(3), 363–406.

Ericsson, K. A., & Lehmann, A. C. (1996). Expert and exceptional performance: Evidence of maximal adaptation to task constraints. *Annual Review of Psychology, 47*, 273–305.

Ericsson, K. A., & Smith, J. (1991). Prospects and limits of the empirical study of expertise: An introduction. In K. A. Ericsson & J. Smith (Eds.), *Toward a general theory of expertise: Prospects and limits* (pp. 1–38). Cambridge, UK: Cambridge University Press.

Ericsson, K. A., & Staszewski, J. (1989). Skilled memory and expertise: Mechanisms of exceptional performance. In D. Klahr & K. Kotovsky (Eds.), *Complex information processing: The impact of Herbert A. Simon* (pp. 235–267). Hillsdale, NJ: Lawrence Erlbaum Associates.

Faraj, S., & Sproull, L. (2000). Coordinating expertise in software development teams. *Management Science, 46*(12), 1554–1568.

Feltovich, P. J., Johnson, P. E., Moller, J. H., & Swanson, L. C. S. (1984). The role and development of medical knowledge in diagnostic expertise. In W. J. Clancey & E. H. Shortliffe (Eds.), *Readings in medical artificial intelligence*. Reading, MA: Addison-Wesley.

Feltovich, P. J., Prietula, M. J., & Ericsson, K. A. (2006). Studies of expertise from psychological perspectives. In K. A. Ericsson, N. Charness, P. J. Feltovich, & R. R. Hoffman (Eds.), *Cambridge handbook of expertise and expert performance* (pp. 41–67). New York: Cambridge University Press.

Feltovich, P. J., Spiro, R. J., & Coulson, R. L. (1997). Issues of expert flexibility in contexts characterized by complexity and change. In P. J. Feltovich, K. M. Ford, & R. R. Hoffman (Eds.), *Expertise in context* (pp. 125–146). Menlo Park, CA: AAAI Press/MIT Press.

Fiore, S. M., McDaniel, R., Rosen, M. A., & Salas, E. (2007). Developing narrative theory for understanding the use of story in complex problem solving environments. Paper presented at the 8th International Conference on Naturalistic Decision Making, San Jose, CA.

Flavell, J. H. (1979). Metacognition and cognitive monitoring: A new area of cognitive-developmental inquiry. *American Psychologist, 34*(10), 906–911.

Gentner, D. R. (1988). Expertise in typewriting. In M. T. H. Chi, R. Glaser, & M. Farr (Eds.), *The nature of expertise* (pp. 1–22). Hillsdale, NJ: Lawrence Erlbaum Associates.

Glaser, R. (1987). Thoughts on expertise. In C. Schooler & K. W. Schaie (Eds.), *Cognitive functioning and social structure over the life course* (pp. 81–94). Norwood, NJ: Ablex.

Glaser, R., & Chi, M. T. H. (1988). Overview. In M. T. H. Chi, R. Glaser, & M. Farr (Eds.), *The nature of expertise* (pp. xv–xxviii). Hillsdale, NJ: Lawrence Erlbaum Associates.

Gobet, F., & Simon, H. A. (1996). Templates in chess memory: A mechanism for recalling several boards. *Cognitive Psychology, 31,* 1–40.

Graham, S., & Golan, S. (1991). Motivational influences on cognition: Task involvement, ego involvement, and depth of information processing. *Journal of Educational Psychology, 83*(2), 187–194.

Hambrick, D. Z. (2003). Why are some people more knowledgeable than others? A longitudinal study of knowledge acquisition. *Memory and Cognition, 31*(6), 902–917.

Hammond, K. R. (1996). *Human judgment and social policy: Irreducible uncertainty, inevitable error, unavoidable injustice.* New York: Oxford University Press.

Hatano, G., & Inagaki, K. (1986). Two courses of expertise. In H. W. Stevenson & H. Azuma (Eds.), *Child development and education in Japan* (pp. 262–272). New York: Freeman.

Hayes, J. R. (1989). *The complete problem solver.* Hillsdale, NJ: Lawrence Erlbaum Associates.

Hobus, P. P., Schmidt, H. G., Boshuizen, H. P., & Patel, V. L. (1987). Contexual factors in the activation of first diagnostic hypotheses: Expert–novice differences. *Medical Education, 21,* 474–476.

Hoffman, R. R., Feltovich, P. J., & Ford, K. M. (1997). A general conceptual framework for conceiving of expertise and expert systems. In P. J. Feltovich, K. M. Ford, & R. R. Hoffman (Eds.), *Expertise in context* (pp. 543–580). Menlo Park, CA: AAAI Press/MIT Press.

Hogarth, R. M. (2001). *Educating intuition.* Chicago: University of Chicago Press.

Holladay, C. L., & Quifiones, M. A. (2003). Practice variability and transfer of training: The role of self-efficacy generality. *Journal of Applied Psychology, 88*(6), 1094–1103.

Hollenbeck, J. R., Ilgen, D. R., LePine, J. A., Colquitt, J. A., & Hedlund, J. (1998). Extending the multilevel theory of team decision making: Effects of feedback and experience in hierarchical teams. *Academy of Management Journal, 41*(3), 269–282.

Hollenbeck, J. R., Ilgen, D. R., Sego, D. J., Hudlund, J., Major, D. A., & Phillips, J. (1995). Multilevel theory of team decision making: Decision performance in teams incorporating distributed expertise. *Journal of Applied Psychology, 80,* 292–316.

Holyoak, K. J. (1991). Symbolic connectionism: toward third-generation theories of expertise. In K. A. Ericsson & J. Smith (Eds.), *Toward a general theory of expertise: Prospects and limits* (pp. 301–335). Cambridge, UK: Cambridge University Press.

Huguenard, B. R., Prietula, M. J., & Lerch, F. J. (1990). Fragility of expertise: A study in reactive scheduling. *SIGCHI Bulletin, 21*(3), 36–40.

Hutton, R. J. B., & Klein, G. (1999). Expert decision making. *Systems Engineering, 2*(1), 32–45.

Karniol, R., & Ross, M. (1977). The effect of performance-relevant and performance-irrelevant rewards on children's intrinsic motivation. *Child Development,* 482–487.

Kitsantas, A., & Zimmerman, B. J. (2002). Comparing self-regulatory processes among novice, non-expert, and expert volleyball players: A microanalytic study. *Journal of Applied Sport Psychology, 14*, 91–105.

Klein, G. (1993). A recognition primed decision (RPD) model of rapid decision making. In G. Klein, J. Orasanu, R. Calderwood, & C. E. Zsambok (Eds.), *Decision making in action* (pp. 138–147). Norwood, NJ: Ablex.

Klein, G. (1998). *Sources of power: How people make decisions.* Cambridge, MA: MIT Press.

Klein, G. A., Orasanu, J., & Calderwood, R. (Eds.). (1993). *Decision making in action: Models and methods.* Westport, CT: Ablex.

Krampe, R. T., & Ericsson, K. A. (1996). Maintaining excellence: Deliberate practice and elite performance in young and older pianists. *Journal of Experimental Psychology: General, 125*(4), 331–359.

Krampe, R. T., & Charness, N. (2006). Aging and expertise. In K. A. Ericsson, N. Charness, P. Feltovich, & R. Hoffman (Eds.), *Cambridge Handbook of Expertise and Expert Performance* (in press). New York: Cambridge University Press.

Larkin, J., McDermott, J., Simon, D. P., & Simon, H. A. (1980). Expert and novice performance in solving physics problems. *Science, 208*, 1335–1342.

Lesgold, A. M., Rubinson, H., Feltovich, P. J., Glaser, R., Klopfer, D., & Wang, Y. (1988). Expertise in a complex skill: Diagnosing X-ray pictures. In M. T. H. Chi, R. Glaser, & M. Farr (Eds.), *The nature of expertise* (pp. 311–342). Hillsdale, NJ: Lawrence Erlbaum Associates.

Libby, R., Trotman, K. T., & Zimmer, I. (1987). Member variation, recognition of expertise, and group performance. *Journal of Applied Psychology, 72*(1), 81–87.

Locke, E. A., & Latham, G. P. (2002). Building a practically useful theory of goal setting and task motivation: A 35-year odyssey. *American Psychologist, 57*, 705–717.

Logan, G. D. (1988). Toward an instance theory of automatization. *Psychological Review, 95*(4), 492–527.

London, M., & Smither, J. W. (1999). Empowered self-development and continuous learning. *Human Resource Management, 38*(1).

Lorenzet, S. J., Salas, E., & Tannenbaum, S. I. (2005). Benefiting from mistakes: The impact of guided errors on learning, performance, and self-efficacy. *Human Resource Development Quarterly, 16*(3).

Mieg, H. A. (2001). *The social psychology of expertise: Case studies in research, professional domains, and expert roles.* Mahwah, NJ: Lawrence Erlbaum Associates.

Mieg, H. A. (2006). Social and sociological factors in the development of expertise. In K. A. Ericsson, N. Charness, R. Hoffman, & P. J. Feltovich (Eds.), *The Cambridge handbook of expertise and expert performance* (pp. 743–760). New York: Cambridge University Press.

Miller, G. (1956). The magical number seven, plus or minus two: Some limits on our capacity for processing information. *Psychological Review, 63*(2), 81–97.

Moors, A., & De Houwer, J. (2006). Automaticity: A theoretical and conceptual analysis. *Psychological Bulletin, 132*(2), 297–326.

Newell, A., & Simon, H. A. (1972). *Human problem solving.* Englewood Cliffs, NJ: Prentice Hall.

Oberauer, K. (2006). Is the focus of attention in working memory expanded through practice? *Journal of Experimental Psychology: Learning, Memory and Cognition, 32*(2), 197–214.

Orasanu, J., & Connolly, T. (1993). The reinvention of decision making. In G. Klein, J. Orasanu, R. Calderwood, & C. E. Zsambok (Eds.), *Decision making in action: Models and methods* (pp. 3–20). Norwood, CT: Ablex.

Pintrich, P. R. (2000). Multiple goals, multiple pathways: The role of goal orientation in learning and achievement. *Journal of Educational Psychology, 92*(3), 544–555.

Pritchard, R. D. (Ed.). (1995). *Productivity measurement and improvement: Organizational case studies*. Westport, CT: Praeger.

Quillian, M. A. (1969). The teachable language comprehender: A simulation program and theory of language. *Communications of the ACM, 12*(8), 459–476.

Quiñones, M. A. (1995). Pretraining context effects: Training assignment as feedback. *Journal of Applied Psychology, 80*(2), 226–238.

Quiñones, M. A., Ford, J. K., & Teachout, M. S. (1995). The relationship between work experience and job performance: A conceptual and meta-analytic review. *Personnel Psychology, 48*, 887–910.

Randel, J. M., Pugh, H. L., & Reed, S. K. (1996). Differences in expert and novice situation awareness in naturalistic decision making. *International Journal of Human–Computer Studies, 45*(5), 579–597.

Salas, E., & Klein, G. A. (Eds.). (2001). *Linking expertise and naturalistic decision making*: Mahwah, NJ: Lawrence Erlbaum Associates.

Salthouse, T. A. (1986). Perceptual, cognitive, and motoric aspects of transcription typing. *Psychological Bulletin, 99*, 303–319.

Salthouse, T. A. (1991). Expertise as the circumvention of human processing limitations. In K. A. Ericsson & J. Smith (Eds.), *Toward a general theory of expertise: Prospects and limits* (pp. 286–300). Cambridge, UK: Cambridge University Press.

Schunn, C. D., & Anderson, J. R. (1999). The generality/specificity of expertise in scientific reasoning. *Cognitive Science, 23*(3), 337–370.

Schunn, C. D., McGregor, M. U., & Saner, L. D. (2005). Expertise in ill-defined problem-solving domains as effective strategy use. *Memory and Cognition, 33*(8), 1377–1387.

Seijts, G. H., & Latham, G. P. (2006). Learning goals or performance goals: Is it the journey or the destination? *Ivey Business Journal, 1–6*.

Shaffer, L. H. (1975). Multiple attention in continuous verbal tasks. In P. M. Rabbitt & S. Dornic (Eds.), *Attention and performance* (Vol. 5, pp. 157–167). London: Academic Press.

Shanteau, J., Friel, B. M., Thomas, R. P., & Raacke, J. (2005). Development of expertise in a dynamic decision-making environment. In T. Betsch & S. Haberstroh (Eds.), *The routines of decision making* (pp. 251–270). Mahwah, NJ: Lawrence Erlbaum Associates.

Shanteau, J., Weiss, D. J., Thomas, R. P., & Pounds, J. (2003). How can you tell if someone is an expert? Empirical assessment of expertise. In S. L. Schneider & J. Shanteau (Eds.), *Emerging perspectives on judgement and decision research* (pp. 620–639). Cambridge, UK: Cambridge University Press.

Shiffrin, R. M. (1996). Laboratory experimentation on the genesis of expertise. In K. A. Ericsson (Ed.), *The road to excellence: The acquisition of expert performance in the arts and sciences, sports and games* (pp. 337–345). Mahwah, NJ: Lawrence Erlbaum Associates.

Simon, H. A., & Chase, W. G. (1973). Skill in chess. *American Scientist, 61*, 393–403.

Simonton, D. K. (1996). Creative expertise: A life-span developmental perspective. In K. A. Ericsson (Ed.), *The road to excellence: The acquisition of expert performance in the arts and sciences, sports and games* (pp. 227–253). Mahwah, NJ: Lawrence Erlbaum Associates.

Simonton, D. K. (2003). Expertise, competence, and creative ability: The perplexing complexities. In R. J. Sternberg & E. L. Grigorenko (Eds.), *The psychology of abilities, competencies, and expertise* (pp. 213–239). Cambridge, UK: Cambridge University Press.

Snowden, D. (1999). Story telling: An old skill in a new context. *Business Information Review, 16*(1), 30–37.

Sohn, Y. W., & Doane, S. M. (2003). Roles of working memory capacity and long-term working memory skill in complex task performance. *Memory and Cognition, 31*(3), 458–466.

Sohn, Y. W., & Doane, S. M. (2004). Memory processes of flight situation awareness: Interactive roles of working memory capacity, long-term working memory, and expertise. *Human Factors, 46*(3), 461–475.

Sonnentag, S. (2000). Excellent performance: The role of communication and cooperation processes. *Applied Psychology: An International Review, 49*(3), 483–497.

Sonnentag, S., & Kleine, B. M. (2000). Deliberate practice at work: A study with insurance agents. *Journal of Occupational and Organizational Psychology, 73*, 87–102.

Stein, E. W. (1992). A method to identify candidates for knowledge acquisition. *Journal of Management Information Systems, 9*, 161–178.

Stein, E. W. (1997). A look at expertise from a social perspective. In P. J. Feltovich, K. M. Ford, & R. R. Hoffman (Eds.), *Expertise in context* (pp. 181–194). Menlo Park, CA: AAAI Press/MIT Press.

Sternberg, R. J. (1996). Costs of expertise. In K. A. Ericsson (Ed.), *The road to excellence: The acquisition of expert performance in the arts and sciences, sports and games* (pp. 347–353). Mahwah, NJ: Lawrence Erlbaum Associates.

Sternberg, R. J. (1997). Cognitive conceptions of expertise. In P. J. Feltovich, K. M. Ford, & R. R. Hoffman (Eds.), *Expertise in context* (pp. 149–162). Menlo Park, CA: AAAI Press/MIT Press.

Sternberg, R. J. (1998). Abilities are forms of developing expertise. *Educational Researcher, 27*(3), 11–20.

Sternberg, R. J., & Frensch, P. A. (1991). On being an expert: A cost-benefit analysis. In R. R. Hoffman (Ed.), *The psychology of expertise: Cognitive research and empirical AI* (pp. 191–203). Mahwah, NJ: Lawrence Erlbaum Associates.

Van Gog, T., Paas, F., & Van Merrienboer, J. J. G. (2005). Uncovering expertise-related differences in troubleshooting performance: Combining eye movement and concurrent verbal protocol data. *Applied Cognitive Psychology, 19*, 205–221.

Vicente, K. J., & Wang, J. H. (1998). An ecological theory of expertise effects in memory recall. *Psychological Review, 105*(1), 33–57.

Vise, D. A. (2005, April 28). Gates cites hiring woes, criticizes visa restrictions. *Washington Post*, p. E05.

Voss, J. F., & Post, T. A. (1988). On the solving of ill-structured problems. In M. T. H. Chi, R. Glaser, & M. Farr (Eds.), *The nature of expertise* (pp. 261–285). Hillsdale, NJ: Lawrence Erlbaum Associates.

Wagner, R. K., & Stanovich, K. E. (1996). Expertise in reading. In K. A. Ericsson (Ed.), *The road to excellence* (pp. 189–225). Mahwah, NJ: Lawrence Erlbaum Associates.

Weiss, D. J., & Shanteau, J. (2003). Empirical assessment of expertise. *Human Factors, 45*(1), 104–114.

Winner, E. (1996). The rage to master: The decisive role of talent in the visual arts. In K. A. Ericsson (Ed.), *The road to excellence: The acquisition of expert performance in the arts and sciences, sports and games* (pp. 271–301). Mahwah, NJ: Lawrence Erlbaum Associates.

Zeitz, C. M. (1997). Some concrete advantages of abstraction: How experts' representations facilitate reasoning. In P. J. Feltovich, K. M. Ford, & R. R. Hoffman (Eds.), *Expertise in context* (pp. 43–65). Menlo Park, CA: AAAI Press/MIT Press.

Zimmerman, B. J. (2006). Development and adaptation of expertise: The role of self-regulatory processes and beliefs. In K. A. Ericsson, N. Charness, R. Hoffman, & P. J. Feltovich (Eds.), *The Cambridge handbook of expertise and expert performance* (pp. 705–722). New York: Cambridge University Press.

Zimmerman, B. J., Bandura, A., & Martinez-Pons, M. (1992). Self-motivation for academic attainment: The role of self-efficacy beliefs and personal goal setting. *American Educational Research Journal, 29*, 663–676.

Zimmerman, B. J., & Campillo, M. (2003). Motivating self-regulated problem solvers. In J. E. Davidson & R. J. Sternberg (Eds.), *The psychology of problem solving* (pp. 233–262). New York: Cambridge University Press.

Zsambok, C. E., & Klein, G. (Eds.). (1997). *Naturalistic decision making*. Mahwah, NJ: Lawrence Erlbaum Associates.

4

An Updated Review of the Multidimensionality of Training Outcomes: New Directions for Training Evaluation Research

J. Kevin Ford
Michigan State University

Kurt Kraiger
Colorado State University

Stephanie M. Merritt
University of Missouri–St. Louis

Kraiger, Ford, and Salas (1993) argued that to advance the science and practice of training evaluation, it was necessary to move toward a conceptually based classification scheme of learning based on a multidimensionality perspective. They examined learning taxonomies from educational and cognitive science disciplines (e.g., Bloom, 1956; Gagne, 1984; Krathwohl, Bloom, & Masia, 1964) and developed a classification scheme of learning outcomes that included three major learning outcome categories: cognitive, skill based, and affective.

For each of these three categories, Kraiger et al. (1993) reviewed relevant theory and research from a variety of disciplines to identify key learning constructs. Cognitive learning outcomes included verbal knowledge, knowledge organization, and cognitive strategies. Skill-based outcomes included issues of compilation and automaticity. Affective outcomes included issues of attitude change and motivational shifts in terms of mastery goals, self-efficacy, and goal direction. Once the constructs were described, measurement issues relevant to each of these learning constructs were discussed and methods for training evaluation proposed.

It has been over 15 years since this classification scheme was proposed to provide the training field with a multidimensional perspective to learning outcomes. Although the classification scheme was focused on training evaluation, the researchers stated that the ultimate goal was to spur additional research to advance our understanding of training effectiveness. As discussed by others (e.g., Cannon-Bowers & Salas, 2001; Kraiger, 2003), training evaluation addresses the question of whether (or not) training worked, whereas training effectiveness addresses the question of why it worked (or not). Identifying specific learning outcomes linked to desired training outcomes is critical not only for evaluating training but also for understanding the individual, training design, and work environmental factors that have the greatest impact on learning and training transfer outcomes (Goldstein & Ford, 2002).

The purpose of this chapter is threefold. First, we examined training research on evaluation since 1993 by analyzing the 125 research studies that have cited Kraiger et al. (1993). This investigation was used to identify key trends in training evaluation research. Second, we examined the literature for new evaluation methodologies that have been created since 1993. In particular, we focused on two cognitive outcomes (mental models and metacognition) and two affective outcomes (goal orientation and attitude strength). In this way, we could track innovative advances in research on these constructs and discuss the implications of these advances for improving training evaluation and training effectiveness research. The chapter concludes with research directions relevant to increasing our evolving understanding of learning outcomes.

Four Trends in Learning Outcomes Research

An examination of the 125 studies citing Kraiger et al. (1993) reveals four research trends. First, it is clear that more researchers are increasingly taking a multidimensional perspective to learning. A majority of the empirical studies in our sample cited Kraiger et al. in their introduction as justifying the need for taking a multidimensional approach to learning. For example, Kozlowski et al. (2001) stated,

> Kraiger et al. (1993) have called for research that elaborates the nomological network around cognitive, affective, and behavioral training outcomes. By examining a full spectrum of outcomes, and their theoretical influences, we begin elaborating linkages among individual differences, training interventions, learning, performance and adaptability for complex dynamic tasks. (p. 3)

A second example comes from Yi and Davis (2001), who justified their outcome measures by stating that consistent with Kraiger et al. (1993), they measured cognitive, skill-based, and affective dimensions through a multiple-choice knowledge test, a variety of skill-based problems, and affective reactions scales, respectively. Practice-oriented articles have also noted the need to take a broader approach. For example, in a *Public Personnel Management* article, Ivancevich and Gilbert (2000) noted that the Kraiger et al. framework

> provides diversity management training researchers and advocates with a model that requires that cognitive, skill based or affective outcomes be assessed. This model, which highlights outcomes, could provide a starting framework for enabling an evaluation of what a diversity training program is attempting to achieve. (p. 84)

The second major trend occurring in the literature is that empirical research has emphasized cognitive and affective learning outcomes relative to skill-based outcomes. This trend is not surprising because Kraiger et al.'s paper (1993) was one of the first "cognitively oriented" training evaluation papers and stressed the need to shift away from a strong behavioral emphasis to a more general understanding of learning, including cognitive and affective change. This cognitive-affective focus is consistent with the current zeitgeist of much of the I/O field and a break from historical trends in which training researchers emphasized the importance of primarily measuring behavioral change (Kraiger & Ford, 2007). Yet, although Kraiger et al. promoted the use of additional measures of cognitive and affective outcomes, they also called for more construct-relevant measures of skill development. One good example of a study on skill development was conducted by Yeo and Neal (2004). They described quadratic effects that they found relevant to rate of performance improvement as learners transitioned to the compilation phase of skill acquisition. There is a need for more studies that investigate better ways of measuring skill acquisition and retention.

A third trend is increased sophistication in measuring cognitive learning outcomes. Researchers are going beyond verbal or declarative knowledge (i.e., measuring learning through multiple-choice tests of basic knowledge) to measuring procedural or more strategic knowledge and knowledge structures such as mental models. For example, a number of studies have measured mental models (knowledge structure) as an indicator of learning and as a predictor of training transfer (e.g., Day, Arthur, & Gettman, 2001; Kozlowski et al., 2001; Marks, Sabella, Burke, & Zaccaro, 2002; Mathieu, Heffner, Goodwin, Salas, & Cannon-Bowers, 2000). Sandberg, Christoph, and Emans (2001) emphasized the importance of not only assessing declarative knowledge but also measuring "strategic knowledge" (which Kraiger et al., 1993, described as procedural knowledge) defined as mental activities facilitating knowledge acquisition, organization, and application.

The fourth trend concerns the measurement of affective outcomes. A number of researchers cited the importance of measuring affective outcomes other than trainee reactions to the quality of the training received. For example, Hsieh and Chao (2004) noted the need to incorporate affective changes, such as increases in motivation, as indicators of training effectiveness. Nevertheless, as noted by Colquitt, LePine, and Noe (2000) in their meta-analysis, many researchers continue to measure reactions to or satisfaction with training and fail to incorporate additional attitudinal outcomes. Even among those who did adopt a broader approach to affective outcomes, posttraining self-efficacy was the only motivational outcome that has been researched with any frequency. Alternative attitudinal indicators of learning have been largely ignored.

As with any chapter, there is a need to focus our attention to a few key issues. Based on the analysis above, we decided to focus on advances in our understanding of cognitive and affective learning outcomes. In discussing cognitive outcomes, we make a renewed call for research beyond basic declarative knowledge as important indicators of learning. In regard to affective outcomes, we focus on the need to broaden our efforts beyond reaction measures and measures of self-efficacy to issues of changes in goal orientation, attitude strength, and implicit attitudes as a function of training.

Cognitive Learning Outcomes

Kraiger et al. (1993) stated that knowledge acquisition has traditionally been focused on verbal knowledge as assessed by achievement tests administered at the end of training. Research in the cognitive sciences has highlighted the complex and dynamic nature of the knowledge acquisition process, with the acquisition of verbal knowledge serving as a foundation for cognitive skill development (e.g., Anderson, 1982). For more advanced learners, it may be more useful to measure the level of procedural knowledge (knowledge of the how, what, and why) that a trainee has obtained.

Concurrent with an increase in a trainee's verbal and procedural knowledge is the development of more meaningful structures for organizing knowledge. These structures allow people to draw inferences, make predictions, understand phenomena, and decide which actions to take (Johnson-Laird, 1983). Kraiger et al. (1993) described the emerging research on mental models, which trainees can use to describe task functions and forms, explain the integration of various tasks, and anticipate future task requirements (Rouse & Morris, 1986).

Kraiger et al. (1993) also stressed the importance of measuring higher order learning as indicated by the development and application of cognitive strategies by trainees. As knowledge continues to be compiled and organized in memory, more elegant task strategies can emerge. Therefore, the use of executive functions and strategy development could serve as capstones for training evaluation. In particular, Kraiger et al. focused on metacognition, defined as the knowledge of one's own cognition and the regulation of cognitive processes such as planning, monitoring, and revising goal-appropriate behavior.

Studies Examining Procedural Knowledge and Mental Models

Multiple studies have moved beyond measuring simple declarative knowledge. A systematic set of studies by Kozlowski and his colleagues (Bell & Kozlowski, 2002a, 2002b; Kozlowski & Bell, 2006) has distinguished between what they call basic (declarative) knowledge and strategic (procedural) knowledge. They also linked these knowledge differences to two different transfer outcomes: basic performance and strategic performance. For example, using confirmatory factor analysis, Bell and Kozlowski (2002b) showed that declarative and procedural knowledge scales were indeed measuring two different latent aspects of knowledge acquisition. They also found that the level of procedural knowledge was a predictor of performance on the more complex generalization task, whereas declarative knowledge was not. More research distinguishing between these two types of knowledge is needed to build further the nomological network of knowledge outcomes.

As noted by Yi and Davis (2001), as trainees gain in procedural knowledge, they refine the cognitive structures used to organize and access that knowledge. Jonassen (1995) emphasized that the ability to reliably and validly measure changes in users' mental models can help us to assess the degree to which advanced knowledge and problem-solving skills were acquired during training. Several potentially useful criteria have emerged for assessing the quality and utility of individual mental models (Jonassen). These criteria include model coherence, personal relevance, integration, fidelity with the real world, imagery, complexity, applicability, and inferential ability. Consequently, it is not surprising that the measurement of mental models as an indicator of learning has expanded and become more mainstream. For example, Kaplan and Black (2003) used mental models and the concept of animation to allow trainees to understand how the differentiation of model elements (water temperature, soil density, terrain, etc.) interacts and causally impacts outcome variables (floods, mudslides, erosion, etc.). Mental-model quality has also been found to predict outcomes over and above more traditional measures of knowledge acquisition. For example, Davis, Curtis, and Tschetter (2003) found that the quality of a trainee's structural knowledge (operationalized as closeness to an expert model) provided an incremental prediction of posttraining self-efficacy beyond measures of declarative knowledge.

Kraiger et al. (1993) discussed two major strategies for measuring mental models. First, model elements could be mapped by having the learners arrange elements using a free sort task (e.g., Champagne, Klopfer, Desena, & Squires, 1981; Eccles & Tenenbaum, 2004). Second, the mapping process could be accomplished by submitting the judgments to a clustering algorithm often referred to as a *structural assessment*. The most commonly used structural assessment algorithm, Pathfinder (Schvaneveldt, Durso, & Dearholt, 1885), has been used in a number of studies (e.g., Curtis & Davis, 2003; Davis et al., 2003; Day et al., 2001; Kraiger, Salas, & Cannon-Bowers, 1995; Stout, Kraiger, & Salas, 1997).

One newer measurement method popularized in education fields is that of concept mapping (Daley, Shaw, Balistrieri, Glasenapp, & Piacentine, 1999; Yin, Vanides, Ruiz-Primo, Ayala, & Shavelson, 2005). The process of concept mapping involves having participants create action-based links between elements in the mental model. More work is needed in the training field of using concept-mapping methods for examining knowledge structures. Operationally, researchers need to consider if links are hierarchically structured as well as how constrained to make the number of links between elements (e.g., see Shavelson, Lang, & Lewin, 1993; Yin et al., 2005).

A shift from individual mental models to team mental models has been observed since the Kraiger et al. (1993) publication. Many researchers have investigated the pre- and posttraining effects of mental models on team performance and/or team process (Marks, Zaccaro, & Mathieu, 2000; Mathieu et al., 2000; Mohammed & Dumville 2001; Smith-Jentsch, Mathieu, & Kraiger, 2005). Mohammed and Dumville (2001) conducted an analysis of the academic roots of team mental models across several disciplines of study and discussed issues of transactive memory and information sharing. They suggested that how we interact as team members relevant to giving and receiving knowledge can have a dramatic effect on how fast our mental models converge and what they converge toward. Marks et al. (2000) examined how team interaction training influences team members' knowledge structures (measured by a modified form of concept mapping) regarding such outcome variables as effective performance across routine and novel environments. The researchers hypothesized (and found support) that team interaction training (cross-training) as well as leader briefings led to enhanced levels of mental model similarity (sharedness) and accuracy. The enhanced level of knowledge facilitated the development of more effective communication and increased overall team performance. Similarly, Mathieu et al. (2000) investigated the effects of shared mental models on team processes and performance using computer flight-based simulations. They found that team mental models correlated significantly with team performance and that the relationship was fully mediated by team process.

The research literature has evolved to reflect the fact that certain measures of knowledge organization offer greater predictive validity than do traditional measures of knowledge (Mathieu et al., 2000). Researchers have begun to investigate the relationship of environment, communication, task demands, workload, team process, and other factors on mental model formation, similarity, and accuracy. Research has also examined factors impacting related concepts such as transactive memory (Ellis, 2006).

Conceptual Advances and Metacognition

There are conceptual advances in the educational domain that can also be applied to improve our understanding of learning outcomes. In 2001, Anderson et al. created a revision to Bloom's (1956) taxonomy of educational objectives. The original taxonomy focused on cognitive, psychomotor, and affective objectives. It was ordered from simple (concrete) cognitive knowledge to more complex (abstract) knowledge with the assumption that the simpler category was a prerequisite for mastery of the next, more complex level. The structure of the original hierarchical taxonomy included knowledge (knowledge of specifics, knowledge of ways and means of dealing with specifics, and knowledge of principles), comprehension, application, analysis, synthesis, and evaluation.

The revised taxonomy by Anderson et al. (2001) created two dimensions. One dimension was the *structure* of knowledge, skill, or affect. The second dimension was the *process* underlying learning. The new knowledge dimension contains four rather than three main categories. Three of the categories include the substance of the original subcategories of knowledge—factual knowledge, conceptual knowledge, and procedural knowledge. The fourth, new category is labeled *metacognitive knowledge*, which the researchers reserved for knowledge about cognition and an awareness of one's own cognition.

The revised taxonomy is consistent with the call by Kraiger et al. (1993) for training researchers to view metacognition as a learning outcome. Metacognitive skills are essential in the planning, monitoring, and revising of goal-relevant behavior. Examples of metacognitive skills include the understanding of the relationship between task demands and one's skills and the appropriate matching of task strategies to situational contexts.

Kraiger et al. (1993) suggested a number of ways in which the measurement of metacognitive skills can support inferences of learning during training. For example, in contrast to novices, experts are more likely to discontinue a problem-solving strategy that would ultimately prove to be unsuccessful, are more accurate about judging the difficulty of new problems, and are better able to estimate the number of trials they will need to accomplish a task. Thus, an increase in a trainee's ability to identify and discontinue an unsuccessful strategy would indicate learning. In terms of measurement, they discussed verbal protocols (e.g., Glaser, Lesgold, & Gott, 1986; Means & Gott, 1988) as a method to assess trainee understanding of task behavior relevant to a superordinate goal. Questions could be asked to investigate which trainees were generating and testing hypotheses, were operating under goals, or understood whether they were making adequate progress. Questions could also be asked to determine the trainees' awareness of their level of proceduralization, the degree of additional learning needed, and trainees' awareness of mistakes. No published study in our review of the 125 studies since 1993 in the training field examined changes in metacognition as a function of training. We reiterate the call by Kraiger et al. to view metacognition as a potential learning outcome as there have been conceptual and operational advances in this area.

Anderson and colleagues' (2001) revised taxonomy suggests that metacognitive knowledge should be thought of as including three aspects—strategic knowledge (e.g., knowledge of the use of heuristics), knowledge about cognitive tasks (including appropriate contextual and conditional knowledge), and self-knowledge (awareness of one's own knowledge level, including strengths and weaknesses). With enhanced metacognitive knowledge, learners can better adapt the ways in which they think and operate both across and within situations (Krathwohl, 2002). There has been increased interest in helping learners become more knowledgeable of, and responsible for, their own cognition and thinking (Pintrich, 2002). Research supports the proposition that as learners become more aware of their own thinking and become more knowledgeable about cognition in general, they tend to learn better (see Bransford, Brown, & Cocking, 1999).

Pintrich (2002) discussed the revised taxonomy with a special focus on metacognitive knowledge in learning, teaching, and assessment. He distinguished between metacognitive knowledge and self-regulatory processes. As discussed, metacognitive knowledge is viewed as consisting of knowledge of general strategies that might be used for different tasks, knowledge of the conditions under which these strategies might be used, knowledge of the extent to which the strategies are effective, and knowledge of self. These forms of knowledge are distinct from metacognitive control and self-regulatory processes that learners use to monitor, control, and regulate their learning.

The implication of metacognition for training is that the skills most critical to higher order thinking or critical thinking are metacognitive rather than simply cognitive (see Kuhn, 2000). Thus, training programs designed to produce experts should focus heavily on the development of effective metacognitive skills. For example, Bransford et al. (1999) showed that metacognitive knowledge was positively related to skill transfer across settings. Formal questionnaires and interviews have been used in the education field to assess learning (metacognitive) strategies as well as student knowledge about different tasks and contexts (e.g., see Baker & Cerro, 2000; Pintrich et. al., 2000). These methods are directly applicable when examining workplace training efforts. As noted by Airasian and Miranda (2002), knowledge of cognitive strategies, cognitive tasks, and self requires different ways of thinking about assessment than simply measuring knowledge of content.

Affectively Based Learning Outcomes

Kraiger et al. (1993) argued that an emphasis on behavioral or cognitive measurement at the expense of attitudinal and motivational issues provides an incomplete profile of learning. They proposed a broader range of motivationally and attitudinally based outcomes that could be measured and used to infer that learning had occurred during training.

Affectively based measures of training evaluation are a class of variables encompassing topics such as attitudes, motivations, and goals. Attitudes or preferences may be either the direct target of learning or an indirect target of change. In other words, change in the affective outcome might be the major goal of the training program (e.g., diversity training), or these changes might indirectly support the acquisition of knowledge and skills. Since 1993, there have been advances in the conceptualization and measurement of motivation and attitudes that have implications for improving training evaluation methodologies.

Motivational Outcomes

Kraiger et al. (1993) discussed three constructs relevant to motivational learning outcomes: motivational dispositions, self-efficacy, and goals. The primary emphasis was on changes in preexisting or enduring motivational orientations. Trainees enter training environments with not only preexisting knowledge and skills, but also preexisting attitudes toward themselves, the content matter, and the value of training. These predispositions and motivations may be affected by training in such a way that the accomplishment of the primary training objective (i.e., knowledge or skill acquisition) would be facilitated. For example, changes in these motivational constructs might enable greater persistence or focus during training, or facilitate transfer.

One learning outcome that has been the focus of considerable subsequent research is what Kraiger et al. (1993) labeled "motivational disposition." Drawing primarily on the work of Carolyn Dweck (Dweck, 1986; Dweck & Elliott, 1983), we noted that (a) persons tended to display either a mastery orientation (concern for learning or mastering the task at hand) or a performance orientation (concern for doing well or garnering positive evaluations from peers or superiors); (b) what has been labeled a *motivational disposition* is actually a goal orientation (or tendency) and, as such, may be malleable via interventions such as training; and (c) the optimal goal orientation depends on the training material, the level of instruction, and the instructional context. Here, we focus on this motivational disposition as an important motivational learning outcome because recent advances in research on goal orientation have great potential for increasing our understanding of learning outcomes.

Since 1993, a number of researchers have used goal orientation in studies on training (e.g., Bell & Kozlowski, 2002a; Chen, Gully, Whiteman, & Kilcullen, 2000; Colquitt & Simmering, 1998; Ford, Smith, Weissbein, Gully, & Salas, 1998; Radosevich, Vaidyanathan, Yeo, & Radosevich, 2004; Stevens & Gist, 1997). Although goal orientation has proven to be a popular construct in the training literature, few studies have examined it as a learning outcome. More typically, goal orientation has been studied as a predictor variable that may have direct or interactive effects on learning and other outcomes, including cognitive activity, motivation, and transfer (Fisher & Ford, 1998; Ford et al., 1998; Schmidt & Ford, 2003). Several key studies are summarized below.

Two studies examined the impact of goal orientation on trainee practice. Ford et al. (1998) measured mastery and performance orientation as individual difference variables prior to a 2-day training session. Participants received training on a complex, PC-based, decision-making program that simulated naval radar tracking. Participants completed multiple training scenarios and completed measures of metacognitive activity and self-efficacy. Finally, participants completed a knowledge test and separate transfer task. Their results showed that pretraining mastery orientation was related to metacognitive activity and learning, which were in turn related to transfer performance. Participants' performance orientation was related negatively to self-efficacy after training, which in turn was predictive of transfer performance.

Stevens and Gist (1997) examined the impact of an end-of-training goal orientation intervention on posttraining (transfer) outcomes. Rather than measure trainees' goal orientations, Stevens and Gist attempted to manipulate them by advising trainees to view a final practice session as either a chance to improve their newly trained skills (mastery) or an opportunity to achieve their best outcomes (performance). The goal orientation condition had a significant impact on both interim skill maintenance activities and transfer intention after training, with participants who received the mastery orientation coaching reporting greater transfer intent and greater use of strategies taught in training to achieve the intended outcomes of the training. This study indicates that interventions (and, thus, training content) can affect individuals' goal orientations.

In the Ford et al. (1998) and Stevens and Gist (1997) studies, goal orientation was viewed as an indirect predictor of knowledge- or skill-based training outcomes. In other words, goal orientation affected trainees' acquisition of knowledge or skill via its effects on trainees' cognitive and motivational states. Neither study measured goal orientation as a primary end-of-training outcome. One study that did view goal orientation as a primary outcome was conducted in the sports psychology domain (Wallhead & Ntoumanis, 2004). In contrast to students who experienced a traditional, instructor-led, physical education class, students in an experimental condition featuring self-referenced evaluation, greater autonomy, and private recognition of accomplishment showed a decrease in performance orientation and an increase in mastery orientation relative to precourse levels. Thus, the experiences that the trainees had in the experimental condition led to desired changes in goal orientations. The effect of situations on individuals' goal orientations has been an emerging topic in the goal orientation literature and has implications for the use of goal orientation as a learning outcome, as is discussed further below.

Just as there has been considerable research activity on the correlates and outcomes of trainee goal orientation, there has also been considerable theoretical and scaling activity. One major subject of interest has been the identification of the process by which goal orientation affects outcomes. In this regard, an important theoretical (and methodological) contribution was made by Button, Mathieu, and Zajac (1996), who determined several behavioral and cognitive tendencies that may ensue from holding a performance or mastery orientation. For example, performance-oriented individuals may avoid challenges, attribute failure to low ability, and experience deterioration of performance or cognitive withdrawal over time. In contrast, mastery-oriented individuals may seek challenging tasks, interpret failure as useful feedback, and self-regulate learning so as to improve in performance over time. These tendencies are proposed to mediate the relationship of goal orientation with other learning outcomes, such as the acquisition of knowledge or skills.

A second major topic of theoretical interest concerns the dimensionality of goal orientation. Whereas Dweck (1986) implied that mastery and performance orientation were anchors of a bipolar continuum, Button et al. (1996) suggested that the two were separate dimensions that were "neither mutually exclusive, nor contradictory" (p. 28). Thus, one could demonstrate either or both orientations, depending on the strength of the relative individual traits and situational conditions. In support of this conceptualization, Button et al. developed and provided preliminary validation evidence for a two-dimensional measure of goal orientation with both dispositional and situational components (see below).

Concurrently, Elliot and Harackiewicz (1996) proposed a trimodal model of goal orientation, partitioning performance orientation into two dimensions: a performance approach dimension (which resembles prior conceptualizations of performance orientation) and a performance avoidance dimension characterized by a desire to avoid negative evaluations by others. In this model, mastery orientation is consistent with an incremental view of task-related ability (i.e., one can improve through practice and feedback), whereas performance approach and performance avoidance orientations are related to views of task-related ability as relatively fixed. In the latter case, if individuals believe that their task-related ability is not likely to change through short-term training interventions, they are more likely to adopt goals related to impression management than performance improvement (VandeWalle, Cron, & Slocum, 2001).

Finally, some educational psychologists have begun to move past chronic goal orientation models and have begun to focus on achievement goals (e.g., Elliot & Harackiewicz, 1994; Harackiewicz, Barron, Tauer, & Elliot, 2002). Achievement goals are situationally specific goals related to the immediate context (such as a particular class or training program). Although achievement goals may be related to developing competence (mastery), demonstrating competence to others (performance approach), or avoiding negative evaluations or cognitive effort (performance avoidance) (similar to the trimodal goal orientation model), they are defined more by the situational requirements or payoffs for learning than by stable individual differences (see also Breland & Donovan, 2005). Researchers are currently interested in identifying the amount of variance in goal orientations that can be attributed to the person and to the situation.

There have been considerable efforts in the past decade to develop measures of goal orientation. In a recent review of the goal orientation literature, DeShon and Gillespie (2005) reported that a majority of the studies measuring goal orientation used an existing measure. Of those studies using an existing measure, the most common instruments were those by Button et al. (1996; 13 studies), VandeWalle (1997; seven studies), and Elliot and Church (1997; seven studies). Other recently developed instruments have been published by Dowson and McInerney (2004), Midgley et al. (1998), and Zweig and Webster (2004b).

As noted by DeShon and Gillespie (2005), although different instruments may share the same name, they may not be measuring identical constructs. For example, the Button et al. (1996) scale assesses only mastery and performance approach orientations, whereas the VandeWalle (1997) scale measures mastery, performance approach, and performance avoidance dimensions. DeShon and Gillespie also commented on the surprising lack of evidence of convergence among scales and the lack of construct validity data in general (although Midgley et al., 1998, and Zweig & Webster, 2004a, 2004b, appear to be exceptions). Therefore, the choice of goal orientation measures should be highly dependent on whether the scale developers and the research agree on how many dimensions reflect goal orientation and whether goal orientation is best viewed as a disposition or trait, a temporary goal state, or a mental framework for approaching learning tasks. Considerably more research is needed to establish relations among measures and, more importantly, between the measures and underlying constructs.

The debate regarding whether goal orientation is a stable disposition or a motivational tendency that can be affected by situational characteristics has tremendous implications for the utility of goal orientation in the assessment of learning outcomes. If goal orientation is viewed as a relatively stable disposition, then it should be utilized as a secondary learning outcome. In other words, if goal orientation is a trait, its main utility in the learning process is in the facilitation of knowledge and skill acquisition or intention to transfer. In other words, it is more relevant to investigations of training effectiveness than training evaluation. On the other hand, if goal orientation can be greatly affected by the situation, change in trainee goal orientation may constitute a primary learning outcome in itself and thus be relevant to training evaluation. Each of these possibilities is discussed further below.

If goal orientation is viewed as a trait, the primary benefits of measuring goal orientation should accrue before training. Trainees' goal orientations should be assessed, and the structure of the training program should be adapted in order to motivate learners of each orientation. There has been preliminary work showing that when the motivational climate of a classroom matches the goal orientation of learners, learners report greater intrinsic motivation and satisfaction (e.g., Ferrer-Caja & Weiss, 2002; Standage, Duda, & Ntoumanis, 2003). However, more research is necessary in order to determine how knowledge of trainees' goal orientations should affect the design or delivery of training. The question of *how* to provide different climates for different types of learners has not been adequately addressed. In addition, more research is necessary in order to determine how best to tailor instructional strategies to the goal orientations of learners in heterogeneous training groups.

If goal orientation is viewed as highly state dependent, pre-post changes in trainees' goal orientations may be considered primary indicators of learning. We have already noted the paucity of studies that have used goal orientation as an outcome variable. This scarcity may reflect the fact that the conceptualization of goal orientation as a statelike tendency is a relatively recent development. However, the notion that goal orientation is malleable raises several interesting questions regarding the use of goal orientation as a training outcome.

For example, mastery orientation is typically positively related to desired outcomes such as learning and performance. However, to date, these benefits are primarily limited to training contexts—more focused cognitive activity, enhanced self-regulation of learning, and so on (e.g., Fisher & Ford, 1998; Radosevich et al., 2004; Schmidt & Ford, 2003). Much less is known about the impact of a mastery orientation on activities outside of the training context, such as on-the-job performance. Although mastery orientation is often viewed more positively than performance orientation, it is possible that these effects are specific to the learning environment. Whereas a mastery orientation tends to lead to greater learning during training, a performance approach orientation might result in greater on-the-job performance following the training session.

Furthermore, the most effective goal orientation to instill in trainees may depend on the specific job in question. For example, mastery orientation may be most appropriate for jobs requiring creativity (e.g., research and development), a performance approach orientation may be best for competitive jobs (e.g., stock trader), and a performance avoidance orientation may be best for jobs requiring monitoring or vigilance (e.g., air traffic controller). More research is needed to determine what job or task characteristics might moderate the relationship between each goal orientation and performance.

As a final note regarding the use of goal orientation as a primary learning outcome, we observe that situational specificity is a double-edged sword. Care should be taken that training be designed with high fidelity relative to the actual job environment. Failure to consider issues related to the fidelity of the training context may result in a failure to transfer a newly trained goal orientation to the job.

Finally, there is a need to continue to examine critically the core constructs of mastery and performance orientation. Although there is mounting evidence that goal orientations can be measured, there remains doubt as to what is actually being measured. Tan and Hall (2005) reported that two common goal orientation measures are significantly affected by social desirability effects. Breland and Donovan (2005), Elliot and Harackiewicz (1996; Harackiewicz et al., 2002), and others argued for greater consideration of situation-specific goal structures, whereas Brophy (2005), citing research evidence, questioned whether learners set performance goals when not prompted to do so by academic researchers. DeShon and Gillespie (2005) recently proposed a dynamic self-regulation model called *motivated action theory* as an alternative to prior goal orientation models. Motivated action theory is less dependent on dispositional models of goal behavior and more focused on the role of goal setting and self-regulation in achievement situations.

We would add that although we are heartened by the number of training studies employing goal orientation variables, there is a need for a clearer understanding of the construct. Although there is agreement that mastery and performance orientations are not two ends of one continuum, still unanswered is the question of the extent to which goal orientation is an enduring trait, a malleable disposition, or a momentary goal state that is primarily determined by the requirements and consequences of learning. Additionally, more research is needed on the relationship between goal orientation and other stable individual differences such as cognitive ability and personality (cf. Klein & Lee, 2006; Phillips & Gully, 1997; Zweig & Webster, 2004a).

Attitudinal Outcomes

Kraiger et al. (1993) recommended that when attitudinal learning outcomes are of interest, attitude strength should be assessed in addition to the more traditional focus on attitude direction. Strong attitudes are more persistent over time and more resistant to change than are weak attitudes, and strong attitudes are more closely linked to cognition and behavior (Krosnick & Petty, 1995, as cited in Bizer & Krosnick, 2001). There is also more research on implicit rather than explicit attitudes that may have relevance for training evaluation research.

Attitude Strength

The strength of an attitude is not always captured by the score on a self-report measure of attitude direction. Endorsements of attitude statements may reveal that the individual accepts the statement but not firmly enough that there are any future consequences. For example, a participant may indicate that he or she "strongly agrees" with the statement "It is important to wear a safety helmet in construction zones," yet if the attitude is weak, it might not persist over time or be related to helmet-wearing behavior. Therefore, Kraiger and colleagues (1993) suggested that in addition to the level of an attitude, researchers should also consider explicitly measuring attitude strength as a learning outcome. A posttraining increase in attitude strength may reflect a change from conformity to active identification with training goals. In addition, those who experience an increase in attitude strength throughout the course of training may be more likely to devote attention to new information relevant to the attitude in question and more likely to demonstrate behavioral transfer of training than are those who have weaker attitudes (see Chaiken & Stangor, 1987).

The review of empirical studies citing Kraiger et al. (1993) suggested that researchers have not incorporated these suggestions into their research.

Although several studies measured self-efficacy as a learning outcome, few incorporated other types of attitudinal outcomes and none assessed attitude strength. We reiterate that attitudinal outcomes including attitude strength may be important indicators of learning.

Kraiger et al. (1993) identified attitude accessibility, centrality, and conviction as three central components of attitude strength. Several additional factors have since been identified by attitude researchers. Krosnick, Boninger, Chuang, Berent, and Carnot (1993) identified 10 dimensions of attitude strength that have been particularly well studied in the literature: attitude extremity, affective intensity, certainty, importance, interest in relevant information, knowledge, accessibility, direct behavioral experience, latitudes of rejection and noncommitment, and affective-cognitive consistency. Each of these dimensions and their respective definitions (as defined by Krosnick et al., 1993) are displayed in Table 4.1.

Empirical evidence has supported the multidimensionality of attitude strength (e.g., Bizer & Krosnick, 2001; Krosnick et al., 1993). For example, Ajzen (2001) found that attitude extremity, ambivalence, and response latency were related to the resistance-to-change feature of attitude

TABLE 4.1

Ten Common Attitude Strength Factors

Extremity	The extent to which an individual's attitude deviates from the midpoint of the favorable-unfavorable dimension.
Intensity	The strength of the emotional reaction provoked by the attitude object in an individual.
Certainty	The degree to which an individual is confident that an attitude toward an object is correct.
Importance	The extent to which an individual cares about and is personally invested in a particular attitude.
Interest in relevant information	The extent to which an individual is motivated to gather information about an attitude object.
Knowledge	The amount of information that is available in memory regarding one's attitude.
Accessibility	The strength of the object–evaluation link in memory.
Direct experience	The degree to which one has participated in behavioral activities related to an object and the amount of contact one has had with it.
Latitudes of rejection and noncommitment	The size of the region of the pro-con attitude dimension that an individual finds objectionable, and the latitude of noncommitment is the region that an individual sees as neither objectionable nor acceptable.
Affective-cognitive consistency	The match between one's feelings about an object and one's beliefs about the attributes of that object.

Source: Adapted from J. A. Krosnick, D. S. Boninger, Y. C. Chuang, M. K. Berent, & C. G. Carnot. (1993). Attitude strength: One construct or many related constructs? *Journal of Social and Personality Psychology, 65,* 1132–1151. Published by the American Psychological Association. Adapted with permission.

strength, whereas attitude certainty, importance, strength, knowledge, attention, and frequency of thought were not. Bizer and Krosnick (2001) found evidence that attitude importance and attitude accessibility are distinct constructs, with attitude importance affecting accessibility. Holbrook, Berent, Krosnick, Visser, and Boninger (2005) found that the relationship between attitude importance and attitude knowledge is dependent upon selective exposure and selective elaboration of relevant information. Holland and van Knippenberg (2003) found that attitude accessibility was unrelated to attitude centrality. This body of research suggests that although attitude strength may be an important moderator of the attitude direction–behavior link, the construct itself could be better understood (Crano & Prislin, 2006). As research advances, we may be able to identify the number of attitude strength dimensions and to untangle those dimensions from their antecedents and consequences.

Attitude strength may be used as a primary learning outcome. An increase in attitude strength might reflect increased buy-in for training goals such as increasing the use of safety equipment or improving one's sensitivity in interpersonal relationships. In addition, an increase in attitude strength should presumably predict training transfer. When attitudinal outcomes are of interest, attitude strength should be measured pre- and posttraining in order to identify changes that have occurred during training.

When measuring attitude strength, it would seem reasonable to select multiple dimensions for measurement. Given the conceptual ambiguity regarding the number of dimensions reflecting attitude strength and the relationships among those dimensions, assessment of multiple dimensions may provide the best picture of how training is affecting attitude strength. Research suggests that the outcome of interest should be carefully considered when selecting which dimensions should be used. For example, when an attitude's resistance to change is of interest (e.g., in sexual harassment or diversity training), attitude accessibility might be the most relevant dimension to assess (Pfau et al., 2004).

Implicit Attitudes

Since 1993, attitude researchers have devoted increased attention to implicit, or subliminal, attitudes as differentiated from explicit or stated attitudes. This research contends that people can hold two sets of attitudes—implicit and explicit (cf. Greenwald & Banaji, 1995)—which may or may not be congruent (Wilson, Lindsey, & Schooler, 2000).

Research has shown that implicit, or automatically activated, attitudes can shape people's reactions to attitude objects and can drive their behaviors (Dovidio, Kawakami, Johnson, Johnson, & Howard, 1997; Karpinski & Hilton, 2001; McConnell & Liebold, 2001). These reactions are often outside of conscious control (see Gawronski, LeBel, & Peters, 2007, for a critique of this assumption and others underlying research on implicit attitudes). When a conflict between implicit and explicit attitudes occurs, motivation and cognitive capacity are required to "override" the influence of the implicit or automatically activated attitude in favor of the explicit or consciously controlled attitude (see Ajzen, 2001; Smith & Zarate, 1992; Wilson et al., 2000). Furthermore, Wilson et al. (2000) have suggested that when attitudes change, the new attitude may not completely replace the old attitude. Instead, the previous attitude may remain as an implicit attitude, whereas the new attitude assumes the role of explicit attitude.

Three major methods for measuring implicit attitudes have been proposed. All three of these methods are based on the priming of object attitudes and use response latencies to determine the extent to which attitudes have been automatically activated. Each technique is briefly summarized below (for a more detailed explanation of subliminal priming techniques, see Bargh & Chartrand, 2000).

First, Fazio, Sanbonmatsu, Powell, and Kardes (1986) introduced a "semantic priming technique" (SPT) that is based on the well-established finding that when an element is primed, it is retrieved from memory more quickly than when it is not primed. Fazio et al. (1986) proposed that to measure one's attitude toward an object, words or pictures representing the attitude object should be paired with adjectives with either positive or negative connotations (e.g., *brilliant* or *terrible*). The participant's instructions are to identify the meaning of each adjective as either "good" or "bad" as quickly as possible. If the respondent's attitude toward the attitude object is positive, then the respondent should be able to identify a subsequent "good" adjective faster than a subsequent "bad" adjective due to the priming effect. The validity of SPT has been generally supported in the literature (e.g., Bargh, Chaiken, Govender, & Pratto, 1992; Fazio, 1993; Fazio, Jackson, Dunton, & Williams, 1995).

Although the SPT assesses the degree to which an implicit attitude toward an attitude object is positive or negative, a second approach called the Implicit Association Test (IAT; Greenwald, McGhee, & Schwartz, 1998) contrasts implicit attitudes toward two attitude objects and results in a judgment of which of the two objects is implicitly preferred. The IAT typically consists of pictures or words representing two attitude objects (e.g., *dog* and *cat*) and words representing "pleasant" or "unpleasant" (e.g., *wonderful* or *disgusting*). The IAT consists of several blocks of trials; however, only two blocks are critical. In the first block, respondents are instructed that if the stimulus presented is *either* the first attitude object or an unpleasant word, they respond by pressing a certain key. If the stimulus presented is either the second attitude object or a pleasant word, they respond by pressing a different key. In the second block, the pairings are reversed such that the first attitude object is paired with *pleasant* and the second attitude object is paired with *unpleasant*. A pairing of the preferred object with "pleasant" words should be easier (and therefore faster) than a pairing of the preferred object with "unpleasant" words. The magnitude of the difference in response times is taken to indicate the degree of implicit preference for one attitude object over the other.

A third method for measuring implicit attitudes is the Lexical Decision Task (LDT; Wittenbrink, Judd, & Park, 1997). The LDT requires respondents to distinguish words from nonwords as quickly as possible. Each word or nonword is preceded by a subliminal prime that either is neutral (e.g., *ABCD*) or reflects one of two attitude objects in question (e.g., *computer* or *typewriter*). The facilitation or inhibition effect observed for the two attitude object primes relative to the neutral prime reveals the respondent's implicit attitudes toward the attitude objects. For example, participants who identified negative words more quickly following an attitude object prime than when following the neutral prime would be classified as having more negative implicit attitudes toward that object. Participants who identified positive words more quickly following an attitude object prime than when following a neutral prime are classified as having positive implicit attitudes toward that attitude object. Tests for significant differences in the degree of facilitation or inhibition for the two attitude objects can be used to determine whether implicit attitudes toward one object are more positive than attitudes toward the other.

One implication of the research on implicit and explicit attitudes is that explicit statements of attitudes may not completely reveal one's deep-seated attitudes. Explicit attitudes may differ from implicit attitudes when respondents are either *unable* or *unwilling* to report their implicit attitudes. Thus, changes in explicit attitudes as a function of training may not be measuring true change, and changes in implicit attitudes should also be considered.

Further, trainees may be *unable* to report their implicit attitudes when these attitudes are outside of conscious awareness. However, these implicit attitudes may still drive posttraining behavior. For example, even when a training program results in a change in explicit attitude, the old attitude may still remain implicitly. Because overriding implicit attitudes requires cognitive resources, under cognitively demanding conditions such as those often faced in the work setting, the individual's behavior may be driven by the old attitude as opposed to the new one. Thus, it may be important to measure the extent to which implicit attitudes, as well as explicit attitudes, have changed during the course of training. In some cases, measurement of implicit attitudes may more accurately predict the extent to which training transfer occurs than explicit measures of attitudes.

In settings such as safety or diversity training, trainees may also be *unwilling* to report their true attitudes (e.g., Amodio, Harmon-Jones, &

Devine, 2000; Devine, Plant, Amodio, Harmon-Jones, & Vance, 2002; Fazio et al., 1995). Most of the research on implicit and explicit attitudes has focused on racial attitudes, but socially desirable responding on attitude measures might be a problem in the assessment of other types of attitudes as well. For example, due to fears of management retaliation, trainees may be motivated to provide the "correct" answers to explicit attitude measures rather than responses that represent their "true" feelings. Some researchers have proposed that measures of implicit attitudes may provide a way to circumvent the pressures for social conformity in order to provide a "pipeline" to the individual's true attitudes (Devine, 2001; Fazio et al., 1995); however, this recommendation should be considered with caution (e.g., Brendl, Markman, & Messner, 2001; Gawronski et al., 2007; Karpinski & Hilton, 2001; Olson & Fazio, 2004).

Researchers must also make decisions about *how* they will measure implicit attitudes. For example, a training program might be designed with the goal of reducing employee resistance to using a new computer program. Implicit attitudes toward the new computer program could be assessed via any of the three techniques discussed above. The SPT would result in an index of how positively or negatively trainees implicitly evaluated the new computer program following training. In contrast, the IAT and the LDT would provide researchers with a comparison of trainees' implicit attitudes toward the new computer program versus the old computer program. Even if posttraining implicit attitudes toward the new computer program were positive, transfer of training might be poor if the trainees' implicit attitudes toward the old computer program were *more* positive. Because cognitive resources are required to override implicit attitudes, trainees might revert to the old program when under cognitive load. Therefore, when making decisions about measurement, it is important to consider whether a contrast between two attitude objects is desirable.

When deciding whether to use the IAT or LDT, researchers might consider the potential for socially desirable responding. In cases in which social desirability is of particular concern, researchers might wish to use the LDT as opposed to the IAT. Because the LDT primes are presented subliminally, there is little opportunity for participants to respond in socially desirable ways.

An Example

Rudman, Ashmore, and Gray (2001) provided a creative illustration of the assessment of implicit and explicit attitudes before and after a diversity training program. In a series of two studies, Rudman et al. (2001) investigated the effectiveness of a semester-long prejudice and conflict seminar taught by an African American professor. Changes in the implicit and explicit attitudes of students enrolled in this diversity seminar were compared with changes in the implicit and explicit attitudes of students enrolled in a semester-long psychology methods course taught by a White professor. No differences in presemester racial implicit or explicit attitudes were found between the two classes. The attitudinal learning that occurred during the course of the prejudice seminar was assessed using two implicit and two explicit measures in a pretest, posttest design.

Two IATs were employed to measure implicit attitudes. One IAT assessed implicit *prejudice* (an affective construct), and the other assessed implicit *stereotyping* (a cognitive construct). The prejudice IAT presented respondents with seven White male names and seven Black male names paired with pleasant and unpleasant words. The stereotyping IAT paired the Black and White male names with attributes that were negatively stereotypical of African Americans (e.g., *lazy* and *hostile*) and positively stereotypical of White Americans (e.g., *ambitious* and *calm*). Trainees' explicit attitudes were measured using self-report scales. Explicit prejudice was assessed using the Modern Racism Scale (McConahay, 1986), and explicit stereotyping was assessed using a self-report measure in which respondents reported the percentages of White and Black males that they believed possessed each of several traits presented (Kawakami, Dion, & Dovidio, 1998).

Rudman and colleagues (2001) calculated effect sizes of the differences in pre- and posttraining scores on each of these four measures as well as between-group effect sizes. Their results indicated that the training was successful; implicit prejudice and stereotyping ($d = .74, .86$, respectively) and explicit prejudice and stereotyping ($d = .47, .91$, respectively) were reduced following the seminar for participants in the experimental group. The results also indicated significant differences between the control group and the experimental group, with the experimental group showing greater decreases in prejudice and stereotyping.

Along with the differential relationships discussed above, correlations found between implicit and explicit measures suggest that implicit and explicit attitudes may be distinct. In addition, Rudman et al. (2001) found that implicit and explicit measures related differently to elements of the training course. For example, perceptions that the seminar increased one's awareness of, and motivation to overcome, one's personal biases were significantly related to decreases in explicit prejudice and stereotyping but unrelated to changes in implicit prejudice and stereotyping. This relationship is consistent with the conceptualization of explicit attitudes as subject to conscious control. These results support the conclusion that different training experiences might have differential effects on implicit and explicit attitudes and that the measurement of both implicit and explicit attitudinal training outcomes is not redundant.

Future Research and Concluding Comments

Consistent with Kraiger et al. (1993), this chapter has advocated a construct-oriented approach to the conceptualization of learning outcomes and the development of training evaluation measures. The review shows that the field has made a number of strides to enhance our understanding of learning within a training context. There are more attempts to measure multiple learning concepts and to examine interrelationships among learning outcomes. We now have more evidence of convergent and divergent validity of some (but not all) learning constructs. In addition, there is an increased level of sophistication in the measurement of cognitive learning outcomes such as procedural (strategic) knowledge and knowledge structures. Research has also begun to examine learning constructs across levels of analysis to include team- as well as individual-level outcomes.

This chapter has also identified areas for which additional research efforts could be placed. Table 4.2 provides a summary of a number of potential research topics and research questions generated through the review and analysis presented above. Table 4.2 is not exhaustive of the research that needs to be done on learning outcomes, but provides an initial starting point for training researchers. Note too that we have focused our review primarily on cognitively and affectively based learning outcomes, so additional reflection and research are needed on measuring skill-based outcomes.

For example, there has been little effort to examine metacognition as a learning outcome. This outcome would seem to be quite important when examining how an individual's skills in regulating or evoking appropriate task strategies change over time. Change in metacognition might be most expected in long training programs or in multiple training programs focused on building a particular skill or competency (e.g., quality control in manufacturing settings or truck driver safety training). As noted in Table 4.2, research questions on metacognition include the determination of when the development of metacognitive skills is critical to develop in trainees and what specific interventions are more likely to enhance metacognitive functioning in trainees.

In addition, we need additional research on trainee motivational dispositions (and states) and attitudes. For example, we must take what we have learned about the multidimensionality of attitude strength and apply that to understanding changes in attitude as a function of training. We also need further research on applying the concept of implicit attitudes where the goal of training is to affect attitude change (e.g., sexual harassment training). Such research could examine the relative sensitivity of measures of implicit and explicit attitudes and the extent to which both types of measures predict behavior on the job.

TABLE 4.2

Research Topics Related to the Multidimensionality of Training Outcomes

Focus of Chapter	Potential Research Topics and Questions
Trends in learning research	• Validate construct valid measures of skill development • Validate measures of motivational changes (beyond self-efficacy)
Cognitive learning outcomes	• What are the theoretical and empirical linkages between the acquisition of declarative and procedural knowledge? • What is the convergent validity between different measures of mental models (e.g., Pathfinder versus cognitive mapping) or between different scoring criteria (e.g., expert overlap versus coherence) for the same measure? • When are metacognitive skills critical to develop? What interventions are likely to enhance metacognitive skills? How generalizable are these changes in metacognition to other training, learning, or performance environments? • If metacognitive skills are executive-level functions beyond the immediate awareness of learners, how can metacognitive activity (or skills) be measured validly?
Affectively based learning outcomes	• What are the relationships among different goal orientation measures (state and trait) and between these measures and latent goal orientation factors? What is the impact of different trait goal orientation (e.g., mastery versus performance orientation) on the effectiveness of training programs? • To what extent is learner goal orientation a viable outcome of training programs? Does goal orientation shift, broaden, or narrow in response to training? To what extent does the strength of individual (trait) goal orientation enhance or inhibit changes to state goal orientation through training? • What is the relationship between different goal orientations affected through training and subsequent job performance? That is, can goal orientation as a learning outcome predict transfer of training? Is this relationship moderated by characteristics of the job or work environment? • What are the theoretical and empirical linkages among the multidimensional measures of attitude strength and how are they relevant to affectively based measures of learning? • To what extent are implicit attitude measures relevant to consider as affectively based measures of learning? • What is the relative sensitivity of measures of implicit and explicit attitudes when the focus of training is on attitude change (e.g., sexual harassment training)? To what extent are these measures sustained over time and do both types of measures predict behavior in situations relevant to the training context?

Finally, we note the importance of continuing to investigate relationships among different types of learning outcomes and between learning outcomes and on-the-job behavior. Modern learning theory posits that the acquisition of declarative knowledge precedes the acquisition of procedural or strategic knowledge, so we should be able to find these same time-based relationships among our learning measures. To do so is not just of theoretical interest but of practical importance as well. Consider a 4-day leadership training program in which participants first learn core learning concepts (step 1), then behaviors related to building and articulating a vision or guiding followers (step 2), followed by strategies related to how and when each new behavior should be applied (step 3). Measures of declarative knowledge at step 1 should predict scores on measures of procedural knowledge at step 2 or strategic knowledge at step 3. If they do not, there is either a weakness in the measure or a fundamental incongruence in the different components of training that must be identified and rectified. Alternatively, if the measure at step 1 is a valid predictor of measures at later steps, the initial measure can serve as a diagnostic tool to identify participants who are not yet ready to advance to later stages of training.

Another benefit of understanding conceptual and empirical linkages between different learning outcomes is that we can advance our understanding of the extent to which different cognitive and affective outcomes mediate training–learning relationships. For example, efforts to teach safety behaviors may only be effective if trainees come to hold implicit attitudes favoring safety, or develop the metacognitive skills to recognize when they are or are not employing appropriate behaviors.

It is also important that learning outcomes be linked to actual behaviors on the job. Doing so helps one to recognize that not all learning outcomes that can be measured should be measured. On the other hand, it is valuable to know when precise changes in learners predict outcomes valued by organizations. For example, it is helpful to understand how two measures of shared mental models (positional goal interdependencies and cue strategy associations) are related to tower safety and efficiency in an air traffic control environment (Mathieu et al., 2005). Given our emerging understanding of the complex relationship between training activity and transfer (e.g., Holladay & Quiñones, 2003; Schmidt & Bjork, 1992), understanding the extent to which different types of learning outcomes predict distal criteria such as generalization, maintenance, and adaptability will inform theory and practice regarding transfer of training. We have some research (e.g., Kozlowski et al., 2002; Kozlowski and Bell, 2006) that has begun to examine the conditions under which different learning constructs (e.g., declarative and procedural knowledge) are related to different behavioral change measures of transfer (e.g., skill generalizability and adaptability). We look forward to further efforts to build upon our emerging nomological network of relationships. We echo the conclusion of Kraiger et al. (1993) in our hopes that this chapter can play a part in spurring additional research in training that advances our understanding of training evaluation and training effectiveness.

Acknowledgment

Thanks to John Lamia for his help in coding and analyzing the articles on learning outcomes.

References

Airasian, P. W., & Miranda, H. (2002). The role of assessment in the revised taxonomy. *Theory Into Practice, 41*, 249–254.

Ajzen, I. (2001). Nature and operation of attitudes. *Annual Review of Psychology, 52*, 27–58.

Amodio, D. M., Harmon-Jones, E., & Devine, P. G. (2003). Individual differences in the activation and control of affective race bias as assessed by startle eyeblink response and self-report. *Journal of Personality and Social Psychology, 84*(4), 738–753.

Anderson, J. R. (1982). Acquisition of a cognitive skill. *Psychological Review, 89*, 369–406.

Anderson, L. W., Krathwohl, D. R., Airasian, P. W., Cruikshank, D. A., Mayer, R. E., Pintrich, P. R., et al. (2001). *A taxonomy for learning and assessing: A revision of Bloom's taxonomy of educational objectives.* New York: Longman.

Baker, L., & Cerro, L. (2000). Assessing metacognition in children and adults. In G. Schraw & J. Impara (Eds.), *Issues in the measurement of metacognition* (pp. 99–145), Lincoln, NE: Buros Institute of Mental Measurements, University of Nebraska Press.

Bargh, J. A., Chaiken, S., Govender, R., & Pratto, F. (1992). The generality of the automatic activation effect. *Journal of Personality and Social Psychology, 62*, 893–912.

Bargh, J. A., & Chartrand, T. L. (2000). The mind in the middle: A practical guide to priming and automaticity research. In H. T. Reiss & C. M. Judd (Eds.), *Handbook of research methods in social and personality psychology* (pp. 253–285). New York: Cambridge University Press.

Bell, B. S., & Kozlowski, S. W. J. (2002a). Goal orientation and ability: Interactive effects on self-efficacy, performance, and knowledge. *Journal of Applied Psychology, 87*, 497–505.

Bell, B. S., & Kozlowski, S. W. J. (2002b). Adaptive guidance: Enhancing self-regulation, knowledge and performance in technology-based training. *Personnel Psychology, 55*, 267–306.

Bizer, G. Y., & Krosnick, J. A. (2001). Exploring the structure of strength-related features: The relation between attitude importance and attitude accessibility. *Journal of Personality and Social Psychology, 81*, 566–586.

Bloom, B. (1956). *Taxonomy of learning objectives: The cognitive domain.* New York: Donald McKay.

Bransford, J., Brown, A., & Cocking, R. (1999). *How people learn: Brain, mind, experience, and school.* Washington, DC: National Academy Press.

Breland, B. T., & Donovan, J. J. (2005). The role of state goal orientation in the goal establishment process. *Human Performance, 18,* 23–53.

Brendl, C. M., Markman, A. B., & Messner, C. (2001). How do indirect measures of evaluation work? Evaluating the inference of prejudice in the Implicit Association Test. *Journal of Personality and Social Psychology, 81,* 760–773.

Brophy, J. (2005). Goal theorists should move on from performance goals. *Educational Psychologist, 40*(3), 167–176.

Button, S. B., Mathieu, J. E., & Zajac, D. M. (1996). Goal orientation in organizational research: A conceptual and empirical foundation. *Organizational Behavior and Human Decision Processes, 67,* 26–48.

Cannon-Bowers, J. A., & Salas, E. (2001). Reflections on shared cognition. *Journal of Organizational Behavior,* 195–202.

Chaiken, S., & Stangor, C. (1987). Attitudes and attitude change. *Annual Review of Psychology, 38,* 575–630.

Champagne, A. B., Klopfer, L. E., Desena, A. T., & Squires, D. A. (1981). Structural representations of students' knowledge before and after science instruction. *Journal of Research in Science Technology, 18,* 97–111.

Chen, G., Gully, S. M., Whiteman, J., & Kilcullen, R. N. (2000). Examination of relationships among trait-like individual differences, state-like individual differences, and learning performance. *Journal of Applied Psychology, 85,* 835–847.

Colquitt, J. A., LePine, J. A., & Noe, R. A. (2000). Trainee attributes and attitudes revisited: A meta-analytic structural equation modeling analysis of research on training motivation. *Journal of Applied Psychology, 85,* 678–706.

Colquitt, J. A., & Simmering, M. J. (1998). Conscientiousness, goal orientation, and motivation to learn during the learning process: A longitudinal study. *Journal of Applied Psychology, 83,* 654–665.

Crano, W. D., & Prislin, R. (2006). Attitudes and persuasion. *Annual Review of Psychology, 57,* 345–374.

Curtis, M.B., & Davis, M.A. (2003). Assessing knowledge structure in accounting education: An application of Pathfinder associative networks. *Journal of Accounting Education, 21,* 185–195.

Daley, B. J., Shaw, C. R., Balistrieri, T., Glasenapp, K., & Piacentine, L. (1999). Concept maps: A strategy to teach and evaluate critical thinking. *Journal of Nursing Education, 38,* 42–47.

Davis, M. A., Curtis, M. B., & Tschetter, J. D. (2003). Evaluating cognitive training outcomes: Validity and utility of structural knowledge assessment. *Journal of Business and Psychology, 18,* 191–206.

Day, E. A., Arthur, W., & Gettman, D. (2001). Knowledge structures and the acquisition of a complex skill. *Journal of Applied Psychology, 86,* 1022–1033.

Devine, P. (2001). Implicit prejudice and stereotyping: How automatic are they? Introduction to the special section. *Journal of Personality and Social Psychology, 81,* 757–759.

Devine, P. G., Plant, E. A., Amodio, D. M., Harmon-Jones, E., & Vance, S. L. (2002). The regulation of explicit and implicit race bias: The role of motivations to respond without prejudice. *Journal of Personality and Social Psychology, 82,* 835–848.

DeShon, R. P., & Gillespie, J. Z. (2005). A motivated action theory account of goal orientation. *Journal of Applied Psychology, 90*, 1096–1127.

Dovidio, J. F., Kawakami, K., Johnson, C., Johnson, B., & Howard, A. (1997). On the nature of prejudice: Automatic and controlled processes. *Journal of Experimental Social Psychology, 33*, 510–540.

Dowson, M., & McInerney, D. M. (2004). The development and validation of the Goal Orientation and Learning Strategies Survey (GOALS-S). *Educational and Psychological Measurement, 64*, 290–310.

Dweck, C. S. (1986). Mental processes affecting learning. *American Psychologist, 41*, 1040–1048.

Dweck, C. S., & Elliott, E. S. (1983). Achievement motivation. In E. M. Hetherington (Ed.), *Handbook of child psychology* (Vol. 4, pp. 643–691). New York: Wiley.

Eccles, D. W., & Tenenbaum, G. (2004). Why an expert team is more than a team of experts: A social-cognitive conceptualization of team coordination and communication in sport. *Journal of Sport and Exercise Psychology, 26*, 542–560.

Elliot, A. J., & Church, M. A. (1997). A hierarchical model of approach and avoidance achievement motivation. *Journal of Personality, 71*, 369–396.

Elliot, A. J., & Harackiewicz, J. M. (1996). Approach and avoidance goals and intrinsic motivation: A mediational analysis. *Journal of Personality and Social Psychology, 70*, 461–475.

Ellis, A. (2006). System breakdown: The role of mental models and transactive memory in the relationship between acute stress and team performance. *Academy of Management Journal, 49*, 576–589.

Fazio, R. H. (1993). Variability in the likelihood of automatic attitude activation: Data reanalysis and commentary on Bargh, Chaiken, Govender, and Pratto (1992). *Journal of Personality and Social Psychology, 64*, 753–758.

Fazio, R. H., Jackson, J. R., Dunton, B. C., & Williams, C. J. (1995). Variability in automatic activation as an unobtrusive measure of racial attitudes: A bona fide pipeline? *Journal of Personality and Social Psychology, 69*, 1013–1027.

Fazio, R. H., Sanbonmatsu, D. M., Powell, M. C., & Kardes, F. R. (1986). On the automatic activation of attitudes. *Journal of Personality and Social Psychology, 50*, 229–238.

Ferrer-Caja, E., & Weiss, M. R. (2002). Cross-validation of a model of intrinsic motivation with students enrolled in high school elective courses. *Journal of Experimental Education, 71*, 41–65.

Fisher, S. L., & Ford, J. K. (1998). Differential effects of learner effort and goal orientation on two learning outcomes. *Personnel Psychology, 51*, 397–420.

Ford, J. K., Smith, E. M., Weissbein, D. A., Gully, S. M., & Salas, E. (1998). Relationships of goal orientation, metacognitive activity, and practice strategies with learning outcomes and transfer. *Journal of Applied Psychology, 83*, 218–233.

Gagne, R. M. (1984). Learning outcomes and their effects: Useful categories of human performance. *American Psychologist, 39*, 377–385.

Gawronski, B., LeBel, E. P., & Peters, K. R. (2007). What do implicit measures tell us? *Perspectives on Psychological Science, 2*, 181–193.

Glaser, R., Lesgold, A., & Gott, S. (1986, July). Implications of cognitive psychology for measuring job performance. Paper presented for the Committee on the Performance of Military Personnel, National Academy of Sciences, Washington, DC.

Goldstein, I. L., & Ford, J. K. (2002). *Training in organizations* (4th ed.). Belmont, CA: Wadsworth/Thompson.

Greenwald, A. G., & Banaji, M. R. (1995). Implicit social cognition: Attitudes, self-esteem, and stereotypes. *Psychological Review, 102*, 4–27.

Greenwald, A. G., McGhee, D. E., & Schwartz, J. L. K. (1998). Measuring individual differences in implicit cognition: The implicit association test. *Journal of Personality and Social Psychology, 74*, 1464–1480.

Harackiewicz, J. M., Barron, K. E., Tauer, J. M., & Elliot, A. J. (2002). Predicting success in college: A longitudinal study of achievement goals and ability measures as predictors of interest and performance from freshman year through graduation. *Journal of Educational Psychology, 94*, 562–575.

Holbrook, A. L., Berent, M. K., Krosnick, J. A., Visser, P. S., & Boninger, D. S. (2005). Attitude importance and the accumulation of attitude-relevant knowledge in memory. *Journal of Personality and Social Psychology, 88*, 749–769.

Holladay, C. L., & Quiñones, M. A. (2003). Practice variability and transfer of training: The role of self-efficacy generality. *Journal of Applied Psychology, 88*, 1094–1103.

Holland, R. W., & van Knippenberg, A. (2003). From repetition to conviction: Attitude accessibility as a determinant of attitude certainty. *Journal of Experimental Social Psychology, 39*, 594–601.

Hsieh, A. T., & Chao, H. Y. (2004). A reassessment of the relationship between job specialization, job rotation and job burnout: An example of Taiwan's high-technology industry. *International Journal of Human Resource Management, 15*, 1108–1123.

Ivancevich, J. M., & Gilbert, J. A. (2000). Diversity management: Time for a new approach. *Public Personnel Management, 29*, 75–92.

Johnson-Laird, P. (1983). *Mental models.* Cambridge, MA: Harvard University Press.

Jonassen, D. H. (1995). Operationalizing mental models: Strategies for assessing mental models to support meaningful learning and design-supportive learning environments. *CSCL Proceedings*, 182–186.

Kaplan, D. E., & Black, J. B. (2003). Mental models and computer based scientific inquiry learning: Effects of mechanistic cues on adolescent representation and reasoning about causal systems. *Journal of Science Education & Technology, 12*, 483–493.

Karpinski, A., & Hilton, J. L. (2001). Attitudes and the Implicit Association Test. *Journal of Personality and Social Psychology, 81*, 774–788.

Kawakami, K., Dion, K. L., & Dovidio, J. F. (1998). Racial prejudice and stereotype activation. *Personality and Social Psychology Bulletin, 24*, 407–416.

Klein, H. J., & Lee, S. (2006). The effects of personality on learning: The mediated role of goal setting. *Human Performance, 19*, 43–66.

Kozlowski, S. W. J., & Bell, B. S. (2006). Disentangling achievement orientation and goal setting: Effects on self-regulatory processes. *Journal of Applied Psychology, 91*, 900–916.

Kozlowski, S. W. J., DeShon, R. P., Schmidt, A. M., & Chambers, B. A. (2002). Effects of feedback and goal orientation on individual and team regulation, learning, and performance. In S. W. J. Kozlowski (Chair), *Advances in training effective-*

ness: Traits, states, learning processes, and outcomes. Symposium presented at the 17th Annual Conference of the Society for Industrial and Organizational Psychology, Toronto, Ontario, Canada.

Kozlowski, S. W. J., Gully, S. M., Brown, K. G., Salas, E., Smith, E. M., & Nason, E. R. (2001). Effects of training goals and goal orientation traits on multidimensional training outcomes and performance adaptability. *Organizational Behavior and Human Decision Processes, 85*, 1–31.

Kraiger, K. (2003). Perspectives on training. In W. C. Borman, D. R. Ilgen, & R. J. Klimoski (Eds.), *Comprehensive handbook of psychology: Volume 12. Industrial and organizational psychology* (pp. 171–192). Hoboken, NJ: John Wiley.

Kraiger, K., & Ford, J. K. (2007). The history of training in industrial/organizational psychology. In L. Koppes (Ed.), *The science and practice of industrial and organizational psychology: Historical aspects from the first 100 years.* Mahwah, NJ: Lawrence Erlbaum Associates.

Kraiger, K., Ford, J. K., & Salas, E. D. (1993). Application of cognitive, skill-based, and affective theories of learning outcomes to new methods of training evaluation. *Journal of Applied Psychology, 78*, 311–328.

Kraiger, K., Salas, E., & Cannon-Bowers, J. (1995). Measuring knowledge organization as a method for assessing learning during training. *Human Factors, 37*, 804–816.

Krathwohl, D. R. (2002). A revision of Bloom's taxonomy: An overview. *Theory Into Practice, 41*, 212–218.

Krathwohl, D. R., Bloom, B. S., & Masia, B. B. (1964). *Taxonomy of educational objectives: The classification of educational goals.* White Plains, NY: Longman.

Krosnick, J. A., Boninger, D. S., Chuang, Y. C., Berent, M. K., & Carnot, C. G. (1993). Attitude strength: One construct or many related constructs? *Journal of Personality and Social Psychology, 65*, 1132–1151.

Krosnick, J. A., & Petty, R. E. (1995). Attitude strength: An overview. In R. E. Petty & J. A. Krosnick (Eds.), *Attitude strength: Antecedents and consequences* (pp. 1–24). Hillsdale, NJ: Lawrence Erlbaum Associates.

Kuhn, D. (2000). Metacognitive development. *Current Directions in Cognitive Science, 9*, 178–181.

Marks, M. A., Sabella, M. J., Burke, C., & Zaccaro, S. J. (2002). The impact of cross training on team effectiveness. *Journal of Applied Psychology, 87*, 3–13.

Marks, M. A., Zaccaro, S. J., & Mathieu, J. E. (2000). Performance implications for leader briefings and team-interaction training for team adaptation to novel environments. *Journal of Applied Psychology, 85*, 971–986.

Mathieu, J. E., Heffner, T. S., Goodwin, G. F., Salas, E., & Cannon-Bowers, J. A. (2000). The influence of shared mental models on team process and performance. *Journal of Applied Psychology, 85*, 273–283.

McConahay, J. B. (1986). Modern racism, ambivalence, and the Modern Racism Scale. In J. F. Dovidio & S. L. Gaertner (Eds.), *Prejudice, discrimination, and racism* (pp. 91–125). San Diego, CA: Academic Press.

McConnell, A. R., & Liebold, J. M. (2001). Relations between the Implicit Association Test, explicit racial attitudes, and discriminatory behavior. *Journal of Experimental Social Psychology, 37*, 435–442.

Means, B., & Gott, S. P. (1988). Cognitive task analysis as a basis for tutor development: Articulating abstract knowledge representations. In J. Psotka, L. D. Massey, & S. A. Mutter (Eds.), *Intelligent tutoring systems: Lessons learned* (pp. 35–57). Hillsdale, NJ: Lawrence Erlbaum Associates.

Midgley, C., Kaplan, A., Middleton, M., Maehr, M. L., Urdan, T., Anderman, L. H., et al. (1998). The development and validation of scales assessing students' achievement goal orientations. *Contemporary Educational Psychology, 23,* 113–131.

Mohammed, S., & Dumville, B. C. (2001). Team mental models in a team knowledge framework: Expanding theory and measurement across disciplinary boundaries. *Journal of Organizational Behavior, 22,* 89–106.

Olson, M. A., & Fazio, R. H. (2004). Reducing the influence of extrapersonal associations on the Implicit Association Test: Personalizing the IAT. *Journal of Personality and Social Psychology, 86,* 653–667.

Pfau, M., Compton, J., Parker, K. A., Wittenberg, E. M., An, C., Ferguson, M., et al. (2004). The traditional explanation for resistance versus attitude accessibility: Do they trigger distinct or overlapping processes of resistance? *Human Communication Research, 30,* 329–360.

Phillips, J. M., & Gully, S. M. (1997). Role of goal orientation, ability, need for achievement, and locus of control in the self-efficacy and goal-setting process. *Journal of Applied Psychology, 82,* 792–802.

Pintrich, P. (2002). The role of metacognitive knowledge in learning, teaching and assessing. *Theory Into Practice, 41,* 119–225.

Pintrich, P. R., Wolters, C., & Baxter, G. (2000). Assessing metacognition and self-regulated learning. In G. Schraw & J. Impara (Eds.), *Issues in the measurement of metacognition* (pp. 43–97). Lincoln, NE: Buros Institute of Mental Measurements.

Radosevich, D. J., Vaidyanathan, V. T., Yeo, S., & Radosevich, D. M. (2004). Relating goal orientation to self-regulatory processes: A longitudinal field test. *Contemporary Educational Psychology, 29,* 207–229.

Rouse, W. B., & Morris, N. M. (1986). On looking into the black box: Prospects and limits in the search for mental models. *Psychological Bulletin, 100,* 349–363.

Rudman, L. A., Ashmore, R. D., & Gray, M. L. (2001). "Unlearning" automatic biases: The malleability of implicit prejudice and stereotypes. *Journal of Personality and Social Psychology, 81,* 856–868.

Sandberg, J., Christoph, N., & Emans, B. (2001). Tutor training: A systematic investigation of tutor requirements and an evaluation of a training program. *British Journal of Education Technology, 32,* 69–90.

Schmidt, A., & Ford, K. (2003). Learning within a learner control training environment: The interactive effects of goal orientation and metacognitive instruction on learning outcomes. *Personnel Psychology, 56,* 405–429.

Schmidt, R. A., & Bjork, R. A. (1992). New conceptualizations of practice: Common principles in three paradigms suggest new concepts for training. *Psychological Science, 3,* 207–217.

Schvaneveldt, R. W., Durso, F. T., & Dearholt, D. W. (1985). *Pathfinder: Scaling with network structures.* Las Cruces: New Mexico State University, Computing Research Laboratory.

Shavelson, R. J., Lang, H., & Lewin, B. (1993). *Indirect approaches to knowledge representation of high school science: On concept maps as potential authentic assessments in science.* Los Angeles: National Center for Research on Evaluation, Standards, and Student Testing, U.S. Department of Education.

Smith, E. R., & Zarate, M. A. (1992). Exemplar-based model of social judgment. *Psychological Review, 99*, 3–21.

Smith-Jentsch, K., Mathieu, J., & Kraiger, K. (2005). Investigating linear and interactive effects of shared mental models on safety and efficiency in a field setting. *Journal of Applied Psychology, 90*, 523–535.

Standage, M., Duda, J., & Ntoumanis, N. (2003). Predicting motivational regulations in physical education: The interplay between dispositional goal orientations, motivational climate and perceived competence. *Journal of Sport Sciences, 21*, 631–647.

Stevens, C. K., & Gist, M. E. (1997). Effects of self-efficacy and goal-orientation training on negotiation skill maintenance: What are the mechanisms? *Personnel Psychology, 50*, 955–978.

Stout, R. J., Kraiger, K., & Salas, E. (1997). The role of trainee knowledge structures in aviation team environments. *International Journal of Aviation Psychology, 7*, 235–250.

Tan, J. A., & Hall, R. J. (2005). The effects of social desirability bias on applied measures of goal orientation. *Personality & Individual Differences, 38*, 1891–1902.

VandeWalle, D. (1997). Development and validation of a work domain goal orientation instrument. *Educational and Psychological Measurement, 57*, 995–1015.

VandeWalle, D., Cron, W. L., & Slocum, J. W., Jr. (2001). The role of goal orientation following performance feedback. *Journal of Applied Psychology, 86*, 629–640.

Wallhead, T. L., & Ntoumanis, N. (2004). Effects of a sport education intervention on students' motivational responses in physical education. *Journal of Teaching in Physical Education, 23*, 4–18.

Wilson, T. D., Lindsey, S., & Schooler, T. Y. (2000). A model of dual attitudes. *Psychological Review, 107*, 101–126.

Wittenbrink, B., Judd, C. M., & Park, B. (1997). Evidence for racial prejudice at the implicit level and its relationship with questionnaire measures. *Journal of Personality and Social Psychology, 72*, 262–274.

Yeo, G. B., & Neal, A. (2004). A multilevel analysis of effort, practice, and performance: Effects of ability, conscientiousness, and goal orientation. *Journal of Applied Psychology, 89*, 231–247.

Yi, M. Y., & Davis, F. D. (2001). Improving computer training effectiveness for decision technologies: Behavior modeling and retention enhancement. *Decision Sciences, 32*, 521–545.

Yin, Y., Vanides, J., Ruiz-Primo, M., Ayala, C., & Shavelson, R. (2005). Comparison of two concept-mapping techniques: Implications for scoring, interpretation, and use. *Journal of Research in Science Teaching, 42*, 166–184.

Zweig, D., & Webster, J. (2004a). What are we measuring? An examination of the relationships between the big-five personality traits, goal orientation, and performance intentions. *Personality and Individual Differences, 36*, 1693–1708.

Zweig, D., & Webster, J. (2004b). Validation of a multidimensional measure of goal orientation. *Canadian Journal of Behavioral Science, 36*, 232–243.

Section 2

Emerging Issues for Design and Delivery

Our enhanced understanding of learning and motivational processes; the effects of individual differences and expertise; and the changing nature of work combine to create several emerging issues that will influence the design and delivery of training over the coming decade and beyond. For example, advances in our understanding of cognition and its role in learning provide key principles that should influence research on training design and the development of new and improved instructional techniques. Moreover, consider that training is increasingly delivered via technology and is often distributed in time and space (i.e., computer-based, Web-based, or distributed training systems). These forms of training design and delivery place emphasis on motivated and self-directed learners, who need to be actively engaged yet effectively guided through the learning process.

Chapter 5, "Cognitive Science-Based Principles for the Design and Delivery of Training," by Cooke and Fiore, updates and expands on the 1989 Frontiers Series chapter authored by Howell and Cooke that has had an important influence on developments in training research. This new chapter draws on recent advances in cognitive science and links them to training, outlining the cognitive-based principles that should be incorporated in training design and delivery.

Chapter 6, by Mayer, is entitled "Research-Based Solutions to Three Problems in Web-Based Training." The penetration of computer technology into all facets of the workplace, the enhanced connectivity of the Internet, and the increasing pressures to reduce costs and improve response times have combined to push e-learning as a revolution in organizational-training delivery. Unfortunately, however, e-learning applications have been driven more by available technologies than by sound instructional principles. Mayer brings an educational psychologist's perspective to instructional design and illustrates how the cognitive science principles highlighted in the prior chapter can be very profitably applied in research to improve the design of Web-based instruction.

In Chapter 7, "Synthetic Learning Environments: On Developing a Science of Simulation, Games, and Virtual Worlds for Training,"

Cannon-Bowers and Bowers take a look at the technological future of training. Organizations increasingly depend on technology, and the art and science of simulation, games, and virtual "synthetic" worlds have the potential to provide engaging and effective training for complex skills. However, although technological advances continue to proliferate in the development of new training media, technologies are merely delivery systems, not an integrated instructional design. This chapter discusses available and emerging technologies that can be used to create sophisticated synthetic, gaming, and simulation-based instruction, and the theory and research needed to guide the design of synthetic learning environments.

Chapter 8 by Bell and Kozlowski, "Toward a Theory of Learner-Centered Training Design: An Integrative Framework of Active Learning," shifts attention to the critical role of the learner and learning processes in training design. The increasing use of technology to deliver training has made the learner a much more active participant in the learning process and has prompted a growing interest in techniques that actively engage individuals in their learning. Research suggests that these techniques, known collectively as active learning, not only offer the potential to enhance learning, retention, and adaptability but also may be well suited for the learner-centered and unstructured learning environments common in today's organizations. This chapter develops a theoretical framework to enhance understanding of the key characteristics of active learning, the mechanisms by which it operates, and its implications for designing effective training systems.

5

Cognitive Science-Based Principles for the Design and Delivery of Training

Nancy J. Cooke
Arizona State University and Cognitive Engineering Research Institute

Stephen M. Fiore
University of Central Florida

The Cognitive World of Work: Howell and Cooke's Perspective

Cognition is defined by Ulric Neisser (1976) as the "activity of knowing: the acquisition, organization, and use of knowledge" (p. 1). This is just one of many definitions, most of which implicate the products or processes of thought. Although cognition has been a topic of broad interest since the time of Plato and Aristotle (Herrmann & Chaffin, 1988), the current cognitive paradigm dates back to the mid-20th century and the confluence of several pivotal ideas, chief of which was the computer metaphor of thought or *information processing*. There was also a simultaneous realization that the current behaviorist paradigm was limited in several ways. George Miller (2003) dated the conception of the cognitive revolution in psychology back to September 11, 1956, a day on which several seminal talks on information theory were given at the Massachusetts Institute of Technology. Since then, the paradigm has been influenced by numerous disciplines, including psychology, linguistics, neuroscience, philosophy, and computer science.

Certainly after nearly half of a century of research on cognition, there is much to say about training. Therefore, in this chapter we describe some of what cognitive science has to say about the design and delivery of training. This is not the first word on this topic. There have been several central reviews (e.g., Evans & Patel, 1992; Wilson, Jonassen, & Cole, 1993) pertaining to the application of cognition to education and training.

We take, however, as our starting point a 1989 chapter in this same series authored by Howell and Cooke entitled "Training the Human Information Processor."

There were several points made in the Howell and Cooke (1989) chapter that are as relevant today as they were 20 years ago. There is first the premise that "machines will become increasingly involved in what we now consider uniquely human intellectual functions: those that require cognition or thought" (Howell & Cooke, p. 122). This trend continues today as machines replace workers in service industries, assuming the roles of travel agents, tax accountants, telephone operators, and bank tellers, to name a few, and as they continue to take on job functions ranging from data processing to copy editing and navigation.

Another theme from the 1989 Howell and Cooke chapter is that ironically, even though machines take on these human intellectual functions, the human's task in many cases becomes increasingly intellectual. So the end result is not an offloading of cognitive tasks to the machine, but a transformation of the task to something requiring even more cognition on the part of the human than ever before. This continues to be the case today, as is exemplified in the control of commercial aircraft via human and automated systems (e.g., Hoeft, Kochan, & Jentsch, 2006) and, more recently, in unmanned aerial vehicles (Cooke & Pedersen, in press). In this latter context, humans in the cockpit have been entirely replaced by automation, but in many respects the job of the *remote pilot* of these systems is even more complicated—especially in a cognitive sense.

Finally, the 1989 Howell and Cooke chapter promotes cognitive approaches and training tools for the training of cognitive tasks. The claim was made by Howell and Cooke that the domain of training had been slow to adopt the cognitive paradigm or to at least expand its behaviorist repertoire to include cognitive concepts. The case was made then that you cannot ignore the *K* in *KSAs* (knowledge, skills, and abilities). Twenty years later, cognitive principles are providing the basis of many training strategies.

There were also proposals for applying methods from cognitive psychology to training. Methodologies for task analysis and knowledge elicitation were highlighted as critical hurdles that must be overcome in order to apply cognitive concepts to training. Some other cognitive concepts with potential training application mentioned in the 1989 Howell and Cooke chapter include training for automaticity, organizing structures for working and long-term memory, mental models, metacognition, expert systems, intelligent tutors, and organizers. Are these concepts as important today as they were 20 years ago? Has progress been made in the cognitive training arena? What is new in cognition that has application to training? In this chapter, we address cognitively based principles for the design and delivery of training, providing a representative update on the state of the field since 1989.

Relevant Changes Since 1989

The mainstream view of cognition depicts mental activity as something that is not directly observable, but that can be indirectly inferred, modeled, and measured through observable behavior. For example, one may not be able to observe a prosecuting lawyer's thought processes as she strategizes about a line of questioning for a witness on the stand. But one could infer her line of thinking based upon her subsequent actions. Of course, there are other events that may occur (unexpected objections and/or directions from the judge) that may create a disconnect between the behavior and the inferred cognition. One might talk to the prosecutor and ask her to "think aloud" as she views a replay of the trial proceedings. In this case, verbal behavior would be used to infer cognition, and although we might get closer to cognition, there may still be some gap between the actual cognition and the verbal report. Much of the work in cognitive science over the last 50 years has involved systematic observations of behavior like this that can provide insight into cognition and, in particular, mechanistic theories of cognition.

What have been the main changes in cognitive science over the last 20 or so years? Cognitive science has grown in many ways, but one of the features that characterizes the last decade or so is the growth in neuroscience and methodologies for imaging the brain and its activity. These new methodologies have allowed cognitive scientists to more deeply explore the connection between cognition and the brain, a connection that was acknowledged but not emphasized in early information-processing theories (Kandel & Squire, 2000).

Cognitive science has also broadened its scope, now including the study of emotion and its relation to cognition (Lane & Nadel, 1999). The study of cognition has also begun to move outside of the head and into the surrounding context or environment and the human's activity and interactions with that context (Clancey, 1997; Heft, 2001). Other people and cultures are also part of the environment, and this has been recognized in studies of cross-cultural cognition (Nisbett, Peng, Choi, & Norenzayan, 2001), social cognition (Fiske & Taylor, 1991), and team cognition (Salas & Fiore, 2004). Sometimes, these changes can progress to the point of challenging the information-processing paradigm, but at the very least, they have increased its scope.

The importance of cognition in the workplace continues to increase and creates new situations for cognitive activity. Seldom are people working alone in a backroom, but their work products are complexly intertwined with those of others. They continue to do cognitive tasks (e.g., software design, proposal writing, and marketing plans), but they do them in an increasingly collaborative fashion. Therefore, there are new tools to facilitate collaboration (e.g., Microsoft Word's Track Changes feature) that themselves require additional cognitive overhead (Olson, Malone, & Smith, 2001). The workers, although they collaborate extensively, may not all be in one place. Therefore, there is a need for technology that allows for distributed work, distance education, telecommuting, and, in the military, distributed mission training, once again taxing the worker's cognitive resources (Fiore, Salas, Cuevas, & Bowers, 2003).

Consider the list of electronic devices that must be rattled off by the flight attendant prior to a plane's takeoff. The world of work has in a very short time become quite dependent on technology from the Internet and Blackberries to cell phones and e-mail—technology has completely changed our work habits and in many cases has increased the number or complexity of cognitive tasks. On the one hand, it is difficult to remember work before e-mail, and we recognize the benefits in this form of asynchronous communication. On the other hand, managing e-mail has become a new cognitive work task—sometimes taking a significant chunk of our workday. Similarly, the availability of technology has changed the nature of our work. We do not use specialists for tasks such as typing, graphics design, typesetting, travel arrangements, banking, and purchasing, but the average worker has now, through the convenience of technology, taken on all of these new tasks.

Technology has also breached training, with visualization, virtual reality, gaming, and simulation playing bigger roles. But how does the technology itself impact training? Are there cognitive costs associated with training technology that must be borne beyond the costs in learning the material? Consider the first time you used a computer mouse or an in-vehicle navigation system. As technological skills become more widespread in society and as human–computer interfaces improve, the "start-up" costs of learning new technologies should decline. However, there are still likely to be costs.

Finally, our society has generally changed as it has moved from the information age to the knowledge society (Drucker, 1994). Not only does the trainee need to contend with new technology, but he or she also needs to adapt and be open to continuous, lifelong learning. In this knowledge society, reengineering and multiskilling are valued. Individuals continually reinvent themselves in terms of their place in the workforce. In this new, cognitively complex, and dynamic setting, there has been no greater need for training. In the remainder of the chapter, we discuss a number of these aforementioned issues.

Cognitively Based Training

How has training incorporated principles, theories, and methods of cognitive psychology? In 1989, the examples were scarce and were primarily drawn from educational or instructional applications such as intelligent tutors and learning geometry proofs or human factors examples such as training for automatization, training troubleshooting skill, and training for judgment and decision making. In this section, we describe how it is that cognitive psychology is having an increasing impact on understanding training in complex settings. There are two broad epistemological issues that have been fueling relevant cognitive research. On the one hand are researchers (Clancey, 2002; Mayer, 2001) who have emphasized "learner-centered" approaches to system development. On the other hand is the continuing influence of ecological factors or context in understanding human performance. We discuss each of these in turn and then follow this with specific examples of how research and theory from the cognitive and learning sciences have been informing training research.

Learner-Centered Research and the Influence of Context on Cognition

As cognitive psychology attempts to broaden its impact, we have seen a greater focus on training research and development taking a "learner-centered" perspective. In this context, researchers are reacting to studies that have emphasized either the technology or the system over and above the human. The learner-centered camp suggests that organizational training can be best supported when research focuses on the capabilities of the learner such that the emphasis is on how the trainee constructs knowledge and how training systems can be an aid to knowledge construction (see Mayer, 2001). Here, research attends to the learner's cognitive processes when interacting with, for example, technology-based learning environments.

A related movement is that of *human-centered work system design*, an effort that emerged out of expert systems research in the 1980s and that has since evolved into research in a variety of complex domains (Clancey, 2002), including semiautonomous missions to the moon for NASA (e.g., Clancey, 2004; Sierhuis & Clancey, 2002). This approach applies analyses to work practice in order to better understand how the human interacts with, and is impacted by, his or her systems. More specifically, "rather than abstracting human behavior as work processes or tasks ... [this models] people's activities comprehensively and chronologically throughout the day" (Sierhuis & Clancey, p. 32).

The cognitive and learning sciences have long debated how contextual factors influence human cognition and the degree to which this must be taken into account when investigating human behavior, for example learning. Within psychology, competing methods and theories for understanding the complex phenomena associated with human learning can be generally classified into one of two primary approaches. First is *in vitro research*, the term used to describe laboratory studies on standardized tasks. Next is *in vivo research*, used to describe research conducted in natural contexts so as to capture the influence of contextual factors. Emerging primarily from ecological psychology (e.g., Gibson, 1966), this latter approach argues that human behavior must be understood in its relation to the environment and notes how significantly our environment affects our cognition. Gibson (1966) theorized that one cannot disentangle the human from the larger system that is the environment. Therefore, the environment must always be part of the analysis if we are to adequately understand humans within this system. From a more methodological perspective, Hoffman and Deffenbacher (1993) argued that both epistemological and ecological factors must be simultaneously considered in order to truly understand humans in context.

In sum, our understanding of cognition has increased substantially, particularly as we have come to understand how contextual factors influence and interact with the learner. These have forced cognitive scientists to consider human cognition more broadly and recognize the complexities inherent in human information processing when it is considered outside the laboratory. Below, we describe how these dimensions of learning have influenced training.

From Knowledge Elicitation to Training

In their 1989 chapter, Howell and Cooke described cognitive task analysis and knowledge elicitation methodologies as primary hurdles in cognitively based training. These methods are needed to provide training content, to set training objectives based on expert KSAs or mission-essential competencies (MECs; Colegrove & Alliger, 2002), to uncover novice misconceptions along the way, and to assess the knowledge state (Goldsmith, Johnson, & Acton, 1991). Since 1989, many summaries and taxonomies of knowledge elicitation methods have been written (e.g., Cooke, 1994, 1999; Hoffman, Shadbolt, Burton, & Klein, 1995), new methodologies have emerged (e.g., cognitive work analysis; Vincente, 1999), and these methodologies have been called upon in recent training research and applications.

The basic premises are that expertise in a domain is highly dependent on the knowledge of specific facts and rules (Glaser & Chi, 1988) and that techniques are needed to make this information more explicit so that it can be conveyed in training. We also know that expert knowledge differs from novice knowledge, not just in content but also in its organization (e.g., Glaser, 1989). One way to approach training, then, is to view it as the facilitation of the novice's journey to expertise and how isolated bits of knowledge evolve to become the tightly coupled network of expert knowledge.

There are many examples of the use of various knowledge elicitation techniques to reveal expert knowledge and in many cases contrast it with novice knowledge. For example, Connor (2005) used similarity ratings and Pathfinder, a network scaling technique, to elicit and represent anesthesiologists' knowledge about the decision to extubate a patient. Connor assessed anesthesiology expertise by comparing elicited novice knowledge network structures to expert structures. She found that the degree to which the novice conceptual structure deviated from that of the expert structure correlated negatively with oral exam scores. Neville, Fowlkes, Walwanis Nelson, and Bergondy-Wilhelm (2003) similarly used interview methods to elicit and assess team coordination knowledge of naval flight officers.

New techniques such as latent semantic analysis (LSA; Deerwester, Dumais, Furnas, Landauer, & Harshman, 1990) are developing in such a way that they have applications to knowledge assessment. For instance, LSA is a statistical approach to quantifying meaning in text that is based on the surrounding context in a large database. LSA has been applied to the assessment of meaning and expert–novice differences in student essays (Foltz, 1996) and team communication patterns (Kiekel, Cooke, Foltz, & Shope, 2001). In this way, LSA can be used to assess level of expertise reflected in text of discourse and the need for further training.

The same kinds of methods have been used to identify novice misconceptions or gaps in understanding that can be targeted for training. For example, Feltovich, Spiro, and Coulson (1993) uncovered misconceptions among medical students for some complex concepts covered in their coursework and blamed this gap on instruction that does not promote active learning. Likewise, Sarter and Woods (1993) found that experienced pilots did not have a full understanding of their Flight Management System (FMS). These kinds of knowledge gap analyses provide targets of opportunity for training.

In summary, various cognitive methodologies have been applied to elicit knowledge from experts and novices. We have also been able to use this information to assess the knowledge state of an individual and to uncover gaps or misunderstandings that can guide training. It is less clear, however, how to use the information about expert knowledge to design training for novices. How do we bootstrap expertise?

There are a few examples. In some cases, the knowledge of how an expert approaches a problem may suggest that there is a disconnect between current training practices and expertise, leaving the door open to modifications of the existing training program. In some cases, even experts seem to deviate from stated practice. Staszewski and Davison (2000) capitalized on this disconnect and based a U.S. Army training program in land mine detection on expert strategies making use of auditory pattern recognition. They found huge improvements in an operator's ability to detect land mines (e.g., from 16% to 87% detection for the most difficult-to-detect mines) when training was modified in accordance with the pattern detection strategies gleaned from an analysis of expertise.

Although there is promise, the procedure for translating elicited knowledge, KSAs, and MECs into training material remains ill defined. Why not, for example, spoon-feed the KSAs of an expert to a novice to facilitate the development of expertise? This is different from Stazsewski's approach (Staszewski & Davison, 2000), which involved active practice at detection guided by expert strategies. There are many who agree with Ericsson and Charness (1994) that expertise comes only with this kind of deliberate practice. Deliberate practice means that the practice is set up to address training objectives and that progress toward the objectives is continually assessed as it becomes increasingly challenging. So rather than spoon-feed the trainee expert knowledge (i.e., facts and rules), this approach suggests that what is needed is the sculpting of experiences that facilitate the novice to expert transition. In terms of chess expertise, a longtime drosophila of cognitive psychology, this approach might favor training that provides specific moves or games as part of practice as opposed to one that teaches the recognition and interpretation of meaningful chess patterns. Although memory for chess patterns has been shown to distinguish experts from novices, it is not clear that the chess patterns are causally implicated in chess expertise. Instead, they may simply be a by-product of experience.

Perceptual Learning

Training that targets perceptual learning can benefit from an understanding of the role that *knowledge, skills* (e.g., visual scanning), and individual *abilities* play in mediating the perceptual process and interacting with training interventions.

This distinction between skills and abilities can be understood by comparison to findings in tasks requiring significant perceptual processes. In radiology, researchers documented the importance of both learnable perceptual skills such as contrast sensitivity (e.g., Sowden, Davies, & Roling, 2000) and spatial abilities predicting success in the field (e.g., Berbaum,

Smoker, & Smith, 1985). By attempting to disentangle the abilities from the skills involved in a perceptual learning task, training research may not only gain a more fundamental understanding of the task but also be better able to devise training that is targeted to the appropriate areas. Along these lines, Fiore, Scielzo, and Jentsch (2004) examined knowledge acquisition in the X-ray security screening task and showed how the training content may differentially influence learning dependent upon the particular abilities of the learner. They found that when trained with simple stimuli (i.e., X-ray images containing only a threat target) as opposed to with cluttered bags, participants low in visuospatial ability performed better on test items that were cluttered. The opposite pattern was found for participants high in visuospatial ability.

With respect to training search skills, research suggests that strategic search skills can develop, that is, skills allowing one to quickly identify features useful for discrimination, and this may be moderated by visuospatial abilities (Alderton, Cross, & Doane, 2002). Similarly, in industrial applications, researchers have emphasized training perceptual search processes in complex operations. For example, Wang, Lin, and Drury (1997) showed how search strategies are learnable in a soldering task. Wang et al. (1997) found that participants were better able to find problems on simulated solder joint arrays when trained with systematic search strategies (i.e., in regular eye movements across the circuit board). More recently, researchers have used simulations in conjunction with eye tracking to determine if search skills could be trained when modeled on expert scan paths in an aircraft inspection task. Sadasivan, Greenstein, Gramopadhye, and Duchowski (2005) captured training content by extracting the expert's scan while performing in the simulator, and they used this to produce what they termed *feed-forward* training of the expert scan path. They found that this improved novices' performance and led to their adopting a slower search strategy, presumably due to more deliberate processes being engaged. Finally, in medical research, Guerlain and colleagues (2003) found that video-based training can lead to improvements of perceptual skills associated with laparoscopic surgery. In a study with medical students shown examples of steps involved in the surgery, significant improvements were found in what they termed *perceptual rule-based skills*.

In sum, a growing body of research is demonstrating how theory and methods of cognitive psychology can be adopted and applied to examine training of perceptual processes and related skills in a variety of complex domains. Future research needs to continue to increase the impact of such studies by, for example, broadening the scope beyond that of primarily medical research.

Training Thinking Skills

In the years following the 1989 Howell and Cooke chapter that emphasized the importance of cognition in training, there have been a number of efforts directed at training thinking skills or high-level cognitive skills, including decision making, planning, coordination, situation assessment, diagnosis or troubleshooting, and metacognition. One characteristic of this kind of training that coincides with findings on the domain specificity of expert knowledge and skill is that the training of thinking skills occurs within the context of the domain. As we pointed out in our discussions of context and cognition, it is for this reason that there is extensive use of exercises, scenarios, and simulations.

Training Mental Models

A mental model is knowledge specific to a system or task that can be applied in order to understand or make predictions in that context. Mental models have been investigated in training paradigms as a possible mediator of task performance in individuals (e.g., Smith-Jentsch, Campbell, Milanovich, & Reynolds, 2001), or in teams, in which the notions of shared mental models and cross-training are usually adopted (e.g., Marks, Sabella, Burke, & Zaccaro, 2002; Smith-Jentsch, Mathieu, & Kraiger, 2005). Overall, these studies indicate that higher sharedness of mental models leads to better team performance.

Mental models are also widely used as a diagnostic measure evaluating the possibility of novices to construct operational schemas more in line with those of experts in such domains as computer-based training (e.g., Azevedo & Cromley, 2004; Fiore, Cuevas, & Oser, 2003; Fiore, Cuevas, Scielzo, & Salas, 2002), team communication (e.g., Marks, Zaccaro, & Mathieu, 2000), and decision making (e.g., Chermack, 2003; Pollock, Paton, Smith, & Violanti, 2003). For example, Fiore et al. (2002) found that participants with mental models more similar to an expert model performed better on tasks devised to tap the integration of knowledge in a command-and-control setting. These studies show the importance of developing accurate mental models in order to achieve high performance in that accurate mental models are not only an indicator of training success but also a predictor of operational performance.

Metacognition Training

Metacognition, a term describing knowledge about one's own knowledge, has been researched in a number of training paradigms. These examine factors such as the impact that metacognitive awareness has on comprehension and subsequent skill development and transfer (e.g., Ford, Smith, Weissbein, Gully, & Salas, 1998; Keith & Frese, 2005). For example, error management training shows that it is beneficial to encourage error and error remediation training to improve transfer (e.g., Keith & Frese). Such findings illustrate both metacognition mediating performance differences and the importance of encouraging self-regulatory processing during training. Theoretical developments in decision making and metacognition have led to a model of learning transfer that focuses on the active role of the learner (e.g., Ford et al., 1998). Training metacognitive processes has shown to be critical in operational environments such as aviation and crew training (e.g., Jentsch, Bowers, & Salas, 1999), showing that training metacognition led to better decision making. Overall, metacognitive activity in decision making has been shown to be positively related to knowledge acquisition, skilled performance at the end of training, and self-efficacy, thereby improving performance on transfer tasks. More recently, Freeman, LeClerc, and Richardson (2005) applied cognitive concepts of critical thinking and metacognition to the design of the Diagnostic Assessment and Training System (DATS) for maintenance. The theoretical framework guided the interviews and analysis required for identifying the training requirements. Freeman and Cohen (1994) explained how the training of such metacognitive skills can be useful for dynamic decision making and situation assessment.

Case-Based Reasoning Training

Somewhat related to both mental models and metacognition is case-based reasoning (CBR) approaches to training. Arising out of research in understanding how prior experience serves present and future problem solving, CBR has been applied to a number of differing venues. More specifically, CBR arises mainly from the field of cognitive science, focusing on skill development, and situational hypothesis generation based upon knowledge acquired from past experience (Shiu & Pal, 2004; Sormo, Cassens, & Aamodt, 2005). That is, CBR refers to the process of developing an explanation, based on a cyclic manipulation of "explanation patterns" (e.g., Schank, 1986; Shiu & Pal). Explanation patterns can be either specific or generalized cases of events and are related to providing creative or tweaked answers (Schank & Leake, 1989). A typical processing cycle is composed of retrieving similar cases, integrating solutions from previous cases, adapting the solutions to solve the novel problem, and retaining the solution if validated (see Kim, 2004; McSherry, 2001).

Training Decision Making

Pliske, McCloskey, and Klein (2001) developed training inspired by the naturalistic decision making (NDM) movement and the recognition-primed decision model (Klein, 1993) that explains expert decision making not analytically, but rather in terms of sizing up the situation and recognizing a solution. The NDM approach examines decision making in the context of real tasks and is in direct contrast to the analytic approaches using comparatively sterile problems (e.g., Kahneman, Slovic, & Tversky, 1982) that were described by Howell and Cooke (1989). More recently, decision making has been trained in the context of scenarios and simulations through the use of games, critiques, and exercises for specific aspects of decision making such as coming up with decision requirements or communicating the intent of a decision. More generally, Fallesen and Pounds (2001) described a systematic approach for developing training programs based on an understanding of natural strategies for decision making. The context in which cognition occurs has also been represented well by several new training techniques. The U.S. Army in conjunction with the Institute for Creative Technologies (Gordon, van Lent, van Velsen, Carpenter, & Jhala, 2004) has used high-quality video scenarios combined with interactive training technologies to train leadership skills, especially critical thinking and decision making. In this case, the context is of movie quality and the scenarios are engaging. In another study, Brooks, Switzer, and Gugerty (2003) used a process control simulation to test a training that emphasized situation awareness strategies of the expert operators. Compared to control conditions, this situation awareness training resulted in improved operator performance.

Team-level cognitive decision skills have also been trained. Team Dimensional Training (Smith-Jentsch, Zeisig, Acton, & McPherson, 1998) is a training approach used to improve communication and coordination on board naval ships that was implemented under the Tactical Decision Making Under Stress (TADMUS) program. The training took place in the context of an exercise with cycles of prebriefing, performance, diagnosis, and debriefing interventions. This training targeted group-level decision making that involved knowledge sharing and coordination. Team dimensional training was found to be successful, with interventions improving decision-making performance. Similarly, Cohen and Thompson (2001) described the cognitive skills necessary to function effectively as a team in complex, dynamic, and uncertain environments and then identified methods for training these skills.

Since 1989, the targets of training, whether mental models, metacognition, cases, or NDM, have become more context dependent. Although the training of thinking skills appears to be a useful approach for cognitively based training, it is not clear how well the scenario-specific skills transfer to other scenarios, tasks, or domains. A better understanding of the generality of this training is a critical issue for future research.

Computational Modeling and Training

Not only have recent findings in cognitive psychology from perceptual skills to higher level thinking skills been applied to training, but also in the last 15 years these findings have inspired a flurry of work on computational modeling of human cognition (Pew & Mavor, 1997). Such models summarize findings and make explicit the structures and processes of cognitive theories and, thus, help advance our understanding of human cognition. Moreover, these models, implemented as computer programs (i.e., *computational* cognitive modeling), can serve as engines for a variety of training interventions.

Some of the earliest implementations of cognitive models were in the form of intelligent tutoring systems (Anderson, Boyle, Corbett, & Lewis, 1990), that is, the cognition of the typical student would be modeled as well as that of the typical instructor or expert. The models would be used by the larger system as a basis for assessing and diagnosing the cognitive strengths and weaknesses underlying student performance. These systems were *intelligent* in the sense that the instruction was adapted to the individual learner on the basis of a student's interactions with the system and the interpretation of those interactions by the models. The expert model was also relevant here and could serve as the end state in the learning process. The adaptive control of thought—rational (ACT-R) cognitive modeling architecture, one approach to computational cognitive modeling (Anderson, Matessa, & Lebiere, 1997), has served as the basis for several tutoring systems, including a list-processing (LISP) tutor and a geometry tutor (Anderson, Boyle, & Reiser, 1985). Other forms of cognitive modeling have been implemented as intelligent interfaces for just-in-time learning (Rouse, Geddes, & Curry, 1987–1988).

In short, this is an exciting area of research that has tremendous potential for dynamic training environments. Important areas of future research within this context include understanding how cognitive models can be developed to serve as synthetic teammates or as opposite, adversarial forces (e.g., Gluck et al., 2005). Similarly, future research will help us understand how such artificial entities can then serve a training role by providing input from other individuals in the context of a simulation. Generally, as cognitive modeling architectures become more sophisticated, the possibilities increase for the use of the models in training applications.

Summary

Although this is only a sampling of the many areas in which cognition is impacting training, it is clear that tremendous strides have been made. In particular, despite the fact that many of the same challenges identified in Howell and Cooke (1989) still exist today, a number of important gains have been made in incorporating cognitive psychology into training research. Similarly, a number of the future directions that were identified 20 years ago have been realized. Along these lines, we turn next to a discussion of a set of emerging and exciting areas of research that have the potential to significantly impact learning and performance at work.

Future Directions for Applying Cognitive Psychology to Training

In this final section, we discuss some important directions for the continued application of the cognitive and learning sciences to organizational training. Two factors are driving these developments. First is the increasing complexity of the technology continually being developed and adopted within organizations. Second is the increasing sophistication of the tools and methods being developed by those trying to understand human learning and performance. What is important to recognize is that we are addressing training for organizational systems at a level of complexity that we have not considered before. Thus, training research is increasingly relying on coordinated scientific efforts ignoring traditional boundaries and cutting across disciplines.

We turn next to a brief discussion of some of these multidisciplinary efforts involving cognitive psychology bearing on the future of training research. First we discuss some of the burgeoning research on individual differences in cognition that has the potential to be adapted and explored within training research. Then we discuss some of the theoretical and practical developments coming out of the use of simulations and games for training. We then discuss recent research on the application of the computational sciences and neurosciences to augmenting human learning and performance in complex environments. Following this we discuss the implications of such approaches for team cognition and collaborative applications.

Individual Differences in Training Contexts

Given the ubiquitous use of technologies within training programs, an important emerging area of inquiry is that of individual differences and the potential for interaction between the trainee and the training system. Individual differences, aptitudes, or skills potentially may interact with training protocols and affect performance outcomes (e.g., Gully, Payne, Kiechel Koles, & Whiteman, 2002). These performance outcomes that are differentially impacted upon by specific aptitudes are also referred to as *aptitude–treatment interactions* (ATIs; e.g., McInerney, McInerney, & Marsh, 1997). In training paradigms, individual differences that are typically looked at are verbal ability (e.g., Cuevas, Fiore, & Oser, 2002; Mayer & Gallini, 1990; Mayer & Sims, 1994) and visuospatial ability (e.g., Fiore et al., 2004), but also contextual dispositions such as motivation can be taken into consideration (e.g., Smith-Jentsch, Jentsch, Payne, & Salas, 1996). Specifically, the individual characteristic of goal orientation has been shown to account for the cognitive, motivational, and affective processes of self-regulation (Bell & Kozlowski, 2002; Gully & Chen, this volume; Kozlowski et al., 2001). Generally, individual differences have also been shown to interact with skill acquisition in a variety of task contexts (e.g., Ackerman, 1992; Bell, Gardner, & Woltz, 1997; Sohn, Doane, & Garrison, 2006).

Working memory can be seen as a form of individual difference in that different working memory capacities can differentially impact learning (e.g., Unsworth & Engle, 2005) or performance on various tasks (e.g., Brumback, Low, Gratton, & Fabiani, 2005; Long & Prat, 2002). Working memory is usually described as the amount of information that can be processed at once, comprising both verbal and spatial information and the management and integration of this information (e.g., Daily, Lovett, & Reder, 2001; Lovett, Daily, Reder, & Sun, 2001). Overall, there are three main categories of research on working memory and individual differences. First, working memory capacity has been researched as it impacts attention processes (Bleckley, Durso, Crutchfield, Engle, & Khanna, 2003; Kane & Engle, 2000; Tuholski, Engle, & Baylis, 2001). With respect to the potential for ATIs, these studies suggest that low working memory capacity hinders the ability of successfully attending to diverse stimuli. Second, working memory is also looked at in conjunction with the ability to make judgments (e.g., Dougherty & Hunter, 2003; Sprenger & Dougherty, 2006) or the amount of information that can be pulled from long-term memory in order to help with making judgments (e.g., Unsworth & Engle, 2006). Finally, working memory subcomponents such as spatial memory (e.g., Hegarty, Montello, Richardson, & Ishikawa, 2006), verbal memory, or both (e.g., Capon, Handley, & Dennis, 2003; Pulos & Denzine, 2005) are looked at in relation to the ability to reason and/or manage spatial tasks.

The importance of ATIs has led a number of computer-based training protocols to take into consideration such individual aptitudes. Specifically, intelligent tutoring systems are designed to take into consideration individual aptitudes and adapt according to these differences (e.g., Katz et al., 1998; Mitchell, 2000). With respect to learning in groups and differences within such groups, from an individual differences perspective, recent studies highlight the influence of "mixed-ability" collaborative groups. For example, Hmelo, Nagarajan, and Day (2000) found that high- and low-knowledge groups navigated the problem space differently and constructed different representations of the problem (see also Faulkner, Joiner, Littleton, Miell, & Thompson, 2000).

In sum, these results suggest that individual differences are directly related to the manner in which trainees acquire knowledge and/or develop strategies for acquiring knowledge. As such, training research must explore how factors such as collaborative learning or the use of technologies in training interact with cognitive processes to impact training efficacy. Finally, based upon our emerging understanding of individual differences across a variety of cognitive processes, we must better attend to the potential to link, for example, cognitive modeling techniques to training paradigms to produce adaptive training environments supporting the idiosyncratic needs of the learner.

Multimedia and Multimodalities

Multimedia training is characterized by a multimedia message, and acquiring knowledge from it results in multimedia learning (Mayer, 2001, this volume). The important problems that multimedia training needs to consider are broad, but generally can be grouped into three main categories: (a) multimedia design, or the manner in which modalities are employed; (b) the individual characteristics of the trainees; and (c) the manner in which a multimedia message depletes cognitive resources.

Many studies have manipulated the presence or absence of modalities in training varying multimedia to determine the best combinations in terms of learning outcomes (e.g., Fiore et al., 2003; Leahy, Chandler, & Sweller, 2003; Mayer & Sims, 1994; Moreno & Mayer, 2002). A major factor affecting multimedia learning is the manner in which cognitive capacity is tasked. Cognitive load theory, conceptualized by Sweller and colleagues (e.g., Sweller, 1994), holds that there are characteristics of information that make material more or less difficult to learn. Overall, learning may be differentially affected by the burden placed on working memory from either intrinsic cognitive load arising from the training's content or extrinsic cognitive load due to training system design factors (e.g., Sweller). Overall, studies have shown a number of benefits that multimedia training can have on learning, and most of these benefits are reflected in Mayer's (2001) principles of multimedia learning.

Individual factors and dispositions also play a factor in the acquisition of multimedia information. Verbal ability (e.g., Cuevas et al., 2002; Mayer & Gallini, 1990) and spatial ability (e.g., Mayer & Sims, 1994) do seem to play a role in multimedia learning, as well as working memory capacity (e.g., Gyselinck, Cornoldi, Dubois, de Beni, & Ehrlick, 2002).

Finally, multimedia training will allow certain latitude in letting learners *navigate* throughout the multimedia content. This dynamic learning component is seen as being closely related to metacognitive skills because it involves the ability to effectively monitor one's learning to make use of hyperlinks, giving the learner a sense of ownership (e.g., Niederhauser, Reynolds, Salmen, & Skolmoski, 2000; Squires, 1999). Metacognition has also been researched in multimedia computer-based training paradigms (e.g., Cuevas et al., 2002; Fiore et al., 2002), underlining the importance of cognitive self-regulation during the acquisition phase of multimedia information. Fiore and colleagues have shown, for example, how general metacognitive predispositions are related to metacognition in more complex multimedia learning (Fiore et al., 2002) and how metacognitive accuracy is related to actual task performance in a multimedia training context (Cuevas et al.).

Simulation and Games for Training

As discussed previously, an important issue with respect to cognition and learning is how contextual factors impact retention and transfer. Another relevant issue related to contextual learning is how context has been implemented in the field of simulation and training (Cannon-Bowers & Bowers, this volume). Here, we have real-world situations modeled so as to recreate the contextual factors associated with a given operational environment. Primarily driven by military research in the latter portions of the 20th century, simulation is becoming more and more prevalent in organizational learning contexts. In this section, we discuss some of the theoretical issues and directions the field is taking as well as advances that have been made.

First, research in simulation and training does not speak about context as a unidimensional concept. Instead, the discussions center on the construct of *fidelity* within simulations and how certain elements of the learning must be similar to the target environment. Importantly, research highlights how only some components of the simulation need to be faithful to the operational setting being simulated in training. Researchers have noted that the use of simulations with high physical fidelity had little, if any, impact on the actual operational job tasks (Taylor et al., 1999). Others have shown how low-fidelity PC-based simulations can be used to train complex skills at the individual and team levels (Gopher, Weil, & Bareket, 1994; Jentsch & Bowers, 1998; Taylor et al.). Most generally, fidelity needs to be determined by the behavioral and cognitive requirements of the task (Salas & Burke, 2002). As can be seen, this notion of fidelity aligns with what we suggested regarding context. Further, fidelity researchers argue that it is the mental process to which we must be faithful as opposed to only emphasizing the physical environment. *Cognitive or psychological fidelity* is the term used to describe a requirement for the learning environment to faithfully reproduce the mental processes necessary for a given task (see Cooke & Shope, 2004; Durlach & Mavor, 1995; Kozlowski & DeShon, 2004).

A number of recent studies explore the combinatory effect of collaboration and simulation technologies, and cognitive scientists are using enhanced simulations and displays to facilitate collaborative learning on a variety of tasks. These tools help the learner discover relations, and they transform more abstract aspects of a task into a more concrete form (e.g., Suthers et al., 2001). Nonetheless, relatively little is known about the importance of these methodologies for organizational training. We can glean promising data from studies investigating simulation technology in other collaborative environments. For example, Suthers and Hundhausen (2001) documented the efficacy of diagrammatic presentation to facilitate argument construction (see also Goodman, Soller, Linton, & Gaimari, 1998; Stenning & Oberlander, 1995). Similarly, three-dimensional (3D) images in collaborative problem solving facilitate a group's ability to generate alternative interpretations while assisting them to visualize complex task components (Grabowski, Litynski, & Wallace, 1997).

More recently, the simulation industry has taken note of, and attempted to incorporate the tools and techniques of, the computer game industry. Often referred to as the *serious games movement,* some (Sawyer, 2002; Zyda, 2005) have suggested that this began with the National Research Council (1997) policy paper on how to link the entertainment and defense industries. Serious games are defined as "a mental contest, played with a computer in accordance with specific rules, that uses entertainment to further government or corporate training, education, health, public policy, and strategic communication objectives" (Zyda, 2005, p. 25). Additionally, serious games integrate three critical elements—story, art, and software—with pedagogy to create a product that is designed to be entertaining, challenging, and educational (Sawyer, 2002). The movement is fueled to a large degree by the perception that the next generation of workers will be more demanding in their requirements for entertaining training. These so-called digital natives (Prensky, 2001) have been raised in an entirely digital world, and they are not only comfortable with but also accustomed to computer-based interactions.

Others (Jenkins, Klopfer, Squire, & Tan, 2003) have noted that many popular games such as The Sims have been successfully entertaining players while simultaneously informing them. As Blackman (2005) noted, many in industry recognize the importance of this trend; for example, a project lead in a major aerospace company "gets it." He observed that in a few short years, the workforce would consist of a generation of people brought up on video games. Do you give them a stack of dry manuals to read through or an interactive application that tests their skills and abilities with instant feedback, rewarding and "punishing" in creative and entertaining ways? (p. 16)

Although there has been little controlled experimentation to date that demonstrates the idea that games-based training is as efficacious as (or more efficacious than) traditional training, there are some suggestive data. For example, research on perceptual and pattern recognition skills found that action video games improved performance on unrelated tasks drawing upon visuospatial abilities (Green & Bavelier, 2003).

Finally, in the military and elsewhere, we have started to see a blurring of performance development (i.e., training) and performance support. Network-centric warfare, for instance, has removed the soldier from the battlefield, which is no longer a battlefield per se but a distributed information space made up of sensors, weapons, and command-and-control units. Simulations and training exercises for this new form of battle are difficult to distinguish from the real thing. It is not difficult to provide high-fidelity simulations of network-centric warfare, just as a simulation of a teleconference or emergency response communications would, at least at one level, be seamless with reality. As technologies and computational power become increasingly available, the very training systems devised to scaffold learning are likely to become performance tools that support the actual tasks. In these settings, transfer of training from simulator to real task should be less of a question. The military mantra of "Train as We Fight" has become reality.

Team Cognition and Collaboration

Today's workplace is dominated by team tasks. No longer can these tasks be accomplished by a single individual, but instead the synergy of multiple, specialized experts is required. How can cognitive psychology speak to team training? Crew resource management (Helmreich, Merritt, & Wilhelm, 1999; Salas, Burke, Bowers, & Wilson, 2001) for aviation crews and team training for command-and-control teams have been the forerunners in this area. However, there has been little to draw on from cognitive psychology. That is now changing as the fields of social psychology, small-group decision making, business management, and collaborative software development merge with cognitive psychology to address team-training applications.

Recent efforts in the area of team cognition have attempted to define and develop measures for shared understanding and team situation awareness (Cooke, Salas, Cannon-Bowers, & Stout, 2000). For example, Fiore, Fowlkes, Martin-Milham, and Oser (2000) used knowledge structure assessment techniques to explore differences in the way experts may represent task-relevant knowledge related to situation awareness. They compared pilot and navigator teams in a complex cognitive task (i.e., low-level navigation in the T-39 trainer) so as to identify an organizing framework with which to train situation awareness–related behaviors. Based upon the identified structures, Fiore et al. (2000) made recommendations for how such a framework could serve as a means to organize training programs and guide measurement and feedback within such training. These are necessary first steps in the development of metrics for assessing team cognition. More recently, measures and metrics used for assessing individual cognition have been applied to teams with some success (e.g., Cooke et al., 2003; Mathieu, Goodwin, Heffner, Salas, & Cannon-Bowers, 2000), but it is becoming clear that entirely new methods may be better suited to the emergent cognition of teams. For example, there has been a recent flurry of activity on team communication and its use as a source of data for assessing team cognition (Kiekel et al., 2001).

One of the thrusts in this growing area has been to automate the assessment of team cognition and to embed assessment tools within the task or simulation so that team performance is not disrupted. This embedded assessment is made possible because team cognition is readily observable through communication in the course of much team performance. Not only does communication behavior make automated and embedded assessment possible, but also it is highly desirable for high-tempo team decision-making environments in which team performance could be corrected as soon as a lapse, error, or inefficient process was noted. In summary, one future direction for cognitively based training is to direct assessment toward teams and to do so in real time. As for individuals, however, there is a gap in the connection between knowledge elicitation and assessment and training programs. Future research should be directed at applying theories of team cognition and methods for online assessment to team training.

Augmented Cognition and Diagnosing Brain Function

Augmented cognition is a programmatic effort initiated by the U.S. Department of Defense to develop technologies capable of diagnosing and understanding cognitive processes in complex operational settings. The goal of such technology is the eventual dynamic scaffolding of cognition so as to optimize human performance. More generally, the research and development address noninvasive techniques for measuring cortical activation that can be linked to a variety of higher and lower level cognitive processes (Schmorrow & Kruse, 2002; St. John, Kobus, Morrison,

& Schmorrow, 2004). Measurements of the latter form typically require expensive imaging technologies such as functional magnetic resonance imaging (fMRI). Through the augmented cognition efforts, techniques such as functional optical imaging via near-infrared (fNIR) offer less invasive techniques for real-time assessment during performance on operational tasks. These measures are the individual analogs of real-time measures of team cognition.

Such technologies attempt to measure a "cognitive state" as it relates to a task function with the subsequent modification of a system (e.g., multi-modal mitigation where an interface changes to better support the user). This includes not only measurements such as arousal or workload but also measurements of, for example, the subcomponents of working memory (e.g., spatial processing). Generally, understanding the relation between cognitive states and complex task performance is essential for the development of effective training and system design. Because many of today's tasks require one to monitor multiple system parameters, each potentially composed of input from differing modalities, and often require the integration of this information, these differing task components uniquely impact brain subsystems.

Importantly, the theories from cognitive science are maturing in such a way that they can better inform these approaches. For example, researchers in ergonomics have been developing studies on the underlying neurology supporting operational tasks within the burgeoning discipline of *neuroergonomics* (e.g., Hancock & Szalma, 2003; Parasuraman, 2003). Here, the goal is to use the theories emerging from the cognitive sciences and knowledge of brain function to better design learning and performance systems.

Given the well-documented findings associated with the underlying neurology of the brain subsystems, attempts by these developing fields to use imaging and associated techniques to understand human–system interaction and workload can only be facilitated by adapting and/or refining validated models from the cognitive neurosciences. These programs are in the early stages of development, but the engineering systems and computational methods will soon be at appropriate levels of sophistication to meet these goals. In sum, as the relationship between humans and systems continues to increase in complexity, the challenge will be to more closely link theories and findings from the cognitive and neurosciences to training and system design.

Summary

There are many multidisciplinary approaches looming on the horizon that lend themselves well to cognitively based training. Taking these emerging technologies as a starting point and projecting ahead another

15 years, we anticipate that the future should see training programs tailored to the knowledge, skills, and abilities of the individual learner. In addition, training should be contextually rich and should involve deliberate practice in this context. This requirement will be met by continued use of simulation, gaming environments, and multimedia. Finally, metrics for assessing training needs will consider all aspects of human behavior, including biological and neural indices at the individual level and communication and interaction patterns at the team level.

Conclusions

The points made by Howell and Cooke in 1989 regarding the increasing need to bring cognition to the forefront of training hold today, despite numerous changes in the study of cognition and in technology that impact training. But since 1989, cognition has simultaneously made inroads inside of the head through advances in neuroscience and outside of the head through advances in contextual inquiry and ecological psychology. At the same time, technology has become fully integrated into work lives as the learner strives to keep pace with Drucker's (1994) knowledge society. These changes only serve to intensify the relationship between cognition and training and the need for scientifically based connections between the two. With these developments, it should come as no surprise, then, that the cognitive sciences have had a significant impact on training design and delivery over the last 20 years.

The last 15 years have resulted in significant advances in knowledge elicitation methodology still crucial for the design and delivery of training, as well as our understanding of how knowledge develops with expertise. Cognitive science developments in perceptual learning, the acquisition of higher level thinking skills, and computational modeling of cognition have similarly impacted training applications. Most importantly, in the last 15 years, the connection between the cognitive sciences and training applications has been strengthened.

There are also exciting new developments in cognitive science that leverage multidisciplinary contributions to science and technology in order to advance training practices and technologies. In this chapter, we described a few of the developments on the forefront of this movement. These include deeper consideration of individual differences in training; opportunistic use of multimedia, simulation, and games for advancing training technologies; and new metrics for training assessment that range from brain-based measures of individual workload to communication-based measures of team cognition. The next 15 years should see exciting new developments pertinent to training as the cognitive sciences advance and incorporate new findings in neuroscience and ecological psychology for a multidimensional and more complete understanding of the learner.

There are also gaps that remain to be addressed in the next 15 years (Table 5.1). Although the connection between cognition and training has strengthened, more is needed to translate findings and methods in cognitive science to the practice of training. For instance, although methods have been developed for the elicitation of training-relevant material (e.g., KSAs and MECs), it is still not clear how to integrate these materials into a training program. Another gap concerns generality or transfer of training. With an increasing appreciation of the context of work comes more specific training scenarios that recreate that context for learning. However, how well does learning in context transfer out of context? As Table 5.1 indicates, although there has been progress, there is much more research to be done.

In sum, research and development in cognition and training have grown closer over the last 15 years. We anticipate that the next 15 years will bring new theories, findings, methods, and technologies to address these gaps and to move forward in forging a connection between cognition and training.

TABLE 5.1

Research Needs to Strengthen the Connection Between Cognition and Training

- Additional methods and tools for eliciting, assessing, and diagnosing cognition of the individual or team, especially focusing on cognition relevant to interaction with advanced technology, complex systems-of-systems, and methods that can be administered unobtrusively and in real time.
- Methods and tools that facilitate the transition between cognition and design of training.
- A better understanding of how training in context transfers out of context and the factors that are most relevant to that transfer.
- A better understanding of how individual differences and group composition impact training efficacy directly and indirectly through other factors.
- Research on the role of individual and group differences (e.g., cognitive self-regulation) in multimedia environments.
- A better understanding of how simulation can be used to train collaboration.
- Research on the use of gaming as training. Does training transfer to the target tasks, and what are the factors that facilitate or hinder such transfer?
- An appreciation of the relevant training issues in the blurring of the distinction between training and operations such as in command-and-control settings for network-centric warfare.
- More closely linked theories and findings from the cognitive neurosciences to training and system design.

Acknowledgments

Writing this manuscript was partially supported by AFRL Grant No. FA8650-04-6442 and AFOSR Grant No. FA9550-04-1-0234 awarded to the first author and by Grant No. SBE0350345 from the National Science Foundation and Grant No. N000140610118 from the Office of Naval Research awarded to the second author. We thank Leah Rowe and Sandro Scielzo for their assistance with portions of the literature review.

References

Ackerman, P. L. (1992). Predicting individual differences in complex skill acquisition: Dynamics of ability determinants. *Journal of Applied Psychology, 77,* 598–614.

Alderton, D. L., Cross, G. W., & Doane, S. M. (2002). Training for optimal strategic skills. *Proceedings of the 46th Annual Meeting of the Human Factors Society* (pp. 2054–2058). Baltimore: Human Factors Society.

Anderson, J. R., Boyle, C. F., Corbett, A. T., & Lewis, M. W. (1990). Cognitive modeling and intelligent tutoring. *Artificial Intelligence, 42,* 7–49.

Anderson, J. R., Boyle, C. F., & Reiser, B. J. (1985). Intelligent tutoring systems. *Science, 456–462.*

Anderson, J. R., Matessa, M., & Lebiere, C. (1997). ACT-R: A theory of higher level cognition and its relation to perception. *Human-Computer Interaction, 12,* 439–462.

Azevedo, R., & Cromley, J. G. (2004). Does training on self-regulated learning facilitate students' learning with hypermedia? *Journal of Educational Psychology, 96*(3), 523–535.

Bell, B. G., Gardner, M. K., & Woltz, D. J. (1997). Individual differences in undetected errors in skilled cognitive performance. *Learning and Individual Differences, 9,* 43–61.

Bell, B. S., & Kozlowski, S. W. J. (2002). Goal orientation and ability: Interactive effects on self-efficacy, performance, and knowledge. *Journal of Applied Psychology, 87,* 497–505.

Berbaum, K., Smoker, W. R. K., & Smith, W. L. (1985). Measurement and prediction of diagnostic performance during radiology residence. *American Journal of Roentgenology, 145,* 1305–1311.

Blackman, S. (2005). Serious games ... and less! *ACM SIGGRAPH Computer Graphics, 39, 1,* 12–16.

Bleckley, M. K., Durso, F. T., Crutchfield, J. M., Engle, R. W., & Khanna, M. M. (2003). Individual differences in working memory capacity predict visual attention allocation. *Psychonomic Bulletin & Review, 10,* 884–889.

Brooks, J. O., Switzer, F. S., & Gugerty, L. (2003). Effects of situation awareness training on novice process control plant operators. *Proceedings of the Human Factors and Ergonomics Society 47th annual meeting* (pp. 606–609). Santa Monica, CA: Human Factors and Ergonomics Society.

Brumback, C. R., Low, K. A., Gratton, G., & Fabiani, M. (2005). Putting things into perspective: Individual differences in working-memory span and the integration of information. *Experimental Psychology, 52*, 21–30.

Capon, A., Handley, S., & Dennis, I. (2003). Working memory and reasoning: An individual differences perspective. *Thinking & Reasoning, 9*, 203–244.

Chermack, T. J. (2003). Mental models in decision making and implications for human resource development. *Advances in Developing Human Resources, 5*, 408–422.

Clancey, W. J. (1997). *Situated cognition: On human knowledge and computer representations.* Cambridge: Cambridge University Press.

Clancey, W. J. (2002). Simulating activities: Relating motives, deliberation, and attentive coordination. *Cognitive Systems Research, 3*, 471–499.

Clancey, W. J. (2004). Roles for agent assistants in field science: Understanding personal projects and collaboration. *IEEE Transactions on Systems, Man and Cybernetics, Part C: Applications and Reviews, 34*(2), 125–137.

Cohen, M. S., & Thompson, B. B. (2001). Training teams to take initiative: Critical thinking in novel situations. In E. Salas (Ed.), *Advances in cognitive engineering and human performance research.* Greenwich, CT: JAI.

Colegrove, C. M., & Alliger, G. M. (2002, April). Mission essential competencies: Defining combat readiness in a novel way. Paper presented at the SAS-038 NATO working group meeting, Brussels.

Connor, O. O. (2005). Assessing clinical expertise in anesthesiology. Unpublished M.A. thesis, New Mexico State University.

Cooke, N. J. (1994). Varieties of knowledge elicitation techniques. *International Journal of Human-Computer Studies, 41*, 801–849.

Cooke, N. J. (1999). Knowledge elicitation. In F. T. Durso (Ed.), *Handbook of applied cognition* (pp. 479–509). Chichester, UK: Wiley.

Cooke, N. J., Kiekel, P. A., Salas, E., Stout, R. J., Bowers, C., & Cannon-Bowers, J. (2003). Measuring team knowledge: A window to the cognitive underpinnings of team performance. *Group Dynamics: Theory, Research and Practice, 7*, 179–199.

Cooke, N. J., & Pederson, H. K. (In press). Human factors of unmanned aerial vehicles. In J. A. Wise, V. D. Hopkin, & D. J. Garland (Eds.), *Handbook of aviation human factors* (2nd ed.). Hillsdale, NJ: Lawrence Erlbaum Associates.

Cooke, N. J., Salas, E., Cannon-Bowers, J. A., & Stout, R. (2000). Measuring team knowledge. *Human Factors, 42*, 151–173.

Cooke, N. J., & Shope, S. M. (2004). Designing a synthetic task environment. In S. G. Schiflett, L. R. Elliott, E. Salas, & M. D. Coovert (Eds.), *Scaled worlds: Development, validation, and application* (pp. 263–278). Surrey, UK: Ashgate.

Cuevas, H. M., Fiore, S. M., & Oser, R. L. (2002). Scaffolding cognitive and metacognitive processes in low verbal ability learners: Use of diagrams in computer-based training environment. *Instructional Science, 30*, 433–464.

Daily, L. Z., Lovett, M. C., & Reder, L. M. (2001). Modeling individual differences in working memory performance: A source activation account. *Cognitive Science, 25*, 315–353.

Deerwester, S., Dumais, S. T., Furnas, G. W., Landauer, T. K., & Harshman, R. (1990). Indexing by latent semantic analysis. *Journal of the American Society for Information Science, 41*, 391–407.

Dougherty, M. R. P., & Hunter, J. (2003). Probability judgment and subadditivity: The role of working memory capacity and constraining retrieval. *Memory & Cognition, 31*, 968–982.

Drucker, P. F. (1994, November). The age of social transformation. *Atlantic Monthly*, 53–80.

Durlach, N. I., & Mavor, A. (Eds.). (1995). *Virtual reality: Scientific and technological challenges*. Washington, DC: National Academy of Science Press.

Ericsson, K. A., & Charness, N. (1994). Expert performance: Its structure and acquisition. *American Psychologist, 49*, 725–747.

Evans, D. A., & Patel, V. L. (1992). Advanced models of cognition for medical training and practice. *Proceedings of the NATO ASI Series F: Computer and Systems Sciences, 97*.

Fallesen, J. J., & Pounds, J. (2001). Identifying and testing a naturalistic approach for cognitive skill training. In E. Salas & G. Klein (Eds.), *Linking expertise and naturalistic decision making* (pp. 55–70). Mahwah, NJ: Lawrence Erlbaum Associates.

Faulkner, D., Joiner, R., Littleton, K., Miell, D., & Thompson, L. (2000). The mediating effect of task presentation on collaboration and children's acquisition of scientific reasoning. *European Journal of Psychology of Education, 15*, 417–430.

Feltovich, P. J., Spiro, R. J., & Coulson, R. L. (1993). Learning, teaching, and testing for complex conceptual understanding. In N. Frederiksen, R. J. Mislevy, & I. I. Bejar (Eds.), *Test theory for a new generation of tests* (pp. 181–217). Mahwah, NJ: Lawrence Erlbaum Associates.

Fiore, S. M., Cuevas, H. M., & Oser, R. L. (2003). A picture is worth a thousand connections: The facilitative effects of diagrams on mental model development and task performance. *Computers in Human Behavior, 19*, 185–199.

Fiore, S. M., Cuevas, H. M., Scielzo, S., & Salas, E. (2002). Training individuals for distributed teams: Problem solving assessment for distributed mission research. *Computers in Human Behavior, 18*, 125–140.

Fiore, S. M., Fowlkes, J., Martin-Milham, L., & Oser, R. L. (2000). Convergence or divergence of expert models: On the utility of knowledge structure assessment in training research. *Proceedings of the 44th annual meeting of the Human Factors and Ergonomic Society* (Vol. 2, 427–430). Santa Monica, CA: Human Factors and Ergonomics Society.

Fiore, S. M., Salas, E., Cuevas, H. M., & Bowers, C. A. (2003). Distributed coordination space: Toward a theory of distributed team process and performance. *Theoretical Issues in Ergonomic Science, 4*(3–4), 340–363.

Fiore, S. M., Scielzo, S., & Jentsch, F. (2004). Stimulus competition during perceptual learning: Training and aptitude considerations in the X-ray security screening process. *International Journal of Cognitive Technology, 9*, 34–39.

Fiske, S. T., & Taylor, S. E. (1991). *Social cognition* (2nd ed.). Reading, MA: Addison-Wesley.

Foltz, P. W. (1996). Latent semantic analysis for text-based research. *Behavior Research Methods, Instruments and Computers, 28*, 197–202.

Ford, J. K., Smith, E. M., Weissbein, D. A., Gully, S. M., & Salas, E. (1998). Relationships of goal orientation, metacognitive activity, and practice strategies with learning outcomes and transfer. *Journal of Applied Psychology, 83*, 218–233.

Freeman, J. T., & Cohen, M. S. (1994). *Training metacognitive skills for situation assessment.* Paper presented at the Proceedings of the 1994 Symposium on Command and Control Research and Decision Aids.

Freeman, J., LeClerc, J., & Richardson, A. X. (2005). A diagnostic assessment and training system for maintenance technicians. In *Proceedings of the American Society of Naval Engineers Human Systems Integration Symposium* (CD-ROM). Alexandria, VA: American Society of Naval Engineers.

Gibson, J. J. (1966). *The ecological approach to visual perception.* Boston: Houghton Mifflin.

Glaser, R. (1989). Expertise and learning: How do we think about instructional processes now that we have discovered knowledge structures? In D. Klahr & K. Kotovsky (Eds.), *Complex information processing: The impact of Herbert A. Simon* (pp. 269–282). Hillsdale, NJ: Lawrence Erlbaum Associates.

Glaser, R., & Chi, M. T. H. (1988). Overview. In M. T. H. Chi, R. Glaser, & M. J. Farr (Eds.), *The nature of expertise* (pp. xv–xxviii). Hillsdale, NJ: Lawrence Erlbaum Associates.

Gluck, K. A., Ball, J. T., Gunzelmann, G., Krusmark, M. A., Lyons, D. R., & Cooke, N. J. (2005). *A prospective look at a synthetic teammate for UAV applications.* Arlington, VA: Infotech@Aerospace.

Goldsmith, T. E., Johnson, P. J., & Acton, W. H. (1991). Assessing structural knowledge. *Journal of Educational Psychology, 83*, 88–96.

Goodman, B., Soller, A., Linton, F., & Gaimari, R. (1998). Encouraging student reflection and articulation using a learning companion. *International Journal of Artificial Intelligence in Education, 9*, 237—255.

Gopher, D., Weil, M., & Bareket, T. (1994). Transfer of skill from a computer game trainer to flight. *Human Factors, 36*, 387–405.

Gordon, A., van Lent, M., van Velsen, M., Carpenter, P., & Jhala, A. (2004, July 25–29). Branching storylines in virtual reality environments for leadership development. *Proceedings of the Sixteenth Innovative Applications of Artificial Intelligence Conference (IAAI-04)*, San Jose, CA.

Grabowski, M., Litynski, D. M., & Wallace, W. (1997). The relationship between three-dimensional imaging and group decision making: An exploratory study. *IEEE Transactions on Systems, Man, and Cybernetics—Part A: Systems and Humans, 27*, 402–411.

Green, C. S., & Bavelier, D. (2003). Action video game modifies visual selective attention. *Nature, 423*, 534–537.

Guerlain, S., Green, K. B., LaFollette, M., Mersch, T., Mitchell, B., Poole, G. R., et al. (2003). Training anatomy recognition through repetitive viewing of laparoscopic surgery video clips. *Proceedings of the 47th Annual Human Factors and Ergonomics Society Conference* (pp. 391–394). Santa Monica, CA: Human Factors and Ergonomics Society.

Gully, S. M., Payne, S. C., Kiechel Koles, K. L., & Whiteman, J. A. K. (2002). The impact of error training and individual differences on training outcomes: An attribute–treatment interaction perspective. *Journal of Applied Psychology, 87,* 143–155.

Gyselinck, V., Cornoldi, C., Dubois, V., de Beni, R., & Ehrlick, M. F. (2002). Visuo-spatial memory and phonological loop in learning from multimedia. *Applied Cognitive Psychology, 16,* 665–685.

Hancock, P. A., & Szalma, J. L. (2003). The future of ergonomics. *Theoretical Issues in Ergonomic Science, 44,* 238–249.

Heft, H. (2001). *Ecological psychology in context: James Gibson, Roger Barker, and the legacy of William James's radical empiricism.* Mahwah, NJ: Lawrence Erlbaum Associates.

Hegarty, M., Montello, D. R., Richardson, A. E., & Ishikawa, T. (2006). Spatial abilities at different scales: Individual differences in aptitude-test performance and spatial-layout learning. *Intelligence, 34,* 151–176.

Helmreich, R. L., Merritt, A. C., & Wilhelm, J. A. (1999). The evolution of crew resource management. *International Journal of Aviation Psychology, 9*(1), 19–32.

Herrmann, D. J., & Chaffin, R. (1988). *Memory in a historical perspective.* New York: Springer Verlag.

Hmelo, C. E., Nagarajan, A., & Day, R. S. (2000). Effects of high and low prior knowledge on construction of a joint problem space. *Journal of Experimental Education, 69,* 36–56.

Hoeft, R. M., Kochan, J. A., & Jentsch, F. (2006). Automated systems in the cockpit: Is the autopilot, "George," a team member? In C. A. Bowers, E. Salas, & F. Jentsch (Eds.), *Creating high-tech teams: Practical guidance on work performance and technology.* Washington, DC: American Psychological Association.

Hoffman, R. R., & Deffenbacher, K. A. (1993). An analysis of the relations of basic and applied science. *Ecological Psychology, 5,* 315–352.

Hoffman, R. R., Shadbolt, N. R., Burton, A. M., & Klein, G. (1995). Eliciting knowledge from experts: A methodological analysis. *Organizational Behavior and Human Decision Processes, 62,* 129–158.

Howell, W. C., & Cooke, N. J. (1989). Training the human information processor: A look at cognitive models. In I. L. Goldstein & Associates (Eds.), *Training and development in organizations* (pp. 121–182). New York: Jossey-Bass.

Jenkins, H., Klopfer, E., Squire, K., & Tan, P. (2003). Entering the education arcade. *Computers in Entertainment, 1*(1), 1–11.

Jentsch, F., & Bowers, C. (1998). Evidence for the validity of PC-based simulations in studying aircrew coordination. *International Journal of Aviation Psychology, 8,* 243–260.

Jentsch, F., Bowers, C., & Salas, E. (1999, May). Developing a metacognitive training program for followership skills. *Proceedings of the 10th International Symposium on Aviation Psychology.* Columbus: Ohio State University.

Kahneman, D., Slovic, P., & Tversky, A. (Eds.). (1982). *Judgment under uncertainty: Heuristics and biases.* New York: Cambridge University Press.

Kandel, E. R., & Squire, L. R. (2000). Neuroscience: Breaking down scientific barriers to the study of brain and mind. *Science, 10,* 1113–1120.

Kane, M. J., & Engle, R. W. (2000). Working-memory capacity, proactive interference, and divided attention: Limits on long-term memory retrieval. *Journal of Experimental Psychology: Learning, Memory, and Cognition, 26,* 336–358.

Katz, S., Lesgold, A., Hughes, E., Peters, D., Eggan, G., Gordin, M., et al. (1998). Sherlock 2: An intelligent tutoring system built on the LRDC framework. In C. P. Bloom & R. B. Loftin (Eds.), *Facilitating the development and use of interactive learning environments* (pp. 227–258). Mahwah, NJ: Lawrence Erlbaum Associates.

Keith, N., & Frese, M. (2005). Self-regulation in error management training: Emotion control and metacognition as mediators of performance effects. *Journal of Applied Psychology, 90*, 677–691.

Kiekel, P. A., Cooke, N. J., Foltz, P. W., & Shope, S. M. (2001). Automating measurement of team cognition through analysis of communication data. In M. J. Smith, G. Salvendy, D. Harris, & R. J. Koubek (Eds.), *Usability evaluation and interface design* (pp. 1382–1386). Mahwah, NJ: Lawrence Erlbaum Associates.

Kim, K. J. (2004). Toward global optimization of case-based reasoning systems for financial forecasting. *Applied Intelligence, 21*, 239–249.

Klein, G. A. (1993). A recognition-primed decision (RPD) model of rapid decision making. In G. A. Klein, J. Orasanu, R. Calderwood, & C. E. Zsambok (Eds.), *Decision making in action: Models and methods* (pp. 138–147). Norwood, NJ: Ablex.

Kozlowski, S. W. J., & DeShon, R. P. (2004). A psychological fidelity approach to simulation-based training: Theory, research, and principles. In E. Salas, L. R. Elliott, S. G. Schflett, & M. D. Coovert (Eds.), *Scaled worlds: Development, validation, and applications* (pp. 75–99). Burlington, VT: Ashgate.

Kozlowski, S. W. J., Gully, S. M., Brown, K. G., Salas, E., Smith, E. A., & Nason, E. R. (2001). Effects of training goals and goal orientation traits on multidimensional training outcomes and performance adaptability. *Organizational Behavior and Human Decision Processes, 85*, 1–31.

Lane, R. D., & Nadel, L. (1999). *Cognitive neuroscience of emotion*. New York: Oxford University Press.

Leahy, W., Chandler, P., & Sweller, J. (2003). When auditory presentations should and should not be a component of multimedia instruction. *Applied Cognitive Psychology, 17*, 401–418.

Long, D. L., & Prat, C. S. (2002). Working memory and Stroop interference: An individual differences investigation. *Memory & Cognition, 30*, 294–301.

Lovett, M. C., Daily, L. Z., Reder, L. M., & Sun, R. (2001). A source activation theory of working memory: Cross-task prediction of performance in ACT-R. *Cognitive Systems Research, 1*, 99–118.

Marks, M. A., Sabella, M. J., Burke, S. C., & Zaccaro, S. J. (2002). The impact of cross-training on team effectiveness. *Journal of Applied Psychology, 22*, 3–13.

Marks, M. A., Zaccaro, S. J., & Mathieu, J. E. (2000). Performance implications of leader briefings and team-interaction training for team adaptation to novel environments. *Journal of Applied Psychology, 85*, 971–986.

Mathieu, J. E., Goodwin, G. F., Heffner, T. S., Salas, E., & Cannon-Bowers, J. A. (2000). The influence of shared mental models on team process and performance. *Journal of Applied Psychology, 85*, 273–283.

Mayer, R. E. (2001). *Multimedia learning*. Cambridge, UK: Cambridge University Press.

Mayer, R. E., & Gallini, J. K. (1990). When is an illustration worth ten thousand words? *Journal of Educational Psychology, 82*, 715–726.

Mayer, R. E., & Sims, V. K. (1994). For whom is a picture worth a thousand words? Extensions of a dual-coding theory of multimedia. *Journal of Educational Psychology, 86,* 389–401.

McInerney, V., McInerney, D. M., & Marsh, H. W. (1997). Effects of metacognitive strategy training within a cooperative group learning context on computer achievement and anxiety: An aptitude–treatment interaction study. *Journal of Educational Psychology, 89,* 686–695.

McSherry, D. (2001). Interactive case-based reasoning in sequential diagnosis. *Applied Intelligence, 14,* 65–76.

Miller, G. (2003). The cognitive revolution: A historical perspective. *TRENDS in Cognitive Sciences, 7,* 141–144.

Moreno, R., & Mayer, R. E. (2002). The instructive animation: Helping students build connections between words and pictures in multimedia learning. *Journal of Educational Psychology, 84,* 444–452.

Mitchell, C. M. (2000). Horizons in pilot training: Desktop tutoring systems. In N. Sarter & R. Amalberti (Eds.), *Cognitive engineering in the aviation domain.* Mahwah, NJ: Lawrence Erlbaum Associates.

National Research Council. (1997). *Modeling and simulation: Linking entertainment and defense.* Washington, DC: National Academy of Sciences Press.

Neisser, U. (1976). *Cognition and reality.* New York: Freeman.

Neville, K., Fowlkes, J. E., Walwanis Nelson, M. M., & Bergondy-Wilhelm, M. L. (2003). A cognitive task analysis of coordination in a distributed tactical team: Implications for expertise acquisition. *Proceedings of the Human Factors and Ergonomics Society 47th annual meeting* (pp. 359–364). Santa Monica, CA: Human Factors and Ergonomics Society.

Niederhauser, D. S., Reynolds, R. E., Salmen, D. J., & Skolmoski, P. (2000). The influence of cognitive load on learning from hypertext. *Journal of Educational Computing Research, 23,* 237–255.

Nisbett, R. E., Peng, K., Choi, I., & Norenzayan, A. (2001). Culture and systems of thought: Holistic versus analytic cognition. *Psychological Review, 108,* 291–310.

Olson, G. M., Malone, T. W, & Smith, J. B. (Eds.). (2001). *Coordination theory and collaboration technology.* Mahwah, NJ: Lawrence Erlbaum Associates.

Parasuraman, R. (2003). Neuroergonomics: Research and practice. *Theoretical Issues in Ergonomic Science, 44,* 5–20.

Pew, R. W., & Mavor, A. S. (1997). *Representing human behavior in military simulations: Interim report.* Report from Panel on Modeling Human Behavior and Command Decision Making: Representations for Military Simulations. Washington, DC: National Research Council.

Pliske, R. M., McCloskey, M. J., & Klein, G. (2001). Decision skills training: Facilitating learning from experience. In E. Salas & G. Klein (Eds.), *Linking expertise and naturalistic decision making* (pp. 37–53). Mahwah, NJ: Lawrence Erlbaum Associates.

Pollock, C., Paton, D., Smith, L. M., & Violanti, J. M. (2003). Training for resilience. In D. Paton, J. M. Violanti, & L. M. Smith (Eds.), *Promoting capabilities to manage posttraumatic stress: Perspectives on resilience.* Springfield, IL: Thomas.

Prensky, M. (2001). *Digital game based training.* New York: McGraw-Hill.

Pulos, S., & Denzine, G. (2005). Individual differences in planning behavior and working memory: A study of the tower of London. *Individual Differences Research, 3*, 99–104.

Rouse, W. B., Geddes, N. D., & Curry, R. E. (1987–1988). An architecture for intelligent interfaces: Outline of an approach to supporting operators of complex systems. *Human Computer Interaction, 3*, 97–122.

Sadasivan, S., Greenstein, J. S., Gramopadhye, A. K., & Duchowski, A. T. (2005). Use of eye movements as feedforward training for a synthetic aircraft inspection task. In *CHI'05 Proceedings of the ACM* (pp. 141–149). New York: Association for Computing Machinery.

Salas, E., & Burke, S. (2002). Simulation for training is effective when … *Quality and Safety in Health Care, 11*, 119–120.

Salas, E., & Fiore, S. M. (Eds.). (2004). *Team cognition: Understanding the factors that drive process and performance.* Washington, DC: American Psychological Association.

Salas, E., Burke, C. S., Bowers, C. A., & Wilson, K. A. (2001). Team training in the skies: Does crew resource management (CRM) training work? *Human Factors, 43*(4), 641–674.

Sarter, N. B., & Woods, D. D. (1993). *Pilot interaction with cockpit automation: Operational experiences with the flight management system.* NASA Contractor Report 177617. Washington, DC: NASA.

Sawyer, B. (2002). *Serious games: Improving public policy through game-based learning and simulation.* Woodrow Wilson International Center for Scholars. Retrieved March 22, 2008, from http://wwics.si.edu/subsites/game/index.htm

Schank, R. C. (1986). *Explanation patterns: Understanding mechanically and creatively.* New York: Lawrence Erlbaum Associates.

Schank, R., & Leake, D. (1989). Creativity and learning in a case-based explainer. *Artificial Intelligence, 40*, 353–385.

Schmorrow, D. D., & Kruse, A. A. (2002). Improving human performance through advanced cognitive system technology. In *Proceedings of the Interservice/Industry Training, Simulation and Education Conference* (I/ITSEC'02), Orlando, FL.

Shiu, S., & Pal, S. (2004). Case-based reasoning: Concepts, features and soft computing. *Applied Intelligence, 21*, 233–238.

Sierhuis, M., & Clancey, W. J. (2002, September/October). Modeling and simulating work practice: A method for work systems design. *IEEE Intelligent Systems*, pp. 32–41.

Smith-Jentsch, K. A., Campbell, G. E., Milanovich, D. M., & Reynolds, A. M. (2001). Measuring teamwork mental models to support training needs assessment, development, and evaluation: Two empirical studies. *Journal of Organizational Behavior, 22*, 179–194.

Smith-Jentsch, K. A., Jentsch, F. G., Payne, S. C., & Salas, E. (1996). Can pretraining experiences explain individual differences in learning? *Journal of Applied Psychology, 81*, 110–116.

Smith-Jentsch, K. A., Mathieu, J. E., & Kraiger, K. (2005). Investigating linear and interactive effects of shared mental models on safety and efficiency in a field setting. *Journal of Applied Psychology, 90*(3), 523–535.

Smith-Jentsch, K. A., Zeisig, R. L., Acton, B., & McPherson, J. A. (1998). Team dimensional training: A strategy for guided team self-correction. In J. A. Cannon-Bowers & E. Salas (Eds.), *Making decisions under stress: Implications for individual and team training* (pp. 271–297) Washington, DC: American Psychological Association.

Sohn, Y. W., Doane, S. M., & Garrison, T. (2006). The impact of individual differences and learning context on strategic skill acquisition and transfer. *Learning and Individual Differences, 16,* 13–30.

Sormo, F., Cassens, J., & Aamodt, A. (2005). Explanation in case-based reasoning-perspectives and goals. *Artificial Intelligence Review, 24*(2), 109–143.

Sowden, P. T., Davies, I. R. L., & Roling, P. (2000). Perceptual learning of the detection of features in X-ray images: A functional role for improvements in adults' visual sensitivity? *Journal of Experimental Psychology: Human Perception & Performance, 26,* 379–390.

Sprenger, A., & Dougherty, M. R. (2006). Differences between probability and frequency judgments: The role of individual differences in working memory capacity. *Organizational Behavior and Human Decision Processes, 99,* 202–211.

Squires, D. (1999). Educational software for constructivist learning environments: Subversive use and volatile design. *Educational Technology, 39*(3), 48–54.

St. John, M., Kobus, D. A., Morrison, J. G., & Schmorrow, D. (2004). Overview of the DARPA augmented cognition technical integration experiment. *International Journal of Human–Computer Interaction, 17*(2), 131–150.

Staszewski, J. J., & Davison, A. (2000). Mine detection training based on expert skill. In V. A. C. Dubey, J. F. Harvey, J. T. Broach, & R. E. Dugan (Eds.), *Proceedings of SPIE* (Vol. 4038, pp. 90–101). Bellingham, WA: SPIE.

Stenning, K., & Oberlander, J. (1995). A cognitive theory of graphical and linguistic reasoning: Logic and implementation. *Cognitive Science, 19,* 97–140.

Suthers, D., Connelly, J., Lesgold, A., Paolucci, M., Toth, E., Toth, J., et al. (2001). Representational and advisory guidance for students learning scientific inquiry. In K. Forbus & P. J. Feltovich (Eds.), *Smart machines in education: The coming revolution in educational technology* (pp. 7–35). Menlo Park, CA: AAAI/ MIT Press.

Suthers, D., & Hundhausen, C. (2001). Learning by constructing collaborative representations: An empirical comparison of three alternatives. In P. Dillenbourg, A. Eurelings, & K. Hakkarainen (Eds.), *European perspectives on computer-supported collaborative learning: Proceedings of the First European Conference on Computer-Supported Collaborative Learning* (pp. 577–584). Maastricht, The Netherlands: Universiteit Maastricht.

Sweller, J. (1994). Cognitive load theory, learning difficulty and instructional design. *Learning and Instruction, 4,* 295–312.

Taylor, H. L., Lintern, G., Hulin, C. L., Talleur, D. A., Emanuel, T. W., Jr., & Phillips, S. I. (1999). Transfer of training effectiveness of a personal computer aviation training device. *International Journal of Aviation Psychology, 9*(4), 319–335.

Tuholski, S. W., Engle, R. W., & Baylis, G. C. (2001). Individual differences in working memory capacity and enumeration. *Memory & Cognition, 29,* 484–492.

Unsworth, N., & Engle, R. W. (2005). Individual differences in working memory capacity and learning: Evidence from the serial reaction time task. *Memory & Cognition, 33,* 213–220.

Unsworth, N., & Engle, R. W. (2006). A temporal-contextual retrieval account of complex span: An analysis of errors. *Journal of Memory and Language, 54,* 346–362.

Vincente, K. J. (1999). *Cognitive work analysis: Toward safe, productive, and healthy computer-based work.* Mahwah, NJ: Lawrence Erlbaum Associates.

Wang, M. J. J., Lin, S. C., & Drury, C. G. (1997). Training for strategy in visual search. *Industrial Ergonomics, 20,* 101–108.

Wilson, B. G., Jonassen, D. H., & Cole, P. (1993). Cognitive approaches to instructional design. In G. M. Piskurich (Ed.), *The ASTD handbook of instructional technology* (pp. 21.1–21.22). New York: McGraw-Hill.

Zyda, M. (2005). From visual simulation to virtual reality to games. *IEEE Computer, 38*(9), 25–32.

6

Research-Based Solutions to Three Problems in Web-Based Training

Richard E. Mayer
University of California, Santa Barbara

The design of Web-based training should be based on scientific research and grounded in a cognitive theory of how people learn. In this chapter, I examine three classic problems in the design of Web-based lessons: (a) The material is presented in a way that is insensitive to the learner's cognitive-processing system, (b) the content is inherently difficult for the learner, and (c) the material is presented in a way that is unfriendly to the learner. On the basis of the cognitive theory of multimedia learning (Mayer, 2001, 2005a; Mayer & Moreno, 2003) and on a body of scientifically rigorous empirical research involving approximately 80 experimental comparisons (Mayer, 2001, 2005b, 2005c, 2005d), I describe solutions to each e-learning problem. When the material is presented in an insensitive way, the solutions include weeding (in which extraneous words, sounds, and graphics are eliminated), decaptioning (in which presentations consist of animation and narration rather than animation, narration, and on-screen text), signaling (in which essential words and graphics are highlighted), aligning (in which corresponding words and graphics are presented near rather than far from each other on the page or screen), and synchronizing (in which corresponding narration and animation are presented simultaneously rather than successively). When the content is difficult, the solutions include segmenting (in which a lesson is broken into segments that can be paced by the learner rather than given as a continuous presentation), pretraining (in which the learner is given pretraining in the names and characteristics of the key concepts before the lesson), and off-loading (in which material is presented as graphics and spoken text rather than graphics and printed text). When the material is presented in an unfriendly way, the solutions include personalizing (in which the words are presented in a conversational style using *I* and *you* rather than formal style) and articulating (in which the words are spoken in a clear human voice rather than a machine voice). Well-designed Web-based training can result in large improvements in learners' performance on tests of transfer in which they are able to use what was taught to solve new problems.

Before examining the research-based solutions to the insensitivity problem, the difficulty problem, and the unfriendliness problem, I briefly explore the learner-centered approach to research on Web-based training, the cognitive theory approach to research on Web-based training, and the evidence-based approach to research on Web-based training.

Taking a Learner-Centered Approach to Research on Web-Based Training

Is Web-based training a good idea? For example, do people learn better on the Web than in conventional formats? In my opinion, this seemingly reasonable question is not a fruitful one. It is somewhat like asking whether books are useful educational devices. The question assumes a technology-centered approach in which we begin with a cutting-edge technology and try to use it for instructional purposes. However, as Clark (2001) has argued, the instructional medium does not cause learning, but rather the instructional method fosters learning. In short, the consensus among educational psychologists is that media research—for example, testing whether one medium is better than another—is not a useful enterprise.

In contrast, in taking a learner-centered approach, we begin with an understanding of how people learn, and then try to adapt technology to support the learner's cognitive processing during learning. In this way, technology can provide cognitive tools that assist the learner's natural learning processes. Thus, the goal of research on instructional technology should be to determine which features (or instructional methods) support which kinds of learning for which kinds of learners. In this review I empirically examine the effects of 10 instructional methods intended to foster learning based on a cognitive theory of learning. In short, my focus is on instructional methods rather than on instructional media.

Taking a Cognitive Theory Approach to Research on Web-Based Training

Web-based training should be designed to assist human learning, so it should be consistent with cognitive theories of how people learn. For example, three important learning principles derived from cognitive science theories of human learning are (a) the dual-channel principle—people have separate channels for processing visual-pictorial material and auditory-verbal material; (b) the limited-capacity principle—people can process only a limited amount of material in each channel at any one time; and (c) the active-processing principle—deep learning occurs when people engage in appropriate cognitive processing during learning such as selecting relevant material for further processing, organizing the selected material into a coherent mental structure, and integrating it with existing knowledge. Each of these principles has important implications for instructional design because we want to prime active cognitive processing without overloading cognitive processing in either channel.

Figure 6.1 shows a cognitive theory of multimedia learning based on these three principles. The multimedia training consists of graphics and printed words, which enter the learner's cognitive system through the eyes, and sounds such as spoken words, which enter the learner's cognitive system through the ears. By paying attention to some of the incoming material (indicated by the *selecting images* and *selecting words* arrows in the figure), relevant images and words are transferred to working memory for further processing. The next step is to mentally organize the selected words and images into coherent mental structures (indicated by the *organizing images* and *organizing words* arrows). Finally, the learner must mentally integrate the verbal and pictorial models with each other and with prior knowledge (indicated by the *integrating* arrow) and store the result in the long-term memory. Meaningful learning occurs when learners are able to engage in all five of these cognitive processes (i.e., learners use all five of the arrows in the figure).

Based on this framework as well as cognitive load theory (Paas, Renkl, & Sweller, 2003; Sweller, 1999, 2005), there are three forms of cognitive processing: (a) extraneous processing—cognitive processing that does not promote learning and is caused by poor instructional design; (b) essential (or intrinsic) processing—cognitive processing that is intended to mentally represent the essential material and is caused by the difficulty

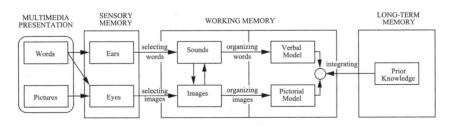

FIGURE 6.1
Cognitive theory of multimedia learning.

of the essential material; and (c) generative (or germane) processing—cognitive processing that is intended to mentally organize and integrate the essential material and is caused by attempts to make sense of the presented material. Given the severe limits on the learner's cognitive-processing capacity, when most of the cognitive capacity must be devoted to extraneous processing, little capacity is left for essential processing so the learner will perform poorly on retention and transfer tests. In contrast, when extraneous processing is reduced but essential processing takes most of the available cognitive capacity, the learner will not be able to engage in generative processing and therefore is expected to perform well on retention but poorly on transfer. Finally, if extraneous processing is reduced and essential processing is managed, the learner will have cognitive capacity available for generative processing, leading to good performance on both retention and transfer. In short, the goals of effective instructional design are to reduce extraneous processing, manage essential processing, and foster generative processing.

Taking an Evidence-Based Approach to Research on Web-Based Training

Much of the literature in Web-based training is not based on empirical evidence, but rather is based on the opinions and wisdom of experts. In some cases, the evidence takes the form of "best practices"—descriptions of exemplary Web-based training programs (Rossett, 2002). Although I respect the craft knowledge of experts and I appreciate exemplary training programs, I think psychologists also have something important to offer—namely, a set of research methods that can answer fundamental questions about what works (O'Neil, 2005). For this reason, I advocate an evidence-based approach to research on Web-based training.

One approach to Web-based training research is to set up a Web-based course and record every action of every learner in a log file. What is wrong with this seemingly comprehensive methodology? Although observational studies can provide useful and rich empirical data, they are not designed to determine whether one instructional method is more effective than another. Observational research can show that various variables are correlated with one another, but not that one variable causes another. The problem with observational studies such as this type is that they do not allow us to answer fundamental questions about how to design effective Web-based training.

In contrast, experimental methods are the gold standard when it comes to testing whether one instructional method is more effective than another (Phye, Robinson, & Levin, 2005). In a consensus review of scientific research methodologies in education commissioned by the National Research Council, Shavelson and Towne (2002) stated that "randomized trials (we also use the term "experiment") are the ideal for establishing whether one or more factors caused change in an outcome" (p. 110). The hallmark of experimental research is random assignment of learners to treatments and control of extraneous variables between treatments. I have taken an experimental approach in the research reported in this chapter because my focus is on comparing one instructional method against another. In my opinion, the field would benefit from a larger research base of experimental studies comparing instructional methods in Web-based training. This base—coupled with insights gleaned from observational studies—could form the basis for evidence-based practice.

Insensitivity Problem: The Training Lesson Is Insensitive to the Learner's Cognitive System

Consider a Web-based training lesson designed to explain the process of chemical equilibrium when two chemicals are mixed. It consists of four windows running in real time, including an animation of the chemical process, a graph of the amounts of resulting chemicals, a video of someone mixing the chemicals, and a talking head of the instructor. What is wrong with this lesson? It is insensitive to the information-processing limitations of the learner, because it presents too much material at one time. Humans are limited in the amount of information they can process at any one time. Even though a lot of material can be presented on the screen, the learner is able to look at only part of the screen at a time. When the learner spends time looking at irrelevant material (such as the instructor's talking head) or scanning the screen to find which window to focus on, the learner is engaging in extraneous processing. Lessons that are insensitive to the processing capacity of the learner can result in cognitive overload.

When a Web-based lesson contains unneeded material or features that require too much extraneous processing, the learner may not have enough remaining cognitive capacity to make sense of the incoming material. *Extraneous processing* refers to cognitive processing during learning that does not support learning of the core material. In some Web-based training scenarios, the lesson may contain extraneous material or features that prime extraneous processing in the learner. Given that cognitive capacity is limited, learners who engage in a large amount of extraneous processing do not have enough capacity to engage in the cognitive processing needed for learning—which can be called *intrinsic* and *generative processing*. In this section, I explore five techniques for reducing extraneous processing—weeding, decaptioning, signaling, aligning, and synchronizing.

Weeding

Weeding is an instructional design technique of eliminating extraneous words and pictures from a multimedia lesson—including extraneous facts, stories, equations, illustrations, video, music, and sounds. Suppose you click on an icon for *lightning* and you receive a 140-second narrated animation explaining the steps in lightning formation. To spice up this somewhat dry lesson, we intersperse short video clips depicting spectacular lightning storms that light up the sky along with narration describing interesting facts about lightning. Is this addition a good idea? According to the cognitive theory of multimedia learning, people can process only a small amount of material in each channel at one time. The added irrelevant visual and verbal material requires processing capacity, and may interfere with processing of the step-by-step explanation of lightning formation. A solution to this problem of extraneous material in a Web-based lesson is to weed it out. For example, Mayer, Heiser, and Lonn (2001, Experiment 3) reported that students performed better on a transfer test after receiving a concise version of the narrated animation rather than an embellished version. In another attempt to spice up the lightning lesson, we could add background music and environmental sounds, such as blowing wind or cracking ice. Moreno and Mayer (2000, Experiments 1 & 2) found that students performed better on transfer tests after receiving a concise lesson rather than one that was embellished with music and sounds.

In a series of five experimental tests, Harp and Mayer (1997, Experiment 1; 1998, Experiments, 1, 2, 3, & 4) found that students learned best from a concise lesson that contained illustrations and text explaining lightning formation than from an embellished lesson that added interesting photos and stories about lightning. In a series of three experimental tests, Mayer, Bove, Bryman, Mars, and Tapangco (1996) found that students learned as well from a summary that contained illustrations and text explaining the steps in lightning formation as from a longer version that contained many details. Finally, in a set of two experiments, Mayer and Jackson (2005, Experiments 1 & 2) found that adding quantitative details (such as formulas and mathematical computations) to a multimedia lesson explaining ocean waves hurt performance on a transfer test.

TABLE 6.1

Evidence-Based Techniques for Overcoming Three Problems in Web-Based Training

Technique	Tests	Effect Size
Overcoming the Insensitivity Problem: Reduce Extraneous Processing		
Weeding: Eliminate extraneous words and pictures.	13 of 14	0.98
Decaptioning: Remove unneeded captions from a narrated animation.	5 of 5	0.72
Signaling: Add organizational cues such as an outline, headings, and highlighting.	3 of 3	0.60
Aligning: Place corresponding words and pictures near each other on the screen or page.	5 of 5	1.12
Synchronizing: Present corresponding segments of animation and narration at the same time.	8 of 8	1.31
Overcoming the Difficulty Problem: Manage Essential Processing		
Segmenting: Break narrated animation into learner-controlled segments.	3 of 3	0.98
Pretraining: Provide pretraining on the names, locations, and behavior of each component.	5 of 5	0.79
Off-loading: Present words as narration rather than on-screen text.	14 of 14	1.06
Overcoming the Unfriendliness Problem: Foster Generative Processing		
Personalizing: Present words in conversational style rather than formal style.	10 of 10	1.30
Articulating: Narrate with human voice rather than machine voice.	3 of 3	0.78

Overall, in 13 out of 14 experiments, people learned better from concise multimedia lessons than from embellished ones (Harp & Mayer, 1997, Experiment 1; Harp & Mayer, 1998, Experiments, 1, 2, 3, & 4; Mayer et al., 1996, Experiments 1, 2, & 3; Mayer, Heiser, et al., 2000a, Experiment 3; Mayer & Jackson, 2005, Experiments 1 & 2; Moreno & Mayer, 2001, Experiments 1 & 2). As shown in Table 6.1, the median effect size for weeding is 0.98.

Decaptioning

What can be done to increase the effectiveness of a narrated animation? You might be tempted to add on-screen text, such as captions along the bottom of the screen that mimic what the narrator is saying. A rationale for adding captions is that they allow learners to choose the presentation form they prefer—in other words, auditory learners can listen to the narration, whereas visual learners can read the captions. However, according to the cognitive theory of multimedia learning, adding on-screen text (i.e., captions) to a narrated animation is likely to create unnecessary cognitive processing because the learner will try to attend to and reconcile the two verbal streams. In addition, the learner will have to split attention between the caption and the animation because it is not possible to look at both at the same time. In short, the on-screen text is redundant. Using redundant on-screen text is insensitive to the learner's cognitive-processing capacity because it encourages extraneous processing.

The solution to this problem is *decaptioning*—removing unneeded captions from a narrated animation. For example, in a series of three studies involving lightning (Mayer, Heiser, et al., 2001, Experiments 1 & 2; Moreno & Mayer, 2002a, Experiment 2) and two studies involving a computer-based environmental science game (Moreno & Mayer, 2002b, Experiments 2a & 2b), students performed better on transfer tests after receiving narration and animation rather than narration, animation, and on-screen text. As shown in Table 6.1, the median effect size for *decaptioning* was 0.72. Decaptioning is actually a special case of weeding in which irrelevant material is deleted from a lesson. Similar results were also reported by Mousavi, Low, and Sweller (1995, Experiments 1 & 2); Kalyuga, Chandler, and Sweller (1999, Experiment 1; 2000, Experiment 1); and Craig, Gholson, and Driscoll (2002, Experiment 2). My support for decaptioning should not be taken to mean that all redundant on-screen text should always be eliminated. In some cases it may be pedagogically sound to insert some on-screen text such as when the learners are nonnative speakers or hearing impaired, when the material is technical or the terms are hard to pronounce, when learners may need to refer back to the text, or when small amounts of on-screen text are placed next to corresponding portions of the screen to direct the learner's attention.

Signaling

Sometimes it is not possible to weed out extraneous material in a lesson, so an alternative technique is to insert cues that draw the learner's attention to the essential material. For example, consider a Web-based lesson explaining how airplanes achieve lift. The lesson's narration describes how lift is related to the wing being more curved on the top than the bottom, air traveling faster on the top than the bottom of the wing, and air pressure being less on the top than the bottom wing. The lesson's animation depicts these three steps in the explanation. The lesson also contains extraneous information such as the following: "The wingspan of a 747 is more than 200 feet; that's taller than a 15-story building."

What can be done to draw the learner's attention to the essential material? First, we can add a preview sentence containing "First, how the top of the wing is *shaped* differently than the bottom; second, how quickly *air flows* across the top surface; and third, how the *air pressure* on the top of the wing compares to that on the bottom of the wing." Second, we can add headings keyed to the preview sentence such as "1. Curvature: Wing is more curved (longer distance) on top than on bottom"; "2. Air speed: Air travels faster (longer distance in same time) above wing than below"; and "3. Pressure: Pressure (amount of air per surface area) is less above wing than below." Third, we can verbally emphasize key terms such as the headings and the italicized words. These techniques, which can be called *signaling,* had a strong positive effect on learning; people who received the signaled version of the airplane lesson scored higher on a transfer test than did those who received the nonsignaled version (Mautone & Mayer, 2001, Experiments 1a & 1b). Similarly, adding signaling to a lesson on lightning improved transfer test performance (Harp & Mayer, 1998, Experiment 3a).

Overall, in three out of three experiments, people learned better with signaled than nonsignaled lessons, yielding a median effect size of 0.60, as shown in Table 6.1 (Harp & Mayer, 1998, Experiment 3a; Mautone & Mayer, 2001, Experiments 1a & 1b). I use the term *signaling* to refer to the technique of adding verbal cues that show how the material is organized, including an outline, headings, and highlighted words. Signaling is intended to reduce the amount of extraneous processing performed by the learner during learning.

Aligning

Insensitivity to the learner's cognitive capacity also occurs when the on-screen text is presented far away from the corresponding portion of an on-screen graphic. For example, text and pictures are misaligned when the upper-right portion of the screen shows negative symbols moving to the bottom of the cloud and the very bottom of the screen contains text, "[N]egative particles fall to the bottom of the cloud." This situation primes a form of extraneous processing in which the learner must scan the screen to see the connection between the on-screen text and the relevant portion of the graphic.

Aligning is a technique for reducing extraneous cognitive processing in which corresponding words and images are presented near each other on the screen or page. For example, in a series of four experiments on lightning involving text and illustrations as well as on-screen text and animation, students performed better when corresponding words and pictures were near rather than far from one another on the screen (Mayer, Steinhoff, Bower, & Mars, 1995, Experiments 1, 2, & 3; Moreno & Mayer, 1999, Experiment 1). Mayer (1989, Experiment 2) reported similar results with a lesson on brakes.

Overall, in five out of five experimental tests, students who received the aligned presentation performed better on a transfer test than those who received the misaligned presentation. Table 6.1 shows that the median effect size attributable to aligning was 1.12. Similar results were reported by Chandler and Sweller (1991, Experiment 1); Sweller, Chandler, Tierney, and Cooper (1990, Experiment 1); and Tindall-Ford, Chandler, and Sweller (1997, Experiment 1).

Synchronizing

Finally, another form of insensitivity to the learner's cognitive capacity occurs when an animation is out of synch with the corresponding narration. For example, suppose that you opened an electronic encyclopedia and clicked on the entry for *pump*. First you click on the "speaker" icon and hear a 45-second narration describing how a bicycle tire pump works. Then, you click on the "movie" and see a 45-second animation depicting the same process. Why is this an insensitive way to present information? According to the cognitive theory of multimedia learning, meaningful learning occurs when the learner makes connections between corresponding segments of the animation and narration, and then stores the integrated representation in working memory. When the narration and animation are presented successively, the learner has to mentally hold the verbal representation in working memory until the corresponding images from the animation are presented. Given the limits on working memory capacity, the learner does not have the cognitive capacity to hold the entire script in working memory. Thus, it is less likely that the learner will be able to have corresponding portions of the animation and narration in working memory at the same time.

Synchronizing refers to the technique of presenting corresponding segments of animation and narration at the same time. For example, in a multimedia lesson on bicycle tire pumps, Mayer and Anderson (1991, Experiments 1 & 2a; 1992, Experiment 1) presented the animation and narration successively or simultaneously. Even though students in both groups received identical material, the simultaneous group performed better than the successive group on transfer tests. Similar results were obtained using animation and narration on brakes (Mayer & Anderson, 1992, Experiment 2; Mayer, Moreno, Boire, & Vagge, 1999, Experiment 2), lightning (Mayer et al., 1999, Experiment 1), and lungs (Mayer & Sims, 1994, Experiment 2).

Overall, in eight out of eight experiments, people performed better on transfer tests when they received simultaneous rather than successive animation and narration. As shown in Table 6.1, this technique of synchronizing yielded a median effect size of 1.31.

Research Agenda for the Insensitivity Problem

Future research on the insensitivity problem is needed to address empirical and theoretical issues. On the empirical front, it is important to know whether people learn to overcome the five design flaws discussed in this section as they gain more experience (and expertise) with the material. For example, Kalyuga (2005) summarized research on the expertise reversal effect—instructional methods that help low-knowledge learners tend to hinder high-knowledge learners. It would also be useful to understand the conditions under which redundant on-screen text can aid in learning.

On the theoretical front, there is a need for an independent measure of cognitive load. According to the cognitive theory of multimedia learning, poor instructional design can lead to extraneous processing that creates cognitive overload. Although poor test performance is a useful indirect measure of the effects of overload, it would be helpful to also have a direct measure of cognitive load during learning.

Difficulty Problem: The Training Content Is Inherently Difficult for the Learner

Even if a lesson was so well designed that the need for extraneous processing was completely eliminated, learners might still be overwhelmed by the processing demands required to understand the essential material. In short, the training material might be so inherently complex that the learner is not able to hold all of the needed material in working memory at the same time. I refer to this situation as the *difficulty problem.*

According to the cognitive theory of multimedia learning, an important challenge of instructional designers is to manage essential processing—cognitive processing required to mentally represent the essential presented material. In this section, I explore three techniques intended to manage essential processing—segmenting, pretraining, and off-loading.

Segmenting

In some Web-based training situations, a narrated animation about a complex topic is presented at a fast rate, and the learner's task is to build a mental representation of the key elements and relations. For example, a 140-second narrated animation on lightning formation contains 16 major events such as "Cool moist air moves over a warmer surface and becomes heated," which are depicted in animation and spoken by the narrator's voice. This scenario can lead to the difficulty problem because the explanation of lightning formation is complex.

What can be done to help the learner engage in the necessary essential processing? One approach—which I called *segmenting*—is to break the narrated animation into meaningful segments and allow the learner to have control over the pace of presentation. For example, the lightning lesson can be broken into 16 segments, each describing one major event. When on segment is finished, a Continue button appears on the screen. When the learner clicks on the Continue button, the next segment is presented, and so on. In this way, the learner can fully digest one segment before moving on to the next one, thus helping manage essential processing.

Mayer and Chandler (2001, Experiment 2) found that learners who were allowed to view the lightning lesson as a series of learner-controlled segments performed better on subsequent transfer tests than students who viewed the lightning lesson as a continuous presentation. Similar results were obtained by Mayer, Dow, and Mayer (2003, Experiments 2a & 2b) in a lesson involving electric motors. Overall, in three out of three experiments, segmenting led to better transfer performance than continuous presentation, with a median effect size of 0.98, as shown in Table 6.1.

Pretraining

Suppose that a learner opens a multimedia encyclopedia and clicks on *brakes*. On the screen, a 50-second narrated animation appears explaining the causal chain:

> When the driver steps on the car's brake pedal, a piston moves forward inside the master cylinder. The piston forces brake fluid out of the master cylinder and through the tubes to the wheel cylinders. In the wheel cylinders, the increase in fluid pressure makes a smaller set of pistons move. These smaller pistons activate the brake shoes. When the brake shoes press against the drum, both the drum and the wheel stop or slow down.

This scenario can lead to the difficulty problem because the learner must mentally represent component models (i.e., the name, location, and behavior) of each part (i.e., the pedal, piston in master cylinder, fluid in tubes, smaller set of pistons in wheel cylinders, brake shoes, drum, and wheel) and a causal model (e.g., stepping on the pedal causes the piston to move forward). The learner has to represent the parts and the causal relations among them, but the information is presented at a fast pace. The learner has the task of building a causal model but also must identify each of the components within the model such as the piston in the master cylinder.

How can we overcome the difficulty problem? One approach is to provide pretraining concerning the name, location, and behavior of the components. Thus, when the learner is given the narrated animation, it is easier to build a causal model because the learner does not have to concurrently build component models for each part. For example, one kind of pretraining for the brakes lesson involves showing each part on the screen, saying its name, and showing the states it can be in. For example, when the learner clicks on the piston in the master cylinder, the computer screen highlights this component and runs an animation of the piston moving forward and back. Next to the component, the screen says, "This is the piston in the master cylinder. It can move back or forward."

In a series of two experiments involving the brakes lesson, students who received pretraining in the names, locations, and behavior of each part performed better on a transfer test than those who did not receive pretraining (Mayer, Mathias, & Wetzell, 2002, Experiments 1 & 2). Similar results were obtained in a study involving a tire pump (Mayer, Mathias, et al., 2002, Experiment 3) and a computer-based geology simulation game (Mayer, Mautone, & Prothero, 2002, Experiments 2 & 3).

Overall, in five out of five experiments, students who received pretraining outperformed those who did not. As shown in Table 6.1, pretraining produced a median effect size of 0.79. Pollock, Chandler, and Sweller (2002, Experiments 1 & 3) reported similar results.

Off-Loading

Let's begin with a 140-second animation of the steps in lightning formation that contain captions at the bottom of the screen describing the events in the animation. This situation can lead to the difficulty problem because the learner's visual channel is overloaded with essential processing—that is, the learner must try to read the words and view the animation at the same time.

Off-loading involves presenting the words that accompany an animation as narration rather than as on-screen text. In this way, some processing demands on the visual information channel are off-loaded onto the verbal information-processing channel. In three experiments involving the lightning passage, people learned better from animation and narration than from animation and on-screen text, even though exactly the same words were presented at exactly the same time in the animation (Mayer & Moreno, 1998, Experiment 1; Moreno & Mayer, 1999, Experiments 1 & 2). Off-loading also had positive effects on learning about brakes (Mayer & Moreno, Experiment 2) and electric motors (Mayer, Dow, et al., 2003; Experiment 1), and in learning within a computer-based environmental science game (Moreno & Mayer, 2002a, Experiments 1a, 1b, 1c, 2a, & 2b; Moreno, Mayer, Spires, & Lester, 2001, Experiments 1, 4a, 4b, 5a, & 5b).

Overall, in 14 of 14 experimental tests conducted in our lab, people performed better on transfer tests after receiving animation and narration than animation and on-screen text. Table 6.1 shows that the median effect size of off-loading was 1.06. Similar results were also reported by Craig et al. (2002, Experiment 2); Jeung, Chandler, and Sweller (1997, Experiments 1, 2, & 3); Kalyuga et al. (1999, Experiment 1; 2000, Experiment 1); and O'Neil et al. (2000, Experiment 1).

Research Agenda for the Difficulty Problem

Research is needed on both the empirical front and the theoretical front. Although further replications of the off-loading technique are not needed, it would be useful to determine whether the technique (as well as the others reviewed so far) holds up over longer term training programs and in authentic training environments. In addition, more work is needed on pinpointing the best way to provide pretraining, and on the optimal size for a segment in segmenting.

On the theoretical front, it would be useful to have direct measures of cognitive load in order to determine whether these techniques actually help to manage cognitive load during learning.

Unfriendliness Problem: The Training Lesson Is Unfriendly to the Learner

Consider a training program intended to help industrial engineers learn to design assembly line processes. The program explains the major principle for designing assembly line processes in straightforward language. What is wrong with this approach? A major shortcoming is that it may not encourage the learner to actively make sense of the presented material—that is, it may fail to foster generative processing in the learner. Simply presenting information may not be sufficient to promote learning because learners need to engage in active cognitive processing such as attending to relevant material, mentally organizing the material into a coherent cognitive representation, and mentally integrating new incoming material with relevant existing knowledge. When the learner has the cognitive capacity to engage in active cognitive processing during learning but does not do so, there is a need to use instructional design features that will prime these processes.

When a Web-based lesson is presented in an unfriendly way, the learner is less likely to develop a social relation with the instructor and therefore less likely to process the material deeply during learning. This is the premise underlying social agency theory.

Generative processing refers to deep cognitive processing of the incoming material during learning, including paying attention to relevant portions of the presented material, mentally organizing the selected material in a coherent cognitive representation, and mentally integrating incoming material with appropriate existing knowledge. In some Web-based training scenarios, the material may be well designed so it does not overload the learner's cognitive system, but the learner still does not use that available capacity for active cognitive processing during learning. In this section, I explore two ways to promote generative processing during learning—personalizing and articulating.

Personalizing

As part of a Web-based training program on health issues, suppose a learner clicks on *lungs* and receives a 60-second narrated animation describing how the human respiratory system works. The script of the presentation is as follows:

> There are three phases in respiration: inhaling, exchanging, and exhaling. During inhaling, the diaphragm moves down, creating more space for the lungs; air enters through the nose or mouth, moves down through the throat and bronchial tubes to tiny air sacs in the lungs. During exchange, oxygen moves from the air sacs to the bloodstream running nearby, and carbon dioxide moves from the bloodstream to the air sacs. During exhaling, the diaphragm moves up, creating less room for the lungs; air travels through the bronchial tubes and throat to the nose and mouth, where it leaves the body.

The learner hears these words while watching an on-screen animation depicting each of the steps in respiration.

What is wrong with this straightforward explanation of how something works? One problem is that the script is written in formal style, with third person constructions that the learner may interpret as unfriendly. According to cognitive theories of communication, people try harder to understand what a speaker is saying when they feel that they are in a conversation with the speaker (Grice, 1975; Mayer, Fennell, Farmer, & Campbell, 2004; Reeves & Nass, 1996). That is, learners try harder to make sense of the presented explanation when they feel that the speaker is a social partner—someone with whom they are having a conversation rather than someone who is presenting a monologue.

How can we prime this conversational schema in learners? One technique is to have the computer's voice speak in conversational style rather than formal style. In particular, personalization involves using first and second person constructions (e.g., *I* and *you*) instead of third person constructions (e.g., *the*). For example, we can personalize the script for the lungs by substituting *your* for *the* in each of 11 places. In a series of three experiments, learners who received the personalized version of the lungs presentation performed better on subsequent transfer tests than did learners who received the nonpersonalized version (Mayer et al., 2004, Experiments 1, 2, & 3). Apparently, a very modest change toward conversational style can be enough to encourage learners to work harder to make sense of the presented material.

Next, consider a 140-second narrated animation that explains the process of lightning formation. The speaker begins by saying, "Cool moist air moves over a warmer surface and becomes heated. The warmed moist air near the earth's surface rises rapidly. As the air in this updraft cools, water vapor condenses into water droplets and forms a cloud." Along with the narration, the screen displays an animation depicting the events described by the speaker. As you can see, the narration about lightning formation is in formal style. We can personalize the narration by adding some sentences that directly address the learner. For example, right before these sentences, the speaker says, "Let me tell you what happens when lightning forms. Suppose you are standing outside, feeling the warm rays of the sun heating up the earth's surface around you." Right after these sentences, the speaker says, "Congratulations. You have just witnessed the birth of your own cloud." In a set of two experiments, learners performed better on transfer tests after receiving the personalized version than the nonpersonalized version of the lightning presentation (Moreno & Mayer, 2000b, Experiments 1 & 2).

Finally, consider a computer-based educational game aimed at helping people learn principles of environmental science. In the game, called Design-a-Plant, the learner watches as Herman-the-Bug is transported to a distance planet with distinct environmental conditions such as strong winds and rain. The learner's job is to design a plant that would survive on the planet, including selecting appropriate roots, stem, and leaves. For example, Herman says,

> This program is about what type of plant survives on different planets. For each planet, a plant will be designed. This goal is to learn what

type of roots, stem, and leaves allow the plants to survive in each environment. Some hints are provided throughout the program.

Then, the learner sees whether the plant survives and receives explanations from Herman-the-Bug. For example, Herman says, "In very rainy environments, plant leaves have to be flexible so they are not damaged by the rainfall. What really matters for the rain is the choice between thick and thin leaves." As you can see, Herman is an example of an animated pedagogical agent—an on-screen character who interacts with the learner.

What can be done to improve this game? We can help make Herman-the-Bug seem more like a social partner by changing the way he speaks from formal style to conversational style. In short, we can personalize the speech of the animated pedagogical agent by using first and second person constructions (using *I* and *you*). For example, the personalized version of Herman's introduction to the game is

> You are about to start a journey where you will be visiting different planets. For each planet, you will need to design a plant. Your mission is to learn what type of roots, stem, and leaves allow your plant to survive in each environment. I will be guiding you through by giving out some hints.

Similarly, the personalized version of the rainy-planet explanation is "This is a very rainy environment, and the leaves of your plant have to be flexible so they're not damaged by rainfall. What really matters for the rain is your choice between thick leaves and thin leaves." In a series of five experimental tests, people who learned with the personalized version of the Design-a-Plant game performed better on subsequent transfer tests than did those who learned with the nonpersonalized version (Moreno & Mayer, 2000b, Experiments 1, 2, 3, 4, & 5; Moreno & Mayer, 2004, Experiments 1a & 1b). When training programs include animated pedagogical agents, it is best for them to speak in conversational style rather than formal style. In a complementary study, Wang et al. (2005) reported that students learned better from a Web-based industrial engineering game called Virtual Factory when the on-screen animated pedagogical agent made polite suggestions (e.g., "You may want to click the Enter key") rather than direct suggestions (e.g., "Click the Enter key").

Overall, in 10 out of 10 experimental tests, students learned better from Web-based instruction when the scripts were in conversational style rather than formal style (Mayer et al., 2004, Experiments 1, 2, & 3; Moreno & Mayer, 2000b, Experiments 1, 2, 3, 4, & 5; Moreno & Mayer, 2004, Experiments 1a & 1b). I refer to this instructional design technique as *personalizing*. As shown in Table 6.1, the median effect size for personalizing was 1.30.

Articulating

The goal of personalization (e.g., using conversational style) is to help create a feeling of social partnership between the learner and the Web-based instructor, which in turn primes the learner to work harder to make sense of the presented material. Are there other features of Web-based training that might also promote this kind of social partnership? In some Web-based training programs, the on-screen agent or instructor speaks in a machine-simulated voice. A problem with a machine voice is that it might hinder the learner's feeling of working with a social partner, and reduce the learner's willingness to try to make sense of what the voice is saying. In contrast, these problems may be reduced if the on-screen agent or instructor speaks in a friendly human voice. In a series of two experiments, Atkinson, Mayer, and Merrill (2005, Experiments 1 & 2) provided worked examples that explained how to solve proportional reasoning word problems. An on-screen agent named Peddy-the-Parrott provided a step-by-step narration of computational steps shown on the screen. Learners performed better on subsequent transfer tests when Peddy spoke in a human voice rather than in a machine voice. Similarly, Mayer, Sobko, and Mautone (2003, Experiment 2) reported that students learned better from a narrated animation explaining lightning formation when the speaker had a human voice rather than a machine voice.

Overall, in three out of three experiments (Atkinson et al., 2005, Experiments 1 & 2; Mayer, Sobko, et al., 2003, Experiment 3), people learned better when the speaker had a human voice rather than a machine voice. I refer to this instructional design technique as *articulating*. Table 6.1 shows that the median effect size for articulating was 0.78.

Research Agenda for the Unfriendliness Problem

Research is needed on both the empirical front and the theoretical front. First, on the empirical front, although there is some preliminary evidence for the personalization and voice principles, more research is needed to determine the conditions under which these principles are most effective. In addition, it would be worthwhile to explore other social cues that might prime deeper learning, such following up on Wang et al.'s (2005) finding favoring politeness of animated pedagogical agents. However, not all social cues appear to have the same positive effects. For example, having the image of the speaker on the screen during a Web-based lesson did not result in a strong and consistent improvement in transfer test performance across nine experimental tests

(Atkinson, 2002, Experiments 1a, 1b, & 2; Craig et al., 2002, Experiment 1; Mayer, Dow, et al., 2003; Experiment 4; Moreno et al., 2001, Experiments 4a, 4b, 5a, & 5b). More research is needed to determine the pedagogical role of the speaker's image on-screen, including the role of gestures and facial expressions.

Second, on the theoretical front, the experiments reported in this review are based on social agency theory—the idea that social cues can create a feeling of social partnership that leads to deeper cognitive processing. There is a need for more direct evidence that social cues such as personalization or a human voice prime a feeling of social partnership and lead to deeper processing. It would be useful to have direct measures of the feeling of social partnership and the depth of cognitive processing during learning.

Looking Ahead

In addition to the cognitive issues described in this chapter, four additional challenges for effective Web-based training involve the needs for implementing technology-supported training programs that are sensitive to the organizational culture (i.e., cultural issues), that maintain learner motivation during training (affective issues), that foster social presence during training (social issues), and that promote metacognitive strategies that apply to realistic tasks (metacognitive issues). First, more research is needed on understanding the conditions that lead to successful implementations of technology-supported training. Preliminary studies suggest that technology-based solutions to organizational problems work best when they fit into existing organizational culture and practices. For example, recent studies show that paper remains a central feature of organizations in spite of attempts to mandate high-tech alternatives, because paper better serves the needs of workers for some tasks (Brown & Duguid, 2000; Sellen & Harper, 2002). Rather than searching for technology-based training as a way of replacing current training practices, it may be useful to determine what multimedia training can do well to supplement existing training (Chambers, Cheung, Madden, Slavin, & Gifford, 2006).

Second, more research is needed on how to maintain learners' motivation during online training. Clark and Feldon (2005) exposed the myth that Web-based training is more motivating for students; instead, Web-based training often leads to high dropout rates. Research is needed on how to use the affordances of technology-based training to help motivate learners, including more effective use of feedback and individualized guidance.

Third, more research is needed on how to create a sense of social partnership between the learner and the computer. Nass and Brave (2005) have shown how voice can be used to promote positive affect in the learner. More research is needed on the appropriate use of conversational style, politeness, and voice as vehicles for improving learner affect concerning the training program (Mayer, 2005d). Another promising venue is the use of video in which an author describes his or her ideas directly to the learner, because making the author visible may help to interest the learner.

Fourth, more research is needed on how to use technology-supported training to foster the metacognitive skills needed to perform authentic tasks, including metacognitive skills such as monitoring how well you understand and predicting how well you would perform on a task. People have difficulty in working with multiple sources of information and in judging the quality of information they find, so they need explicit training in how to use documents (Rouet, 2006). Overall, learners need guidance in how to learn and use online information, and technology-supported learning environments can be designed to provide the needed guidance (Azevedo & Cromley, 2004). In short, research is needed in how to promote metacognitive skills.

In summary, future research should be broadened to address the cultural, social, affective, and metacognitive aspects of Web-based training in addition to the fundamental cognitive issues.

Conclusions

The purpose of the brief review presented in this chapter is to show that it is possible to derive research-based principles for the design of Web-based training. Most of the work summarized here is based on short-term learning episodes in a well-controlled laboratory environment. Future research should examine how well these techniques work in longer term training programs in authentic environments.

It is now possible for Web-based training to go beyond standard presentations of text, narration, and graphics. More advanced technologies include games, simulations, and animated pedagogical agents, as well as digital libraries, immersive virtual reality, and user modeling. Research is needed to determine which features of these technologies tend to benefit learning. For example, what are the features of an effective simulation or game? What is the appropriate conversational style for an animated pedagogical agent? Is it helpful to adjust the presentation style to accommodate visual and verbal learners? These are examples of the types of research questions suggested by the introduction of advanced instructional technologies.

Consistent with Clark (2001), the theme of this chapter is that technology does not cause learning, but rather instructional methods can foster learning. The goal of research on Web-based training should not be to determine whether one form of technology is better than conventional instruction (e.g., whether simulations are good for learning). Rather, the goal of research on Web-based training should be to determine how various features of a Web-based training lesson affect learning, for example whether students learn better from simulations when they are free to explore on their own (pure discovery) or when they are asked to make predictions and run experiments with simulations (guided discovery).

Although Web-based training is becoming commonplace, high-quality research on Web-based training is not. What is needed is an empirical research base from which to derive practical design principles as well as a theory of how people learn. In short, Web-based training should be based on research evidence and on a cognitive theory of how people learn. This vision of evidence-based and theory-grounded practice motivates the development of an empirical research base in which various instructional methods are extensively tested.

Author Note

Preparation of this chapter was supported by a grant from the Office of Naval Research. The author's address is Richard E. Mayer, Department of Psychology, University of California, Santa Barbara, CA 93106. E-mail: mayer@psych.ucsb.edu.

References

Atkinson, R. K. (2002). Optimizing learning from examples using animated pedagogical agents. *Journal of Educational Psychology, 94,* 416–427.

Atkinson, R. K., Mayer, R. E., & Merrill, M. M. (2005). Fostering social agency in multimedia learning: Examining the impact of an animated agent's voice. *Contemporary Educational Psychology, 30,* 117–139.

Azevedo, R., & Cromley, J. G. (2004). Does training in self-regulated learning facilitate students' learning with hypermedia? *Journal of Educational Psychology, 96,* 523–535.

Brown, J. S., & Duguid, P. (2000). *The social life of information.* Cambridge, MA: Harvard Business School Press.

Chambers, B., Cheung, A. C. K., Madden, N. A., Slavin, R. E., & Gifford, R. (2006). Achievement effects of embedded multimedia in a success for all reading program. *Journal of Educational Psychology, 98,* 232–237.

Chandler, P., & Sweller, J. (1991). Cognitive load theory and the format of instruction. *Cognition and Instruction, 8,* 293–332.

Clark, R. C. (2001). *Learning from media: Arguments, analysis, and evidence.* Greenwich, CT: Information Age.

Clark, R. E., & Feldon, D. F. (2005). Five common but questionable principles of multimedia learning. In R. E. Mayer (Ed.), *Cambridge handbook of multimedia learning* (pp. 97–116). New York: Cambridge University Press.

Craig, S. D., Gholson, B., & Driscoll, D. M. (2002). Animated pedagogical agents in multimedia educational environments: Effects of agent properties, picture features, and redundancy. *Journal of Educational Psychology, 94,* 428–434.

Grice, H. P. (1975). Logic and conversation. In P. Cole & J. Morgan (Eds.), *Syntax and semantics* (Vol. 3, pp. 41–58). New York: Academic Press.

Harp, S. F., & Mayer, R. E. (1997). The role of interest in learning from scientific text and illustrations: On the distinction between emotional interest and cognitive interest. *Journal of Educational Psychology, 89,* 92–102.

Harp, S. F., & Mayer, R. E. (1998). How seductive details do their damage: A theory of cognitive interest in science learning. *Journal of Educational Psychology, 90,* 414–434.

Jeung, H., Chandler, P., & Sweller, J. (1997). The role of visual indicators in dual sensory mode instruction. *Educational Psychology, 17,* 329–343.

Kalyuga, S. (2005). The prior knowledge principle in multimedia learning. In R. E. Mayer (Ed.), *Cambridge handbook of multimedia learning* (pp. 325–338). New York: Cambridge University Press.

Kalyuga, S., Chandler, P., & Sweller, J. (1999). Managing split-attention and redundancy in multimedia instruction. *Applied Cognitive Psychology, 13,* 351–371.

Kalyuga, S., Chandler, P., & Sweller, J. (2000). Incorporating learner experience into the design of multimedia instruction. *Journal of Educational Psychology, 92,* 126–136.

Mautone, P. D., & Mayer, R. E. (2001). Signaling as a cognitive guide in multimedia learning. *Journal of Educational Psychology, 93,* 377–389.

Mayer, R. E. (1989). Systematic thinking fostered by illustrations in scientific text. *Journal of Educational Psychology, 81,* 240–246.

Mayer, R. E. (2001). *Multimedia learning.* New York: Cambridge University Press.

Mayer, R. E. (2005a). Cognitive theory of multimedia learning. In R. E. Mayer (Ed.), *Cambridge handbook of multimedia learning* (pp. 31–48). New York: Cambridge University Press.

Mayer, R. E. (2005b). Principles for managing essential processing in multimedia learning: Segmenting, pre-training, and modality principles. In R. E. Mayer (Ed.), *Cambridge handbook of multimedia learning* (pp. 169–182). New York: Cambridge University Press.

Mayer, R. E. (2005c). Principles for reducing extraneous cognitive processing in multimedia learning: Coherence, signaling, redundancy, spatial contiguity, and temporal contiguity principles. In R. E. Mayer (Ed.), *Cambridge handbook of multimedia learning* (pp. 183–200). New York: Cambridge University Press.

Mayer, R. E. (2005d). Principles of multimedia learning based in social cues: Personalization, voice, and image principles. In R. E. Mayer (Ed.), *Cambridge handbook of multimedia learning* (pp. 201–212). New York: Cambridge University Press.

Mayer, R. E., & Anderson, R. B. (1991). Animations need narrations: An experimental test of a dual-coding hypothesis. *Journal of Educational Psychology, 83,* 484–490.

Mayer, R. E., & Anderson, R. B. (1992). The instructive animation: Helping students build connections between words and pictures in multimedia learning. *Journal of Educational Psychology, 84,* 444–452.

Mayer, R. E., Bove, W., Bryman, A., Mars, R., & Tapangco, L. (1996). When less is more: Meaningful learning from visual and verbal summaries of science textbook lessons. *Journal of Educational Psychology, 88,* 64–73.

Mayer, R. E., & Chandler, P. (2001). When learning is just a click away: Does simple user interaction foster deeper understanding of multimedia messages? *Journal of Educational Psychology, 93,* 390–397.

Mayer, R. E., Dow, G., & Mayer, R. E. (2003). Multimedia learning in an interactive self-explaining environment: What works in the design of agent-based microworlds? *Journal of Educational Psychology, 95,* 806–813.

Mayer, R. E., Fennell, S., Farmer, L., & Campbell, J. (2004). A personalization effect in multimedia learning: Students learn better when words are in conversational style rather than formal style. *Journal of Educational Psychology, 96,* 389–395.

Mayer, R. E., Heiser, H., & Lonn, S. (2001). Cognitive constraints on multimedia learning: When presenting more material results in less understanding. *Journal of Educational Psychology, 93,* 187–198.

Mayer, R. E., & Jackson, J. (2005). The case for conciseness in scientific explanations: Quantitative details can hurt qualitative understanding. *Journal of Experimental Psychology: Applied, 11,* 13–18.

Mayer, R. E., Mathias, A., & Wetzell, K. (2002). Fostering understanding of multimedia messages through pre-training: Evidence for a two-stage theory of mental model construction. *Journal of Experimental Psychology: Applied, 8,* 147–154.

Mayer, R. E., Mautone, P., & Prothero, W. (2002). Pictorial aids for learning by doing in a multimedia geology simulation game. *Journal of Educational Psychology, 94,* 171–185.

Mayer, R. E., & Moreno, R. E. (1998). A split-attention effect in multimedia learning: Evidence for dual processing systems in working memory. *Journal of Educational Psychology, 90,* 312–320.

Mayer, R. E., & Moreno, R. (2003). Nine ways to reduce cognitive load in multimedia learning. *Educational Psychologist, 38,* 43–52.

Mayer, R. E., Moreno, R., Boire, M., & Vagge, S. (1999). Maximizing constructivist learning from multimedia communications by minimizing cognitive load. *Journal of Educational Psychology, 91,* 638–643.

Mayer, R. E., & Sims, V. K. (1994). For whom is a picture worth a thousand words? Extensions of a dual-coding theory of multimedia learning? *Journal of Educational Psychology, 86,* 389–401.

Mayer, R. E., Sobko, K., & Mautone, P. D. (2003). Social cues in multimedia learning: Role of speaker's voice. *Journal of Educational Psychology, 95,* 419–425.

Mayer, R. E., Steinhoff, K., Bower, G., & Mars, R. (1995). A generative theory of textbook design: Using annotated illustrations to foster meaningful learning of science text. *Educational Technology Research and Development, 43,* 31–43.

Moreno, R., & Mayer, R. E. (1999). Cognitive principles of multimedia learning: The role of modality and contiguity. *Journal of Educational Psychology, 91,* 358–368.

Moreno, R., & Mayer, R. E. (2000a). A coherence effect in multimedia learning: The case for minimizing irrelevant sounds in the design of multimedia messages. *Journal of Educational Psychology, 92,* 117–125.

Moreno, R., & Mayer, R. E. (2000b). Engaging students in active learning: The case for personalized multimedia messages. *Journal of Educational Psychology, 92,* 724–733.

Moreno, R., & Mayer, R. E. (2002a). Verbal redundancy in multimedia learning: When reading helps listening. *Journal of Educational Psychology, 94,* 156–163.

Moreno, R., & Mayer, R. E. (2002b). Learning science in virtual reality multimedia environments: Role of methods and media. *Journal of Educational Psychology, 94,* 598–610.

Moreno, R., & Mayer, R. E. (2004). Personalized messages that promote science learning in virtual environments. *Journal of Educational Psychology, 96,* 165–173.

Moreno, R., Mayer, R. E., Spires, H. A., & Lester, J. C. (2001). The case for social agency in computer-based teaching: Do students learn more deeply when they interact with animated pedagogical agents? *Cognition and Instruction, 19,* 177–213.

Mousavi, S. Y., Low, R., & Sweller, J. (1995). Reducing cognitive load by mixing auditory and visual presentation modes. *Journal of Educational Psychology, 87,* 319–334.

Nass, C., & Brave, S. (2005). *Wired for speech.* Cambridge, MA: MIT Press.

O'Neil, H. F. (Ed.). (2005). *What works in distance learning: Guidelines.* Greenwich, CT: Information Age Publishing.

O'Neil, H. F., Mayer, R. E., Herl, H. E., Niemi, C., Olin, K., & Thurman, R. A. (2000). Instructional strategies for virtual aviation training environments. In H. F. O'Neil & D. H. Andrews (Eds.), *Aircrew training and assessment* (pp. 105–130). Mahwah, NJ: Lawrence Erlbaum Associates.

Paas, F., Renkl, A., & Sweller, J. (2003). Cognitive load theory and instructional design: Recent developments. *Educational Psychologist, 38,* 1–4.

Phye, G. D., Robinson, D. H., & Levin, J. (2005). *Empirical methods for evaluating educational interventions.* San Diego: Elsevier Academic Press.

Pollock, E., Chandler, P., & Sweller, J. (2002). Assimilating complex information. *Learning and Instruction, 12,* 61–86.

Reeves, B., & Nass, C. (1996). *The media equation.* New York: Cambridge University Press.

Rossett, A. (2002). *The ASTD e-learning handbook: Best practices, strategies, and case studies for an emerging field*. New York: McGraw-Hill.

Rouet, J-F. (2006). *The skills of document use*. Mahwah. NJ: Lawrence Erlbaum Associates.

Sellen, A. J., & Harper, R. H. R. (2002). *The myth of the paperless office*. Cambridge, MA: MIT Press.

Shavelson, R. J., & Towne, L. (Eds.). (2002). *Scientific research in education*. Washington, DC: National Academy Press.

Sweller, J. (1999). *Instructional design in technical areas*. Camberwell, Australia: ACER Press.

Sweller, J. (2005). Implications of cognitive load theory for multimedia learning. In R. E. Mayer (Ed.), *Cambridge handbook of multimedia learning* (pp. 19–30). New York: Cambridge University Press.

Sweller, J., Chandler, P., Tierney, P., & Cooper, M. (1990). Cognitive load and selective attention as factors in the structuring of technical material. *Journal of Experimental Psychology: General, 119,* 176–192.

Tindall-Ford, S., Chandler, P., & Sweller, J. (1997). When two sensory modalities are better than one. *Journal of Experimental Psychology: Applied, 3,* 257–287.

Wang, N., Johnson, W. L., Mayer, R. E., Rizzo, P., Shaw, E., & Collins, H. (2005). The politeness effect: Pedagogical agents and learning gains. In C-K. Looi, G. McCalla, B. Bredewg, & J. Breuker (Eds.), *Artificial intelligence in education: Supporting learning through intelligent and socially informed technology*. Amsterdam: IOS Press.

7

Synthetic Learning Environments: On Developing a Science of Simulation, Games, and Virtual Worlds for Training

Jan Cannon-Bowers
University of Central Florida

Clint Bowers
University of Central Florida

It has been argued that the United States' position as a global economic leader depends largely on the degree to which a workforce of educated, adaptive, and motivated individuals can be developed and maintained (Stein, 2000). This challenge is intensified by the availability and sophistication of technology that is now commonplace in many jobs. Fortunately, the same technology that has increased requirements for better skilled and prepared workers is also providing unprecedented opportunities to improve the education and training process. Applied prudently and intelligently, technology holds great promise as a means to improve education and training at all levels. However, attempts to exploit technology in learning systems are likely to fail if they are not based on the *science of learning*, a situation that is all too common in instructional system design. Moreover, poorly implemented systems will cause educators and trainers to abandon technologies that could be very effective if applied correctly.

The purpose of this chapter is to focus attention on a subset of technology-enabled instructional systems—simulations, games, and virtual worlds—which we refer to collectively as *synthetic learning environments* (SLEs). Our goal is to establish a framework that will help integrate past results and provide a roadmap for future research into these techniques. To do this, we first make a case for why SLEs hold promise as particularly effective learning tools in the workplace, and what makes them unique among training media. We then describe a framework presented recently by Sugrue and Clark (2000) and use it as a means to specify and organize pertinent variables and associated research questions that must be addressed in order to optimize the use of SLEs in training.

Before we proceed, it is first important to define what we mean by the terms we are using in this chapter: simulations, games, virtual worlds, and synthetic learning environments. We use the term *SLEs* to describe a variety of technology-based training media or approaches that have as an essential feature the ability to augment, replace, create, and/or manage a learner's actual experience with the world by providing realistic content and embedded instructional features. Included in this definition are simulations, games, and virtual worlds.

Training *simulations* (also referred to as *simulators* or *simulation-based training*) are systems that attempt to provide realistic training by incorporating "a working representation of reality ... [that] may be an abstracted, simplified, or accelerated model of process" (Galvao, Martins, & Gomes, 2000, p. 1692). Importantly, what is being simulated is not necessarily the physical aspects of the system, but can be the underlying structure of the task or problem (e.g., in business simulations), so that the cognitive processes involved in accomplishing the task are represented. In a generic sense, the term *game* refers to an activity that provides entertainment, especially one that involves competitive engagement and/or adherence to a set of rules. Vogel and her colleagues (2006) suggested that the essential characteristics of a computer game are goals, interactivity, and feedback. Galvao and colleagues (2000) included rules and competition as other important characteristics of games. When the primary goal of the game is to train users (instead of, or in addition to, just entertaining them), the terms *serious game*, *educational game*, or *game-based training* have been used.

Due to advances in computing power, there is also an emerging interest in using *virtual worlds* as training environments. These environments typically involve a large number of geographically distributed players who all interact with and within an elaborate, shared cue set (the "virtual world"). Many of these virtual worlds are *persistent*. That is, actions continue and the world changes whether or not any given player is involved, and players may enter and exit the world at will. In a sense, virtual worlds are very elaborate simulations (composed of many interacting models) that allow for complex interactions among players as well as between players and objects in the world.

It is crucial to note that the constructs of game, simulation, and virtual world are not orthogonal; they are actually overlapping. For example, it is quite possible to have a simulation that has gaming features (e.g., one that mimics a real process and also contains rules, competition, challenges) or one that does not, a game that provides educational content but is not a simulation (e.g., a matching game to teach vocabulary or a card game to teach strategy), or a virtual world that may or may not include gaming features or connection to a real process. However, for training purposes—that is, to impart an explicit set of competencies in adult learners—we believe that the most useful environment is one that contains some type of underlying simulation of the task and/or environment. Moreover, to be effective training devices, all of these systems require embedded instructional features. Hence, SLEs may be stand-alone simulations or provide persistent, complex virtual worlds, and they may or may not include gaming features. The essential characteristic of an SLE in our view is that it provides deliberate, well-managed, sufficiently realistic *synthetic experience* as a means to enhance learning and performance.

A Case for Using SLEs in Training

As noted, it is generally agreed that the nature of work is changing in modern organizations. The modern workforce—across jobs and at all levels—must be adaptable, be able to make decisions, be able to communicate effectively, demonstrate effective interpersonal skills, and commit to lifelong learning (Stein, 2000). SLEs provide a unique opportunity to achieve these objectives, in some cases more effectively and cheaply than other forms of instruction. To understand fully the potential of SLEs, it is important to explain the theoretical justification for why they are expected to be viable teaching tools, and briefly review past empirical work regarding their effectiveness.

Theoretical justification for the proposition that SLEs are a potent medium in which to design instruction can be found in several lines of research into how people learn (see Cannon-Bowers & Bowers, 2008). In their recent summary on this topic, Cannon-Bowers and Bowers (2008) began with seminal work by Glaser (1989), suggesting that the knowledge of beginners in a domain is disconnected and isolated, with relatively superficial understanding of central concepts or terms. These disconnected concepts gradually become more integrated through experience and also better structured or organized. Similarly, research into learning and expertise suggests that experts may begin to build and store "condition action rules" so that eventually "a specific pattern (the condition) will trigger a stereotypic" response (Chi, Glaser, & Farr, 1988, p. xvii). It is argued, therefore, that expertise may consist of a well-organized repertoire of instances, indexed in a way that makes them easily and quickly accessible when appropriately triggered by external stimuli (cf. Gobet & Simon, 1996; Logan, 1988).

In addition, the notion that experts recognize meaningful patterns in the problem space and "chunk" information into meaningful units or clusters has been replicated across domains (DeGroot, 1965; Egan &

Schwartz, 1979; Lesgold, 1988). Importantly, these patterns are formed and reinforced through experience. Other researchers have argued that the modern workplace requires adaptive expertise, that is, the ability to adapt to novel or changing job demands through a deeper conceptual under-standing of the domain (see Smith, Ford, & Kozlowski, 1997).

Among the (many) implications of these conclusions for the design of effective learning systems, the notion that learning should occur in a meaningful or relevant context is perhaps most pertinent here. This asser-tion is based on the conclusions noted above. Specifically, effective learn-ing leads one to recognize patterns, use these as the basis for knowledge organization, and recognize that this knowledge is conditionalized (i.e., specific to a context). New learning, in turn, must be integrated into this existing world knowledge. Many other lines of inquiry into the science of learning also converge on the conclusion that *experiential learning* (i.e., learning through experience) is a fundamental human process (e.g., Kolb, 1984; Kolb, Boyatzis, & Mainemelis, 2001).

What Is Unique About SLEs?

Technology offers opportunities to enable the development of learning environments that are consistent with principles noted above. Moreover, in many cases, simulation environments offer a number of unique advan-tages as compared to training with actual equipment or in the actual job environment; these include that they: (a) can be used as practice environ-ments for tasks that are too dangerous to be practiced in the real world, (b) can provide increased opportunities for practice on tasks that occur infrequently (e.g., emergency procedures), (c) are available when actual equipment cannot be employed, (d) can contain embedded instructional features (e.g., feedback) that enhance the instructional experience, and (e) can represent significant cost savings compared with training on oper-ational equipment.

From a theoretical standpoint, SLEs also provide several other chal-lenges (or opportunities) that must be addressed (or exploited). These include the following:

- SLEs are most often *instructorless*, that is, the trainee engages in learning without the direct involvement of an instructor or teacher (Brown, 2001). In fact, this feature is a defining attribute of many SLEs. The implication for researchers and designers is that neces-sary instructional features must be carefully conceptualized and embedded in SLE design.
- SLEs can be incredibly engaging—even fun—learning situations. Indeed, the desire to use video games to teach is at least partly

driven by the fact that they can captivate learners' attention and are inherently motivating. The challenge for research and design in this regard is to exploit the motivational aspects of SLEs while ensuring that they effectively train targeted material.

A Conceptual Framework for Studying SLE Design

Given that SLEs hold great potential as sound training solutions, it is not surprising that a growing body of work suggests that they can be effective (see Fletcher & Tobias, 2006; Gredler, 2004; Green & Bavelier, 2003; Vogel, Greenwood-Ericksen, Cannon-Bowers, & Bowers, 2006). For example, several studies have supported the contention that management simulations can be effective training environments for graduate students and professionals (e.g., Gredler; Scherpereel, 2005). Other research suggests that simulations are effective in improving both the technical and nontechnical skills of pilots (Goeters, 2002; Goettl & Shute, 1996; Jentsch & Bowers, 1998; Roessingh, 2005). There are also studies to suggest that SLEs can help train clinicians (Abell & Galinsky, 2002; Lane, Slavin, & Ziv, 2001; Pederson, 2003), military personnel (Pleban, Matthews, Salter, & Eakin, 2002; Ricci, Salas, & Cannon-Bowers, 1996), firemen (Spagnolli, Varotto, & Mantovani, 2003), and survey interviewers (Link, Armsby, Hubal, & Guinn, 2006).

In contrast, several studies have failed to find an advantage in using SLEs (Cameron & Dwyer, 2005; Ellis, Marcus, & Taylor, 2005; Fletcher & Tobias, 2006), making it clear that more work needs to be done if these environments are to realize their potential. Perhaps what is most unfortunate (and debilitating from a designer's standpoint) about the state of knowledge regarding SLE design is that it is not entirely clear from reading the literature *why* the SLE in any particular study was or was not effective. Moreover, little, if any, design guidance can be extracted from past research to aid instructional designers and trainers in developing or selecting effective systems. A notable exception is the work by Tobias and Fletcher (2007), which represents an initial attempt to provide pedagogically sound guidance for educational games. This work notwithstanding, we believe that most often the design of SLEs tends to be more of an art than a science, with developers at a loss to translate educational concepts into a format that can be inserted meaningfully into the SLE. The result is that the use of SLEs for training is suboptimized.

Although there are many reasons for this, we see one as particularly problematic: namely, research studies in this area are most often conducted at the *training system level*. By this, we mean that the training system itself—with all sorts of embedded assumptions, strategies, features, and variables—is what is tested, usually in its entirety. In some cases, one or two features of the SLE are isolated for investigation, but many times this is not even done. The result is that the underlying mechanisms or causes of observed outcomes are not known; instead, all that can be concluded is that this particular system did (or did not) work, but it is unclear exactly why.

To remedy this, a more systematic approach is needed that aims to elucidate and investigate, in an organized way, the host of variables that can have an impact on instructional effectiveness for a particular SLE application. One way to conceptualize a systematic program of this sort is to rely on an overriding framework that can organize pertinent variables within the instructional design space. In this regard, Sugrue and Clark (2000) recently summarized many years of research from a number of perspectives, and concluded that there are six major cognitive underpinnings of instruction: (a) interpretation of the targeted performance goal; (b) encoding of task-relevant declarative knowledge and/or retrieval of task-relevant declarative and procedural knowledge; (c) compilation and execution of new procedural knowledge, that is, production rules relating sequences of actions and decisions to task goals and conditions; (d) monitoring of performance; (e) diagnosis of sources of error in performance; and (f) adaptation of goal interpretation, retrieval and encoding of declarative knowledge, or retrieval and compilation of procedural knowledge to improve performance (p. 217).

Obviously, a comprehensive view of SLE design must also include other classes of variables that can impinge on their ultimate success, namely, those associated with learner characteristics and the training context. Space limitations prevent us from including these variables here; interested readers are encouraged to consult other sources (e.g., see Kozlowski, Toney, et al., 2001, for an excellent summary).

To provide a useful guiding framework for specifying research needs in SLE design, we modified the Sugrue and Clark (2000) model slightly to include the components *trigger effective learning strategies and motivation* and *provide feedback*, which were not highlighted in the original list but are, we believe, important enough to deserve explicit attention. Hence, we propose a modified version of Sugrue and Clark's framework, which includes six major phases of instruction that must be considered in studying and designing instruction. These can be summarized as follows:

1. Elaborate on the goal of instruction and trigger effective learning strategies and motivation.
2. Provide information related to the task (declarative knowledge).
3. Provide appropriate practice environments (declarative knowledge and skill).

4. Monitor ongoing trainee performance.

5. Diagnose trainees' level of mastery and performance deficiencies.

6. Provide feedback and adapt instruction or provide remediation.

Conceptualizing the instructional design process in these terms provides a viable mechanism in which to couch a research agenda for SLEs; therefore, the tables of research tasks that follow are organized around these six instructional events. Our goal in constructing the tables was to focus on variables that we believe must be addressed to optimize SLE design, concentrating on the unique impact of them on SLEs (as opposed to providing comprehensive summaries of past work). In addition, we have highlighted (in bold) a subset of these variables that we propose will have the highest payoff in terms of improving SLE design; as such, they represent a viable research agenda that can guide future efforts.

Phase 1: Elaborate Instructional Goals and Trigger Instructional Strategies and Motivation

The first of Sugrue and Clark's (2000) instructional events that needs to be supported in learning involves elaboration of the instructional goal. In this area, we believe that researchers must be concerned not only with communicating the goal of instruction to the learner but also with triggering effective instructional strategies and motivational processes that will increase the likelihood that instruction will be successful. Table 7.1 delineates the variables and research questions associated with goal elaboration and learning strategies and motivation that require attention with respect to SLE research and design. We propose that there are actually two ways in which SLE design can affect these variables. First, SLEs can be designed to trigger strategies in learners that have been demonstrated to be effective in past work, and/or they can be designed to have a direct impact on motivational variables that appear to facilitate learning. These are described in more detail in the sections that follow.

Triggering Effective Learning Strategies

A great deal of attention has been paid in recent years to better understanding the mechanisms by which learners adopt strategies that improve their own learning. A driving set of research questions with respect to SLEs concerns how to best induce or trigger these strategies by incorporating them into the design of the learning environment.

TABLE 7.1

Research Issues Associated With Goal Elaboration, Learning Strategies, and Motivation

Variable	Definition and/or Description	Sample Research Issues
Triggering Effective Learning Strategies		
Metacognition and self-regulation	Awareness of one's own cognitive processes, and ability to understand, control, and manipulate these	• Possibility to elicit metacognition in SLEs • Incorporation of metacognitive strategies into SLE design • Support of self-regulation through SLE design
Training goals	Degree to which trainees seek to develop competence by acquiring new skills and mastering novel situations	• Potential to induce a mastery orientation (frame) embedded within the SLE • Impact of typical gaming features (e.g., competition, and emphasis on score) on mastery orientation • Mechanisms to counteract potential game-induced performance orientation
Enhancing Motivation to Learn		
Meaningfulness of material	Degree to which trainees perceive relevance of training content to themselves and/or their jobs	• Mechanisms for communicating the relevance of targeted material that can be built into SLEs • Possibility of increasing perceived relevance through SLE design
Expectations for training	Nature of expectations that trainees have for what the training situation will be like and what it might yield	• Impact of expectations for SLEs (either positive or negative) on their effectiveness • Impact of experience with video games on expectations and outcomes

Metacognition and Self-Regulation

Central to most theories of learning and motivation is the notion that learners must actively participate in their own learning process. In fact, *metacognition* (Bransford, Brown, & Cocking, 1999) is broadly defined as having insight into one's own learning process. It includes a learner's knowledge about learning, of his or her own strengths and weaknesses, and of the demands of the learning task at hand. Metacognition also includes *self-regulation*, which generally refers to the more micro process of monitoring one's own progress toward learning goals (Kanfer & Ackerman, 1989; Kozlowski, Toney, et al., 2001). Self-regulated learning emphasizes cognitive, affective, and behavioral processes including planning, goal setting, self-monitoring, self-assessment, and self-efficacy. Moreover, evidence suggests that self-regulation skills can be successfully trained and that such training aids in learning (see Greiner & Karoly, 1976; Smith et al., 1997; Volet, 1991).

Several possibilities exist to employ the concept of self-regulation in SLE design. First, it may be possible to incorporate early material into the training itself that promotes self-monitoring (for example, by scripting self-assessments into the scenario or incorporating them into the course of game play). Smith et al. (1997) also suggested that self-regulation can be enhanced by encouraging trainees to adopt mastery goals or manipulating the learner's control over the learning process. These possibilities are explored further in subsequent sections.

Training Goals

Learning researchers make a distinction between mastery (or learning) goals, which emphasize the acquisition of knowledge and skills in trainees, and performance goals, which emphasize the demonstration of competence by trainees (see Ames & Archer, 1988; Kozlowski, Toney, et al., 2001). Although research indicates that goal orientation is an individual difference on the part of trainees (Dweck, 1986), it has also been shown to be a malleable characteristic that can be manipulated through induction or situational features (see Kozlowski, Gully, et al., 2001; Kozlowski, Toney, et al., 2001). Moreover, triggering mastery goals in trainees has been shown to enhance a number of important learning process variables. Kozlowski, Toney, et al. (2001) summarized these as use of better learning strategies by trainees, increased resilience to negative effects of failure in training, and more positive attitudes toward learning.

Performance goals, on the other hand, have generally been found to have negative (or no) consequences for learning except when the task is simple and clear feedback can be provided (Latham & Locke, 1991). However, evidence suggests that learning and performance goals may not be mutually exclusive (Button, Mathieu, & Zajac, 1996) and that each may have advantages at different phases of the learner's development (Kanfer, 1996). Specifically, learning goals may be more beneficial in early phases of training when trainees are susceptible to the effects of poor performance and strategy exploration is desired, whereas performance goals may be better later to sustain interest and motivation (Kozlowski, Toney, et al., 2001).

The issue of training goals is pertinent to SLEs (particularly educational games) in the following sense: The (inherent) tendency for games to "keep score" and emphasize competition may actually trigger a performance-oriented strategy because the learner's attention is directed toward how he or she is performing. In fact, a hallmark (albeit anecdotal) of popular games is that players are motivated to succeed despite repeated failure.

In early phases of training, evidence suggests that this tendency could be detrimental to deeper processing. Hence, further effort to understand how gaming features such as competition and scorekeeping affect goal orientation, learning, and performance is needed.

Moreover, the possibility that various inductions designed to elicit mastery-oriented behavior can be embedded into SLEs is a topic worthy of attention. For example, it may be possible to counteract the impact of scorekeeping by introducing a general mastery-oriented *frame* (induced prior to training). In this regard, Kozlowski and Bell (2006) demonstrated that although not as potent as goal content, mastery goal frames do benefit learning strategies. In addition, these researchers found that mastery-oriented goal frames in combination with performance goal content were better than performance frames coupled with performance goal content. More generally, SLE designs that encourage trainees to self-monitor (Carver & Scheier, 1982; Kozlowski, Toney, et al., 2001; Schunk, 1990) and build self-efficacy (Bandura, 1991; Gist & Mitchell, 1992) should be investigated.

Enhancing Motivation to Learn

Several classes of variables have been shown to be effective in enhancing motivation to learn and training outcomes. In this section, we are interested in learning-related perceptions that trainees hold with respect to the training situation itself. Our contention is that SLEs can (and should) be designed to modify these perceptions early in training in a way that increases the likelihood of training success.

Meaningfulness of Material

It is almost impossible to find modern instructional researchers or theorists who do not believe that learning is enhanced when it occurs in a context that is meaningful to learners (Bransford et al., 1999), particularly when dealing with adult learners. Instead, disagreements regarding this principle are really a matter of degree. In fact, many researchers converge on the conclusion that learning is enhanced when students are presented with relevant, meaningful learning goals and problems (e.g., see Bransford et al.; Clark & Wittrock, 2000; Cognition and Technology Group at Vanderbilt [CTGV], 2000; Perkins & Unger, 1999).

Related to meaningfulness of material is the notion of perceived value and instrumentality of training. Eccles and colleagues (e.g., Durik, Vida, & Eccles, 2006; Eccles, 2005) argued that subjective task values can affect learner motivation. Several types of subjective task values are important: attainment value (i.e., the importance of doing well on a particular task), intrinsic value (i.e., enjoyment experienced by engaging in a task), and utility value (i.e., perceived usefulness of achieving a task).

In general, SLEs should fare well as training approaches that provide meaningful material and perceived value to trainees because of their inherent reliance on realistic content and/or stimuli. In fact, this characteristic of SLEs may make them useful to train a wider range of learning tasks than has been typical in the past. For example, rather than viewing SLEs as simply practice environments (i.e., to build hands-on skills), researchers may perceive SLEs as having a greater role in fundamental knowledge acquisition within a domain. Viewed in this way, SLEs could provide a backdrop with which to impart declarative and procedural knowledge underlying complex performance, as well as skill-building environments.

Expectations for Training

Researchers have suggested that preconceived attitudes toward training are effective predictors of subsequent training outcomes (Cannon-Bowers, Salas, Tannenbaum, & Mathieu, 1995; Smith-Jentsch, Jentsch, Payne, & Salas, 1996). This is potentially a troublesome finding for researchers interested in implementing SLEs. Specifically, it might be that the introduction of an SLE (especially a game, but even a simulation or virtual world) is so different from the trainee's experience that it colors his or her expectations about how effective it can be, adversely influencing downstream learning. Indeed, some trainees may not readily accept the use of a game to train serious knowledge and skill. Although there is virtually no research with which to evaluate this hypothesis, it is clear that some students are at least dubious about being educated in computer-based environments (Bohlin & Hunt, 1995; Chiou, 2001) and that learning expectations do affect outcomes in computer-mediated instruction (Garland & Noyes, 2004). Similarly, even if the trainee has positive expectations about the outcomes of this type of learning, the effects might also be mitigated by negative attitudes of instructors or coaches who are adjunct to the learning experience (MacArthur & Malouf, 1991).

Conversely, if trainees are led to believe that they are going to play an educational game, their own experience with video games could have an impact on what they expect the game to be. If the educational game fails to meet trainee expectations (for reasons that have nothing to do with its efficacy as a learning device), its effectiveness could suffer. The implications of trainee expectations in SLE design will not be fully understood until sufficient research is done. However, in the short term we believe that attempts to train with SLEs should be prefaced with a deliberate attempt to both understand and adjust trainee expectations prior to training.

Phase 2: Present Information

An important instructional event described by Sugrue and Clark (2000) is presenting information. In the past, the choices of presentation strategy were far more limited in this regard than they are today. Hence, it is important to focus attention on how technology might be used to effectively present information, and even how it could improve upon traditional methods. In this regard, we believe that some information presentation strategies can also influence motivation to learn (having both a cognitive and affective focus), whereas others are more directly useful as mechanisms to support acquisition of knowledge (cognitive focus). Our summary of important variables in each of these areas is shown in Table 7.2.

TABLE 7.2

Research Issues Associated With Presenting Information

Variable	Definition/Description	Sample Research Issues
Cognitively Focused Information Presentation Strategies		
Examples and worked-out examples	Exemplary problems presented with or without solutions from an expert	• Best use of examples and worked-out examples in SLEs • Impact of example formats on learning • Incorporation of examples into story or scenario
Scaffolding	A temporary supporting framework that bridges the gap between what learners can and cannot do	• Best scaffolding strategies and techniques to support learning in SLES • Designing scaffolds to target lower ability trainees • Optimal fading strategy for scaffolds in learning
Cognitively and Affectively Focused Information Presentation Strategies		
Story and narrative	Elements that contribute to the background story: characters, plot, backstory, story arc, conflict, and so on	• Impact of story or narrative structure on learning • Elements of story most important to motivation and instruction • Use of narrative elements to guide learning and self-regulation
Active participation	Degree to which the learner is cognitively and behaviorally engaged in the learning process	• Ensuring high degrees of active participation in learning through SLE design • Providing needed guidance to support learner control • Impact of active participation on emotional and motivational processes in SLEs

Cognitively Focused Information Presentation Strategies

As noted, we believe that SLEs have generally been underutilized as mechanisms to impart declarative knowledge. However, several lines of research have identified strategies for presenting declarative and procedural knowledge that can be incorporated into SLE design. These are described in the following sections.

Examples and Worked-Out Examples

With respect to the use of examples to support learning, Anderson and Schunn (2000) argued that the use of examples is a primary mechanism for learners to acquire procedural knowledge. This view contends that when a learner confronts a new problem (and hence has a goal to solve the problem), he or she needs to be shown an example of the solution. Anderson and Schunn went on to explain that to be successful, the example must be understood—in terms of its relevance both to the current problem and to what exactly is being conveyed. These factors place a premium on the explanations that accompany examples in learning.

The use of worked-out examples, where learners are given an example of a problem that has been solved by an expert, has also been studied extensively. According to Sweller, van Merriënboer, and Paas (1998; also see Sweller, 1999), learning is enhanced and time to train reduced when worked-out examples are substituted for practice problems because they reduce the cognitive load on the user (also see Paas, Renkl, and Sweller, 2003; Sweller, 2006). Recent studies also indicate that this effect holds for trainees with less prior knowledge in a domain (where necessary schemas are not available to guide problem solving) but is reversed for trainees with extensive prior knowledge (Kalyuga, Chandler, Tuovinen, & Sweller, 2001).

There is also evidence to suggest that when learners are required to generate an organization of examples in learning, transfer of learning is enhanced (DiVesta & Peverly, 1984). One explanation for this finding is that trainee-generated organization of examples may be more decontextualized than instructor-provided examples (Clark & Voogel, 1985; Smith et al., 1997), leading to more adaptive performance.

Given these findings, it seems likely that examples and worked-out examples comprise a promising strategy. SLEs provide a viable mechanism in which to embed and manipulate examples and worked-out examples in learning. The challenge for researchers will be to determine how best to incorporate these into the SLE for maximum benefit. Here again, we believe that the most successful strategies will be those that are naturally embedded into the scenario or story.

Scaffolding

The notion that a simulated learning environment must incorporate appropriate scaffolds for learners as a means to guide them through the learning process has received some attention in the literature. For example, Bransford et al. (1999) discussed the use of technology to scaffold experience. They used the analogy of "training wheels" as a means to explain how computerized tools can be used to support learning that students would otherwise be unable to accomplish. According to Puntambekar and Hübscher (2005), instructional scaffolds enable novices to solve a problem or accomplish a task that they would not be able to complete on their own. Further, these researchers asserted that a crucial feature of scaffolds is fading, that is, removing the support so that the learner can take control.

Hannafin, Land, and Oliver (1999) described several methods and mechanisms for scaffolding, including conceptual, metacognitive, procedural, and strategic ones. Scaffolds can take graphic form or include explicit representations of tacit aspects of the task. For example, Cuevas, Fiore, and Oser (2002) demonstrated a positive impact of scaffolding (in the form of diagrams) on both cognitive and metacognitive processes in learning. Moreover, adaptive scaffolding has been shown to improve students' ability to self-regulate (Azevedo, Cromley, & Seibert, 2004).

With respect to SLE design, there are vast opportunities to scaffold learner performance, including adaptive scaffolds that change and fade over time. In particular, graphically based scaffolds are a natural choice in SLEs because they can be embedded relatively easily and unobtrusively. The precise nature and implementation of scaffolding in SLEs merit further inquiry.

Cognitively and Affectively Focused Information Presentation Strategies

Besides having the obvious benefit of improving the comprehension and retention of knowledge, we believe that some of the information presentation strategies studied by past researchers also have motivational value. That is, they not only guide the trainee's acquisition of knowledge but also do so in a way that keeps the trainee involved and motivated to learn.

Active Participation

Most modern instructional theorists and educational researchers have converged on the conclusion that active participation by learners is a crucial feature of instructional design. For example, Chi (2000) contended that there is abundant evidence (albeit indirect in some cases) that learners benefit from active involvement in learning. Anderson and Schunn (2000) asserted that procedural knowledge is acquired through analogy—learners make reference to past problems while actively attempting to solve new ones. Further, Mayer (2001) pointed out an important distinction between behavioral activity and cognitive activity in learning, arguing that cognitive activity is what is crucial for learning to occur, so that even learners who appear to be actively participating (i.e., as manifest in their behavior) may not be learning unless cognitive activity is also taking place. Moreover, according to Bell and Kozlowski (2008), active learning is a key strategy for developing adaptive expertise and promoting transfer of learning.

However, considerable research has also shown that active learning must be supported (i.e., giving learners complete control without some guidance has not yielded favorable results; see Brown, 2001; Steinberg, 1989). Recently, Kozlowski and colleagues (Bell & Kozlowski, 2008; Kozlowski, Toney, et al., 2001) expanded the definition of *active learning* to include cognitive, emotional, and motivational processes that characterize the way in which trainees focus attention, direct effort, and manage emotion in learning. Bell and Kozlowski reviewed popular approaches to active learning and then tested important components independently. Among other things, they found that a more active, exploratory approach to learning (as opposed to proceduralized instruction) benefited transfer of training but not performance during training.

As with other variables we have discussed, an important consideration in SLE design is how to achieve an appropriate degree of active learning. More work along the lines of Bell and Kozlowski (under review) is needed.

Story and Narrative

Although much of the research related to SLEs is focused on relatively concrete aspects of the environments, such as learning content or fidelity, there is an emerging interest in some of the "softer" elements of design, such as narrative. It seems reasonable to hypothesize that likely mediating factors such as presence (i.e., the feeling of being present in the virtual environment) and engagement (see below) are directly affected by the richness of the narrative or story that underlies the simulation. In fact, one way to help learners to perceive relevance and meaningfulness may be by building compelling stories as the backdrop for training. This is related to the notion of scenario design, but in this sense it refers more to the degree to which the learning environment can spark the learner's interest and foster greater effort.

Further, in environments where there is not a teacher or coach to provide guidance, narrative elements might be an important factor in guiding the learner through the experience (Laurillard, Stratford, Luckin, Plowman, & Taylor, 2000; Plowman, 2005). As such, there is an emerging interest in combining tools derived from narrative theory with guidance from learning theory to create effective computer-presented learning stories (Voithofer, 2004). Although the research in this area is sparse, there are some data to suggest that specific narrative elements can aid in computer-presented learning (Plowman; Wolfe, 2002). Clearly, there is a need for a much more rigorous program of research to better understand this issue.

Phase 3: Develop Practice Environments

Another crucial instructional event included in Sugrue and Clark's (2000) framework is creating practice environments for instruction. In this regard, the work cited above (as well as work by other researchers) converges on the conclusion that skill development is enhanced when learners are provided a realistic context in which to practice targeted material. This principle has extensive implications for the design of SLEs. However, current knowledge in exactly how to create effective simulation-based practice environments is not specific enough to provide robust guidelines for designers.

In this area, we actually see three related categories of variables. There are those that contribute to the realism of the experience (and presumably enhance generalizability and transfer), there are those that provide incentives for engaging in the learning system (and therefore motivate trainees), and there are those that contribute to both realism and motivation. Table 7.3 summarizes major variables needing further investigation in these categories.

Factors That Contribute to Realism

If our underlying thesis—that SLEs are effective (at least in part) because they provide synthetic experience to trainees—is correct, then the issue of how realistic the simulation is becomes a driving question. However, as described below, it may not be realism per se that is crucial; rather, it may be more a question of the adequacy of the simulation for achieving the specific learning objectives that is most important.

Fidelity

An important issue related to the design of SLEs has to do with the fidelity of models and simulations that underlie the system (i.e., the degree to which the simulation is a faithful representation of the real phenomenon or task; Andrews & Bell, 2000). The underlying issue here is related to the

TABLE 7.3

Research Issues Associated With Developing Practice Environments

Variable	Definition	Sample Research Issues
Factors That Contribute to Realism		
Fidelity (physical)	Degree to which SLE is a faithful representation of the real phenomenon or task	• Optimal degree of physical fidelity given learning objectives • Use of multiple modalities in the SLE
Scenario and case design	Controlled vignettes designed to trigger appropriate behavior based on learning objectives	• Essential features of effective scenarios • Principles of scenario and case design to optimize learning • Determining the appropriate level of challenge in scenario events
Features That Contribute to Realism and Motivation		
Authenticity (cognitive and emotional)	Degree to which SLE causes learners to engage in cognitive and emotional processes similar to those in the real world	• Optimal degree of authenticity in the synthetic experience to improve learning • Role of emotional authenticity in learning and transfer • Mechanisms to enhance authenticity in SLEs
Immersion, emotional intensity, and engagement	Degree to which learner feels he or she is a part of the synthetic experience; emotional intensity of the experience	• Better understanding of the constructs of immersion, engagement, and presence in SLEs • Impact of immersion and emotional intensity on training effectiveness in SLEs • Mechanisms to enhance engagement
Features That Provide Incentives		
Reward and social status	Degree to which the SLE provides intrinsic motivation and/or relies on reward and public recognition to motivate	• Maximizing intrinsic motivation in SLEs • Optimal use of rewards and competition to motivate learning • Impact of public recognition and social status on motivation
Embodiment and personalization	Manner in which learners are represented within the virtual or simulated game world	• Impact of embodiment on learning in an SLE • Impact of personalization of the avatar on motivation and engagement

transfer of specific knowledge and skill to the actual operational or job environment (Andrews & Bell). Specifically, if trainees are learning how to apply a particular skill, then the training (simulated) environment must respond in a manner that is similar to what would occur in the real world.

Otherwise, the trainee will receive incorrect feedback and perhaps learn the wrong things. In this regard, Hays and Singer (1989) distinguished between physical fidelity (i.e., the degree to which physical features of the simulation are represented, such as knobs and buttons) and cognitive fidelity (i.e., the degree to which the simulation faithfully represents conceptual aspects of the actual task). To be consistent with other work, we are using the term *authenticity* to refer to cognitive fidelity (see below). Hence, the issue with respect to fidelity is how closely the physical training environment must mimic the real world.

Recently, Kozlowski and DeShon (2004) described a comprehensive approach for conceptualizing a somewhat different but related construct—psychological fidelity. These researchers expanded the traditional approach to fidelity from a simple consideration of realism to a more complex consideration of the psychological constructs and processes responsible for effective performance (including cognitive, motivational, and behavioral ones). This approach is promising particularly because it can be used to develop lower fidelity (e.g., PC-based) simulations that are sufficient to achieve instructional goals.

Scenario and Case Design

A central question in designing simulation-based practice environments involves the design of scenarios or cases as the backdrop for instruction. Working in a team training environment, Cannon-Bowers, Salas, and colleagues (Cannon-Bowers, Burns, Salas, & Pruitt, 1998; Oser, Cannon-Bowers, Salas, & Dwyer, 1999; Salas & Cannon-Bowers, 2001) developed a method whereby specific trigger events are scripted into a scenario based on the learning objectives to be accomplished. These trigger events are designed to elicit desired behavior, to allow trainees to practice targeted skills, and to provide an opportunity to measure performance and deliver specific feedback (Salas & Cannon-Bowers). To date, the event-based approach to training has been successfully demonstrated in several settings (Dwyer, Oser, Salas, & Fowlkes, 1999; Fowlkes, Dwyer, & Oser, 1998). In a similar vein, Schank, Berman, and Macpherson (1999) advocated a strategy for developing goal-based scenarios or cases.

The design of scenarios must also consider the level of challenge in trigger events or activities. Several studies have found that incorporating *challenges* into learning has motivational benefits (Barron et al., 1995; CTGV, 2000). However, challenges that are beyond the capability of trainees may also be frustrating and actually impair progress. Related to this, Kozlowski, Toney, et al. (2001) recently summarized the implications of sequencing, complexity, variability, workload, and built-in errors of training tasks in embedded training systems, all of which have implications for how scenarios are designed.

Features That Contribute to Realism and Motivation

As noted, we believe that some variables related to the nature of practice environments contribute not only to their realism but also to how much they motivate trainees to use them. A description of these follows.

Authenticity

We use the term *authenticity* to refer to the cognitive and emotional fidelity of a synthetic environment (as opposed to physical fidelity, discussed previously). In past work, Jonassen (2000) discussed the notion of authenticity by pointing out that it does not necessarily mean that the instruction is developed around specific, real-world tasks. Rather, authenticity can best be thought of as the degree to which the learning environment causes learners to engage in cognitive processes that are similar to those in the real world (see Honebein, Duffy, & Fishman, 1993; Petraglia, 1998).

Importantly, authentic learning environments are proposed to be engaging to learners because they provide realistic, challenging problems to solve (e.g., CTGV, 2000). Hence, we contend that SLEs viewed as authentic will have learning value through enhanced motivation and direct learning effects. For this reason, the question is not whether authenticity is important; rather, it is what degree of authenticity is required to support learning and what contributes to an authentic experience.

Immersion, Emotional Intensity, and Engagement

Another issue that is related to motivation is the degree of immersion or presence experienced by the learner. *Immersion* is defined as the experience of feeling a part of the synthetic experience (Stanney, 2002) and is hypothesized by some to be a psychological state resulting from a participant's intense feelings of "presence" in the virtual world (Gerhard, Moore, & Hobbs, 2004). It has also been hypothesized that training effectiveness in virtual environments may be influenced by the degree to which trainees experience feelings of immersion or engagement (Knerr, Breaux, Goldberg, & Thurman, 2002). Research to support or refute this claim needs to be conducted.

Moreover, the tendency to experience immersion seems to be an individual difference (Kaber, Draper, & Usher, 2002), meaning that some people may be predisposed to benefit from immersive environments in training

(Knerr et al., 2002). Related to this, some limited evidence exists to suggest that the emotional intensity of the training experience may contribute to learning. For example, Morris, Hancock, and Shirkey (2004) found that adding context-relevant stress to a low-fidelity military simulation increased overall mission success (interpreted as an indication of motivation) but not necessarily skill acquisition.

A related topic is the idea of *flow*. Csikszentmihalyi (1990) described flow as an experience where an individual becomes so engaged in an activity that time becomes distorted, self-consciousness is forgotten, and external rewards disappear. Instead, people engage in complex, goal-directed behavior because it is inherently motivating. From a pedagogical standpoint, it is not clear whether or how this notion of flow in an SLE may affect the learning process. However, from a strictly time-on-task perspective (i.e., the amount of time engaging instructional content), it would follow that intense engagement should benefit learning.

Features That Provide Incentives

A final category of practice environment features that we discuss is not so much related to realism in the experience but can be considered adjunct features that can be added to the environment to enhance motivation directly through increased incentives.

Reward and Social Status

Decades of research into motivation, and especially intrinsic motivation, generally show that externalizing the reward for engaging in a behavior can reduce a person's intrinsic motivation to engage in it (cf. Deci, Koestner, & Ryan, 1999; Ryan & Deci, 2000). However, researchers have also found that under certain conditions, externalized rewards and competition can increase intrinsic motivation (Reeve & Deci, 1996). In particular, when an activity is seen as challenging, it allows the user to gain feelings of competence, and is not perceived as being controlling (i.e., forced on the user), intrinsic motivation does not suffer. In addition, when the user places importance on doing well, competition generates affective involvement in the activity and increases personal meaningfulness (Epstein & Harackiewicz, 1992).

In SLEs (and particularly games), reward and social status are typically integral to the game experience. Hence, it is important to better understand how these processes may affect learning in an SLE. The findings cited above (particularly Reeve & Deci, 1996) suggest that appropriately designed external rewards may not interfere with intrinsic motivation. Simply observing the popularity of video games (albeit anecdotal evidence) would bear out this possibility. Empirical investigation of this hypothesis is needed.

Embodiment and Personalization

User "embodiment" has become a topic of interest in recent years as the development of collaborative computer systems and virtual worlds has increased. The notion of *embodiment* refers to the mechanism of representation of the user in the virtual world. According to Gerhard et al. (2004), the notion of embodiment stems from philosophical writings about the meaning of the physical body. These researchers have argued that avatars that represent the user in the virtual world are important in establishing the user's identity in the world. In addition, avatars provide a basis for conversation and social interaction (Slater, Sadagic, Usoh, & Schroeder, 2000), which increases the sense of engagement in the simulation. In a learning system context, Moreno and Mayer (2004) found that personalizing the interaction with the student in a virtual environment improved learning and retention of science content. Baylor's (2001) work on intelligent agents and mentors similarly indicates a measurable impact of personalization and presentation style on learning outcomes. Hence, it appears that increasing a students' level of embodiment and personalization can increase engagement and learning in an SLE.

Phases 4, 5, and 6: Monitor, Diagnose, and Adapt Instruction

The final three instructional events delineated by Sugrue and Clark (2000) are monitoring student performance during learning, diagnosing the causes of effective and ineffective performance, and adapting instruction accordingly. Implicit in this series of activities is the notion that learners must receive feedback that helps to inform them of their progress and gives them information about how to improve if necessary. We have combined these processes into Table 7.4, with explanations following.

Monitoring Performance

Dynamic Assessment

With respect to monitoring learner performance, an issue that needs attention involves how to dynamically collect performance data during learning. In this regard, Anderson and Schunn (2000) concluded that there is great

TABLE 7.4

Research Issues Associated With Monitoring, Diagnosing, and Adapting

Variable	Definition and/or Description	Sample Research Issues
Monitoring Performance		
Dynamic assessment	Automated techniques and strategies for collecting and interpreting performance information during learning	• Methods for developing cognitively diagnostic measures within SLEs • Specification of metrics that can be tracked by the learning system • Instrumentation of the SLE to capture necessary performance data
Diagnosing Performance		
Diagnostic models	Learner performance models that interpret dynamically collected performance data for comparison to an expert model	• Design of diagnostic models for dynamically interpreting and diagnosing ongoing performance • Modeling of expert performance to provide a comparison for ongoing trainee behavior
Providing Feedback and Adapting Instruction		
Feedback (online and post training)	Information provided to learners regarding their performance as well as their progress in achieving learning objectives	• Most important features of feedback displays in SLEs • Establishing conditions under which immediate or delayed feedback is more effective • Investigating the timing, sequence, and nature of feedback in SLEs
Automated guidance and coaching	Aiding learners by organizing and structuring knowledge, identifying and clarifying misconceptions, and prompting reflection	• Best strategies for incorporating computer-generated coaching in SLE design • Mechanisms for providing adaptive guidance to trainees • Optimizing the utility of feedback to aid self-regulation, self-efficacy, and learning

potential for applying cognitive theory to the issue of diagnosing learner performance. However, the difficulty is in finding behavioral (observable) indicants that allow such theories to be applied. Moreover, only limited efforts to instrument learning environments have been accomplished so that such information can be collected dynamically (e.g., Cannon-Bowers et al., 1998). More work in this area is needed. In particular, unobtrusive methods to collect and interpret data such as keystrokes, button or mouse actions, eye movements, verbal responses, protocol analysis, and even facial expression and gesturing must be further developed.

Diagnosing Performance

Diagnostic Models

Once collected, learner performance data must be interpreted in a manner that allows conclusions about learner mastery to be drawn. This implies two capabilities: First is the ability to interpret dynamically collected performance data in a manner that allows meaningful diagnosis to occur, and second is the ability to develop a means to compare this "observed" performance to an expert standard. Again working in the intelligent tutoring arena (e.g., Gott & Lesgold, 2000) have used cognitive task analysis methods to establish "expert" models of performance. Embedded into the instructional system, such models provide a basis for real-time comparison of current student performance (which is organized into dynamic student models) with what would be expected by an expert. Gott and Lesgold (2000) emphasized that this ability is enhanced when progressively sophisticated models of the expert (i.e., that describe not only ultimate performance but also important waypoints in learning) are employed. Further work is necessary to codify a set of guidelines and develop tools to aid in model development.

Providing Feedback and Adapting Instruction

Providing Feedback

A tremendous amount of work has been done regarding how to provide feedback to enhance learning and transfer, with issues such as the frequency, specificity, and timing of feedback of central interest (see Kozlowski, Toney, et al., 2001, for a good summary). Clearly, feedback is the central mechanism by which learners can regulate their own performance and understand how to improve. According to Bransford et al. (1999), opportunities for feedback should be frequent and/or continuous.

It has also been suggested that feedback must help learners to understand how to *change* their performance in order to improve (i.e., simply providing learners with knowledge of results is insufficient because it may not suggest ways to improve performance; Bransford et al., 1999). In this regard, Kozlowski, Toney, et al. (2001) distinguished the information properties of feedback from its interpretation properties. Further, these researchers contended that feedback can be interpreted in several ways— it can be evaluative (e.g., positive or negative), attributional (e.g., internal or external), or used to provide appropriate guidance. They presented specific principles for each type of feedback, and specific propositions for how feedback should be constructed and delivered over the course of training.

Recently, it has also been argued that feedback strategies that promote deeper processing are superior to achieve transfer of learning. For example, intermittent feedback may help trainees to be less dependent on continuous reinforcement (Schmidt & Bjork, 1992; Shute & Gawlick, 1995). Mathan and Koedinger (2005) found that a feedback strategy based on guiding trainees through error detection and correction resulted in a deeper conceptual understanding of domain principles and better transfer of skills over time.

Clearly, SLEs offer unprecedented opportunities to provide feedback in real time and to control the amount and timing of feedback that a trainee receives. In addition, even when online feedback is not possible or appropriate (for example, when reflection in trainees is desired—see Smith-Jentsch et al., 1996), SLEs can be useful in collecting and interpreting performance data that are crucial to postexercise feedback sessions. Research is needed to better understand how to make full use of this capability; propositions offered by Kozlowski, Toney, et al. (2001) provided needed direction in this area.

Another important issue regarding feedback that is more specific to SLEs is that it is delivered in a way that does not interfere with the trainee's feelings of immersion. By this, we mean that efforts to deliver feedback need to be constructed so that they are well integrated into the scenario or story. Failing to do this may cause cognitive and/or emotional disruption that is detrimental to learning.

Adaptive Guidance and Coaching

Coaching has been implicated as a means to enhance learning for understanding (e.g., see Bransford et al., 1999; Jonassen, 2000). For example, as part of an effort to develop intelligent practice environments for troubleshooting skills, Gott and Lesgold (2000) implemented an intelligent coach, which gave adaptive feedback that was based on cognitive task analysis results indicating the manner in which expertise develops in this domain. Likewise, Bell and Kozlowski (2002) improved outcomes by providing adaptive (performance-based) guidance to trainees that helped them to understand future directions that must be taken for improvement. Further, Smith et al. (1997) argued that appropriate guidance is necessary to augment discovery learning environments so that they are more efficient and effective.

More work is needed to determine how and when adaptive coaching and guidance can be incorporated into SLEs, and to address the technical issues associated with modeling performance so that guidance can be tailored to the specific needs of the trainee. Once again, there is also an issue of how to embed guidance naturally into an SLE so that it is not disruptive. The coaching metaphor may be useful in this regard.

Conclusions

Obviously, much work needs to be done in order to realize the full potential of SLEs in workplace learning. In this regard, we recommend three areas in need of attention: (a) development of a research agenda for this area, (b) an enhanced research strategy for conducting and reporting research, and (c) concerted efforts to overcome the challenges inherent in completing empirical work in this area. These are discussed further in the following paragraphs.

For reasons discussed previously, our strongest recommendation is for researchers to establish and adopt a research agenda to guide future work in this area. We believe that the framework we presented here can provide a reasonable first attempt at this (although we realize that it would benefit from further development). In fact, the highlighted variables in the tables represent what we view as the research priorities and, as such, can provide a viable research agenda in this area. In selecting these variables, we tried to focus on features that we believe would have a high payoff in terms of improved learning but were relatively straightforward to implement. For example, understanding better the manner in which scorekeeping, competition, and other features foster or inhibit training goals could be a highly effective way to improve learning for a relatively small cost (in terms of design changes). In other cases, we selected variables for which SLEs provide a unique opportunity (e.g., authenticity and narrative) to study the impact of that feature. Taken together, these variables provide a good start at "charting the territory" in terms of designing research studies.

A second set of recommendations has to do with changing how research in this area is conducted so as to contribute to meaningful advances in the field. Specifically, we offer several recommendations for future research that we believe can help establish a true science of SLEs: (a) Adopt a *systems view* when conducting research by incorporating factors that surround the training system, as well as those within the training system itself; (b) identify variables that may be *causal* factors in the SLE design, and include these as part of the investigation (i.e., manipulate and or control them if possible); (c) include *more information* in empirical studies (description of the participants, learning tasks, and organization) even if none of these factors is being manipulated so that future researchers can better interpret results and assess generalizability; and (d) move toward a establishing a *taxonomy* or common language for describing tasks to help determine generalizability of results based on underlying task demands. All of these factors will contribute to the ability of results to be interpreted, generalized, and incorporated into a theoretical framework (such as the one proposed in this chapter) that can systematically advance the field.

Finally, we acknowledge a number of challenges in conducting this type of research. First of all, access and availability of high-quality SLEs for testing are often limited. The cost and time needed to develop viable SLEs for use in research programs often exceed available resources. One possible solution to this problem is for research groups to team with industry so that development efforts can become an opportunity for investigation. In addition, establishing multidisciplinary teams (including artists, programmers, writers, producers, and training specialists) across typical university boundaries may allow researchers to reduce the costs associated with test bed development.

Overall, we are optimistic about the future of SLEs in workplace training. Certainly, they offer great potential as a means to train the modern workforce. Indeed, SLEs provide unique advantages that enable them to address the complex, higher order skills that are required to be successful in many jobs. Our hope is that serious researchers take up the challenge of better understanding how to develop and deploy SLEs for training.

References

Abell, M., & Galinsky, M. (2002). Introducing students to computer-based group work practice. *Journal of Social Work Education, 38*, 39–54.

Ames, C., & Archer, J. (1988). Achievement goals in the classroom: Students' learning strategies and motivation processes. *Journal of Educational Psychology, 80*, 260–267.

Anderson, J., & Schunn, C. (2000). Implications of the ACT-R learning theory: No magic bullets. In R. Glaser (Ed.), *Advances in instructional psychology: Educational design and cognitive science* (Vol. 5, pp. 1–33). Mahwah, NJ: Lawrence Erlbaum Associates.

Andrews, D. H., & Bell, H. H. (2000). Simulation-based training. In S. Tobias & J. D. Fletcher (Eds.), *Training and retraining: A handbook for business, industry, government, and the military* (pp. 357–384). New York: Macmillan.

Azevedo, R., Cromley, J., & Seibert, D. (2004). Does adaptive scaffolding facilitate students' ability to regulate their learning with hypermedia? *Contemporary Educational Psychology, 29*, 344–370.

Bandura, A. (1991). Human agency: The rhetoric and the reality. *American Psychologist, 46*, 157–162.

Barron, B., Vye, N., Zech, L., Schwartz, D., Bransford, J., Goldman, S., et al. (1995). Creating contexts for community-based problem solving: "The Jasper Challenge Series." In C. N. Hedley, P. Antonacci, & M. Rabinowitz (Eds.), *Thinking and literacy: The mind at work* (pp. 47–71). Hillsdale, NJ: Lawrence Erlbaum Associates.

Baylor, A. L. (2001). Agent-based learning environments for investigating teaching and learning. *Journal of Educational Computing Research, 26*, 249–270.

Bell, B. S., & Kozlowski, S. W. J. (2002). Adaptive guidance: Enhancing self-regulation, knowledge, and performance in technology-based training. *Personnel Psychology, 55,* 267–306.

Bell, B. S., & Kozlowski, S. W. J. (2008). Active learning: Effects of coretraining design elements on self-regulatory processes, learning, and adaptability. *Journal of Applied Psychology, 93,* 296–316.

Bohlin, R., & Hunt, N. (1995). Course structure effects on students' computer anxiety, confidence and attitudes. *Journal of Educational Computing Research, 13,* 263–270.

Bransford, J. D., Brown, A. L., & Cocking, R. R. (Eds.). (1999). *How people learn: Brain, mind, experience, and school.* Washington, DC: National Academy Press.

Brown, K. G. (2001). Using computers to deliver training: Which employees learn and why? *Personnel Psychology, 54,* 217–296.

Button, S., Mathieu, J., & Zajac, D. (1996). Goal orientation in organizational research: A conceptual and empirical foundation. *Organizational Behavior and Human Decision Processes, 67,* 26–48.

Cameron, B., & Dwyer, F. (2005). The effect of online gaming, cognition and feedback type in facilitating delayed achievement of different learning objectives. *Journal of Interactive Learning Research, 16,* 243–258.

Cannon–Bowers, J. A., & Bowers, C. A. (2008). Synthetic learning environments. In J. M. Spector, M. David Merrill, J. J. G. van Merriënboer, & M. P. Driscoll (Eds.), *Handbook of research on educational communications and technology* (3rd ed., pp. 317–328). Mahwah, NJ: Lawrence Erlbaum Associates.

Cannon-Bowers, J. A., Burns, J., Salas, E., & Pruitt, J. (1998). Advanced technology in scenario-based training. In J. Cannon-Bowers & E. Salas (Eds.), *Making decisions under stress: Implications for individual and team training* (pp. 365–374). Washington, DC: APA Books.

Cannon-Bowers, J. A., Salas, E., Tannenbaum, S. I., & Mathieu, J. E. (1995). Toward theoretically-based principles of training effectiveness: A model and initial empirical investigation. *Military Psychology, 7,* 141–164.

Carver, C., & Scheier, M. (1982). Control theory: A useful conceptual framework for personality-social, clinical, and health psychology. *Psychological Bulletin, 92,* 111–135.

Chi, M. T. H. (2000). Self-explaining: The dual processes of generating inference and repairing mental models. In R. Glaser (Ed.), *Advances in instructional psychology: Educational design and cognitive science* (Vol. 5, pp. 161–238). Mahwah, NJ: Lawrence Erlbaum Associates.

Chi, M. T. H., Glaser, R., & Farr, M. J. (Eds.). (1988). *The nature of expertise.* Hillsdale, NJ: Lawrence Erlbaum Associates.

Chiou, J. (2001). Horizontal and vertical individualism and collectivism among college students in the United States, Taiwan, and Argentina. *Journal of Social Psychology, 141,* 667–678.

Clark, R., & Voogel, A. (1985). Transfer of training principles for instructional design. *Educational Communication & Technology Journal, 33,* 113–123.

Clark, R., & Wittrock, M. C. (2000). Psychological principles in training. In S. Tobias & J. D. Fletcher (Eds.), *Training and retraining: A handbook for business, industry, government, and the military* (pp. 51–84). New York: Macmillan.

Cognition and Technology Group at Vanderbilt (CTGV). (2000). Adventures in anchored instruction: Lessons from beyond the ivory tower. In R. Glaser (Ed.), *Advances in instructional psychology: Educational design and cognitive science* (Vol. 5, pp. 35–99). Mahwah, NJ: Lawrence Erlbaum Associates.

Csikszentmihalyi, M. (1990). *Flow: The psychology of optical experience.* New York: Harper Perennial.

Cuevas, H., Fiore, S., & Oser, R. (2002). Scaffolding cognitive and metacognitive processes in low verbal ability learners: Use of diagrams in computer-based training environments. *Instructional Science, 30,* 433–464.

Deci, E. L., Koestner, R., & Ryan, R. M. (1999). A meta-analytic review of experiments examining the effects of extrinsic rewards on intrinsic motivation. *Psychological Bulletin, 125,* 627–668.

DeGroot, A. (1965). *Thought and choice in chess.* The Hague: Mouton.

DiVesta, F. J., & Peverly, S. T. (1984). The effects of encoding variability, processing activity, and rule-example sequence on the transfer of conceptual rules. *Journal of Educational Psychology, 76,* 108–119.

Durik, A., Vida, M., & Eccles, J. (2006). Task values and ability beliefs as predictors of high school literacy choices: A developmental analysis. *Journal of Educational Psychology, 98*(2), 382–393.

Dweck, C. S. (1986). Motivation processes affecting learning. *American Psychologist, 41,* 1040–1048.

Dwyer, D. J., Oser, R. L., Salas, E., & Fowlkes, J. E. (1999). Performance measurement in distributed environments: Initial results and implications for training. *Military Psychology, 11,* 189–215.

Eccles, J. (2005). Subjective task value and the Eccles et al. model of achievement-related choices. In A. J. Elliot & C. S. Dweck (Eds.), *Handbook of competence and motivation* (pp. 105–121). New York: Guilford.

Egan, D. E., & Schwartz, B. J. (1979). Chunking in recall of symbolic drawings. *Memory & Cognition, 7,* 149–158.

Ellis, R., Marcus, G., & Taylor, R. (2005). Learning through inquiry: Student difficulties with online course-based material. *Journal of Computer Assisted Learning, 21,* 239–252.

Epstein, J. A., & Harackiewicz, J. M. (1992). Winning is not enough: The effects of competition and achievement motivation on intrinsic interest. *Personality and Social Psychology Bulletin, 18,* 128–138.

Fletcher, J. D., & Tobias, S. (2006, February). *Using computer games and simulations for instruction: A research review.* Paper presented at the Society for Applied Learning Technology, Orlando, FL.

Fowlkes, J., Dwyer, D., & Oser, R. (1998). Event-based approach to training. *International Journal of Aviation Psychology, 8,* 209–222.

Galvao, J. R., Martins, P. G., & Gomes, M. R. (2000). Modeling reality with simulation games for a cooperative learning. In J. A. Joines, R. R. Barton, K. Kang, & P. A. Fishwick (Eds.), *Proceedings of the 2000 Winter Simulation Conference* (pp. 1692–1698). Piscataway, NJ: IEEE.

Garland, K., & Noyes, J. (2004). The effects of mandatory and optional use on students' ratings of a computer-based learning package. *British Journal of Educational Technology, 35,* 263–273.

Gerhard, M., Moore, D., & Hobbs, D. (2004). Embodiment and copresence in collaborative interfaces. *International Journal of Human–Computer Studies, 61,* 453–480.

Gist, M., & Mitchell, T. (1992). Self-efficacy: A theoretical analysis of its determinants and malleability. *Academy of Management Review, 17,* 183–211.

Glaser, R. (1989). Expertise in learning: How do we think about instructional processes now that we have discovered knowledge structure? In D. Klahr & D. Kotosfky (Eds.), *Complex information processing: The impact of Herbert A. Simon* (pp. 269–282). Hillsdale, NJ: Lawrence Erlbaum Associates.

Gobet, F., & Simon, H. A. (1996). Recall of random and distorted positions: Implications for the theory of expertise. *Memory and Cognition, 24,* 493–503.

Goeters, K. (2002). Evaluation of the effects of CRM training by the assessment of non-technical skills under LOFT. *Human Factors and Aerospace Safety, 2,* 71–86.

Goettl, B., & Shute, V. (1996). Analysis of part-task training using the backward-transfer technique. *Journal of Experimental Psychology: Applied, 2,* 227–249.

Gott, S. P., & Lesgold, A. M. (2000). Competence in the workplace: How cognitive performance models and situated instruction can accelerate skill acquisition. In R. Glaser (Ed.), *Advances in instructional psychology: Educational design and cognitive science* (Vol. 5, pp. 239–327). Mahwah, NJ: Lawrence Erlbaum Associates.

Gredler, M. E. (2004). *Games and simulations and their relationships to learning.* Mahwah, NJ: Lawrence Erlbaum Associates.

Green, C., & Bavelier, D. (2003). Action video game modifies visual selective attention. *Nature, 423,* 534–537.

Greiner, J., & Karoly, P. (1976). Effects of self-control training on study activity and academic performance: An analysis of self-monitoring, self-reward, and systematic-planning components. *Journal of Counseling Psychology, 23,* 495–502.

Hannafin, M., Land, S., & Oliver, K. (1999). Open learning environments: Foundation, methods, and models. In C. M. Reigeluth (Ed.), *Instructional-design theories and models: A new paradigm of instructional theory* (Vol. 2, pp. 115–140). Mahwah, NJ: Lawrence Erlbaum Associates.

Hays, R. T., & Singer, M. J. (1989). *Simulation fidelity in training system design.* New York: Springer-Verlag.

Honebein, P. C., Duffy, T. M., & Fishman, B. J. (1993). Constructivism and the design of learning environments: Context and authentic activities for learning. In T. M. Duffy, J. Lowyck, & D. H. Jonassen (Eds.), *Designing environments for constructive learning* (pp. 87–108). New York: Springer-Verlag.

Jentsch, F., & Bowers, C. A. (1998). Evidence for the validity of PC-based simulations in studying aircrew coordination. *The International Journal of Aviation Psychology, 8*(3), 243–260.

Jonassen, D. H. (2000). Revisiting activity theory as a framework for designing student-centered learning environments. In D. H. Jonassen & S. M. Land (Eds.), *Theoretical foundations of learning environments* (pp. 89–121). Mahwah, NJ: Lawrence Erlbaum Associates.

Kaber, D. B., Draper, J. V., & Usher, J. M. (2002). Influence of individual differences on application design for individual and collaborative immersive virtual environments. In K. Stanney (Ed.), *Handbook of virtual environments: Design, implementation, and applications* (pp. 379–402). Mahwah, NJ: Lawrence Erlbaum Associates.

Kalyuga, S., Chandler, P., Tuovinen, J., & Sweller, J. (2001). When problem solving is superior to studying worked examples. *Journal of Educational Psychology, 93,* 579–588.

Kanfer, R. (1996). Self-regulatory and other non-ability determinants of skill acquisition. In P. M. Gollwitzer & J. A. Bargh (Eds.), *The psychology of action: Linking cognition and motivation to behavior* (pp. 404–423). New York: Guilford.

Kanfer, R., & Ackerman, P. (1989). Motivation and cognitive abilities: An integrative/aptitude treatment interaction approach to skill acquisition. *Journal of Applied Psychology, 74,* 657–690.

Knerr, B. W., Breaux, R., Goldberg, S. L., & Thurman, R. A. (2002). National defense. In K. Stanney (Ed.), *Handbook of virtual environments: Design, implementation, and applications* (pp. 857–872). Mahwah, NJ: Lawrence Erlbaum Associates.

Kolb, D. A. (1984). *Experiential learning: Experience as the source of learning and development.* Englewood Cliffs, NJ: Prentice Hall.

Kolb, D. A., Boyatzis, R. E., & Mainemelis, C. (2001). Experiential learning theory: Previous research and new directions. In R. J. Sternberg & L. Zhang (Eds.), *Perspectives on thinking, learning, and cognitive styles: The educational psychology series* (pp. 227–247). Mahwah, NJ; Lawrence Erlbaum Associates.

Kozlowski, S. W. J., & Bell, B. S. (2006). Disentangling achievement orientation and goal setting: Effects on self-regulatory processes. *Journal of Applied Psychology, 91*(4), 900–916.

Kozlowski, S. W. J., & DeShon, R. P. (2004). A psychological fidelity approach to simulation-based training: Theory, research, and principles. In E. Salas, L. R. Elliott, S. G. Schiflett, & M. D. Coovert (Eds.), *Scaled worlds: Development, validation, and applications* (pp. 75–99). Burlington, VT: Ashgate.

Kozlowski, S., Gully, S., Brown, K., Salas, E., Smith, E., & Nason, E. (2001). Effects of training goals and goal orientation traits on multidimensional training outcomes and performance adaptability. *Organizational Behavior and Human Decision Processes, 85,* 1–31.

Kozlowski, S., Toney, R., Mullins, M., Weissbein, D., Brown, K., & Bell, B. (2001). Developing adaptability: A theory for the design of integrated-embedded training systems. In E. Salas (Ed.), *Advances in human performance and cognitive engineering research* (pp. 59–123). Stamford, CT: Elsevier Science/JAI.

Lane, J., Slavin, S., & Ziv, A. (2001). Simulation in medical education: A review. *Simulation & Gaming, 32,* 297–314.

Latham, G., & Locke, E. (1991). Self-regulation through goal setting. *Organizational Behavior and Human Decision Processes, 50,* 212–247.

Laurillard, D., Stratfold, M., Luckin, R., Plowman, L., & Taylor, J. (2000). Affordances for learning in a non-linear narrative medium. *Journal of Interactive Media in Education,* (2). Retrieved February 20, 2008, from http://www-jime.open.ac.uk/00/2/

Lesgold, A. (1988). Toward a theory of curriculum for use in designing intelligent instructional systems. In H. Mandl & A. Lesgold (Eds.), *Learning issues for intelligent tutoring systems* (pp. 114–137). New York: Springer-Verlag.

Link, M., Armsby, P., Hubal, R., & Guinn, C. (2006). Accessibility and acceptance of responsive virtual human technology as a survey interviewer training tool. *Computers in Human Behavior, 22*, 412–426.

Logan, G. D. (1988). Toward an instance theory of automatization. *Psychological Review, 95*, 492–527.

MacArthur, C., & Malouf, D. (1991). Teachers' beliefs, plans, and decisions about computer-based instruction. *Journal of Special Education, 25*, 44–72.

Mathan, S., & Koedinger, K. (2005). Fostering the intelligent novice: Learning from errors with metacognitive tutoring. *Educational Psychologist, 40*(4), 257–265.

Mayer, R. E. (2001). *Multimedia learning*. Cambridge: Cambridge University Press.

Moreno, R., & Mayer, R. E. (2004). Personalized messages that promote science learning in virtual environments. *Journal of Educational Psychology, 96*, 165–173.

Morris, C., Hancock, P., & Shirkey, E. (2004). Motivational effects of adding context relevant stress in PC-based game training. *Military Psychology, 16*, 135–147.

Oser, R., Cannon-Bowers, J., Salas, E., & Dwyer, D. (1999). Enhancing human performance in technology-rich environments: Guidelines for scenario-based training. In W. B. Rouse (Ed.), *Human/technology interaction in complex systems* (Vol. 9, pp. 175–202). Stamford, CT: Elsevier Science/JAI.

Paas, F., Renkl, A., & Sweller, J. (2003). Cognitive load theory and instructional design: Recent developments. *Educational Psychologist, 38*, 1–4.

Pederson, P. B. (2003). *"Walking the talk": Simulations in multicultural training*. Alexandria, VA: Association for Multicultural Counseling and Development.

Perkins, D. N., & Unger, C. (1999). Teaching and learning for understanding. In C. M. Reigeluth (Ed.), *Instructional-design theories and models: A new paradigm of instructional theory* (Vol. 2, pp. 91–114). Mahwah, NJ: Lawrence Erlbaum Associates.

Petraglia, J. (1998). *Reality by design: The rhetoric and technology of authenticity in education*. Mahwah, NJ: Lawrence Erlbaum Associates.

Pleban, R., Matthews, M., Salter, M., & Eakin, D. (2002). Training and assessing complex decision making in a virtual environment. *Perceptual and Motor Skills, 94*, 871–882.

Plowman, L. (2005). Getting the story straight: The role of narrative in teaching and learning with interactive media. In P. Gardenfors & P. Johansson (Eds.), *Cognition, education, and communication technology* (pp. 55–76). Mahwah, NJ: Lawrence Erlbaum Associates.

Puntambekar, S., & Hübscher, R. (2005). Tools for scaffolding students in a complex learning environment: What have we gained and what have we missed? *Educational Psychologist, 40*, 1–12.

Reeve, J., & Deci, E. L. (1996). Elements of the competitive situation that affect intrinsic motivation. *Personality and Social Psychology Bulletin, 22*, 24–33.

Ricci, K., Salas, E., & Cannon-Bowers, J. (1996). Do computer-based games facilitate knowledge acquisition and retention? *Military Psychology, 8*, 295–307.

Roessingh, J. (2005). Transfer of manual flying skills from PC-based simulation to actual flight: Comparison of in-flight measured data and instructor ratings. *International Journal of Aviation Psychology, 15*, 67–90.

Ryan, R. M., & Deci, E. L. (2000). Self-determination theory and the facilitation of intrinsic motivation, social development and well-being. *American Psychologist, 55*, 68–78.

Salas, E., & Cannon-Bowers, J. A. (2001). The science of training: A decade of progress. *Annual Review of Psychology, 52*, 471–499.

Schank, R. C., Berman, T. R., & Macpherson, K. A. (1999). Learning by doing. In C. M. Reigeluth (Ed.), *Instructional-design theories and models: A new paradigm of instructional theory* (Vol. 2, pp. 161–181). Mahwah, NJ: Lawrence Erlbaum Associates.

Scherpereel, C. (2005). Changing mental models: Business simulation exercises. *Simulation & Gaming, 36*, 388–403.

Schmidt, R. A., & Bjork, R. A. (1992). New conceptualizations of practice: Common principles in three paradigms suggest new concepts for training. *Psychological Science, 3*, 207–217.

Schunk, D. (1990). Goal setting and self-efficacy during self-regulated learning. *Educational Psychologist, 25*(1), 71–86.

Shute, V., & Gawlick, L. (1995). Practice effects on skill acquisition, learning outcome, retention, and sensitivity to relearning. *Human Factors, 37*(4), 781–803.

Slater, M., Sadagic, A., Usoh, M., & Schroeder, R. (2000). Small-group behaviour in a virtual and real environment: A comparative study. *Presence: Teleoperators and Virtual Environments, 9*, 37–51.

Smith, E. M., Ford, J. K., & Kozlowski, S. W. J. (1997). Building adaptive expertise: Implications for training design. In M. A. Quinones & A. Dudda (Eds.), *Training for a rapidly changing workplace: Applications of psychological research* (pp. 89–118). Washington, DC: APA Books.

Smith-Jentsch, K. A, Jentsch, F. G., Payne, S. C., & Salas, E. (1996). Can pretraining experiences explain individual differences in learning? *Journal of Applied Psychology, 81*, 909–936.

Spagnolli, A., Varotto, D., & Mantovani, G. (2003). An ethnographic, action-based approach to human experience in virtual environments. *International Journal of Human-Computer Studies, 59*, 797–822.

Stanney, K. (Ed.). (2002). *Handbook of virtual environments: Design, implementation, and applications.* Mahwah, NJ: Lawrence Erlbaum Associates.

Stein, S. (2000). *Equipped for the future content standards: What adults need to know and be able to do in the 21st century.* Washington, DC: National Institute for Literacy.

Steinberg, E. R. (1989). Cognition and learner control: A literature review, 1977–1988. *Journal of Computer Based Instruction, 16*(4), 117–121.

Sugrue, B., & Clark, R. E. (2000). Media selection for training. In S. Tobias & J. D. Fletcher (Eds.), *Training and retraining: A handbook for business, industry, government, and the military* (pp. 208–234). New York: Macmillan.

Sugrue, B., & Clark, R. E. (2000). Media selection for training. In S. Tobias & J. D. Fletcher (Eds.), *Training and retraining: A handbook for business, industry, government, and the military* (pp. 208–234). New York: Macmillan.

Sweller, J. (1999). *Instructional design.* Melbourne: ACER Press.

Sweller, J. (2006). The worked example effect and human cognition. *Learning and Instruction, 2*, 165–169.

Sweller, J., van Merriënboer, J., & Paas, F. (1998). Cognitive architecture and instructional design. *Educational Psychology Review, 10*, 251–296.

Tobias, S., & Fletcher, J. D. (2007). What research has to say about designing computer games for learning. *Educational Technology, 47*(5), 20–29.

Vogel, J. F., Vogel, D. S., Cannon-Bowers, J. A., Bowers, C. A., Muse, K., & Wright, M. (2006). Computer gaming and interactive simulations for learning: A meta-analysis. *Journal of Educational Computing Research, 34*(3), 229–243.

Vogel, J. J., Greenwood-Ericksen, A., Cannon-Bowers, J. A., & Bowers, C. A. (2006). Using virtual reality with and without gaming attributes for academic achievement. *Journal of Research on Technology in Education, 39*(1), 105–118.

Voithofer, R. (2004). Teaching computers to tell learning stories: Using critical narrative theory to frame design and evaluation strategies for online educational experiences. *Journal of Educational Multimedia and Hypermedia, 13*, 47–72.

Volet, S. (1991). Modelling and coaching of relevant metacognitive strategies for enhancing university students' learning. *Learning and Instruction, 1*, 319–336.

Wolfe, C. (2002). Learning and teaching on the World Wide Web. *Applied Cognitive Psychology, 16*, 863–864.

8

Toward a Theory of Learner-Centered Training Design: An Integrative Framework of Active Learning

Bradford S. Bell
Cornell University

Steve W. J. Kozlowski
Michigan State University

The dynamicity and complexity of the current business landscape mean that, now more than ever, organizations must rely on workplace learning and continuous improvement to gain and sustain competitive advantage (Salas & Cannon-Bowers, 2001). However, the same trends that are driving the renewed emphasis on workplace learning have also introduced new training challenges. Traditionally, training has focused on developing routine expertise, or providing employees with competencies that directly transfer to the job. Yet, the changing nature of work has increasingly shifted attention toward the development of adaptive expertise, or competencies that are not only specialized but also flexible enough to be modified to changing circumstances. Although our understanding of how to develop adaptability remains limited, emerging research suggests that training designs that selectively influence cognitive, motivational, and affective self-regulatory processes to induce an active approach to learning may hold promise for developing adaptive capabilities (for a review, see Kozlowski, Toney, et al., 2001, and chapters by Mayer and Cannon-Bowers & Bowers, this volume).

Companies also face the challenge of delivering training on demand and to a workforce that is increasingly distributed across the globe. The result has been a steady increase in the utilization of e-learning because of its capacity to deliver just-in-time training to employees anytime and almost anywhere. For example, in 2004 nearly 58% of all training days at IBM were conducted through e-learning, and the company's on-demand learning database has grown to include 54,000 courses. One important implication of putting training online is that employees are being given unprecedented control over their learning (Bell & Kozlowski, 2002). As Brown and Ford (2002) stated, "[O]nce the computer program is set up, the burden for active learning switches to the learner" (p. 194). Yet, research has consistently demonstrated that many learners do not make good use of this control (DeRouin, Fritzsche, & Salas, 2004). This creates a training dilemma and highlights the need for strategies that can help employees effectively leverage the control offered by online training programs.

There is also an emerging trend within organizations of replacing formal, classroom training with more informal, job-embedded training. As Kozlowski, Toney, et al. (2001) stated, "It [training] is shifting from an off-site single episode to a systematic series of learning experiences that are *integrated* in the workplace and *embedded* in work technology" (p. 60; italics in original). Integrated-embedded training has the potential to offer many advantages, including improved efficiency and cost control as well as enhanced transfer of competencies from training to the workplace. However, embedded training is often more informal and self-directed, which places greater responsibility on employees to manage their own learning. It is essential, therefore, to understand the process of self-directed learning and identify instructional strategies that can be used to help support employees' learning activities outside the classroom. As Salas and Cannon-Bowers (2001) noted, there is a need for research "that helps us get a better understanding of what, how, and when on-the-job training works" (p. 491).

A key theme that underlies developments in the areas of adaptive expertise, technology-based training, and embedded training is the inherent shift from a traditional, proceduralized approach to training, which tends to treat the trainee as a passive recipient of information, to a learner-centered approach that makes the learner an active participant in the learning process—an active learning approach. The active learning approach aims to stimulate and shape a combination of cognitive, motivational, and emotion self-regulatory processes that characterize how people focus their attention, direct their effort, and manage their emotions during learning (Kozlowski, Toney, et al., 2001). Recent research indicates that these self-regulatory processes may play a critical role not only in the development of adaptive expertise but also in enabling individuals to successfully navigate learner-controlled training contexts, such as e-learning and informal, on-the-job training (DeRouin et al., 2004; Ivancic & Hesketh, 2000). Although a number of discrete active learning interventions have been developed and tested over the past decade, with few exceptions (Clark, 2001; Mayer, this volume) very little work has integrated across these interventions to identify their common training components and the process pathways by which they exert effects on learning outcomes.

As a result, our understanding of the active learning approach and how to leverage it to address these emerging challenges remains limited.

The goal of this chapter, therefore, is to develop an integrative conceptual framework of active learning, and we do this by focusing on three primary issues. First, we define the active learning approach and contrast it to more traditional, passive instructional approaches. We argue that the active learning approach can be distinguished from not only more passive approaches to instruction but also other forms of experiential learning based on its use of formal training components to systematically influence trainees' cognitive, motivational, and emotion self-regulatory processes. Second, we examine how specific training components can be used to influence each of these process domains. Through a review of prior research, we extract core training components that cut across different active learning interventions, map these components onto specific process domains, and consider the role of individual differences in shaping the effects of these components (aptitude–treatment interactions [ATIs]). A final issue examined in this chapter concerns the outcomes associated with the active learning approach. Despite its considerable versatility, the active learning approach is not the most efficient or effective means of responding to all training needs. Thus, we discuss the impact of the active learning approach on different types of learning outcomes in order to identify the situations under which it is likely to demonstrate the greatest utility. We conclude the chapter by highlighting research and practical implications of our integrated framework, and we outline an agenda for future research on active learning.

Theoretical Foundation of the Active Learning Approach

Prior research has typically conceptualized the active learning approach by comparing it to more passive approaches to learning, which some refer to as *transmission* or *conduit models of learning* (Iran-Nejad, 1990; Schwartz & Bransford, 1998). The active learning approach is distinct in two fundamental respects. First, the active learning approach provides individuals with significant control over their learning. Whereas passive approaches to learning have the instructional system (e.g., the instructor, or the computer program) assume most of the responsibility for important learning decisions, the active learning approach gives the learner primary responsibility for managing his or her learning (e.g., sequencing his or her learning activities, monitoring, and judging progress). The important distinction is one of internal versus external regulation of learning (Iran-Nejad, 1990).

Second, the active learning approach is grounded in the constructivist vision of learning, which argues that learning is an inductive process in which individuals explore and experiment with a task to infer the rules, principles, and strategies for effective performance (Mayer, 2004; Smith, Ford, & Kozlowski, 1997). In contrast, passive approaches to learning are based on conduit or transmission models of learning, which assume that individuals acquire knowledge by having it transmitted to them by some external source (e.g., a teacher or text) (Schwartz & Bransford, 1998). The important distinction is one of active knowledge construction versus the internalization of external knowledge.

The notion that the learner should be actively involved in the learning process is not exclusive to the active learning approach; it is a theme that can be found in a number of educational philosophies and approaches, including experiential learning and action learning (Kolb, 1984; Revans, 1982). However, the active learning approach is unique in that it extends beyond simply "learning by doing" and utilizes formal training components to systematically shape and support trainees' learning processes. In particular, the active learning interventions that have been developed in recent years, such as error training, mastery training, and guided exploration, combine multiple training components intended to selectively influence the nature, quality, and focus of self-regulatory activity (Debowski, Wood, & Bandura, 2001; Keith & Frese, 2005; Kozlowski, Gully, et al., 2001; Kozlowski, Toney, et al., 2001). Self-regulation can be defined as processes "that enable an individual to guide his/her goal directed activities over time and across changing circumstances," including the "modulation of thought, affect, behavior, or attention" (Karoly, 1993, p. 25). Although previous research has shown that active learning interventions can enhance important learning outcomes, particularly adaptive transfer, it has not provided much insight into the self-regulatory mechanisms through which these interventions have their effects. One reason is that very little of this work has attempted to directly test these mechanisms (Keith & Frese, 2005). Moreover, in the few cases where processes have been modeled, the focus on multifaceted active learning interventions makes it difficult to precisely map pathways between the training components that comprise these interventions and the process targets (Kozlowski & Bell, 2006).

Thus, a primary goal of the current chapter is to identify the core training components that comprise active learning interventions and more clearly elucidate the process pathways through which these components have their effects. In the following section, we use the Adaptive Learning System (ALS) framework developed by Kozlowski, Toney, et al. (2001) to highlight the role that training design can play in shaping trainee self-regulation. The ALS was developed as a theoretically based model to guide the design of training interventions that actively and selectively stimulate self-regulatory processes as a means to enhance learning, performance, and performance adaptation. Although the model is application oriented, it serves as a useful theoretical framework for examining how the training components embedded in active learning interventions may influence relatively distinct self-regulatory pathways to drive training effectiveness. The different elements of the ALS framework are presented in Figure 8.1 and discussed below.

The ALS

Self-Regulation System

At the core of the ALS is the dynamic process of self-regulation. In training contexts, the self-regulatory system can be divided into three general domains. The first, *practice behaviors*, defines what individuals do during training. The primary focus is on how individuals allocate effort (i.e., motivation) during practice aimed at skill improvement, although one should not overlook pre- and postpractice behaviors such as studying, strategic planning, and reviewing feedback, which are equally important forms of effort allocation (Cannon-Bowers, Rhodenizer, Salas, & Bowers, 1998). The second domain, *self-monitoring*, represents the cognitive component of the self-regulation system. It is concerned with how trainees focus their cognitive attention and reflect on their progress toward desired objectives (Carver & Scheier, 1990; Karoly, 1993). The final self-regulatory component highlighted in the model is *self-evaluation reaction*, which focuses on trainees' affective (i.e., emotion-based) reactions to goal progress. Kozlowski, Toney, et al. (2001) highlighted two primary aspects of self-reactions critical in learning contexts: self-efficacy and causal attributions. High levels of self-efficacy and appropriate attributions are essential if self-regulatory activities are to be engaged or maintained (Kanfer & Ackerman, 1989).

Training Strategy

A training strategy is composed of specific training components that form a training intervention. That is, interventions are constructed from a combination of manipulations designed to actively leverage the different domains of the self-regulation system discussed above. Kozlowski, Toney, et al. (2001) reviewed three primary training components. First, *training design* refers to the nature of the experience that is created for the trainee through the provision of information and type of practice available during learning. Some of the training design features that have been shown to have important implications for self-regulation during learning

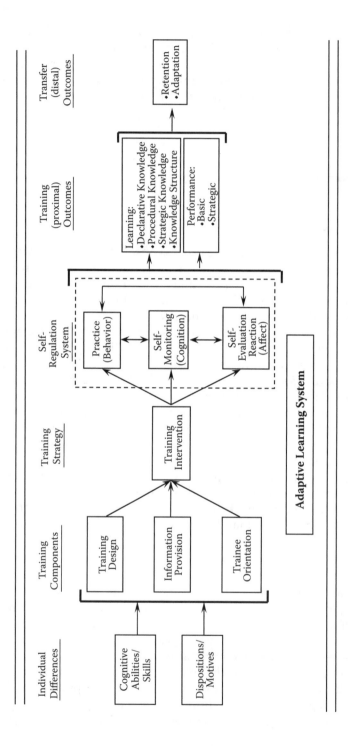

FIGURE 8.1

Theoretical model of adaptive learning design. (From Kozlowski, S. W. J., Toney, R. J., Mullins, M. E, Weissbein. D. A., Brown, K. G., & Bell, B. S. (2001). Developing adaptability: A theory for the design of integrated-embedded training systems. In E. Salas (Ed.), *Advances in human performance and cognitive engineering research* (Vol. 1, pp. 59–123). Amsterdam: JAI/Elsevier Science. © 1999, 2006 by S. W. J. Kozlowski. All rights reserved worldwide. Adapted and used with permisison.)

include the sequencing and pacing of training (Kozlowski & Bell, 2006) and errors during learning (Frese et al., 1991). *Information provision* refers to the feedback provided to trainees that influences their interpretation of past progress. There are many conditions that influence how feedback impacts learning, including the type of feedback given (e.g., descriptive vs. normative), trainees' ability and performance levels, and feedback sign (i.e., positive or negative; Kluger & DeNisi, 1996). In addition to feedback, information provision refers to guidance provided to trainees that can be designed to influence their preparation for future learning efforts (Bell & Kozlowski, 2002). The final training component is *trainee orientation*, or the motivational and attributional frames that affect the way the trainee perceives the training experience. The type of orientation an individual adopts in an achievement situation is influenced by both dispositional and situational influences that are independent and additive (Archer, 1994; Boyle & Klimoski, 1995; Chen, Gully, Whiteman, & Kilcullen, 2000). The situational factors that drive trainees' motivational orientation can be divided into two categories: instructional goals and general training frames. Instructional goals are the explicit directions provided to train-ees, whereas general training frames do not focus explicitly on goals or objectives, but rather are general statements made by trainers that influ-ence trainees' goal orientation. Goals and training frames that emphasize learning and task mastery, as opposed to performance and the demon-stration of competence, can enhance self-regulation, learning, and adapt-ability (Kozlowski & Bell, 2006; Kozlowski, Gully, et al., 2001).

Training Outcomes

Through its effects on the self-regulation system, training strategy exerts an influence on multidimensional training outcomes (Kraiger, Ford, & Salas, 1993). Proximal training outcomes are outcomes that arise directly from training and are exhibited immediately at its completion. Kozlowski, Toney, et al. (2001) argued that these outcomes can be divided into two categories: learning and performance. Learning outcomes represent the more abstract cognitive indicators of learning, such as different types of knowledge (e.g., declarative or strategic) and knowledge organization. Performance outcomes reflect the behavioral manifestations of learning. The performance domain can be further divided into basic and strategic performance (Bell & Kozlowski, 2002). Basic performance captures the information-processing and decision-making aspects of a task domain, whereas strategic performance involves the more complex behavioral rou-tines that underlie adaptability to dynamic task environments.

These proximal training outcomes affect trainees' ability to transfer what they have learned to tasks that occur following training. Transfer can be broken down into two main types: near (or analogical) and far (or adaptive) transfer. Near transfer represents the transfer of skills to problems similar to those encountered in training (Frese, 1995). Far transfer, however, "involves using one's existing knowledge base to change a learned procedure, or to generate a solution to a completely new problem" (Ivancic & Hesketh, 2000, p. 1968). Some training strategies are better suited than others for promoting far transfer, based on their ability to stimulate specific self-regulatory patterns that lead to the development of strategic knowledge and skills, which underlie adaptability (Bell & Kozlowski, 2008; Keith & Frese, 2005).

Individual Differences

Finally, the different abilities and dispositional tendencies that individuals bring with them to the training setting are also important. We know that a number of individual differences, including cognitive ability, goal orientation, anxiety, and locus of control, directly influence learning outcomes (Colquitt, LePine, & Noe, 2000). Yet, the low degree of structure and the lack of external guidance that often characterize technology-based and informal training programs suggest that individual differences may be particularly potent in these contexts (Brown, 2001). Accordingly, it is important to understand how both cognitive abilities and motivation- and emotion-based traits interact with different training strategies to impact the process and outcomes of active learning (Gully, Payne, Kiechel, & Whiteman, 2002; Keith & Frese, 2005). To the extent that we can more precisely map these potential ATIs, we will advance our understanding of how to design training to more effectively meet the needs of different learners.

Application of the ALS

The ALS is predicated on developing training interventions that systematically influence self-regulatory processes to facilitate learning and performance. In that function, the model and approach have been effective. For example, Kozlowski, Gully, et al. (2001) used the model to develop a mastery training strategy composed of multiple training components, including learning goals, a mastery-oriented training frame, and the progressive sequencing of knowledge and skill development. Kozlowski, Gully, et al. found that the mastery training strategy not only had a positive impact on trainees' self-efficacy but also led to greater and more coherent knowledge, better training performance, and enhanced adaptability. Bell and Kozlowski (2002) also used the ALS model to develop an adaptive guidance intervention, which leverages the information provision component of the model to support trainees' self-regulatory processes in learner-controlled, online training environments. Specifically, adaptive guidance assesses trainees' learning in real time and provides personalized study and practice recommendations. Bell and Kozlowski (2002) found that this supplemental information not only enhanced trainees' self-regulation (e.g., self-efficacy, and attentional focus) but also facilitated learning and adaptive transfer.

Elaborating the Training Components and Process Pathways of Active Learning

The studies by Kozlowski, Gully, et al. (2001) and Bell and Kozlowski (2002) demonstrate the value of the ALS as a guiding framework for the design of effective training interventions. However, one limitation associated with studying complex, multifaceted interventions is that it is difficult or impossible to isolate the effects of specific training components or to identify the process pathways through which they operate. For example, in the Kozlowski, Gully, et al. study described above, it is unclear which of the different training components (e.g., learning goals, mastery-oriented training frame, and/or goal proximity) account for the effects of the mastery training strategy. The results may be explained by a single component, the independent additive contributions of several components, or the interactive effects of two or more of the components; we do not know. Further, one is unable to compare the relative impact of the different components on specific learning processes and outcomes, which is critical information for designing future strategies that will be optimally efficient and effective. Last, decomposing a complex intervention allows one to isolate the precise processes or mechanisms by which specific training components exert their effects. For example, Kozlowski, Gully, et al. (2001) examined several self-regulatory variables as mediators of the effects of their mastery training strategy. However, because the training components embedded in this strategy were not teased apart, it is impossible to align different process pathways with specific training components.

To begin to address these research gaps, a recent study by Kozlowski and Bell (2006) sought to tease apart the key elements of mastery training. In particular, we examined the independent and integrated effects of three training components drawn from the achievement orientation and goal-setting domains—goal frame (i.e., learning or performance orientation induction), goal content (i.e., tangible learning or performance goals), and goal proximity (i.e., proximal or distal tangible goals)—on trainees' cognitive and affective self-regulatory activities. The results revealed that all three components had significant effects, although goal content was a more potent driver of self-regulatory activity compared to frame or goal proximity. Further, we found that congruent learning frame and content relative to congruent performance frame and content were more beneficial for trainees' self-regulatory activity, incongruent combinations of goal frame and content were better than congruent performance frames and content, and effects for the incongruent combinations cutting across the domains were asymmetrical. Finally, we found evidence that distal learning goals were generally more effective for self-regulation than proximal learning goals.

Although this research begins to disentangle the common and distinctive effects of different mastery training components on trainees' self-regulatory activities, it is limited in its narrow focus on only those components embedded in the mastery training strategy and the processes targeted by this strategy. If our goal is to develop a broader theory of active learning, we need to expand our focus and explore the training components and processes that underlie a broader range of active learning interventions. By identifying those areas in which these different interventions converge, we can begin to map the core elements of the active learning approach. In the following section, we present a conceptual framework of active learning, which is aimed at integrating research on different active learning interventions so as to extract a set of core training components and highlight the self-regulatory processes through which these components impact learning and adaptability.

Active Learning: An Integrative Framework

Our review of several exemplars of the active learning approach revealed three core training components that cut across these interventions. As shown in Table 8.1, these three core training components are the nature of instruction, motivational induction, and emotion control, each of which targets a relatively distinct set of cognitive, motivational, or emotional self-regulatory processes. First, all of these interventions use an exploratory instructional approach to engage learners' cognitive self-regulatory processes, such as metacognition. In some strategies, such as enactive exploration, trainees are provided with very little guidance and are explicitly instructed to explore the task (Heimbeck, Frese, Sonnentag, & Keith, 2003). In others, such as guided exploration, the emphasis is on more systematic or preplanned exploration (Debowski et al., 2001). Thus, although the level of structure may vary, there is agreement on the use of an exploratory instructional approach to stimulate cognitive self-regulation. Second, most of the interventions incorporate a motivational induction designed to shape the orientation that trainees take toward the training task. As discussed above, trainee orientation can be influenced by both instructional goals and general training frames, and the interventions shown in

TABLE 8.1

Active Learning Interventions: Core Training Components, Key Process Targets, and Individual Difference Considerations

Intervention	Studies	Instruction	Motivational Induction	Emotion Control
			Core Training Components	
Exploratory and discovery learning	Frese et al. (1988) Kamouri, Kamouri, and Smith (1986) McDaniel and Schlager (1990)	*Exploratory learning:* • Limited guidance and structure • Exploration and discovery inductive learning process		
Guided exploration	Bell and Kozlowski (2002) Debowski, Wood, and Bandura (2001) Wood, Kakebeeke, Debowski, and Frese (2000)	*Exploratory learning:* • Limited guidance and structure • Exploration and discovery • Inductive learning process	*Error framing:* • Errors encouraged • Errors framed as essential for learning	*Emotion control statements:* • Statements designed to reduce anxiety and frustration • Promote personal control
Error training and enactive exploration	Frese et al. (1991) Gully, Payne, Kiechel, and Whiteman (2002) Heimbeck, Frese, Sonnentag, and Keith (2003) Keith and Frese (2005)	*Guided exploration:* • Guidance on educational decisions • Systematic and preplanned exploration	*Practice framing:* • Practice framed as opportunity for learning • Progressive achievement to build self-efficacy	*Guided practice:* • Guided enactments of practice strengthen satisfaction with progress
Mastery training	Chillarege, Nordstrom, and Williams (2003) Kozlowski, Gully et al. (2001) Kozlowski and Bell (2006) Martocchio (1994) Stevens and Gist (1997) Tabernero and Wood (1999)	*Exploratory learning:* • Minimal to moderate guidance • Exploration and experimentation encouraged • Active practice emphasized	*Mastery goals and framing:* • Mastery goals • Errors framed as essential for learning. • Task ability framed as acquirable skill	*Self-evaluative guidance:* • Training framed as learning opportunity to reduce performance anxiety • Emphasis on self-management and personal control

(continued on next page)

TABLE 8.1 (continued)

Active Learning Interventions: Core Training Components, Key Process Targets, and Individual Difference Considerations

	Core Training Components		
	Instruction	Motivational Induction	Emotion Control
Individual difference considerations	• Cognitive ability • Openness to experience	• Trait goal orientation • Conscientiousness	• Cognitive ability • Trait anxiety
Key process targets	• Cognition • Metacognition • Controlled and effortful processing • Mental models	• Motivation • State goal orientation • Intrinsic motivation • Self-efficacy • Effort and persistence	• Emotion • Emotion regulation • Satisfaction or negative affect • Anxiety • Attributions
Key training outcomes	*Proximal outcomes:* • Strategic knowledge • Strategic performance	*Distal outcomes:* • Adaptive transfer	

Source: Bell, B. S., & Kozlowski, S. W. J. (2008). Active learning: Effects of core training design elements on self-regulatory processes, learning, and adaptability. *Journal of Applied Psychology, 93,* 296–316. Published by the American Psychological Association. Adapted with permission.

Table 8.1 evidence use of both strategies. Mastery training, for example, uses mastery goals that encourage trainees to focus their effort on developing their task competence rather than performing well (Kozlowski, Gully, et al., 2001). In contrast, error training incorporates instructions that encourage trainees to make errors and frame errors as instrumental for learning (Frese et al., 1991). These instructions, like the mastery goals, are designed to induce a mastery orientation and drive important motivational processes, such as intrinsic motivation and self-efficacy. Finally, because giving learners control over their instruction can increase stress and anxiety (Kanfer & Heggestad, 1999; Keith & Frese, 2005), many active learning interventions also incorporate a training design element aimed at helping trainees to regulate their emotions. Although a common element of active learning interventions, the specific emotion control strategies that have been employed are quite varied, including emotion control statements and different forms of guidance.

In Figure 8.2, we present an integrated conceptual model of active learning. Our goal in the following sections is to provide a more detailed examination of each of the three training components highlighted in the model and to highlight the relatively distinct self-regulatory pathways that each is designed to influence. In addition, we consider potential ATIs, where the effects of the training design components vary across trainees with different personal characteristics.

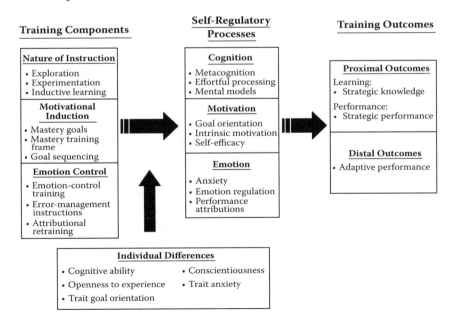

FIGURE 8.2
Integrated conceptual model of active learning.

Instruction

A fundamental distinction between active and passive approaches to learning concerns the nature of instruction. In the active learning approach, the dominant pedagogical approach is *exploratory* or *discovery learning*, which refers to the acquisition of new information through activities initiated and controlled by the learner (Kamouri, Kamouri, & Smith, 1986). Exploratory learning methods facilitate an inductive learning process in which individuals must explore and experiment with the task to infer and learn the rules, principles, and strategies for effective performance (Kamouri et al., 1986; Pearn & Downs, 1989; Smith et al., 1997). Exploration can be encouraged by creating an open (unstructured) learning environment and/or by explicitly encouraging trainees to engage in exploratory behaviors. In contrast, more traditional, passive approaches to learning are characterized by a much more deductive instructional approach that explicitly instructs individuals on the complete task and its concepts, rules, and strategies. This type of learning is often referred to as *proceduralized* or *expository instruction*, because it provides trainees with detailed, step-by-step instructions and all the commands necessary for task performance (e.g., Dormann & Frese, 1994; Frese et al., 1988, 1991; Nordstrom, Wendland, & Williams, 1998).

It is important to recognize that pure exploratory or discovery learning and expository methods represent two ends of a continuum representing varying degrees of structure and guidance. Although pure exploratory learning remains a common active learning approach, it has also been criticized in recent years. Mayer (2004), for example, argued that instructional researchers have made the mistake of equating active teaching methods (e.g., hands-on activities and group discussions) with active learning. He suggested that the key to active learning is not learners' behavioral activity per se but, rather, their cognitive activity (e.g., selecting, organizing, and integrating knowledge). Moreover, he argued that on this latter criterion, pure exploratory methods often fall short. For instance, in pure exploratory learning, students may fail to come into contact with to-be-learned principles and, therefore, have nothing to integrate into their knowledge base. Mayer supported his position by reviewing research over the past 3 decades that has consistently shown that guided exploration leads to greater learning and transfer than pure exploration (see also Smith et al., 1997). Research on the topic of learner control has reached a similar conclusion, arguing that learners need guidance to help them make effective use of the control they are given (e.g., DeRouin et al., 2004; Reeves, 1993). The key point is that an appropriate mixture of exploration and guidance can balance the need for learners to be active during learning while also ensuring they make appropriate learning choices. Growing attention is being focused on incorporating guidance into active learning strategies (e.g., Bell & Kozlowski, 2002), although more research is needed on how much and what kind of guidance to provide in different learning contexts.

Nonetheless, when exploratory methods are appropriately designed, they can serve as a useful means of engaging trainees' cognitive self-regulatory processes. Below, we discuss the effects of exploratory learning on three important cognitive learning processes: metacognition, effortful processing, and mental models.

Metacognition

Metacognition involves exerting control over self-monitoring and self-regulatory processes, and includes planning, monitoring, and revising goal-appropriate behavior (Brown, Bransford, Ferrara, & Campione, 1983). Researchers have suggested that metacognition is critical for enabling learners to successfully orchestrate their own learning (Bransford, Brown, & Cocking, 1999; Keith & Frese, 2005). Cannon-Bowers et al. (1998), for example, argued that metacognition "assists learners in becoming active in their education instead of being passive recipients of instruction" (p. 296). In addition, metacognitive skills enable learners to recognize changes in task demands, devise new solutions, and evaluate the effectiveness of the implemented solution, all of which are critical elements of adaptability (Ford, Smith, Weissbein, Gully, & Salas, 1998; Ivancic & Hesketh, 2000).

One of the keys to building metacognitive skills is giving individuals an opportunity to engage in self-directed learning (Holyoak, 1991; Sweller, Mawer, & Ward, 1983). The learner control inherent in exploratory learning prompts individuals to engage in planning, test their hypotheses, monitor their learning progress, and develop and revise learning strategies (Frese et al., 1988). Proceduralized instruction does not offer the opportunity to engage in metacognitive activities because individuals are provided with the correct task solution and exploration is restricted (Keith & Frese, 2005). Further, Salomon and Globerson (1987) argued that when there is a perception that a particular authority "knows best," individuals will often forgo any mindful examination of information.

A recent study by Keith and Frese (2005) examined metacognition as an important cognitive self-regulatory process in error management training. Specifically, the authors argued that errors stimulate metacognitive activities by prompting individuals to diagnose their mistakes, devise and implement solutions, and monitor their effectiveness. Keith and Frese found that error management stimulated more metacognitive activity than error-avoidant training. Further, the authors found that this increase in metacognitive activity partially accounted for the positive relationship between error management training and adaptive transfer. A recent study by Bell and Kozlowski (2008) also provides evidence for the importance of metacognition in active learning. In this study, we hypothesized that guided exploration would stimulate greater metacognitive activity than more structured, proceduralized instruction. Our findings provided support for this hypothesis and also revealed that metacognitive activity positively predicted not only trainees' self-evaluation activity but also their intrinsic motivation and self-efficacy.

Effortful Processing

Exploratory learning may also increase the amount of cognitive effort that individuals devote to learning a task. In part, this may be due to the fact that exploratory learning increases the number of errors that occur during learning (Ivancic & Hesketh, 1995). Not only do errors serve a surprise function that attracts individuals' attention, but also cognitive resources are required to diagnoses and recover from errors (Schönpflug, 1985). Exploratory learning may also require greater cognitive attention than proceduralized instruction because more effort is required to solve problems (Ivancic & Hesketh, 1995). Tuovinen and Sweller (1999), for instance, compared the mental effort involved in using exploration or worked-examples practice to learn a database program. They found that exploratory learning required significantly higher levels of mental effort than worked-examples practice, especially for individuals with no previous domain familiarity. This increase in cognitive effort may be important because extending the length of time a skill is practiced using more effortful, controlled processing has been shown to foster schema extraction and the learning of principles (Sweller, 1988) and prevent the premature automatization of a skill (Frese & Altmann, 1989).

Mental Models

Finally, exploratory learning may influence the coherence and breadth of trainees' knowledge structures. Because individuals must develop a solution to the task on their own, the knowledge they acquire through exploratory learning becomes better integrated into their existing knowledge (Egan & Greeno, 1973; Frese et al., 1988). Individuals begin with a rudimentary conceptualization of the system, which guides their initial exploration. The more it is possible to integrate new information into these already existing conceptualizations, the better they are able to learn (Frese et al., 1988; Volpert, 1987). The knowledge is also more flexible because the effortful processing that occurs during exploratory learning leads to acquisition of knowledge at a higher level of regulation (Frese & Zapf, 1994; Salomon & Perkins, 1989). Proceduralized instruction, on the other hand, is often based on a very concrete representation of problem-solving actions, which may encourage individuals to represent the problem domain at an inappropriate level of abstraction (Carlson, Lundy, & Schneider, 1992; Simons & De Jong, 1992).

Exploratory learning also allows individuals to make errors, and, therefore, individuals learn not only from performing the task correctly but also from making mistakes (Ivancic & Hesketh, 1995; Singer & Pease, 1976). Making mistakes leads to the development of a better operative mental model of the task, because as individuals explore the task and make errors, they are able to incorporate potential pitfalls and error-prone areas into their mental model (Frese, 1995; Kozlowski, Gully, et al., 2001). In addition, exploration exposes individuals to a wider range of task material. Although some of this material may not be applicable to the current problem, it may prove useful when individuals are required to transfer their knowledge and skills and solve a novel problem (Kozlowski, Gully, et al.).

ATIs

Although the evidence reviewed above links exploratory learning to several important cognitive self-regulatory processes, research also suggests that a number of individual difference variables may moderate these effects. Snow (1986), for example, highlighted research that suggests that students with lower levels of ability benefit from tightly structured lessons, whereas students with higher levels of ability perform better in less structured, error-filled environments that provide room for independent learning. Similarly, Gully et al. (2002) found that high-ability trainees performed better under "make errors" instructions, whereas low-ability trainees performed better under "avoid errors" instructions. Bell and Kozlowski (2008) also found that high-ability trainees displayed higher levels of metacognitive activity when given guided exploratory learning compared to proceduralized instruction. It has been argued that low-ability trainees do not possess the cognitive resources necessary to make effective use of exploratory learning and errors (Gully et al., 2002). Further, as noted above, research has shown that exploratory learning increases trainees' workload (e.g., Schönpflug, 1985; Tuovinen & Sweller, 1999), which may make it difficult for trainees with limited cognitive resources to devote adequate attention to both learning and self-regulatory activities.

Openness to experience may also moderate the impact of exploratory learning on learners' cognitive activity. Gully et al. (2002), for example, found that openness to experience moderated the impact of error training on several important training outcomes. Individuals high in openness to experience are more curious, imaginative, and broad-minded (Barrick &

Mount, 1991). They also may be more willing to engage in new approaches to learning, which may explain why openness to experience tends to have a positive impact on training proficiency (Barrick & Mount, 1991). Consistent with past research, Gully et al. (2002) found that openness to experience was positively related to trainees' self-efficacy, knowledge, and performance. In addition, Gully et al. found that the positive relationship between openness to experience and training outcomes was particularly strong when training encouraged errors, but that these relationships disappeared when errors were discouraged. Gully et al. suggested that these results may be due to the facts that (a) error training encourages exploration and (b) trainees higher in openness are more likely to engage in exploratory behaviors. In other words, it appears that there is a particularly good fit between individuals high in openness to experience and more active, exploratory approaches to instruction. Proceduralized instruction, however, restricts exploration for trainees high in openness, thereby nullifying the positive effects of openness on training outcomes.

Motivational Induction

In recent years, the achievement goal literature has blended traditional conceptualizations of mastery and performance goals with classic achievement motivation theories, which differentiate between activities that are oriented toward the attainment of success (approach) and those that are oriented toward the avoidance of failure (e.g., Elliot & Church, 1997; Harackiewicz, Barron, Pintrich, Elliot, & Thrash, 2002). The result is three distinct motivational orientations: a *mastery* goal that emphasizes the development of competence and task mastery, a *performance-prove* goal that focuses on the attainment of favorable judgments of competence, and a *performance-avoid* goal that stresses avoiding perceptions of failure and incompetence (Elliot & Church).

A second core element of many active learning interventions involves efforts to shape trainees' motivational orientation, or the achievement goals that trainees adopt with regard to the training task. Research has demonstrated that a variety of situational factors and inductions can be used to manipulate the achievement goals that individuals adopt (Archer, 1994; Boyle & Klimoski, 1995; Tabernero & Wood, 1999). In their ALS framework, Kozlowski, Toney, et al. (2001) divided these situational factors into two categories: instructional goals and general training frames.

Instructional goals are the explicit directions provided to trainees. These instructions suggest the behaviors and actions that trainees should engage in during training and, accordingly, identify the goals trainees should strive to achieve. Although training programs have traditionally been characterized by the assignment of performance goals, there is growing recognition that performance goals are often detrimental for knowledge and skill acquisition because they prompt a performance orientation and shift attention away from learning activities (Kanfer & Ackerman, 1989; Locke, 2000; Seijts, Latham, Tasa, & Latham, 2004). One solution is to provide individuals with mastery goals, which induce a mastery orientation and focus individuals' attention on discovering strategies and deeper comprehension of a task domain rather than on performing well (Kozlowski & Bell, 2006; Locke & Latham, 2002).

The second set of situational factors is general training frames. A mastery orientation can be induced by training instructions that do not focus explicitly on goals. Training settings that emphasize long-term outcomes and effort can induce a mastery orientation. Meece (1994), for example, suggested that training that emphasizes self-improvement and the usefulness of information provided in training will encourage the adoption of a mastery orientation. A mastery orientation can also be induced by instructions that stress self-referenced improvement and the malleability of ability, as opposed to the demonstration of fixed ability (Kozlowski & Bell, 2006; Wood & Bandura, 1989). Moreover, several studies indicate that a powerful means of inducing different motivational orientations involves the framing of errors (e.g., Bell & Kozlowski, 2008; Frese et al., 1991; Kozlowski, Gully, et al., 2001; Martocchio, 1994). Learners are likely to adopt a mastery orientation when errors are framed as a normal and valuable part of the learning process and performance evaluation is deemphasized (Church, Elliot, & Gable, 2001; Debowski et al., 2001; Kozlowski, Gully, et al., 2001; Martocchio, 1994). Thus, active learning strategies frequently incorporate task instructions that encourage learners to make errors and to view mistakes as instrumental for learning and self-improvement. In contrast, more traditional approaches to training, which subscribe to the belief that errors are negative occurrences that will detract from learning, encourage trainees to avoid making mistakes, an approach that is likely to induce a performance-avoid orientation (Church et al., 2001; Gully et al., 2002; Ivancic & Hesketh, 1995).

Brown and Ford (2002) proposed that learners who adopt a mastery orientation are likely to be more active learners than those who adopt either a performance-prove or performance-avoid orientation. At the root of this argument is the differential effects of these orientations on how individuals approach, interpret, and respond to achievement activities. Indeed, a growing body of research has demonstrated a relationship between individuals' motivational orientation and their self-regulatory processes (see Payne, Youngcourt, & Beaubien, 2007, for a review). Below, we discuss the effects of trainees' motivational orientation on their intrinsic motivation and self-efficacy, and also examine the potential role of motivational orientation as a prerequisite for other cognitive and emotional self-regulatory processes.

Intrinsic Motivation

One key difference across the three orientations involves their effects on trainees' intrinsic motivation. A mastery orientation promotes challenging appraisals, encourages task absorption, and supports self-determination and feelings of autonomy, all factors presumed to facilitate intrinsic interest and enjoyment (Dweck, 1986). Performance orientations, on the other hand, produce evaluative pressures and elicit anxiety, processes considered antithetical to intrinsic motivation (McGregor & Elliot, 2002). A meta-analysis by Rawsthorne and Elliot (1999) provided support for these different patterns and revealed that mastery orientation stimulates higher levels of intrinsic motivation than a performance orientation. Research that has further partitioned performance orientation into independent approach and avoidance motivational orientations suggests that only a performance orientation grounded in the avoidance of failure undermines intrinsic motivation (e.g., Elliot & Harackiewicz, 1996). The effect of the performance-approach orientation on intrinsic motivation tends to be equivocal (e.g., Church et al., 2001; Elliot & Church, 1997), which may be explained by the fact that approach orientation is undergirded by both a need for achievement and a fear of failure (Harackiewicz et al., 2002). From these findings, we can conclude that trainees who adopt a mastery orientation should exhibit higher levels of intrinsic motivation, which will in turn lead to greater engagement and effort during learning.

Self-Efficacy

Another difference between the three orientations concerns their effect on trainees' self-efficacy. Research has shown that high levels of mastery orientation tend to buffer individuals from the negative effects of failure, thereby helping to increase or maintain self-efficacy (e.g., Button, Mathieu, & Zajac, 1996; Payne et al., 2007; Phillips & Gully, 1997). In contrast, the evaluative pressures associated with performance orientation tend to lead to anxiety, which undermines self-efficacy and leads to a greater propensity to withdraw from tasks (especially in the face of failure). Colquitt and Simmering (1998), for example, demonstrated that mastery orientation not only leads to higher levels of motivation to learn than performance orientation but also buffers individuals from becoming demotivated in the face of performance difficulties. These findings have led researchers to conclude that trainees with a mastery orientation are likely to be more active, persistent learners (Brown & Ford, 2002; Heimbeck et al., 2003). This may be particularly important in self-directed learning contexts (e.g., technology-based training, or on-the-job training [OJT]), because trainees must self-diagnose and solve any obstacles they encounter during learning.

Supporting Cognitive and Emotional Processes

In addition to influencing intrinsic motivation and self-efficacy, trainees' motivational orientation may also serve as a prerequisite for specific cognitive and emotional self-regulatory processes. Ford et al. (1998), for example, argued that a mastery orientation facilitates the use of deep processing strategies that require cognitive effort but facilitate understanding, whereas a performance orientation is related to more short-term and surface-level processing. Consistent with this rationale, Ford et al. showed that a mastery orientation led to higher levels of metacognitive activity than a performance orientation. Prior research has also demonstrated a significant relationship between individuals' motivational orientation and affective states (Elliot & McGregor, 2001; McGregor & Elliot, 2002). For example, a performance-avoid orientation tends to be associated with higher levels of state anxiety. These findings suggest that a mastery orientation may represent a critical condition for supporting the cognitive and emotional processes of active learning. Indeed, a recent study by Bell and Kozlowski (2008) provides evidence that the motivational pathway of active learning is intertwined with both the cognitive and emotion pathways.

ATIs

The goals that individuals adopt during training are determined by both situational factors and dispositional influences (Brett & VandeWalle, 1999; Button et al., 1996; Chen et al., 2000). That is, individuals possess trait goal orientations that predispose them to adopt a mastery or a performance orientation in learning situations characterized by weak situational cues. Thus, it is possible that these two sources may interact to influence trainee orientation in a particular context. In particular, situational manipulations may be used to compensate for or balance a person's dispositional orientation (Bouffard, Boisvert, Vezeau, & Larouche, 1995; Button et al.; Dweck & Leggett, 1988; Newman, 1998). As Harackiewicz and Elliot (1993) noted, when an individual is characteristically oriented toward mastery (or performance), the external instantiation of such an orientation is likely to have little effect. Thus, mastery frames or goals will likely be a more powerful inducement of mastery orientation among trainees with low trait levels of mastery orientation.

Research by Gully et al. (2002) also suggests that conscientiousness may moderate the effect of specific goal frame manipulations. Specifically, Gully et al. found that individuals high in conscientiousness had higher levels of self-efficacy when they were encouraged to avoid errors, whereas individuals low in conscientiousness had higher levels of self-efficacy when encouraged to make errors. This finding is consistent with the fact that individuals high in conscientiousness tend to be careful, thorough, responsible, organized, achievement oriented, and hardworking (Barrick & Mount, 1991; Martocchio & Judge, 1997). In fact, one of the dimensions of conscientiousness is cautiousness (Costa & McCrae, 1992; Hogan & Ones, 1997), which has been measured by the extent to which individuals avoid mistakes (Goldberg, 1999). Thus, Gully et al. (2002) suggested that goal frames that are based on error encouragement may have negative effects for individuals high in conscientiousness because making mistakes is inconsistent with their natural disposition. Similarly, Bell and Kozlowski (2008) found that individuals who were high on performance-avoid orientation responded better to an error-avoidant condition (i.e., they exhibited less state avoidance and less anxiety) compared to a make-errors condition. Again, the result demonstrated that in some instances, it is better to design training to fit an individual's characteristic disposition than to try to change it.

Emotion Control

Although cognitive and motivational processes have garnered the greatest attention in active learning research, a number of researchers have argued that it is also important to consider the important role of emotion control in self-regulated learning. Simons and De Jong (1992) noted that "becoming an active learner is a difficult and stressful process" (p. 342). In a typical passive training program, trainees are provided with the information (e.g., rules, strategies) necessary for effective performance, which attenuates the standard learning curve. However, active learning approaches focus on improving performance after (as opposed to during) training (Keith & Frese, 2005). In fact, many active learning approaches emphasize the positive function of errors, poor performance, and other challenges in learning. In addition, an instructor is often not present to help guide trainees through these challenges or to provide encouragement. Although the relatively unstructured environment of active learning and the challenges it presents may yield cognitive benefits, the risk is that it may also produce greater levels of frustration, stress, and anxiety. If not controlled, these negative reactions can not only be demotivating but also divert attentional resources away from on-task activities (Wood, Kakebeeke, Debowski, & Frese, 2000).

Kanfer, Ackerman, and Heggestad (1996) defined *emotion control* as "the use of self-regulatory processes to keep performance anxiety and other negative emotional reactions (e.g., worry) at bay during task engagement" (p. 186). Emotion control may be particularly important during learning. As Kanfer and Heggestad (1999) noted, "Learners with poor emotion-control skills, in essence, compound the difficulty of learning a new task by being distracted by worry and anxiety" (p. 297). Negative emotions may be particularly damaging in the early stages of training, when cognitive demands are high (Kanfer & Ackerman, 1989; Kanfer, Ackerman, Murtha, Dugdale, & Nelson, 1994).

Over the years, many different techniques have been developed with the aim of helping individuals control their emotions in learning and performance contexts. These techniques include cue-controlled relaxation (Barrios, 1978; Benson, 1975), cognitive modification (e.g., Horan, Hackett, Buchanan, Stone, & Demchik-Stone, 1977), and guided mental imagery (e.g., Carter & Kelly, 1997; Sapp, 1994). Although these interventions can have a significant influence on individuals' affect and performance, one limitation of many of these programs is that they tend to require a considerable amount of training time. A typical intervention, for example, may involve five or six 2-hour instructional sessions (Rose & Veiga, 1984). These sessions often focus on outlining the physiological and psychological mechanisms of stress, teaching individuals how to identify anxiety or stress cues, and instructing and practicing the particular emotion control skills. In many real-world training environments, this type of time commitment is just not feasible.

As a result, a number of researchers have explored whether it is possible to design emotion control techniques that are less resource intensive yet equally efficacious. A good example is the emotion control strategy developed by Kanfer and Ackerman (1990, 1996), which contains several key elements. First, trainees are told not to worry about their task performance early in training and not to be distracted by the errors that they make. Second, trainees are instructed to increase the frequency of positive thoughts and to reduce the frequency of negative emotions, such as worry or upset following errors (Kanfer & Ackerman, 1996). Individuals receive instruction on the emotion control strategy prior to initial task performance, and between trials they are given emotion control reminders such as "Use the EMOTION CONTROL strategy while performing the task. That is, do not get upset or worry. Adopt a positive, 'CAN DO' attitude. This will improve your performance" (Kanfer & Ackerman, 1990, p. 35). Kanfer and Ackerman (1990) found that trainees exposed to this emotion control strategy exhibited increased performance, reported fewer negative affective reactions, and made fewer attempts to monitor their performance score. In addition, the authors found that the beneficial effects of the emotion control strategy were most pronounced during the early stages of task performance. Once again, this is when task demands are the greatest and poor performance and errors are most likely. As Kanfer and Ackerman (1996) stated, "Emotion-control skills refer to self-regulatory patterns aimed at reducing the diversion of attentional resources to emotional concerns, and are most useful when attentional demands of the task are high" (p. 168).

The key elements of Kanfer and Ackerman's emotion control strategy are not unique and can be found singularly or in combination in a number of active learning strategies. For example, most studies on error training have integrated error management instructions or heuristics (e.g., "There is always a way to leave the error situation") into the strategy (Keith & Frese, 2005, p. 681). These statements are presented repeatedly to learners during the course of training and are designed to reduce the negative emotions that often accompany errors and poor performance. Similarly, mastery training strategies often incorporate instructions designed to help reduce evaluative pressures surrounding performance. For example, the mastery training strategy evaluated by Kozlowski, Gully, et al. (2001) instructed trainees to use their scores as diagnostic feedback that could help them learn the task, rather than as indication of their ability. These instructions may promote more adaptive performance attributions (e.g., feelings of personal control), thereby reducing frustration and anxiety.

Despite this theoretical and empirical evidence, the importance of emotions in active learning has been debated over the years. For example, early research on error management training emphasized the importance of emotion control for reducing the frustration and anxiety that typically accompany errors (Frese et al., 1991). However, Frese (1995) noted difficulty in replicating the positive effects of emotion control and stated, "At this point in time, I have become more sceptical of the emotional hypothesis" (p. 119). However, more recent work has renewed interest in the emotion control component of active learning. In the following sections, we briefly discuss the potential effect of this emotion control component of the active learning approach on two affective self-regulatory processes: state anxiety and attributions.

State Anxiety

Keith and Frese (2005) found that error management training led to higher emotion control (i.e., greater use of emotional regulation strategies) than error-avoidant training and that emotion control positively affected adaptive transfer. Based on this finding, the authors concluded that emotional self-regulation plays an important role in active learning. Another study by Bell and Kozlowski (2008) examined the implications of including emotion control training as part of an active learning strategy. The emotion control training lowered trainees' state anxiety, which in turn led to higher levels of self-efficacy and adaptive performance. These emerging findings suggest that emotion control is an important self-regulatory element of active learning due not only to its direct effects on learning and performance but also to its role in supporting other key self-regulation processes.

Attributions

One process variable that has yet to be examined in active learning research but nonetheless may be important in emotion regulation concerns trainees' performance attributions. Prior research has revealed that negative emotions occur when an individual makes a cognitive appraisal that a substantial imbalance exists between perceived environmental demands and perceived response capability (McGrath, 1970). Attributions play an important role in an individual's perception of his or her response capability. In particular, individuals who perceive greater personal control over their current situation tend to experience lower levels of anxiety. This relates to the fact that individuals who perceive that they can respond to environmental demands tend to experience less anxiety. DuCette and Wolk (1973), for example, found that individuals with a more internal locus of control were more likely to believe they could meet situational demands and, therefore, experienced less anxiety than individuals with a more external locus of control.

A major risk in giving individuals control over their learning and encouraging them to make errors is that they will get trapped in an error state, feel helpless, and withdraw from the task. Recognizing this, the emotion control strategies highlighted above include components designed to help shape learners' attributions. For example, emotion control statements such as "There is always a way to leave the error situation" are aimed, in part, at countering feelings of helplessness and increasing individuals' perceptions of control. By instructing individuals to adopt a "can-do" attitude, Kanfer and Ackerman's (1990) emotion control intervention also influences individuals' attributions. Accordingly, future research should consider trainees' attributions, in particular their locus of control, as an important process involved in emotional regulation during active learning.

ATIs

It is important to highlight that Kanfer and Ackerman (1990) found that their emotion control strategy had positive effects for low-ability trainees but did not benefit high-ability trainees. They suggested that low-ability individuals benefited the most from the strategy because they were more likely to make errors, perform poorly, and, therefore, experience negative affect. In addition, a number of researchers (e.g., Kanfer & Ackerman, 1990; Reason, 1990; Wood et al., 2000) have argued that emotions, such as stress and anxiety, increase cognitive load and divert attentional resources away from the task at hand. Whereas high-ability individuals may have ample cognitive resources to split between performing a task and monitoring their emotions, low-ability individuals have more limited cognitive resources. As a result, any diversion of their resources away from the task probably has a significant and negative impact on their performance. Overall, these findings suggest that cognitive ability may moderate the effects of emotion control strategies, such that their impact will be greater for low-ability individuals because of their increased susceptibility to negative emotions and the significant impact that any type of distraction will have on their performance.

A second important individual difference to consider is trait anxiety. Research has shown that individuals differ in terms of their natural, or trait, level of anxiety (e.g., Gaudry, Vagg, & Spielberger, 1975; Spielberger, 1985). Whereas some individuals are relatively immune to anxiety and stress, other individuals are prone to such emotions. Put simply, some individuals are more likely than others to experience high levels of state anxiety. These differences in trait anxiety, therefore, may play an important role in determining the impact of an emotion control strategy. Individuals who are anxiety prone are more likely to react negatively to events, such as errors, and be distracted by the worry and anxiety that accompany them. In contrast, individuals who have relatively low levels of trait anxiety will be less likely to develop anxiety and, therefore, be distracted by their emotions. As a result, an emotion control strategy should be especially important for individuals high in trait anxiety, because of their enhanced susceptibility to state anxiety.

Outcomes of the Active Learning Approach

Although it is clear that the active learning approach has the potential to enhance trainees' knowledge and performance, it is also important to recognize that the effects of this approach are not uniform across all types of learning outcomes or at all periods of time. In particular, most active learning strategies are designed to improve outcomes after, as opposed to during, training. Error training, for example, often leads to lower levels of training performance because trainees experiment, make errors, and sometimes arrive at wrong solutions (Keith & Frese, 2005). The benefits of error training typically do not emerge until one examines trainees' performance in the long run or the transfer of knowledge and skills to new problems (Bell & Kozlowski, 2008; Hesketh, 1997). Similarly, mastery inductions often lead to lower levels of performance in the short term because trainees are focused on developing rather than demonstrating their competence. Again, it is often not until one examines trainees' transfer performance that the benefits of mastery training become evident. An important implication of these findings is that assessments of trainees' skills during or immediately following training may not provide an accurate indication of the utility of active learning strategies. In the sections that follow, we further examine the implications of the active learning approach for different types of training outcomes by considering the distinction between basic and strategic outcomes and analogical and adaptive transfer.

Basic Versus Strategic Outcomes

Several researchers have argued that the effectiveness of the active learning approach may depend on the complexity of the skills being trained. Clark and Voogel (1985), for example, argued that more basic, proceduralized skills lend themselves to training by errorless learning and more traditionally behavioristic techniques, whereas more cognitively based and complex skills that require conceptual knowledge or the development of a mental model and strategies are better suited to exploratory learning. Similarly, Heimbeck et al. (2003) predicted and found benefits for error training on difficult but not easy tasks. They suggested that performance in easy tasks does not benefit from error management training because easy tasks require only basic skills and typically involve few errors. Overall, active learning approaches are likely to yield little benefit over more traditional, proceduralized approaches when the goal is the development of basic declarative knowledge and skills (e.g., McDaniel & Schlager, 1990). However, on more complex tasks where performance depends on the development of strategic competencies, the active learning approach is typically superior to traditional forms of instructions (Frese, 1995).

Analogical Versus Adaptive Transfer

The active learning approach may also be more effective for specific types of transfer. For example, numerous studies have shown that exploratory learning and proceduralized instruction produce similar levels of analogical or near transfer (e.g., Dormann & Frese, 1994; McDaniel & Schlager, 1990), which involves the application of trained skills to problems analogous to those encountered during training. However, exploratory learning has also been shown to be superior to proceduralized instruction for facilitating adaptive transfer (Bell & Kozlowski, 2008; Frese et al., 1988; Kamouri et al., 1986), or the transfer of skills to novel problems. Similarly, Keith and Frese (2005) argued that error training should be particularly effective for promoting adaptive transfer because trainees learn to deal with unexpected problems. Indeed, they found that error management and error-avoidant training led to similar levels of analogical transfer, but error management training resulted in higher levels of adaptive transfer. Finally, Kozlowski, Gully, et al. (2001) found that mastery training enhanced trainees' adaptive performance through its positive effects on their knowledge coherence and self-efficacy. Although these findings emerged from research on specific active learning strategies, the overall body of evidence suggests that although the benefits of the active learning approach for analogical transfer are negligible, it leads to higher levels of adaptive transfer than more traditional instruction.

A Research Agenda

As highlighted at the outset of this chapter, substantial changes in the nature of work and organizations have occurred in recent years (Salas & Cannon-Bowers, 2001). These changes have forced organizations to rethink the nature of training as it has become clear that many of our traditional training tools and principles are not well suited for developing the adaptive competencies required for success in an increasing number of jobs. Moreover, training today is increasingly being delivered via technology-based methods and embedded in the work environment, placing greater demands on employees to manage their own learning. These and other trends have stimulated interest in the concept of active learning, not only because of its role in developing complex and adaptive skills but also because of its importance in the process of self-directed learning. A number of recent studies have been instrumental in demonstrating the utility of active learning strategies for enhancing trainee self-regulation, learning, and adaptability. Yet, a comprehensive theory of active learning remains elusive, and many important questions persist.

The goal of this chapter was to develop a comprehensive and integrative framework of active learning. In the preceding sections, we discussed the different elements of this framework, including the core training components that cut across different active learning interventions; the cognitive, motivational, and emotion self-regulatory pathways these components influence; the individual differences that moderate the effects of the training components; and the anticipated outcomes of the active learning approach. Although we believe this is an important first step toward developing a theory of active learning and learner-centered training design, we also recognize that much more work is needed. In this final section of the chapter, we use the framework to highlight several potentially fruitful areas of future research in the area of active learning.

Core Training Components and Individual Differences

As argued throughout this chapter, it is important that future research move beyond testing multifaceted active learning strategies to examining the effects of the core training components on self-regulatory processes and training outcomes. This is not to say that we should avoid intervention-based research, but it will be important to ensure that new interventions are conceptually linked to the core components so we understand their training design features and the process pathways through which these interventions operate. Through the elaboration of the components embedded in different active learning strategies, results across studies will be more readily compared and integrated, thereby facilitating the development of a theory of active learning.

Future research on active learning must also continue to adopt an aptitude–treatment perspective. A number of recent studies have provided valuable insight into the effects of individual differences on how learners interact with active learning interventions (e.g., Gully et al., 2002; Heimbeck et al., 2003), but to date the focus has been limited to cognitive ability and a small set of dispositional traits (e.g., conscientiousness). More research is needed to not only expand this focus to include previously unexamined individual differences, such as trait anxiety or self-regulatory focus, but also explore how these individual differences interact with specific training components to influence particular self-regulatory processes.

Elaborating Process Pathways

In this chapter, we have also argued for greater emphasis on understanding the processes that define active learning and the process pathways through which the different training components exert their effects on learning, performance, and adaptability. In this regard, it is important to note that some of these active learning mechanisms have received more attention than others. In the cognitive domain, for example, recent research has firmly established metacognition as an important self-regulatory process underlying active learning (e.g., Bell & Kozlowski, 2008; Keith & Frese, 2005; Schmidt & Ford, 2003). However, other potentially important cognitive self-regulatory processes, such as effortful processing and mental models, have received very little attention. Similarly, significant research has demonstrated that intrinsic motivation and self-efficacy are important mediators of the effects of mastery inductions on learning and performance (e.g., Kozlowski, Toney, et al., 2001; Phillips & Gully, 1997; Rawsthorne & Elliot, 1999), but the effects of emotion control strategies on trainees' emotional regulation and emotion states have not been widely studied. Accordingly, it will be important to expand the scope of self-regulatory processes examined in future active learning research.

Relative to the cognitive and motivational components of active learning, the emotion component has received much less support over the years (Frese, 1995). Although a few recent studies have provided evidence that emotional regulation is important in the active learning approach (e.g., Bell & Kozlowski, 2008; Keith & Frese, 2005), we lack a solid understanding of how to effectively utilize emotion control strategies in training. For example, in situations where anxiety levels do not reach a level where they cause significant decrements in performance, encouraging trainees to focus on regulating their emotions may have little utility and in fact may be harmful due to decreased attentional resources and on-task focus.

More research is needed to better identify those situations in which it is critical to incorporate an emotion control strategy into training. Different methods of implementing emotion control strategies should also be examined. For example, Heimbeck et al. (2003) argued that it may be most appropriate to implement emotion control interventions only after trainees have acquired a foundation of knowledge and skills, but Kanfer and Ackerman (1990) suggested that there may be utility in gradually phasing out these interventions over the course of training. It is important to determine whether one of these competing recommendations is more effective than the other.

Unpacking Adaptation

One of the themes underlying research on active learning is the prospect that it enables adaptive expertise (Smith et al., 1997), the ability to flexibly adjust one's learning when the task becomes more difficult, complex, and dynamic. One general finding is that adaptive learning often appears to slow or inhibit training performance, but the payoff appears when capabilities have to be applied to a changed task. Some active learning research has helped to identify self-regulatory constructs that underlie adaptive performance. For example, at the individual level, Kozlowski, Gully, et al. (2001) showed that knowledge structure coherence and self-efficacy were predictive of adaptive performance after declarative knowledge, training performance, and cognitive ability had been controlled. They reasoned that knowledge coherence allowed trainees to extrapolate what they had learned to a changed task situation, and self-efficacy enabled trainees to persist in spite of the difficulties they encountered when the task changed. However, as a general rule, the process of adaptation has not yet been a central focus in most active learning research. We think the process framework we have outlined in this chapter can be extended to better unpack the underpinnings of adaptive performance.

Work by LePine, Colquitt, and Erez (2000) has shown that conscientiousness, which is generally regarded as a positive contributor to task performance, inhibits individual adaptation when a task has changed. Similar to the findings by Gully et al. (2002), it appears that the dependability and persistence aspects of conscientiousness prevent an individual from exploring alternative actions when what had been successful no longer works. In addition, more recent work by LePine (2005) has shown that when teams have to adapt to an unexpected change, those teams that were more performance oriented failed to adapt well, whereas those teams that were more mastery oriented were better able to detect the need to change and to discover an appropriate adaptive strategy. In this vein, recent research by Chen, Wallace, and Thomas (2005) modeled self-regulatory processes to link end-of-training outcomes and adaptive performance. Although neither of these studies was directly relevant to active learning interventions, they suggest a promising extension to the paradigm that would begin to probe the process of adaptation that warrants further investigation.

Conclusion

More than a decade of research has shown that active learning interventions, such as error training, mastery training, and guided exploration, are useful tools for promoting learning, performance, and, in particular, adaptability (Smith et al., 1997). However, what is less well understood is how these interventions work—which training components are essential to their success, and what are the process mechanisms through which they operate? In addition, it remains unclear for whom these interventions are most effective. This chapter advances recent research on active learning (e.g., Keith & Frese, 2005; Kozlowski & Bell, 2006) by shifting the theoretical focus from one of intervention design (e.g., Kozlowski, Toney, et al., 2001) to one providing an integrative framework that identifies the core training components of active learning interventions, maps these components onto self-regulatory process pathways that drive important training outcomes, and highlights possible aptitude–treatment interactions that detail how different trainees may interact with specific components of active learning interventions. Ultimately, we hope that this effort will stimulate future theory development and empirical research aimed at better understanding active learning and advancing the science of learner-centered training design.

References

Archer, J. (1994). Achievement goals as a measure of motivation in university students. *Contemporary Educational Psychology, 19*, 430–446.
Barrick, M. R., & Mount, M. K. (1991). The Big Five personality dimensions and job performance: A meta-analysis. *Personnel Psychology, 44*, 1–26.
Barrios, B. A. (1978). Cue controlled relaxation as a generalizable coping skill. *Psychology, 15*, 14–17.

Bell, B. S., & Kozlowski, S. W. J. (2002). Adaptive guidance: Enhancing self-regulation, knowledge, and performance in technology-based training. *Personnel Psychology, 55,* 267–306.

Bell, B. S., & Kozlowski, S. W. J. (2008). Active learning: Effects of core training design elements on self-regulatory processes, learning, and adaptability. *Journal of Applied Psychology, 93,* 296–316.

Benson, H. (1975). *The relaxation response.* New York: Avon.

Bouffard, T., Boisvert, J., Vezeau, C., & Larouche, C. (1995). The impact of goal orientation on self-regulation and performance among college students. *British Journal of Educational Psychology, 65,* 317–329.

Boyle, K., & Klimoski, R. J. (1995, May). *Toward an understanding of goal orientation in a training context.* Paper presented at the 10th Annual Conference of the Society for Industrial/Organizational Psychology, Orlando, FL.

Bransford, J. D., Brown, A. L., & Cocking, R. R. (Eds.). (1999). *How people learn: Brain, mind, experience, and school.* Washington, DC: National Academy Press.

Brett, J. F., & VandeWalle, D. (1999). Goal orientation and goal content as predictors of performance in a training program. *Journal of Applied Psychology, 84,* 863–873.

Brown, A. L., Bransford, J. D. Ferrara, R. A., & Campione, J. C. (1983). Learning, remembering, and understanding. In J. H. Flavell & E. M. Markman (Eds.), *Handbook of child psychology* (Vol. 3, pp. 77–166). New York: Wiley.

Brown, K. G. (2001). Using computers to deliver training: Which employees learn and why? *Personnel Psychology, 54,* 271–296.

Brown, K. G., & Ford, J. K. (2002). Using computer technology in training: Building an infrastructure for active learning. In K. Kraiger (Ed.), *Creating, implementing, and managing effective training and development* (pp. 192–233). San Francisco: Jossey-Bass.

Button, S. B., Mathieu, J. E., & Zajac, D. M. (1996). Goal orientation in organizational research: A conceptual and empirical foundation. *Organizational Behavior and Human Decision Processes, 67,* 26–48.

Cannon-Bowers, J. A., Rhodenizer, L., Salas, E., & Bowers, C. A. (1998). A framework for understanding pre-practice conditions and their impact on learning. *Personnel Psychology, 51,* 291–320.

Carlson, R. A., Lundy, D. H., & Schneider, W. (1992). Strategy guidance and memory aiding in learning a problem-solving skill. *Human Factors, 34,* 129–145.

Carter, J. E., & Kelly, A. E. (1997). Using traditional and paradoxical imagery interventions with reactant intramural athletes. *The Sports Psychologist, 11,* 175–189.

Carver, C. S., & Scheier, M. F. (1990). Origins and functions of positive and negative affect: A control-process view. *Psychological Review, 97,* 19–35.

Chen, G., Gully, S. M., Whiteman, J., & Kilcullen, R. N. (2000). Examination of relationships among trait-like individual differences, state-like individual differences, and learning performance. *Journal of Applied Psychology, 85,* 835–847.

Chen, G., Thomas, B., & Wallace, J. C. (2005). A multilevel examination of the relationships among training outcomes, mediating regulatory processes, and adaptive performance. *Journal of Applied Psychology, 90,* 827–841.

Toward a Theory of Learner-Centered Training Design 295

Chillarege, K. A., Nordstrom, C. R., & Williams, K. B. (2003). Learning from our mistakes: Error management training for mature learners. *Journal of Business and Psychology, 17*, 369–385.
Church, M. A., Elliot, A. J., & Gable, S. L. (2001). Perceptions of classroom environment, achievement goals, and achievement outcomes. *Journal of Educational Psychology, 93*, 43–54.
Clark, R. E. (2001). *Learning from media: Arguments, analysis, and evidence.* Greenwich, CT: Information Age.
Clark, R. E., & Voogel, A. (1985). Transfer of training principles for instructional design. *Educational Communication and Technology Journal, 33*, 113–123.
Colquitt, J. A., LePine, J. A., & Noe, R. A. (2000). Toward an integrative theory of training motivation: A meta-analytic path analysis of twenty years of research. *Journal of Applied Psychology, 85*, 678–707.
Colquitt, J. A., & Simmering, M. J. (1998). Conscientiousness, goal orientation, and motivation to learn during the learning process: A longitudinal study. *Journal of Applied Psychology, 83*, 654–665.
Costa, P. T., Jr., & McCrae, R. R. (1992). *Revised NEO Personality Inventory (NEO-PI-R) and NEO Five-Factor Inventory (NEO-FFI) professional manual.* Odessa, FL: Psychological Assessment Resources.
Debowski, S., Wood, R. E., & Bandura, A. (2001). Impact of guided exploration and enactive exploration on self-regulatory mechanisms and information acquisition through electronic search. *Journal of Applied Psychology, 86*, 1129–1141.
DeRouin, R. E., Fritzsche, B. A., & Salas, E. (2004). Optimizing e-learning: Research-based guidelines for learner-controlled training. *Human Resource Management, 43*, 147–162.
Dormann, T., & Frese, M. (1994). Error training: Replication and the function of exploratory behavior. *International Journal of Human-Computer Interaction, 6*, 365–372.
DuCette, J., & Wolk, S. (1973). Cognitive and motivational correlates of generalized expectancies for control. *Journal of Personality and Social Psychology, 26*, 420–429.
Dweck, C. S. (1986). Mental processes affecting learning. *American Psychologist, 41*, 1040–1048.
Dweck, C. S., & Leggett, E. L. (1988). A social-cognitive approach to motivation and personality. *Psychological Review, 95*, 256–273.
Egan, D. E., & Greeno, J. G. (1973). Acquiring cognitive structure by discovery and rule learning. *Journal of Educational Psychology, 64*, 85–97.
Elliot, A. J., & Church, M. A. (1997). A hierarchical model of approach and avoidance achievement motivation. *Journal of Personality and Social Psychology, 72*, 218–232.
Elliot, A. J., & Harackiewicz, J. M. (1996). Approach and avoidance achievement goals and intrinsic motivation: A mediational analysis. *Journal of Personality and Social Psychology, 70*, 461–475.
Elliot, A. J., & McGregor, H. (2001). A 2 x 2 achievement goal framework. *Journal of Personality and Social Psychology, 80*, 501–519.
Ford, J. K., Smith, E. M., Weissbein, D. A., Gully, S. M., & Salas, E. (1998). Relationships of goal orientation, metacognitive activity, and practice strategies with learning outcomes and transfer. *Journal of Applied Psychology, 83*, 218–233.

Frese, M. (1995). Error management in training: Conceptual and empirical results. In C. Zucchermaglio, S. Bagnara, & S. U. Stuchy (Eds.), *Organizational learning and technological change* (pp. 112–124). New York: Springer-Verlag.

Frese, M., Albrecht, K., Altmann, A., Lang, J., Papstein, P. V., Peyerl, R., et al. (1988). The effects of an active development of the mental model in the training process: Experimental results in a word processing system. *Behaviour and Information Technology, 7,* 295–304.

Frese, M., & Altmann, A. (1989). The treatment of errors in learning and training. In L. Bainbridge & S. A. R. Quintanilla (Eds.), *Developing skills with new technology* (pp. 65–86). Chichester, UK: Wiley & Sons.

Frese, M., Brodbeck, F., Heinbokel, T., Mooser, C., Schleiffenbaum, E., & Thiemann, P. (1991). Errors in training computer skills: On the positive function of errors. *Human–Computer Interaction, 6,* 77–93.

Frese, M., & Zapf, D. (1994). Action as the core of work psychology: A German approach. In H. C. Triandis, M. D. Dunnette, & L. M. Hough (Eds.), *Handbook of industrial and organizational psychology* (2nd ed., Vol. 4, pp. 271–340). Palo Alto, CA: Consulting Psychologists.

Gaudry, E., Vagg, P., & Spielberger, C. D. (1975). Validation of the state-trait distinction in anxiety research. *Multivariate Behavioral Research, 10,* 331–341.

Goldberg, L. R. (1999). A broad-bandwidth, public-domain, personality inventory measuring the lower-level facets of several five-factor models. In I. Mervielde, I. Deary, F. DeFruyt, & F. Ostendorf (Eds.), *Personality psychology in Europe* (Vol. 7, pp. 7–28). Tilburg, The Netherlands: Tilburg University Press.

Gully, S. M., Payne, S. C., Kiechel, K. L., & Whiteman, J. K. (2002). The impact of error training and individual differences on training outcomes: An attribute-treatment interaction perspective. *Journal of Applied Psychology, 87,* 143–155.

Harackiewicz, J. M., Barron, K. E., Pintrich, P. R., Elliot, A. J., & Thrash, T. M. (2002). Revision of achievement goal theory: Necessary and illuminating. *Journal of Educational Psychology, 94*(3), 638–645.

Harackiewicz, J. M., & Elliot, A. J. (1993). Achievement goals and intrinsic motivation. *Journal of Personality and Social Psychology, 65,* 904–915.

Heimbeck, D., Frese, M., Sonnentag, S., & Keith, N. (2003). Integrating errors into the training process: The function of error management instructions and the role of goal orientation. *Personnel Psychology, 56,* 333–361.

Hesketh, B. (1997). Dilemmas in training for transfer and retention. *Applied Psychology: An International Review, 46,* 317–339.

Hogan, J., & Ones, D. S. (1997). Conscientiousness and integrity at work. In R. Hogan, J. Johnson, & S. Briggs (Eds.), *Handbook of personality psychology* (pp. 849–870). San Diego, CA: Academic Press.

Holyoak, K. J. (1991). Symbolic connectionism: Toward third-generation theories of expertise. In K. A. Ericsson & J. Smith (Eds.), *Toward a general theory of expertise* (pp. 301–336). Cambridge, UK: Cambridge University Press.

Horan, J. J., Hackett, G., Buchanan, J. D., Stone, G. I., & Demchik-Stone, D. (1977). Coping with pain. A component analysis of stress inoculation. *Cognitive Therapy and Research, 1,* 211–221.

Iran-Nejad, A. (1990). Active and dynamic self-regulation of learning processes. *Review of Educational Research, 60,* 573–602.

Ivancic, K., & Hesketh, B. (1995). Making the best of errors during training. *Training Research Journal, 1*, 103–125.

Ivancic, K., & Hesketh, B. (2000). Learning from error in a driving simulation: Effects on driving skill and self-confidence. *Ergonomics, 43*, 1966–1984.

Kamouri, A. L., Kamouri, J., & Smith, K. H. (1986). Training by exploration: Facilitating the transfer of procedural knowledge through analogical reasoning. *International Journal of Man-Machine Studies, 24*, 171–192.

Kanfer, R., & Ackerman, P. L. (1989). Motivation and cognitive abilities: An integrative/aptitude-treatment interaction approach to skill acquisition. *Journal of Applied Psychology—Monograph, 74*, 657–690.

Kanfer, R., & Ackerman, P. L. (1990). *Ability and metacognitive determinants of skill acquisition and transfer* (Air Force Office of Scientific Research Final Report). Minneapolis, MN: Air Force Office of Scientific Research.

Kanfer, R., & Ackerman, P. L. (1996). A self-regulatory skills perspective to reducing cognitive interference. In I. G. Sarason, G. R. Pierce, & B. R. Sarason (Eds.), *Cognitive interference: Theories, methods, and findings* (pp. 153–171). Mahwah, NJ: Lawrence Erlbaum Associates.

Kanfer, R., Ackerman, P. L., & Heggestad, E. D. (1996). Motivational skills and self-regulation for learning: A trait perspective. *Learning and Individual Differences, 8*, 185–209.

Kanfer, R., Ackerman, P. L., Murtha, T. C., Dugdale, B., & Nelson, L. (1994). Goal setting, conditions of practice, and task performance: A resource allocation perspective. *Journal of Applied Psychology, 79*, 826–835.

Kanfer, R., & Heggestad, E. D. (1999). Individual differences in motivation: Traits and self-regulatory skills. In P. L. Ackerman, P. C. Kyllonen, & R. D. Roberts (Eds.), *Learning and individual differences: Process, trait, and content determinants* (pp. 293–309). Washington, DC: American Psychological Association.

Karoly, P. (1993). Mechanisms of self-regulation: A systems view. *Annual Review of Psychology, 44*, 23–52.

Keith, N., & Frese, M. (2005). Self-regulation in error management training: Emotion control and metacognition as mediators of performance effects. *Journal of Applied Psychology, 90*, 677–691.

Kluger, A., & DeNisi, A. (1996). The effects of feedback interventions on performance: A historical review, a meta-analysis, and a preliminary intervention theory. *Psychological Bulletin, 119*, 254–284.

Kolb, D. A. (1984). *Experiential learning*. Englewood Cliffs, NJ: Prentice Hall.

Kozlowski, S. W. J., & Bell, B. S. (2006). Disentangling achievement orientation and goal setting: Effects on self-regulatory processes. *Journal of Applied Psychology, 91*, 900–916.

Kozlowski, S. W. J., Gully, S. M., Brown, K. G., Salas, E., Smith, E. M., & Nason, E. R. (2001). Effects of training goals and goal orientation traits on multidimensional training outcomes and performance adaptability. *Organizational Behavior and Human Decision Processes, 85*, 1–31.

Kozlowski, S. W. J., Toney, R. J., Mullins, M. E., Weissbein, D. A., Brown, K. G., & Bell, B. S. (2001). Developing adaptability: A theory for the design of integrated-embedded training systems. In E. Salas (Ed.), *Human/technology interaction in complex systems* (Vol. 10). Greenwich, CT: JAI.

Kraiger, K., Ford, J. K., & Salas, E. (1993). Application of cognitive, skill-based, and affective theories of learning outcomes to new methods of training evaluation. *Journal of Applied Psychology, 78*, 311–328.

LePine, J. A. (2005). Adaptation in teams in response to unforeseen change: Effects of goal difficulty and team composition in terms of cognitive ability and goal orientation. *Journal of Applied Psychology, 90*, 1153–1167.

LePine, J. A., Colquitt, J. A., & Erez, A. (2000). Adaptability to changing tasks contexts: Effects of general cognitive ability, conscientiousness, and openness to experience. *Personnel Psychology, 53*, 563–593.

Locke, E. A. (2000). Motivation, cognition, and action: An analysis of studies of task goals and knowledge. *Applied Psychology: An International Review, 49*, 408–429.

Locke, E. A., & Latham, G. P. (2002). Building a practically useful theory of goal setting and task motivation: A 35-year odyssey. *American Psychologist, 57*, 705–717.

Martocchio, J. J. (1994). Effects of conceptions of ability, and academic achievement. *Journal of Applied Psychology, 79*, 819–825.

Martocchio, J. J., & Judge, T. A. (1997). Relationship between conscientiousness and learning in employee training: Mediating influences of self-deception and self-efficacy. *Journal of Applied Psychology, 82*, 764–773.

Mayer, R. E. (2004). Should there be a three-strikes rule against pure discovery learning? The case for guided methods of instruction. *American Psychologist, 59*, 14–19.

McDaniel, M. A., & Schlager, M. S. (1990). Discovery learning and transfer of problem-solving skills. *Cognition and Instruction, 7*, 129–159.

McGrath, J. E. (1970). *Social and psychological factors in stress.* New York: Holt, Rinehart & Winston.

McGregor, H., & Elliot, A. J. (2002). Achievement goals as predictors of achievement related processes prior to task engagement. *Journal of Educational Psychology, 94*, 381–395.

Meece, J. (1994). The role of motivation in self-regulated learning. In D. H. Schunk & B. J. Zimmerman (Eds.), *Self-regulation of learning and performance* (pp. 25–44). Hillsdale, NJ: Lawrence Erlbaum Associates.

Newman, R. S. (1998). Students' help seeking during problem solving: Influences of personal and contextual achievement goals. *Journal of Educational Psychology, 90*, 644–658.

Nordstrom, C. R., Wendland, D., & Williams, K. B. (1998). "To err is human": An examination of the effectiveness of error management training. *Journal of Business and Psychology, 12*, 269–282.

Payne, S. C., Youngcourt, S. S., & Beaubien, J. M. (2007). A meta-analytic examination of the goal orientation nomological net. *Journal of Applied Psychology, 92*, 128–150.

Pearn, M., & Downs, S. (1989). *Adapting to new technology by developing skilled learners.* Paper presented at the 4th West European Congress on the Psychology of Work and Organisation: Working With Change, Cambridge, UK.

Phillips, J. M., & Gully, S. M. (1997). Role of goal orientation, ability, need for achievement, and locus of control in the self-efficacy and goal-setting process. *Journal of Applied Psychology, 82*, 792–802.

Rawsthorne, L. J., & Elliot, A. J. (1999). Achievement goals and intrinsic motivation: A meta-analytic review. *Personality and Social Psychological Review, 3,* 326–344.

Reason, J. (1990). *Human error.* New York: Cambridge University Press.

Reeves, T. C. (1993). Pseudoscience in computer-based instruction: The case of learner control research. *Journal of Computer-Based Instruction, 20,* 39–46.

Revans, R. W. (1982). *The origins and growth of action learning.* Bromley, UK: Chartwell-Bratt.

Rose, R. L., & Veiga, J. F. (1984). Assessing the sustained effects of a stress management intervention on anxiety and locus of control. *Academy of Management Journal, 27,* 190–198.

Salas, E., & Cannon-Bowers, J. A. (2001). The science of training: A decade of progress. *Annual Review of Psychology, 52,* 471–499.

Salomon, G., & Globerson, T. (1987). Skill is not enough: The role of mindfulness in learning and transfer. *International Journal of Research in Education, 11,* 623–638.

Salomon, G., & Perkins, D. N. (1989). Rocky roads to transfer: Rethinking mechanisms of a neglected phenomenon. *Educational Psychologist, 24,* 113–142.

Sapp, M. (1994). The effects of guided imagery on reducing the worry and emotionality components of test anxiety. *Journal of Mental Imagery, 18,* 165–180.

Schmidt, A. M., & Ford, J. K. (2003). Learning within a learner control training environment: The interactive effects of goal orientation and metacognitive instruction on learning outcomes. *Personnel Psychology, 56,* 405–429.

Schönpflug, W. (1985). Goal directed behavior as a source of stress: Psychological origins and consequences of inefficiency. In M. Frese & J. Sabini (Eds.), *Goal directed behavior: The concept of action in psychology* (pp. 172–188). Hillsdale, NJ: Lawrence Erlbaum Associates.

Schwartz, D. L., & Bransford, J. D. (1998). A time for telling. *Cognition and Instruction, 16,* 475–522.

Seijts, G. H., Latham, G. P., Tasa, K., & Latham, B. W. (2004). Goal setting and goal orientation: An integration of two different yet related literatures. *Academy of Management Journal, 47,* 227–239.

Simons, P. R., & De Jong, F. P. C. M. (1992). Self-regulation and computer-aided instruction. *Applied Psychology: An International Review, 41,* 333–346.

Singer, R. N., & Pease, D. (1976). A comparison of discovery learning and guided instructional strategies on motor skill learning, retention, and transfer. *Research Quarterly, 47,* 788–796.

Smith, E. M., Ford, J. K., & Kozlowski, S. W. J. (1997). Building adaptive expertise: Implications for training design strategies. In M. A. Quinones & A. Ehrenstein (Eds.), *Training for a rapidly changing workplace: Applications of psychological research* (pp. 89–118). Washington, DC: American Psychological Association.

Snow, R. E. (1986). Individual differences in the design of educational programs. *American Psychologist, 41,* 1029–1039.

Spielberger, C. D. (1985). Assessment of state and trait anxiety: Conceptual and methodological issues. *Southern Psychologist, 2,* 6–16.

Stevens, C. K., & Gist, M. E. (1997). Effects of self-efficacy and goal-orientation training on negotiation skill maintenance: What are the mechanisms? *Personnel Psychology, 50,* 955–978.

Sweller, J. (1988). Cognitive load during problem solving: Effects on learning. *Cognitive Science, 12*, 257–285.

Sweller, J., Mawer, R., & Ward, M. (1983). Development of expertise in mathematical problem solving. *Journal of Experimental Psychology: General, 112*(4), 639–661.

Tabernero, C., & Wood, R. E. (1999). Implicit theories versus the social construal of ability in self-regulation and performance on a complex task. *Organizational Behavior and Human Decision Processes, 78*, 104–127.

Tuovinen, J. E., & Sweller, J. (1999). A comparison of cognitive load associated with discovery learning and worked examples. *Journal of Educational Psychology, 91*, 334–341.

Volpert, W. (1987). Psychological regulation of work activities. In U. Kleinbeck & J. Rutenfranz (Eds.), *Enzyklopädie der Psychologie: Themenbereich D, Serie III, Band 1. Arbeitspsychologie.* Göttingen, Germany: Hogrefe.

Wood, R., & Bandura, A. (1989). Impact of conceptions of ability on self-regulatory mechanisms and complex decision-making. *Journal of Personality and Social Psychology, 56*, 407–415.

Wood, R. E., Kakebeeke, B. M., Debowski, S., & Frese, M. (2000). The impact of enactive exploration on intrinsic motivation, strategy, and performance in electronic search. *Applied Psychology: An International Review, 49*, 263–283.

Section 3

The Organizational Context, Levels, and Time

Having elucidated learning processes and indicated how effective learning can be stimulated through sound, evidence-based instructional design, we now shift attention to a multilevel perspective that considers learning and development in the broader context of the organization. For example, although formal training is an important aspect of learning in organizations, there are many informal ways that employees enhance their knowledge and skills. And, although "training" is essentially a discrete event, employees have the potential to be proactive learners across the life span. Moreover, consider that learning, although a fundamentally psychological process at the individual level, is also multilevel and can be meaningfully captured as collective phenomena that emerge across levels and over time as team and organizational learning. Finally, we conclude the section with a consideration of the interplay between macro and micro approaches to training effectiveness, and the way forward to better integration across the organizational system.

Chapter 9 by Tannenbaum, Beard, McNall, and Salas, "Informal Learning and Development in Organizations," considers the role of unstructured, unsystematic, informal learning that occurs on the job. Although organizations make considerable investments in formal training and development, the majority of what employees learn in organizations is tacit and transmitted informally. Remarkably, these informal processes are not leveraged by organizations—they are unmanaged. This chapter develops a conceptual framework focusing on the individual and the organization in an effort to identify how informal learning can be better shaped, leveraged, and utilized by organizations.

In Chapter 10, "'Learning' a Living: Continuous Learning for Survival in Today's Talent Market," Malloy and Noe consider the many challenges and pressures facing employees in today's competitive talent market. The employer–employee relationship in force for much of the 20th century has changed, and changed radically. That once stable relationship is unstable, temporary, and continuing to evolve. This chapter builds a model of continuous learning that goes beyond the more typical focus on individual factors to also integrate organizational context factors and broader labor market influences in an effort to better understand the forces and processes that influence employee efforts to maintain and build their human capital and to navigate a successful career across the turbulent landscape of today's talent market.

Shifting focus to Chapter 11, "Building an Infrastructure for Organizational Learning: A Multilevel Approach," Kozlowski, Chao, and Jensen consider collective learning as an emergent process across levels and time, and the means by which it can be supported, shaped, and amplified. Individuals learn, but they often do so in collective contexts; certainly this is the case in organizations. Although there is a huge literature on "organizational learning," this literature is chaotic, encompassing everything from macro culture to meso collaborative learning to individual learning processes. This chapter surveys the multifaceted conceptualizations of organizational learning, and then uses multilevel theory to build a conceptual model that integrates informal learning, formal learning, and emergent learning outcomes across the micro, meso, and macro levels of the organizational system. They characterize the organizational infrastructure needed for stimulating, capturing, and transmitting learning as a phenomenon that encompasses all levels of the organization.

Chapter 12 by Mathieu and Tesluk takes "A Multilevel Perspective on Training and Development Effectiveness." No one doubts that we know far more now about what constitutes training effectiveness in organizations than ever before. However, we have seen relatively few system-level, integrated models that provide us with an overall perspective that incorporates a full range of macro and micro antecedents, processes, and outcomes. This chapter reviews the relatively distinct micro human resource management (HRM) and macro strategic human resource management (SHRM) literatures, integrating the different perspectives. Their resulting multilevel framework enhances understanding of training effectiveness as a system-wide phenomenon. A compelling real-world illustration and set of research directions complete the package.

9

Informal Learning and Development in Organizations

Scott I. Tannenbaum
The Group for Organizational Effectiveness, Inc.

Rebecca L. Beard
The Group for Organizational Effectiveness, Inc.

Laurel A. McNall
The College at Brockport State University of New York

Eduardo Salas
University of Central Florida

Why Study Informal Learning?

Organizations focus the majority of their "learning" budget on formalized training programs. Accordingly, a great deal of research has been conducted to determine how best to design, deliver, and evaluate training programs (see Salas & Cannon-Bowers, 2001; Tannenbaum & Yukl, 1992). Unfortunately, formal training programs alone are insufficient to ensure organizational and individual readiness. There is an increasing awareness that informal learning is at least as important as formal learning in organizational settings (Birdi, Allan, & Warr, 1997; Day, 1998; Enos, Kehrhahn, & Bell, 2003; Lohman, 2000; Skule, 2004).

Jobs have become more complex and challenging (Thayer, 1997). Job demands (Cascio, 1995) and competency requirements are changing more rapidly due to organizational, competitive, and technological advances (London & Mone, 1999), which creates challenges for traditional, classroom training. Ellinger (2005) found that the introduction of new technology or new processes and downsizing were catalysts for informal learning. To stay competitive and increase quality, organizations must use many forms of employee development (Noe, Wilk, Mullen, & Wanek, 1997).

303

Moreover, research (Chao, 1997) has revealed that the majority of learning in organizations does not occur in formalized training settings and that "informal socialization strategies and unstructured training are believed to be more influential than their formal counterparts" (p. 132). Most learning occurs more naturally and informally. For example, Tannenbaum (1997) found that in seven different organizations, individuals consistently attributed less than 10% of their personal development to formal training. This finding was replicated in samples in Japan, Korea, and China (Flynn, Eddy, & Tannenbaum, 2005).

A study by the Center for Workforce Development (1998) found that 70% of what people know about their jobs they learn informally from the people with whom they work. Moreover, for every hour of formal training an individual experiences, a 4-hour spillover of informal learning is common (Stamps, 1998). Employees are continually learning informally; even the employment of formal training leads to further informal learning.

Given the prevalence and increasing importance of informal learning, it is imperative to understand the nature, components, and features of informal learning. Only then can we help organizations encourage, support, and promote informal learning, and guide individuals to gain the greatest benefit from their organizational experiences. Although researchers have begun to study informal learning more diligently, there are many opportunities for additional research. Several authors have argued that we have an incomplete or underdeveloped understanding of how informal learning works in organizations (Boud & Middleton, 2003; Skule, 2004). Given the importance of informal learning and the relative paucity of knowledge about it, informal learning research has the potential to produce more meaningful advancements over the next 10 years than does research on formal training programs.

Challenges in Understanding Informal Learning

Unfortunately, it is more difficult to study informal learning than formal learning. In part, this may be due to the essence of informal learning. The lack of a formal setting for learning implies that there is usually less structure involved in the process. Informal learning is often regarded as being "part of the job" or a mechanism for "doing the job properly" and is thus rendered invisible as a type of learning (Boud & Middleton, 2003). Chao (1997) pointed out that there is limited empirical research on informal training because of the wide variety of organizational experiences that qualify as examples of it and that individuals may not view unstructured training as a true learning experience.

Formal learning experiences typically have defined start and end points. They are usually based on predefined learning goals or desired outcomes. In contrast, informal learning occurs on a continual but sporadic basis, usually without a predefined set of learning objectives. This presents some obvious challenges for designing and conducting informal learning research studies. For example, when there are no preestablished learning objectives, it can be far more difficult to establish meaningful dependent variables or outcome measures to assess the effectiveness of an intervention.

In addition, there is not complete agreement about how best to define informal learning. Related concepts such as continuous learning (London & Smither, 1999b), experiential learning (Kolb, 1984), self-directed learning (Clardy, 2000), action learning (Yorks, O'Neil, & Marsick, 1999), and incidental learning (Watkins & Marsick, 1992) share some characteristics with informal learning. Given the overlap between and ambiguity of developmental constructs (D'Abate, Eddy, & Tannenbaum, 2003), greater clarity would be beneficial.

This chapter draws upon the existing literature related to informal learning. We first present a dynamic model that attempts to identify the components that contribute to effective informal learning. This provides a foundation for the next part of the chapter, where we examine the organizational and individual factors that can influence informal learning and present a few key research questions and propositions for future research. Finally, we present a high-level view of the informal learning domain and identify five metaresearch needs.

A Dynamic Model of Informal Learning

According to Kolb (1984), learning is defined as "the process whereby knowledge is created through the transformation of experience" (p. 38). Various definitions exist regarding informal learning. It has been described as learning that is unstructured, experiential, and noninstitutional, driven by people's choices, preferences, and intentions (Marsick & Volpe, 1999); involves a process that is neither determined nor designed by the organization, regardless of the formality of the goals and objectives to which the learning is directed (Stamps, 1998); results from the natural opportunities that occur in a person's working life when the person controls his or her own learning (Ellinger, 2005) but does not require intent—learners may not set out intentionally to learn something (Ellinger, 2004); and occurs from opportunities that lead to "teachable moments," where the timing is best for a learning opportunity to occur—usually when an individual encounters a problem where the learning is immediately helpful in accomplishing the goal (Brinkerhoff & Gill, 1994).

For the purposes of this chapter, we assume that informal learning has several common characteristics:

- Is predominately learner directed and self-guided (i.e., individually not organizationally controlled).
- Reflects at least some intent for development, growth, learning, or improvement (i.e., it is not simply incidental learning).
- Involves some action and doing, and is not purely educational (e.g., not reading or training).
- Does not occur in a formal learning setting (e.g., not classroom or e-learning).

As such, this eliminates learning related activities such as formal training, e-learning, and organizationally driven mentoring programs as well as incidental learning from direct consideration in this chapter. However, some research from those domains is cited when it can help shed light on the dynamics of informal learning.

Classic training models such as the instructional system design model (Reigeluth, 1983) often assume a linear process. However, as noted earlier, informal learning experiences are less structured and more dynamic than formal training. The beginning and completion points are often unclear or undefined. Therefore, a linear model may not accurately capture the dynamic nature of informal learning.

We present a dynamic model of informal learning (see Figure 9.1). The model contains four informal learning components, as noted below. These components do not occur in isolation and therefore must be understood as part of a larger context of organizational and individual characteristics that can encourage or impede the informal learning process (Dechant, 1999; London & Smither, 1999a). The four informal learning components are as follows:

- *Intent to learn, improve, and develop*: recognizing or being personally aware of the need to improve oneself, acquire knowledge, or build expertise.
- *Experience and action*: engaging in an action or an experience that involves the individual actively doing something.
- *Feedback*: receiving feedback related to an event or action. Feedback can come from the task itself or from others; it can be directed toward the learner or occur vicariously.
- *Reflection*: engaging in thoughtful consideration to seek understanding about one's experiences.

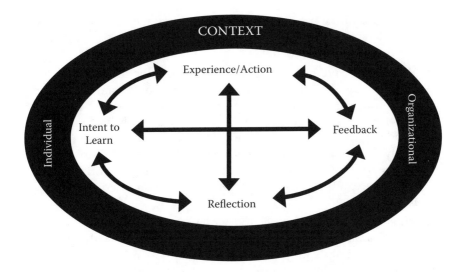

FIGURE 9.1
Dynamic model of informal learning.

A person can enter the informal learning process at any point in the model and may experience one or more of the components, one or more times. For example, a person may decide that she needs to become more skilled in a given area (intent), so she asks a colleague how she has been doing (feedback), performs some work that involves that skill (experience and action), and then thinks about how she performed and how she might handle that situation in the future (reflection).

Alternatively, a person may be participating in a project and receive feedback that causes him to reflect on his experience. Upon reflection, he decides he needs to learn more to be able to contribute most effectively, performs additional related work, and reflects again on what happened. The model implies that, unlike formalized learning, in practice, informal learning does not follow a preestablished sequence. Each component, however, contributes to the effectiveness of informal learning.

The Importance of the Four Components

It is our contention that informal learning is most effective when all four components are involved, with some components occurring more than once. What happens when one or more of the components are missing?

- When *intent* is missing, an individual may not recognize or take advantage of a potential learning opportunity. Individuals who lack intent may be less likely to reflect upon their experiences or seek feedback as a conscious means of learning. When one is conscious of the need to learn and improve, action and reflection are often part of a natural, iterative process. Without intent, learning is primarily incidental.

- When *experience* or *action* is missing, the person loses the chance to learn by doing; test his or her ideas, understanding, and assumptions; practice skills; and receive direct feedback from the experience. Although people can learn vicariously, without first-hand experience individuals may be more prone to assume incorrectly that they are "fully ready." They can find it easier to dismiss advice or attribute problems to the person who is involved in the experience, rather than accept it as a lesson that can be applicable to them as well.

- When *feedback* is missing, individuals may fail to take advantage of a potentially valuable learning experience. Without feedback, individuals may misread a situation or misinterpret cues; they may also develop or operate under false assumptions. They may falsely assume that their own understanding or competence assessment is accurate, or, conversely, may incorrectly lose confidence or interest if they fail to recognize their own progress.

- When *reflection* is missing, individuals may fail to uncover insights from their experiences. They are less likely to learn from, absorb, and internalize learning from experience. When individuals act without reflecting, they can fail to see connections and consequences, resulting in less than complete understanding.

As experiencing one component can trigger another, missing any component can also be detrimental because it may short-circuit the informal learning process. For example, if I take an action and receive no feedback, I may be less likely to reflect upon the experience.

Below is a description of each of the four factors in our model and a rationale for how and why each component contributes to informal learning.

Intent to Learn, Improve, and Develop

Self-awareness of developmental needs plays a key element in workplace development (Maurer & Tarulli, 1994; McCauley & Hezlett, 2002). One component in our model of informal learning is intent to learn. Intentions can be thought of as a form of goal that direct and regulate individuals' actions (Locke & Latham, 1990). An assumption we made when defining the domain of informal learning is that intent to learn or improve is what differentiates informal learning from incidental learning. A supervisor or other organizational representative may help an individual identify a goal for learning, but for it to be considered informal learning, the learning process has to be driven by the individual (Marsick & Volpe, 1999). Intent in this context implies motivation or recognition of a need, and motivation has been shown to be related to training effectiveness and learning (Colquitt, LePine, & Noe, 2000).

Intent may arise for several reasons. For example, intent may be based on a personal insight arising from self-reflection; may result from critical or encouraging feedback (e.g., from a colleague, or 360-degree feedback results); may be due to a perceived gap between goals and accomplishments or between perceived capabilities and needed capabilities; occur as a result of advice, mentoring, and/or coaching; or perhaps be driven by an aspiration for career advancement. Intent is often triggered by an event or experience. Sometimes, intent may be induced and feel mandatory (e.g., to redress an imbalance between required readiness and actual readiness). At other times, it is perceived as voluntary (e.g., not required by the situation; Clardy, 2000). An intention to learn does not necessarily mean that the individual has a formally stated or documented intent or goal (Stamps, 1998), although she could (e.g., as captured in a personal development plan).

Experience and Action

Action, planned or unplanned, is a central component in our model of informal learning. According to McCauley and Hezlett (2002), experience is "the medium through which learning occurs" (p. 317), and new experiences are required for development to occur within the workplace. Experiences are where individuals can test or apply new ideas based on their learning goals and prior reflection. The application of new ideas or concepts is a key component in training because it helps promote skill building. Van der Sluis-den Dikken and Hoeksema (2001) argued that managers learn optimally in situations in which their typical behavior no longer works, because they need to try out new behaviors, which compels them to "sink or swim" (p. 170). Unanticipated or serendipitous events can sometimes heighten one's attention. Nonroutine events or results may require heightened attention, encourage reflection, and trigger the informal learning process (Watkins & Marsick, 1992).

Triggers for informal learning can include many different types of activities. Leslie, Aring, and Brand (1998) suggested that some of the most common triggers for informal learning include work activities such as meetings, customer interactions, supervision, shift changes, peer-to-peer communications, teaming, and executing one's job. Lohman (2003) found that new assignments, new leadership roles, and following policies and procedures were triggers for informal learning among schoolteachers. Ellinger (2005) studied employees who were described as exemplary facilitators of learning and committed lifelong learners. Catalysts for informal learning incidents included participating in cross-functional meetings, seeing a need to change the way things are done, being given challenging assignments, addressing current job responsibilities, implementing a high-priority project, assuming a new position and new responsibilities, being given required performance expectations on a development plan, receiving a poor performance evaluation, receiving feedback, and just needing help.

Feedback

Learning from experience is not automatic—experiences vary in their learning potential. Moreover, an individual may only learn part of what he could have learned from an experience or, worse yet, may acquire the wrong lesson from an experience (McCall, 2004). Feedback provides individuals with information needed to learn the appropriate lesson from their experiences. Feedback can come from the task itself or from others. In an informal learning context, feedback can be directed at the learner (e.g., "Next time, you should check the equipment before starting that procedure") or can occur vicariously, such as when one person talks about the consequences of her actions in front of others ("When I failed to check the equipment one time, we had to shut down the system right after start-up").

Direct feedback can be sought by asking others about one's own performance. Vicarious feedback can be uncovered by asking people about their experiences and the consequences of their actions.

Feedback has been established as critical for learning but has shown mixed results for improving performance (Kluger & DeNisi, 1996). What is clear is that goal setting in combination with performance feedback has a powerful effect on performance (Bandura & Cervone, 1983; Locke, Frederick, Lee, & Bobko, 1984). However, not all feedback is equally effective in promoting learning and improving performance. Actionable feedback, focused on the task level, that contains examples or specific recommendations for improvement has been shown to be most effective (Cannon & Witherspoon, 2005; Kluger & DeNisi, 1996).

Reflection

Reflection is the final component of our definition of informal learning. It is the element that provides an understanding of the connection between action and outcome and helps to motivate individuals to seek further experiences and learning.

According to Barmeyer (2004), "In the heart of all learning, lies the way in which experience is processed, in particular, the critical reflection of the experience" (p. 580). Reflection involves a conscious attempt to make sense of one's experiences, which can involve self-critiquing or recognizing why something is working or not working, either while the experience is happening or after it has occurred (Schon, 1987). Reflecting on an experience while it is happening may enable an individual to self-correct on a real-time basis, whereas reflecting on experiences after they occur may promote future learning.

Marsick and Volpe (1999) noted that reflection involves looking back on what occurred, measuring the results against desired outcomes, and assessing the consequences. It is difficult to learn from experience if the appropriate connections are not made between action and outcome. Reflection provides the opportunity for individuals to learn from their mistakes and to reduce the likelihood of those situations recurring (Cannon & Edmonson, 2001; West, 1996). Reflection can involve asking oneself (or trusted others) key questions (Brooks, 1999) to help sort through and make sense of one's experiences or perhaps reframe a problem. During this process, individuals may challenge some implicit assumptions and revise existing mental models or form new ones. Reflection can guide subsequent actions (e.g., "Let me try that next time and see how it works").

Brooks (1999) argued that organizational members can develop critically reflective learning by engaging in a variety of work and educational experiences, modeling, practicing critical questioning, getting feedback, and participating in policy-making and policy implementation.

However, Scanlan and Chernomas (1997) noted that the literature on reflection is anecdotal and research is needed to assess whether reflection improves learning. In addition, Newell (1992) pointed out that it may be difficult for people to recall and retrieve accurate descriptions of their experiences. Research is needed to clarify how to encourage reflection that promotes effective learning.

As noted earlier, the four components of informal learning occur within a larger context. In the next section, we examine this context and the factors that influence informal learning.

The Context in Which Informal Learning Occurs

There is consistent support for the idea that informal learning occurs within the context of performing one's job or work activities (Leslie et al., 1998; Marsick & Volpe, 1999; Stern & Somerlad, 1999) when natural events provide opportunities to learn (Boud & Middleton, 2003). However, what can be learned from experience is influenced both by the context in which the event occurs and "what the individual brings to it" (McCall, 2004, p. 128). In this section, we examine the organizational and individual factors that may influence the effectiveness of informal learning. We briefly describe what is known about each factor and what we need to learn about them as they relate to informal learning. For each factor, we highlight a few research questions and propositions that should be examined in future research. These are summarized in Table 9.1.

Organizational (Situational) Factors

There are several organizational or situational factors that may influence the effectiveness of informal learning. These include organizational climate, learning opportunities, time, support and encouragement, and enablers (tools and processes).

Organizational Climate

Research on structured training experiences demonstrates that an organizational climate that signals that the organization values training can have a positive affect on training effectiveness. Climate has been shown to be related to the transfer of trained behaviors (Colquitt et al., 2000; Rouiller & Goldstein, 1993; Tracey, Tannenbaum, & Kavanagh, 1995), to the effectiveness of feedback (Silverman, Pogson, & Cober, 2005), and to the degree to which technical updating occurs (Kozlowski & Hults, 1987). Signs that formal training is valued include the availability of training, recognition, and rewards for those who participate in training; discussion of training during career conversations; reminders about the importance of training; and posttraining conversations about training with trainees.

   Although there is strong evidence that climate can influence training effectiveness, research is needed to better understand how climate can support informal, on-the-job learning. Future research should seek to identify which signals promote the importance of informal learning. What is it that suggests to employees that it is appropriate to reflect upon and discuss work experiences as an expected means of ongoing learning? Given the dynamic, sporadic, and self-guided nature of informal learning, some of the organizational signals that promote the importance of informal learning may be different than those that promote formal learning. For example, we would propose that the discussion of learning opportunities when assignments are issued should help build intent, the use of team debriefs should encourage feedback seeking, and leaders who occasionally "think aloud" about their experiences should encourage reflection.

TABLE 9.1

Research Questions and Propositions

Organizational (Situational) Factors

Organizational Climate

Research question: What organizational "signals" promote the importance of informal learning?

Proposition: Some signals that promote informal learning would include the following: The discussion of learning opportunities when assignments are issued, the use of team debriefs, and leaders who "think aloud" about their experiences should influence intent, feedback seeking, and reflection, respectively.

Learning Opportunities

Research question: What characteristics of on-the-job experiences create the greatest opportunity for informal learning?

Proposition: Experiences that require the acquisition or use of a new skill, with sufficient tolerance for deviation, and the opportunity to acquire feedback should stimulate informal learning, but many of the ideal characteristics will be unique to particular job types, learning needs, and preferences.

Time

Research question: How can organizations enable informal learning when employees are under increasing time pressures and have limited "free time"?

Proposition: Designated informal learning times such as brown-bag discussions and team debriefs can stimulate greater intent to learn, reflection, and feedback-seeking behaviors among time-crunched employees.

Support and Encouragement

Research question: What is the best way to encourage supervisors and peers to support informal learning?

Proposition: Individuals who are taught the components of informal learning, how to recognize when opportunities exist, and how to employ effective learning techniques will engage in more informal learning, and will be more likely to support others' informal learning.

Enablers: Tools and Processes

Research question: When and where is providing structure beneficial for informal learning?

Proposition: The appropriate use of learning tipsheets, work assignment scorecards, diaries, and self-guided learning contracts should increase the likelihood that employees seek learning opportunities and reflect on their experiences.

Strategic View of Informal Learning

Research question: What is the right mix of formal and informal learning?

Proposition: Organizations that rely predominantly on formal learning will demonstrate less readiness and resilience than those that promote a more balanced portfolio of formal and informal learning opportunities.

(continued on next page)

TABLE 9.1 (continued)

Research Questions and Propositions

Individual Factors

Learner Motivation

Research question: How does learner motivation relate to the four components of the informal learning model?

Proposition: Individuals with greater motivation to improve and learn (intent), motivation to find or take advantage of informal learning opportunities (action), motivation to reflect (reflection), and motivation to seek feedback (feedback) will engage in and benefit more from informal learning opportunities.

Personality Characteristics

Research question: How do various personality factors affect willingness to try new ideas or take on developmental assignments, intent and motivation to learn, feedback seeking, and reflection?

Proposition: Individuals with an internal locus of control will be more likely to consciously seek out and engage in informal learning experiences, seek feedback, and reflect on their experiences.

Proposition: Individuals with higher self-esteem will be more likely to accept a challenging assignment and more comfortable seeking out feedback about their performance, but less likely to perceive a personal learning need.

Proposition: Individuals with a learning goal orientation will be more likely to see experiences as informal learning opportunities and more likely to pursue and accept challenging or stretch assignments that offer the chance for informal learning.

Proposition: Individuals who are high on conscientiousness are more likely to address perceived learning needs and seek out learning opportunities; however, in organizations where formal learning is the norm, they may be less likely to see informal learning as sufficient or valuable.

Self-Awareness

Research question: How do metacognitive skills and enhanced self-awareness operate during informal learning?

Proposition: Effective informal learners process information about their experiences differently than less effective informal learners, demonstrating greater self-awareness and clearer metacognitive processes.

Feedback Orientation

Research question: How do we encourage the tendency to seek out and value feedback as a means of informal learning?

Proposition: For jobs where ongoing informal learning is critical, hiring individuals with greater feedback orientation will not result in better short-term performance but should result in better long-term learning and performance, and may help create a more learning-oriented culture.

Self-Efficacy

Research question: How does self-efficacy operate in informal learning settings?

Proposition: Individuals with a strong self-efficacy about informal learning will demonstrate greater resilience, and will be more likely to persevere during and learn from challenging situations.

Learning Opportunities

Action is at the heart of experiential learning (Kolb, 1984). On-the-job experiences that allow for, or in some cases necessitate, learning are critical for stimulating on-the-job growth. Key on-the-job experiences can provide individuals with a laboratory in which to experiment and test their skills. In fact, without the chance to practice and test learned behaviors, new skills will atrophy (Arthur, Bennett, Stanush, & McNelly, 1998).

Self-learners typically prefer environments where there are ample opportunities for individual learning (Confessore & Kops, 1998), and the availability of stimulating experiences should heighten self-learners' motivation to learn. Research has identified some of the types of on-the-job experiences that may promote ongoing development, particularly for those in leadership positions (McCall, Lombardo, & Morrison, 1988). Participating in these experiences should stimulate informal learning.

Opportunities for informal learning can be influenced by the relationships an individual has with coworkers. For example, a manager who trusts an employee is more likely to provide her with a learning opportunity (Lovin, 1992). Coworkers who trust one another should be more likely to provide each other with constructive feedback.

Although there is no doubt that learning opportunities are essential for informal learning, some questions remain about how best to identify, structure, and provide on-the-job experiences to optimize informal learning. For example, future research should examine the characteristics of on-the-job experiences that create the greatest opportunity for informal learning and seek to learn how these promote informal learning. What is it about an experience that stimulates informal learning? A range of methods can be used to examine how employees view informal learning opportunities, including interviews, diaries, blogs, and think-aloud protocols. A key question is "Are there any characteristics that universally stimulate informal learning?" We would propose that experiences that require the acquisition or use of a new skill, with sufficient tolerance for deviation, and the opportunity to acquire feedback should stimulate informal learning but that many of the ideal characteristics will vary for different jobs, learning needs, and preferences.

Time

There is an increasing emphasis on efficiency and productivity in most organizations. Organizations employ lean staffing levels and operate with larger spans of control than in the past. As a result, individuals have less "free" time to learn, and supervisors have less time to support on-the-job learning (Hagel & Brown, 2005). Yet, sufficient time is critical for informal learning (Marsick & Volpe, 1999; Sambrook & Stewart, 2000). Noe and

Wilk (1993) found that situational constraints, such as lack of time, were negatively related to participation in development activities. Moreover, time-related pressures have been found to be a common inhibitor to informal learning (Lohman, 2000).

According to Edland and Svenson (1993), time pressure can lead to a tendency to lock in on a particular strategy and decrease one's ability to find alternative strategies for problem solving. Consequently, human judgments often become less accurate under time pressure. This suggests that it may be harder to learn when there is no time to reflect or get feedback.

It is clear that lack of time can inhibit informal learning and that individuals are facing greater time pressures. As it is unlikely that time pressures will dissipate, future research needs to examine how best to mitigate or overcome those time pressures. To what extent can the provision of designated informal learning "times" such as brown-bag discussions and team debriefs stimulate greater intent to learn, reflection, and feedback-seeking behaviors among time-pressured employees?

Support and Encouragement

Supervisor support has consistently been shown to be a positive influence on training effectiveness (Birdi et al., 1997; Colquitt et al., 2000; Facteau, Dobbins, Russell, Ladd, & Kudisch, 1995) and can be beneficial in promoting self-directed learning (Maurer & Tarulli, 1994). For example, Facteau et al. (1995) found that if employees believe their supervisor supports training, they will be more motivated to attend and learn from training. Birdi et al. (1997) found a positive relationship between manager support and participation in voluntary development activities. Likewise, Noe and Wilk (1993) found that social support from managers and peers for development activities influenced participation in development activities. It seems that supervisor support leads to a more open environment that encourages learning and admission of errors (Edmonson, 1996).

How support is provided can make a difference. For example, learners who are guided toward self-discovery have better developmental experiences than those who are simply given answers (Eddy, D'Abate, Tannenbaum, Givens-Skeaton, & Robinson, 2006). Self-learners generally prefer the use of a participative leadership style (Confessore & Kops, 1998).

Senior management support has also been shown to enhance informal learning (Ashton, 2004; Ellinger, 2005; Sambrook & Stewart, 2000; Skule, 2004). However, the results related to peer support are less definitive (McCauley & Hezlett, 2002).

Supervisor support helps ensure transfer of training and can be a key element in promoting informal learning. The research on peer support is less clear, but there can be little doubt that peers influence one another under many circumstances. Given the importance of social support in learning, future research should seek to better understand how supervisor and peer support can encourage informal learning, and determine how best to prepare supervisors to promote effective informal learning. We would propose that individuals who are taught the components of, opportunities for, and techniques of effective informal learning will engage in more informal learning, and will be more likely to support others' informal learning.

Enablers: Tools and Processes

Some formality and informality are present in all learning situations, but the degree and interrelationships between formal and informal attributes vary across situations (Malcolm, Hodkinson, & Colley, 2003). Many learning approaches, such as classroom training, are highly structured, and structure can be a helpful instructional aid. However, there is some evidence that in some circumstances, too much structure might stifle learning. For example, Snow and Lohman (1984) found that for more able learners, greater structure inhibits their natural learning process, whereas less structure is viewed as challenging. On the other hand, for less able learners, less structure can produce anxiety. Brooks (1999) speculated that "when individuals are told exactly how to carry out an assignment, critical reflection can be stifled" (p. 74).

Informal learning is by definition a less structured approach to personal development than is classroom learning. Some researchers have suggested that organizations can help provide some beneficial structure to informal learning through the use of various tools and processes (Lohman, 2000; Marsick, Volpe, & Watkins, 1999). For example, some organizations use learning contracts where individuals identify their needs, set learning goals, decide on assessment criteria, and locate appropriate strategies and resources to ensure their personal development.

Errors can be a stimulant for learning (Kay, 2007). Most classroom learning experiences are structured so that learners avoid errors. In contrast, individuals naturally make errors in their work environment with some regularity. Although these can be learning opportunities, attention on "mistakes" may lead individuals to be more cautious. Research has suggested that a training strategy that incorporates errors in a structured or guided manner can be beneficial (Lorenzet, Salas, & Tannenbaum, 2005). Although it may not make sense to guide people to make errors on the job, it may be possible to improve the likelihood that individuals learn from naturally occurring errors on the job.

In some cases, structure can aid the learning process, but it may also stifle learning. Research is needed to clarify how, when, and what types of tools and other processes can be used to provide support that fosters rather than inhibits informal learning. Under what circumstances is it beneficial to provide greater structure for informal learning? For example, we would propose that the appropriate use of learning tipsheets, work assignment scorecards, diaries, and self-guided learning contracts should increase the likelihood that employees seek learning opportunities and take the time to reflect on their experiences.

Strategic View of Informal Learning

Informal learning is not intended to replace training or other formal learning mechanisms. Ideally, informal learning is part of a portfolio of learning opportunities available to individuals within an organization. There are times when formal learning may take precedence (e.g., when safety is at stake, we cannot rely on informal learning) and times when informal learning may be most beneficial (e.g., when change is so rapid and continual that formal training cannot keep up).

To maximize the benefit of their learning portfolio, organizations need to take a more strategic, balanced view of their offerings (Tannenbaum, 2002). Several questions emerge when we consider informal learning from this strategic perspective. For example, what is the right mix of formal and informal offerings? Under what circumstances can informal learning substitute for formal learning, and vice versa? If a company has an outstanding formal training curriculum, does that reduce the need for informal learning? Given the pace of change in organizations, we would propose that organizations that rely predominantly on formal learning will demonstrate less readiness and resilience than those with a more balanced portfolio of formal and informal learning opportunities.

Individual Factors

There are many individual factors that influence the effectiveness of informal learning. These include learner motivation, personality characteristics, self-awareness, feedback orientation, and self-efficacy.

Learner Motivation

Motivation to learn refers to trainees' desire to learn from the training material (Colquitt et al., 2000). Noe (1986) proposed a model of motivational influences on training effectiveness. Motivation levels can influence training effectiveness at multiple points, including motivation to attend, motivation to learn, and motivation to transfer. Research from the formal training literature provides ample evidence that learner motivation is positively related to learning outcomes, including declarative knowledge, skill acquisition, reactions to training, and transfer of training (Colquitt et al., 2000).

It is clear that motivation is advantageous in formal training environments. Research on motivation to learn in an informal learning context has been more limited. An exception to this work by Lohman (2003) who found several factors that motivated informal learning: teachers' initiative, self-efficacy, commitment to lifelong learning, and interest in their content area.

Given the self-directed nature of informal learning, learner motivation should be even more influential in informal learning than it is in formal, structured training. Research should help clarify how motivation works with regard to informal learning including its antecedents, covariates, and consequences. For example, how does motivation relate to the four components of the informal learning model? What is the relationship between motivation to improve and learn, motivation to find or take advantage of informal learning opportunities, motivation to reflect, and motivation to seek feedback? We would propose that learner motivation is related to each of the four components of the informal learning model. Many of the organizational factors that were previously discussed in this chapter are likely to operate as antecedents of learner motivation, encouraging or discouraging employees from engaging in and building competence from on-the-job experiences.

Personality Characteristics

Personality variables are critical factors in training effectiveness. They have been shown to display moderate to strong relationships with motivation to learn and learning outcomes (Colquitt et al., 2000). There are several personality characteristics that may be related to informal learning.

Locus of Control

Locus of control refers to the degree to which an individual believes the occurrence of reinforcements is under his or her control (Rotter, 1996). Noe (1986) argued that individuals with an internal locus of control would be more likely to believe they can improve their skills and hence are more likely to participate in developmental activities than those with an external locus of control. Colquitt et al. (2000) found that individuals with an internal locus of control were typically more motivated to learn. We would propose that individuals with an internal locus of control are more likely to consciously engage in informal learning experiences, seek feedback, and reflect on their experiences.

Self-Esteem

According to Gist and Mitchell (1992), self-esteem is a trait that reflects an individual's affective evaluation of the self. A person with high self-esteem may be more likely to engage in developmental activities such as mentoring (Turban & Dougherty, 1994). We would propose that individuals with higher self-esteem are more likely to accept a challenging assignment and more comfortable seeking out feedback about their experiences, but may be less likely to perceive a need for learning.

Goal Orientation

People's theories about how ability can or cannot be enhanced exert powerful effects on the goals they pursue and the behaviors they exhibit (Dweck & Leggett, 1988). Individuals who believe that attributes are fixed are more likely to set performance goals. In contrast, individuals who believe that personal attributes can be developed are more likely to set learning goals. Learning goal–oriented people are motivated by competence development and will select challenging tasks that foster learning. Colquitt and Simmering (1998) found that highly learning-oriented individuals had higher motivation to learn, both initially and when getting feedback during the learning process, whereas performance orientation was negatively related to motivation to learn. Kozlowski et al. (2001) found that learning orientation was positively related to self-efficacy, which in turn was related to adaptive performance. Moreover, Silverman et al. (2005) noted that learning goal orientation should influence the effectiveness of feedback. Individuals with a learning goal orientation may be more likely to see experiences as informal learning opportunities and more likely to pursue and accept challenging or stretch assignments that offer the chance for informal learning.

Conscientiousness

Highly conscientious people view themselves as dependable, thorough, hardworking, and achievement oriented (Digman, 1990) and, as a result, set high performance standards and strive for excellence (Costa & McCrae, 1992). Martocchio and Judge (1997) found that highly conscientious people had higher self-efficacy, which was positively related to learning. Colquitt and Simmering (1998) found that learners high in conscientiousness exhibited higher motivation levels both initially and when getting feedback during the learning process. Colquitt et al. (2000) found that conscientiousness was positively related to motivation to learn (as did Turner in 2005), but, surprisingly, their meta-analysis revealed that conscientiousness was negatively related to skill acquisition.

Individuals who are high on conscientiousness are often more motivated to learn. Thus, we propose that they are more likely to address perceived learning needs and seek out learning opportunities; however, in organizations where formal learning is the norm, they may be less likely to perceive informal learning as sufficient or valuable.

Self-Awareness

Awareness has been conceptualized as the first step in reflection by Scanlan and Chernomas (1997), who also pointed out that research is needed to determine how psychological defense processes affect reflective thinking and the ability to learn. Individuals can develop a self-serving bias, attributing success to internal factors and failure to external factors (Miller & Ross, 1975). People are not good at viewing themselves objectively and tend not to view themselves or others' perceptions of them accurately (Brown, 1991). However, Renner and Renner (2001) found that people's biases can be reduced through training focused on increasing metacognitive abilities. For people to maximize what they learn from their experiences, it is critical that they build metacognitive skills, which include self-awareness, because learners with good metacognitive skills are able to monitor and direct their own learning processes.

Metacognitive skills and enhanced self-awareness should play a key role in enabling individuals to benefit from informal learning. Research that further clarifies how these mental processes work during informal learning opportunities should be helpful. For example, how does self-awareness influence intent to learn? Are individuals with stronger self-awareness more likely to recognize the need for informal learning and seek feedback? Do they consciously decide to approach a situation differently based on a more accurate self-assessment of similar situations in the past?

Research that compares effective and less effective informal learners could provide useful insights to drive subsequent training efforts. We propose that effective informal learners process information about their experiences differently than less effective informal learners, demonstrating greater self-awareness and clearer metacognitive processes. Moreover, training that builds metacognitive skills, particularly as those skills relate to informal learning, should increase the quantity and effectiveness of reflection during informal learning and increase the likelihood that individuals recognize informal learning opportunities as they emerge.

Feedback Orientation

Silverman et al. (2005) noted that feedback orientation, or the tendency to seek out and value feedback, influences the effectiveness of feedback. Individuals with a feedback-seeking orientation are more likely to detect discrepancies between their self-perceptions and others' perceptions of their behavior and to subsequently correct the behavior that others believe needs improvement (Ashford & Tsui, 1991). They found that managers' willingness to seek negative feedback was associated with a more accurate knowledge of how others evaluate their work.

Whether or not an individual is able to learn from feedback depends on both cognitive and emotional dynamics (Cannon & Witherspoon, 2005) such as self-perception, self-efficacy, and self-serving bias. Individuals who perform poorly may not seek feedback to preserve their self-image and manage others' impressions of them, causing a "feedback gap" (Moss & Sanchez, 2004). The personal factors that may encourage feedback avoidance include a predisposition to seek positive feedback, fear of receiving a negative evaluation, high self-esteem, high concern about public image, and high need for approval. Hence, individuals tend to avoid feedback when they have performed badly but seek it when they have performed well (Moss & Sanchez). Individuals may be reluctant to seek feedback in situations where they may experience threats or embarrassment (Argyris, 1982).

Feedback is one of the key components of the informal learning process. Greater understanding about feedback orientation should provide insights into informal learning. How can we encourage the tendency to seek out and value feedback as a means of informal learning? How can we maximize informal learning for individuals who demonstrate feedback avoidance? We would propose that hiring individuals with greater feedback orientation will not result in better short-term job performance but, for jobs where ongoing informal learning is critical, should result in better long-term learning and performance, and may help create a more learning-oriented culture.

Self-Efficacy

Self-efficacy is "the belief in one's capability to organize and execute the courses of action required to produce given attainments" (Bandura, 1997, p. 3). Researchers have consistently found that self-efficacy is related to learning (Colquitt et al., 2000; Maurer & Tarulli, 1994; Warr & Bunce, 1995). Colquitt et al. (2000) found that pretraining self-efficacy was strongly related to motivation to learn and moderately related to declarative knowledge, skill acquisition, and job performance. Self-efficacy is related to higher quality learning strategies (Kurtz & Borkowski, 1984), task persistence (Zimmerman & Ringle, 1981), and skill acquisition (Schunk, 1984). Hellervik, Hazucha, and Schneider (1992) stated that "one might plausibly suggest that self-efficacy can contribute substantially to an individual's ability to formulate strong intentions" (p. 865).

Clearly, in formal training settings, a belief that one will be able to learn and perform effectively is related to motivation to learn and subsequent learning and performance. Research should examine the role of self-efficacy in informal learning. Does it operate differently? For example, some people might have high self-efficacy for learning in a structured training environment, perhaps as a result of prior strong academic performance, but lower self-efficacy about their ability to learn informally. If so, what can be done to build informal learning self-efficacy or the belief that one can effectively learn from experience without a formal training structure? We would propose that individuals with a strong self-efficacy about informal learning will approach informal learning opportunities differently, demonstrating greater resilience and a willingness to persevere during and learn from challenging situations.

Other Characteristics

Other individual characteristics may influence informal learning, including education and management level (McCauley & Hezlett, 2002). Birdi et al. (1997) found that more educated employees were more active in work-based developmental activities on work time, voluntary job-related learning on their own time, and career planning activities. Higher level employees undertook more work-based development activities and career planning activities. Employees who worked in shifts took part in significantly fewer development activities.

Age may also be a factor in learning. Colquitt et al. (2000) found that age was linked to motivation to learn and learning (i.e., older trainees demonstrated lower motivation, learning, and posttraining self-efficacy). In addition, Warr and Bunce (1995) found that younger people had better learning scores in an "open" learning program.

Demographic variables such as education and age may influence interest in and openness toward learning. Future research should examine how best to encourage informal learning among groups that may be less likely to gravitate toward learning activities.

Looking Forward: The Informal Learning Research Domain

As noted in the beginning of this chapter, it can be challenging to conduct research on informal learning, because informal learning does not have preestablished learning goals or clearly defined start and end points. Formal training programs are often studied or evaluated as an event with clear before, during, and after periods. Traditional dependent variables in training research include trainee reactions, learning, performance, and sometimes results. Common independent variables include characteristics of the training and the trainees.

Studying and evaluating informal learning are more challenging. The variables of interest are not as well specified, the start and end points are blurrier, and the goals are not as clearly identified. In Figure 9.2, we attempt to summarize the potential informal learning research domain. The figure highlights five metaresearch needs that have been alluded to throughout this chapter (labeled 1 to 5). In the center of the figure is the dynamic informal learning process with its four components. To the left are the two sets of contextual variables, organizational characteristics and individual characteristics. To the right are two sets of potential outcomes, organizational outcomes and individual outcomes.

Desired organizational outcomes from effective informal learning include better organizational readiness to perform and compete, enhanced employee engagement and retention, establishment of a learning culture or norms that encourage continuous learning, and greater organizational agility to learn and adjust quickly to changing needs and demands.

Potential individual outcomes of effective informal learning include learning or knowledge and skill acquisition, improved job performance, enhanced commitment (including the belief that the organization cares about their development and an intention to remain with the company), increased motivation to learn, stronger self-efficacy, and greater personal adaptability.

The five metaresearch needs are labeled 1 to 5. The first two needs are to understand how (1) organizational and (2) individual characteristics influence the quantity, quality, and nature of informal learning processes. Several specific research questions and propositions related to these themes are listed in Table 9.1. The third research need is to better understand the informal learning process (3), including natural and desirable patterns among the four components of action, feedback, reflection, and intent. The last two needs are to examine how the quantity, quality, and nature of informal learning processes result in desired (4) organizational and (5) individual outcomes.

Future research could examine informal learning as an event, for example by collecting critical incidents of specific informal learning opportunities. Informal learning could also be examined as a series of events, for example through journaling of learning triggers and experiences over a period of time. It can be studied at the individual level of analysis, for example by examining how providing informal learning tools influences individual outcomes. Alternatively, informal learning can be studied at a higher level of analysis, for example by examining the quantity and nature of informal learning activities within different teams or business units and how those are related to team- or unit-level outcomes.

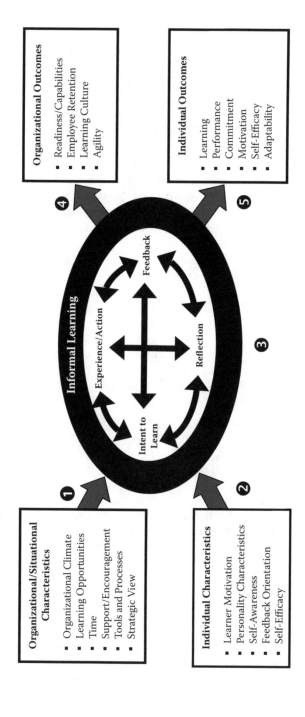

FIGURE 9.2
Informal learning research domain and themes.

Concluding Remarks

Organizations and individuals cannot rely on training and other formal learning experiences to meet all their developmental needs. Informal learning is an essential component of employee development. Unfortunately, simply providing people with "experience" does not ensure that learning or other desired outcomes will result. There is a need to better understand the informal learning process, including its antecedents and consequences. Numerous research opportunities exist, some of which we articulated in this chapter. Given the importance and prevalence of informal learning, we hope that future research will explore this domain, advancing our collective knowledge about informal learning and enabling individuals and organizations to gain the maximum value from their on-the-job learning opportunities.

References

Argyris, C. (1982). *Reasoning, learning and action: Individual and organizational.* San Francisco: Jossey-Bass.

Arthur, W., Bennett, W., Stanush, P. L., & McNelly, T. L. (1998). Factors that influence skill decay and retention: A quantitative review and analysis. *Human Performance, 11*, 57–101.

Ashford, S. J., & Tsui, A .S. (1991). Self-regulation for managerial effectiveness: The role of active feedback seeking. *Academy of Management Journal, 34*, 251–280.

Ashton, D. N. (2004). The impact of organizational structure and practices on learning in the workplace. *International Journal of Training and Development, 8*(1), 43–53.

Bandura, A. (1997). *Self-efficacy: The exercise of control.* New York: Freeman.

Bandura, A., & Cervone, D. (1983). Self-evaluative and self-efficacy mechanisms governing the motivational effects of goal systems. *Journal of Personality and Social Psychology, 45*, 1017–1028.

Barmeyer, C. I. (2004). Learning styles and their impact on cross-cultural training: An international comparison in France, Germany and Quebec. *International Journal of Intercultural Relations, 28*, 577–594.

Birdi, K., Allan, C., & Warr, P. (1997). Correlates of perceived outcomes of four types of employee development activity. *Journal of Applied Psychology, 82*, 845–857.

Boud, D., & Middleton, H. (2003). Learning from others at work: Communities of practice and informal learning. *Journal of Workplace Learning, 15*, 194–202.

Brinkerhoff, R. O., & Gill, S. J. (1994). *The learning alliance: Systems thinking in human resource development.* San Francisco: Jossey-Bass.

Brooks, A. K. (1999). Critical reflection as a response to organizational disruption. In V. J. Marsick & K. E. Watkins (Eds.), *Informal learning on the job* (pp. 66–79). Baton Rouge, LA: Academy of Human Resource Development.

Brown, J. D. (1991). Accuracy and bias in self-knowledge. In C. R. Snyder & D. R. Forsyth (Eds.), *Handbook of social and clinical psychology* (pp. 158–178). New York: Pergamon.

Cannon, M. D., & Edmonson, A. C. (2001). Confronting failure: Antecedents and consequences of shared beliefs about failure in organizational work groups. *Journal of Organizational Behavior, 22,* 161–177.

Cannon, M. D., & Witherspoon, R. (2005). Actionable feedback: Unlocking the power of learning and performance improvement. *Academy of Management Executive, 19,* 120–134.

Cascio, W. F. (1995). Whither industrial and organizational psychology in a changing world of work? *American Psychologist, 50,* 928–939.

Center for Workforce Development. (1998). *The teaching firm: Where productive work and learning converge.* Newton, MA: Education Development Center.

Chao, G. T. (1997). Unstructured training and development: The role of organizational socialization. In J. K. Ford (Ed.), *Improving training effectiveness in work organizations* (pp. 129–151). Mahwah, NJ: Lawrence Erlbaum Associates.

Clardy, A. (2000). Learning on their own: Vocationally oriented self-directed learning projects. *Human Resource Development Quarterly, 11*(2), 105–125.

Colquitt, J. A., LePine, J. A., & Noe, R. A. (2000). Toward an integrative theory of training motivation: A meta-analytic path analysis of 20 years of research. *Journal of Applied Psychology, 85,* 678–707.

Colquitt, J. A., & Simmering, M. S. (1998). Conscientiousness, goal orientation, and motivation to learn during the learning process: A longitudinal study. *Journal of Applied Psychology, 83,* 654–665.

Confessore, S. J., & Kops, W. J. (1998). Self-direct learning and the learning organization: Examining the connection between the individual and the learning environment. *Human Resource Development Quarterly, 9,* 365–375.

Costa, P. T., & McCrae, R. R. (1992). *Revised NEO personality inventory and the NEO five-factor inventory.* Odessa, FL: Psychological Assessment Resources.

D'Abate, C. P., Eddy, E. R., & Tannenbaum, S. I. (2003). What's in a name? A literature-based approach to understanding mentoring, coaching, and other constructs that describe developmental interactions. *Human Resource Development Review, 2,* 360–384.

Day, N. (1998). Informal learning gets results. *Workforce, 77,* 30–36.

Dechant, K. (1999). How managers learn in the knowledge area. In V. J. Marsick & K. E. Watkins (Eds.), *Informal learning on the job* (pp. 42–51). Baton Rouge, LA: Academy of Human Resource Development.

Digman, J. M. (1990). Personality structure: Emergence of the five-factor model. *Annual Review of Psychology, 41,* 417–440.

Dweck, C. S., & Leggett, E. L. (1988). A social-cognitive approach to motivation and personality. *Psychological Review, 95,* 256–273.

Eddy, E. R., D'Abate, C. P., Tannenbaum, S. I., Givens-Skeaton, S., & Robinson, G. (2006). Key characteristics of effective and ineffective developmental interactions. *Human Resource Development Quarterly, 17,* 59–84.

Edland, A., & Svenson, O. (1993). Judgment and decision making under time pressure. In O. Svenson & A. J. Maule (Eds.), *Time pressure and stress in human judgment and decision making* (pp. 27–38). New York: Plenum.

Edmonson, A. (1996). Learning from mistakes is easier said than done: group and organizational influences on the detection and correction of human error. *Journal of Applied Behavioral Science, 32*(1), 5–28.

Ellinger, A. D. (2004). The concept of self-directed learning and its implications for human resource development. *Advances in Developing Human Resources, 6*(2), 158–177.

Ellinger, A. D. (2005). Contextual factors shaping informal workplace learning in a workplace setting: The case of reinventing itself company. *Human Resource Development Quarterly, 16*(3), 389–415.

Enos, M. D., Kehrhahn, M. T., & Bell, A. (2003). Informal learning and the transfer of learning: How managers develop proficiency. *Human Resource Development Quarterly, 14*, 369–387.

Facteau, J. D., Dobbins, G. H., Russell, J. E. A., Ladd, R. T., & Kudisch, J. D. (1995). The influence of general perceptions of the training environment on pretraining motivation and perceived training transfer. *Journal of Management, 21*, 1–25.

Flynn, D., Eddy, E., & Tannenbaum, S. I. (2005). The impact of national culture on the continuous learning environment: Exploratory findings from multiple countries. *Journal of East-West Business, 12*, 85–107.

Gist, M. E., & Mitchell, T. R. (1992). Self-efficacy: A theoretical analysis of its determinants and malleability. *Academy of Management Review, 17*, 183–211.

Hagel, J., & Brown, J. S. (2005). *The only sustainable edge: Why business strategy depends on productive friction and dynamic specialization.* Boston: Harvard Business School Press.

Hellervik, L. W., Hazucha, J. F., & Schneider, R. J. (1992). Behavior change: Models, methods, and a review of evidence. *Handbook of Industrial and Organizational Psychology, 3*, 823–895.

Kay, R. H. (2007). The role of errors in learning computer software. *Computers & Education, 49*, 441–459.

Kluger, A. N., & DeNisi, A. S. (1996). The effects of feedback interventions on performance: A historical review, a meta-analysis, and a preliminary feedback intervention theory. *Psychological Bulletin, 119*, 254–284.

Kolb, D. (1984). *Experiential learning.* Englewood Cliffs, NJ: Prentice Hall.

Kozlowski, S. W. J., Gully, S. M., Brown, K. G., Salas, E., Smith, E. M., & Nason, E. R. (2001). Effects of training goals and goal orientation traits on multidimensional training outcomes and performance adaptability. *Organizational Behavior and Human Decision Processes, 85*, 1–31.

Kozlowski, S. W. J., & Hults, B. M. (1987). An exploration of climates for technical updating and performance. *Personnel Psychology, 40*, 539–563.

Kurtz, B. E., & Borkowski, J. G. (1984). Children's meta-cognition: Exploring relations among knowledge, process and motivational variables. *Journal of Experimental Child Psychology, 37*, 335–354.

Leslie, B., Aring, M. K., & Brand, B. (1998). Informal learning: The new frontier of employee development and organizational development. *Economic Development Review, 15*, 12–18.

Locke, E. A., Frederick, E., Lee, C., & Bobko, P. (1984). Effect of self-efficacy, goals, and task strategies on task performance. *Journal of Applied Psychology, 69*, 241–251.

Locke, E. A., & Latham, G. P. (1990). *A theory of goal setting and task performance.* Englewood Cliffs, NJ: Prentice Hall.

Lohman, M. C. (2000). Environmental inhibitors to informal learning in the workplace: A case study of public school teachers. *Adult Education Quarterly, 50*, 83–101.

Lohman, M. C. (2003). Work situations triggering participation in informal learning in the workplace: A case study of public school teachers. *Performance Improvement Quarterly, 16*, 29–54.

London, M., & Mone, E. M. (1999). Continuous learning. In D. R. Ilgen & E. D. Pulakos (Eds.), *The changing nature of work performance: Implications for staffing, personnel actions, and development* (pp. 119–153). San Francisco: Jossey-Bass.

London, M., & Smither, J. W. (1999a). Empowered self-development and continuous learning. *Human Resource Management, 38*, 3–15.

London, M., & Smither, J. W. (1999b). Career-related continuous learning: Defining the construct and mapping the process. In K. M. Rowlands & G. R. Ferris (Eds.), *Research in personnel and human resources management* (Vol. 17, pp. 81–121). Greenwich, CT: JAI.

Lorenzet, S. J., Salas, E., & Tannenbaum, S. I. (2005). Benefiting from mistakes: The impact of guided errors on learning, performance, and self-efficacy. *Human Resource Development Quarterly, 16*, 301–322.

Lovin, B. K. (1992). Professional learning through workplace partnerships. In H. K. M. Baskett & V. J. Marsick (Eds.), *Professionals' ways of knowing* (pp. 61–69). San Francisco: Jossey-Bass.

Malcolm, J., Hodkinson, P., & Colley, H. (2003). The interrelationships between informal and formal learning. *Journal of Workplace Learning, 15*, 313–318.

Marsick, V. J., & Volpe, M. (1999). The nature and need for informal learning. In V. J. Marsick & M. Volpe (Eds.), *Informal learning on the job* (pp. 1–9). Baton Rouge, LA: Academy of Human Resource Development.

Marsick, V. J., Volpe, M., & Watkins, K. E. (1999). Theory and practice of informal learning in the knowledge era. In V. J. Marsick & M. Volpe (Eds.), *Informal learning on the job* (pp. 80–95). Baton Rouge, LA: Academy of Human Resource Development.

Martocchio, J. J., & Judge, T. A. (1997). Relationship between conscientiousness and learning in employee training: Mediating influences of self-deception and self-efficacy. *Journal of Applied Psychology, 82*, 764–773.

Maurer, T. J., & Tarulli, B. A. (1994). Investigation of perceived environment, perceived outcome, and person variables in relationship to voluntary development activity by employees. *Journal of Applied Psychology, 79*, 3–14.

McCall, M. W. (2004). Leadership development through experience. *Academy of Management Executive, 18*(3), 127–130.

McCall, M. W., Lombardo, M. M., & Morrison, A. M. (1988). *The lessons of experience: How successful executives develop on the job.* New York: Lexington.

McCauley, C. D., & Hezlett, S. A. (2002). Individual development in the workplace. In N. Anderson, D. S. Ones, H. K. Sinangil, & C. Viswesvaran (Eds.), *Handbook of industrial, work and organizational psychology* (Vol. 1, pp. 313–335). Thousand Oaks, CA: Sage.

Miller, D., & Ross, M. (1975). Self-serving biases in attribution of causality: Fact or fiction? *Psychological Bulletin, 92*, 213–225.

Moss, S. E., & Sanchez, J. I. (2004). Are your employees avoiding you? Managerial strategies for closing the feedback gap. *Academy of Management Executive, 18*(1), 32–44.

Newell, R. (1992). Anxiety, accuracy, and reflection: the limits of professional development. *Journal of Advanced Nursing, 17*, 1326–1333.

Noe, R. A. (1986). Trainee attributes and attitudes: Neglected influences on training effectiveness. *Academy of Management Review, 11*, 736–749.

Noe, R. A., & Wilk, S. L. (1993). Investigation of the factors that influence employees' participation in development activities. *Journal of Applied Psychology, 78*, 291–302.

Noe, R. A., Wilk, S. L., Mullen, E. J., & Wanek, J. E. (1997). Employee development: Issues in construct definition and investigation of antecedents. In J. K. Ford (Ed.), *Improving training effectiveness in work organizations* (pp. 153–189). Mahwah, NJ: Lawrence Erlbaum Associates.

Reigeluth, C. M. (1983). *Instructional design theories and models: An overview of their current status*. Hillsdale, NJ: Lawrence Erlbaum Associates.

Renner, C. H., & Renner, M. J. (2001). But I thought I knew that: Using confidence estimation as a debiasing technique to improve classroom performance. *Applied Cognitive Psychology, 15*, 23–32.

Rotter, J. B. (1966). Generalized expectancies for internal versus external control of reinforcement. *Psychological Monographs, 33*, 300–303.

Rouiller, J. Z., & Goldstein, I. L. (1993). The relationship between organizational transfer climate and positive transfer of training. *Human Resources Development Quarterly, 4*, 377–390.

Salas, E., & Cannon-Bowers, J. (2001). The science of training: A decade of progress. *Annual Review of Psychology, 52*, 471–499.

Sambrook, S., & Steward, J. (2000). Factors influencing learning in European learning-oriented organizations: Issues for management. *Journal of European Industrial Training, 24*(2), 209–221.

Scanlan, J. M., & Chernomas, W. M. (1997). Developing the reflective teacher. *Journal of Advanced Nursing, 25*, 1138–1143.

Schon, D. A. (1987). *Educating the reflective practitioner*. San Francisco: Jossey-Bass.

Schunk, D. H. (1984). Self-efficacy perspective on achievement behavior. *Educational Psychologist, 19*, 48–58.

Silverman, S. B., Pogson, C. E., & Cober, A. B. (2005). When employees at work don't get it: A model for enhancing individual employee change in response to performance feedback. *Academy of Management Executive, 19*, 135–147.

Skule, S. (2004, April 13). Learning conditions at work: A framework to understand and assess informal learning in the workplace. *International Journal of Training and Development*, pp. 8–17.

Snow, R. E., & Lohman, D. F. (1984). Toward a theory of cognitive aptitude for learning from instruction. *Journal of Educational Psychology, 76*, 247–376.

Stamps, D. (1998). Learning ecologies. *Training, 35*, 32–38.

Stern, E., & Somerlad, E. (1999). *Workplace learning, culture and performance*. London: Cromwell.

Tannenbaum, S. I. (1997). Enhancing continuous learning: Diagnostic findings from multiple companies. *Human Resource Management, 36,* 437–452.

Tannenbaum, S. I. (2002). A strategic view of organizational training and learning. In K. Kraiger (Ed.), *Creating, implementing, and maintaining effective training and development: State-of-the-art lessons for practice* (pp. 10–52). San Francisco: Jossey-Bass.

Tannenbaum, S. I., & Yukl, G. (1992). Training and development in work organizations. *Annual Review of Psychology, 43,* 399–441.

Thayer, P. W. (1997). A rapidly changing world: Some implications for training systems in the year 2001 and beyond. In M. A. Quinones & A. Ehrenstein (Eds.), *Training for a rapidly changing workplace.* Washington, DC: American Psychological Association.

Tracey, J. B., Tannenbaum, S. I., & Kavanagh, M. J. (1995). Applying trained skills on the job: The importance of the work environment. *Journal of Applied Psychology, 80,* 239–252.

Turban, D. B., & Dougherty, T. W. (1994). Role of protégé personality in receipt of mentoring and career success. *Academy of Management Journal, 37*(3), 688–702.

Turner, J. E. (2005). Proactive personality and the Big Five as predictors of motivation to learn. *Dissertation Abstracts International, 65,* 9-B.

Van der Sluis-den Dikken, L., & Hoeksema, L. H. (2001). The palette of management development. *Journal of Management Development, 20*(2), 168–179.

Warr, P., & Bunce, D. (1995). Trainee characteristics and the outcomes of open learning. *Personnel Psychology, 42,* 347–375.

Watkins, K. E., & Marsick, V. J. (1992). Towards a theory of informal and incidental learning in organizations. *International Journal of Lifelong Education, 11,* 287–300.

West, M. A. (1996). Reflexivity and work group effectiveness: A conceptual integration. In M. A. West (Ed.), *Handbook of work group psychology* (pp. 555–579). Chichester, UK: Wiley.

Yorks, L., O'Neil, J., & Marsick, V. J. (Eds.). (1999). *Action learning: Successful strategies for individual, team, and organizational development.* Thousand Oaks, CA: Sage.

Zimmerman, B. J., & Ringle, J. (1981). Effects of model persistence and statements of confidence on children's efficacy and problem solving. *Journal of Educational Psychology, 73,* 485–493.

10

"Learning" a Living: Continuous Learning for Survival in Today's Talent Market

Janice C. Molloy
Michigan State University

Raymond A. Noe
The Ohio State University

Lifelong learning, continuous learning, adaptability, career resilience, continuous improvement, self-development, recycling… The message has been crystal clear: The employer–employee relationship has changed (e.g., Arthur & Rousseau, 1996; Rousseau, 2005), as evidenced by the frequency with which individuals' employers are changing (e.g., Bureau of Labor Statistics, 2004; Light, 2005) and the fact that a temporary agency (Manpower, Incorporated) has been and continues to be the largest employer in the United States ("The 2006 Fortune 500," 2006; Hall, 2002).

It remains to be seen what name historians—and future generations—will use to refer to this era of fundamental transformation in the employment relationship. Whether this period is said to be characterized by a "transition to a knowledge-based economy," "the advent of global sourcing," or the "start of the digital age," the bottom line is that the demand for talent has been—and will continue to be—anything but stable. Indeed, individuals' work-related knowledge, skills, and abilities are subject to continuous obsolescence and displacement (Howard, 1995). As such, the survival and adaptability of individuals in today's talent market depend on their "learning" a living, that is, refining and adding to their skill sets throughout their careers to adapt to ever-changing requirements (e.g., see Hall, 1996, 2002; London & Mone, 1999). Gone are the times when career-related learning referred to a choice made only once and early in one's career. Today, individuals make many continuous-learning choices as they navigate the "permanent whitewater" (Vaill, 1996) of today's talent market.

The purpose of this chapter is to build on extant models of continuous learning (e.g., Hall, 2002; London & Smither, 1999; Mitchell & Krumboltz, 1990) by depicting a model of continuous learning that includes both individual-difference and social-environmental factors. Although social-environmental factors have typically been omitted from continuous-learning conceptualizations, the addition of such factors appears warranted given the maturity of the literatures on continuous learning (e.g., London, 1983; London & Smither) and career-related learning antecedents (e.g., Colquitt, LePine, & Noe, 2000; Maurer, Weiss, & Barbeite, 2003; Noe, 1996). Such focus on social-environmental factors may help to further illuminate the underlying processes and predict variance surrounding participation in continuous learning.

At the outset, it is important to note that continuous learning is defined here as *career-related acquisition of knowledge, skills, and abilities, occurring as a result of either systematic planning or chance events, which may facilitate adaptation to talent market dynamics.* In contrast to the many depictions (e.g., Hall, 2002; London & Mone, 1999; London & Smither, 1999; Morrison & Hall, 2002) that focus on the learning resulting from a high-involvement, systematic career exploration process (e.g., Greenhaus, 1987; Greenhaus, Callahan, & Godshalk, 1994), the definition above encompasses both high-involvement decision processes and chance events—including those Bandura (1982) termed "fortuitous encounters." Inclusion of both high-involvement decision processes and chance events appears warranted given that fortuitous encounters may have a significant impact on not only learning opportunities but also subsequent career paths (e.g., see Bandura, 2001; Granovetter, 1973, 1983).

This chapter is organized as follows: The first section provides a brief review of the continuous-learning literature. Next, a model of continuous learning is presented that includes individual-difference variables as well as social network and environmental characteristics as antecedents. The chapter concludes with a discussion and detailed research agenda.

Continuous Learning

As Sessa and London (2006) noted, the literature on continuous learning is fractured, being found in the broader human resource management, education, vocational behavior, and psychology literatures, with little cross-citation between fields. Moreover, London and Mone (1999) observed that in addition to the investigation of factors that influence individuals' participation in continuous learning, the literature describes continuous learning at the group and organization levels as well. Given that the focus of this chapter is on individuals' continuous learning, only that literature that concerns the individual perspective is discussed.

The literature on career-related learning at the individual level is voluminous (Wheelock & Catlahan, 2006). As such, Hall (2002) divided the literature into two broad topic categories: In Hall's terms, "big C" refers to literature that has evolved over the past century (e.g., Parsons, 1909) and that focuses on the initial culminating event of career choice—vocational choice. In contrast, "little c" literature began to emerge in the 1970s (e.g., Paxton, 1976) and focuses on the everyday decisions and choices individuals make to participate in learning after their initial vocational choice has been made. The focus of this section is on the "little c" literature. Specifically, decision-making processes regarding individuals' continuous learning and outcomes of such learning are discussed.

Nature of Decision Processes

Two types of continuous-learning decision processes are depicted in the literature: high-involvement and planned-happenstance models. High-involvement models imply that individuals engage in self-reflection and information seeking regarding their personal values and goals, carefully consider relevant information, and arrive at deliberate, conscious continuous-learning choices (Greenwald & Leavitt, 1984; Hastie & Dawes, 2000). In contrast, planned-happenstance models (Mitchell & Krumboltz, 1990) focus on individuals recognizing and incorporating chance events into their lives. High-involvement and planned-happenstance models are discussed in the following sections.

High-Involvement Models

Evaluation of the continuous-learning models in both the human resource management and career literatures suggests the majority of models depict or imply that the continuous-learning decision process is characterized by high involvement and choices that are deliberate and conscious. Such depictions emphasize concepts related to goal-setting theory (e.g., Klein, Wesson, Hollenbeck, & Alge, 1999; Latham, 1988) and the ability of individuals to self-regulate and control behavior (e.g., Carver & Scheier, 2000). For example, the career management process (e.g., Greenhaus, 1987; London, 1983; London & Noe, 1997) involves individuals' engagement in feedback seeking and self-reflection in order to establish personal insight, refine personal and career identities, and identify learning goals (e.g., Greenhaus, 1987; Greenhaus et al., 1994; Hall & Mirvis, 1995; London). Further, such a reflective process is explicitly discussed as a precursor of continuous learning in Hall (2002), London and Mone (1999), London and Smither (1999), Morrison and Hall (2002), Senge (1994), and Sessa and London (2006).

One example of high-involvement continuous learning is the stage model of continuous learning developed by London and Smither (1999). London and Smither depicted three distinct phases of continuous learning: prelearning (recognizing the learning need), learning (acquiring new skills and knowledge, and monitoring learning), and application of learning (using, evaluating, and reaping the benefits of learning). The prelearning phase is described as the recognition of "a gap between capabilities and the requirements of the current job or future career goals" (London & Smither, p. 93). It is important to note that, in contrast to other models, London and Smither did mention "serendipity" in their discussion (p. 88). However, their model does not describe a mechanism by which serendipitous life or work events influence continuous learning. Further, the discussion regarding serendipitous events suggests that such events "may set off a more deliberate continuous learning cycle" and may encourage the "self-determined continuous learner" to "establish a more systematic learning process" (London & Smither, pp. 88–89).

Planned-Happenstance Models

In contrast to high-involvement models, planned-happenstance models focus on individuals recognizing and capitalizing on chance events in their lives (Mitchell & Krumboltz, 1990). Consistent with Bandura (1982), the premise of such models is that chance encounters play a prominent role in shaping career paths. The models are based on the notion that although the occurrence of such chance events may be uncontrollable, perhaps individual differences in the likelihood of such events occurring and factors influencing how individuals react to such events may be identified. Although with the exception of Bright, Pryor, and Harpham (2005), there have been few empirical studies, several terms have been used to describe these "unplanned, accidental, or otherwise situational, unpredictable, or unintentional events or encounters that have an impact on career development and behavior" (Rojewski, 1999, p. 269). Such terms include "random" (Noe, 1996), "planned happenstance" (Mitchell & Krumboltz), "fortuitous encounters" (Bandura, 1982), and "coincidence, happenstance, serendipity, fate, or the hand of god" (Guindon & Hanna, 2002, p. 195).

Our literature review identified two models that incorporate planned happenstance: Krumboltz's (1994) social cognitive career theory and Lent, Brown, and Hackett's (1994) social-cognitive model. Similar to the high-involvement models discussed earlier, they are based on Bandura's (2001) social learning theory and the triadic interaction of the individual, behavior, and the environment. In contrast with the high-involvement decision processes that focus on establishing person–environment fit interactions within a contained system, planned-happenstance models consider the exogenous factors impacting continuous-learning decisions.

Krumboltz's (1994) social cognitive career theory highlights four factors influencing career-related choice behavior: genetic endowment, environmental conditions and events, previous learning experiences, and task-approach skills. The primary emphasis is on the influence of factors outside the control of the individual (e.g., cultural, political, and economic considerations) on educational, occupational, and social conditions. Task-approach skills and the wide variety of individual difference in task-approach preferences are also discussed. For instance, Krumboltz (1994) suggested that some individuals have the necessary cognitive ability, internal locus of control, conscientiousness, and career salience to use a sophisticated, high-involvement task approach to career planning, whereas many individuals do not have the required abilities for or interest in such a process. In addition, Krumboltz (1994) emphasized that some individuals have a greater ability to capitalize on chance encounters—for example, the persistence to follow through on leads or the capacity to see the potential good in involuntary changes (e.g., a downsized individual may view his or her situation as offering the opportunity to find a more interesting position). Mitchell, Levin, and Krumboltz (1999) identified five individual differences that likely influence the probability that an individual will capitalize on chance encounters; these include curiosity, persistence, flexibility, optimism, and risk taking.

Lent et al.'s (1994) model also includes contextual influences on continuous learning. In this model, contextual influences are defined as any factors outside an individual's control, including both background contextual factors (e.g., gender, race, and socioeconomic status) and current contextual factors (e.g., current availability of jobs within a given occupation, personal financial resources, and health status). In the model, background contextual factors directly influence "big C" vocational choices, and current contextual factors moderate "little c" continuous-learning and ongoing career choices.

Outcomes of Continuous Learning

The previous section reviewed the different types of decision processes individuals likely use with regard to continuous learning. Below, we provide a brief discussion of outcomes of continuous learning. Although continuous learning is receiving greater emphasis due to the relatively recent instability of talent markets, it has been discussed in the literature for 80 years. During this time, continuous learning has been depicted as leading to a variety of spiritual, economic, and psychological outcomes.

In terms of spiritual outcomes, Lindeman (1926) and Jacks (1929) framed continuous learning within the context of the Protestant work ethic (e.g., Weber, 1904), discussing such learning as an honorable pursuit required to further one's alignment with his or her divine calling. Fifty years later, an economic emphasis emerged as continuous learning was depicted as being related to valuable individual (advancement and employment stability within the firm) and organizational outcomes (the ability to maintain full-employment policies, minimize costly turnover, and adapt to changing business requirements) (e.g., London, 1983; Paxton, 1976). During this period, the primary emphasis of continuous learning was on organization-initiated and organization-sponsored training and development. For example, a related chapter in Goldstein (1989) by London and Bassman (1989) focused on preparing individuals impacted by downsizing for redeployment within the organization. Later, when redeployment within the organization was not as common after downsizing, Arthur and Rousseau (1996) advocated for continuous learning as a way for individuals to enhance their employability and prepare for a "boundaryless" career across organizations.

Finally, the notion of psychological success as an outcome of continuous learning emerged with Hall's (1996) description of "protean" careers, which involve both continuous learning and widely varying roles that span multiple organizations. Hall (1996) suggested the underlying motivation for continuous learning in protean careers is based on the psychological contract as occurring between the self and one's work (rather than between the self and an organization). Hall's depiction of psychological success transcends job satisfaction and task involvement, focusing instead on the extent to which careers and deeply held values are aligned. Hall and Chandler's (2005) work on the career as a "calling" suggests that such alignment of work with personal values may give work spiritual meaning. Such a view echoes Terkel's (1972) summary of interviews with a cross section of Americans; Terkel suggested that for some individuals, work involves a "search for daily meaning as well as daily bread, for recognition as well as cash, and for astonishment rather than torpor" (p. ix).

Summary

This section provided a brief overview of the literature on continuous-learning choices and outcomes. Extant models focusing on high-involvement and planned-happenstance decision processes were discussed. The model depicted in the following section builds on the research discussed in this section. Specifically, the planned-happenstance models support this chapter's focus on the influence of social-environmental factors on continuous learning.

Continuous-Learning Model

A model of continuous learning is presented in Figure 10.1. The model builds in part upon the work of Lent et al. (1994) and Mitchell and Krumboltz (1990), which focuses on the way environmental factors influence continuous-learning decisions. Consistent with our definition of continuous learning (e.g., Sessa & London, 2006) and with notions of the protean career (Hall, 1996), the model shown here is iterative. That is, although continuous learning may well provide individuals with the means to develop professionally in a traditional sense, the model's feedback loop suggests that individuals may also periodically backtrack in their careers, moving from expert back to novice. Such transitions may be self-initiated in response to personal preferences or instead may be a response to a loss of employment (see London & Smithers, 1999).

As shown in Figure 10.1, the model depicts continuous learning as a process in which social network characteristics, individual differences, and environmental characteristics influence the extent to which an individual participates in career-related learning. The model further suggests that an individual may choose to participate in such learning as a result of either (a) high-involvement processes such as career exploration (e.g., Greenhaus, 1987), or (b) chance events such as necessity (e.g., due to downsizing) or fortuitous encounters with individuals in one's social network. For those inclined toward high-involvement decision making, continuous-learning choices are thought to be based in part on the individual's perception that his or her knowledge and skills do not "fit" with those demanded by the talent market (either a current employer or other employers the individual finds attractive).

The extent to which an individual's initial intention to participate in continuous learning actually results in such participation is thought to be moderated by two variables: career salience and competing commitments. Career salience is viewed as the importance one places on his or her work and career role relative to other roles (Greenhaus, 1971), and competing commitments include the full set of work and nonwork commitments the individual must manage (Kegan & Lahey, 2001). Finally, although participation in learning is typically depicted as enhancing the value of the individual's human capital (i.e., the individual receives a return on the learning investment), the model depicted here suggests that the relationship between learning and human capital is moderated by both economic (e.g., industry and regional economic conditions) and technological dynamics (e.g., technological advances may lead to skill obsolescence).

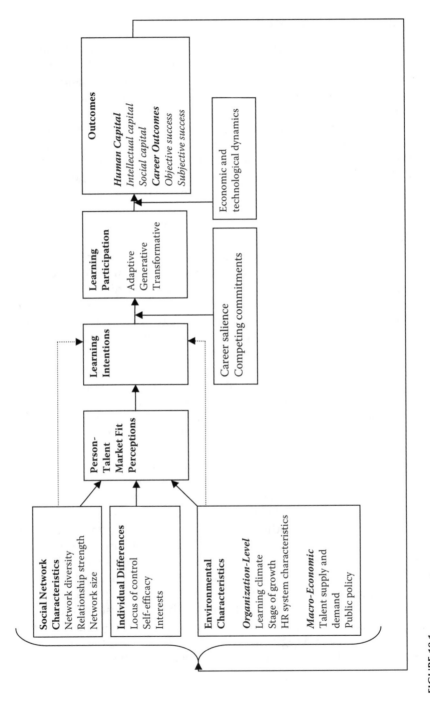

FIGURE 10.1
Continuous learning model.

Antecedents

Social Network Characteristics

The first category of continuous-learning antecedents includes social network characteristics. Development networks, a type of social network explored by Higgins and Kram (2001), are typically composed of five to seven individuals whom a protégé identifies as having provided career-related instrumental and/or psychosocial support at a certain point in time (Higgins & Kram). Higgins and Kram suggested network diversity and relationship strength would influence the mentoring protégés receive; and empirical research (Higgins, 2001) supports these suggestions. Siebert, Kraimer, and Liden (2001) also provided empirical support for associations between social network characteristics (network diversity, relationship strength, and network size).

In contrast to the studies on development networks, other empirical studies have explored the impact of broader social networks on career outcomes. Specifically, Eby, Butts, and Lockwood (2003) suggested that network diversity (e.g., the inclusion of individuals within and external to one's current employer) and network size are associated with positive subjective and objective career outcomes. Ng, Eby, Sorensen, and Feldman's (2005) meta-analysis of predictors of career success also suggested network size is likely associated with career outcomes. Given the findings from research on both development networks and broader social networks, the model depicted here includes the following social network characteristics: network diversity, relationship strength, and network size.

Network diversity refers to the extent to which relationships within the network provide either "new" or redundant information to the individual. Two characteristics that directly influence the amount of new information a network can provide are (a) the range and number of different social systems from which the relationships stem, and (b) the extent to which the members of the network interact (Brass, 1984). For instance, an individual embedded within a closely knit company town likely does not have a diverse network, that is, any new relationships with other individuals living and working within this environment likely yield redundant information. In contrast, an individual living in a diverse metropolitan area who commutes to work and has an active lifestyle likely interacts with individuals who provide "new" information based upon their unique perspectives and hobbies.

Relationship strength refers to the strength of the interpersonal bonds or "ties" (Granovetter, 1973, 1983) maintained by individuals in the network. Strong ties are characterized by strong emotional attachment, reciprocity, and frequent communications (Krackhardt, 1992); in such relationships, individuals are highly motivated to assist each other. Finally, *network size* refers to the number of individuals the individual interacts with across a wide range of social systems (e.g., work, family, church, and neighbor-hood; Burt, 1992).

Individual Differences

From a psychological perspective, locus of control and self-efficacy are included in the model based on research showing their influence on training and development motivation (e.g., Colquitt et al., 2000; Gully & Chen, this volume; Noe & Wilk, 1993) and career management behav-iors (e.g., Noe, 1996; Sturges, Conway, Guest, & Liefogghe, 2005; Sturges, Guest, Conway, & Davey, 2002). These variables likely influence contin-uous learning in the extent to which an individual not only perceives the ability to navigate the talent market in a broad sense (i.e., through high-involvement career-planning processes) but also capitalizes on any chance encounters. For example, if when talking with a friend an indi-vidual learns about upcoming workshops in an emerging technology, this person is more likely to investigate the logistical details of the workshop and attend if he or she has high task-specific self-efficacy for technology and an internal locus of control.

Interests, an additional psychological individual-difference variable shown in the model, are defined as preferences for activities. Dawis and Lofquist (1984) suggested that interests are influenced by both the individ-ual's abilities and personality. Although there is a long history of research on interests relating to career choice (e.g., Dawis & Lofquist; Holland, 1966; Parsons, 1909; Super, 1980), interests have received less attention in the continuous-learning literature. This lack of attention could be a remnant of traditional notions of employment in which individuals were perhaps more likely to participate in organization-sponsored and organization-initiated training, regardless of their personal interest. Interests are included in the model shown here as they likely influence the particu-lar content of the continuous learning one finds attractive—whether that content is applicable in a job at a current or potential employer. That is, in accordance with the nature of contemporary employment relationships, individuals' continuous-learning intentions may be influenced not only by talent market demands but also by their interests and desire for psy-chological success (Hall, 1996).

Environmental Characteristics

As shown in Figure 10.1, environmental factors influencing continuous learning include both organization-level and macroeconomic charac-teristics. First, consistent with extant models, interfirm differences such as learning climate (e.g., Salas & Cannon-Bowers, 2001) likely influence learning intentions and assessments of person–talent market fit. Further, other interfirm differences such as organization age and stage of growth or decline may also influence continuous learning. For example, a growing biotech firm may provide a more supportive learning climate than an employer in a declining market. Specifically, individuals in growing organizations may be more likely to find an organizational emphasis on learning and training (e.g., Delery & Doty, 1996) than would individuals in organizations focused primarily on survival, minimizing costs, and decreasing the asset base. As such, individuals in growing firms may choose to participate in continuous learning in order to keep pace with the change within both their current employer and other firms within their talent market. In contrast, individuals in declining organizations may find themselves participating in continuous learning due to necessity, for example as a result of downsizing.

In terms of macroeconomic antecedents, consistent with human capital theory and related research, macroeconomic factors influencing decisions to participate in career management activities may include unemployment levels (e.g., Cahill, 2000), trends toward global sourcing (Cascio, 2002), and public policy initiatives such as tax incentives, initiatives to enhance the competitiveness of the workforce, and public policy regarding employment and workforce readiness (e.g., Jacobs & Hawley, 2005; Mangum, 2005). For example, some countries (e.g., the United Kingdom and Germany) have government policies supporting continuous (or lifelong) learning in order to enhance national competitiveness (Morley, 2004).

Person–Talent Market Fit

Fit has long been studied in industrial-organizational psychology and is based on goodness-of-fit models that, within the Lewin (1931) tradition, consider congruence between individual and contextual variables. Seminal works include Shaffer's (1953) depiction of person–job fit; Dawis and Lofquist's (1984) theory of work adjustment and the related perceived environment congruence construct (Bretz & Judge, 1994); and Schneider's (1987) attraction–selection–attrition model, which suggests that over time individuals gravitate toward organizations and jobs congruent with their values. Although various types of fit (e.g., person–job, person–organization, person–group, and person–environment) have been studied, our model of continuous learning suggests that subjective assessments of person–talent market fit also guide continuous learning decisions.

Person–talent market fit is defined here as the extent to which individuals perceive congruence between their abilities and the requirements posed by their current or prospective employer(s). Assessments of person–talent market fit are thought to be influenced by an individual's social network, psychological individual-difference variables, and environmental characteristics. Such a depiction is consistent with the high-involvement career assessment processes (e.g., Greenhaus, 1987) discussed earlier. Further, some of these antecedents may also *initiate* fit assessments; for instance, an individual employed at an organization that is beginning to decline may begin to evaluate his or her person–talent market fit in anticipation of downsizing. Assessments of person–talent market fit differ from other fit assessments in that, unlike other fits in which congruence is "good" and facilitates action (e.g., application and job acceptance), perceptions of person–talent market fit likely do *not* encourage action. Instead, consistent with Simmering, Colquitt, Noe, and Porter's (2003) study of learning motivation in response to developmental feedback, it is suggested that *misfit* is more likely than fit to initiate participation in continuous learning.

Continuous-Learning Intentions

The model depicts three modes through which an individual may arrive at decisions to participate in continuous learning. First, the influence of person–talent market fit assessments on learning depicts one scenario in which individuals may arrive at decisions to participate in continuous learning based on high-involvement career planning processes (e.g., Greenhaus, 1987). Conversely, chance events may influence continuous learning in two ways. First, participation in social interactions (i.e., the presence of social networks) may expose individuals to fortuitous encounters that encourage learning. For example, an individual with a diverse social network composed of strong relationships may develop an interest in new careers or topics as a result of these relationships. In addition, the potential for some chance events (e.g., organizational downsizing or regional economic trends) to influence learning intentions through necessity is depicted in Figure 10.1 by the relationship (portrayed with a dotted arrow) between environmental characteristics and learning intentions. For example, an individual impacted by a downsizing may choose to pursue new learning in order to ease their redeployment.

Types of Continuous Learning

Consistent with Sessa and London (2006), our model depicts three types of continuous learning: adaptive, generative, and transformative learning. Each type of learning differs depending on the extent to which it relates to the individual's current career role(s). Adaptive learning, for example, is purely reactionary in nature, occurring in response to environmental demands. As such, the adaptive learning content is related to the individual's current role. Generative learning also occurs in relation to one's current role but involves proactive anticipation of future job and organization requirements. As such, generative learning is most likely among individuals with an internal locus of control and high task-specific self-efficacy (Sessa & London, 2006). For example, an individual high in career-related self-efficacy is likely to anticipate environmental changes and engage in new, generative learning in order to prepare for the impact of such changes on their current role(s).

In contrast, transformative learning is defined as learning that does not relate directly to the individuals' current role(s). For example, an electrician participating in nursing courses would be engaging in transformative learning. As suggested above, such transformative learning may result from fortuitous encounters (e.g., the individual may be accompanying a friend who is taking the course), necessity (e.g., the individual may be learning about the equipment that nurses use in order to prepare for a contract involving hospitals), or a high-involvement career management process (e.g., the individual may be switching to a nursing career given boredom in his or her current role, a long-standing interest in working with elders, and/or talent market and demographic dynamics).

Moderators of the Learning Intentions and Learning Participation Relationship

Consistent with the theory of planned behavior (Ajzen, 2002; Ajzen & Fishbein, 2004), the relationship between intentions to participate in learning and actual participation in such learning is likely moderated by career salience and competing commitments. *Career salience* refers to the importance an individual places on the roles of work and career in comparison with other life roles (Greenhaus, 1971). Consistent with the model depicted here, individuals low in career salience may tend to engage in continuous learning to a lesser extent than those high in career salience, as individuals low in career salience may not believe that continuous learning is especially valuable to them. In contrast, individuals high in career salience may have a strong predisposition toward career-related learning, as these individuals highly value the outcomes associated with such learning.

With regard to the second moderator, competing commitments to a variety of targets within and outside the work domain have long been recognized (Becker, 1992; Kegan & Lahey, 2001; Reichers, 1985). Such commitments, even when they are not in direct conflict, may still vie for an individual's limited emotional and attentional resources (Kanfer & Ackerman, 1989) as well as their time and energy (Naylor, Pritchard, & Ilgen, 1980). Individuals with multiple work or nonwork commitments that require much time and effort may find it difficult to engage in continuous learning even if they strongly intend to do so (e.g., as a result of high career salience).

Outcomes

A proximal outcome of continuous learning is the development of human and social capital, both of which are defined here at the individual level. Consistent with Becker (1964), *human capital* is defined as an individual's knowledge, skills, and experiences. Social capital, in contrast, is based upon connections with others; we define *social capital* as the individual's interpersonal relationships with others, along with the resources embedded in such relationships (Seibert, Kraimer, & Liden, 2001). Through engagement in continuous learning, individuals likely broaden and perhaps increase the diversity of their social networks. In turn, as noted by Granovetter (1973, 1983), these "weak ties" in the social network may increase the likelihood of the individual encountering fortuitous circumstances.[1] As such, social capital may be related to both subjective (e.g., new friendships) and objective (e.g., assistance with job search) outcomes.

In the model shown here, continuous learning is depicted as potentially influencing both objective and subjective career outcomes. Depictions of objective outcomes included money and advancement, and have expanded to include job mobility (e.g., Heslin, 2005). Similarly, subjective career outcomes, including such elements as purpose, job satisfaction, and career satisfaction, have expanded to emphasize work–life balance (Finegold & Mohrman, 2001) and a provision of a sense of meaning (Wrzesniewski & Dutton, 2002) or contribution (Hall & Chandler, 2005). The depiction of both objective and subjective outcomes reflects Hughes' (1958) and Schein's (1978) statement that objective and subjective success are not necessarily highly correlated. That is, individuals may be "successful" in objective, worldly terms (e.g., as determined from personnel records or by expert raters) but not in subjective terms (i.e., as defined by the individual). Therefore, consistent with the work of Friedman and Greenhaus (2000), the dimensions of subjective career success considered here would include elements such as time for self, challenge, and/or opportunities for socialization.

Moderators of the Learning and Outcome Relationship

An implied assumption in the human resource literature is that participation in continuous learning typically *enhances* human capital. We believe this is a limitation of the continuous-learning literature because it fails to acknowledge that some types of learning may not be valued by the talent market, and may be in fact detrimental to the individual's objective career success. Our model addresses this limitation by incorporating economic and technological dynamics as moderators of the relationship between continuous learning and learning outcomes. Inclusion of economic and technological dynamics in the model acknowledges that (a) economic and technological dynamics can decrease the value of any continuous learning an individual engages in, and (b) both individual and "expert" (e.g., government agency or professional organization) predictions regarding which skills will be in demand (and therefore what learning will be valuable) are far from certain. That is, like financial investments, investment in continuous learning is risky and outcomes are unknown.

For example, technological advances may result in discontinuous changes that in turn fundamentally alter business models. As a result, skills in the previous technology may no longer be in demand or especially valued by the talent market. An industry-specific example would be the film industry, which faced the shift from film to digital imaging. A consequence of this shift was that individuals who had invested in the development of silver halide technology and manufacturing skills were left with a skill set that was no longer in demand. As a non-industry-specific example, current trends suggest that individuals who have pursued learning in Web programming may find that software advances have decreased the demand for Web programmers; thus, this work is being exported, and the demand for these skills within the United States has decreased. This being the case, at the present time continuous learning related to Web programming (although it may lead to short-term favorable outcomes such as pride and enjoyment of learning) does not enhance human capital.

Although uncommon in the human resource management literature, the view that learning may not lead to favorable outcomes is consistent with anthropological views of adaptation, which are that (a) adaptations are not deliberately planned, (b) the primary adaptation that humans engage in is learning, and (c) the outcomes associated with adaptations cannot be predicted ex ante (Pelissier, 1991). As Darwin (1905) noted, "God plays a game of chance" (p. 456). That is, at the time that the adaptation occurs (e.g., learning), it is unclear whether the adaptation will facilitate, hamper, or not affect the organism's survival. This uncertainty is due to the lack of knowledge about how other organisms and the environment are changing or may change. For example, a change viewed as adaptive for the existing environment (e.g., a photographic scientist learning about film-based technology) may actually be a maladaptive change for future environments (e.g., a world dominated by digital photography). This analogy relates to lifelong learning in that when individuals invest in lifelong learning, it is unclear how this learning may facilitate, hamper, or not influence the individual's fit with his or her current employer and the broader talent market. Therefore, the model depicts external factors (i.e., economic and technological dynamics) as potentially altering (increasing or decreasing) the value of specific continuous-learning investments.

Discussion

The model depicted in Figure 10.1 differs from other contemporary models of continuous learning in that it (a) utilizes a talent market context rather than an organizational context; (b) incorporates chance events in addition to high-involvement career management processes; (c) depicts various types of continuous learning; (d) incorporates factors influencing participation in learning (e.g., competing commitments); and (e) incorporates factors influencing learning outcomes (i.e., macroenvironmental and technological dynamics). These differences are discussed below.

First, the context for our model is the talent market. Extant models suggest that individuals' points of reference for decisions regarding continuous learning are embedded in an organization, typically the current employer. That is, the organization's strategy and staffing projections are considered to be the primary points of reference for continuous-learning decisions (as well as perceptions of skill misfit). In contrast, we suggest that individuals use not only their current employer but also potential future employers as points of reference for continuous-learning decisions. Further, given the emergence of protean careers and unstable talent markets, consideration of a talent market context (in addition to or instead of an organizational context) may enhance our understanding of and ability to predict continuous learning.

Second, extant models often focus on engagement in learning as an outcome of a high-involvement decision process. As such, individuals are often portrayed as having prespecified learning goals that align with their long-term career goals. In contrast, consistent with the work of Lent et al. (1994) and Mitchell and Krumboltz (1990), the model shown in Figure 10.1 is applicable across a variety of decision processes. Specifically, it is suggested that in addition to participation in a high-involvement decision-making process such as career exploration, fortuitous events and necessity may also motivate individuals to participate in continuous learning. The focus here is not to minimize the importance of career management or suggest that some individuals do not participate in career exploration, but rather to acknowledge that such processes require time, motivation, and ability (Petty & Cacioppo, 1986); thus, given the variance individuals likely have in career salience (Greenhaus, 1971) as well as the broad range of competing commitments individuals manage (Kegan & Lahey, 2001), it is likely that many individuals use a less deliberate approach in making continuous-learning decisions.

Third, consistent with Sessa and London (2006), the model shown here includes various types of continuous learning in addition to the generative learning implied in extant models. The incorporation of adaptive and transformative learning in depictions of the continuous-learning process may spur additional research related to these learning modes. Fourth, learning intentions likely vary depending on factors such as career salience and competing commitments; moreover, learning intentions do not necessarily lead to one's actual participation in continuous learning. To date, there has been little research on the underlying psychological processes related to the formation of continuous-learning intentions.

Finally, extant models view continuous learning as a "good thing" for the individual; that is, learning is viewed as contributing to the individual's knowledge, skills, and experiences in ways that tend to enhance his or her ability to manage the ever-changing skill sets demanded by employers. As such, the assumption is that continuous learning enhances human capital, providing individuals (e.g., the "self-determined" learner; London & Smither, 1999) with more control over their future in accordance with the contemporary employment relationship (e.g., Arthur & Rousseau, 1996). We further suggest that perhaps the contemporary employment relationship is presently being interpreted as "As long as I continue to learn and grow, there will be a good job for me (probably not a job at my current employer, but a job that uses my skills)." On the other hand, our inclusion of moderators of the learning–outcomes relationship suggests that the enhanced personal control and increased human capital resulting from continuous learning may be illusory or mythical to some extent. As history confirms, the lack of certainty surrounding continuous learning and full employment can be attested to by individuals ranging from former print press operators and blacksmiths to former television repair technicians, carburetor specialists, and phone switchboard operators, to former photographic film scientists and computer programmers.

This section discussed the ways in which our model of continuous learning differs from extant models. However, it is also important to keep in mind a fundamental element that our model and other extant models share, namely, the notion of intraindividual change. That is, contemporary continuous-learning models reinforce the notion of plasticity of individuals' knowledge, skills, and abilities. Further, these models also reflect the fact that individuals' interests may change over time—as do the specific knowledge, skills, and experiences demanded by the talent market. The following section discusses future research opportunities within the domain of continuous learning.

Future Research Agenda

First, it is important to note that the accumulated knowledge and wisdom regarding learning in organizations (e.g., Salas & Cannon-Bowers, 2001; Tannenbaum & Yukl, 1992) are impressive. Our evaluation of this research through the lens of continuous learning, however, suggests that although we understand a great deal about the "learning participant" (i.e., the individual involved in a learning activity), we know relatively little about the "continuous learner." In the following paragraphs, suggestions for future research on both continuous learners and the continuous-learning process are discussed.

Continuous Learners

The iterative nature of our continuous-learning model suggests that engagement in continuous learning is recurring or periodic. Yet it is unclear to what extent our voluminous knowledge regarding the learning participant generalizes to continuous learners. That is, to what extent does our knowledge of the influence of individual differences on engagement in and outcomes of training and development extend to continuous learning?

To explore this question, the term *continuous learner* will need to be defined, and this is not an easy task given the plethora of continuous-learning constructs. One preliminary definition of the continuous learner might be as follows: *an individual who consistently acquires career-related knowledge, skills, and worldviews (as a result of either systematic planning or chance events) that may facilitate adaptation to talent market dynamics.* This definition includes behaviors as well as intended outcomes, yet more specificity is needed to make the definition workable. Scholars will want to explore the antecedents, behaviors, and outcomes to be included in such a definition, along with the trade-offs associated with alternative definitions.

One consideration is the dimensionality of learning included in definitions of the continuous learner. In evaluating extant constructs relating to continuous learning, we found that three dimensions are commonly depicted: formal versus informal learning, organization- versus self-initiated learning, and current- versus future-job-oriented learning. We suggest that in defining the continuous learner or creating a typology of continuous learners, other dimensions should be considered, including firm-specific versus generalized skill learning, self- versus organization payment for learning, and type of learning (e.g., Sessa & London, 2005).

Nature of Continuous-Learning Catalyst

Another stream of research could consider the nature of antecedents stimulating individuals to consider continuous learning. This chapter has suggested that catalysts for continuous learning may include high-involvement career management, fortuitous encounters happened upon through social networks, and necessity resulting from environmental factors. However, it is unclear if this is a comprehensive taxonomy, and perhaps a typology could be created. Further, there is the need to understand what individual difference and outcome variables are associated with participation in continuous learning associated with high-involvement career management and individuals capitalizing on fortuitous encounters. Moreover, how training participation and transfer motivation may differ between individuals attending training based on necessity resulting from environmental factors (e.g., downsizings) compared to individuals who attend training based on individual differences (e.g., interests) has yet to be explored.

Social Network Characteristics

Higgins and Kram (2001) described various social networks as based upon two characteristics: an individual's network diversity and the strength of the relationships within the network. Further, Higgins and Kram suggested that one's social network is associated with certain mentoring processes and outcomes. Table 10.1 lists the four types of networks defined by Higgins and Kram along with types of learning as defined by Sessa and London (2006). With regard to future research on continuous-learning processes, such research could determine how the typology of social network and mentoring outcomes developed by Higgins and Kram might be adapted for continuous learning. More specifically, research could investigate whether the various social network configurations depicted in Table 10.1 are associated with either "fortuitous learning" resulting from chance events or the particular types of learning identified by Sessa and London.

For example, the receptive networks described in Table 10.1 are characterized by weak relationships with individuals having similar backgrounds and interests. Such weak relationships are not likely to influence an individual's attitudes toward topics such as career options. Further, as

TABLE 10.1

Social Networks and Continuous Learning

Network Type	Likelihood of Fortuitous Events Resulting in Continuous Learning	Associated Type of Learning
Receptive (homogeneous, weak relationship ties)	Low	Adaptive (in reaction to environment)
Opportunistic (diverse, weak relationship ties)	High	Generative (new knowledge and conditions)
Traditional (homogeneous, strong relationship ties)	Medium	Adaptive (in reaction to environment)
Entrepreneurial (diverse, strong relationship ties)	High	Transformative (discontinuous learning, perhaps enabling potential career change)

Source: Inspired by Higgins and Kram (2001) and Sessa and London (2006).

suggested earlier, the homogeneity of the receptive network is not likely to expose the individual to fortuitous encounters or a diversity of ideas. Therefore, perhaps the type of learning most likely to occur in such environments is adaptive learning, that is, incremental learning related to the individual's current role. In contrast, individuals in entrepreneurial networks are likely to have strong relationships with diverse individuals, for example, relationships with those engaged in a wide range of occupations or employed within various industries. As noted in Table 10.1, such diverse relationships are more likely than the homogeneous relationships in receptive networks to lead to fortuitous events and/or expose the individual to new ideas; moreover, the supportive context characteristic of entrepreneurial networks may provide an ideal context for the consideration of significant changes such as an alternative career path. Accordingly, entrepreneurial networks may be more likely than other network types to be associated with transformative learning.

As social network analytical approaches are refined and related research continues to develop, a rich understanding of the social influences on continuous learning may emerge that may enhance the external validity of continuous-learning models. That is, whereas extant models consider continuous learning within an organizational context, refinements in social network analysis allow for continuous learning to be evaluated within the social and talent market contexts in which such learning occurs. Such analysis is likely to aid our understanding and prediction of continuous-learning participation and outcomes.

Scholars studying social networks have begun to identify implications for understanding continuous learning (e.g., Hatala, 2006). For example, Higgins (2001) found that those with entrepreneurial networks (described in Table 10.1 as involving diverse social networks and strong relationships) were more likely than other network types to make discontinuous career changes. However, little is known about the mechanisms through which individual-difference, social network, and environmental characteristics interacted with or influenced the continuous learning and career change. For example, to what extent does person–talent market fit (or misfit) tend to be associated with learning intentions and learning participation?

In terms of the continuous-learning patterns associated with the other social network types listed in Table 10.1, little is known. For example, what types of learning (adaptive, generative transformative) are associated with various network types? How do the antecedents depicted in the model interact with talent market fit perceptions to influence continuous-learning intentions, participation, and outcomes? Further, little is known about how the size and density of each type of social network described in Table 10.1 influence talent market fit perceptions and related outcomes. To address these questions, perhaps the innovative methods Seibert et al.

(2001) used with university alumni to examine social capital and career outcomes could be adapted to study continuous learning.

Further, although it can be argued that evaluation of potential relationships between psychological individual-difference variables and social network characteristics is counter to the sociological emphasis on the influence of social class and background variables on such factors (e.g., Wasserman & Galaskiewicz, 1994), Burt, Janotta, and Mahoney (1998) suggested (based on administration of personality and social network assessments to MBA students and a field study in a financial services firm) that there are systematic patterns in social network structure explained by personality characteristics. This study may be useful as a starting point for research on how personality may influence both social network characteristics and individuals' ability to leverage fortuitous encounters. However, this line of research should be pursued with caution given the nature of the sociological and human resource perspectives. Chandler and Kram (2006) provided insights regarding potential reconciliation of the theoretical tensions between sociological and psychological views of social networks.

Individual Differences

With regard to individual differences, the significant question concerns the extent to which knowledge regarding participation in specific training and/or development activities (Colquitt et al., 2000; Gully & Chen, this volume; Noe & Wilk, 1993) generalizes to repeated participation in learning throughout one's career. To explore this question, longitudinal research designs will be required. Consistent with MacCallum (1998), we suggest that perhaps the human resources field could benefit from the use of archival data sets, specifically the National Longitudinal Survey of Youth (Bureau of Labor Statistics, 2002). This study is sometimes referred to as the study of the "Class of 1976," as data collection began when high school seniors were administered a comprehensive battery of personality, career interest, and ability tests in that year. Each subsequent year, data on a variety of topics (including education levels, training participation, job search methods, employment status, and job and life satisfaction) have been included in the study.

In terms of additional data sets that may aid the study of individual differences and continuous learning, a comprehensive study of the children of the class of 1976 now entering the workforce is available, with data tied to specific class members of the class of 1997 for intergenerational analysis (Bureau of Labor Statistics, 2002). A comprehensive study of the high school class of 1997 (designed to mirror the Class of 1976 study) is also available (Bureau of Labor Statistics, 2002). For all three studies, data are gathered and released once each year.

Although these data sets have been used extensively in the sociology and economics literatures (MacCallum, 1998), to our knowledge they have not been widely utilized in the human resource management literature. Such data could be used to test some of the relationships suggested in Figure 10.1. For instance, continuous learners could be identified and logistic analysis conducted to explore the extent to which the individual-difference variables suggested by extant research (e.g., Gully & Chen, this volume) predict continuous-learning group membership. It may also be possible to determine the extent to which continuous learners experience career success (in terms of both subjective and objective measures). Although we do not consider such data sets to be a panacea for longitudinal studies specifically established to study continuous learning, such data may serve as a valuable starting point for understanding how continuous learners differ from others in terms of relatively stable individual differences, background, and response to environmental factors.

Environmental Antecedents

Welbourne and Andrews (1996) evaluated initial public offering documentation to identify human resource system characteristics and studied firm outcomes associated with various human resource systems. To understand the influence of the organizational context on continuous learning, a similar approach could be utilized using annual reports or the "careers" sections of company Web sites to categorize firms using Delery and Doty's (1996) market and internal human resource system types. Specifically, Delery and Doty noted the existence of training and development systems as one of seven human resource characteristics differentiating market and internal human resource systems. Market human resource systems are consistent with the talent market context associated with Figure 10.1 (i.e., employees and human resource strategists consider continuous learning from talent market rather than organizational perspective). In contrast, internal human resource systems are characteristic of an organizational context for both employee and human resource strategist decisions regarding continuous-learning investments. The type of human resource system and the associated context likely have implications for the type of learning (adaptive, generative, or transformative) individuals participate in; whether the learning is self-initiated or organization initiated; and who pays for the learning (e.g., registration fees, and payment of wages, or lack thereof, while attending). Perhaps such research would find systematic differences in the continuous-learning participation and outcomes of individuals employed at firms with internal versus market human resource systems.

In addition, in terms of macroeconomic variables, the Class of 1976 data (Bureau of Labor Statistics, 2002) could be used to explore the extent to which national and regional economic conditions explain variation in career outcomes (and possibly continuous learning) during the various economic cycles occurring in the United States since 1976.

To summarize, future research on continuous learners and the continuous-learning process may be aided by the use of archival data sets (e.g., MacCallum, 1998) as well as by leveraging the research on social-environmental influences on development (e.g., Higgins, 2001). Continuous-learning studies may also be aided by research on contingent employees who rapidly cycle through continuous-learning processes (e.g., Ellingson, Gruys, & Sackett, 1998), as well as by research on the individual-difference variable of adaptability (e.g., LePine, Colquitt, & Erez, 2000) and the outcomes of adaptive performance (e.g., Pulakos & Arad, 2000).

Summary

Human resource scholars have positioned continuous learning as part of boundaryless (Arthur & Rousseau, 1996), protean (Hall, 1996) careers for over a decade. Continuous learning, which may occur as a result of either systematic career planning or chance events, has become a significant means by which individuals may thrive in today's dynamic talent markets. In order to depict both planned and chance events within the continuous-learning process, this chapter presented a model of continuous learning that includes not only psychological individual-difference variables but also social network and macroeconomic characteristics as antecedents of continuous learning. In contrast with extant models (e.g., London & Mone, 1999; London & Smither, 1999; Morrison & Hall, 2002), the model shown here utilizes a talent market context rather than an organizational context. Incorporation of such elements as the talent market context and social network and macroenvironmental characteristics may enhance our understanding of the underlying psychological and social processes involved in continuous learning as well as the factors that influence continuous-learning outcomes.

In discussing career adaptability, Morrison and Hall (2002) stated that "there is not a topic more critical to the study of successful careers than the issue of how people reinvent and redefine themselves, in ways that bring them psychological success" (p. 233). We agree, and we view the study of continuous learning—or the way individuals reinvent and redefine themselves as they "learn" a living—to be of primary importance to scholars, practitioners, and individuals navigating the dynamics of today's talent market.

Note

1. The interested reader may also want to see Burt's (1992) work on a related concept, "structural holes," a term referring to the absence of interassociations among an individual's network members. Further, Wasserman and Galaskiewicz (1994) provided a comprehensive description of network diversity and relationship strength as well as measurement and analytical approaches.

References

The 2006 Fortune 500. (2006). *Fortune, 151*(9), 42–47.

Ajzen, I. (2002). Perceived behavioral control, self-efficacy, locus of control, and the theory of planned behavior. *Journal of Applied Social Psychology, 32,* 665–683.

Ajzen, I., & Fishbein, M. (2004). Questions raised by a reasoned action approach: Reply to Ogden (2003). *Health Psychology, 23,* 431–434.

Arthur, M., & Rousseau, D. (1996). *The boundaryless career.* New York: Oxford University Press.

Bandura, A. (1982). The psychology of chance encounters and life paths. *American Psychologist, 37,* 747–755.

Bandura, A. (2001). Social cognitive theory: An agentic perspective. In S. T. Fiske, D. L. Schacter, & C. Zahn-Waxler (Eds.), *Annual review of psychology* (Vol. 52, pp. 1–26). Palo Alto, CA: Annual Reviews.

Becker, G. (1964). *Human capital.* New York: Columbia University Press.

Becker, T. (1992). Foci and bases of commitment: Are they distinctions worth making? *Academy of Management Journal, 35,* 232–244.

Brass, D. (1984). A social network perspective on human resource management. *Research in Personnel and Human Resources Management, 13,* 39–79.

Bretz, R., Jr., & Judge, T. (1994). Person–organization fit and the theory of work adjustment: Implications for satisfaction, tenure, and career success. *Journal of Vocational Behavior, 44,* 32–54.

Bright, J., Pryor, R., & Harpham, L. (2005). The role of chance events in career decision making. *Journal of Vocational Behavior, 66,* 561–575.

Bureau of Labor Statistics. (2002). *The NLS79 user's guide National Longitudinal Surveys of Labor Market Experience, youth cohort: Children and young adults 1979–2002.* Columbus: Center for Human Resource Research, Ohio State University.

Bureau of Labor Statistics. (2004). Younger boomers: Nearly 10 jobs by age 36. *MLR: The Editor's Desk.* Retrieved October 25, 2005, from http://www.bls.gov/opub/ted/2002/aug/wk4/art03.htm

Burt, R. (1992). *Structural holes: The social structure of competition.* Cambridge, MA: Harvard University Press.

Burt, R., Janotta, J., & Mahoney, J. (1998). Personality correlates of structural holes. *Social Networks, 13,* 332-367.

Cahill, M. (2000). Truth or macroeconomic consequences: Theoretical implications of the decline and rise of job references in the United States. *Journal of Post-Keynesian Economics, 22,* 451–475.

Carver, C., & Scheier, M. (2000). Autonomy of self-regulation. *Psychological Inquiry, 11*(4), 284–292.

Cascio, W. F. (2002). Changes in workers, work, and organizations. In W. C. Borman, D. R. Ilgen, & R. J. Klimoski (Eds.), *Handbook of psychology: Vol. 12. Industrial and organizational psychology* (pp. 401–422). Hoboken, NJ: John Wiley.

Chandler, D., & Kram, K. (2006). Mentoring and developmental networks in the new career context. In H. Gunz & M. Peiperl (Eds.), *Handbook of career studies.* Thousand Oaks, CA: Sage.

Colquitt, J., LePine, J., & Noe, R. (2000). Toward an integrative theory of training motivation: A meta-analytic path analysis of 20 years of research. *Journal of Applied Psychology, 85*(5), 678–707.

Darwin, C. (1905). *The origin of species.* Oxford, UK: Oxford University Press.

Dawis, R., & Lofquist, L. (1984). *A psychological theory of work adjustment.* Minneapolis: University of Minnesota Press.

Delery, J., & Doty, D. (1996). Modes of theorizing in strategic human resource management. *Academy of Management Journal, 39*(4), 802–834.

Eby, L., Butts, M., & Lockwood, A. (2003). Predictors of success in the era of the boundaryless career. *Journal of Organizational Behavior, 24,* 698–708.

Ellingson, J., Gruys, M., & Sackett, P. (1998). Factors related to the satisfaction performance of temporary employees. *Journal of Applied Psychology, 83,* 913–921.

Finegold, D., & Mohrman, S. (2001). *What do employees really want: Perceptions vs. reality.* Report presented at the World Economic Forum 2001 annual meeting. Los Angeles: Korn/Ferry International.

Friedman, S., & Greenhaus, J. (2000). *Work and family—allies or enemies? What happens when business professionals confront life choices.* Oxford, UK: Oxford University Press.

Goldstein, I. (Ed.). (1989). *Training and development in organizations.* San Francisco: Jossey-Bass.

Granovetter, M. (1973). The strength of weak ties. *American Journal of Sociology, 6,* 1360–1380.

Granovetter, M. (1983). The strength of weak ties: A network theory revisited. *Sociological Theory, 1,* 201–233.

Greenhaus, J. (1971). An investigation of the role of career salience in vocational behavior. *Journal of Vocational Behavior, 1,* 209–216.

Greenhaus, J. (1987). *Career management.* Hinsdale, IL: Dryden Press.

Greenhaus, J., Callahan, G., & Godshalk, V. (1994). *Career management.* Fort Worth, TX: Dryden Press.

Greenwald, A., & Leavitt, C. (1984). Audience involvement in advertising: Four levels. *Journal of Consumer Research, 11,* 581–592.

Guindon, M., & Hanna, F. (2002). Coincidence, happenstance, serendipity, fate, or the hand of god: Case studies in synchronicity. *Career Development Quarterly, 50,* 195–209.

Hall, D. (1996). *The career is dead, long live the career.* San Francisco: Jossey-Bass.

Hall, D. (2002). *Careers in and out of organizations.* Thousand Oaks, CA: Sage.

Hall, D., & Chandler, D. (2005). Psychological success: When the career is a calling. *Journal of Organizational Behavior, 26*(2), 155–176.

Hall, D., & Mirvis, P. (1995). Careers as lifelong learning. In A. Howard (Ed.), *The changing nature of work* (pp. 323–362). San Francisco: Jossey-Bass.

Hastie, R., & Dawes, R. (2000). *Rational choice in an uncertain world.* Thousand Oaks, CA: Sage.

Hatala, J. (2006). Social network analysis in human resource development: A new methodology. *Human Resource Development Review, 5*(1), 45–71.

Heslin, P. (2005). Conceptualizing and evaluating career success. *Journal of Organizational Behavior, 26*(2), 113–136.

Higgins, M. (2001). Changing careers: The effects of social context. *Journal of Organizational Behavior, 22*(6), 595–618.

Higgins, M., & Kram, K. E. (2001). Reconceptualizing mentoring at work: A developmental network perspective. *Academy of Management Review, 26*(2), 264–289.

Holland, J. (1966). *The psychology of vocational choice.* Waltham, MA: Blaisdell.

Howard, A. (Ed.). (1995). *The changing nature of work.* San Francisco: Jossey-Bass.

Hughes, E. (1958). *Men and their work.* Glencoe, NY: Free Press.

Jacks, L. P. (1929). Continuity of earning and living throughout life. *Journal of Adult Education, 1*(1), 7–10.

Jacobs, R., & Hawley, J. (2005). Emergence of workforce development: Definition, conceptual boundaries, and future perspectives. In R. MacLean & D. Wilson (Eds.), *International handbook of technical and vocational education and training* (pp. 201–243). Bonn, Germany: UNESCO UNEVOC.

Kanfer, R., & Ackerman, P. (1989). Motivation and cognitive abilities: An integrative/aptitude treatment interaction approach to skill acquisition. *Journal of Applied Psychology, 74,* 657–690.

Kegan, R., & Lahey, L. (2001). The real reason people won't change. *Harvard Business Review, 79*(10), 85–92.

Klein, H. J., Wesson, M. J., Hollenbeck, J. R., & Alge, B. J. (1999). Goal commitment and the goal-setting process: Conceptual clarification and empirical synthesis. *Journal of Applied Psychology, 84,* 885–897.

Krackhardt, D. (1992). The strength of strong ties: The importance of philos in organizations. In N. Nohria & R. Eccles (Eds.), *Networks and organizations: Structure, form, and action* (pp. 216–239). Boston: Harvard Business School Press.

Krumboltz, J. (1994). Improving career development theory from a social-learning perspective. In M. L. Savickas & R. W. Lent (Eds.), *Convergence in career development theories* (pp. 9–32). Palo Alto, CA: Consulting Psychologists Press.

Latham, G. (1988). Human resource training and development. In M. R. Rosenzweig & L. W. Porter (Eds.), *Annual review of psychology* (Vol. 39, pp. 545–582). Palo Alto, CA: Annual Reviews.

Lent, R., Brown, S., & Hackett, G. (1994). Toward a unified social cognitive theory of career and academic interest, choice, and performance. *Journal of Vocational Behavior, 45,* 79–122.

LePine, J., Colquitt, J., & Erez, A. (2000). Adaptability to changing task contexts: Effects of general cognitive ability, conscientiousness, and openness to experience. *Personnel Psychology, 53*(3), 563–593.

Lewin, K. (1931). The conflict between Aristotelian and Galilean modes of thought in contemporary psychology. *Journal of General Psychology, 5,* 141–177.

Light, A. (2005). Job mobility and wage growth: Evidence from the National Longitudinal Survey of the High School Class of 1976. *Monthly Labor Review, 23*(2), 33–39.

Lindeman, E. (1926). *The meaning of adult education.* New York: New Republic.

London, M. (1983). Toward a theory of career motivation. *Academy of Management Review, 8,* 620–630.

London, M., & Bassman, E. (1989). *Retraining midcareer workers for the future workplace.* In I. Goldstein (Ed.), *Training and development in organizations.* San Francisco: Jossey-Bass.

London, M., & Mone, E. (1999). Continuous learning. In D. R. Ilgen & E. D. Pulakos (Eds.), *The changing nature of performance: Implications for staffing, motivation, and development* (pp. 119–153). San Francisco: Jossey-Bass.

London, M., & Noe, R. (1997). London's career motivation theory: An update on measurement and research. *Journal of Career Assessment, 5*(1), 61–80.

London, M., & Smither, J. (1999). Career-related continuous learning: Defining the construct and mapping the process. In G. R. Ferris (Ed.), *Research in personnel and human resources management* (Vol. 17, pp. 81–121). Stamford, CT: JAI.

MacCallum, R. (1998). Commentary on quantitative methods in I/O research. *Industrial-Organizational Psychologist, 35*(4), 8–14.

Mangum, G. (2005). Job training policy in the United States. *Industrial & Labor Relations Review, 59*(1), 169–170.

Maurer, T., Weiss, E., & Barbeite, F. (2003). A model of involvement in work-related learning and development activity: The effects of individual, situational, motivational, and age variables. *Journal of Applied Psychology, 88*(4), 707–725.

Mitchell, K., Levin, A., & Krumboltz, J. (1999). Planned happenstance: Constructing unexpected career opportunities. *Journal of Counseling and Development, 77,* 115–124.

Mitchell, L., & Krumboltz, J. (1990). Social-learning approach to career decision-making: Krumboltz's theory. In D. Brown, L. Brooks, & Associates (Eds.), *Career choice and development.* San Francisco: Jossey Bass.

Morley, M. (2004). Contemporary debates in European human resource management: Context and content. *Human Resource Management Review, 14*(4), 353–365.

Morrison, R., & Hall, D. (2002). Career adaptability. In D. Hall (Ed.), *Careers in and out of organizations* (pp. 205–234). Thousand Oaks, CA: Sage.

Naylor, J., Pritchard, R., & Ilgen, D. (1980). *A theory of behavior in organizations.* New York: Academic Press.

Ng, T., Eby, L., Sorensen, K., & Feldman, D. (2005). Predictors of objective and subjective career success: A meta-analysis. *Personnel Psychology, 58,* 212–240.

Noe, R. (1996). Is career management related to employee development and performance? *Journal of Organizational Behavior, 17,* 119–133.

Noe, R., & Wilk, S. (1993). Investigation of the factors that influence employees' participation in development activities. *Journal of Applied Psychology, 78*(2), 291–303.

Parsons, F. (1909). *Choosing a vocation*. Boston: Houghton Mifflin.

Paxton, D. (1976). Employee development: A lifelong learning approach. *Training and Development Journal*, 30(12), 24–27.

Pelissier, C. (1991). *The anthropology of teaching and learning* (Annual Review of Anthropology, Vol. 20). New York: Elsevier.

Petty, R., & Cacioppo, J. (1986). *The elaboration likelihood model of persuasion*. New York: Academic Press.

Pulakos, E., & Arad, S. (2000). Adaptability in the workplace: Development of a taxonomy of adaptive performance. *Journal of Applied Psychology*, 85(4), 612–624.

Reichers, A. (1985). A review and reconceptualization of organizational commitment. *Academy of Management Review*, 10, 465–476.

Rojewski, J. (1999). The role of chance in the career development of individuals with learning disabilities. *Learning Disability Quarterly*, 22(4), 267–278.

Rousseau, D. (2005). *I-deals: Idiosyncratic deals employees bargain for themselves*. Armonk, NY: M. E. Sharpe.

Salas, E., & Cannon-Bowers, J. (2001). The science of training: A decade of progress. In S. T. Fiske, D. L. Schacter, & C. Zahn-Waxler (Eds.), *Annual review of psychology* (Vol. 52, pp. 471–499). Palo Alto, CA: Annual Reviews.

Schein, E. (1978). *Career dynamics: Matching individual and organizational needs*. Reading, MA: Addison-Wesley.

Schneider, B. (1987). The people make the place. *Personnel Psychology*, 40, 437–454.

Seibert, S., Kraimer, M., & Liden, C. (2001). A social capital theory of career success. *Academy of Management Journal*, 44(2), 219–237.

Senge, P. (1994). *The fifth discipline: The art and science of the learning organization*. New York: Doubleday.

Sessa, V., & London, M. (2006). *Continuous learning in organizations: Individual, group, and organizational perspectives*. Mahwah, NJ: Lawrence Erlbaum Associates.

Shaffer, R. (1953). Job satisfaction as related to need satisfaction in work. *Psychological Monographs: General and Applied*, 67(14; whole no. 364), 1–29.

Simmering, M., Colquitt, J., Noe, R., & Porter, S. (2003). Conscientiousness, autonomy fit, and development: A longitudinal study. *Journal of Applied Psychology*, 88(5), 954–964.

Sturges, J., Conway, N., Guest, D., & Liefogghe, A. (2005). Managing the career deal: The psychological contract as a framework for understanding career management, organizational commitment, and work behavior. *Journal of Organizational Behavior*, 26(7), 821–838.

Sturges, J., Guest, D., Conway, N., & Davey, K. (2002). A longitudinal study of the relationship between career management and organizational commitment. *Journal of Organizational Behavior*, 23(6), 731–748.

Super, D. (1980). A life span, life space approach to career development. *Journal of Vocational Behavior*, 13, 282–298.

Tannenbaum, S., & Yukl, G. (1992). Training and development in work organizations. In M. R. Rosenzweig & L. W. Porter (Eds.), *Annual review of psychology* (Vol. 43, pp. 399–442). Palo Alto, CA: Annual Reviews.

Terkel, S. (1972). *Working: Americans talk about what they do all day and how they feel about it*. New York: New Press.

Vaill, P. B. (1996). *Learning as a way of being: Strategies for survival in a world of permanent white water*. San Francisco: Jossey-Bass.

Wasserman, S., & Galaskiewicz, J. (Eds.). (1994). *Advances in social network analysis: Research in the social and behavioral sciences*. Thousand Oaks, CA: Sage.

Weber, M. (1904). *The Protestant ethic and the spirit of capitalism*. New York: Charles Scribner's Sons.

Welbourne, T., & Andrews, A. (1996). Predicting the performance of initial public offerings: Should human resource management be in the equation? *Academy of Management Journal, 29*(4), 891–919.

Wheelock, L., & Catlahan, J. (2006). Mary Parker Follett: A rediscovered voice informing the field of Human Resource Development. *Human Resource Development Review, 5*(2), 96–125.

Wrzesniewski, A., & Dutton, J. (2002). Crafting a job: Revisioning employees as active crafters of their work. *Academy of Management Review, 26*(2), 179–202.

11

Building an Infrastructure for Organizational Learning: A Multilevel Approach

Steve W. J. Kozlowski
Michigan State University

Georgia T. Chao
Michigan State University

Jaclyn M. Jensen
The George Washington University

Organizational environments are increasingly turbulent, chaotic, and unpredictable, thereby creating demands for organizational flexibility, agility, and adaptability (Terreberry, 1968). Organizations have responded to these pressures in a multitude of ways. They have made structural changes to organize work around teams (Lawler, Mohrman, & Ledford, 1995), to push expertise closer to the source of problems, to enable more rapid decision making, and to empower flexible action. They have made investments in information technology to manage knowledge acquisition, retention, and transfer (Argote, McEvily, & Reagans, 2003). Furthermore, they have invested in human capital to increase their collective knowledge stock and capacities (Davenport, 1999).

A key theme running through these responses is the need for learning and adaptive capabilities operating at multiple levels of the organizational system. Learning has been specified as a key individual capability that enables adaptation (Smith, Ford, & Kozlowski, 1997). The concept of learning has also been applied to teams (Edmondson, 2002; Kozlowski, Gully, Nason, & Smith, 1999) and organizations (Cyert & March, 1963) with respect to their capacity to acquire capabilities and to adapt to changes in their environments. Indeed, organization learning, from its early roots in the development of the science of organizational behavior, and particularly over the last decade, has evolved to become a multidisciplinary, vibrant, and diverse area of inquiry.

What is organizational learning, and how can it be enhanced? The answer from the literature is diffuse. Since its inception as a concept in the 1960s, organizational learning has been very broadly conceptualized across different levels of analysis—often at the macro or organizational level; more rarely at the meso, work unit, or team level; and frequently at the micro or individual level (see Fiol & Lyles, 1985, for a review). Indeed, the particular level of interest is often not explicitly specified, and an explanation can wander across multiple levels. Organizational learning has been viewed as informal processes that promote knowledge acquisition (e.g., organizational culture, socialization, and mentoring) and as more formal systems that capture and compile such knowledge (e.g., knowledge management and information systems). Moreover, the different and unique ways that organizational learning has been conceptualized cut across multiple disciplines and literatures that tend to be insular. The result is a very broad, fuzzy, and multifaceted concept that has much intellectual appeal. However, it also has limited operational utility so that the question posed at the beginning of this paragraph cannot easily be answered.

The conceptual challenge is a multilevel one. The process of *learning* can be reasonably well defined as an individual-level psychological phenomenon, but it is ill defined and more amorphous when applied to higher levels of conceptualization. It is rooted in individual learning, but it is also much more than just a simple aggregate or summation of individual learning. Indeed, because learning is fundamentally psychological, the conceptual meaning and theoretical mechanisms of collective learning have to incorporate individual learning (as the theoretical origin), but they also have to encompass higher level processes and linkages that capture how learning by individuals is combined, translated, and amplified to emerge as an analogous phenomenon at the collective level (Kozlowski & Klein, 2000).

The goal of this chapter is to bring a multilevel conceptualization to bear on this diffuse area of theory and research, with the goal of articulating how an *integrated infrastructure* can be created to foster learning across multiple levels of the organizational system. There are three primary points of contribution. First, we believe that the broad and diverse conceptualizations of organizational learning are amorphous and that making progress toward developing tools that can shape organizational learning requires specifics. Second, we believe that an appropriate point of departure for identifying those specifics is to focus on the informal and formal processes that shape how individuals learn in organizations; individual learning is the foundation for collective learning. Third, by applying principles of multilevel theory, we can understand how learning by individuals coalesces, amplifies, and crystallizes as collective learning and ways to leverage and shape the emergence of collective learning as a multilevel phenomenon.

At the onset, we want to be clear that we are not conducting a comprehensive review of the literature on organizational learning. Rather, we offer a perspective, one that we think differs from more typical perspectives that tend to be primarily macro. We develop an integrative framework that provides a foundation for understanding organizational learning as a multilevel phenomenon. We pay primary attention to the individual level because it is the origin of learning as a psychological process with knowledge and skill outcomes, and the team level because work teams comprise the proximal social context that shapes and amplifies the emergence of learning as a collective phenomenon (Kozlowski & Klein, 2000). In our approach, organizational learning is enhanced by construction of a coherent infrastructure that aligns fundamental levels of the organizational system using both formal and informal developmental processes. These processes are often disconnected or misaligned. Our approach is designed to integrate them into an infrastructure that can provide operational utility for a multilevel conceptualization of the foundation for organizational learning.

We begin by highlighting seminal perspectives on organizational learning in order to identify the dimensions that structure our approach. We then develop our conceptual framework. We first briefly highlight fundamental principles of multilevel theory relevant to conceptualizing learning as a collective phenomenon, paying particular attention to organizational-level contextual effects that shape learning processes at the team and individual levels and to composition and compilation forms of emergence that are important for conceptualizing collective learning. We next elucidate our framework, focusing first on the informal processes that energize learning and then on the formal training, development, and leadership interventions that can leverage learning. We then consider the necessity for system alignment so that learning can be leveraged to higher levels to promote the emergence of collective learning. We close the chapter with implications of our conceptualization for research.

Organizational Learning

Theoretical musings on organizational learning have proliferated from its inception in the early 1960s to the present time; however, the field is fragmented, and there is considerable debate on the nature of organizational learning (Roth, 2008). It is a very broad, fuzzy concept that encompasses many distinct areas of inquiry, ranging from the use of human and machine metaphors to a sort of mystical process (Friedman, Lipshitz, & Popper, 2005). For example, Ashby (1960) characterized it using an organizational brain metaphor, whereas others have relied on an information-processing perspective (e.g., organizational memory; Huber, 1991; March, 1991). It has been viewed as organizational culture (Fiol & Lyles, 1985), organizational development (Argyris, 1990, 1999), adaptation (Chakravarthy, 1982; March, 1991; Meyer, 1982), change (Dutton & Duncan, 1983; Mintzberg & Waters, 1982), and communities of practice (Brown & Duguid, 1991; Lave & Wenger, 1991). This diversity in the conceptualization of organizational learning and its practice has yielded an amorphous literature and broad research streams subject to many differing interpretations (Ulrich, Jick, & von Glinow, 1993): "[T]he concept of the learning organization has become a management Rorschach test. One sees whatever one wants to see" (p. 57). The research has not been cumulative, nor is there much synthesis across different research groups (Huber, 1991).

We begin with Fiol and Lyles' (1985) rudimentary definition of organizational learning as "the process of improving actions through better knowledge and understanding" (p. 803). It is not just the sum of each individual's learning but also the associations, cognitive systems, and memories that are developed and shared by past and present members of the organization (Fiol & Lyles, 1985). Whereas an individual learns through processing information, an organization learns if it acquires knowledge that it recognizes as potentially useful to the organization (Huber, 1991). Although the literature on organizational learning lacks a unifying theory with integrated research, several key dimensions can be gleaned in the seminal exemplars of organizational learning that we believe are useful for crafting our integrative framework. They include key dimensions tapping formal versus informal processes of learning, the distinction between learning as a process versus learning outcomes, distinctions between individual and collective learning, and exploration versus exploitation as distinctly different forms of collective learning. These dimensions are briefly highlighted below.

Learning can occur through *formal or informal processes*. Brown and Duguid (1991) submitted that people actually perform work in ways that are fundamentally different from work described by formal manuals, training programs, and organizational charts. Formal systems often prescribe algorithms, decision trees, or standard operating procedures to guide work; yet actual work is often performed with improvisations, experimentation, and "work-arounds." Brown and Duguid posited that much of an organization's learning and innovation is a result of informal interactions among an organization's communities-of-practice. These communities or networks of individuals work together to solve problems or explore opportunities that challenge current situated knowledge. Araujo (1998) extended this concept to include individuals outside the formal boundaries of an organization. Thus, informal communities can include customers, suppliers, professional peers, and others who may not share an organization's mission but can still contribute to that organization's learning. Organizations that recognize these informal processes can maximize their effectiveness by aligning formal structures and resources to support them. Organizational learning from aligned formal and informal processes can produce high-level learning that results in new cognitive frameworks (Hedberg, 1981), changes in organizational assumptions and values (e.g., double-loop learning; Argyris & Schön, 1978), and more integrated and proactive interpretive schemes (Bartunek, 1984; Daft & Weick, 1984).

Organizational learning can also be distinguished as a *process* or as an *outcome*. As a process, organizational learning involves the acquisition of patterns of cognitive associations and structures that are developed through experience by individuals that are then apprehended at the group or organizational level (Duncan & Weiss, 1979; Hedberg, 1981). Thus, as a process, learning involves interaction and experience with the environment that yield insight, meaning, and understanding. As an outcome, collective learning is captured by changes in knowledge and its representation (e.g., collective knowledge pool, and shared knowledge structure; Ellis & Bell, 2005; Kozlowski & Bell, 2008) that may then manifest in subsequent behavioral actions intended to improve organizational effectiveness and performance (Daft & Weick, 1984). Fiol and Lyles (1985) stressed that the distinction between process and outcome is important because the process of learning and subsequent action may not be well matched. The process of organizational learning generates new organizational knowledge that may or may not be translated into behavioral development or change. For example, in 1979 Steve Jobs toured Xerox's research facilities to observe developments on the Alto computer. Although Xerox engineers created knowledge essential to today's personal computers, the management culture was unable to translate this knowledge into a successful consumer product. However, Steve Jobs and Apple Computers were successful in applying this knowledge to organizational action (Cringely, 1996). Thus, organizational learning requires alignment of process and outcomes to make best use of the new knowledge.

Distinctions between *individual* and *collective* levels of learning can be traced back to Cyert and March's (1963) notion that organizational learning was the aggregate of emergent learning across individuals. Since then, scholars have debated on how learning may be *organizational*. Duncan and Weiss (1979) asserted that only individuals can learn, but they can also communicate their knowledge across a system. Fiol and Lyles (1985) and Levitt and March (1988) emphasized that organizational learning is more than the sum of individual knowledge and that new knowledge can emerge from the interactions of individuals; this is the essence of collective learning as a process of emergence. In this regard, Cohen and Levinthal (1990) introduced the term "absorptive capacity" to describe a firm's ability to exploit new knowledge by assimilating it into the existing knowledge base and using it as a competitive advantage. A firm's absorptive capacity is more than the sum of individuals' absorptive capacities because it can be influenced by firm-level attributes such as investment in research and development. Furthermore, a firm's absorptive capacity relies on communication structures within an organization and between the organization and its external environment. Thus, macro characteristics define the context that can promote (or inhibit) learning as an emergent process of individual knowledge acquisition, amplification and crystallization through human interaction, and exploitation via firm-level action.

Given the importance of the concept of organizational learning for organizations that face ever-changing, turbulent, and unpredictable environments, the domain—though rich in ideas—has a relatively limited empirical foundation, particularly with respect to human processes and actionable knowledge. We will use the dimensions of organizational learning highlighted above to structure our framework. Next, we consider basic issues in multilevel theory.

Collective Learning: Multilevel Considerations

There are four key multilevel considerations that are important to highlight, because they influence the way we construct our framework and the processes that we address. First, higher level contextual effects can influence lower level processes, so that learning at a lower level is shaped and constrained. Second, lower level processes like individual learning can have emergent or collective, higher level manifestations. Third, system coherence in the form of compatible alignments within levels (formal technostructure and informal enabling processes) and across levels (top-down and bottom-up linkages) provides a theoretical conduit to shape, leverage, and amplify collective learning. And, fourth, there are different forms of emergence that are often shaped by the context—composition and compilation (Kozlowski & Klein, 2000)—and that have implications for achieving system coherence. We briefly elaborate each of these points, illustrating points 1 through 3 in Figure 11.1 and point 4 in Figure 11.2.

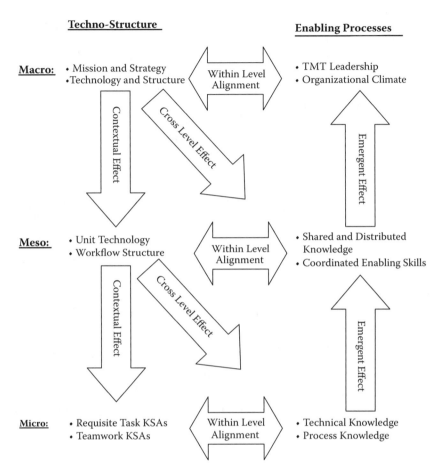

FIGURE 11.1
A multilevel and cross-level model of organizational system alignment.

Contextual Effects

Collective learning is a multilevel phenomenon, shaped by contextual factors such as organizational strategy, structure, technology, and culture that emanate from the top down. It is noteworthy that these factors are often regarded as aspects or representations of organizational learning (Fiol & Lyles, 1985). For example, the contextual factors of organizational strategy, structure, and technology can create a press for innovation that, when supported by an aligned climate, prompts individuals to be on the technical cutting edge (Kozlowski & Hults, 1987), a cross-level effect. As illustrated in Figure 11.1, higher level context factors can also directly shape lower level factors that are embedded under them. So, for example, macro technology and structure will tend to constrain meso technology and structure (House, Rousseau, & Thomas-Hunt, 1995). It is also possible for macro factors (e.g., updating policies) to have direct effects on individuals (e.g., continuing education efforts), but the meso context is most proximal and thus the most potent contextual effect on individual perception and action (Kozlowski & Hults, 1987).

Emergence

On the other hand, collective learning is also shaped by emergent processes that emanate from the bottom up. "A phenomenon is emergent when it originates in the cognition, affect, behaviors, or other characteristics of individuals, is amplified by their interactions, and manifests as a higher-level, collective phenomenon" (Kozlowski & Klein, 2000, p. 55). Emergent processes amplify, combine, and crystallize individual learning such that it manifests as a collective phenomenon. For example, individual learning in the context of team interaction can yield parallel, multilevel learning processes (DeShon, Kozlowski, Schmidt, Milner, & Wiechmann, 2004) and emergent forms of knowledge representation such as team mental models (Cannon-Bowers, Salas, & Converse, 1993) and transactive memory (Wegner, 1986). Thus, collective learning is fundamentally rooted in the processes and outcomes of individual learning—teams and organizations don't learn, individuals do (Kozlowski & Salas, 1997)—but individual learning can combine in different ways and emerge as different forms of collective learning.

System Coherence

However, collective learning is not merely an aggregate of individual learning. Collective knowledge, skills, and other capabilities for coping with uncertainty and change take on additional meaning at collective levels, and are inextricably entwined with technostructural aspects of the organizational system. For example, the demands of unit-level technology and workflow structure have to have corresponding within-level alignments with team knowledge (both shared and distributed) and team coordination, or the team will not be able to effectively exploit the capabilities of the technical system. Informal processes and learning tend to occur spontaneously. However, there is no guarantee that informal learning processes yield capabilities that translate into meaningful team and organizational learning. Formal systems such as training and leadership can shape, align, and strengthen informal learning processes. Thus, key to our conceptualization is an alignment between formal and informal systems at multiple levels of the organization (within level) and across multiple levels of the organization (between level). Formal organizational systems and informal processes, when aligned, can encourage, enhance, capture, and amplify individual learning, thereby creating an organizational learning system.

Emergent Forms

Kozlowski and Klein (2000) posited that "collective phenomena may emerge in different ways under different contextual constraints and patterns of interaction" (p. 59). Figure 11.2 illustrates two qualitatively distinct, ideal forms of emergence—*composition* and *compilation*—that they contrasted as opposing forms bracketing other alternatives on a continuum of emergence types. They characterized the composition form of emergence as relevant when a higher level phenomenon emerges through shared and convergent processes (i.e., when the same elemental content is shared in common by all team members). In other words, composition represents the same construct at the lower and higher levels of analysis. It is both structurally (i.e., same content) and functionally equivalent (i.e., fills the same linking function) at both levels of analysis (Kozlowski & Klein, 2000; Morgeson & Hofmann, 1999). In contrast, they characterized the compilation form of emergence as relevant when a higher level phenomenon emerges through divergent processes (i.e., when elemental content possessed by team members is different, yet creates a meaningful pattern).

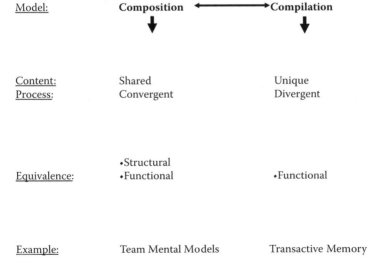

Model:	Composition ←————→ Compilation	
Content:	Shared	Unique
Process:	Convergent	Divergent
Equivalence:	•Structural •Functional	•Functional
Example:	Team Mental Models	Transactive Memory

FIGURE 11.2
Composition and compilation forms of emergence.

In other words, compilation represents a configuration like puzzle pieces; each element is distinct but when combined correctly creates a meaningful pattern. Compilation constructs are functionally equivalent, but not structurally equivalent across levels (Kozlowski & Klein, 2000; Morgeson & Hofmann, 1999).

As a composition example, scholars have hypothesized that team members working together on an interdependent task develop shared mental models that allow them to anticipate coordination needs (Cannon-Bowers et al., 1993). Team mental models represent a collective construct in which team members share identical knowledge; the construct is parallel at the individual and team levels. As a compilation example, scholars have hypothesized that team members may develop a networked memory system—transactive memory. In this example, each team member possesses unique knowledge, but each team member also shares knowledge of each other member's distinct expertise. This allows team members to collectively access knowledge as necessary by tapping the appropriate team member in the network (Mohammed & Dumville, 2001). Note that team members do not possess the same knowledge, but the transactive memory system performs the same linking function at the individual and team levels; transactive memory is configural.

The Foundation: Informal Learning Processes

Newcomer Socialization

Informal mechanisms of learning will focus on newcomer socialization. *Newcomer socialization* is defined as a process by which an employee who is new to the organization or to a particular business unit learns to fit into that group and is perceived as a valued member. Some of this learning may be formalized in orientation and training programs, but much is informally learned through everyday experiences on the job (Chao, Kozlowski, Major, & Gardner, 1994). Research on newcomer socialization (often referred to as *organizational socialization*) has contributed to our understanding of how individuals learn and adjust to their jobs, work groups, and organizations. As an informal learning process, socialization serves many purposes, involves many resources, and taps many content areas.

Socialization theory and research have generally focused on the individual fitting into an organization. The notion of fit has been refined to acknowledge different levels of fit between an individual and that person's job, group or team, and organization (Kristof, 1996). Generally, it is the adjustment of the individual that is the center of organizational socialization research. Theory, however, has recognized that an organization can learn from a new organizational member; thus, learning is a two-way process. Van Maanen and Schein (1979) described an investiture socialization tactic that essentially has an organization adjusting to a newcomer. This case may be seen when an organization seeks new ideas and leadership by bringing in "new blood" with the hire of a chief executive from outside the organization. In addition, Huber (1991) described how organizations can "graft" new people and their knowledge onto the existing organizational knowledge base. March (1991) cautioned that rapid socialization of newcomers may come at a cost to the organization. One of the strengths of new hires is the diversity of ideas and perspectives that are not encumbered by the organization. When new hires accept organizational perspectives and roles, they may be less likely to teach the organization different ways and ideas. Thus, March brought up an apparent paradox with organizational socialization. Swift socialization can efficiently transform an organizational newcomer into an organizational insider. This may be a desirable purpose for organizational assimilation and team building; but it may not be desirable for organizational learning. Future research should examine how organizations can maximize their learning from newcomers before they are fully assimilated into the organization.

Most of the organizational socialization literature is focused at the individual level. Newcomers learn how to perform their jobs, they learn about other organizational members, and they may learn how to adjust their attitudes and behaviors to be successful organizational members. Several resources may be tapped for this learning. Ostroff and Kozlowski (1992) found that newcomers rely primarily on observation and experimentation to learn about task mastery, role responsibilities, getting along with coworkers, and the organizational culture. Thus, newcomers are proactive in this learning process. Three particular sources for information—the supervisor, team, and mentor—deserve special attention. Supervisors are often charged with the task of assimilating newcomers into the organization and have power to directly influence the newcomer. Team members are also often charged with the same assimilation task, and although they may not have superior power over the newcomer; their interactions with a newcomer may be critical in time and influence. Last, some newcomers may find mentors in an organization who can serve as a professional advisor or coach. These three sources for information are primary interpersonal processes in organizational socialization and learning.

A newcomer's relationship with a supervisor develops very quickly. Liden, Wayne, and Stilwell (1993) measured newcomer expectations about their supervisors within the first week of the relationship. These early expectations were significant predictors of their relationship 6 months later. Thus, initial newcomer perceptions can have lasting effects. Major, Kozlowski, Chao, and Gardner (1995) found that a good relationship between a newcomer and supervisor or between a newcomer and his or her team was able to ameliorate the negative effects of unmet job expectations. Morrison (1993) found supervisors were primary sources for technical information, role expectations, and getting feedback. In contrast, a newcomer's coworkers were primary sources for normative and social information. Thus, different resources were used to learn different lessons. These resources for learning also can be associated with different outcomes. For example, newcomers who learned more from their supervisors were more likely to be satisfied, well adjusted to the job, and committed to the organization (Ostroff & Kozlowski, 1992).

Socialization research has only recently considered the mutual influence between organizational newcomers and team members (Kozlowski & Bell, 2003). Chen and Klimoski (2003) found that a newcomer's experiences influence a team's expectations for that person. In return, the team's expectations can affect the newcomer's role performance. Furthermore, Chen (2005) found that the newcomer's early performance can affect subsequent overall team performance. Thus, one individual's performance can impact higher levels of performance. The extent to which new employees affect organizational outcomes will help define an organization's learning.

Traditionally, a mentor is defined as a senior organizational member who helps develop the career of a junior organizational member (i.e., protégé). It is an intense professional relationship where a mentor personally coaches, advises, protects, and befriends a protégé. A mentor's position and experience can offer a wealth of information that is unavailable through most other sources (Ostroff & Kozlowski, 1993). Information based on speculations, rumors, and organizational politics can be as valuable as conventional information related to work procedures and performance expectations. Furthermore, a mentor's senior position can promote and protect a protégé's experimentations or efforts to change the organization. Thus, an organization is more likely to learn from a protégé with an encouraging mentor than from someone without such support. Lankau and Scandura (in press) described how the personal learning from mentors can enhance the development of social capital within an organization. Informal mentoring can create powerful informal ties between organizational members that transcend formal organizational structures. Managerial systems and organizational values can be communicated through storytelling and narratives that are shared in mentoring. Chao (2007) integrated mentoring and organizational socialization by describing a network of mentors who can help a protégé. Multiple mentors can expand a protégé's information base when one mentor is able to provide information and support that another mentor cannot. For example, one mentor with technical expertise can help a protégé's job performance, whereas another mentor with a large professional network can help a protégé's career visibility. Building a network of mentors can help the protégé learn different lessons from different experts.

Given that supervisors, coworkers, and mentors can serve as powerful socialization agents, more research is needed to understand how this process can be effectively managed by organizations. For example, can supervisors and coworkers be trained to be effective socialization agents? This training may include diagnosing a newcomer's learning needs, providing multiple sources of support that can reinforce one another, and aligning informal and formal processes with organizational goals and values. Furthermore, supervisors and coworkers can also be trained to explore how a newcomer's knowledge base can contribute to organizational knowledge. Results from such research may identify an optimal balance between individuals learning from the organization and organizations learning from an individual; see March's (1991) contrast of exploitation versus exploration in organizational learning.

The different lessons in organizational socialization highlight the different content areas. What is learned? Chao, O'Leary-Kelly et al. (1994) developed six dimensions of organizational socialization: performance proficiency, people, politics, language, goals and values, and history. Performance proficiency is a vital dimension because a newcomer must learn to be proficient on the job if he or she is interested in keeping that job. People and politics are important for the newcomer to learn to work well with others. The last three dimensions characterize a particular organization and how members define themselves as part of that organization. Thus, an organizational member understands the organization's goals and values, is knowledgeable about the organization's past, and is able to communicate with other organizational members using specific jargon, acronyms, and abbreviations that nonmembers may not know. Chao, O'Leary-Kelly et al. (1994) found that individuals who learned more about their organization, in terms of these six content dimensions, were more likely to be satisfied and successful on the job.

Learning in these content areas may be explicit or implicit. Currently, all socialization research involves explicit learning—learning that the newcomer is aware of. However, much of what is learned may be implicit, tacit knowledge. Chao (1997) recognized that organizational socialization can operate at the unconscious level through implicit learning. Learning about people and organizational politics are most likely to be affected by implicit learning because this knowledge can be gained from observations, social judgments, and interactions. Similarly, knowledge about performance proficiency and organizational goals and values can be explicit if there is a strong culture with clear performance expectations; or it may be more implicit if these areas are not well specified, or there is a perceived gap between what is espoused and what is practiced. Tacit knowledge created by implicit socialization learning can represent a default type of socialization. Newcomers learn a lot from observation (Ostroff & Kozlowski, 1992), but they cannot control the events they observe. Thus, the lessons learned from incidental learning conditions may or may not be to an organization's advantage. Nonanka (1994) described how tacit knowledge is passed from one organizational member to another through a socialization process. From an organizational learning perspective, this is an important mode of knowledge conversion. However, because tacit knowledge is difficult to formalize and articulate, most theories of organizational learning do not incorporate aspects of tacit knowledge and socialization.

Team Learning

Some reviewers have observed that much of the research on team learning conducted thus far has focused on the outcome representations of team learning, such as team mental models and transactive memory (see Figure 11.3), with relatively little attention devoted to characterizing the process by which individual learning emerges and manifests as collective learning (Kozlowski & Bell, 2008; Kozlowski & Ilgen, 2006). There are, however, some notable exceptions worth highlighting because they will help to identify the individual and team processes that should be targeted by interventions.

Edmondson (1999), for example, conducted a qualitative and quantitative examination of team learning in a field setting. Her research showed that when the team context supported experimentation and risk taking, team members exhibited more team-learning behaviors that, in turn, were related to higher team performance. More specifically, her model postulated team psychological safety as a key contextual construct—a climate-like shared perception among team members that the team was a psychologically safe setting for interpersonal risk taking—that promoted team-learning behaviors as the basic elements of team learning as a process. Teams that perceived more psychological safety engaged in more learning behaviors such as sharing information, requesting assistance, seeking feedback, and discussing mistakes. Edmondson's work also showed that team psychological safety was influenced by a supportive organizational context and coaching by the team leader. There are two important points to highlight from this research: first, that contextual alignment across levels of the organizational system was instrumental to enabling team-learning processes (Kozlowski & Salas, 1997); and second, that team learning as a process not only has its roots in individual characteristics (here, behavioral action) but also encompasses cognition and motivational aspects (Kozlowski & Bell, 2008).

In an effort to better unpack and reveal the processes underlying team learning, DeShon et al. (2004) focused on dynamic self-regulation and a

Organization Learning System

		Informal Processes OL Foundation	Formal Processes OL Infrastructure	OL Outcomes

Macro		▪ Exploitation / Exploration
		▪ Enabling Processes
			▪ Exploitation / Exploration
			   Techno-Structure
				▪ Exploitation / Exploration
				   Vertical Transfer

Meso		▪ Team Development ▪ Team Learning	▪ Team Leader Training ▪ Team Training Techniques	▪ Shared Mental Models ▪ Transactive Memory ▪ Knowledge Pool & Distribution
Micro		▪ Socialization and Mentoring ▪ Implicit Learning	▪ Distributed Learning Systems ▪ Active, Embedded Training	▪ Task-Relevant Knowledge ▪ Enabling Process Knowledge

FIGURE 11.3

A multilevel foundation and infrastructure for organizational learning.

parallel process of team regulation as a fundamental process mechanism accounting for learning, motivation, and performance in teams. There are several theories of *self*-regulation that, although distinctive, share key features. Goals serve an energizing function and direct effort toward goal accomplishment. Some level of performance results, and, through feedback, a person compares his goal to his performance. During learning, the resulting level of performance is generally lower than the desired end state. This negative discrepancy prompts a self-evaluation of progress and reactions. If progress is deemed satisfactory, a person will likely feel capable and confident of success (i.e., self-efficacy), and will revise her learning strategies, redouble efforts, and iteratively persist toward goal accomplishment. If progress is judged to be unsatisfactory, self-efficacy will be undermined and a person will likely be distracted by frustration, off-task thoughts, and anxiety that will interfere with her subsequent motivation and learning.

DeShon et al. (2004) noted that extant models of self-regulation focus on the accomplishment of a single goal at any given point in time. They argued that interdependent team tasks, however, necessitate multiple goal regulation—individual and team. In other words, learning and performing in a team necessitate dynamic regulation around an individual goal–feedback loop relevant to one's role on the team *and* regulation around a team goal–feedback loop when a person must assist a teammate, correct a teammate's error, or otherwise devote resources to the collective goal. DeShon et al. (2004) reasoned that this dynamic process of multiple goal regulation and resource allocation within individual team members would, over time, result in the emergence of a multilevel homology with parallel regulatory processes accounting for learning and performance at both the individual and team levels of analysis. Their evaluation of the multiple goals and multiple levels of regulation provided a rare empirical assessment and support for their homologous model. Other research has also usefully employed regulatory processes as a theoretical foundation to model skill transfer and adaptation following training in dyads (Chen, Wallace, & Thomas, 2005) and to propose a broad-based model of team motivation (Chen & Kanfer, 2006). Although the findings by Chen et al. (2005) did not support a strict homology across levels, the research did show that regulation was a promising conceptual tool for modeling the link between learning and subsequent performance adaptation.

There are two important points to highlight from this work by DeShon et al. (2004) and others. First, team learning is emergent—fundamentally rooted in individual cognition, motivation, and behavior—but shaped and amplified by interaction over time to manifest at the collective level. In other words, trying to treat team learning as a solely collective concept is not meaningful because such an approach neglects the underpinnings of the process. Rather, one needs to understand team learning as a process encompassing multiple levels. Second, regulation is a potentially useful and potent leverage point for influencing team learning. Influencing team learning, by necessity, means multiple levels of intervention or infrastructure creation.

Team Development

Given the high interest in work teams, it is remarkable that there are relatively little good descriptive data on the development of work teams (Kozlowski & Bell, 2003). Most of the work on this topic has been shaped by classic stage models of development (e.g., Tuckman, 1965), which have tended to focus on laboratory or other minimal social groups (i.e., groups independent of an organizational context, with no distinct roles or interaction demands, and with few shared goals), or by the punctuated equilibrium model (PEM; Gersick, 1988), which examined eight work groups and eight student project groups. There are a variety of stage models, but they all share much in common and are well represented by Tuckman's classic model of forming, storming, norming, and performing. During the forming stage, members are uncertain about the group, their goals and roles, and how they will work together. As many voices offer differing ideas and approaches, members become frustrated and enter a storming stage as they compete to shape social structure to reduce uncertainty. With time, the team enters a norming stage as members begin to resolve their differences, develop norms to guide interactions, and ameliorate social uncertainty. Finally, with social structure in place, team members are able to focus on the task at hand, and the team enters the performing stage. Although there are little hard descriptive data to substantiate this and other stage models, they have intuitive appeal and are the biggest class of team development models (Kozlowski et al., 1999).

In contrast to the process of linear progression that undergirds stage models, Gersick (1988) concluded that the groups in her sample exhibited a simpler pattern of development. Her groups were all project groups with a distinct timeline—a deadline—by which the project was to conclude. She observed that groups initially formed and created a work structure that persisted until approximately halfway to the project deadline. At that point, the initial inertia was broken, and there was a major discontinuous shift—the punctuated equilibrium—as the team structure, member roles, and activities were reorganized. This revised structure then guided group interactions until project completion.

Although stage models and the PEM are often contrasted as competing models of group development, Chang, Bordia, and Duck (2003) showed that aspects of both models described team development processes of lab teams depending on the content examined and the timing used—smaller time units and a focus on group processes and structure related to linear development, and larger time units and a focus task approach related to the PEM. Indeed, some models have integrated aspects of both approaches. For example, Morgan, Salas, and Glickman (1993) proposed a nine-stage model: preforming, forming, storming, norming, and performing-I; and reforming (i.e., the punctuated equilibrium), followed by performing-II, conforming, and de-forming. A key feature of the model is the conceptual distinction between task work (i.e., task-relevant knowledge and skills) and teamwork (i.e., knowledge and skills that enhance coordination and the integration of action among members).

The normative theory of team development and performance compilation by Kozlowski and colleagues (1999) also draws on both models. In their theory, knowledge and skill development is viewed as a progressive process across four phases; with each phase focused on distinct content, learning processes, and outcomes; and with transitions across phases and emergent levels as target skills compile at the individual, dyadic, and team network levels. During phase 1, team formation, individual team members acquire interpersonal knowledge about teammates' abilities, personalities, and values and an orientation to the team in terms of goal commitment, norms, and climate. They transition to a task compilation phase in which individual team members develop self-regulation skills of goal setting, performance monitoring, self-efficacy, and resilience, and establish their task proficiency. They are then able to shift to the dyadic level in the role compilation phase as they define their responsibilities, establish coordination patterns, and routinize task interactions. Finally, they transition to the team compilation phase, where through team experimentation and regulation, the team continuously improves its work processes and develops a repertoire of skills to enable adaptation. This conceptualization is useful, because it links back to regulation, which is garnering evidence as the theoretical engine of individual and team learning, motivation, and performance. Thus, interventions that target regulatory processes in teams are a potentially potent means to build an infrastructure to influence team-level and higher level learning processes.

Infrastructure Design: Formal Interventions

Prompting Individual Learning

Active Learning

In the prior section, we reviewed theory and research that establish regulatory processes as the theoretical engine for individual and team learning, performance, and adaptation. Bell and Kozlowski (this volume) describe active learning as a conceptual approach to learner-centered training design. The premise underlying active learning techniques is that trainees learn best when they are situated in the to-be-learned work context, or close approximations to it, and when they are actively engaged and self-directed in extracting relevant inferences relative to more passive, proceduralized approaches to training. Although the active learning approach encompasses a wide range of discrete training techniques, Bell and Kozlowski (this volume) argue that the techniques can be unified under an integrated theoretical framework. Their model posits that active learning methods operate via one or more self-regulatory process pathways—cognitive, motivational, or affective—and that each of these process pathways is primarily influenced by a corresponding core training design element: instruction (guided exploration), motivational induction (error framing), and emotion control (emotion regulation strategy), respectively.

Bell and Kozlowski (2008) provided empirical support for their active learning conceptual framework. In addition to tracing the process pathways, their work demonstrated the importance of individual differences in cognitive ability and goal orientation in understanding how learners reacted to the different core design elements. For example, learners with high cognitive ability responded better to guided exploration, compared to proceduralized training, because they could gain more from their metacognitive processing as they explored the task domain. Thus, this evolving line of theory and research on active learning has the potential to be tailored to the individual characteristics, preferences, and progress of learners (Bell & Kozlowski, this volume; Gully & Chen, this volume).

Embedded Training

From the perspective of building an infrastructure for organizational learning, Bell and Kozlowski's integrated theoretical model of active learning is consistent with a companion model—the adaptive learning system (ALS; Kozlowski, Toney, et al., 2001)—that is predicated on designing active learning interventions that can be embedded in computer-based workplace technology or in close approximations to the workplace such as synthetic learning environments (SLEs; Cannon-Bowers & Bowers, this volume). The ALS model specifies three design components—training design, information provision, and trainee orientation—that influence the nature of the learning experience, characteristics of feedback, and motivational frame placed on trainees, respectively. The theoretical rationale of the model is that these design components can be combined to selectively influence the nature and quality of self-regulation as learners study and practice, monitor their progress, and reflect and react to their learning experience over time. The framework has been used to construct several effective active learning techniques, including adaptive guidance (Bell & Kozlowski, 2002), mastery training (Kozlowski & Bell, 2006; Kozlowski, Gully, et al., 2001), and mastery feedback (Nowakowski & Kozlowski, 2004, 2005).

In summary, we have developed a conceptual foundation that is beginning to unpack the core design elements and specific self-regulatory process pathways that undergird active learning and the development of adaptive capabilities. We have empirical research that supports the theoretical framework and evidences meaningful interactions for each core element and individual differences. With further research, we anticipate refinement of the process pathways and the nature of the aptitude–treatment interactions, which will enable the design of more precise and tailored training experiences. And, we have a more pragmatic companion model that has demonstrated effectiveness for designing active learning interventions. Altogether, this work provides a conceptual foundation and operational tools for embedding learning in work technology, simulations, or SLEs (Bell, Kanar, & Kozlowski, 2008). It provides the basics for building a learning infrastructure in organizations.

Distributed Learning Systems

In addition to embedding training in the workplace, new and emerging technologies make it increasingly feasible and cost-effective to distribute learning in space and time—the concept of distributed learning systems (DLS; Fiore & Salas, 2007). Kozlowski and Bell (2007) have formulated a theoretical framework to guide the design of such systems. The theoretical core of their approach is that DLS design should be guided by the complexity of the targeted knowledge and skill sets, and the corresponding learning processes that have to be stimulated for the targeted skills to be acquired. Simpler knowledge and skill sets, such as declarative and procedural knowledge, entail more basic learning processes, such as memorization and static practice, which can be delivered through less interactive and immersive, low-bandwidth, and low-cost technologies. More complex skill sets that entail these more basic skills, but also necessitate strategic and adaptive knowledge, require commensurately more complex learning processes, such as exploration, experimentation, and dynamic practice. For these latter skills, a DLS needs to be more realistic, immersive, and interactive, which means higher bandwidth, computing power, and cost. The point is that, when combined with the prior models that can be used to design a tailored, learner-centered experience, this approach can help guide the design of the technology infrastructure needed to distribute learning across an organizational system.

Prompting Team Learning

Generic Versus Context-Specific Competencies

One of the big challenges for team training is that it can be difficult and costly to train an entire team together at once. On the other hand, training individuals absent the team context may fail to deliver necessary competencies. Cannon-Bowers, Tannenbaum, Salas, and Volpe (1995) tackled this problem by developing a typology that classified team competencies into those that are transportable (i.e., generic and generalizable across different task and team contexts) and those that are context driven (i.e., specific to a team task and context). Thus, transportable competencies like interpersonal skills can be trained individually, whereas context-specific competencies like backup and error correction that enable coordination should be delivered to intact teams in their task and team setting (Salas & Cannon-Bowers, 1997; Salas, Wilson, Priest, & Guthrie, 2006). Research has shown that training on generic teamwork competencies yields improvements in team planning, coordination, communication, and problem solving (Ellis, Bell, Ployhart, Hollenbeck, & Ilgen, 2005).

Vertical Transfer

Taking a similar approach but applying multilevel theory, Kozlowski, Brown, Weissbein, Cannon-Bowers, and Salas (2000) addressed the question of whether team skills should be trained at the individual or team level by focusing on processes of vertical transfer. *Vertical transfer* refers to the upward propagation of training effects across levels of the organizational system (i.e., the collective emergence of learning), in contrast to the more typical training focus on horizontal transfer (i.e., transfer of training from the training to the performance context). Kozlowski et al. (2000) reasoned that the level of training delivery should be determined by the nature of team performance emergence, that is, whether team performance emerges from individual cognition, motivation, and action through composition or compilation processes. Although this summary is a simplification, in general, they argued that simpler forms of team workflow design in which team members perform parallel or additive tasks are composition in form, and, thus, training could be delivered at the individual level because team performance was pooled with individual performance; whereas more complex workflows that entail distinct roles, distributed expertise, coordination, and synchronization are compilation in form, and, thus, training should be delivered to intact teams in their work context (or close approximations) to ensure vertical transfer.

Team-Training Techniques

Once it has been determined that team training should be delivered at the team level, there is a wide range of effective techniques that can be employed (see Salas & Cannon-Bowers, 1997, for a comprehensive review). Because the key challenge for compilation tasks is training team members to understand how distinct individual knowledge and action combine to yield team performance, context-specific team-training techniques tend to focus on learning the roles of teammates (i.e., cross-training), providing practice experience in realistic contexts (i.e., simulation training), or emphasizing skills that enable coordination and synchronization (i.e., adaptability training, coordination training, or crew resource management [CRM] training). In a recent meta-analytic investigation, Klein et al. (2005) summarized empirical evidence showing that each of these approaches is effective. Cross-training team members on each others' role requirements (6 studies, 13 effects) yielded a 95% confidence interval (CI) of .376–.556 centered on .471. Simulation-based training (37 studies, 81 effects) yielded a 95% CI of .384–.504 centered on .446. And, team adaptation–coordination–CRM training (16 studies, 30 effects) yielded a 95% CI of .479–.698 centered on .600. These effect estimates were not corrected for unreliability, suggesting that they are conservative. Thus, we have the necessary theoretical models and operational tools to design and deliver effective team-training experiences (Salas, Stagl, & Burke, 2004). Moreover, the increasing penetration of computer technology and interactivity into all facets of the workplace allows generalization of the principles of active learning and embedded training to team-level simulations and SLEs (Bell & Kozlowski, 2008; Salas et al., 2006).

Team Leadership, Development, and Regulation

A primary theme of this section has been to identify theories and operational tools that deploy training into the work setting. Thus far, the interventions discussed incorporate a technology component as a primary means to deliver information or experience, but it is also possible to use software in the form of people skills (i.e., knowledge of behavioral science principles) to intervene and shape experiences in the work setting. Kozlowski and colleagues (Kozlowski, Gully, McHugh, Salas, & Cannon-Bowers, 1996; Kozlowski, Gully, Salas, & Cannon-Bowers, 1996; Kozlowski, Watola, Jensen, Kim, & Botero, in press) have provided an evolving series of models that comprise a theory of team leadership where the key purpose of the leader is to develop an expert team, capable of regulating its activity and adapting to its operating environment.

By focusing on the middle range of the team level and context, rather than treating leadership as a more general set of dimensions applicable across all levels and contexts, the theory is able to achieve some precision in its prescription of appropriate leader actions, and the contingencies that should drive them. The theory is multilevel (it considers individuals, teams, and the surrounding organizational context) and dynamic (it considers task dynamics driven by the team's environment and developmental dynamics driven by team members learning progressively more complex skills). The theory conceptualizes the leader as a critical agent for (a) harnessing task dynamics to a regulatory process to prompt development targeted skills, and (b) transitioning the team to focus development on progressively more complex skill sets as capabilities are acquired. Thus, it is an integration of work that conceptualizes regulation as the theoretical engine of individual and team learning (DeShon et al., 2004) and the theory of team development that conceptualizes team skill compilation as a learning process across levels and time (Kozlowski et al., 1999).

Here, we briefly sketch the two key dynamic features of the theory. First, the surrounding context is viewed as a source of variation in task complexity that makes corresponding demands on the team to align its processes to resolve the task demands. Moreover, task demands are not viewed as fixed but rather as cycles that naturally vary in terms of the load placed on team member resources. Marks, Mathieu, and Zaccaro (2001) offered a similar perspective in their portrayal of team tasks as "episodic" patterns of transition (preparation), action (engagement), and transition (reflection). Kozlowski and colleagues (Kozlowski, Gully, McHugh et al., 1996; Kozlowski, Gully, Salas et al., 1996; Kozlowski et al., 2009) characterized this pattern as "cyclical," but the intent to capture variations in the ebb and flow of task demands is the same. Kozlowski and colleagues conceptualized the leader's function as one of explicitly linking regulation to the task cycles. During preparation, the leader should guide team members to set goals and plan strategies for the upcoming engagement. As the team engages the task, the leader monitors performance relative to the goal and strategy, and provides advice for minor or major adjustments to individual action or team processes as necessary to maintain team performance. As an engagement concludes, the leader guides the team in reflection on their performance, diagnosis of areas for improvement, and intentions for further skill development. The process is iterative across subsequent task cycles, with the leader seeking opportunities to build targeted skills in the work setting.

Second, as targeted skills are acquired at a particular phase of development, the leader helps transition team members to (a) focus development on more complex skill sets and (b) progress from an individual focus to a collective one as capabilities are acquired. This developmental progression tracks the skill compilation process posed by Kozlowski et al. (1999). The team formation phase is characterized by individual team members identifying with the team and committing to its mission; the task and role development phase centers on individuals developing proficiency on their tasks and role; the team development phase is characterized by the development of teamwork, cooperation, and coordination; and the team improvement phase centers on the ability of the team to regulate and adapt on its own.

Subsequent conceptual development has started to identify the specific competencies team leaders have to possess to operationalize the prescriptions of the model (Watola & Kozlowski, 2005). Moreover, although there are no direct tests of the theory in its entirety, there is support for the theoretical engine of regulatory processes (e.g., Chen et al., 2005; DeShon et al., 2004) and for team developmental progression (Chang et al., 2003; DeShon, Kozlowski, Schmidt, Wiechmann, & Milner, 2001). Research to more directly evaluate the regulatory functions of team leadership is in progress (Kozlowski, Jundt, Curran, & Kuljanin, 2007). Moreover, this is just one approach; there are other approaches that have been proposed that are complementary with one or more of the processes specified in our approach (e.g., Hackman & Wageman, 2005; Klein, Ziegert, Knight, & Xiao, 2006; Zaccaro, Rittman, & Marks, 2001). Thus, we believe that leaders have the potential to be key agents for prompting the individual and team learning that underpins learning at higher collective levels. We also believe that this potential has been relatively neglected.

Aligning the Organizational System: Leveraging the Infrastructure

Contextual Alignment

Organizational systems theory has long held the assumption that key features of the system context need to be in alignment or congruent (i.e., contingent fit) with organizational goals, strategy, technology, structure, and processes (e.g., Likert, 1961; Miles, Snow, Meyer, & Coleman, 1978; Thompson, 1967). Alignment serves to marshal resources, facilitate desirable behavior, and constrain undesirable behavior, thereby guiding the system toward goal accomplishment as an adaptive, regulating entity (Katz & Kahn, 1978). Facilitating factors could be in the form of explicit goals, feedback, and incentives that are consistent with organizational goals and strategy. Constraints could be in the form of explicit structures, policies, and practices designed to prevent deviant behavior. Explicit factors are those formal aspects of organizational design that are more or less the purview of rational management. However, facilitators and inhibitors can also be in the form of informal social organizational factors and processes, such as organizational climate, norms, and leadership, which are generally more challenging to align with the formal system (Katz & Kahn, 1978; Likert, 1961). Not coincidentally, this also represents a perspective that is widely applied to organizational learning (Fiol & Lyles, 1985). Consistent with the foundation of organizational systems theory and organizational learning, we view system alignment as critical for leveraging and amplifying the knowledge and skill capacities of individuals and teams that are provided by our infrastructure approach. Key alignments are illustrated in Figure 11.1.

The literature on organizational training identifies a number of contextual factors that influence the motivation to learn (pretraining), learning during training, and transfer of trained knowledge and skills back to the work setting (Baldwin & Ford, 1988; Ford & Weissbein, 1997). These factors are generally clustered into (a) situational constraints (i.e., insufficient money, time, equipment, and information) and (b) mediating perceptions of the context that represent how members of the organization "make sense" of the setting (i.e., organizational climate, transfer climate, and support from leaders and peers). Both clusters are viewed as either hindering or supporting motivation to learn and interfering with or facilitating the opportunity to apply skills (Kozlowski & Farr, 1988; Mathieu & Martineau, 1997; Noe & Wilk, 1993; Rouiller & Goldstein, 1993; Tracey, Tannenbaum, & Kavanagh, 1995).

Vertical Transfer

The contextual alignment sketched above applies to the traditional focus in training research on transfer of skills from a training setting to the workplace, what Kozlowski et al. (2000) characterized as horizontal transfer. Although Kozlowski et al. (2000) summarized and acknowledged the importance of contextual alignment for supporting horizontal transfer, building on Kozlowski and Salas (1997) and incorporating multilevel theory, they asserted that processes of vertical transfer—the propagation of trained knowledge and skills upward—comprise an important and unexplored aspect of training effectiveness. This goes directly to the challenge of characterizing organizational learning as an emergent, higher level phenomenon with roots in individual and team learning.

Kozlowski and Salas (1997) developed an integrative framework that was designed to highlight the importance of system alignment for promoting propagation of training effects to higher levels of analysis. There are three key conceptual themes underlying their model: level, focal content, and congruence. These themes structure Figure 11.1. Level is concerned with establishing the targeted level at which the effects of learning are desired and dealing with the complexities when the target is at a higher level than the intervention. Focal content addresses the nature of the knowledge and skill domain where learning is to be targeted for improvement. Technostructural factors are linked to manifestations of technology and structural design that manifest in the system. Enabling processes capture the more intangible social-psychological and human interaction mechanisms that operationalize a given technology system. Congruence characterizes the nature of top-down contextual effects (embedding consistency) and cross-level effects (cross-content influences), within level alignment (alignment across content), and the bottom-up emergent effects that represent the emergence of collective learning across levels of the system.

One key element missing from the Kozlowski and Salas (1997) conceptualization is an explicit recognition that different forms of emergence—composition versus compilation—may necessitate different types of system alignment (Kozlowski et al., 2000). Composition forms of emergence are the result of processes of convergence that constrain elemental content to be similar across levels (i.e., isomorphism). The processes that yield composition are linear and additive so that each bit of similar content at the lower level contributes to the higher level. Composition processes are likely to be robust when the system is aligned. For composition processes, *system alignment* refers to the consistency of fit; the context is composed of features that are consistent with and support the elemental content. This view of alignment is similar to March's (1991) notion of the *exploitation* aspect of organizational learning. For example, an organization might array its learning infrastructure to promote total quality management (TQM). There would be policies, rewards, and management support for TQM, and it would be a prominent strategic imperative of the organizational climate. Socialization and training would be rapid, so that desired perspectives and knowledge would be assimilated without deviation. Production personnel would be socialized to the importance of TQM. Embedded, active learning interventions would convey knowledge of the core principles and methodology to meet specific standards. Coworkers and leaders would support skill development and application so that individuals would all have TQM knowledge and skill sets. Deviations would be discouraged. As TQM knowledge emerges at the team level, members would share team mental models aligned with TQM practices. Similar knowledge and skills would emerge as a property of the collective.

In contrast, compilation forms of emergence are the result of processes of divergence that create a pattern, configuration, or meaningful whole at the higher level from distinct differences in elemental content at the lower level (i.e., discontinuity). The processes that yield compilation are nonlinear and more complex than composition, so the form of alignment is likely more complex as well. For compilation processes, *system alignment* refers to contingencies among contextual factors (e.g., if-then conditional linkages, moderating relations, and temporal entrainment) that constrain a particular pattern or configuration. This view of alignment is similar to March's (1991) notion of the *exploration* aspect of organizational learning. For example, an organization might array its learning infrastructure to promote the development of adaptive teams. There would be policies, rewards, and management support for innovation, risk taking, and experimentation, and agility would be a prominent strategic imperative of the organizational climate. Socialization and training would proceed more slowly, so that novel perspectives and knowledge held by newcomers could be explored and acquired by the collective prior to assimilation. Training and skill acquisition would more likely be an active role of the team leader, developing unique team member skills, roles, and responsibilities in context. Different team members would possess distinct knowledge and skills that could be combined to fit task contingencies. As basic skills compiled, the leader would shift the locus of development to skill integration among members. Transactive memory would emerge, enabling team members to access unique expertise as needed without having to share all knowledge in common. The team would evolve into a self-regulating, experimenting, and adaptive entity.

Team Networks

A final aspect of aligning the organizational system involves leveraging the infrastructure to facilitate informal processes that promote organizational learning. Araujo (1998) described how informal networks are composed of interlocking and shifting relationships within and across organizations. These networks may bear little resemblance to formal organizational charts and structures. Interactions within a network allow individuals to share, synthesize, and interpret information in a variety of contexts. New ideas and solutions provide an opportunity for vertical transfer, and the knowledge may be adopted in formal organizational structures and practices.

From an organizational socialization perspective, learning is shaped by a number of people formally or informally tied to the newcomer. Morrison (2002) examined newcomer relationships with organizational insiders and found different networks were related to different outcomes. Specifically, informational networks were instrumental to a newcomer's learning, whereas friendship networks were tied to the newcomer's assimilation into the organization. Future research can examine how different networks contribute to an individual's socialization and an organization's learning from newcomers. For example, teams represent a dense network where each team member is tightly linked to all other team members. Research is needed to understand how a network's density might require newcomers to quickly adapt to the team or how the network's density might discourage team members from learning much from or adapting to a newcomer.

Informal networks can bridge structural holes in formal reporting relationships. These informal ties can be critical communication links to transmit organizational knowledge. Organizations may be able to promote these links by fostering a culture that rewards mentoring or exploration. New research on organizational socialization can also be designed within different organizational strategies of exploitation and exploration (March, 1991). Organizations focused on exploiting their current strengths may benefit from swift socialization in dense networks. In this case, a newcomer learns what organizational insiders already know and can contribute improvements to existing products and strategies. Conversely, organizations focused on exploring new products or strategies may benefit from slower socialization in loosely coupled networks. In this case, a newcomer is expected to bring new ideas and knowledge into the organization that can contribute to knowledge creation for original innovations.

Research Agenda and Conclusion

Our basic thesis for this chapter is simple. Organizational learning is an important concept for understanding organizational effectiveness, given the unpredictable dynamics of change that characterize contemporary organizational environments. The concept of organizational learning is richly conceived, diverse, and multidisciplinary. It is vibrant but also amorphous, and it is mostly considered at the macro level of the organizational system. These points make it difficult to conceptualize and to study empirically. Thus, the area of inquiry is characterized by lots of interesting ideas and approaches, but not very many well-developed, systematically evaluated, operational tools to promote and guide organizational learning.

Our approach was designed to get at specifics. We used multilevel theory as our conceptual framework and focused on areas of inquiry where there are well-developed theories and systematic empirical research, that is, on the foundations and origins of organizational learning in the learning of individuals and teams. Thus, we focused on organizational learning as informal, emergent processes of individual and team learning, and on the formal infrastructure and system alignment that can be used to leverage and shape the emergence of collective learning. As we noted at the onset of the chapter, we offer a multilevel theoretical perspective applied to organizational learning—not a representation of the literature. Indeed, we think our perspective differs markedly from the literature (if it were even possible to typify it!). However, we believe that the approach we have taken is useful for identifying tractable research issues so that researchers can begin making systematic progress toward conceptual clarity, theory development, application, and operational value.

Research Agenda

Informal Learning

Table 11.1 highlights research issues developed throughout the chapter that we briefly summarize in this section. We constructed our framework bottom-up, first focusing on informal learning processes in organizations. Newcomer or organizational socialization is the dominant informal learning process whereby individuals entering the organization (or transitioning across major boundaries) are assimilated to new features of their context. Although it is often referred to as *organizational* socialization, the entire organization is not encountered. Rather, socialization takes place in the more proximal context of the work group, composed of coworkers and supervisors.

Research suggests that insiders—supervisors in particular—have the potential to be key agents of newcomer socialization (Major et al., 1995; Ostroff & Kozlowski, 1992), but this issue has received little research attention. More importantly, socialization research has not always been sensitive to the proximal context of the work group, instead conceptualizing socialization as an organizational phenomenon (Van Maanen & Schein, 1979), although some research shows that organizational socialization tactics wane over time whereas proximal work group influences remain significant (Chao, Kozlowski, et al., 1994). Finally, from an organizational learning perspective, understanding the influence of newcomers in teams and their influence on team-level outcomes represents a new and exciting research direction (Chen, 2005; Chen & Klimoski, 2003). In particular, March's (1991) systematic simulation of exploitation–exploration yielded conclusions that slower socialization would yield more collective learning relative to fast assimilation. The appropriate balance of exploitation–exploration ought to be contingent on the context. Stable bureaucracies are likely to be better aligned by a balance tilted toward exploitation, whereas innovative systems are more likely to be better aligned by a balance tilted toward exploration. We think this is a very promising research issue.

Team learning is an area of increasing research interest and an area that is at the juncture of the individual and organizational levels. Thus, it has the potential to be a key level for developing the conceptual underpinnings of organizational learning *and* a key leverage point for prompting organizational learning. We believe that the most pressing issue with respect to team learning is developing conceptual clarity. Much research

TABLE 11.1

Research Agenda

	Informal Learning
Socialization	• Research is needed to examine the effectiveness of training insiders, especially supervisors, to be effective socialization agents.
	• Research is needed that is sensitive to the proximal context of socialization, the work team—not just research on how insiders influence newcomer socialization but also research on how newcomers influence insiders and the unit.
	• Research is needed to identify the optimal balance or trade-offs of exploitation and exploration during socialization (prior to equilibrium) and congruence with the context.
Team learning	• Learning as a process and its outcomes have to be distinct.
	• Conceptual development is needed to clarify different representations of the collective knowledge pool.
	• Research is needed to better link distinct individual and team learning *processes* to learning *outcomes*.
	• Research is needed on the dynamic processes of individual and team regulation and the emergence of collective skill.
Team development	• Descriptive research (longitudinal) is needed on work team development.
	• Research is needed to test normative models of team development: task cycles and regulatory processes within phases and skill compilation across levels across phases.
	Formal Interventions
Active learning	• Continuing research is needed to elaborate and refine the self-regulatory process pathways that link intervention elements to multidimensional learning and performance outcomes.
	• Continuing research is needed to map interactions between learner characteristics and intervention elements.
	• There is a need to generalize the approach to the team level.
Embedded training	• Continuing research is needed to refine the development of specific active learning interventions.
	• Research is needed to evaluate the effectiveness of embedding training capabilities in work technology.
	• There is a need to generalize the approach to the team level.
Distributed training	• Research is needed to evaluate the effectiveness of calibrating DLS technology design to the underlying model of learning.
	• Need to generalize to teams and multiteam systems.
Team training	• Continuing work to meta-analyze the effectiveness of team-training techniques.
	• There is a need for conceptual consolidation.
Team leadership	• Research is needed to evaluate the normative models of team leadership, specifically the ability of the leader to prompt self-regulation and to shape team development.
System alignment and vertical transfer	• Research is needed on configurations of system alignment and to evaluate vertical transfer emergence models.
	• Research is needed on exploitation–exploration and vertical transfer.
	• Research needed on intrateam and between-team networks as a means to promote collective propagation.

treats team learning as types of collective knowledge representations (e.g., transactive memory, and team mental models). Other theorists have asserted that conceptual progress for understanding team learning hinges on distinguishing the dynamic *process* of knowledge and skill acquisition from outcomes that capture knowledge representation (Kozlowski & Bell, in press). With respect to knowledge representations, there is well-developed theory and research to support team mental models, and less well-developed but still promising research on transactive memory (Kozlowski & Ilgen, 2006). Although measurement issues abound and there is plenty of developmental work needed, these two forms of collective knowledge get most of the research attention. Many other alternative forms of collective knowledge emergence are conceivable (Kozlowski & Klein, 2000), but have been neglected. We think this has promise. Finally, although initial research on team regulation as a learning process to account for team learning, performance, and adaptation has been promising (Chen et al., 2005; DeShon et al., 2004), more attention needs to be paid to the specific regulatory process pathways by which effects manifest and on the dynamic interplay between self-regulation and team regulation during the emergence of team knowledge, skilled behavior, and performance (DeShon et al., 2004).

Team development has the potential to be an extraordinarily useful point in the life cycle of a team at which to intervene, yet much of the formal effort to build teams occurs after teams have passed through the developmental phases—a missed opportunity (Kozlowski & Bell, 2003). Early intervention is likely to have a much bigger payoff, but the problem is that we have very little good descriptive data on the natural developmental progression of work teams. Good longitudinal descriptive research (no manipulations necessary!) is sorely needed. It would help inform theory development, especially the issues of phase shifts, timing, and temporal dynamics. Finally, basic research to evaluate the critical mechanisms underlying task cycles and developmental transition and progression proposed by normative models is needed. Because these models are complex, it is likely that research will have to isolate specific processes (e.g., task episodes or progression) and study them separately (e.g., DeShon et al., 2001; Marks & Panzer, 2004).

Formal Interventions

In our framework, formal interventions are designed to prompt and shape learning to augment informal processes and to leverage learning toward targeted outcomes at multiple levels. We begin with a focus on active learning as a foundation because it is rooted in theories of self-regulation that have relevance and applicability at higher levels of conceptualization. Bell and Kozlowski (this volume) present a detailed agenda for research on active learning, so we merely highlight key points here. The primary research needs are to (a) further refine the linkages between active learning design elements, self-regulatory process pathways, and learning outcomes; and (b) map the interactions between individual differences and active learning design elements and their effects on self-regulation. Both of these issues are relevant to improving the delivery of active learning experiences and, in particular, to tailoring the techniques to individuals and their progress as they learn—individualized training on demand.

Embedded training is theoretically related to active learning, but with a more pragmatic emphasis on the design of techniques that selectively stimulate self-regulation to influence its focus and quality during active learning. As research refines the integrative active learning model, those theoretical advances will need to be incorporated into the ALS model to improve intervention design. Moreover, as the stable of effective active learning techniques that can be embedded in technology expands, evaluation of their generality out of controlled lab simulations and into work technology systems needs to be undertaken. Do they work as effectively in work systems? How effectively can they be deployed and distributed in a broader DLS technology network? These are pragmatic questions, but they are critical questions to answer if we are to be able to realize the promise of these approaches. Finally, the other important research opportunity is to begin to generalize active learning techniques and embedded training to the team level. Virtually all of the research on these models has been conducted at the individual level. Do the same processes manifest in the team-learning context?

There is a wide range of team-learning techniques that have evidence of effectiveness for specific applications (Salas & Cannon-Bowers, 1997). Choosing among the many techniques can be a challenge, although recent efforts to statistically summarize the research on team-training effectiveness using meta-analysis are very promising (Salas, DiazGrandos et al., 2009). We encourage more of this work. Moreover, we would also encourage conceptual integration. The integrated active learning model identified a parsimonious set of core design elements that accounted for a wide array of distinct active learning interventions, and the pathways by which they exhibit their effects (Bell & Kozlowski, this volume). By taking a similar approach, it might be possible to consolidate the wide array of team-training techniques into a smaller set of intervention clusters linked to process mechanisms. That would simplify meta-analyses and would also promote theoretical parsimony.

Normative models of team leadership focus on the role functions of the team leader in harnessing the task cycles (discussed under team development), linking them to a regulatory cycle (setting goals, monitoring performance, intervening as necessary, and guiding process feedback) to build targeted skills, and shifting the locus of skill development as individual and team skills compile. As discussed above, the basic underpinnings of the normative model with respect to task cycles and skill compilation are in need of more research attention, although initial research is promising (Kozlowski & Bell, 2008). However, specific to the models of team leadership, we need to evaluate how effectively the regulatory cycles can be prompted by leader functions or actions. We think leaders (or other agents) have high potential to leverage learning in the workplace, whether augmented by technology or not. If so, they are key to prompting developmental processes that underpin collective learning at higher levels of the organizational system. This is uncharted territory.

With the basic underpinnings of an infrastructure in place at the individual and team levels, research attention also has to extend to system alignment for qualitatively different emergence processes, and the ways the vertical transfer can be fostered so that collective learning propagates throughout the organizational system. The two primary forms of vertical transfer discussed by Kozlowski and colleagues (2000) are the composition and compilation forms. However, it should be noted that those two ideal types anchor the ends of a quasi-continuum of more specific types of emergence (Kozlowski & Klein, 2000). There are fairly specific propositions attached to each form of emergence and their implications for needs assessment, training design and delivery, and evaluation that have not been evaluated. Evaluation of the basic forms of vertical transfer, and the more specific alternatives, is warranted.

In this chapter, we proposed that composition forms of emergence are more likely to be associated with (or would characterize) more effective system alignment when the organizational system is designed to promote exploitation as the form of organizational learning, whereas compilation forms of emergence are more likely to be associated with (or would characterize) more effective system alignment when the organizational system is designed to promote exploration as the form of organizational learning (March, 1991). We think this idea has conceptual merit and would help to guide system design.

Finally, networks within and across teams may provide a way to research how learning emerges across members within a team and how collective learning propagates across the organizational system. Networks provide an approach for conceptualizing how knowledge from learning is accessed and synthesized from diverse sources, shared across nodes, and compiled to emerge as part of the vertical transfer process. It is likely that both formal networks (i.e., task structure links) and informal networks (i.e., interpersonal links) are implicated.

Dense team networks may force more rapid newcomer socialization, which could limit the degree to which a team can learn from newcomers before they are socialized. However, it is also possible that dense team networks could enable more rapid propagation of knowledge across team members once useful knowledge has been acquired and identified by a member. Thus, research on the effects of network density, both formal and informal, on intrateam socialization and learning is warranted.

At the higher level, parallel research is needed on how linkages across teams may similarly facilitate or inhibit collective learning. Moreover, if network connections enable collective learning as would be expected, research would be needed to address how gaps or structural holes in the unit network could be bridged to enable more uniform emergence of collective learning.

Conclusion

Organizational learning has been discussed in the literature on organizational behavior since at least the early 1960s, but, although the concept is conceptually rich, it has not served as a major driver of research. We think that a big part of the limited research impact of organizational learning is the relative lack of more specific theories and interventions needed to provide process engines and actionable tools to guide the process, respectively. In this chapter we have proposed a multilevel framework in an effort to provide a conceptual and operational foundation to fill this gap. We hope that this chapter will help guide researchers to see the myriad promising ways that the underpinnings of organizational learning can be investigated and that as a result our field will begin to gain a better grasp on this important domain of applied psychology and organizational behavior.

References

Araujo, L. (1998). Knowing and learning as networking. *Management Learning, 29,* 317–336.

Argote, L., McEvily, B., & Reagans, R. (2003). Managing knowledge in organizations: An integrative framework and review of emerging themes. *Management Science, 49,* 571–582.

Argyris, C. (1990). *Overcoming organizational defenses: Facilitating organizational learning.* Boston, MA: Allyn & Bacon.

Argyris, C. (1999). *On organizational learning.* Oxford, UK: Blackwells.

Argyris, C., & Schön, D. A. (1978). *Organizational learning: A theory of action perspective.* Reading, MA: Addison-Wesley.

Ashby, W. R. (1960). *Design for a brain: The origin of adaptive behavior.* London: Chapman and Hall.

Baldwin, T. T., & Ford, J. K. (1988). Transfer of training: A review and directions for future research. *Personnel Psychology, 41*, 63–105.

Bartunek, J. M. (1984). Changing interpretive schemes and organizational restructuring: The example of a religious order. *Administrative Science Quarterly, 29*, 355–372.

Bell, B. S., Kanar, A. M., & Kozlowski, S. W. J. (2008). Current issues and future directions in simulation-based training in North America. *International Journal of Human Resource Management, 19*, 1416–1434.

Bell, B. S., & Kozlowski, S. W. J. (2002). Adaptive guidance: Enhancing self-regulation, knowledge and performance in technology-based training. *Personnel Psychology, 55*, 267–306.

Bell, B. S., & Kozlowski, S. W. J. (2007). Advances in technology-based training. In S. Werner (Ed.), *Managing human resources in North America* (pp. 27–42). Oxon, UK: Routledge.

Bell, B. S., & Kozlowski, S. W. J. (2008). Active learning: Effects of core training design elements on self-regulatory processes, learning, and adaptability. *Journal of Applied Psychology, 93*, 296–316.

Brown, J. S., & Duguid, P. (1991). Organizational learning and communities-of-practice: Toward a unified view of working, learning, and innovation. *Organization Science, 2*, 40–57.

Cannon-Bowers, J. A., Salas, E., & Converse, S. A. (1993). Shared mental models in expert team decision making. In N. J. Castellan (Ed.), *Individual and group decision making: Current issues* (pp. 221–246). Hillsdale, NJ: Lawrence Erlbaum Associates.

Cannon-Bowers, J. A., Tannenbaum, S. I., Salas, E., & Volpe, C. E. (1995). Defining team competencies and establishing team training requirements. In R. Guzzo & E. Salas (Eds.), *Team effectiveness and decision making in organizations* (pp. 333–380). San Francisco: Jossey-Bass.

Chakravarthy, B. S. (1982). Adaptation: A promising metaphor for strategic management. *Academy of Management Review, 7*, 735–744.

Chang, A., Bordia, P., & Duck, J. (2003). Punctuated equilibrium and linear progression: Toward a new understanding of group development. *Academy of Management Journal, 46*, 106–117.

Chao, G. T. (1997). Organizational socialization in multinational corporations: The role of implicit learning. In C. L. Cooper & S. E. Jackson (Eds.), *Creating tomorrow's organizations: A handbook for future research in organizational behavior* (pp. 43–57). New York: John Wiley.

Chao, G. T. (2007). Mentoring and organizational socialization: Networks for work adjustment. In B. R. Ragins & K. E. Kram (Eds.), *The handbook of mentoring at work: Theory, research and practice* (pp. 179–196). Thousand Oaks, CA: Sage.

Chao, G. T., Kozlowski, S. W. J., Major, D. A., & Gardner, P. D. (1994, April). *The effects of organizational tactics and contextual factors on newcomer socialization and learning outcomes.* Paper presented at the Ninth Annual Conference of the Society of Industrial and Organizational Psychology, Nashville, TN.

Chao, G. T., O'Leary-Kelly, A. M., Wolf, S., Klein, H. J., & Gardner, P. D. (1994). Organizational socialization: Its content and consequences. *Journal of Applied Psychology, 79*, 730–743.

Chen, G. (2005). Newcomer adaptation in teams: Multilevel antecedents and outcomes. *Academy of Management Journal, 48*, 101–116.

Chen, G., & Kanfer, R. (2006). Toward a systems theory in motivated behavior in work teams. *Research in Organizational Behavior, 27*, 223–267

Chen, G., & Klimoski, R. J. (2003). The impact of expectations on newcomer performance in teams as mediated by work characteristics, social exchanges, and empowerment. *Academy of Management Journal, 46*, 591–607.

Chen, G., Wallace, J. C., & Thomas, B. (2005). Multilevel examination of the relationships among training outcomes, mediating regulatory processes, and adaptive performance. *Journal of Applied Psychology, 90*, 827–841.

Cohen, W. M., & Levinthal, D. A. (1990). Absorptive capacity: A new perspective on learning and innovation. *Administrative Science Quarterly, 35*, 128–152.

Cringely, R. X. (1996). *Accidental empires: How the boys of Silicon Valley make their millions, battle foreign competition, and still can't get a date.* New York: HarperCollins.

Cyert, R. M., & March, J. G. (1963). *A behavioral theory of the firm.* Englewood Cliffs, NJ: Prentice Hall.

Daft, R. L., & Weick, K. E. (1984). Toward a model of organizations as interpretation systems. *Academy of Management Review, 9*, 284–295.

Davenport, T. O. (1999). *Human capital: What it is and why people invest it.* San Francisco: Jossey-Bass.

DeShon, R. P., Kozlowski, S. W. J., Schmidt, A. M., Milner, K. R., & Wiechmann, D. (2004). A multiple goal, multilevel model of feedback effects on the regulation of individual and team performance. *Journal of Applied Psychology, 89*, 1035–1056.

DeShon, R. P., Kozlowski, S. W. J., Schmidt, A. M., Wiechmann, D., & Milner, K. R. (2001, April). Developing team adaptability: Shifting regulatory focus across levels. In S. W. J. Kozlowski & R. P. DeShon (Chairs), *Enhancing team performance: Emerging theory, instructional strategies, and evidence.* Symposium presented at the 16th Annual Conference of the Society for Industrial and Organizational Psychology, San Diego, CA.

Duncan, R. B. & Weiss, A. (1979). Organizational learning: Implications for organizational design. In B.M. Staw (Ed.) *Research in Organizational Behavior* (pp. 75–123). Greenwich, CT: JAI Press.

Dutton, J., & Duncan, R. (1983, May). *The creation of momentum for change through the process of organizational sensemaking.* Unpublished manuscript, Graduate School of Business Administration, New York University.

Edmondson, A. C. (1999). Psychological safety and learning behavior in work teams. *Administrative Science Quarterly, 44*(2), 350–383.

Edmondson, A. C. (2002). The local and variegated nature of learning in organizations: A group-level perspective. *Organization Science, 13*, 128–146.

Ellis, A. P. J., & Bell, B. S. (2005). Capacity, collaboration, and commonality: A framework for understanding team learning. In L. L. Neider & C. A. Shriesheim (Eds.), *Understanding teams: A volume in research in management* (pp. 1–25). Greenwich, CT: Information Age.

Ellis, A. P. J., Bell, B. S., Ployhart, R. E., Hollenbeck, J. R., & Ilgen, D. R. (2005). An evaluation of generic teamwork skills training with action teams: Effects on cognitive and skill-based outcomes. *Personnel Psychology, 58*, 641–672.

Fiol, C. M., & Lyles, M. A. (1985). Organizational learning. *Academy of Management Review, 10*(4), 803–813.

Fiore, S. M., & Salas, E. (2007). *Where is the learning in distance learning? Toward a science of distributed learning and training.* Washington, DC: APA Books.

Ford, J. K., & Weissbein, D. A. (1997). Transfer of training: An updated review and analysis. *Performance Improvement Quarterly, 10*, 22–41.

Friedman, V. J., Lipshitz, R., & Popper, M. (2005). The mystification of organizational learning. *Journal of Management Inquiry, 14*, 19–30.

Gersick, C. J. G. (1988). Time and transition in work teams: Toward a new model of group development. *Academy of Management Journal, 31*, 9–41.

Hackman, J. R., & Wageman, R. (2005). A theory of team coaching. *Academy of Management Review, 30*, 269–287.

Hedberg, B. (1981). How organizations learn and unlearn. In P. C. Nystrom &. W. H. Starbuck (Eds.), *Handbook of organizational design* (Vol. 1, pp. 3–27). New York: Oxford University Press.

House, R., Rousseau, D. M., & Thomas-Hunt, M. (1995). The meso paradigm: A framework for the integration of micro and macro organizational behavior. *Research in Organizational Behavior, 16*, 71–114.

Huber, G. P. (1991). Organizational learning: The contributing processes and the literatures. *Organization Science, 2*, 88–115.

Katz, D., & Kahn, R. L. (1978). *The social psychology of organizations.* New York: John Wiley.

Klein, C., Salas, E., Badum, A., DiazGranados, D., Burke, C. S., Goodwin, G. F., et al. (2005). *Meta-analytic investigations of the relationships between team training and development strategies and team processes, outputs, and team member affective outcomes.* Unpublished manuscript.

Klein, K. J., Ziegert, J. C., Knight, A. P., & Xiao, Y. (2006). Dynamic delegation: Shared, hierarchical, and deindividualized leadership in extreme action teams. *Administrative Science Quarterly, 51*, 590–621.

Kozlowski, S. W. J., & Bell, B. S. (2003). Work groups and teams in organizations. In W. C. Borman, D. R. Ilgen, & R. J. Klimoski (Eds.), *Handbook of psychology: Industrial and organizational psychology* (Vol. 12, pp. 333–375). London: Wiley.

Kozlowski, S. W. J., & Bell, B. S. (2006). Disentangling achievement orientation and goal setting: Effects on self-regulatory processes. *Journal of Applied Psychology, 91*, 900–916.

Kozlowski, S. W. J., & Bell. B. S. (2007). A theory-based approach for designing distributed learning systems. In S. M. Fiore & E. Salas (Eds.), *Where is the learning in distance learning? Toward a science of distributed learning and training* (pp. 15–39). Washington, DC: APA Books.

Kozlowski, S. W. J., & Bell, B. S. (2008). Team learning, development, and adaptation. In V. I. Sessa & M. London (Eds.), *Group learning* (pp. 15–44). Mahwah, NJ: Lawrence Erlbaum Associates.

Kozlowski, S. W. J., Brown, K. G., Weissbein, D. A., Cannon-Bowers, J., & Salas, E. (2000). A multi-level perspective on training effectiveness: Enhancing horizontal and vertical transfer. In K. J. Klein & S. W. J. Kozlowski (Eds.), *Multilevel theory, research, and methods in organizations: Foundations, extensions, and new directions* (pp. 157–210). San Francisco: Jossey-Bass.

Kozlowski, S. W. J., & Farr, J. L. (1988). An integrative model of updating and performance. *Human Performance, 1,* 5–29.

Kozlowski, S. W. J., Gully, S. M., Brown, K. G., Salas, E., Smith, E. A., & Nason, E. R. (2001). Effects of training goals and goal orientation traits on multidimensional training outcomes and performance adaptability. *Organizational Behavior and Human Decision Processes, 85,* 1–31.

Kozlowski, S. W. J., Gully, S. M., McHugh, P. O., Salas, E., & Cannon-Bowers, J. (1996). A dynamic theory of leadership and team effectiveness: Developmental and task contingent leader roles. In G. R. Ferris (Ed.), *Research in personnel and human resource management* (Vol. 14, pp. 253–305). Greenwich, CT: JAI.

Kozlowski, S. W. J., Gully, S. M., Nason, E. R., & Smith, E. M. (1999). Developing adaptive teams: A theory of compilation and performance across levels and time. In D. R. Ilgen & E. D. Pulakos (Eds.), *The changing nature of work performance: Implications for staffing, personnel actions, and development* (pp. 240–292). San Francisco: Jossey-Bass.

Kozlowski, S. W. J., Gully, S. M., Salas, E., & Cannon-Bowers, J. A. (1996). Team leadership and development: Theory, principles, and guidelines for training leaders and teams. In M. Beyerlein, D. Johnson, & S. Beyerlein (Eds.), *Advances in interdisciplinary studies of work teams: Team leadership* (Vol. 3, pp. 251–289). Greenwich, CT: JAI.

Kozlowski, S. W. J., & Hults, B. M. (1987). An exploration of climates for technical updating and performance. *Personnel Psychology, 40,* 539–563.

Kozlowski, S. W. J., & Ilgen, D. R. (2006). Enhancing the effectiveness of work groups and teams (Monograph). *Psychological Science in the Public Interest, 7,* 77–124.

Kozlowski, S. W. J., Jundt, D. K., Curran, P., & Kuljanin, G. (2007). Leadership regulatory functions: Leveraging learning, skill development, and adaptation. In S. W. J. Kozlowski (Chair), *Leadership: Learning, development, and adaptation.* Symposium presented at the 67th annual convention of the Academy of Management Association, Philadelphia.

Kozlowski, S. W. J., & Klein, K. J. (2000). A multilevel approach to theory and research in organizations: Contextual, temporal, and emergent processes. In K. J. Klein & S. W. J. Kozlowski (Eds.), *Multilevel theory, research, and methods in organizations: Foundations, extensions, and new directions* (pp. 3–90). San Francisco: Jossey-Bass.

Kozlowski, S. W. J., & Salas, E. (1997). An organizational systems approach for the implementation and transfer of training. In J. K. Ford, S. W. J. Kozlowski, K. Kraiger, E. Salas, & M. Teachout (Eds.), *Improving training effectiveness in work organizations* (pp. 247–287). Mahwah, NJ: Lawrence Erlbaum Associates.

Kozlowski, S. W. J., Toney, R. J., Mullins, M. E., Weissbein, D. A., Brown, K. G., & Bell, B. S. (2001). Developing adaptability: A theory for the design of integrated-embedded training systems. In E. Salas (Ed.), *Advances in human performance and cognitive engineering research* (Vol. 1, pp. 59–123). Amsterdam: JAI/Elsevier Science.

Kozlowski, S. W. J., Watola, D., Jensen, J. M., Kim, B., & Botero, I. (2009). Developing adaptive teams: A theory of dynamic team leadership (pp. 109–146). In E. Salas, G. F. Goodwin, & C. S. Burke (Eds.), *Team effectiveness in complex organizations: Cross-disciplinary perspectives and approaches* (pp. 113–155). New York: Routledge Academic.

Kristof, A. L. (1996). Person-organization fit: An integrative review of its conceptualizations, measurement, and implications. *Personnel Psychology, 49,* 1–49.

Lankau, M. J., & Scandura, T. A. (2007). Mentoring as a forum for learning in organizations. In B. R. Ragins & K. E. Kram (Eds.), *The handbook of mentoring at work: Theory, research and practice* (pp. 94–122). Thousand Oaks, CA: Sage.

Lave, J., & Wenger, E. (1991). *Situated legitimate peripheral participation.* Cambridge: Cambridge University Press.

Lawler, E. E., Mohrman, S. A., & Ledford, G. E. (1995). *Creating high performance organizations: Practices and results of employee involvement and total quality management in Fortune 1000 companies.* San Francisco: Jossey-Bass.

Levitt, B., & March, J. G. (1988). Organizational learning. *Annual Review of Sociology, 14,* 319–340.

Liden, R. C., Wayne, S. J., & Stilwell, D. (1993). A longitudinal study on the early development of leader-member exchanges. *Journal of Applied Psychology, 78,* 662–674.

Likert, R. (1961). *New patterns of management.* New York: McGraw-Hill.

Major, D. A., Kozlowski, S. W. J., Chao, G. T., & Gardner, P. D. (1995). A longitudinal investigation of newcomer expectations, early socialization outcomes, and the moderating effects of role development factors. *Journal of Applied Psychology, 80,* 418–431.

March, J. G. (1991). Exploration and exploitation in organizational learning. *Organization Science, 2,* 71–87.

Marks, M. A., Mathieu, J. E., & Zaccaro, S. J. (2001). A temporally based framework and taxonomy of team processes. *Academy of Management Review, 26,* 356–376.

Marks, M. A., & Panzer, F. J. (2004). The influence of team monitoring on team processes and performance. *Human Performance, 17*(1), 25–41.

Mathieu, J. E., & Martineau, J. W. (1997). Individual and situational influences on training motivation. In J. K. Ford & Associates (Eds.), *Improving training effectiveness in work organizations* (pp. 193–222). Mahwah, NJ: Lawrence Erlbaum Associates.

Meyer, A. (1982). Adapting to environmental jolts. *Administrative Science Quarterly, 27,* 515–537.

Miles, R. E., Snow, C. C., Meyer, A. D., & Coleman, H. J., Jr. (1978). Organizational strategy, structure, and process. *Academy of Management Review, 3,* 546–562.

Mintzberg, H., & Waters, J. (1982). Tracking strategy in an entrepreneurial firm. *Academy of Management Journal, 25,* 465–499.

Mohammed, S., & Dumville, B. C. (2001). Team mental models in a team knowledge framework: Expanding theory and measurement across disciplinary boundaries. *Journal of Organizational Behavior, 22,* 89–106.

Morgan, B. B., Salas, E., & Glickman, A. S. (1993). An analysis of team evolution and maturation. *Journal of General Psychology, 120,* 277–291.

Morgeson, F. P., & Hofmann, D. A. (1999). The structure and function of collective constructs: Implications for multilevel research and theory development. *Academy of Management Review, 24*(2), 249–265.

Morrison, E. W. (1993). Newcomer information seeking: Exploring types, modes, sources, and outcomes. *Academy of Management Journal, 36,* 557–589.

Morrison, E. W. (2002). Newcomers' relationships: The role of social network ties during socialization. *Academy of Management Journal, 45,* 1149–1160.

Noe, R. A., & Wilk, S. L. (1993). Investigation of the factors that influence employees' participation in development activities. *Journal of Applied Psychology, 78,* 291–303.

Nonanka, I. (1994). A dynamic theory of organizational knowledge creation. *Organization Science, 5,* 14–37.

Nowakowski, J. M., & Kozlowski, S. W. J. (2004, April). Goal orientation and feedback seeking during learning: Processes and prospects. In B. S. Bell (Chair), *Advances in research on individual differences in training contexts.* Symposium presented at the 19th Annual Conference of the Society for Industrial and Organizational Psychology, Chicago.

Nowakowski, J. M., & Kozlowski, S. W. J. (2005, April). Effects of feedback content on goal-directed behavior and self-regulation. In J. M. Nowakowski & S. W. J. Kozlowski (Chairs), *Feedback interventions and feedback seeking: Implications for self-regulation.* Symposium presented at the 20th Annual Conference of the Society for Industrial and Organizational Psychology, Los Angeles.

Ostroff, C., & Kozlowski, S. W. J. (1992). Organizational socialization as a learning process: The role of information acquisition. *Personnel Psychology, 45,* 849–874.

Ostroff, C., & Kozlowski, S. W. J. (1993). The role of mentoring in the information gathering processes of newcomers during early organizational socialization. *Journal of Vocational Behavior, 42,* 170–183.

Roth, G. (2008). The order and chaos of the learning organization. In T. G. Cummings (Ed.) *Handbook of Organizational Development,* (pp. 475–498). Thousand Oaks, CA: Sage.

Rouiller, J. Z., & Goldstein, I. L. (1993). The relationship between organizational transfer climate and positive transfer of training. *Human Resource Development Quarterly, 4,* 377–390.

Salas, E., & Cannon-Bowers, J. A. (1997). Methods, tools, and strategies for team training. In M. A. Quinones & A. Ehrenstein (Eds.), *Training for a rapidly changing workplace: Applications of psychological research* (pp. 249–279). Washington, DC: American Psychological Association.

Salas, E., DiazGranados, D., Klein, C., Burke, C. S., Stagl, K. C., Goodwin, G. F., & Halpin, S. M. (2009). Does team training improve team performance? A meta-analysis. *Human Factors, 50,* 903–933.

Salas, E., Stagl, K. C., & Burke, C. S. (2004). 25 years of team effectiveness in organizations: Research themes and emerging needs. *International Review of Industrial and Organizational Psychology, 19*, 47–91.

Salas, E., Wilson, K. A., Priest, H. A., & Guthrie, J. W. (2006). Design, delivery, and evaluation of training systems. In G. Salvendy (Ed.), *Handbook of human factors and ergonomics* (3rd ed., pp. 472–512). Hoboken, NJ: John Wiley.

Smith, E. M., Ford, J. K., & Kozlowski, S. W. J. (1997). Building adaptive expertise: Implications for training design. In M. A. Quinones & A. Dudda (Eds.), *Training for a rapidly changing workplace: Applications of psychological research* (pp. 89–118). Washington, DC: APA Books.

Terreberry, S. (1968). The evolution of organizational environments. *Administrative Science Quarterly, 12*(4), 590–613.

Thompson, J. D. (1967). *Organizations in action: Social science bases of administrative theory.* New York: McGraw-Hill.

Tracey, J. B., Tannenbaum, S. I., & Kavanagh, M. J. (1995). Applying trained skills on the job: The importance of the work environment. *Journal of Applied Psychology, 80*, 239–252.

Tuckman, B. W. (1965). Developmental sequence in small groups. *Psychological Bulletin, 63*, 384–399.

Ulrich, D., Jick, T., & von Glinow, M. A. (1993). High-impact learning: Building and diffusing learning capability. *Organizational Dynamics, 22*, 52–66.

Van Maanen, J., & Schein, E. (1979). Toward a theory of organizational socialization. *Research in Organizational Behavior, 1*, 209–264.

Watola, D. J., & Kozlowski, S. W. J. (2005). Leader competencies for developing adaptve teams. In D. V. Day & S. M. Halpin (Chairs), *Leader development theory and research in the United States Army.* Symposuim presented at the 20th Annual Conference of the Society for Industrial and Organizational Psychology, Los Angeles, CA.

Wegner, D. M. (1986). Transactive memory: A contemporary analysis of the group mind. In B. Mullen & G. R. Goethals (Eds.), *Theories of group behavior* (pp. 185–205). New York: Springer-Verlag.

Zaccaro, S. J., Rittman, A. L., & Marks, M. A. (2001). Team leadership. *Leadership Quarterly, 12*(4), 451–483.

12

A Multilevel Perspective on Training and Development Effectiveness

John E. Mathieu
University of Connecticut

Paul E. Tesluk
University of Maryland

In today's highly competitive and global environment, the difference between being a market leader versus a failure is razor thin. Both academic researchers (e.g., Hatch & Dyer, 2004) and business leaders (e.g., Welsh, 2005) have submitted that the difference between organizational success and failure often comes down to how well organizations can attract, develop, align, and retain their human capital. Indeed, the resource-based view of firm performance argues that organizations have a competitive advantage to the extent that they can leverage valuable resources more readily than their competitors. This theory of organizations has been widely adopted by theorists and researchers in the area of strategic human resource management (SHRM). Whereas various models of SHRM exist, they share a common theme in that it is critical to align specific human resource management (HRM) facets (e.g., selection, training, performance management, and reward systems) with the strategic direction of the organization. In other words, the overall guiding strategic model of the organization sets the context within which the effectiveness of various human resources (HR) components can be gauged. This direction, then, filters down throughout the multiple levels of the firm and needs to be managed.

Training and development represent critical components within an organization's HRM system. Indeed, in an era of increasing emphasis on creating "learning organizations" that provide ample learning and development opportunities and encourage continuous-learning behavior by employees, training and development take on significant importance (Maurer, Weiss, & Barbeite, 2003). In addition, there is evidence that investment in training and development activities and in creating a learning culture is associated with firm financial performance (Aragon-Sanchez, Barba-Aragon, & Sanz-Valle, 2003; Ellinger, Ellinger, Yang, & Howton, 2002).

The purpose of this chapter is to articulate a multilevel view of the effectiveness of training and development programs in organizations. We intentionally use the label *training and development*. Training has traditionally referred to planned efforts to facilitate the learning of specific knowledge, skills, and/or behaviors for a specific job (Goldstein, 1993), whereas development is more typically defined in terms of activities (e.g., workshops, seminars, courses, and assignments) that focus on knowledge, skills, and behaviors that provide long-term professional and organization growth and effectiveness (Noe, Wilk, Mullen, & Wanek, 1997). As the changing nature of work brings with it greater expansion of job requirements, and roles and knowledge and skill sets require more frequent updating (Koroly & Panis, 2004), we see the distinction between training and development as less relevant and believe that it is more useful to consider these interrelated and complementary sets of activities together.

We begin with a brief outline of the key attributes of multilevel theory, in general, and how it applies to the issue of training effectiveness in particular. We follow this with an overview of the resource-based view (RBV) of firm competitiveness along with insights from the SHRM literature and their implications for developing and managing human capital. We then outline how researchers have tended to adopt "single-level" views of HR effectiveness, in terms of either "macro" or "micro" approaches. In so doing, we argue that the effectiveness of training and development should be approached from a multilevel perspective that yields insights in terms of dynamic processes and related leverage points for interventions. Here, we detail not only the importance of top-down influences (i.e., vertical alignment of HRM systems) but also how bottom-up influences combine to impact the effectiveness of a training and development initiative. We then offer an example of how a leadership training and development program embodies this multilevel approach illustrating both the top-down and bottom-up influences and their importance in understanding training effectiveness, and we conclude with directions for future research.

Multilevel Theory and Training and Development Effectiveness

The fields of organizational behavior, HRM, and industrial-organizational psychology have been increasingly developing multilevel theories of work behavior over the past two decades. Multilevel theories suggest that any outcome of interest is the result of a confluence of influences emanating from different levels of analysis (House, Rousseau, & Thomas-Hunt, 1995; Kozlowski & Klein, 2000; Rousseau, 1985). The overall logic is that entities are nested in most organizational arrangements, such as individuals in workgroups, which in turn are nested in larger organizational units such as departments, districts, or strategic business units, which in turn are nested in organizations. Further, organizations are nested in strategic groups, which in turn are nested in overall performance environments.

Hackman (2003) aptly applied this multilevel philosophy and advanced the notion of *bracketing*. The bracketing idea implies that to more fully understand the dynamics of a phenomenon of interest, one should consider influences that emanate from at least one layer "within" and at least one layer "outside of" the focal level. The overarching point, however, is that once the salient nesting arrangements have been identified, they represent potentially important sources of influence for study as well as leverage points for management. As a general rule, variables from more proximal layers are likely to exert greater influence on some focal outcome than are variables from more distal layers. Moreover, influences from variables more removed from the focal level are potentially mediated by variables in more proximal layers, although this does not preclude direct effects of variables from distal layers (see Kozlowski & Klein, 2000; Mathieu, 1991; Rousseau, 1985, for more along these lines). Across layers, influences may be positive (e.g., supportive teammates, and organizational climate) or negative (e.g., caustic teammates, and situational constraints), or exhibit complex interactions. Notably, the knowledge, skills, abilities, and other characteristics (KSAOs) associated with entities also can exert both direct effects, and potentially moderate relationships within and across layers in this model, whether those KSAOs refer to individual differences, team composition, or organizations' human capital.

Applying this multilevel thinking to the current context, one can consider the various sources of influence on the effectiveness of a training and development program. Traditionally, the focal level of interest for training effects has been in terms of trainees' reactions to the program, the extent to which they learned or adopted the training content, and the extent to which their behaviors change back on the job. Consequently, factors such as the attributes of the program and characteristics of the trainees are aligned at the same level as are the training criteria. Looking a level *within*, individual learning processes, the structure and flow of the training program over time, and other more "micro" factors will likely play roles in participants' summary reactions, learning, and behavior change. Looking a level *outside*, the degree to which trainees' managers and coworkers endorse the goals of training, the extent to which organizational rewards are aligned with changes stemming from training, and so forth will likely impact the extent to which changes occur and are sustained. In short, the effectiveness of training is a by-product of influences that cut across different levels of analysis.

We are not the first to advance a multilevel view of training effectiveness. Kozlowski, Brown, Weissbein, Cannon-Bowers, and Salas (2000) articulated a multilevel approach that considered processes related to horizontal and vertical training transfer processes (see also Kozlowski & Salas, 1997; Ostroff & Ford, 1989; Quiñones, 2001, for other discussions of multilevel approaches to training effectiveness). Although our framework shares much with that of Kozlowski et al. (2000) and others, they have generally approached the question of training effectiveness from either a "bottom-up" view or a "top-down" view. For instance, Kozlowski et al. detailed how factors at the training level influence effectiveness, and how such effects spread across horizontal levels and, perhaps, combine to yield higher level outcomes. In contrast, Quiñones (2001) discussed how organizational and contextual factors such as organizational climate, the framing of training, and the degree to which organizations provide employees with participation in determining their training and development activities are important factors that influence trainee motivation, self-efficacy, and perceptions of fairness. Here, through our framework and illustrative example, we take a "top-down" approach and feature how organizational-level systems set the tone and the context within which training- and development-related processes evolve as well as a "bottom-up" perspective by articulating mechanisms by which training and development activities can become integrated with other HR practices as part of an SHRM system to impact organizational-level outcomes.

Delery (1998) addressed this levels issue in the context of macro-SHRM research. He argued that the appropriate level of analysis for HRM practices is subject to debate. On one hand, asking about particular facets of each program and summing or averaging them up doesn't necessarily yield an accurate assessment of the quality of a particular practice. For example, if an organization indexes the quality of its training function in terms of how many days of training each person has received, or an average of trainees' reactions, or how large the training budget is, it may well get a biased view of the quality of the entire function. Alternatively, if one merely asks senior managers to provide their general impressions of the quality of "training in general" in their organization, such measures are especially susceptible to ratings biases and may gloss over important details. As we outline below, the different approaches to the evaluation of training effectiveness have adopted different methods of measurement and levels of analysis. Each brings with it certain insights and blinders for our understanding.

Ostroff and Ford (1989) also adopted a multilevel framework tied closely with the long-standing hallmarks of an effective training needs analysis. Traditional training effectiveness frameworks (e.g., Goldstein, 1974;

McGehee & Thayer, 1961) submitted that a precursor to a successful training program is a thorough needs analysis consisting of (a) organizational, (b) requirements, (c) KSAO, and (d) person analyses. In this sense, the traditional needs analysis implicitly adopts a multilevel perspective. In other words, an *organizational analysis* deals with "macro"-type variables, such as the emphasis that an organization has on certain strategic directions, how human resources are developed and configured, and the extent to which the organization is supportive of the goals of training. In this sense, the organizational analysis is a "macro" approach that considers the role of a training program in the context of the organization's strategic direction and the overall manner in which human resources are managed. The *requirements analysis* represents a more circumscribed approach where one begins to target or localize training within the overall organizational system. In other words, the requirements approach deals with organizational subsystems, views jobs in context, and identifies particular opportunities and challenges for successfully implementing a given training program.

The *KSAO analysis* focuses on determining the focal contents of a training program. Here, the attention is devoted to identifying what types of human capital or competencies should be targeted for maximum benefit from the training program. In effect, this approach is designed to specify what it is that will actually be trained. Finally, the *person analysis* focuses on who would benefit the most from the training. This involves an assessment of gaps between employees' current KSAO levels versus desired levels. Here again, the focus is at the micro level with the logic that the training will yield the most overall benefit if it is directed toward people who have the greatest gaps.

One can see that the traditional needs analysis moves from a very macro perspective concerning the value of different forms of human capital, through a focus on subsystem needs, down to detailed analyses of individuals' current and desired KSAO levels (Ostroff & Ford, 1989). In this sense, it truly represents a multilevel perspective of training. Whereas traditionally the focal outcome level has been defined in terms of trainees' reactions, learning, and behavior, for our purposes *we will focus on the effectiveness of any given training program and development*. In other words, our focal unit of analysis is in terms of the extent to which any training program contributes to overall organizational effectiveness. Therefore, variables and processes related to trainees' reactions, learning, and behavior change will occupy a more micro analysis, or what Hackman (2003) called a layer within the focal unit of inquiry. Notably, we also consider how factors that reside beyond any given training program (i.e., the outside levels) come to influence the effectiveness of a given training program. We also consider how a given training program combines with other aspects of the larger HRM system to influence organizational-level outcomes. Consequently, we articulate both micro and macro views of training effectiveness, as well as advance top-down, and bottom-up, processes associated with training effectiveness. Before doing so, however, we first provide a brief overview of how the resource-based view of firm performance, as well as insights from the SHRM management literature, provide a theoretical framework for overlaying this multilevel view of training effectiveness.

Resource-Based View of the Organization

The RBV of the firm, as perhaps best articulated by Barney (1991), has come to occupy a central position in SHRM (Wright, Dunford, & Snell, 2001). In brief, RBV argues that sustained organizational competitive advantage can be derived from resources that a firm controls that are (a) valuable, (b) rare, (c) imperfectly imitable, and (d) not substitutable. Such resources can be tangible as well as intangible, and include HRM capabilities such as organizational processes and routines, management systems, information, and human capital. RBV provides a unifying theoretical framework for aligning SHRM insights with more general percepts of strategic management. In other words, RBV explains "why" SHRM practices offer value for organizational effectiveness.

The key insight from RBV, as applied to SHRM, is that to the extent firm employees possess KSAOs that are suitable for the overall organizational design and strategy (i.e., are thereby valuable), and those same KSAOs are difficult for competitors to obtain (i.e., because they are rare, are not easily copied, and cannot be replaced through other means), a firm will have a competitive advantage in the marketplace. Indeed, Carmeli and Schaubroeck (2005) have found support for this key proposition.

Although traditional HR systems may be able to better identify, attract, and select (e.g., through recruitment and selection systems), as well as retain (e.g., through compensation systems), individuals who possess such rare and valuable skills, they offer relatively little long-term competitive advantage for firms because they are easily copied. Moreover, when the human capital is available in the open market, it becomes less rare and more easily replaced. Consequently, organizational training and development programs offer one of the most potent means to build competitive advantage from an RBV perspective (Hatch & Dyer, 2004; Hitt, Beierman, Shimizu, & Kochhar, 2001).

We should note that competitive advantage may derive from HRM systems beyond that which stems directly from enhanced employee KSAOs. Youndt, Subramaniam, and Snell (2004) differentiated three forms of HR capital: (a) human, which is essentially equivalent to individuals' KSAOs; (b) social, which is defined in terms of employees' exchange relationships, joint activities, or network-type processes; and (c) organizational, defined in terms of management systems, policies, and procedures for orchestrating work processes throughout the system. Here again, we see an implicit multilevel perspective, as the focal level of human capital is in terms of individuals' KSAOs, whereas *social capital* refers to networks or exchange relationships within organizational subsystems, and *organizational capital* is focused upon system-level properties. The dominant perspective in training and development research has been on human capital (i.e., KSAOs). However, as we articulate in greater detail later, training and development initiatives can also impact forms of social capital (e.g., relationships in the form of mentoring initiatives that are part of a leadership training program) and organizational capital (e.g., a training program on performance appraisal and feedback that managers apply to improve performance management practices).

Research and theory in the area of HRM have traditionally adopted either a "micro" or a "macro" approach (Wright & Boswell, 2002). The micro approach has been around for well over a century and focuses on the influence of specific HR programs on individual-level employee outcomes. In contrast, the SHRM heritage is roughly 25 years old, tracing its origins to Walker's (1978) argument that HRM planning should be aligned with organizational strategic planning. The focus of SHRM has generally adopted a macro perspective that focuses on the relationship between the entire HRM system and organizational outcomes. Wright and Boswell (2002) submitted that integrating these two traditions can yield new insights for advancing our understanding of HRM systems from a multilevel perspective. Accordingly, we outline four different approaches for examining the effectiveness of training and development programs from a multilevel perspective, as depicted in Figure 12.1. Each of the four approaches is detailed below. It is the bottom-left and upper-right cells in this 2 × 2 matrix that represent the multilevel approach and that are our focus in the framework and illustrative example.

Micro Approach

The micro approach emanates from the disciplines of human learning and industrial-organizational psychology. In this tradition, the focal influences are in terms of trainees' characteristics and features of

	Focal Level of Influences	
	Specific Training Program	**HRM System**

Individual	**Micro Approach**
	
	The Influence of a Specific Training Program on Targeted Employee KSAOs
		Cross-Level Approach
		
		The Impact of Unit or Organizational Factors on The Effectiveness of Individual Level Training Outcomes
		
		"Regional" Illustration
		
		    Senior executive support
		    Organizational structure and systems
		    Organizational culture
		    Situational constraints
		
		       Top-Down Influences
		
		Influences on participants' pretraining conditions (e.g., motivation, self-efficacy), learning, and transfer

Organizational	**Compilation Approach**
	
	The Combined Influence of the Training and other HR Systems on Organizational Outcomes
	
	"Regional" Illustration
	
	Influences on human capital, social capital, organizational capital outcomes
	
	   Bottom-Up Influences
	
	   Accounting for different forms of HR capital
	   Vertical fit
	   Horizontal fit
	   Differentiation of HRM activities
		Macro Approach
		
		The Relative Influence of The Training System on Organizational Outcomes

(Left margin spanning labels: **Focal Level of Outcome**; rows labeled **Individual** and **Organizational**)

FIGURE 12.1
Multilevel view of training effectiveness.

a particular training and development program, whereas the focal outcomes are in terms of influences on individuals' learning and behavior. Salient attributes of a training program include factors such as the extent that the training incorporates important learning principles into its design (Goldstein & Ford, 2002). These principles might include effective preparation techniques (e.g., the use of advanced organizers, enhancing trainees' expectations), training design (e.g., massed vs. spaced learning, whole vs. part learning, etc.), and reinforcement principles (e.g., feedback, intrinsic and extrinsic rewards for learning, etc.).

The micro approach also focuses attention on instructional approaches (e.g., lecture, simulations, multimedia, and distance learning), the role of the "trainer" (e.g., trainer features and expertise), or aspects of technological guides such as self-administered CD-ROM or Web-based systems, or more immersive approaches such as virtual reality simulations and intelligent tutoring systems (Goldstein & Ford, 2002). Further, this approach views the trainee as an active learner with individual differences, pre-existing capabilities, and motivations. For example, the roles of trainee motivation to learn, individual differences in learning orientation, and other individual differences in individuals' training reactions, learning, and behaviors have been examined (cf. Mathieu & Martineau, 1997; Noe, 1986). Moreover, the micro approach has included aptitude–treatment interactions whereby training program attributes and trainee characteristics are viewed as combining in nonlinear ways to generate training outcomes (see Gully & Chen, this volume).

The overall theme of the micro approach is that the focus is on attributes of a specific training program, design, and delivery along with trainee individual differences, as related to individual-level training and development outcomes. In terms of traditional training evaluation criteria, the salient outcomes for the micro approach include employees' reactions to the training program, the extent to which they have learned or adopted the targeted content, and the extent to which they transfer the trained KSAOs to the job environment. Rarely are programs evaluated in terms of "results"—or the ultimate value of the training program to organizational effectiveness. In the few instances when researchers have included results outcomes, they have typically been in the form of projected utility gains (e.g., Mathieu & Leonard, 1987). Notably, utility analyses such as these implicitly assume that benefits accrued through employees' improved job performance will additively combine to yield organizational utility. Outside of the practitioner literature (e.g., Phillips, 1997), such an assumption, to our knowledge, has never been formally tested.

Summary

The micro approach, generally, tends to approach the question of training and development effectiveness in a vacuum. The implicit assumption is that if trainees react positively to the program, learn the requisite material, and can exhibit the intended new behaviors, the training was successful. Whereas, on one hand, this approach may appear to be quite naïve, as training always occurs in some context, on the other hand this is where "the rubber meets the road" and training actually occurs. No matter how well training might be strategically aligned with the larger system and advantageous RBV principles, if down in the trenches the delivery of that training is simply flawed, no competitive benefits will accrue.

Cross-Level Approach

The cross-level approach to training and development effectiveness was a natural outgrowth of the micro approach. Whereas the focal level for training outcomes remains in terms of trainees' reactions, learning, and behavior, the focal level of influences expands beyond the attributes of the particular program and participants to include features of the larger HRM and surrounding organizational system. This approach is most closely aligned with the organization and job elements of an effective training needs analysis. The guiding theme here is that the training and development program must be aligned with the larger HRM and organization environment if it is to be successful (Tannenbaum, 2002).

Practitioners, theorists, and researchers realized that training does not occur in isolation from the rest of the organization. Trainees come to a program with certain motivations and expectations regarding its potential utility for them (Noe, 1986). The larger HRM system, as well as other organizational systems and processes, may support or undermine the goals of the training. Aspects of the work environment may reinforce or totally negate that which was developed in training. In short, the context matters and may have significant influences on the effectiveness of a given training and development program.

This cross-level approach embodies the growing tradition of modeling top-down relationships in meso designs (cf. Mathieu & Taylor, 2007). The logic of downward cross-level designs is that some feature(s) of the larger context exert influences on lower level processes. In the context of training effectiveness, such influences have generally been examined in terms of their impact on employees' pretraining motivation to learn, the learning processes that occur during the actual training, or their willingness and ability to transfer learning to the work environment (Kozlowski et al., 2000). Mathieu, Tannenbaum, and Salas (1992) investigated the relationship of perceived situational constraints and the effectiveness of a clerical training program. Their results suggested that situational constraints reduced training-related motivation, as well as correlated negatively with individuals' learning. In a follow-up study that employed a true cross-level design, Mathieu, Martineau, and Tannenbaum (1993) found that aggregate situational constraints related negatively to training outcomes.

In an innovative field experiment, Rouiller and Goldstein (1993) found that trainees who were assigned to fast food restaurants that were supportive and reinforced what was learned in training exhibited significantly better transfer than did trainees who were assigned to restaurants that were less accommodating to the training. Similarly, Tracey, Tannenbaum, and Kavanagh (1995) found that a positive training climate facilitated the transfer of manager skills training in a supermarket chain. Tracey, Hinkin, Tannenbaum, and Mathieu (2001) found, in the context of a cross-level field design of management training in a hotel chain, that supportive features of the work environment related positively to both pertaining efficacy and motivation, as well as positively to training reactions and knowledge development. Similar relationships have been observed for other influences from the larger training environment. For example, individuals' choice about whether or not to participate in training has been found to influence pretraining attitudes and/or outcomes (cf. Baldwin, Magjuka, & Loher, 1991; Hicks & Klimoski, 1987). Richman-Hirsch (2001) found that posttraining goal-setting interventions facilitated transfer, particularly when the larger organizational environment was supportive. Tesluk, Farr, Mathieu, and Vance (1995) found that climate for participation and senior managers' attitudes toward employee involvement influenced the degree to which employees generalized the skills learned in employee involvement training to their day-to-day job activities. Elsewhere, Smith-Jentsch, Salas, and Baker (1996) found that the success of an assertiveness training program could be completely undermined by negative supervisor comments back on the job. Finally, Carnevale, Gainer, and Villet (1990) submitted that training transfer is undermined when the goals of the training are not aligned with the strategic direction of the firm. Indeed, organizational efforts designed to reinforce what was learned in training have been shown to facilitate the long-term transfer of training (cf. Richman-Hirsch; Wexley & Baldwin, 1986).

Summary

The cross-level approach to training and development effectiveness maintains the focal level of outcomes at the micro (i.e., individual) level of inquiry. However, the scope of potential influences on such effects is expanded to include factors emanating from higher levels of analysis. In this sense, the cross-level approach better models the multitude of influences, and their combinations, that impact individual processes related to training effectiveness. It also clarifies that such effects may occur before trainees enter a program, during its operation, or later during a transfer phase.

Macro approach

In contrast to the traditional HRM micro approach, SHRM focuses on the entire HRM system as a whole and its relationship with organizational effectiveness (Becker & Huselid, 2006). Consequently, the SHRM approach focuses on both macro outcomes and influences (Bowen & Ostroff, 2004; Jackson & Schuler, 1995; Wright & Snell, 1998). Essentially, work in this tradition has adopted either a *universalistic-* or *contingency-*type approach. The universalistic approach suggests that a given type or combination of HRM practices is likely to be beneficial for all modern-day organizations. Often referred to as high-performance work systems (HPWS), this configuration usually includes features such as (a) internal promotion systems, (b) formal training programs, (c) employee evaluation systems, (d) some form of incentive pay, (e) safety programs, (f) teamwork, and (g) mechanisms for employee participation. The contingency-type approach suggests that certain configurations of HRM practices will be more or less beneficial depending on "some" other organizational factor. Perhaps the most frequently used contingency factor has been the overall business strategy of the firm, most often indexed using Miles and Snow's (1984) typology of (a) *defenders* (narrow and relatively stable product–market domains who devote their primary attention to improving the efficiencies of their existing operations), (b) *prospectors* (continually searching for product and market opportunities and experimenting with potential responses to changing environmental trends), or (c) *analyzers* (who manage a dual focus on one or more relatively stable domains and one or more dynamic domains).

Early work in this macro tradition was in the universalistic approach and sought to test whether the quality of the HRM system related significantly with firm performance. Lee and Miller (1999) obtained some support for a positive relationship between HRM practices and performance in a sample of Korean firms. Similar results were obtained by Guthrie (2001) with a sample of New Zealand firms, and by Richard and Johnson (2001) in a banking sample. Lam and White (1998) found positive relationships between the quality of HRM practices and financial indices of success in a manufacturing sample. Although such positive findings are far from uniform (cf. Becker & Huselid, 1998; Delery & Doty, 1996; Huselid, 1995), the general conclusion has been that high-quality HRM practices are associated with firm effectiveness across a wide variety of settings.

As the research has evolved in this tradition, scholars sought to distinguish the unique and combined influences of different HRM systems, as related to firm performance. Barnard and Rodgers (2000) examined the relative contributions of HRM staffing, employment stability, and employee development practices as related to HPWS in a sample of Singapore-based organizations. They found that employee development practices, extensively represented by the training and development function, comprised the sole contributor to HPWS beyond control variables.

Harel and Tzafrir (1999) collected a national sample of survey responses from public and private sector organizations in Israel. They correlated respondents' perceptions of the effectiveness of different HRM practices (e.g., recruitment, selection, compensation, and training) with organizational effectiveness. Whereas, as a set, the HRM practices correlated significantly with both organizational and market performance criteria, the only practice to exhibit a significant unique effect was training. In contrast, Paul and Anantharaman (2003) obtained significant correlations between the qualities of a wide range of HRM practices and organizational outcomes, as mediated by HRM processes such as teamwork and a customer orientation. Notably, training practices were found to have a direct influence on employees' productivity. Elsewhere, d'Arcimoles (1997) and Aragon-Sanchez and colleagues (2003) found significant positive relationships between the quality of organizational training programs and indicators of financial performance.

Although the universalistic approach has yielded many insights, researchers have sought to identify critical moderators or contingency variables that play a role in system-level effects. Huselid (1995) found a positive correlation between the general level of HRM practices and firm performance. Notably, his findings were more pronounced in instances where the HRM system was well aligned with the overall strategic direction of the organization. The importance of "vertical fit" between the HRM system and the overall organizational strategy has been a central theorem in SHRM theory (Becker & Huselid, 2006; Chadwick & Cappelli, 1999; Delery, 1998). The general logic is that to the extent that the HRM system, as a whole, is well aligned with the strategic orientation of the firm, the organization will be more effective (Schuler & Jackson, 1987; Wright & Snell, 1998). For example, Miles and Snow (1984) argued that certain organizational strategies, such as *defenders* and *analyzers*, place a premium on extensive and formalized training programs. In contrast, they argued that organizations following a *prospector* strategy would more likely seek to acquire external human capital and therefore rely far less on training. Ostroff (2000) found some support for an overall relationship between firm HRM practices and performance. Moreover, she found that different clusters of HRM practices were related to performance depending on the overall business strategy of the firm. Koch and McGrath (1996) found that organizations with effective HRM systems were positively related with labor productivity, and that the relationship was stronger in capital-intensive organizations. However, the bulk of studies seeking to identify general interactions between HRM systems and organizational strategy have failed to produce consistent and encouraging results (for reviews, see Becker & Huselid, 2006; Wright & Boswell, 2002).

Valle, Martin, Romero, and Dolan (2000) conducted an intriguing study focused on the alignment of business strategies and training systems of a sample of 65 Spanish organizations. They empirically indexed organizations' strategic orientations in training along two dimensions: (a) content (i.e., emphasizing individual specialization vs. team-oriented skills), and (b) context (i.e., emphasizing improvement in current performance vs. a future orientation). They also classified organizations' general business strategy in terms of Miles and Snow's (1984) prospector, analyzer, and defender types, each indexed in terms of past, present, and future orientations. Whereas the training content dimension was found to be invariant across the different strategies and times, the context dimension was significantly related to overall organizational present and future strategies. Specifically, Valle et al. (2000) found that although the orientation of training practices was unrelated to past business strategies, it was aligned with present and future temporal orientations.

Considering the research from the macro approach with a particular emphasis on training, Camelo, Martin, Romero, and Valle (2004) submitted that

> it has been found that aspects related to formal training, such as expanding the employee capabilities required by the company, their levels of specialization and diversity of skills, the orientation of learning towards team or group working, the planning of the training process in order to meet future needs or the direct improvement of productivity, are all closely related to the strategies of companies.... Although not all [previous studies] reach the same conclusions, they do appear to support the argument that companies with a strategy based on creative and innovative capacities demand a type of training that is multi-skilled, centered on group working methods and oriented towards the company's identified future needs. (p. 937)

In short, some beneficial features of training and development systems appear to be universally valuable for modern-day organizations. Moreover, when training and development systems are aligned with what have been referred to as HPWS, which are in turn aligned with overall business strategies, the benefits may be especially advantageous.

Summary

The macro approach to SHRM has yielded numerous insights. In particular, it refocused attention from microlevel indices of effectiveness to macro indicators of organizational effectiveness. Reframing the consideration of the value of HRM activities at the organizational level of analysis has enabled scholars and practitioners alike to truly discuss the value of such activities on the same plane as other business decisions such as organizational restructuring efforts, mergers and acquisitions, adopting new technologies, and so forth. This benefit, however, was not without costs.

Treating the entire HRM system as a whole offers few insights in terms of where such benefits are being derived. Consequently, research naturally evolved to comparing the relative competitive advantage of different components of HRM systems. In such investigations, the training and development component has more than held its own. We would argue that this is likely attributable to training and development representing a better means of building and sustaining human capital that is valuable, rare, and imperfectly imitable, as compared to that available to competitors.

Despite the gains from this early SHRM body of research, there was a growing desire to explore the contingency or vertical fit between HRM systems and overall organizational strategy, as related to firm performance. Although some of the initial work was quite promising, the findings have been mixed, which has led researchers to further explore influences from the "next bracket down"—to unpack the overall HRM system in different ways. In other words, researchers from the macro approach began to scrutinize the nature of HRM system configurations, and how such factors may combine to generate benefits at the organizational level of analysis. We turn now to a consideration of that approach.

Compilation Approach

Whereas the initial positive relationships that were observed between HRM systems and organizational effectiveness were encouraging, the "one-size-fits-all" approach did not offer much in terms of theoretical insights or guidelines for practice. Unfortunately, efforts to model general contingencies or interactions between the overall HRM system or its components and other organizational features have been equivocal. Such results motivated scholars to conceptualize the HRM system in more complex fashions such as compilation processes. Kozlowski and Klein (2000) submitted that "in [a] compilation model, the higher-level phenomenon is a complex combination of diverse lower-level contributions" (p. 17). In other words, compilation describes a situation where diverse elements (such as different types of HRM practices) combine in complex and nonlinear ways to yield a gestalt or whole that is not reducible to its constituent parts. This well describes the myriad of ways that HRM practices may combine, as well as the fact that their synthesis is likely to be far more powerful than the individual components would suggest. Although referred to by various labels, essentially these more complex compilation style forms have been referred to in terms of (a) *horizontal fit*, or different bundles of HRM practices; and (b) the *differentiation of subsystem HRM practices* within an organization.

Horizontal Fit

The "horizon 'fit' in SHRM research deals with the internal consistency and complementarity of HRM practices. Specifically, how HRM practices work together as a system to achieve organizational objectives" (Delery, 1998, p. 291). Viewed from a multilevel perspective, the idea here is that the qualities of HRM systems do not necessarily combine in a strictly additive fashion. Rather, there are likely to be more or less effective synergies, profiles, or bundles of HRM practices for different circumstances.

Although the idea of different bundles of coherent HRM practices has great intuitive appeal (Ostroff & Bowen, 2000), in practice it has been fraught with ambiguities (Delery, 1998; Wright & Boswell, 2002). Difficulties surrounding how to best define and index the coherence of HRM practices have led to a wide variety of research strategies, including conceptual groupings, and empirical-based approaches such as clustering and factor-analytic methods. For example, Delery (1998) questioned whether factor-based scales and indices of HRM practices adequately assess HRM systems. Although factor analyses do identify sets of practices items that hang together, they are based on linear combinations that are insensitive to interactive or compensatory-type relationships. In contrast, clustering and other classification methods enable researchers to group organizations on the basis of the profiles or configurations of HRM practices that they employ. Although this approach is far more consistent with the conception of "HRM bundles" of practices, it remains an exploratory method that necessitates many subjective decisions (e.g., how many clusters to retain, what they mean, and how to handle within-cluster differences; see Delery, 1998). Consequently, to date there is no single widely accepted method for identifying coherent HRM bundles of practices. Nevertheless, the idea that HRM practices should be looked at neither as a unified whole nor as component functions in isolation has become firmly entrenched in the current SHRM work.

Lepak and Snell (1999, 2002) advanced a content-based approach and differentiated HRM practices into four general bundles: (a) commitment, (b) productivity, (c) compliance, and (d) collaboration. In effect, they argued that HRM practices do not simply accumulate in a straightforward linear or additive way but, rather, that different combinations of HRM practices yield qualitatively different coherent "bundles" that can be mutually reinforcing. In other words, they articulate a compilation style approach toward HRM systems.

Lepak and Snell's (2002) *commitment bundle* is well aligned with the HPWS style reviewed earlier, and places a premium on building human capital from within (e.g., promotion from within, extensive and continuous training, and long-term employment incentives), enhancing workforce flexibility (e.g., job rotation and cross-training), promoting learning (e.g., developmental feedback and training firm-specific KSAOs), and empowering employees. Clearly, the intention here is to develop a flexible and easily reconfigurable workforce with unique firm-specific KSAOs, who are motivated to achieve strategic goals. In contrast, Lepak and Snell's (1999, 2002) *productivity bundle* focuses on identifying the best employees for current jobs (e.g., extensive multifaceted recruiting, and training in depth for current job requirements), and rewarding them for short-term performance (e.g., evaluations based on efficiency and quantifiable job outputs, and individual-based performance incentives). This approach is consistent with traditional industrial psychology principles of maximizing the fit between individuals' KSAOs and current job requirements, while motivating performance through instrumental incentives.

Lepak and Snell's (1999, 2002) *compliance bundle* echoes aspects of "old-school" Theory X style principles (McGregor, 1960). In this approach, there is a premium on simplifying jobs and motivating short-term performance through hourly pay, compliance with preset work procedures, and standards. Finally, their *collaboration bundle* aligns HRM practices with teamwork, including features such as hiring and building broad-based individual KSAOs (especially those involving teamwork), emphasizing collaboration, and using team-based evaluations and rewards. Notably, although an essential component of all, the characteristics of training, in terms of both content and delivery systems, differed markedly across the four bundles. Moreover, Lepak and Snell (2002) illustrated that different HRM bundles were more suitable for different employment modes (e.g., knowledge-based employment vs. contractual work arrangements).

In summary, the horizontal fit notion has gained prominence among SHRM scholars. The idea that HRM components likely combine in complex ways has great intuitive appeal. More problematic has been the methods of indexing bundles or configurations of practices, and how they combine in complex ways. Nevertheless, we believe that developing a better understanding of this complexity is a key issue for advancing HRM research in general, and training- and development-related research in particular.

Differentiating Subsystem HRM Practices

Commenting on the shortcomings of the macro approach to SHRM, Becker and Huselid (2006) noted,

> Despite the lack of empirical support, we agree that contingencies should continue to play a central role in SHRM theory. But those contingencies should not focus on the ultimate positioning strategy or at the level of Miles and Snow typologies. The point of alignment should be closer to the HR architecture. (p. 901)

Later, they submitted that "the issue is not whether contingencies should play a role in SHRM theory but rather the locus of fit and the nature of that contingency" (Becker & Huselid, 2006, p. 903). In effect, Becker and Huselid (2006), along with others, have advocated a move toward the "lower bracket" of SHRM efforts—to further explore and expand upon organizational subsystems and how they relate to the success of SHRM practices.

Along this vein, Lepak and Snell (1999) submitted that the SHRM literature has generally adopted a holistic view of the HRM system in terms of "the extent to which a set of practices is used across employees in a firm as well as the consistency of these practices across the firm" (p. 32). Alternatively, they argued that HRM practices may well vary within organizations as related to different job types or clusters. Wright and Boswell (2002) noted that "failing to recognize this [differentiation] results in flawed analyses and interpretations of existing results" (pp. 264–265). For example, rather than focusing on the entire HRM system, Delery and Doty (1996) and MacDuffie (1995) concentrated on the HRM practices that pertained to "core jobs" in the organization. Their logic was that some jobs were more critical or "strategic" for overall organizational functioning than were others, and that focusing on the most critical jobs would likely yield the strongest results at the macro level of analysis. Becker and Huselid (2006) argued that "it is not, however, just a question of identifying strategic and nonstrategic jobs. It is equally important to recognize that the HR architecture might have to be differentiated across different strategic capabilities within the same firm" (p. 905).

Lepak and Snell (2002) found numerous significant differences in the extent to which their different HRM bundles were utilized across knowledge-based, job-based, and contractual work arrangements. For example, they found commitment-based HRM bundles were more prominent among knowledge-based jobs than the others. In contrast, the compliance-based HRM bundles were more likely to be used in contractual work arrangements. As the notion that different HRM bundles may be important for different jobs or organizational subsystems has gained acceptance among SHRM researchers, we are reminded of the lessons from training needs analysis: that accurately identifying the critical KSAOs for different people is a key for effectiveness. The takeaway point here is that even HRM bundles are not likely to be "one size fits all." For example, it may well be that performance bundles of HRM activities may be most suitable for production and operations employees in a firm. In contrast, commitment bundles may be better suited for employees in research and development and marketing functional areas of the same firm. Therefore, different HRM bundles are most suitable for different subunits of the organization.

Summary

The differentiation of HRM subsystems is in terms of not only different bundles of practices but also the heterogeneity of HRM practices within organizations. Whether such differentiation is best focused on the organizational subsystem level versus the individual jobs level, or somewhere in between, is debatable and warrants greater scrutiny. We suspect that the answer will likely hinge on the overall organizational design (e.g., functional vs. product-based differentiation), environmental conditions (e.g., relative stability vs. fluidity), and other macro factors. We also anticipate that the best level of inquiry may well differ across organizations. Nevertheless, the important point is that greater insights are likely to follow from tracking the variance of HRM systems within organizations rather than obscuring it in overall summary composites.

Illustrative Example

We illustrate these concepts with profiling a leadership training and development program in a regional medical center (which we refer to as *Regional* throughout the example). We take a 2-year time frame of this newly implemented training and development program to better demonstrate the temporal dynamic associated with the cross-level (i.e., "top-down") and compilation (i.e., "bottom-up") multilevel influences that relate to training and development program effectiveness, and that were introduced above and illustrated in Figure 12.1. To better describe the organizational and contextual factors that have influenced the effectiveness of the training and development program, and to understand the compilation processes by which the training and development program appears to have impacted the organization, we begin with a description of the organization and its strategic setting.

Context

Regional is an over 100-year-old, private, nonprofit medical center that recently moved into a brand-new complex in an effort to expand from a local hospital to a regional medical center after spending its entire history in a downtown location in a small city outside a major metropolitan area. The medical center has approximately 2,000 employees, and its main facility is its 270-bed hospital. Regional is currently undergoing a major $500 million expansion that includes adding new facilities to its main medical park, developing several specialty centers into areas of national prominence, and building new satellite locations to expand its regional coverage of health care services.

In the midst of this expansion, which has been guided by a 10-year strategic and expansion plan, Regional has experienced significant competition from other hospitals and medical centers in the region, which has been reflected in a decline in patient volumes and flattening revenue trends. This has led Regional to institute initiatives designed to increase efficiency through process improvements. Other challenges Regional has encountered include building greater collaboration (e.g., in developing new medical initiatives) with its over 600 medical staff members (mainly physicians) who are not employees but on whom Regional is highly dependent for the delivery of medical services and employee retention (particularly in its mid- to upper-level management positions; director-level positions have experienced a turnover rate of approximately 20% per year over the past 2–3 years).

Leadership Training and Development at Regional

Motivated in large measure by the strategic and operational challenges associated with its movement from a local to a regional health care provider and managing increasing competition, in 2004, Regional decided to provide its middle- to upper-level managers and executives (director level up through president-CEO; approximately 50 individuals) with a comprehensive leadership training and development program. Until this time, managers and executives at Regional had no formal executive or management development or training opportunities available through the organization. The vice president for HR championed the development of a Leadership Institute to not only help develop participants' managerial and leadership skills but also promote greater alignment regarding strategic priorities and "build a common leadership approach" for the organization. Senior executives also hoped that the Leadership Institute would serve as a recruitment and retention tool, especially in helping to reduce the exceptionally high level of turnover among its directors.

The leadership training and development program originated with an organizational needs analysis (e.g., to understand the strategic imperatives of the organization and the general level of support for managers' professional development), a requirements analysis (to understand which levels of management to include in the program), and a KSAO analysis (to identify the leadership and management competencies to include in the program) in the form of semistructured interviews with senior executives, managers, supervisors, and employees. This led to creating a leadership competency model of 22 competencies organized into four broad domains: (a) leading strategically, (b) leading change and transformation, (c) leading on execution and achievement of results, and (d) leading people. The program was designed in a manner consistent with recommendations from leadership development researchers that training and development programs for managers and executives should combine developmental experiences that build knowledge and skills with assessment and feedback and provide participants with means by which they can apply those skills in an environment that supports development goals (Van Velsor, McCauley, & Moxley, 1998). Specifically, the program consisted of three primary components. The first was leadership and management classroom-based training on topics that were based on the competency model and targeted knowledge and skill areas identified in the KSAO analysis as most critical for Regional's managers and executives (e.g., leading and managing change, and understanding the external health care environment and implications for strategy). The second component was 360-degree feedback (in addition to other assessments on interpersonal styles, etc.) on the competencies identified in the leadership at Regional competency model. The third component included one-on-one leadership coaching (initially, 1 hour per quarter; increased to 6 hours in year 2), designed to help participants use their 360-degree feedback to create development plans and to assist in carrying out their plans, and group coaching (i.e., "learning circles"), intended to facilitate participants' transfer of the knowledge and skills covered in the instructional class-based sessions to their job.

Cross-Level Influences

A variety of organizational factors influenced the effectiveness of the leadership training and development program at Regional, including the level of support demonstrated by senior executives, organizational structures and systems, organizational culture, and perceived situational demands. Together, these contextual conditions exerted powerful "top-down" forces impacting participants' training motivation and self-efficacy both before and during the program, as well as training transfer after the program. As we see by tracking the training and development program from one year to the next, they also shaped the evolution of the program and its structure.

Senior Executive Support

Senior executive support at Regional was an important factor in many ways. The CEO, although involved in the design of the program and a participant himself, failed to demonstrate enthusiastic support for the program, particularly at the early stages (e.g., at the program kick-off), which noticeably decreased participants' motivation at the onset. Furthermore, the CEO occasionally made comments during the in-class sessions that many participants felt indicated to them that "senior leadership isn't supportive of what we are being taught in class," which likely affected motivation and transfer. In addition, poor attendance by some of the other top management team members communicated to many participants a lack of senior executive support for the program.

Organizational Structures and Systems

Organizational structures and systems also played an important role during the first year of the Leadership Institute and impacted training effectiveness. For instance, projects that participants developed in courses on project management and teamwork could not be implemented as planned in large part due to stalled development of a planned organization-wide project management infrastructure. This both negatively impacted participants' motivation and harmed transfer because an important component of the training was going to be following an action learning format in the form of applying project management and team leadership skills from the courses to the implementation of the actual projects. As another example of how the organizational structure served as a barrier to training transfer, participants, particularly those in the clinical areas (e.g., directors of nursing), found it nearly impossible to apply many of the performance appraisal, feedback, and development skills they learned in the sessions on performance management because of their incredibly large spans of control due to an organizational structure that was adopted in large measure to demonstrate compliance with "magnet status" criteria.

Organizational Culture

Regional's highly perfectionist and individualistic culture provided a formidable obstacle to the application of many of the skills and knowledge gained through the class sessions, and likely limited the ability of the coaching and learning circle sessions to assist with transfer. For instance, in the small-group, cross-functional learning circle sessions (which where limited to directors, to encourage greater candor and open discussion), many participants frequently commented how they did not feel supported by senior executives (and even frequently not by their peers) if they took initiative or constructively challenged decisions or prevailing viewpoints on topics such as Regional's strategic plan. This was compounded by a strong sense of insecurity on the part of many participants due to the high level of turnover, particularly at the director level of the organization. As one participant phrased it, "[I]f you are seen as going against the grain around here, you are not long in your job." Consequently, although training emphasized building an innovative work environment and provided participants with the frameworks and skills to critically reevaluate their strategy and initiate new projects in areas such as process improvements, the dominant culture was one that implicitly discouraged these behaviors.

Situational Constraints

Health care work environments are demanding, highly dynamic, and often unpredictable, and can present a significant challenge to formalized training and development activities. Participants' perceived lack of time and hectic, often unpredictable schedules were significant obstacles impacting self-efficacy and transfer. The effect of these situational constraints was particularly evident in the individual and group coaching. Many participants had to frequently reschedule their individual coaching sessions, some often missed learning circle meetings, and coaches reported that participants frequently needed assistance with first gaining greater control over their schedules to find time to consider how to apply the skills and knowledge from the training sessions. Although these situational constraints posed formidable challenges to transfer through the individual and group coaching, the opportunity for participants to learn how to potentially manage some of these situational constraints (e.g., prioritizing tasks and meetings, and scheduling "think time" on calendars) through their coaching experiences helped to mitigate the negative effects these situational constraints had on participants' self-efficacy for transfer and perhaps served to both lessen the presence of these situational constraints and reduce participants' perceptions of these factors as constraints on their transfer ability.

Summary

Using this example of a leadership training and development program, we have illustrated potential forms of top-down cross-level influences of organizational and situational factors on training effectiveness. This example is summarized in the upper-right cell of Figure 12.1, where the bulleted context factors we just summarized in this example at Regional influence training outcomes at the individual (i.e., participant) level of analysis. We can draw several conclusions from this example. First, it is important to note that these contextual factors operated at different levels of analyses ranging from the organization level (e.g., culture and senior executive support), where the majority of participants experienced largely similar conditions (although they may be perceived quite differently), to the more immediate work environment (e.g., time constraints, and support from manager), where participants' experiences were more idiosyncratic based on their department or unit, role and responsibilities, manager, and so on. Thus, in theorizing and modeling cross-level influences, researchers need to consider multiple levels of nesting arrangements and where and under what conditions there may be variability in training participants' experiences and exposure to these contextual factors that could influence training motivation, self-efficacy, and transfer. Second, we could have included other organizational and contextual conditions such as level of horizontal alignment of the training and development program with other HR practices such as rewards, and listed additional instances in the set of factors we summarized. Third, as the example highlights, these top-down influences can potentially exert considerable force on training effectiveness through pretraining conditions (e.g., motivation and self-efficacy), learning, and transfer. Our point here is that these cross-level effects are likely to be quite pervasive and critical to understanding and therefore improving training effectiveness.

Compilation Influences

Following the compilation approach and applying it to the context of training and development, the critical question concerning training effectiveness becomes "How does the training and development program impact the organization in an upward or 'bottom-up' manner?" Continuing with our illustrative example below, we show that concepts of identifying and accounting for different forms of HR capital, vertical fit, horizontal fit, and differentiating HRM systems within the organization are important in helping to understand these compilation influences and thereby better predict and support training effectiveness.

Accounting for Different Forms of HR Capital

Applying Kirkpatrick's (1976) classic training criteria framework to evaluating training effectiveness (i.e., trainee reactions, learning, behavioral outcomes, and results), the critical consideration in shifting from the level of the training and development program to organization effectiveness is "How do the learning and changes in participants' behavior (and, if considering development more broadly, perspectives, attitudes, etc.) as a result of the program influence organizational effectiveness (level 4: 'results')?" Drawing from Youndt et al.'s (2004) distinction among different forms of HR capital, the focus here is traditionally on human capital, especially the degree to which the KSAOs gain in the training and development program (as demonstrated through learning criteria) and transferred to the work setting (as demonstrated through behavioral criteria) results in improved performance at the organization level.

Our observations at Regional suggest that although results of the training and development program have been experienced at the department or unit level (e.g., many participants reported applying project management skills to projects in their departments, and using skills and methods on leading teams to engage in team-building efforts within their departments or units), vertical upward transfer to the organization level to date has likely been minimal due to several of the constraints identified earlier at the senior executive level of the organization (e.g., in-fighting between the chief financial officer and chief operations officer prevented many initiatives that could have led to greater collaboration between departments and units).

Although the upward compilation shifting of KSAOs from one level to the next may not have direct effects at the organization level, other forms of HR capital as a result of the leadership training and development program do appear to relate to organizational-level performance. Specifically, the program helped to facilitate various forms of social capital that have benefited interdepartmental collaboration in ways that have yielded beneficial organizational outcomes (e.g., maintaining patient volumes with fewer full time employees (FTEs) by improving ways to manage patient flows across departments; peer support that has been anecdotally linked to a significant decrease in turnover at the director level in year 2 of the program). For instance, the learning circles, originally intended to primarily serve as a mechanism for facilitating training transfer, with their small group, cross-functional structure, were more instrumental in fostering mutual understanding and trust among directors. This social capital was frequently reported as a significant benefit to participants in terms of both aiding their work roles (e.g., for gaining early access to critical information, and support on projects) and providing socioemotional support and the emergence of informal peer mentoring.

A third type of HR capital mentioned by Youndt et al. (2004), organizational capital, in the form of management systems, policies, and procedures for orchestrating teamwork throughout the organization, also benefited from the leadership program. For instance, coursework on performance management highlighted one of the clear limiting factors of Regional's organizational structure—namely, that the current span of control between clinical directors and their nursing and medical staffs was too large to provide direct reports with adequate performance feedback and coaching. Although the structure initially was a barrier to transfer (participants in the clinical areas reported that they could not implement many of the performance management practices they learned), this recognition was in part an impetus to restructure the clinical areas of Regional, thereby allowing performance management systems to be improved.

In short, as this example at Regional demonstrates, training and development programs may have compilation effects on organizational outcomes by building HR capital in ways that go beyond creating human capital in the form of increasing KSAOs that facilitate job performance. Social and organizational capital are potential means by which training and development programs can impact organizational outcomes as well.

Horizontal Fit

The SHRM concept of horizontal fit or the degree of alignment between, in this case, training and development with other HRM systems played a role in the effectiveness of the Leadership Institute at Regional. Initially, there was poor alignment between the leadership training and development program and the other HR systems and practices as they related to the director and executive participants. For instance, the 360-degree feedback, leadership development plans, and coaching components of the program were not aligned with the performance management function as provided by participants' direct managers. Consequently, many participants in the first year of the program felt that they were not adequately supported in, or rewarded for, working toward their development goals by their manager. This changed in year 2 of the program by integrating the performance management function of participants' managers into the 360-degree feedback, leadership development plan, and coaching process by requiring that participants share their development plans with managers and making managers responsible for meeting with their direct reports to review their plans and discuss how participants could achieve their development goals. In addition, the vice president of HR and other senior executives revised their recruitment and selection methods and criteria for managerial and executive-level positions putting greater emphasis on attracting and selecting those with strong learning motivations who would be more likely to gain the most from participating in the Leadership Institute. In short, at Regional there was a clear evolution in the horizontal alignment of the leadership and training program with the HR systems used for directors and executives, and this was identified as benefiting the participants' motivation, the level of learning achieved in the program itself, and transfer.

Vertical Fit

The other relevant concept of fit taken from the SHRM literature that has direct relevance to the potential for training and development programs to exert bottom-up influences of organization outcomes is the alignment of the HRM systems with the organization's strategy (i.e., vertical fit). Again, we see an evolution of fit along this dimension over the course of the training program as it transitioned from year 1 to year 2. Although the design of the initial program began with an organizational analysis to understand Regional's strategy and incorporate strategic priorities in the development of the leadership competency model and the learning objectives of the program, it became apparent that fit between the program and the most urgent strategic priority of strategy execution was not as strong as it needed to be. For instance, sessions on strategy execution, financial management, and process improvement were all added in year 2 to improve participants' KSAOs in these important areas to yield greater efficiencies. In addition, another evolution that helped to facilitate vertical fit was having senior executives introduce sessions by explaining how the content fit with Regional's strategic priorities. Together, these changes helped to tighten the alignment between the program and Regional's strategic needs and consequently year 2 experienced greater vertical transfer.

Differentiating HRM Systems

A final concept that is relevant from the recent SHRM literature for understanding how training and development programs may influence organizational performance is the notion of differentiating HRM systems for specific segments of the organization or types of employees. For instance, a training and development program may be well aligned with the organization's strategy (i.e., vertical fit); however, if it is not targeting the critical positions and/or individuals, then the program may have significantly less impact (Huselid & Becker, 2005). The Leadership Institute at Regional was designed for its upper to middle managers (i.e., directors) and executives (VPs and senior executive officers). With the majority of participants being directors, the focus of the program targeted their needs, which to a large extent centered on execution and implementation. In contrast, the needs of the executives, who struggled more in areas such as leading change and building a cohesive senior leadership team, were not as well incorporated in the year 1 program. Consequently, because the directors' trained skills in the areas such as leading project teams and process improvements were not being supported by a cohesive top management team at the organizational level, the impact of the program on Regional's performance was initially limited. However, this began to change as the program provided greater emphasis through the executive coaching in year 2 on working more extensively with the senior executives on change management and team building.

Another critical distinction between leadership levels at Regional in terms of translating the Leadership Institute program into performance at the organizational level was between participants (directors and executives) and their direct reports (i.e., managers and supervisors, who were not in the program). The distinction became important when it came to implementing process improvements and carrying out new projects that were outgrowths of the Leadership Institute because managers and supervisors were not trained in areas such as process improvement methodologies. To address this, classes on project management, process improvement, and financial management offered in the Leadership Institute to directors and executives provided models for Regional's HR department to develop training programs on similar topics for supervisors and managers, thereby developing Regional's organizational training systems. Regional's Leadership Institute thus began to evolve into a program with more individualized and team coaching being provided to executives on topics focused on strategic direction and managing change, for directors focused on strategy execution, whereas training programs to the next level of leaders immediately below focused on the tools and applications to support strategy execution.

Summary

The example from Regional's experience with its leadership and development program yields several insights gained from taking a multilevel view of training and development effectiveness. As illustrated in the lower-left cell in Figure 12.1, we see that identifying and accounting for different forms of HR capital, vertical fit, and horizontal fit, and understanding how training and development activities are differentiated within the organization, are useful for linking training programs through compilation influence to firm-level outcomes such as the development of human capital, social capital, and organizational capital. The example also illustrates the importance of adopting a multilevel lens to more fully comprehend the dynamic nature of the evolution training and development programs vis-à-vis the organization. The best way to see both the "top-down" (i.e., cross-level approach) and "bottom-up" (i.e., compilation approach) directional arrows is to consider how training and development programs and organizational contexts coevolve. Although the association between training and development programs and organizational development is frequently noted in the literature (e.g., Goldstein, 1993), systematic attempts at studying training and development effectiveness rarely take this approach. A multilevel perspective, and particularly one that captures the dynamic nature of the evolution of training and development programs in conjunction with other HRM systems and organizational strategy, yields greater insights than would otherwise be available.

Summary and Directions for Future Research

In this chapter, we have considered the role of training and development in organizations from a variety of perspectives. Historically, most training research has been focused at the individual level of analysis and sought to optimize "training program–individual difference" combinations in order to drive trainees' reactions, learning, and behavior change. Much has been learned from this approach, and this remains a critical focus for future inquiries. As the composition of the workforce continues to evolve, technology advances, and pressures mount to come up with flexible and cost-efficient delivery systems, the micro approach offers many insights for research and practice. For example, the question of whether generic team-work skills can be taught to individuals via self-administered CD-ROM or Web-based methods is important for organizations that are increasingly moving toward team-based designs (cf. Kirkman, Rosen, Tesluk, & Gibson, 2006; Rapp & Mathieu, 2007). This type of research offers both substantive and practical insights. Nevertheless, it appears beneficial to expand upon the typical micro focus of training investigations and to incorporate important contextual factors.

Whereas knowing whether new technologies and delivery systems can promote the development of targeted KSAO is important, it is equally valuable to know whether the larger system will motivate employees to engage in such efforts and reinforce their application back on the job. Ultimately, it matters little if the optimal training design and delivery system are identified if employees are not motivated to learn and to use the material. In effect, we submit that the greatest insights from the micro approach will come from expanding and incorporating variables from the next "bracket up" into such investigations. In short, as our illustration at Regional demonstrated, we believe that context matters (Johns, 2001). *Accordingly, for future work conducted in the microresearch approach, we recommend that investigators consider contextual influences on*

- participants' pretraining attitudes and motivation,
- the applicability of different training methods and delivery systems, and
- participants' transfer-related processes and outcomes following the program.

The relatively young macro-SHRM heritage has paid large dividends in the past 2 decades. Placing HRM systems on the same plane as other organizational initiatives and decisions has finally gotten HR a "seat at the strategic table"—something that utility analysis efforts were unable to secure in the 1980s. Although broad-brush correlational studies have shown that qualities of overall HRM systems are related significantly to firm performance, such findings have offered little insights as to "why." Subsequent investigations have yielded limited success in terms of arguing for the alignment of overall system properties and organizational strategy, or for the priority of some HRM components over others. Investigations of the latter variety have tended to favor a premium on the training function, but this may well stem from the fact that training is, to varying degrees, involved in virtually all HRM initiatives. It may well be that the macro heritage has sampled too large and diverse organizations for making such comparisons. In other words, there may well be benefit in examining the macro-SHRM themes in smaller organizations that have less differentiated HRM systems and more uniform environments. Again, our illustration at Regional demonstrates that over a relatively short period of time, it is possible to see in smaller to midsize organizations how training and development systems coevolve and become horizontally integrated with other HRM practices and systems. *Accordingly, for future work conducted in the macroresearch approach, we recommend that investigators consider sampling smaller organizations that*

- have fairly uniform HRM systems,
- pursue different organization-wide strategies, and
- compete in environments that have changing characteristics over time.

Current work in the SHRM domain is clearly moving toward more complex compilation and disaggregated approaches. As for the compilation theme, the dominant current approach is in terms of horizontal fit or HRM bundles of practices. Here the idea is that HRM components are likely to augment one another, compensate for one another, and otherwise combine in complex ways. Moreover, there is a growing move toward "drilling down" in organizations and to investigate the substantive variance in HRM systems within organizations. The logic here is that the critical HRM interface likely resides at the subsystem or job level, not at the organizational level of analysis. The case of Regional, with its emphasis on director- and executive-level positions in its leadership development program, is a good example of focusing on subsystems within the organization when examining training and development programs on organization outcomes. *Accordingly, for future work conducted following the compilation approach, we recommend*

- that work continue on efforts to index different types of HRM bundles,

- that researchers should sample organizations that have heterogeneous HRM, and

- that organizations adopt meso designs and examine training- and development-related processes at least at the subunit and organizational levels of analysis.

Conclusion

So where does all this leave us? Curiously, we believe that the micro and macro traditions are moving rapidly toward one another. Micro researchers have been "bracketing up" to consider contextual influences, such as how training works in concert with other HRM components, and what factors from the larger organizational system (or subsystem) influence the effectiveness of training. Meanwhile, macro researchers have been "bracketing down" to examine complex combinations of HRM components in terms of bundles, and to leverage within organizational variance in HRM bundles. Both approaches have reached a "middle ground" from different directions.

The middle ground is a messy, complex arena. HRM components combine in a multitude of ways that are not easily indexed or necessarily directly comparable across situations. Efforts to derive clear additive indices are likely to be suboptimal. To proffer an analogy here, achieving effective bundles of HRM practices is likely to be much more like chemistry than mechanical engineering. In mechanical engineering, one can estimate the degree to which different materials will work together, their load capacities, and the extent to which the ultimate structure will withstand various stresses and strains. In contrast, chemistry deals with complex combinations that are not necessarily decomposable to their constituent parts. Whereas some combinations of elements may be acidic (e.g., external recruiting of top talent yet compensating below industry norms), and others may be explosive (e.g., promotions based on individual achievement in a team-based organization), still others yield powerful compounds (e.g., team-based hiring, training, evaluation, and rewards). Further, the conditions under which the elements are combined have significant influences on the resulting solution. Similarly, achieving the ideal mix of HRM components to shape human capital is likely to be a complex solution that must be viewed in the context of the larger system. And, the same solution is not likely to be uniformly optimal across organizations, nor necessarily even within organizations.

This middle ground is essentially "meso" research (Kozlowski & Klein, 2000; Rousseau, 1985). It represents the crossroads of macro-SHRM and micro-I/O psychology heritages. As the macro-SHRM scholars continue to bracket down a level, whereas the micro-I/O psychologists continue to bracket up a level, we anticipate that far more attention will be focused on this middle ground. It will be messy, challenging, and, we believe, extremely fertile ground to plow. It should offer rich soil for growing the next generation of HRM research, in general, and for better understanding the role of training and development in particular. Notably, this territory may not be easily quantified in a manner sufficient for traditional statistical analyses. Accordingly, as we have tried to highlight in our example at Regional, the field could certainly benefit from some well-conducted case study and qualitative research that illuminates the compilation nature of these processes. In sum, we encourage future researchers to "go there and start digging."

References

Aragon-Sanchez, A., Barba-Aragon, I., & Sanz-Valle, R. (2003). Effects of training on business results. *International Journal of Human Resource Management*, 14(6), 956–980.

Baldwin, T. T., Magjuka, R. J., & Loher, B. T. (1991). The perils of participation: Effects of choice of training on trainee motivation and learning. *Personnel Psychology*, 44, 51–65.

Barnard, M. E., & Rodgers, R. A. (2000). How are internally oriented HRM policies related to high-performance work practices? Evidence from Singapore. *International Journal of Human Resource Management*, 11(6), 1017–1046.

Barney, J. B. (1991). Firm resources and sustained competitive advantage. *Journal of Management*, 17, 99–129.

Becker, B. E., & Huselid, M. A. (1998). High performance work systems and firm performance: A synthesis of research and managerial implications. *Research in Personnel and Human Resources Management*, 16, 53–101.

Becker, B. E., & Huselid, M. A. (2006). Strategic human resources management: Where do we go from here? *Journal of Management*, 32(6), 898–925.

Bowen, D. E., & Ostroff, C. (2004). Understanding HRM-firm performance linkages: The role of the "strength" of the HRM system. *Academy of Management Review*, 29(2), 203–221.

Camelo, C., Martin, F., Romero, P. M., & Valle, R. (2004). Human resources management in Spain: Is it possible to speak of a typical model? *International Journal of Human Resource Management*, 15(6), 935–958.

Carmeli, A., & Schaubroeck, J. (2005). How leveraging human resource capital with its competitive distinctiveness enhances the performance of commercial and public organizations. *Human Resource Management*, 44(4), 391–412.

Carnevale, A. P., Gainer, L. J., & Villet, J. (1990). *Training in America*. San Francisco: Jossey-Bass.

Chadwick, C., & Cappelli, P. (1999). Alternatives to generic strategy typologies in strategic HRM. In P. Wright, L. Dyer, J. Boudreau, & G. Milkovich (Eds.), *Strategic human resources management in the twenty-first century*. Stamford, CT: JAI.

d'Arcimoles, C.-H. (1997). Human resource policies and company performance: A quantitative approach using longitudinal data. *Organizational Studies, 18*, 857–874.

Delery, J. E. (1998). Issues of fit in strategic human resource management: Implications for research. *Human Resource Management Review, 8*(3), 289–309.

Delery, J. E., & Doty, D. H. (1996). Modes and theorizing in strategic human resource management: Tests of universalistic, contingency, and configurational performance predictions. *Academy of Management Journal*, 802–835.

Ellinger, A., Ellinger, A., Yang, B., & Howton, S. (2002). The relationship between the learning organization concept and firms' financial performance: An empirical assessment. *Human Resource Development Quarterly, 13*, 5–21.

Goldstein, I. L. (1974). *Training in organizations*. Belmont, CA: Wadsworth.

Goldstein, I. L. (2003). *Training in organizations* (3rd ed.). Pacific Grove, CA: Brooks/Cole Publishing.

Goldstein, I. L., & Ford, J. K. (2002). *Training in organizations*. Belmont, CA: Wadsworth.

Goldstein, J. (1994). *The unshackled organization: Facing the challenge of unpredictability through spontaneous reorganization*: Portland, OR: Productivity Press.

Guthrie, J. P. (2001). High-involvement work practices, turnover, and productivity: Evidence from New Zealand. *Academy of Management Journal, 44*(1), 180–190.

Hackman, J. R. (2003). Learning more by crossing levels: Evidence from airplanes, hospitals, and orchestras. *Journal of Organizational Behavior, 24*(8), 905–922.

Harel, G. H., & Tzafrir, S. S. (1999). The effect of human resource management practices on the perceptions of organizational and market performance of the firm. *Human Resource Management, 38*(3), 185–199.

Hatch, N. W., & Dyer, J. H. (2004). Human capital and learning as a source of sustainable competitive advantage. *Strategic Management Journal, 25*(12), 1155–1178.

Hicks, W. D., & Klimoski, R. J. (1987). Entry into training programs and its effects on training outcomes: A field experiment. *Academy of Management Journal, 30*, 542–552.

Hitt, M. A., Beierman, L., Shimizu, K., & Kochhar, R. (2001). Direct and moderating effects of human capital on the strategy and performance in professional service firms. *Academy of Management Journal, 44*, 13–28.

House, R., Rousseau, D. M., & Thomas-Hunt, M. (1995). The meso paradigm: A framework for the integration of micro and macro organizational behavior. *Research in Organizational Behavior, 17*, 71–114.

Huselid, M. A. (1995). The impact of human-resource management-practices on turnover, productivity, and corporate financial performance. *Academy of Management Journal, 38*(3), 635–672.

Huselid, M. A., & Becker, B. E. (2005). Improving human resources' analytical literacy lessons. In D. Ulrich, M. Losey, & S. Measinger (Eds.). *The future of human resource management: 64 thought leaders explore the critical HR issues of today and tomorrow* (p. 278). Hoboken, NJ: Wiley.

Jackson, S. E., & Schuler, R. S. (1995). Understanding human-resource management in the context of organizations and their environments. *Annual Review of Psychology, 46,* 237–264.

Johns, G. (2001). In praise of context: Commentary. *Journal of Organizational Behavior,* 22(1), 31–42.

Karoly, L. A., Panis, C. W. (2004). *The 21st Century at work: Forces shaping the future workforce and workplace in the United States,* MG-164. Santa Monica, CA: The RAND Corporation.

Kirkman, B. L., Rosen, B., Tesluk, P. E., & Gibson, C. B. (2006). Enhancing the transfer of computer-assisted training proficiency in geographically distributed teams. *Journal of Applied Psychology, 91,* 706–716.

Kirkpatrick, D. L. (1976). Evaluation. In R. D. Craig (Ed.), *Training and development handbook* (pp. 301–319). New York: McGraw-Hill.

Koch, M. J., & McGrath, R. G. (1996). Improving labor productivity: Human resource management policies do matter. *Strategic Management Journal, 17,* 335–354.

Kozlowski, S. W. J., Brown, K., Weissbein, D., Cannon-Bowers, J. A., & Salas, E. (2000). A multi-level approach to training effectiveness: Enhancing horizontal and vertical transfer. In K. Klein & S. W. J. Kozlowski (Eds.), *Multilevel theory, research and methods in organizations.* San Francisco: Jossey-Bass.

Kozlowski, S. W. J., & Klein, K. J. (2000). A multi-level approach to theory and research in organizations: Contextual, temporal, and emergent processes. In K. J. Klein & S. W. J. Kozlowski (Eds.), *Multilevel theory, research, and methods in organizations* (pp. 3–90). San Francisco: Jossey-Bass.

Kozlowski, S. W. J., & Salas, E. (1997). A multilevel organizational systems approach for the implementation and transfer of training. In J. K. Ford, S. W. J. Kozlowski, K. Kraiger, E. Salas, & M. Teachout (Eds.), *Improving training effectiveness in work organizations.* Mahwah, NJ: Lawrence Erlbaum Associates.

Lam, L., & White, L. P. (1998). Human resources orientation and corporate performance. *Human Resource Development Quarterly, 9,* 351–364.

Lee, J., & Miller, D. (1999). People matter: Commitment to employees, strategy and performance in Korean firms. *Strategic Management Journal, 20,* 579–593.

Lepak, D. P., & Snell, S. A. (1999). The human resource architecture: Toward a theory of human capital allocation and development. *Academy of Management Review, 24*(1), 31–48.

Lepak, D. P., & Snell, S. A. (2002). Examining the human resource architecture: The relationships among human capital, employment, and human resource configurations. *Journl of Management, 28*(4), 517–543.

MacDuffie, J. P. (1995). Human resource bundles and manufacturing performance: Organizational logic and flexible production systems in the world auto industry. *Industrial and labor relations review,* 197–221.

Mathieu, J. E. (1991). A cross-level nonrecursive model of the antecedents of organizational commitment and satisfaction. *Journal of Applied Psychology, 76,* 617–618.

Mathieu, J. E., & Leonard, R. L. (1987). Applying utility concepts to a training program in supervisory skills: A time based approach. *Academy of Management Journal, 30,* 316–335.

Mathieu, J. E., & Martineau, J. W. (1997). Individual and situational influences in training motivation. In J. K. Ford & Associates (Eds.), *Improving training effectiveness in work organizations* (pp. 193–222). Mahwah, NJ: Lawrence Erlbaum Associates.

Mathieu, J. E., Martineau, J. W., & Tannenbaum, S. I. (1993). Individual and situational influences on the development of self-efficacy: Implications for training effectiveness. *Personnel Psychology, 46,* 125–147.

Mathieu, J. E., Tannenbaum, S. I., & Salas, E. (1992). The influences of individual and situational characteristics on measures of training effectiveness. *Academy of Management Journal, 35,* 828–847.

Mathieu, J. E., & Taylor, S. (2007). A framework for testing meso-mediational relationships in organizational behavior. *Journal of Organizational Behavior, 28,* 141–172.

Maurer, T. J., Weiss, E. M., & Barbeite, F. G. (2003). A model of involvement in work-related learning and development activity: The effects of individual, situational, motivational, and age variables. *Journal of Applied Psychology, 88,* 707–724.

McGehee, W., & Thayer, P. W. (1961). *Training in business and industry.* New York: Wiley.

McGregor, D. (1960). *The human side of enterprise.* New York: McGraw-Hill.

Miles, R. E., & Snow, C. C. (1984). Designing strategic human resource systems. *Organizational Dynamics, 13,* 36–52.

Noe, R. A. (1986). Trainees' attributes: Neglected influences on training effectiveness. *Academy of Management Review, 11,* 736–749.

Noe, R. A., Wilk, S. L., Mullen, E. J., & Wanek, J. E. (1997). Employee development: Issues in construct definition and investigation of antecedents. In J. K. Ford & Associates (Eds.), *Improving training effectiveness in work organizations* (pp. 153–189). Mahwah, NJ: Lawrence Erlbaum Associates.

Ostroff, C. (2000). *Human resource management and firm performance.* Tempe: Arizona State University.

Ostroff, C., & Bowen, D. E. (2000). Moving HR to a higher level: HR practices and organizational effectiveness. In K. J. Klein & S. W. J. Kozlowski (Eds.), *Multilevel theory, research, and methods in organizations.* San Francisco: Jossey-Bass.

Ostroff, C., & Ford, J. K. (1989). Assessing training needs: Critical levels of analysis. In I. L. Goldstein (Ed.), *Training and development in organizations* (pp. 25–62). San Francisco: Jossey-Bass.

Paul, A. K., & Anantharaman, R. N. (2003). Impact of people management practices on organizational performance: Analysis of a causal model. *International Journal of Human Resource Management, 14*(7), 1246–1266.

Phillips, J. J. (1997). *Return on investment in training and performance improvement programs.* Woburn, MA: Butterworth-Heinemann.

Quiñones, M. A (2001). Contextual influence on training effectiveness. In M. A. Quiñones & A. Ehrenstein (Eds.), *Training for a rapidly changing workplace* (pp. 177–200). Washington, DC: APA Books.

Rapp, T. L., & Mathieu, J. E. (2007). Evaluating an individually self-administered generic teamwork skills training program across time and levels. *Small Group Research, 38*(4), 532–555.

Richard, O. C., & Johnson, N. B. (2001). Strategic human resource management effectiveness and firm performance. *International Journal of Human Resource Management, 12*(2), 299–310.

Richman-Hirsch, W. L. (2001). Posttraining interventions to enhance transfer: The moderating effects of work environments. *Human Resource Development Quarterly, 12,* 105–120.

Rouiller, J. Z., & Goldstein, I. L. (1993). The relationship between organizational transfer climates and positive transfer of training. *Human Resource Development Quarterly, 4,* 377–390.

Rousseau, D. M. (1985). Issues of level in organizational research: Multi-level and cross-level perspectives. *Research in Organizational Behavior, 7,* 1–37.

Shuler, R. S., & Jackson, S. E. (1987). Linking competitive strategies with human resources practices. *Academy of Management Executive, 1*(3), 207–220.

Smith-Jentsch, K. A., Salas, E., & Baker, D. P. (1996). Training team performance-related assertiveness. *Personnel Psychology, 49*(4), 909–936.

Tannenbaum, S. I. (2002). A strategic view of organizational training and learning. In K. Kraiger (Ed.), *Creating, implementing, and managing effective training and development* (pp. 10–52). San Francisco: Jossey-Bass.

Tesluk, P. E., Farr, J. L., Mathieu, J. E., & Vance, R. J. (1995). Generalization of employee involvement training to the job setting: Individual and situational effects. *Personnel Psychology, 48,* 607–632.

Tracey, J. B., Hinkin, T. R., Tannenbaum, S. I., & Mathieu, J. E. (2001). The influence of individual characteristics and the work environment on varying levels of training outcomes. *Human Resource Development Quarterly, 12,* 5–24.

Tracey, J. B., Tannenbaum, S. I., & Kavanagh, M. J. (1995). Applying trained skills on the job: The importance of the work environment. *Journal of Applied Psychology, 80,* 239–252.

Valle, R., Martin, F., Romero, P. M., & Dolan, S. L. (2000). Business strategy, work processes and human resource training: Are they congruent? *Journal of Organizational Behavior, 21*(3), 283–297.

Van Velsor, E., McCauley, C. D., & Moxley, R. S. (1998). Our view of leadership development. In C. D. McCauley, R. S. Moxley, & E. Van Velsor (Eds.), *Handbook of leadership development* (pp. 1–25). San Francisco: Jossey-Bass.

Walker, J. (1978). Linking human resource planning and strategic planning. *Human Resource Planning, 1,* 1–18.

Welsh, J. (2005). *Winning.* New York: HarperCollins.

Wexley, K. N., & Baldwin, T. T. (1986). Posttraining strategies for facilitating positive transfer: An empirical exploration. *Academy of Management Journal, 29,* 503–520.

Wright, P. M., & Boswell, W. R. (2002). Desegregating HRM: A review and synthesis of micro and macro human resource management research. *Journal of Management, 28*(3), 247–276.

Wright, P. M., Dunford, B. B., & Snell, S. A. (2001). Human resources and the resource based view of the firm. *Journal of Management, 27*(6), 701–721.

Wright, P. M., & Snell, S. A. (1998). Toward a unifying framework for exploring fit and flexibility in strategic human resource management. *Academy of Management Review, 23*(4), 756–772.

Youndt, M. A., Subramaniam, M., & Snell, S. A. (2004). Intellectual capital profiles: An examination of investments and returns. *Journal of Management Studies, 41*(2), 335–361.

Section 4

Reflection and an Agenda for the Future

Important aspects of our goals for this volume are to take stock of the field and to influence the shape of theory development and research by highlighting those areas and issues that are likely to yield solid conceptual advances. Thus, this concluding section of the book reflects upon progress in the field and suggests promising opportunities for future research.

In chapter 13, "Where Have We Been and Where Are We Going?" Thayer and Goldstein—two influential pioneers in training and development—provide their perspectives on the field, its progress, and its prospects. They offer their observations on the chapters in the volume, discuss the promise (and pitfalls) of this work, and suggest directions for the future.

Finally, in chapter 14 by Salas and Kozlowski, "Learning, Training, and Development in Organizations: Much Progress and a Peek Over the Horizon," the editors of the volume provide their perspective on progress, prospects, and possibilities for the future. Each chapter of the volume provides a specific research agenda to guide future research on the topic. This chapter is designed to integrate across the thematic areas and topics to provide a research agenda that is broad and integrative in its identification of profitable opportunities for future effort. Our goal is to guide theory development and research on learning, training, and development in organizations for the next decade and beyond.

13

Where Have We Been, and Where Are We Going?

Paul W. Thayer
North Carolina State University

Irwin L. Goldstein
University of Maryland

Our charge for this chapter is, in part, to see if we have a lot of new material, or "old wine in new bottles." We are expected to go beyond that, however, and our comments will focus on three general themes: ties to the past, implications for theory and conceptual developments, and implications for training in the workplace. Each of the preceding chapters has put differing stress on these themes, and some just touch on one or another.

We will do our best not to repeat what has already been said, except to the extent necessary to make our points clear. Each chapter will be dealt with individually, followed by some general conclusions and predictions. Given the number of chapters, space is limited for each one.

Chapter 1: Individual Differences, Attribute–Treatment Interactions, and Training Outcomes

The beginning of this chapter does a good job of looking back at the lack of attention to trainee attributes. Indeed, McGehee and Thayer (1961) almost completely ignored such differences in referring to man analysis (now person analysis) as part of training needs analyses. *Man analysis* referred to "determining what skills, knowledge, or attitudes an individual employee must develop if he is to perform the tasks which constitute his job in the organization" (McGehee & Thayer, p. 25). Goldstein (1974), in his first edition of *Training in Organizations*, followed the same path and did not mention this area of research. Even when attitudes were mentioned, they referred to those to be trained, not what the individual had before training.

It was not until Noe's article (1986) that predispositions such as locus of control and self-efficacy became prominent variables in training research.

From that point on, the attention to abilities, attitudes, personality traits, demographics, motivations, and cognitive capabilities resulted in a significant change in our research agenda. Indeed, Gully and Chen (chapter 1, this volume) propose a theoretical structure that encompasses just about every individual variable, training intervention, organizational condition, training outcome, and possible interaction. It provides for an aggressive research agenda that might well be pursued. If there is an omission, it has to do with in-training variables that have an effect both on learning and on transfer (Thayer & Teachout, 1995).

The materials provided in this chapter provide a fertile bed for research and conceptual development. Of particular interest is their discussion of intervening mechanisms: information-processing capacity, attentional focus and metacognitive processing, motivation and effort allocation, and emotional regulation and control.

Much more could be done with their model if researchers would broaden the scope of the criteria used so that we learn, for example, the impact of various personality traits not only on learning during training but also on transfer of behaviors and attitudes, and the ultimate impact of those on performance. Contradictory findings for some variables, it seems to us, could well be a function of the criteria used.

There is also the question of how these variables impact training. One way they can impact is as a predictor variable. Self-efficacy can predict training performance; persons who have higher self-efficacy perform better in training programs than persons with low self-efficacy. Such variables can also serve as a training intervention. Thus, Eden and Aviram (1993) found that providing self-efficacy training as a part of a regular training program resulted in persons performing better. They used behavioral role-modeling workshops to boost general self-efficacy in a group of unemployed persons, resulting in enhanced job search activities in individuals with previously low self-efficacy scores. Thus, research indicates that self-efficacy works both as a predictor and as a treatment. Most research in this area is focused on predictor effects. For example, with locus of control, the data show that internals perform better in training. Is it possible to design a training program that would enhance an individual's internal locus of control and improve training on another task? The same question could be asked for a number of the variables discussed in this chapter. If a variable is only useful as a predictor, then the only way an organization can use it is to select people to participate in training. We doubt that organizations would use variables like locus of control to select persons to participate in training. On the other hand, if the variable is useful as a part of a training program, organizations may be more likely to employ it.

Research to date leaves us less optimistic about attribute–treatment inter-actions (ATIs) than Gully and Chen. The most robust ATI finding dating back to 1969 (Cronbach & Snow, 1969) is that individuals who do not score well on a cognitive ability test performed better in treatment where they were given lots of extra explanations. High-ability students did not need that extra information and were able to pursue learning in a much more efficient manner. As noted in Gully and Chen, that effect has been replicated many times and has led to the generalization that high-ability students perform better when they have the opportunity to take responsibility and control learning, whereas low-ability students benefit more from a highly structured learning environment. However, other than this effect and a few others, the search for ATIs has been elusive. Our hunch is that failure to find interactions is a result of not just low statistical power but also the fact that any training population will involve severe restriction of range on many abilities, attitudes, demographics, and other variables. Marked differences on a variable may show some ATIs, but minor ones will go undetected. Theoretically based research may provide precision that will yield more evidence for ATIs, but the yield thus far has been small.

As to the implications for training, the material here is rich. Too few trainers pay more than lip service to individual differences in planning a training intervention. Some don't even bother to determine what trainees know of the subject matter when designing the intervention. Suggesting an assessment of attitudes toward training, the job, the transfer climate, or the like would be met with puzzlement and/or rejection. Much training would be improved if the person analysis done were consistent with the conception included in this chapter.

Despite our pessimism as to ATIs, Gully and Chen make an excellent case for Cronbach's 1957 message that we must integrate experimental and correlational approaches in our research. Most of psychology continues to ignore that message. This chapter makes it clear that training researchers and practitioners cannot.

Chapter 2: Motivation in Training and Development: A Phase Perspective

Fifty years ago, trainers acknowledged the need for motivation for learning, but did little about it. Then, as Beier and Kanfer (Chapter 2, this volume) point out, they became concerned with traits and abilities and situational factors. From there, interest and research have dealt with personal attributes, learn-ing mechanisms, and organizational variables that impinge on the training process. The authors propose a three-stage model that focuses attention on motivation for training, motivation during the training, and motivation to transfer. This provision of differing motivational variables and their interaction highlights the progress we have made in treating motivation and establishes an excellent framework for a comprehensive approach.

Although the previous chapter mentions many of the variables treated here, this one focuses on motivational issues. The detailed discussion of trainee characteristics such as openness to experience, job involvement, conscientiousness, and need for achievement, and the impact of organizational variables such as climate and framing, adds much to our understanding of these issues. Indeed, the first two chapters of this volume make clear that the reason why many of these variables predict training behavior is that they affect motivation to learn.

The discussion of motivation during learning brings a different focus on this issue. In particular, the update on goal orientation and its impact on learning is especially useful. Too many trainers ignore the different effects of goal orientation on complex versus simple tasks, and insist on mastery or performance under all conditions, nor are they aware of the impact of goal orientation on self-regulatory activities during training.

From a research standpoint, the interaction between goal orientation and task complexity and task novelty presents a host of issues we need to understand better. Increased attention to providing encouragement for metacognitive activity is important both for research and for application to training.

In the final section, the importance of special research and application with aging groups, teams, and e-learning was interesting. A major omission, however, here and in the literature is the lack of attention to the waves of migrants now occupying the workforce. Indeed, this country in general is moving toward a time when there will be no majority population. There are both cultural and language issues to be dealt with here by trainers and researchers alike.

Again, the relationship between motivation to learn and its use in promoting effective training programs as an outcome requires further analyses. As noted in the chapter, motivation for learning is one of the most common predictors of the likelihood that a person will participate in training. But the issue for the organization is how to motivate people to participate and learn. Are there effective ways to influence motivation to learn so that people will want to participate in training?

Chapter 3: Experts at Work: Principles for Developing Expertise in Organizations

The Salas and Rosen chapter (Chapter 3, this volume) is quite readable. They review the research and theory on expertise and then turn to the application of what is known through a set of principles. Our knowledge used to be limited to the difference between expert and novice chess players, and the number of trials it took to master a physical skill. The review clearly shows that we have come a long way in understanding the nature of expertise and the factors affecting its development. Although we have known for some years that experts know more about a domain, recent research has shown that experts structure that knowledge differently and at a deeper level. The roles of self-regulation of the environment, one's cognitive and affective states, and the behavioral processes of performance are much better understood today.

Research on the nature of practice, motivation, goal setting, and feedback has accelerated in the past decade or so. Dividing the list into four sections dealing with deliberate and guided practice, continuous learning, motivation, and feedback makes it easier for anyone interested to see the interrelationships of the various principles. Again, we have come a long way.

As to application, the authors' list of 17 principles should be most useful to trainers and researchers alike. Salas and Rosen also pick up and reflect on some of the same themes appearing in the preceding chapter by Beier and Kanfer. Thus, they also note the importance of motivation of the individual in desiring to develop expertise. Indeed, they refer to it as the "rage to master." It is also interesting that these data show that expertise is more a function of time spent in purposeful skill activities than of talent, thus making the motivation question even more important.

They stress that much of the expertise literature involves domains and tasks that are tightly constrained in that they involve a stable task structure and have clear boundaries to the domain. As Salas and Rosen note, this is usually not the case in organizations. Thus, they conclude their chapter with four very important research questions: How do you structure work to develop expertise, what individual characteristics result in expertise, what measure do you need to diagnose expert performance, and what organizational variables facilitate or hinder expertise development?

Researchers can use these questions as the basis for research to refine and expand on the points espoused. Trainers can use the eventual answers as heuristics in the development of their programs.

Chapter 4: An Updated Review of the Multidimensionality of Training Outcomes: New Directions for Training Evaluation Research

Ford and Kraiger (Chapter 4, this volume) review the literature for us and show that quite a few changes have ensued since the seminal paper by Kraiger, Ford, and Salas (1993). These include evaluation technologies such as mental models and metacognition, goal orientation, and attitude strength that go well beyond the emphasis in the past on declarative knowledge, attitudes toward training, and measures of skill. What is most interesting is that the 1993 paper on evaluation technologies resulted in such interesting research across a large variety of topics. Finding that team mental models correlated significantly with team performance is an example. We doubt if there would have been an exploration of such important relationships without the publication of the 1993 paper.

Failure to follow the advice of Kraiger et al. (1993) has left us with little knowledge of the effectiveness of diversity training. The desired outcomes for diversity training have been vague and ambiguous, often resulting in disappointing results. If researchers and advocates considered what they wanted to achieve in terms of cognitive, skill-based, or affective outcomes as suggested here, research might help us understand what diversity programs achieve.

The many examples of criteria will be of use to both researcher and practitioner, and will be especially valuable to the practitioner who is doing formative evaluation. In cognitive assessment, for example, illustrative research is cited involving measurement of procedural knowledge, the quality of mental models, and closeness of fit to expert mental models. We share in their concern for research on changes in metacognition as a potential learning outcome.

As to affective measures, goal orientation is now being studied both as a predictor and as an outcome of training. The fact that it can have an impact on transfer is noteworthy, and demands further research. Breaking goal orientation into three parts (mastery, performance approach, and performance avoidance) can contribute to a better understanding of this variable and permit its use in training to be more effective. Especially important are the results indicating that mastery orientation coaching results in greater transfer and greater use of strategies taught in training.

The relationship of goal orientation to other personal attributes certainly warrants attention, as urged by the authors. Along the same line, the reexamination of feedback interventions (FIs) by Kluger and DeNisi (1996) and Shute (2007) points to the need for research on the effects of various FIs on mastery, performance approach, and performance avoidance orientations. Such work might illuminate a number of inconsistencies as FIs in the literature.

We join Ford and Kraiger in urging work assessing attitude strength as well as direction. The inconsistent relationships between attitudes and behaviors may well be a function of the failure to measure attitude strength. Assessing explicit and implicit attitudes in training, both as predictors and as criteria, seems essential.

Their proposals for research make a great deal of sense to us. Again, we suspect that many of the inconsistent relationships found in training research are a function of using different measures in our evaluation efforts. To the extent possible, criteria in each of the realms described in this chapter should be used in every study of training effectiveness. Sponsors will resist, and considerable ingenuity will be required to devise efficient as well as effective measures so the study does not collapse of its own weight. Practitioners may find several of the criteria described as useful in formative evaluation.

Chapter 5: Cognitive Science-Based Principles for the Design and Delivery of Training

The first Frontiers Series volumes exploring training appeared 20 years ago (e.g., Goldstein, 1989). In that volume, Howell and Cooke (1989) introduced major concepts in cognitive psychology to those interested in training. In that volume, Goldstein (1989) noted that many organizational psychologists had never heard of terms like "advanced organizers," but he speculated that this type of construct was likely to have much more of an impact on training than time-honored behavioral principles such as schedules of reinforcement. In their article, Howell and Cooke introduced the somewhat counterintuitive idea that shifting workplace operations to machines increases rather than decreases the cognitive demands for human beings; routine tasks are performed by machines, and the human is left to cope with the more unpredictable and demanding tasks.

Cooke and Fiore's chapter (Chapter 5, this volume) continues a discussion of these themes. They first note that machines have now become increasingly involved in activities that require complex cognitive thought. These machines have now replaced many activities of service workers such as those of travel agents and telephone operators. But the result is not just off-loading tasks to the machine but also an increased cognitive complexity for the human being. As they note, rarely are persons working alone in a back room, but rather their performance is complexly intertwined with others'. This has enormous implications for training systems in teaching the human how to perform these complex cognitive tasks. Cooke and Fiore track the progress in our understanding of cognitive processes quite nicely, so a review by us is unnecessary.

The description of need for and the various techniques for cognitive task analysis is comprehensive and will be useful to the novice. It is important to note that these systems were in their infancy in 1989, when the previous Frontiers Series volume was published. Cooke and Fiore note the increasing body of research on this topic and correctly point out that we have a long way to go in learning how to apply the results of such analyses.

We were intrigued by their concept of in vitro research used to describe laboratory studies on standardized tasks. They compare this to in vivo research, or research in natural contexts, and note that this permits the capture of contextual factors. Much of the research described in this book makes it clear that we are still mainly in the in vitro stage. Given that many of these concepts did not even exist for the organizational psychologist 20 years ago, this is to be expected. We share their pleasure in the increasing coordinated scientific efforts that cross traditional boundaries and disciplines. The section on future directions highlights these multidisciplinary approaches to training. Many disciplines are becoming involved in complex training, from psychologists of various kinds, to computer scientists, to electronic game creators, and others. There is another nod toward ATI as it relates to working memory. More research is essential here. The issue of fidelity still needs much work if we are to utilize it efficiently in the design of training and development.

Embedding assessments, as illustrated by the discussion of team training, is an exciting development. There have been examples from cashier training and similar individual tasks in the past, but utilization with teams can contribute to both an understanding of the cognitive processes and the factors affecting them.

We suspect that many trainers do not have a good grasp of the material discussed here. Cognition for some involves an understanding—or misunderstanding—of left- and right-brain functions. We need to turn our attention to training our trainers in cognitive science and application, or we will have a decade or two of fads and fashions detrimental to progress in this area.

Chapter 6: Research-Based Solutions to Three Problems in Web-Based Training

Mayer's chapter (Chapter 6, this volume) focuses on Web-based training, an increasingly used vehicle for instruction. He adds to the previous chapter by Cooke and Fiore by noting the severe limits of cognitive capacity. Mayer points out that when cognitive capacity must be devoted to extraneous processing, the learner has little remaining capacity to learn, negatively affecting performance on retention and transfer tests. Mayer disagrees with educational psychologists as to the utility of testing whether one medium is better than another. On the contrary, he believes the goal of instructional technology should be to determine what aspects of instructional support favor what kinds of learning for what kinds of learners. The same point has been made dozens of times over the last 40 years concerning devices such as programmed instruction, computer-assisted instruction, and television and film instruction. Goldstein and Ford (2002) shared this concern and extended it to many of the new devices, including distance learning, intelligent tutoring systems, and virtual reality systems.

Mayer's chapter presents some basic cognitive principles in clear language and shows how research contributes both to cognitive theory and to development of efficient and effective training programs. An example is the finding that in 10 out of 10 experimental tests, students learned better from Web-based training when material was presented in conversational style rather than formal style. The approach should be appealing to researcher and practitioner alike. By starting with design problems, Mayer focuses the attention of practitioners on the relevance of theory to the solution of those problems.

Mayer describes solutions to the problem of material that is insensitive to the learner's cognitive system, and shows how cognitive limitations make learning from elaborate presentations difficult. Reducing extraneous processing as a theoretical notion makes sense to the nonpsychologist designer when solutions are described: weeding, decaptioning, signaling, aligning words and pictures, and synchronizing animation and narration.

Similarly, difficult or complex material puts heavy demands on working memory. Those can be reduced through segmenting, pretraining, and off-loading. Promoting generative processes through personalizing and articulating reduces the problems of unfriendly material.

Thus, this chapter is useful to both theory and practice. We agree with Mayer that direct measures of cognitive overload would help theoretical development. His challenge of providing programs that are sensitive to the organizational culture, provide motivation throughout, add social presence, and promote metacognitive strategies is both daunting and important. An especially important point that Mayer makes is noting that much of the work thus far accomplished is in a well-controlled environment. Similar to the plea by Cooke and Fiore for in vivo research, he urges future research on longer term training in authentic environments.

Chapter 7: Synthetic Learning Environments: On Developing a Science of Simulation, Games, and Virtual Worlds for Training

Cannon-Bowers and Bowers (Chapter 7, this volume) note the growing use of simulations, games and virtual worlds, and synthetic learning environments (SLEs), and encourage their use if based upon sound learning principles. This reemphasizes an important point made in both of the previous chapters. Building upon past systems, they describe six phases of instruction to be considered in designing instruction and in developing a research program. These phases incorporate elaborating goals, triggering learning strategies and motivation, providing declarative knowledge, providing practice, monitoring performance, diagnosing mastery and deficiencies, and providing feedback and remediation.

Simulations and these types of devices have a long history (see Goldstein & Ford, 2002). Cannon-Bowers and Bowers make the point that it is not the physical characteristics of the device but the underlying structure so that activates cognitive processes. In the world of simulators, this concept has for many years been known as *psychological fidelity*. Actually, most of the advantages of SLEs are very similar to those discussed for simulators, and researchers in the area of SLEs would probably benefit from a review of that work. What is different in this chapter is that the authors focus carefully on the types of factors that exploit the motivational possibilities of these devices while still ensuring that they provide effective training.

Although some of this overlaps with previous chapters, the application to SLEs presents a unique set of problems and issues. For example, they refer to how SLE gaming features such as competition and scorekeeping may affect goal orientation and learning, and call for research in this area. The entire chapter touches on each phase and points to both theoretical and practical issues in the use of SLEs in training.

Given the increased use of SLEs and the fact that almost everyone is exposed to and uses some form of technology, this chapter is important. The next generation, as has been noted in this volume, has been conditioned to elaborate games and interactive video experiences. Many will expect flashy training materials. Adherence to the points made here and in the previous chapter will do much to reduce the development of attractive but inefficient SLEs.

Chapter 8: Toward a Theory of Learner-Centered Training Design: An Integrative Framework of Active Learning

Bell and Kozlowski (Chapter 8, this volume) do a fine job of describing the trend toward replacing formal classroom training with more informal job-embedded training. It was startling to learn that 58% of all training days at IBM were conducted through e-learning mainly because of the ability to use such devices for just-in-time training anyplace or anytime. As these authors note, employee control of the processes makes investigating a learning-centered approach very important.

Bell and Kozlowski lay out a clear picture of action learning, stressing the provision of learner control and conceiving learning as an inductive process. It seems ironic that such material is presented in a passive mode, a book chapter. Nevertheless, we found the description of the adaptive learning system (ALS) and action learning models to be sufficiently engaging as to involve us in reacting to their components.

The teasing out of key elements of mastery training, for example, stimulated considerable interest. Differentiating goal frame, goal content, and goal proximity seems obvious, but only after the authors have pointed it out to you and have shown their differential effects and interactions.

The integration provided by their active learning model is comprehensive, and provides a different view than that presented in earlier chapters. Here, however, there is greater stress on self-regulation: cognitive, motivational, and emotional. Mechanisms discussed for enhancing such self-regulation are both old and new. Metacognition has been around for a long time, but we know more about building such skills than we did before.

Although some of the material presented here is repetitive of earlier chapters, such overlap is unavoidable. Fortunately, the treatment differs in that previous research and constructs are integrated into the models presented. We are still uneasy about the repeated stress on ATI, but it may be that the new models and new variables being introduced here and in other chapters will show that ATI is, in fact, a useful rubric. Research will tell.

The research agenda laid out is aggressive and promising. It has both theoretical and practical significance. We especially resonate to the point that considerable research has shown that active learning interventions such as mastery training are useful in promoting positive learning outcomes. As the authors note, we are still not sure how these interventions work, either as to the process mechanisms through which they operate, or for whom they operate best. As noted earlier, this is a common theme in many of these chapters and in the history of training techniques generally. We should also note that with the huge number of such training interventions being introduced, organizations should pay attention to Mayer's concerns over excessive cognitive demands.

Chapter 9: Informal Learning and Development in Organizations

Tannenbaum, Beard, McNall, and Salas had one of the toughest jobs in writing their chapter (Chapter 9, this volume). There is a great deal of talk, but relatively little research or systematic thinking, about informal learning.

Although everyone acknowledges the importance of informal learning and its existence in organizations, little systematic work has been done to define it , build theories about it, or do research on it. Some of the past history on this issue reflects the difficulties. The authors believe there are four essential characteristics of informal learning: self-guidance and self-direction, intent to learn, action beyond reading or listening, and occurrence outside a formal training setting. For learning to occur, there must be intent, action, feedback, and reflection. The description of intent to learn in informal learning is not entirely clear, as the authors state that a supervisor can help define a learning goal, but the learning process must be learner driven. Later they state that intent may occur as the result of advice or coaching. How does one separate out the motivation to learn stemming from a supervisor's "suggestion," and that stemming from a coach? We see the point being made, but the operations to be used in research are not clear in this discussion.

The authors rightfully point to the difficulty of doing research on informal learning because of a lack of a set of learning objectives, making it very hard to select dependent measures to assess the effectiveness of informal learning. Given that, one might ask whether informal learning is really part of training. Training is typically regarded as an activity that contributes to goals of the organization. If so, some informal learning fits under training. Learning to "beat the system," however, may be learned informally, but would not fit under training. In our view, the authors might consider an added restriction on their treatment of informal learning by aligning a learner's goals with those of the organization.

The authors point out that newcomers learn a lot from observation, but what they observe is not under anyone's control. Thus, they may observe and learn things that are not in the best interest of the organization. Is this type of informal learning training? Our guess is that the organization would not want to call it that. On the other hand, newcomer socialization has both formal and informal aspects to it. Thus, many companies offer orientation programs that address many issues such as organizational goals and values, politics, and language. Chao, O'Leary-Kelly, Wolf, Klein, and Gardner (1994), in a study of engineers, managers, and professionals, found that individuals with a stronger understanding of the organizational goals, value, and history showed the strongest relationship to outcomes such as career involvement, job satisfaction, and personal income. This type of research is needed in order to understand what the employee gains from informal as well as formal programs.

We also wonder whether the processes described to enhance informal learning are really different from those involved in formal learning. The processes may occur differently, but are they different? Our attention might best be turned to the ways in which they occur in each case.

In brief, the authors had a most difficult task, and made a good start on defining the field. It might be easier if the issue were structured within the context of training.

Chapter 10: "Learning" a Living: Continuous Learning for Survival in Today's Talent Market

In Chapter 10 (this volume), Molloy and Noe take an entirely different approach to the subject of training. They note that the employer–employee relationship has changed from lifelong partnerships to one of continuous churning in the marketplace. They speculate that with the advent of a knowledge-based economy, a global environment, and the start of the digital age, the demand for talent will be anything but stable. Thus, an individual's survival will depend on his or her participation in continuous learning. These authors are concerned with the individual and his or her development, regardless of the fit with organizational goals or objectives. The concern is with individual adaptation to changing requirements of the job, environment, or personal interests. Of course, anything we learn about continuous learning and its enhancement can be utilized by organizations to further their objectives, but this chapter does not focus on that. The authors do note that several countries, including Germany, have government policies supporting continuous learning. It is also the case, however, that the birth rate in such countries is so low that national policy almost requires training support to be able to meet national competitiveness goals. Many believe that the United States will face similar problems in its future.

Continuous learning involves enhancing knowledge, skills, and abilities (KSAs) on a planned basis or by taking advantage of fortuitous events to meet talent demands of the marketplace and/or changes in individual interests. Especially interesting is the material on individuals capitalizing on chance, uncontrollable events and their significant impact on career development and behavior. The model presented includes many of the variables covered in other models in this book, but distinguishes among three types of continuous learning: adaptive, generative, and transformative. The first two would be of special interest to organizations, but the third might also be of interest to new or drastically changing ones. Outcomes may be either objective gains or individual, subjective feelings or attitudes.

As indicated by Molloy and Noe, their model differs from others in several different ways: emphasis on a talent market rather than organizational contexts, inclusion of chance events, use of various kinds of continuous learning and factors affecting participation, as well as influences on learning outcomes. The last issue is especially noteworthy in that it allows for negative as well as positive outcomes, depending on environmental or technological factors that create discontinuous changes in the job market. A good example of this is the dot-com bust, which resulted in computer science programs enrolling less than half the previous number of students because the job market became so unstable.

The model is quite comprehensive and provides a rich background for research in each of the areas mentioned above. The future research section was made especially valuable because the authors identified data sets from the National Longitudinal Survey of Youth, which could be used to explore the research questions presented. Insights gained here may well affect models portrayed in other chapters.

Chapter 11: Building an Infrastructure for Organizational Learning: A Multilevel Approach

Kozlowski, Chao, and Jensen (Chapter 11, this volume) rightly point out the diffuse and confusing nature of prior treatments of organizational learning. The typical student of training and individual learning may find this chapter more difficult to apprehend because of the numerous organizational concepts introduced.

The authors make comprehension easier, however, by taking us through a number of informal learning processes, such as newcomer socialization. The shaping of the newcomer's attitudes and behaviors is complemented by the impact the newcomer may have on the organization and its members. Similarly, team learning is described as a complex process. The need for research on these processes so that they may work more efficiently is made clear.

In the next section of this chapter, there is considerable discussion of prompting individual and team learning. Although this is repetitive of previous chapters, the primary contribution is to put the material in a different context.

The discussion, on the other hand, of different forms of emergence—composition versus compilation—should have a marked effect on the thinking of the typical trainer. The examples of congruence of the infrastructure with organizational goals are made clear, and its importance emphasized. The "multilevel" aspects of the authors' thinking are clearest in this section.

The authors lay out a broad research program. In conclusion, the authors note the confusing nature of the concept of organizational learning and hope that their research agenda based on a multilevel framework might be helpful in further defining the issues. We wish them considerable success, and we hope that this multilevel analysis for organizational learning achieves the same success as the Kraiger et al. (1993) multilevel approach for evaluation of training outcomes.

Chapter 12: A MultiLevel Perspective on Training and Development Effectiveness

Upon reading the title of this chapter (Chapter 12, this volume), we originally expected a treatment of various means of measuring training and development effectiveness at various levels of the organization. Instead, we were treated to a discussion of the need for such measurement.

Its strength, however, and its attraction to practitioners will be in the detailed example given of a leadership development program in a regional hospital. The authors bring alive concepts such as climate, top-down influences, and horizontal fit. The illustration is clear and should be a reminder to all of us that training systems do not exist in a vacuum and there are many variables besides the strength of the training program that determine success. It is, of course, the reason that many authors point to the need for an organizational analysis as part of the needs assessment process. In the example, these authors provide clear support for that need.

Commentary

Reading these 12 chapters has been an interesting and educational experience. We were unaware of the progress being made in some areas, and were impressed by how far we have come in training and development over the past 15 years or so. There is very little in the way of old wine in new bottles here, but there is some.

More important is the fact that theory and research have advanced so markedly in that time period. Several theories are advanced here, and the wealth of research described is impressive. Indeed, training and development as a science and practice have come of age.

On the other hand, it is clear that there is considerable overlap in terms of the chapters, both in terms of theoretical thinking and in citation of research. Given that, one of the most useful things that these scholars could do is to work toward an integrative theory that pulls all these ideas together. Compare, for example, the models discussed in Chapters 1, 3, 6, 8, 10, and 11. Even though the terms used may be different, there are strong similarities among them. Yes, some work at more than one level, some emphasize individual differences more, some are more concerned with training technology, and so on. Wouldn't it be useful to see if a single integrated model could be developed as a guide to research and theory? Given the richness *within* such a model, there would be ample opportunity for pursuit of individual research interests, and application of findings. Put those chapter figures side by side, and see if it wouldn't make some sense to do that. We don't think we would be risking progress by such a step.

At the same time, we believe our understanding of the impact of the several variables under study is inhibited by the failure to use multiple criteria as described in Kraiger et al. (1993). Several authors mentioned concern with the inconsistencies in findings and suggested that the use of different criteria might account for different findings across studies. Until we consistently follow Kraiger et al.'s advice, we will continue to wonder why the differences, and worse, complicate our models because of differences that may not exist.

We also agree with the plea made by Cooke and Fiore for more in vivo research to permit us to capture contextual factors. Mayer's point that much of his work is thus far accomplished in a well-controlled environment adds to that view. We continue to be intrigued by the idea introduced to us by Howell and Cooke (1989) that as machines take over more and more duties, the human operator ends up in more and more complex situations with cognitive overload. Mayer reminded us that designers can reduce or prevent cognitive overload as they design training programs. We suspect that many of the present e-learning and Web-based learning modules suffer from this problem, resulting in less effective training efforts. Research on this issue is badly needed.

Each set of authors has done an excellent job of laying out a research agenda for the area covered. We will not attempt to gild their lilies.

As to learning styles, we have been unimpressed with the research stemming from Kolb's work, and with the way the concept has been applied. Some speak of styles as if different principles of learning applied depending on the individual's learning style. Given that style is a concept involving preferences, we doubt that is the case and suspect all authors in this volume would agree. If there is any use for this construct as a measure of individual differences, we think it might come from research underway using a measure such as that developed by Towler and Dipboye (2003).

As these authors and current readers continue research and application of the ideas in this book, we hope they will also follow the work stemming from the Association for Psychological Science initiative, Life Long Learning at Work and at Home (L3; Association for Psychological Science, 2008). This effort, chaired by Diane Halpern, Art Graesser, and Milt Hakel, brings researchers from many fields to focus on what we know about learning in all our endeavors. For more information, go to http://psyc.memphis.edu/learning/.

Finally, we believe that training is the ideal research bed for the achievement of Cronbach's (1957) dream. It is clear that we must be aware of the role of individual differences, and of the need to develop lawful relationships among variables. We cannot do one and ignore the other. So, let us pursue Cronbach's vision and unite the two disciplines of psychology, at least in our part of it.

References

Association for Psychological Science. (2008). *Life long learning at work and at home.* Retrieved January 22, 2009, from http://psyc.memphis.edu/learning/.

Chao, G., O'Leary-Kelly, A. M., Wolf, S., Klein, H. J., & Gardner, P. D. (1994). Organizational socialization: Its content and consequences. *Journal of Applied Psychology, 79*, 730–746.

Cronbach, L. J. (1957). The two disciplines of scientific psychology. *American Psychologist, 12*, 671–684.

Cronbach, L. J., & Snow, R. E. (1969). *Individual differences in learning ability as a function of instructional variables.* Final report, School of Education, Stanford University (Contract OEC-4-6001269-1217). Palo Alto, CA: U.S. Office of Education.

Eden, D., & Aviram, A. (1993). Self-efficacy training to speed reemployment: Helping people help themselves. *Journal of Applied Psychology, 78*, 353–360.

Goldstein, I. L. (1974). *Training: Program development and evaluation.* Monterey, CA: Brooks/Cole.

Goldstein, I. L. (Ed.). (1989). *Training and development in organizations.* San Francisco: Jossey-Bass.

Goldstein, I. L., & Ford, J. K. (2002). *Training in organizations.* Belmont, CA: Wadsworth.

Howell, W. C., & Cooke, N. J. (1989). Training the human information processor: A review of cognitive models. In I. L. Goldstein (Ed.), *Training and development in organizations* (pp. 121–182). San Francisco: Jossey-Bass.

Kluger, A., & DeNisi, A. (1996). The effects of feedback interventions on performance: A historical review, a meta-analysis, and a preliminary intervention theory. *Psychological Bulletin, 119*, 254–284.

Kraiger, K., Ford, J. K., & Salas, E. (1993). Application of cognitive, skill-based, and affective theories of learning outcomes to new methods of evaluation. *Journal of Applied Psychology, 78,* 311–328.

McGehee, W., & Thayer, P. W. (1961). *Training in business and industry.* New York: John Wiley.

Noe, R. A. (1986). Trainee attributes and attitudes: Neglected influences on training, effectiveness. *Academy of Management Review, 4,* 736–749.

Shute, V. J. (2007). Focus on formative feedback. *ETS RR -07-11.*

Thayer, P. W., & Teachout, M. S. (1995). *A climate for transfer model.* AL/HR-TP-1995-00, TX: Armstrong Laboratory, Brooks AFB.

Towler, E. J., & Dipboye, R. L. (2003). Development of a learning style orientation measure. *Organizational Research Methods, 6,* 216–235.

14

Learning, Training, and Development in Organizations: Much Progress and a Peek Over the Horizon

Eduardo Salas
University of Central Florida

Steve W. J. Kozlowski
Michigan State University

Organizations have changed dramatically over the last 2 decades as the pace of change has increased and the world has grown smaller. Computer technology penetrates all facets of the workplace. Connectivity afforded by the Internet provides access to information, suppliers, and customers for firms large and small worldwide. Organizations compete globally in an often virtual and multicultural world. The demands created by these changes have pressured organizations to build their human capital— broad, deep, and flexible knowledge and skills—to survive and thrive in this rapidly changing world.

The press to develop human capital has pushed training to the forefront as the means to enhance learning and development in organizations. Training in organizations has evolved at a rapid pace to meet the demands for broad, deep, and flexible skills. There is increased emphasis for fostering continuous learning, just-in-time and on-demand learning applications, optimization of simulation and gaming tools, training team-based and adaptive competencies, and development of blended learning strategies. These demands have stimulated an explosion of research, and significant theoretical and practical advances for training in organizations. Organizations rely more on learning, training, and development initiatives to build human capital and to accomplish competitive goals.

Industrial and organizational psychologists have been at the forefront of the training research explosion and progress in the development of effective applications that has occurred since 1990 (Salas & Cannon-Bowers, 2001). In particular, the first SIOP Organizational Frontiers book on training (Goldstein, 1989) heralded a renaissance in the advancement of psychological theory relevant to the design, delivery, and implementation of training. In many ways, that volume was a touchstone that stimulated and shaped training research conducted during the 1990s and the first part of this decade that has significantly advanced our understanding of the processes of learning and skill acquisition, and the means to stimulate and shape it effectively through training.

The progress that has occurred in the 2 decades since the publication of Goldstein (1989) is well documented in the two *Annual Review of Psychology* articles that showcase many advances in the area (Salas & Cannon-Bowers, 2001; Tannenbaum & Yukl, 1992). These reviews outline several advances in training research, but key ones include (a) the expansion of the criterion domain beyond the classic Kirkpatrick (1957) training criteria to consider multidimensional cognitive, affective-motivational, and behavioral outcomes; (b) the shift from research centered on training evaluation (i.e., did the training work?) to research focused on training effectiveness (i.e., how and why did the training work?); (c) recognition of the importance of pretraining (e.g., motivation to attend) as well as posttraining influences (e.g., supervisory support); (d) legitimization of technology (e.g., mobile tools and simulation) to facilitate learning, and commensurate with the above; and (e) incorporation of theories of cognition, learning, motivation, and performance in an effort to better understand how to optimize the design, delivery, evaluation, and transfer of training. Much had been learned about what matters, what works, and—importantly—why it works. There has been solid theoretical progress; much more sophisticated research; better and more robust studies in context; and actionable, practical, and relevant findings. Yet, although there have been many advances in the science of learning, more progress is needed.

This volume builds on those advances, proposing new areas of theoretical development and highlighting exciting research extensions to be pursued for the next decade and beyond. Our purpose in this concluding chapter is twofold. First, we discuss three theory and research themes that encompass the chapters comprising this book, themes that provide a near-term agenda for research covering the decade ahead. Each chapter provides a comprehensive research agenda, so our intent is not to replicate what the chapter authors have already done so well, but rather to highlight the interplay and integration inherent across chapters with respect to these key themes. Our first purpose is to "guide the science" by offering a map with waypoints to set the research direction for the near term. Second, although peering into the future is often a bit risky, we want to go beyond the chapters to offer a vision of where we think theory and research should evolve in the longer term. We want to "push the envelope of the science"—going beyond what the field knows now and peering toward those things we should explore that are over the horizon. We hope that the observations and conjectures we offer in this chapter motivate novel, deeper, and richer thinking and research in the next decade and beyond. We want to keep the momentum of advances in training research and practice going by providing some direction on where we think it should go next and into the more distal future. Time will tell.

Theory and Research Themes

The chapters in this book encompass three key themes that we believe should drive research on learning, training, and development in organizations: (a) person and process, (b) design and delivery, and (c) context, levels, and time. The themes have different foci, but they are entwined and thread throughout the chapters in this volume. We highlight the themes, make connections to research issues inherent in the chapters in this volume, and explore the interplay among the chapters and themes.

Person and Process

The first key theme that emerges in this volume is the central role of the person—the trainee—and the learning and motivational processes that are inherent in the training enterprise. All training starts (or should start) by considering who the trainee is, that is, by identifying the individual characteristics, motivations, and skills the trainee brings to training. These considerations become the basis for how to design and deliver training—that is, how to shape the processes of learning and motivation. Researchers have suggested that we need to move beyond a narrow examination of cognition ability and job knowledge and focus on other important and enduring trainee characteristics. This means gaining a better understanding of a broad array of diverse individual differences and their unique, combined, synergistic, and countervailing effects on training outcomes (see Gully & Chen, this volume). In addition, in their focus on aptitude–treatment interactions (ATIs), Gully and Chen push for more research to examine how individual differences interact with instructional interventions and the situational context to influence both proximal (learning) and distal (transfer) training outcomes. Although the search for ATIs has been elusive, we believe there are reasons for optimism.

Traditional training has generally taken a "one-size-fits-all" approach, such that the same training intervention is provided to everyone. Recent research shows that this may not be the best approach (Bell & Kozlowski, this volume, 2002, 2008; Cannon-Bowers & Bowers, this volume; Salas & Cannon-Bowers, 2001; Salas, Wilson, Priest, & Guthrie, 2006). That is, more flexible, adjustable, and individualized strategies designed to fit the trainee may be needed in the future. We are much more optimistic than our commentators (Thayer & Goldstein, this volume) on the potential for tailoring and adapting training to better fit the individual difference characteristics, preferences, and progress of learners. We know that individual differences like goal orientation influence how learners approach training, and thus can interact with instructional interventions (Bell & Kozlowski, 2008; Gully & Chen, this volume). We know that cognitive ability and metacognitive skills allow learners to benefit from more open and self-directed learning environments (Bell & Kozlowski, 2008; Gully & Chen, this volume). The more we learn about skill acquisition, the development of expertise, and how to model these processes, the better we will be able to create "adaptive" (Bell & Kozlowski, 2002) and "intelligent" training systems (Salas & Rosen, this volume). Research on intelligent tutoring, for example, is paving the way for this to be a reality in the next decade or so. In the meantime, there are effective ways for training to adapt to fit the progress of individual trainees. This is not an easy undertaking, but our science needs to develop the evidence and provide answers.

To better understand the effects of individual differences and ATIs, we must have a deeper understanding of learning and motivational processes (Beier & Kanfer, this volume; Colquitt, LePine, & Noe, 2000), themes that also arise in Mayer's chapter (this volume) on Web-based training, Cannon-Bowers and Bowers' chapter (this volume) on synthetic learning environments (SLEs), and Bell and Kozlowski's chapter (this volume) on active learning. Beier and Kanfer present a three-stage metamodel of motivation that links motivation to learning, participating, and transferring the skills to the work setting. Moreover, Beier and Kanfer highlight four targets for motivational research that center on an examination of age effects (differences in motivational processes for older and younger workers), e-learning (differences between traditional training and e-learning in terms of trainee motivational processes and contextual supports), emotion (in terms of the role of emotion in motivation during training and transfer), and teams (in terms of how the team context influences motivation during training and how the team setting influences horizontal and vertical transfer).

What is critical is to understand that motivation is intimately entwined in the processes of learning, skill acquisition, and expertise development. This means we must develop a detailed and comprehensive template to guide how trainees evolve from novice to expert and how we can model that process. Salas and Rosen (this volume) outline principles derived from the expertise literature on how to develop expert performance. They provide testable principles that we must examine, compile evidence for, and validate. For research, Salas and Rosen make recommendations centering on individual differences, how to structure experience, the role of the organizational context, and the need for metrics.

Finally, training research cannot possibly elaborate the effects of individual differences, examine ATIs, model learning and motivation, or map the development of expertise without the continued development and elaboration of constructs and validated measures that capture the processes and outcomes of learning. The monograph by Kraiger, Ford, and Salas (1993) opened up training research to consider a broader array of multidimensional—cognitive, affective, and behavioral—outcomes. That stimulated the development of more expansive theoretical models of training, motivation, and learning, *and* that theoretical development spurred a shift from research on training evaluation (did training work?) to research on training effectiveness (why *and* how did training work?). In looking back and forward, Ford, Kraiger, and Merritt (this volume) highlight how far the field has come, link to the themes of person and process, and offer up several new directions to better elaborate learning (e.g., measuring skill development and changes in motivation), cognitive outcomes (e.g., linking declarative and procedural knowledge, clarifying mental model operationalization, and measuring metacognitive processes), and affective outcomes (e.g., clarifying linkages among goal orientation traits, states, and learning; and examining explicit and implicit attitudes vis-à-vis training).

The person—the trainee and his or her characteristics—influences the way that training will be experienced, what will be salient, and how the processes of learning and motivation will unfold. Here, we centered our discussion on person and process, because these considerations need to drive training design and delivery. These considerations go hand in hand, and more attention is needed to this interaction. The next frontier in person- and process-oriented training research is to answer the following set of questions:

1. What are the individual characteristics of highly motivated trainees? What is the profile, or what markers designate the "perfect" learner? What are the individual differences that matter most in skill acquisition, and why?

2. What are the key learning and motivational process pathways by which learning occurs? What is the role of individual differences in prompting these process pathways?

3. Can robust and dynamic diagnostic measures be developed to capture and decompose learning and motivational processes and training outcomes? Can intelligent and adaptive systems be developed to diagnose, guide, and augment complex skill acquisition? How can we promote learning, transfer, and adaptation?

Design and Delivery

The second theme we extracted from the aforementioned chapters is designing directed "experiences" that take advantage of what we know about trainee characteristics and motivational processes to maximize learning and transfer. There are many research-based principles for designing robust and effective instructional strategies (Bell & Kozlowski, this volume; Cannon-Bowers & Bowers, this volume; Cooke & Fiore, this volume; Mayer, this volume). How does one translate these principles and apply them to design effective learning "experiences"? How can learning experiences be shaped by, fit to, and augmented by technology using computers, the Internet, and games? How can learner-centered experiences be created that selectively stimulate metacognition, self-regulation, and appropriate learning and motivational pathways? How can we incorporate and integrate trainee characteristics into the instructional design space? The chapters in this volume and recent research begin to shed light on what we know, where the gaps are, and where research needs to go to enhance training design and delivery.

We can extend our (now admittedly) limited ability to tailor training to learner individual differences (Bell & Kozlowski, 2008) and adapt it to their progress (Bell & Kozlowski, 2002) by better encompassing consideration of learner cognitive capabilities, mechanisms, and limitations (see Cooke & Fiore, this volume; Mayer, this volume). Cooke and Fiore update the seminal chapter on cognitive influences by Howell and Cooke (1989) published in the Goldstein (1989) volume. The prior chapter was instrumental in stimulating a "cognitive revolution" in training research by industrial and organizational psychologists. In this new, updated chapter, Cooke and Fiore describe many multidisciplinary approaches where cognitive principles apply to training design and delivery, and their discussion foreshadows several themes that recur throughout this section: the need to develop tools for tracking and diagnosing cognition during training; integrating individual differences, cognitive processes, and technology-based training design; embedding training in work technology and enhancing transfer; and extending our knowledge base to the team level.

This must be complemented by enhancing our ability to deliver distributed and authentic synthetic experiences (see Cannon-Bowers & Bowers, this volume; Mayer, this volume) that engage the learner. Mayer presents a focused set of research-based principles to enhance the design of Web-based training. His research evidence is organized around reducing the negative effects of three primary problems encountered by the learner—insensitivity, difficulty, and unfriendliness—via a set of design techniques that ameliorate the problems. Mayer illustrates how principles from cognitive theory can improve the design process. His chapter clearly illustrates that the technology does not cause learning, but rather it is appropriate, evidence-based instructional design delivered via technology that fosters learning. Although Mayer's principles are specific to Web-based instruction, the basic approach and concepts are likely applicable to other forms of technology-based instruction as well.

Simulation-based training now offers new ways of creating an environment in which the development of expertise can be accelerated (Salas et al., 2006). Simulation allows us to improve our understanding of the way that experiences created by training interventions stimulate cognitive, motivational, and affective process pathways and the way learner characteristics interact with those interventions in the enactment of the learning experience (Bell, Kanar, & Kozlowski, 2008; Kozlowski et al., 2001; Salas et al., 2006). In this way, as noted by Cannon-Bowers and Bowers (this volume), meaningful synthetic learning environments can be created.

Cannon-Bowers and Bowers (this volume) focus on technology-enabled instructional systems—the use of computer simulations, games, and virtual worlds—that can be used to create synthetic learning environments. They propose a modified six-phase framework adapted from Sugrue and Clark (2000) that puts the learner at the center of the learning process and argue convincingly that the framework provides a point of departure for scholars to study how and why SLEs can be used to stimulate and accelerate authentic learning. Cannon-Bowers and Bowers touch on many themes raised in other chapters throughout this volume. They propose an ambitious and comprehensive research agenda to promote the development of effective SLEs that centers on (a) goal elaboration, learning strategies, and motivation (e.g., prompting learning strategies and motivation to learn); (b) information presentation (e.g., guiding the learner); (c) developing practice environments (e.g., creating realism and engaging the learner); and (d) prompting monitoring, diagnosis, and adaptation (e.g., using dynamic assessment, feedback and diagnosis, and automated coaching and guidance).

The chapter by Bell and Kozlowski on active learning (this volume) likewise touches on our key themes of learner-centered design, individual differences and ATIs, and delineating learning and motivational process pathways as means to improve training design, delivery, and effectiveness. Their theory proposes that a broad array of distinct active-learning techniques can be integrated by focusing on relatively distinct process pathways—cognitive, motivational, and emotional—that are stimulated by core training design components (instruction, motivation, and emotion, respectively) that cut across many active-learning techniques. Moreover, their approach also incorporates individual differences, with cognitive, motivational, and emotional facets presumed to interact with their respective core training design components. And their focus on training effectiveness extends beyond learning and performance to encompass adaptation. Recent empirical research provides support for their integrative theory (Bell & Kozlowski, 2008). Their model provides an evidence-based approach for examining ATIs, elaborating learning and motivational pathways, enhancing training design, and unpacking adaptation.

The design and delivery of training can benefit from an infusion of findings from the cognition, motivation, and emotion literature. Key questions that need to be answered in the design and delivery of training are as follows:

1. We need to go beyond *g*. Research needs to focus more attention on cognition and cognitive processes. What cognitive principles can help promote active and adaptive learning?
2. We need to go beyond goal orientation. Research needs to focus more attention on affective and motivational dispositions *and* on the regulation of emotional states and reactions during learning.
3. What is the role of simulation-based learning, games, and synthetic experiences as forms of mainstream organizational training? They have been pioneered in the military and aviation. They are making their way into medicine. For what purposes are they useful in less specialized organizations? Can they be affordable and effective in business firms?
4. How can we compile and integrate research findings and derive principles from individual differences; cognition, learning, and motivation; and active learning, simulation, and gaming to accelerate expertise development?

Context, Levels, and Time

The organizational context is the "800-pound gorilla" of training. We know it affects everything—pretraining motivation and the mind-set of trainees as they enter a program, motivation during training, and the extent to which trainees strive to acquire trained knowledge and skills— and is a key posttraining factor in facilitating or inhibiting transfer and generalization (Kozlowski & Salas, 1997). Contextual effects are potent and pervasive, playing out at multiple levels of the organizational system (Kozlowski, Brown, Weissbein, Cannon-Bowers, & Salas, 2000; Mathieu & Tesluk, this volume). Contextual effects unfold over time and across levels. Training, learning, and transfer do not occur in a vacuum; the past, present, and future have to be considered. Not all learning is formalized. Much learning occurs on the job—and off it—but is not systematically directed by the organization. Features of the organizational context, in combination with individual differences, are key factors for prompting informal learning (Tannenbaum, Beard, McNall, & Salas, this volume).

Organizational context factors—and contextual factors beyond the boundaries of the organization such as one's social network—interacting with individual differences and experiences are important for stimulating development across the life span (Molloy & Noe, this volume). In addition, contextual factors are key to achieving system alignment that integrates informal and formal learning processes and that is necessary to make learning not merely an individual phenomenon but also a collective one that extends learning across multiple levels of the system to teams and the organization (Kozlowski, Chao, & Jensen, this volume). Finally, integrating training effectiveness across micro and meso levels (Mathieu & Tesluk, this volume) necessitates an understanding of the context, how it influences all aspects of training (before, during, and after), and how it can be studied at multiple levels of analysis.

Tannenbaum and colleagues (this volume) argue that most learning occurs on the job, and, therefore, more attention should be given to informal approaches to learning—learning as you go. This adds a new twist on the concept of learner-centered instruction. Indeed, informal learning is where the trainee "adapts" the learning environment to maximize skill acquisition and where the learning environment provides the needed "instructional goals and strategies." Informal learning focuses attention on the trainee and his or her characteristics from what motivates them to how they self-regulate to how to acquire the skills, and on the organizational factors that promote, shape, and support this informal learning process. Given the importance of this issue, much more systematic science is needed. Tannenbaum and colleagues offer a rich research agenda that is centered on understanding the influence of organizational factors (e.g., how the organizational environment can stimulate it, job experiences that create the best opportunities for it, and how to provide sufficient time and encouragement) and individual factors (e.g., motivation, personality, self-awareness, feedback orientation, and self-efficacy) that promote informal learning.

Building beyond the concept of informal learning on the job, Molloy and Noe (this volume) considered the concept of continuous learning on the job and off the job, deliberately and by chance, and across the span of a career or even multiple careers. This is clearly an expansive learner-centered concept, and its conceptual exploration touches upon all the themes cross-cutting this book: the role of individual differences in knowledge, skills, abilities, life experiences, and prior training, among other factors; and the organizational context, one's broader social network, and the broader labor market and economy as a complex confluence of factors that motivate, shape, and guide a cyclical waxing and waning process of developmental participation that influences one's human capital and career success. Ultimately, training is an organizational responsibility, but in a competitive career marketplace building one's own human capital is the surest way to ensure career success. Molloy and Noe offer an expansive and integrative conceptual model that will serve as a rich source of ideas and research directions as the field moves forward on investigating continuous learning processes.

Continuing on this theme of blending formal and informal learning, Kozlowski, Chao, and Jensen (this volume) tackle the "broad, fuzzy, and multifaceted concept" (p. 362) of organizational learning in an effort to articulate "how an *integrated infrastructure* can be created to foster learning across multiple levels of the organizational system" (p. 362; emphasis in original). Their conceptualization weaves together context and time. The context consists of technostructural influences (e.g., mission and strategy, technology and structure, and KSAs) represented at multiple levels of analysis—micro, meso, and macro—that have top-down and cross-level effects such that high-level contextual factors shape the lower embedded level (Kozlowski & Klein, 2000). Technostructural factors need to be aligned within levels to promote supportive human enabling processes (e.g., leadership and climate, and knowledge and skills) that, over time, propagate and emerge bottom-up to align the organizational system. System alignment allows the development and emergence of an organizational learning (OL) system that integrates informal processes (OL foundation), formal processes (OL infrastructure), and OL outcomes at the macro, meso, and micro levels. Their research agenda encompasses informal learning (socialization, team learning, and team development), formal interventions (active learning, embedded training, distributed training, team training, team leadership, and system alignment and vertical transfer), and their integration. They provide an expansive but tractable integrative multilevel research agenda on organizational learning.

Finally, Mathieu and Tesluk (this volume) consider the effectiveness of training and development initiatives and also adopt a multilevel perspective. Although in that sense there is some obvious overlap with the prior chapter, it is primarily in terms of the multilevel conceptual approach that entails top-down and bottom-up influences. Mathieu and Tesluk review and integrate some very different literatures spanning macro strategic human resource management (SHRM) and micro human resource management (HRM) as they explore alternative approaches to understanding training effectiveness and as they highlight the conceptual value in bridging the very distinct macro and micro perspectives that separate research conducted in these literatures. They illustrate and ground the complex and abstract phenomena in their conceptual model by walking through a real-world example that really helps to make the concepts tangible to the reader. In their research agenda, the authors push macro researchers to encompass more micro, and micro researchers to encompass more macro—that is, to better bracket the meso-middle range that "represents the cross-roads of macro-SHRM and micro-I/O psychology heritages"

(p. 432) of training effectiveness research that will be "messy, challenging, and ... extremely fertile ground to plow" (p. 432). We heartily concur!

Going forward, enhancing research-based understanding on learning, training, and development in organizations necessitates research that considers that pervasive role of context across multiple levels (individual, team, organizational, and beyond), the interplay and interactions that occur within and among levels, and the emergence of learning and effectiveness (shaped by contextual influences) over time. Key questions that need to be answered for context and time include the following:

1. As we shift to more informal learning and see the value of lifelong learning, what learning mechanisms (*both* formal and informal) need to be in place for optimizing skill acquisition in the job context and beyond? How can organizations design contextual supports to prompt informal learning and self-directed development? How can organizations design contextual supports to propagate and leverage the knowledge gained from informal learning?

2. As we consider learning over the life span, how can we blend formal and informal influences that shape development over time? The developmental trajectory of lifelong learning is not likely to be smooth and linear, but rather variable, shifting, and even metamorphic as the dynamics play out over time. How can we capture these dynamics, classify them into modal patterns, and understand their organizational (human capital) and individual (career success) implications?

3. As we seek to capture learning and training effectiveness across contexts, levels, and time, how can we better integrate formal and informal learning processes? How can organizations design interventions and system supports to better align and bridge across levels—macro, meso, and micro? How can organizations develop tracking systems and metrics to better capture learning and effectiveness as emergent phenomena over time?

Over the Horizon

What does the future have in store for learning, training, and development in organizations? What can we learn from other disciplines? What is arising over the horizon that may impact how organizations design and deliver learning, training, and development initiatives in the near and not-so-near future? Many interesting and promising ideas and potential research directions await us. We are optimistic that the future looks bright, exciting, and even surprising; the prospects for innovations are enormous!

In this section, we explore three areas that offer great promise to enhance our understanding of learning and training design and where innovative tools, strategies, and techniques may be developed, with research and time, for practical use. We focus on those areas where there is sufficient maturity of ideas, theories, and promising developments that we can forecast some practical applications that may be just over the horizon. Our goal in these brief sketches of possible future directions is to pique your interest about the possibilities and potential. We first discuss cognitive and computational modeling. Next, we focus our attention on gaming and simulation-based training. Finally, we end with a discussion on cognitive neuroscience.

Cognitive and Computational Modeling

Cognitive modeling developed from a confluence of influences encompassing fields of study that include computer science, cognitive psychology, human factors, artificial intelligence, mathematics, and machine learning, among others. It simulates human mental operations (e.g., problem solving; Anderson, 1990). Although there are many different cognitive models (such as adaptive control of thought—rational [ACT-R]; goals, operators, methods, and selection rules [GOMS]; Soar; cognition as a network of tasks [COGNET]; and executive process interactive control [EPIC]; see Pew & Mavor, 1997, for details), they are all governed by mathematical relationships (or algorithms), and their purpose is to simulate, understand, and predict human behavior and performance on tasks similar to the one being modeled. Cognitive modeling is used in industry, the military, and education.

In recent years, cognitive modeling has been applied to model psychological phenomena such as group and jury decision making, attitudes, social influence, personality, personality dynamics, team dynamics, stereotypes, and causal attributions, among others (Gluck & Pew, 2005). It has been applied to improve the human factors engineering and interface design in manufacturing products (Zachary, Bell, & Ryder, 2008). More specifically, these models have been used to improve the human–computer interface to reduce errors, to build software that reacts to how humans interact with a system, to test psychological theory, and to infer human mental states.

In learning and educational settings, cognitive modeling has been embedded in educational software in order to customize instructions and feedback to the learner. This is a promising use for training—the development of intelligent tutoring and training systems. An intelligent tutoring system (ITS) is a computer-based system that provides tailored instructions and/or feedback to learners, and does this without the presence of or inputs from a "live" instructor. Most ITSs have four components: the interface module (human–computer interaction), the expert module (the desired end state), the student module (the current state of the student), and the tutor module (navigate the student to the desired end state). All of these modules interact to create a dynamic, rich, and robust learning experience. Developing an ITS, however, is not easy because it requires careful and detailed preparations in terms of describing the knowledge and possible behaviors and actions of experts, students, and tutors. ITSs are primarily limited to "closed" or well-defined knowledge systems. However, ITSs have been developed for educational purposes, and they are making their way to more complex settings where higher order skills are needed (see Shute & Psotka, 1996). As we learn more about ITSs, our prediction is that they will make their way to the workplace. These ITSs can provide organizations with powerful tools to deliver training in a robust, effective, and efficient way. Time will tell, but it is worth looking over the horizon for more complex and better ITSs.

Serious Games, Synthetic Experiences, and Simulation-Based Learning

There is no question that serious games, SLEs (Cannon-Bowers & Bowers, this volume), and immersive simulations (e.g., virtual reality) have become a hot topic in training and education. The argument is that these approaches to learning have many motivational virtues: They deeply engage the learner, provide an emotionally and physiologically arousing experience, promote "learning with fun," and realistically create meaningful work scenarios— all noteworthy features for learning. These are "not your father's training systems." However, although the promise is there, much more research is needed to determine what works, when it works, under what conditions, and what KSAs are best suited for these approaches.

We must acknowledge that these approaches are not all created equal. Games use fantasy and challenges for enhancing the opportunities to learn. SLEs (Cannon-Bowers & Bowers, this volume) are immersive simulations that create an engaging experience and mimic the transfer environment in a realistic manner. These approaches are permeating the workplace more and more, but at this stage it is application without a good scientific foundation. Scientific evidence is needed to demonstrate how to use these emerging techniques to meet different training needs in organizations. As one positive step in this direction, Wilson and colleagues (2009) began to link gaming attributes to learning outcomes. They offered a taxonomy that allows for testing how and when specific gaming attributes (e.g., control and fantasy) facilitate learning. As these attributes are evaluated, data and supportive evidence accumulate, and practical guidance develops, the continued development of technology, games, and immersive simulation will become more accessible to organizational training. In time, we predict the tools will get more cost-effective, transportable, adaptable, and acceptable. Attention needs to be given to these emerging learning systems.

Cognitive Neuroscience

Cognitive neuroscience maps the structure and physiology of the brain and nervous system and their activation to human thought, emotion, and behavior. Neuroscientists today focus on describing the human brain and how it functions normally (Posner & DiGirolamo, 2000). They study the biochemical signals that nerves transmit, the evolutionary development of the brain, and many other things. One interesting aspect of what these scientists do is their study of the ways in which the brain processes information—this is what holds promise for learning, development, and training in organizations. For example, cognitive neuroscience might tell us about the "circuiting" and biological mechanisms of learning. We might be able to get a deeper understanding of how trainees are "hardwired" to learn and how variations in the hardwiring influence the rate and effectiveness of learning. There are also research efforts aimed at uncovering how the brain works in context—"in the wild" at work. This field—neuroergonomics—has begun to study the "brain at work" (Parasuraman & Wilson, 2008). Using noninvasive measurement techniques and considering subjective (e.g., self-assessment) as well as objective (e.g., functional near-infrared [fNIR], and eye tracking) measures of task performance, this field has begun to find that brain "activity" can be distinguished when one works on a complex cognitive task in the lab, using simulations, or in the field. This is very promising work with direct application to the design of training methods by providing guidelines for information presentations in formal and informal training. We must stay tuned to progress in this area—neuroergonomics.

Concluding Remarks

No matter what the future brings, one thing we know for sure is that the field of training, learning, and development in organizations does not belong to one discipline. If one looks at the chapters in this volume and the literature that they draw from, one thing is clear—learning and training research is a multidisciplinary science. No one single discipline owns it. Not cognitive science, not educational psychology, not the skill acquisition and expertise scholar, and certainly not industrial and organizational psychology. We believe this is good news and very refreshing. Hopefully, this volume will be one of many forums where several disciplines contribute to advancing the science of learning, training, and development in organizations.

References

Anderson, J. R. (1990). *The adaptive character of thought*. Hillsdale, NJ: Lawrence Erlbaum Associates.

Bell, B. S., Kanar, A. M., & Kozlowski, S. W. J. (2008). Current issues and future directions in simulation-based training in North America. *International Journal of Human Resource Management, 19*, 1416–1434.

Bell, B. S., & Kozlowski, S. W. J. (2002). Adaptive guidance: Enhancing self-regulation, knowledge and performance in technology-based training. *Personnel Psychology, 55*, 267–306.

Bell, B. S., & Kozlowski, S. W. J. (2008). Active learning: Effects of core training design elements on self-regulatory processes, learning, and adaptability. *Journal of Applied Psychology, 93*, 296–316.

Colquitt, J. A., LePine, J. A., & Noe, R. A. (2000). Toward an integrative theory of training motivation: A meta-analytic path analysis of 20 years of research. *Journal of Applied Psychology, 85*(5), 678–707.

Gluck, K. A., & Pew, R. W. (2005). *Modeling human behavior with integrated cognitive architectures: Comparison, evaluation, and validation*. Mahwah, NJ: Lawrence Erlbaum Associates.

Goldstein, I. L. (1989). *Training and development in organizations*. San Francisco: Jossey-Bass.

Howell, W. C., & Cooke, N. J. (1989). Training the human information processor: A review of cognitive models. In I. L. Goldstein (Ed.), *Training and development in organizations*. San Francisco: Jossey-Bass.

Kirkpatrick, D. L. (1959). Techniques for evaluating training programs. *Journal of the American Society of Training Directors, 13*(3–9), 21–26.

Kozlowski, S. W. J., Brown, K. G., Weissbein, D., Cannon-Bowers, J. A., & Salas, E. (2000). A multilevel approach to training effectiveness: Enhancing horizontal and vertical transfer. In K. J. Klein & S. W. J. Kozlowski (Eds.), *Multilevel theory, research and methods in organizations: Foundations, extensions, and new directions* (pp. 157–210). San Francisco: Jossey-Bass.

Kozlowski, S. W. J., & Klein, K. J. (2000). A multilevel approach to theory and research in organizations: Contextual, temporal, and emergent processes. In K. J. Klein & S. W. J. Kozlowski (Eds.), *Multilevel theory, research and methods in organizations: Foundations, extensions, and new directions* (pp. 3–90). San Francisco: Jossey-Bass.

Kozlowski, S. W. J., & Salas, E. (1997). An organizational systems approach for the implementation and transfer of training. In J. K. Ford, S. W. J. Kozlowski, K. Kraiger, E. Salas, & M. Teachout (Eds.), *Improving training effectiveness in work organizations* (pp. 247–287). Mahwah, NJ: Lawrence Erlbaum Associates.

Kozlowski, S. W .J., Toney, R. J., Mullins, M. E., Weissbein, D. A., Brown, K. G., & Bell, B. S. (2001). Developing adaptability: A theory for the design of integrated-embedded training systems. In E. Salas (Ed.), *Advances in human performance and cognitive engineering research* (Vol. 1, pp. 59–123). Amsterdam: JAI/Elsevier Science.

Kraiger, K., Ford, J. K., & Salas, E. (1993). Application of cognitive, skill-based, and affective theories of learning outcomes to new methods of training evaluation. *Journal of Applied Psychology, 78*(2), 311–328.

Parasuraman, R., & Wilson, G. F. (2008). Putting the brain to work: Neuroergonomics past, present and future. *Human Factors, 50*(3), 468–474.

Pew, R. W., & Mavor, A. S. (1997). *Representing human behavior in military simulations: Interim report.* Report from Panel on Modeling Human Behavior and Command Decision Making: Representations for Military Simulations. Washington, DC: National Research Council.

Posner, M. I., & DiGirolamo, G. J. (2000). Cognitive neuroscience: Origins and promise. *Psychological Bulletin, 126,* 873–889.

Salas, E., & Cannon-Bowers, J. A. (2001). The science of training: A decade of progress. *Annual Review of Psychology, 52,* 471–499.

Salas, E., Wilson, K. A., Priest, H. A., & Guthrie, J. W. (2006). Design, delivery, and evaluation of training systems. In G. Salvendy (Ed.), *Handbook of human factors and ergonomics* (3rd ed., pp. 472–512). Hoboken, NJ: John Wiley.

Shute, V. J., & Psotka, J. (1996). Intelligent tutoring systems: Past, present and future. In D. Jonassen (Ed.), *Handbook of research on educational communications and technology* (pp. 570–600). New York: Macmillan.

Sugrue, B., & Clark, R. F. (2000). Media selection for training. In S. Tobias & J. D. Hetcher (Eds.), *Training and retraining: A handbook for business, industry, government, and the military* (pp. 208–234). New York: Macmillan.

Tannenbaum, S. I., & Yukl, G. (1992). Training and development in work organizations. *Annual Review of Psychology, 43,* 399–441.

Wilson, K. A., Bedwell, W. L., Lazzara, E. H., Salas, E., Burke, C. S., Estock, J., Orvis, K. L., & Conkey, C. (2009). Relations between game attributes and learning outcomes: Review and research proposals. *Simulation and Gaming, 40,* 217–266. Zachary, W., Bell, B., & Ryder, J. (2008). Computational representations and method for modeling teams. In E. Salas, G. F. Goodwin, & C. S. Burke (Eds.), *Team effectiveness in complex organizations* (pp. 455–481). New York: Taylor & Francis.

Zachary, W., Bell, B., & Ryder, J. (2008). Computational representations and method for modeling teams. In E. Salas, G. F. Goodwin, & C. S. Burke (Eds.), *Team effectiveness in complex organizations* (pp. 455–481). New York: Taylor & Francis.

Author Index

Subject Index

A

Abstract conceptualization (AC), 31
AC, *see* Abstract conceptualization
Accommodators, 31
Achievement goals, 146
Active experimentation (AE), 31
Active learning, 263–300, 452–453
   Adaptive Learning System, 267–272
      application, 270–271
      individual differences, 270
      practice behaviors, 267
      process pathways of active
         learning, 271–272
      self-regulation system, 267
      training components,
         elaboration of, 271–272
      training outcomes, 269–270
      training strategy, 267–269
   conduit models of learning, 265
   discovery learning, 276
   e-learning, 263
   emotion control, 284, 285
   exploratory learning, 276
   expository instruction, 276
   instructional goals, 280
   integrated embedded training, 264
   integrative framework, 272–289
      analogical versus adaptive
         transfer, 289
      ATIs, 279–280, 283–284, 287–288
      attributions, 286–287
      basic versus strategic outcomes,
         289
      core training components,
         273–274
      effortful processing, 278
      emotion control, 284–288
      instruction, 276–280
      integrated conceptual model,
         275
      intrinsic motivation, 282
      mastery orientation, 275
      mental models, 278–279
      metacognition, 277–278
      motivational induction, 280–284
      outcomes, 288–289
      self-efficacy, 282
      state anxiety, 286
      supporting cognitive and
         emotional processes, 283
   on-the-job training, 282
   performance-avoid goal, 280
   performance-prove goal, 280
   proceduralized instruction, 276
   research agenda, 290–293
      core training components
         and individual differences,
         290–291
      elaborating process pathways,
         291–292
      unpacking adaptation, 292–293
   SLEs and, 243
   technology-based training, 282
   theoretical foundation, 265–267
   transmission models of learning,
      265
ACT-R cognitive modeling, *see*
      Adaptive control of thought—
      rational cognitive modeling
Adaptive control of thought—rational
      (ACT-R) cognitive modeling,
      181, 473
Adaptive expertise, routine expertise
      and, 102
Adaptive Learning System (ALS), 266,
      267–272, 453, *see also* Active
      learning
   application, 270–271
   individual differences, 270
   organizational learning, 381
   practice behaviors, 267